FOOD SERVICE IN INSTITUTIONS

FOOD SERVICE IN INSTITUTIONS

FIFTH EDITION

BESSIE BROOKS WEST, M.A.

Professor Emeritus of Institutional Management
formerly Head of Department
Kansas State University

LEVELLE WOOD, M.S.

Professor Emeritus of Home Economics
formerly Chairman, Division of Institution Management
The Ohio State University

VIRGINIA F. HARGER, M.S., R.D.

Professor of Home Economics
and Head, Institution Management Department
Oregon State University

GRACE SEVERANCE SHUGART, M.S., R.D.

Professor Emeritus of Institutional Management
formerly Head of Department
Kansas State University

John Wiley New York · Santa Barbara
London · Sydney

Library of Congress Cataloging in Publication Data:

Main entry under title:

Food service in institutions.

 Previous editions entered under B. B. West.
 Includes bibliographies and indexes.
 1. Food service. I. West, Bessie Brooks.
II. West, Bessie Brooks. Food service in institutions.
TX946.W415 1977 642'.5 76-26568
ISBN 0-471-93393-7

Printed in the United States of America

10 9

PREFACE

The fifth edition of *Food Service in Institutions* is designed, as were the previous four editions, to be used as a basic text by students in food systems management and as a ready reference by the people actively engaged in the planning, production, and service of meals for larger than family size groups.

Presentation of the content remains under three sections: Quantity Food Service, Organization and Administration, and Physical Facilities. Minor changes have been made in the organization of subject matter in Section 1. Meal Planning and Food Standards have been left in one chapter, while Delivery and Service of Food is a newly added chapter. This seemed appropriate because of the continuing trend toward separation of preparation and service in time and distance, and the resultant need for delivery systems. Less space is given to food products and their preparation, since these areas are well covered in prerequisite courses and in the companion book, *Food for Fifty,* now in its fifth edition.

The updating of chapters on Personnel, Organization and Administration, Sanitation and Safety, and Financial Control emphasizes the importance of applying good management principles and practices in these areas. Since the last edition, an increasing number of federally funded meal programs have been initiated. One result of this legislation is the additional focus placed on the need for good management of foodservice systems.

Rapid developments in food technology, equipment design, personnel policies, and management techniques, adapted to the ever-changing times and needs, necessarily limit the content of this book to trends, principles, basic facts, and some examples of their application to the broad scope of the foodservice industry. It is expected that the users of this text will supplement the subject matter by current research reports, specialized publications, exhibits, and seminars on various aspects of the study course or situation.

We are deeply appreciative of suggestions offered for this revision and for the wide acceptance of former editions.

Bessie Brooks West
LeVelle Wood
Virginia F. Harger
Grace Severance Shugart

CONTENTS

SECTION I
Quantity
Food
Service

SECTION II
Organization
and
Administration

SECTION III
Physical
Facilities

SECTION 1
QUANTITY FOOD SERVICE

1.
FOODSERVICE SYSTEMS AND THEIR DEVELOPMENT

The foodservice industry has expanded rapidly in the past half century, especially in the last two decades, and ranks first in volume of sales among all retail outlets in the United States. A conservative estimate is that one of every four meals is planned, prepared, and served outside the family home. The foodservice industry is broad in scope and varies from systems such as highly competitive and expensive restaurants and hotels to a multiplicity of fast and less costly food outlets such as schools, universities, and hospitals with conservative budgets.

The growth in heavy patronage or use of such foodservices may be attributed in part to changes in the socio-economic trends of the times and an awakened interest in the health and well-being of people. Some factors contributing to changes are: mobility, a shorter workweek with added leisure time, women employed outside the home, urban and apartment living, and general affluency of the population. Also, there has been an increased concern to improve the nutritional status of individuals through education and adequate food for all, especially to meet the needs of certain segments of the populace, for example, schoolchildren, patients in hospitals and nursing homes, and lower-income or other disadvantaged groups.

A report compiled by the National Restaurant Association lists foodservice units under two major groupings.

> **1.** *Commercial* or those establishments which are open to the public, are operated for profit, and which may operate facilities and/or supply meal service on a regular basis for others.

> **2.** *Commercial* (as employee feeding in schools, industrial, and commercial organizations), *Educational, Government,* or *Institutional* Organizations which run their own foodservice operations.[1]

Foodservices in schools, universities, hospitals and other health care facilities, residences for children and retirees (Generation III), camps, community centers, transportation, Armed Forces, industrial plants, and correctional units are in the second group and may or may not show a profit, or even balance out financially at the break-even point. Food is provided primarily as a service to complement their other activities and contribute to the fulfillment of the objectives of the institution. Recent legislation has made possible considerable material assistance and support for the maintenance of improved food standards for some of the foodservices in group 2.

Accurate data on the relative number of meals served in the various types of foodservices are difficult to obtain. NRA statistics show that of total dollar sales and food purchases in the United States in 1971,[2] the Commercial group accounted for $40.0 billion or 83.12 percent of the $48.2 billion received from the sale of food and drink in the total food industry. Also the Commercial group spent $12.7 billion or 70.71 percent of all food purchases. This left 16.88 percent of total food sales volume and 29.29 percent of total purchases by foodservices in group 2. Total retail sales in the foodservice industry are estimated at $62.0 billion for 1975.

The efficient management and supervision of such an extensive array of foodservice systems offers an almost unlimited challenge to students to prepare themselves academically and practically to assume responsibilities in this great industry.

[1] *The National Restaurant Association,* NRA Washington Report, 17, 21 *(1974).*
[2] *The National Restaurant Association,* NRA Washington Report, 17, 21 *(1974).*

Foodservice systems in operation today have become an accepted way of American life, and we tend to regard them as relatively recent innovations. However, they have their roots in the habits and customs that characterize our civilization and date back before the Middle Ages. Certain phases of foodservice systems reached a well-organized form in feudal times in the lands that have exerted the most influence on our customs and habits.

The countries that have most largely determined American food habits and customs are England, France, Germany, Norway, and Sweden. These countries have contributed living habits that would lead naturally to the evolution of institution foodservices. In each the partaking of food was made a social event in which men and women, in fact, the entire family and guests, shared. There was no withdrawal for eating that characterizes the customs of certain peoples, no religious beliefs by which participation in meals with others was barred. The economic level and the type of food eaten were also such as to foster the service of food to groups. Instead of the few grains of parched wheat or corn or the bowl of rice with raw fruit that satisfied some races, these peoples ate meat, regarding as their due a variety of protein foods from various sources. Such foods could not be transported without danger of spoilage, and their preparation required more fire and attention than was readily convenient outside an established kitchen.

In the early days, as in the present, factors affecting the organization and administration of foodservices were the type of institution, the plant in which the service was housed, the personnel available, and the income level or per diem allowance. It will be of interest to consider some of the types of foodservices that existed long ago and contrast them with their modern equivalents. In medieval times quantity food production was the rule rather than the exception in religious orders, royal households, and colleges.

RELIGIOUS ORDERS

Records show that the foodservices in the numerous abbeys that dotted England, in which the work of food preparation and service was carried on by the brethren of the order, reached a much higher standard than the food served in the inn. The vows that had been taken did not destroy the appreciation of good food; the tribute given by the laity and the food grown on the abbey's ground provided liberally for the institution's table. The sense of stewardship was strong enough in the abbots to establish a detailed system of accounting. Records of the religious orders give a fair concept of what was regarded as an adequate food allowance per person and show the early days of cost accounting to have given a fairly effective, if not classified, recording of the data at hand. A specified per capita per diem food allowance seems to have been the rule. The money spent for religious feasts was perhaps the major item in the food expenditures of an otherwise thrifty organization.

The scope of the foodservices undertaken in these institutions is indicated by the space provided for food preparation. The kitchen of the Canterbury Abbey, favorite scene of innumerable pilgrimages, measures 45 feet in diameter. Of greatest architectural interest is the abbot's kitchen in Glastonbury. Within these octagonal walls were served not only the numerous brethren of the order, but also the thousands of pilgrims who flocked to the abbey to worship.

ROYAL AND NOBLE HOUSEHOLDS

The royal household, with its hundreds of retainers, and the households of the nobles, often numbering as many as 150 to 250 persons, also necessitated a foodservice on an institutional basis. There was wide variance in rank and in the subsequent food allowances within these groups. In the provision for these various needs, strict accounting of the cost was necessary, and here, perhaps, is the beginning of the present-day scientific food-cost accounting. The cost record most often referred to is the *Northumberland Household Book.* For this household of more than 140 persons, the serving of 10 different breakfasts is recorded, the best for the earl and his lady, the poorest for the lowest workman or scullion. A similar range is presumed for the other meals. The daily food allowance for breakfast on one level is that given for the "Gentylmen o' th' Chapel, and a Meas of Childer." [3] It includes 3 loaves of bread, 1 1/2 gallons of beer, and 3 pieces of salt fish or 4 white herring.

The kitchens of these medieval households would appall the present-day dietitian by the disregard of all sanitary standards in food storage, preparation, and food handling. A clutter of supplies overflowing from inadequate table and shelf space to the deal floors, handled by children, nosed by dogs, commonly comprised the background for the preparation of elaborate creations for the table. A notable example is shown in Fig. 1.1. Since labor was cheap and readily available a large staff of workers was employed to carry on the task of food preparation. Rank was evident in the division of labor. The head cook might wear a gold chain over handsome cloth-

[3] *William Edward Mead,* The English Medieval Feast, *Houghton Mifflin, Boston, pp. 138–139, 1931.*

FIGURE 1.1   The kitchen, Windsor Castle at Christmas time. Courtesy, Arnold Shircliffe.

ing and present his culinary creations to his employer in person. The pastry cook and the meat cook did not rate as high, but were esteemed for their contributions. The meanest scullion often had scarcely a rag to wear and received as his wage broken bread and the privilege of sleeping on the hearth through the chilly winter nights.

On special occasions, there were feasts of formidable proportions. Although there may be little in common between the menu and the food list of a present-day banquet and those of centuries ago, the rules cited then for public suppers are worthy of thought. We are advised:

in the first place, that it is convenient that a supper be served in due time, not too early, nor too late. . . . The second is convenable place, large, pleasant, and secure. The third is the heart and glad cheer of him that maketh the feast. The fourth is many divers messes, so that who will not of one may taste of another. The fifth are divers wines and drinks. The sixth is courtesy and honesty of servants. The seventh is natural friendship and company of them that sit at the supper. The eighth is mirth of song and instruments of music. . . . The ninth is plenty of light of candles and of prickets and of torches. . . . The tenth is the deliciousness of all that is set on the board. . . . The eleventh is long during of the supper. For men use, after full end of work and travail, to sit long at the supper. For meat eaten too hastily grieveth against night. Therefore at the supper men should eat by leisure and not too hastily. The twelfth is sureness. For without harm and damage every man should be prayed to the dinner. . . . The thirteenth is softness and liking of rest and of sleep. After supper men shall rest, for then sleep is sweet and liking. [4]

With the passage of time, knowledge of the causes of food spoilage led to improved practices in food storage and preparation in these noble households. Advances in the understanding of the laws of physics resulted in the replacement of the open hearth with the iron stove and in a refinement of much of the kitchen equipment. The dress of the employees showed some regard for the tasks they assumed. The convenience in kitchen arrangement and equipment reduced the number of workers required and thus tended to relieve disorder and confusion.

There are no American equivalents of the royal households of other lands. The White House, as the residence of the President of the United States, is the scene of official state entertainment. The State dining room seats a maximum of 120 persons (see Fig. 1.2). One writer states that within the White House kitchen the staff can prepare anything "from an egg to an ox." The following is a typical menu for a diplomatic meal in years past.

Oysters Rockefeller

Claret Consommé

Celery Hearts   Assorted Olives

Whole Wheat Fairy Toast

Broiled Red Snapper   Tartar Sauce

Bread Sticks

Parsley Potato Balls

Sliced Tomatoes and Cucumbers

Broiled Porterhouse Steak

Mushroom Sauce   Mustard Pickles

Spanish Corn   Spinach Goldenrod

Roquefort Cheese Salad Bowl

Buttered Triscuits

Frozen Plum Pudding   Butterscotch Sauce

Lady Fingers

Nuts   Candies   Demitasse

Cigars   Cigarettes

[4] *William Edward Mead,* The English Medieval Feast, *Houghton Mifflin, Boston, pp. 138–139, 1931.*

FIGURE   1.2   *White House State Dining Room set for formal service. Copyright ©*
White House Historical Association. Photograph by George F.
Mobley, National Geographic Society.

The present trend is toward simplification of the menu pattern at the
White House, even for the most formal occasions (see p. 10). This is
in harmony with the generally accepted current food consumption
habits of the American population. A lessened number of items on
one menu, adequate well arranged equipment, and the use of modern management and food production principles, make it easy for a
few qualified kitchen personnel to incorporate most foods into
Gourmet meals. Good food, proper appointments and service contribute much to the success of any size dinner party.

When visiting dignitaries are entertained at state dinners at the
White House, detailed information is obtained in advance regarding
their personal food habits, including dietary restrictions, and any
ethnic or religious food customs that might affect the acceptability
and enjoyment of the meal.

At the White House dinner honoring Queen Elizabeth and
Prince Philip on their Bi-Centennial visit to the United States in July

Dinner

Turtle Soup with Sherry

Robert Mondavi
Pinot Noir
1970

Suprême of Royal Squab
Wild Rice
Sautéed Zucchini

Schramsberg
Blanc de Blancs
1972

Hearts of Palm Salad
Brie Cheese

Praline Mousse

Demitasse

THE WHITE HOUSE
Thursday, January 30, 1975

Courtesy, the White House.

1976, the menu was New England Lobster, Saddle of Veal, Rice Croquettes, Broccoli with Mornay Sauce, Garden Salad, Cheese, Peach Ice Cream Bombe with Red Raspberries, Petit Fours, Wines, Demitasse. Guests were served in an attractively decorated tent dining room on the White House lawn. This menu and service would have been considered improper for a Centennial dinner 100 years ago.

UNIVERSITIES AND COLLEGES

From some time in the twelfth century through the medieval ages hostels existed at the various colleges and universities on the continent and in England as the accepted provision for student living. On the continent the management of these hostels was in the hands of the students. At Oxford, England, hostels originated in the endowments made by men of wealth to provide board and lodging for students unable to pay these costs for themselves. These endowed houses were, at first only slightly but eventually completely, under the direction of the university. In this gradual shift of authority were the beginnings of assumption of responsibility by universities for the living conditions of students. In medieval times the provisions made varied with the halls and changed for any hall from year to year. Reminders of such plans for group feeding by colleges during medieval times are still found in the enormous kitchens in the ancient halls. For example, the kitchen of Christ Church College, Oxford, provides ample room for the roasting of the carcass of an ox in its hearth.

The colonial colleges in the United States were started as counterparts of the universities of Oxford and Cambridge. The provision of residence halls with dining rooms for all students was made a responsibility of the administration, and thriftily and prayerfully was it dispatched by the clergymen who, in general, were in charge of the early colleges. Not always, however, did the provisions meet with student approval. With the development of interest and enthusiasm for German educational procedure, which did not include housing as a school responsibility, many colleges and universities lost interest in student living conditions. This decline in executive interest was accompanied by a marked assumption of the responsibilities of housing and feeding large student groups by sororities and fraternities without faculty supervision. An attendant complication of the whole problem of adequate food provision for the student group was an inevitable result.

The twentieth century has witnessed a shift from the laissez-faire policy adopted earlier by many, if not most, colleges and universities. They now recognize their responsibility for the physical and social well-being of the students and, in many instances, have provided for self-liquidating building programs to furnish adequate facilities for complete living. A diversity of campus foodservices is a familiar pattern. These include residence hall dining rooms that provide all meals for groups living within the respective halls, commons that make similar provision for students living in several halls or off campus, student union buildings with their cafeterias, snack bars, vending, and specialty fast-service units for students and campus personnel and, in some cases, table-service dining rooms open to the public, banquet facilities for serving large groups upon reservation, and other accommodations for special catering.

Gradually, with the influx of students into our colleges and universities after World War II, the more formal seated service and leisurely dining have given way to the speedy informality of self-service in most residence halls. The observance of certain social amenities, formerly a definite part of residence hall dining, seldom is possible today when there are too many students to be seated at one time, and class schedules go "round the clock"; all students cannot be present at a given time. Coeducational residences and dining halls have gained acceptance on many campuses (see Appendix A).

Another trend in large universities with expanding building programs and complex residence hall systems is centralization of services. Buying, storage, prepreparation, and some preparation such as baking may be done in a separate building under centralized management. Prepeeled and cut-for-cooking vegetables, custom-ready salad ingredients, portioned meats, and baked products made in this unit are sent to each of the foodservices on campus. Often recipe development and product acceptance testing are a part of this service also. With increased labor costs, centralization becomes advantageous for all types of foodservices to reduce duplication of personnel and equipment.

The use of the foodservice facilities as laboratories for classes in institution management is a common practice and doubtless has been a contributing factor in the establishment of the high requirements maintained for campus foodservice directors. In addition to teaching the students enrolled in such classes, the director often has the responsibility of supervising student employees. The work schedules and attitudes of these part-time employees present numerous problems not common in other types of foodservice systems.

SOCIAL ORGANIZATIONS

Few modern homes are spacious enough and adequately staffed to provide for the serving of formal dinners to 25 or more guests. Today such dinners and banquets for large groups are commonly held in club rooms or in public establishments planned, equipped, and staffed for such work. It is interesting that concern with the improvement of foodservice facilities for clubs parallels closely similar concern with sanitary measures in the royal households. The recommendations of Mr. Soyer to the Reform Club of London, presented in Fig. 1.3, indicate the approach made in providing for a sanitary and efficient foodservice setup that would utilize the then fairly recent innovations of stoves, water baths, and refrigeration.

Today city clubs, athletic clubs, and country clubs usually at-

FIGURE 1.3 *One of the early plans for an institution kitchen made by Alexis Soyer for the Reform Club of London about 1850.*

tempt to rival the settings of the better hotels, with a similar standard for the foodservice. Not infrequently, however, the dining room is required or expected to defray part of the cost of other services provided for the guests, such as the swimming pool and the recreation rooms, hence the allowance for food may be sharply limited unless subsidized by membership fees. Then, too, the stability of income that characterizes the college residence hall is lacking and often, it seems, the clientele is more critical.

SCHOOL FOODSERVICES

The story of the school lunch is inevitably a part of the larger story of the rapid development of public education. As reforms stemming from the Industrial Revolution began to free society from the supposed necessity of child labor, the number of unemployed children of school age increased, and soon a growth in public concern with education became evident. In order to encourage school attendance, parents and civic-minded townspeople in some European countries banded together to provide school lunches at a low cost. It is reported that canteens for schoolchildren were established in France in 1849 and that in 1865 Victor Hugo started school feeding in England by providing warm luncheons in his own home in Guernsey for children in a nearby school. At some time between these dates, school foodservice began in this country. The Children's Aid Society of New York City opened an industrial school in 1853 as an effort to persuade the children of the slums to seek "instruction in industry and mental training" and offered food to all comers.

Growth in the knowledge of nutrition some decades later placed emphasis on the importance of the wise selection of food and the need for nourishing school lunches at low cost or without charge. Under the notable leadership of Ellen H. Richards, the Boston school committee passed an order that "only such food as was approved by them should be sold in the city schoolhouses." About this same time other men and women likewise concerned with child welfare sponsored similar developments in several urban centers, and the 2 decades that followed brought significant developments in the school-lunchroom movement throughout the country. Naturally the program went forward most rapidly in the large cities, where there were sustaining organizations and informed and concerned public leaders. Later the extension services in the various states, parent-teacher councils, and other organizations championed the cause of rural children and brought about a general and widespread interest in the improvement of the nutrition of school children through the provision of adequate school foodservices. This concern is expressed in the report of the committee of the League of Nations in these words.

Compulsory education has been generally adopted throughout the civilized world. It is agreed that large numbers of school children are not mentally or physically capable of profiting by this universally accepted recognition of the social obligation to educate the mind of every individual. Might it not be well to make such children more physically and mentally fitted to benefit fully from these educational facilities by assuring that their nutritional needs are satisfied? [5]

World Wars I and II brought into focus the need for improved nutrition among the young people, since so many of them were rejected for military service for reasons related to faulty nutrition. Concern was expressed for the future health of the nation if such trends continued. As a direct result, federal legislation was passed in 1933 to provide loans for communities to pay labor costs of lunches served in schools. In 1935 additional assistance was provided by allowing the federal government to donate surplus commodities. With these aids, a noon meal became a common part of the school activities.

The importance attached to such a service is indicated by the rapid development of school feeding that has come about as a result of the National School Lunch Act of 1946. This Act was designed "to

[5] The Relation of Nutrition to Health, Agriculture, and Economic Policy, *Final Report of Mixed Committee, League of Nations, 1937.*

safeguard the health and well-being of the Nation's children, and to encourage the domestic consumption of nutritious agricultural products." Administration of the federal funds has been handled through a cooperative federal-state-local relationship. Statistics show that approximately 87,000 elementary and secondary schools in the United States operated under this program in 1974. These schools served some 24.9 million children daily, 39 percent of whom received free or reduced-price meals. Countless numbers of other schools operate lunchrooms that make hot food available to the children for their noon meal.

The School Breakfast Program was inaugurated on a limited basis in 1968, but it is now available to all schools. The reduced-price Milk Program for preschool and school age children began in 1954. This program has been enlarged to include nonprofit organizations such as child care centers, settlement houses, summer camps, and nursery schools.

The aim of each individual school foodservice program should be to offer a nutritionally adequate lunch that provides one-third to one-half of the child's nutritive requirements for the entire day, at a minimum cost.

The school foodservice program is made more effective through the cooperative efforts of nutritionists, school administrators, and allied groups such as the parent-teacher associations, all of whom are aware of its value in the physical and mental development of the child. By correlating certain phases of the lunch activities with subject matter in other areas of education, it has ceased to be only a "feeding program." The objectives and procedures have broadened to include (1) the promotion of health and nutrition education in all grades, (2) the promotion of good food habits, and (3) the development of good habits of social behavior.

Today a school foodservice is accepted as an integral part of a successful and fully functioning school program. The type of organization and management varies from the simple, one cook-manager operation found in a small independent school to a complex, centrally managed unit in a large city school system. In small schools, the number of workers usually is limited to one or two capable women who are truly interested in the project and a number of part-time student helpers. Adequate equipment is provided in most cases, but often the service has been housed in buildings erected without such functions in mind. If the original building plans called for a school lunchroom, the probably brief time of the lunch period has been considered, and provision for expeditious instead of elegant service will be found. The limitations of a nonprofit income can be noted in the type of menus served and in the adjuncts of the service.

In addition to centralized management, some school systems have established centralized food preparation centers. Items prepared in these centers may be distributed in bulk either hot or refrigerated, to be served in the individual schools.

Traditionally, foodservice in schools was limited to the noon meal but, in recent years, breakfasts and midday snacks have been added. Meals for elderly citizens are served in some schools (see Fig. 1.4).

A progressive school system will provide an effective foodservice that will rank high in respects such as type, adequacy, and nutritive value of menus served, methods of service, purchasing procedures, working hours and wages of paid employees, food-cost control, efficiency of organization and management in the various groups of the service, and provisions in budget and personnel plans for the effective functioning of the foodservice in the future. School foodservice has become big business.

FIGURE   1.4   *An example of the school library serving as a dining area for senior citizens in a small community.*

HOSPITALS

The evolution of foodservices in hospitals is as interesting as their development in schools and colleges. Little or no attempt was made in early times to provide a therapeutic diet for hospital cases. Menus in an eighteenth-century hospital in this country included mush and molasses for breakfast on Monday, Wednesday, and Friday, varied by mush and molasses for supper on Monday, Wednesday, Thursday, and Saturday. Oxtail soup and black bread appeared on occasion.[6]

The accounts for the Pennsylvania Hospital of 150 years ago indicate the simplicity of a day gone by.[7]

In the year 1804, milk, butter, pork, soap, and hay were produced on this hospital's grounds and consumed therein. The matron, among her accomplishments, made rose water for which the sum of $53 was received. Numerous cows, calves, and pigs were sold. Patients paid the hospital for their funeral charges. . . . On the debit side we find the sum of $350 paid for nine months' salary to Francis and Hannah Higgins as steward and matron. It required 1,280 pounds of candles at a cost of $182 to furnish light, and $40 rent was paid to pasture the cows. A year's tobacco cost $2.89. For a hospital population of 419 hospital cases for the year, 838 gallons of molasses, 254 gallons of brandy and spirits, 269 gallons of wine, and 24 1/2 barrels of beer were consumed, among items listed under liquors.

Not until the Crimean War was a beginning made toward the establishment of dietetics as one of the hospital services. Dietitians as well as nurses should honor and revere Florence Nightingale as the pioneer in their profession. Through her efforts a diet kitchen was set up in 1855 to provide clean, nourishing food for the ill and wounded soldiers in Scutari.

The ill-cooked hunks of meat, vilely served at irregular intervals, which had hitherto been the only diet for the sick men were replaced by punctual meals, well-prepared and appetizing, while strengthening extra foods— soups and wines, and jellies ("preposterous luxuries," snarled Dr. Hall)— were distributed to those who needed them. One thing, however, she could not effect. The separation of the bones from the meat was no part of official cookery: the rule was that the food must be divided into equal portions, and

---

[6] Mary I. Barber, History of the American Dietetic Association, J. B. Lippincott, Philadelphia, p. 12, 1959.

[7] Editorial, Journal of the American Dietetic Association, 9, 405 (1934).

if some of the portions were all bone—well, every man must take his chance. The rule, perhaps, was not a very good one; but there it was. "It would require a new Regulation of the Service," she was told, "to bone the meat." [8]

The contribution made by Alexis Soyer, a noted chef, to this newly established diet kitchen is recounted in a magazine article. He offered to serve gratuitously as the superintendent or manager of the kitchen for the barracks hospital. His plan of procedure, as the following quotation shows, was as intelligent and efficient as our modern practice:

My plan would also be, never to act without the sanction of the doctor-in-chief respecting the diets I mean to introduce; and I would not interfere in the slightest degree with any former department, or displace a man from his duty except for incapacity, insubordination, or bad conduct. . . . I should also claim the power of being able to condemn inferior provisions and to substitute better, always without deviating from any army contract which has been, or may be, made by the government, as I do not mean to hold myself responsible for the purchase of any provisions or stores, but merely to give my approval or disapproval of them. . . . By my system of diet every receipt will be printed, framed, and hung up in the kitchen, so that any person, even a soldier (provided he can read), will be able of executing them well, as each receipt will be comprised in a few lines. . . . I shall not think of commencing before I am well acquainted with every one in each department that has reference to the cooking. I shall submit every sample of diets, with a statement of the quantity and kind of ingredients of which they are composed, for the approval and opinion of the medical authorities. [9]

It is not to be wondered that after his effective reorganization of the hospital dietary and culinary department he was asked to instruct the soldiers in cooking their rations to the best advantage.

Changes in hospital foodservices during the last 50 years have been noted by Whitcomb [10] to include the introduction of centralized tray service and mechanical dishwashing, the use of a separate

[8] *Lytton Strachey,* Eminent Victorians, *G. P. Putnam's Sons, New York, p. 152, 1918.*
[9] *Edith Barber, "A Culinary Campaign,"* Journal of the American Dietetic Association, *11, 89–98 (1935).*
[10] *M. Whitcomb, "How Food Service Has Changed in Fifty Years,"* Modern Hospital, *101 (3), 163 (1963).*

kitchen for special diet preparation and then the elimination of such a room, the advent of frozen foods and their use in the menus, and the greater control in all areas of operation. The segregation of staff and workers into separate dining rooms at mealtime has given way in most hospitals to the more economical plan of one dining room for all. Also, pay cafeterias for staff and employees were introduced during this period.

Today hospitals comprise a large group of institutions whose foodservices are so important as to merit special consideration. Within this group some are operated by the federal government, others supported by state, county, or city funds, or by combinations of these sources, others maintained by religious orders, and a large number that are privately owned. Regardless of the source of support, the foodservices in these institutions are unique and complex, requiring a staff of well-qualified dietitians. The main objective of this service is to improve the health of the patient and to restore him to normal activity and state of well-being. A secondary objective is to provide a foodservice for the professional and clerical staffs and other employees in all departments of the hospital in order to maintain happy, well-nourished personnel. Also, the many guests and visitors to patients rightfully expect to find some provision for their meals within the hospital complex.

Food for all groups generally is prepared in a central kitchen. Staff and employees obtain their meals in a pay cafeteria, patronized also by visitors and guests. Free meals are seldom given to any group, since salaries or wages paid are adequate so that meals may be purchased on the premises if desired. Often the regular meal service is supplemented with a coffee shop or vending operation to make food available after meal-service hours.

Patients' food may be distributed by one of several different methods, depending on the physical arrangement of the building, the type of patient, space available, and costs involved (see Chapter 5).

Patient dining rooms for those who are ambulatory or in wheelchairs are found in all types of hospitals, including those for the mentally ill. The therapeutic values of social contacts at mealtime have been recognized, and provisions have been made for such patient dining in a majority of hospitals. Either self- or table service may be used.

The scope of the hospital dietitian's work as an administrator is indicated in the responsibilities listed for the dietitian in a large hospital. She supervises the preparation and service of 7000 meals daily in a 1000-bed hospital; directs a staff of 250, including 20 assistant dietitians, who are administrative assistants, teachers of student nurses, medical students, and patients, or are engaged in dietary calculations for patients. Another dietitian in a small hospital may supervise the preparation and service of 450 meals per day in a 100-bed hospital, direct the work of 10 employees in the foodservice, plan and purchase all food, and personally direct its preparation. She also bears the responsibility of dietary calculations and accounts, and teaches classes in nutrition to the nurses. In addition, the housekeeping responsibilities of the hospital may largely devolve on the dietitian. Her administrative responsibilities are far less in scope than those of the dietitian in the large hospital, but the work in which she must participate directly is much greater and the detail that she must carry is correspondingly increased. Furthermore, she is expected to share in community enterprises that make many additional demands on her time. Regardless of the size of the hospital, the dietitian seeks to direct a foodservice that will meet the varied needs of the patients and personnel whom she serves.

NURSING HOMES AND OTHER
HEALTH CARE CENTERS

The growth of nursing homes nationwide has been phenomenal in the past 40 years as greater attention turned toward the concern for adequate health care of the citizenry. The increased demand for nursing home services is due in great part to population growth, longer life-span, and higher incidence of chronic diseases, especially in the elderly. The advance in medical science and technology for treatment of physical and mental disorders, urban living with condensed family housing units, increased incomes, and health insurance benefits are also contributing factors. It is said that nursing home beds now outnumber general and surgical hospital beds 1.2 million to 1.0 million, with the trend continuing upward.

The term "nursing home" is a broad, umbrella term used to describe several types of long term health care facilities. As a generic term "nursing home" is sometimes applied to extended care facilities, convalescent hospitals/homes, skilled nursing care homes and intermediate nursing care facilities. [11]

[11] Long Term Care Facts, *American Health Care Association (formerly American Nursing Home Association), Washington, D.C., p. 1, 1975.*

The modern nursing home era and the development of the nursing home as a distinct type of health care institution began in 1935 when federal funds to pay for nursing home care for the elderly were made available to the states by the passage of the Social Security Act.

At first the states were restricted from paying for care of patients in public facilities; thus, a number of small private nursing-boarding homes were opened and operated for profit, too often by poorly qualified administrators and personnel.

In 1951 the Kerr-Mills bill made available federal matching funds for nursing home care to states establishing satisfactory licensing and inspection programs. However, limited local welfare budgets and the laxity in enforcement of standards complicated the problem of providing proper medical attention and care to many patients.

An amendment to the Hill-Burton program in 1954 provided financial aid for the construction of facilities for skilled nursing care to meet specified requirements. Many large nursing homes were built, and older small ones were forced to close or modernize and expand in order to meet the standards of the new program.

Medicare and Medicaid legislation (1965) and amendments (1967) established minimum standards for, the inspection of, and staff requirements for nursing homes to permit use of those funds by their patients.

General guidelines for all nursing homes include licensure, meet standards of specific government programs to be certified by them, and one facility may provide one or more levels of care such as nursing care and related medical services, personal care, and residential care.

Nursing homes provide different categories of nursing care and are classified as:

> *Skilled Nursing Facilities (SNF)*—These provide continuous nursing service on a 24-hour basis for convalescent patients. (The phased-out term "extended care facility" is now included in this category.) Registered nurses, licensed practical nurses and nurse's aides and orderlies provide services prescribed by the patient's physician. Emphasis is on nursing care with rehabilitative therapy, physical therapy, occupational therapy and other medical services as needed. The skilled nursing facility is recognized as eligible for both the Medicare and Medicaid pro-

grams, if the facility applies and meets certain conditions of participation.

Intermediate Care Facilities (ICF)—These provide basic medical, nursing and social services in addition to room and board for persons not capable of fully independent living. This category of nursing care is not as intensive as that provided by skilled nursing facilities. This type of facility is recognized for participation in the Medicaid program only.

Other Facilities—Skilled nursing facilities and intermediate care facilities refer to homes certified under specific government programs. Many nursing homes, however, do not participate in these programs. Therefore, they are not classified as such, even though they may provide the same quality of care and categories of services. A facility may provide more than one category of care. The patients may be any age. Many facilities specialize in child care or care of the mentally ill or mentally retarded.[12]

Health care of ill, handicapped, and needy persons in the United States at home and in hospitals or other health care facilities holds unprecedented attention by legislative groups, administrators, patients, and the general public. Constant study of new and pending health-related legislation specifying provision for standard requirements and their implementation by the coordinating Health Systems Agencies is a "must" for all concerned. An example is the Utilization Review Regulations (effective February 1, 1975) for skilled nursing home facilities participating in the Medicare and Medicaid programs. The overall objectives of this regulation are maintenance of high-quality patient care and assurance of appropriate and efficient utilization of facility services.

The quality and amount of appropriate food and supervision of the foodservice are important factors to the successful operation and effectiveness of any nursing home. Small units may employ part-time or consultant dietitians with satisfactory results; otherwise a full-time qualified dietitian is needed to see that this part of nursing home patient care is adequately provided and administered.

[12] Long Term Care Facts, *American Health Care Association (formerly American Nursing Home Association), Washington, D.C., p. 2, 1975.*

meals free of charge or below cost to their employees. This philosophy of subsidizing the meal service has continued in most industrial units and represents a real addition in savings to the employees. The importance of industrial feeding was not fully realized, however, until the period of World War II, when manufacturing plants found that nutritious well-balanced meals contributed much to the health, efficiency, and satisfaction of the employees.

The workers, a majority of whom were women, demanded facilities for obtaining a hot meal while at work. Often new plants were located away from the centers of cities and towns with no restaurants nearby and, with the keen competition for employees, management realized the necessity for providing meal service facilities. Many plants have continued this service as an indispensable part of their operations, either under plant management or on a concessionaire basis. In either case competent trained leadership is necessary to attain the goals of the organization. Dietitians and food managers trained in mass production of quality food products and skilled in management and cost control are an asset to successful operation of these services.

SPACE FEEDING

Man's urge to explore the unknown outer space has created many heretofore undreamed-of problems in the foodservice field. Since April 1957, when seven men were selected to become astronauts for the United States, research has gone forward to determine the type, variety, and form of food best suited to the needs of the space traveler. The most basic concern of the nutritionist and dietitian is the problem of providing suitable, acceptable, and nutritionally adequate meals for man to live effectively for extended periods of time in the weightless environment encountered in outer space. Finkelstein [14] stated:

With the actual orbiting of man in space, knowledge of how to cope with physiologic effects of weightlessness becomes even more urgent. . . . Unfortunately weightlessness for appreciable periods of time has no parallel in human experience on earth. Knowledge of its effect during prolonged periods will come only with actual experience.

Research has continued to try to provide a wider variety in type and form of food for each space trip that would be most convenient

[14] *Beatrice Finkelstein, "Progress in Space Feeding Research,"* Journal of the American Dietetic Association, *40, 528–529 (1962).*

for consumption in weightlessness. Studies are made of the acceptability of the food by the astronauts and the physiological effects on them in relation to the nutrients supplied, as well as the effectiveness of their performance under the controlled environment.

Packaging and storage of foods for space travel must provide protection against conditions such as heat, radiation, moisture pickup, and oxidation. Packages should be of convenient size, light in weight, and edible, yet permit the addition of water for reconstitution. The restrictions imposed by the limitations of space also call for research in equipment designs suitable for storage, preparation, and serving of the food. Weight and available fuel or power are further restrictions.

Obviously, this is an area for future development. Much more research on food and nutrition for the space traveler needs to be accomplished. The challenges are many.

COMMERCIAL FOODSERVICES

Historically the evolution of public eating places was stimulated by the desire for travel, both for spiritual enrichment and commercial gain. It is said that the custom of pilgrimages played no small part in the evolution of French and English inns. The slow rate of transportation often limited the day's trip to 10 miles and necessitated provision for rest and refreshment at frequent intervals. Similarly, the merchant, making the rounds of the villages with his wares, took what he found in primitive institutions to maintain his well-being during his absence from home. The provision for the needs of travelers through inns and taverns was perhaps the earliest but far from the best organized and administered of the forerunners of our present foodservices. The unsanitary conditions under which the food was prepared and served, the monotony of the menus, the meager attempts at serving, and the ignorance of the innkeeper and his slatternly help have been kept vivid by descriptions in the early literature and by the survival of such inns into more recent times.

Early American stagecoach travel, tedious at best, necessitated the establishment of inns where the traveler could rest and eat. These inns, at first, were much like those in England, but there was a leaven of democracy at work that led British visitors to protest that service was lacking and that pleasing deference to guests was not to be expected in a democracy. Perhaps this condition was because in rural sections of the United States the work of the inn was carried on largely as a family enterprise, regarded as wholly worthy by the members. The food served was that made ready for the family group and was plain, ample, and hearty rather than sophisticated and elegant.

It was about this time that the evolution of the restaurant began as a public eating place, separate and apart from provisions for sleeping. The beginning of this concept has been traced to the cook shops of France, which were licensed to prepare *ragoûts* or stews, to be eaten on the premises or taken to inns or homes for consumption. The shops had *écriteur* or menus pasted on the wall or by the door to whet the interest of the passerby. The story goes that one Boulanger, a bouillon maker, decided to add to his list of soups a meat dish with a sauce, contending that this was neither a *ragoût* nor a stew and therefore was no violation of the rights of the *traiteurs*. In the lawsuit that followed, the French lawmakers sustained his point, and his new business was legalized as a restaurant. The word restaurant comes from the French verb, *restauer,* which means "to repair." It is said that the earliest restaurant had this Latin inscription over its doorway: *Venite ad me qui stomacho laboratis et ego restaurabo vos*—Come to me all whose stomachs cry out in anguish, and I shall restore you!

The general appreciation and approval of the French that followed the Revolutionary War doubtless contributed to a ready acceptance by the American public of these new foodservices. This same influence, manifested in the urban centers during the early decades of the nineteenth century, led to highly complicated and elaborate meals such as are indicated by the following account of the planning of a "small, genteel dinner."

"No, indeed, Ma'am! A Bouilli at the foot of the table is indispensable, no dinner without it." "And at the head?" "After the soup, Ma'am, fish, Boiled fish, and after the fish, canvasbacks, the Bouilli to be removed, and Pheasants." "Stop, stop, Henry," cried I, "not so many removes if you please." "Why, ma'am, you said your company was to be a dozen, and I am only telling you what is absolutely necessary. Yesterday at Mr. Woodbury's there was only 18 in company and there were 30 dishes of meat." "But, Henry, I am not a Secretary's lady. I want a small, genteel dinner." "Indeed, ma'am, that is all I am telling you, for side dishes you will have a very small ham, a small turkey, on each side of them partridges, mutton chops, or sweet breads, a macaroni pie, and oyster pie. . . ." "That will do, that will do, Henry. Now for vegetables." "Well, ma'am, stew'd celery, spinach, salsify, cauliflower." "Indeed? Henry, you must substitute potatoes, beets, etc." "Why, ma'am, they will not be genteel, but to be sure if you say so, it must be so. Mrs. Forsyth, the other day, would have a plum-pudding, she will keep to old fashions." "What, Henry, plum-pudding out of fashion?"

"La, yes, ma'am, all kinds of puddings and pies." "Why, what then must I have at the head and foot of the table?" "Forms of ice cream at the head, and a pyramid of anything, grapes, oranges, or anything handsome at the foot." "And the other dishes?" "Jellies, custards, blanc-mange, cakes, sweet-meats, and sugar-plums." "No nuts, raisins, figs, etc., etc.?" "Oh, no, no, ma'am, they are quite vulgar." [15]

The elaborate meals served in most urban hotels were not expected to pay for the outlay involved in their preparation. The bar and the lodgings were counted on to make up the deficit. The introduction of the European plan, which separated the charges for room and board, and later the introduction of the a la carte service of food, were steps toward a rational foodservice in hotels. Through these measures much of the waste that characterized the hotel table was abolished, and the possibility that the foodservice of hotels and inns might be self-supporting became evident. This encouraged the establishment of foodservices separate and distinct from lodging facilities. A further step in simplification came with the introduction of the cafeteria, in which one not only selects what he desires but also serves himself, carries the food-laden tray to the table, and arranges the service there to his liking. The cafeteria, said to have arisen from the need to serve many people at a busy time and sometimes cited as a direct result of the Gold Rush of the Forty-Niners, is regarded as an American innovation. Practically, cafeterias have been important institutions for only the past 50 years. Their popularity in California led to their extension over the country, until today they represent an important phase of the foodservice industry.

Commercial foodservices at the present time range from the most formal a la carte or table d'hôte service used in exclusive restaurants and hotel dining rooms to that available at drive-ins, pizzerias, or soda fountains. Specialty restaurants featuring items such as seafoods, chicken, or prime ribs of beef, or those with foreign food and atmosphere have become more and more popular in recent times. Excellent facilities such as attractive dining rooms, coffee shops, and fast service standup counters have been included in airport terminal buildings since air travel has become so universally accepted. Typical is the ultramodernistic airport restaurant pictured in Fig. 1.5. Rising 70 feet above ground, it affords the 300 diners a 360° view of airport activity. It is international in menu and decor, and the

[15] *Margaret Bayard Smith*, The First Forty Years of Washington Society, *Gaillard Hunt, Scribner's, New York, pp. 359–360, 1906.*

FIGURE 1.5   Host International Gourmet Restaurant, Theme Building, Los Angeles International Airport. Courtesy, Interstate Hosts, Inc., Los Angeles.

82 employees speak a total of 20 different languages to serve well the many foreign travelers and American tourists who patronize the restaurant. The lower section, surrounded by a decorative, concrete, grille screen, houses offices, an employees' cafeteria, and the central commissary that provides food for the gourmet restaurant above, plus 7 other foodservice operations located within the airport complex.

The restaurant industry is defined in its broadest sense to mean all establishments where food is consumed, for a consideration, away from home. Some restaurants are small and simple, catering to a coffee and doughnut trade; others are exclusive, gracious, and charming in setting, modern and adequate in equipment, and formal in service. Many have expanded their services to include sales of bakery products, complete "take-home meals," or other specialty items of the restaurant such as salad dressings, sauces, or jams and jellies.

One trend in the commercial field has been toward speedy types of operations, as evidenced by the rapid growth of the vending business and the "do-it-yourself" types of cafeterias, with no-charge relish and condiment stations in the dining room, to expedite service in the regular serving area. These types of foodservices have developed especially in the wake of freeways and toll systems for fast cross-country travel, and for informal family and youth dining.

SUMMARY

Every citizen of the United States will have some direct personal contact with foodservice in institutions during his lifetime. Through the payment of taxes he contributes to the support of federal, state, county, and municipal foodservices. Examples of these include, as federal projects, feeding units in the military services, veterans' hospitals, and penal institutions; for the state, the foodservices in state hospitals and correctional institutions; for the county, the foodservices in homes for the aged; and for the municipal government, community enterprises such as schools and mess halls for transient relief. In addition, the same citizen may have some of his meals at an industrial food unit and may also utilize commercial operations such as restaurants and hotel and motel dining rooms. He may have membership in a club that serves food or have a son or daughter in college where residence in halls with supervised dining facilities is the stipulated manner of living; at some time he may require the services of a hospital or nursing home; he may seek the services of a caterer for some special function like a wedding reception; and, later in life, he may choose to live in a retirement home and so enjoy another, newer type of foodservice experience. Not every person may need all of these, but each person demands certain experiences for which he will pay accordingly.

The present status of institution foodservices is impressive. The large patronage given the commercial food enterprises exceeds greatly any casual estimate. Statistics on the number of persons in the military services, in hospitals, and in federal, state, or municipal institutions show the enormous scope of necessary foodservices. Then there are also the thousands of students whose nutrition the schools, colleges, and universities accept as a major responsibility. Industry, too, recognizes the importance of feeding its millions.

The professional opportunities arising in this field are unique. College curricula that include specific and definite education for these various services have proved to be necessary for proficiency in this area. Thus equipped, the graduate with further experience should be capable of directing an extensive, highly organized feeding unit in some type of foodservice system, or be prepared to go into one of the many avenues of related nutrition education.

In this cursory survey of the foodservices in various types of institutions, consideration has been given to the points of likeness and of difference among them. It might be well to emphasize that in an institution of any type the foodservice has for its goal *the maintenance of acceptable standards of food preparation that will result in a product of high quality, served in the best condition and manner possible.*

The *purpose* of the organization and administration of the foodservice is not merely to supply food but, instead, *to supply the best possible food, palatable, well-prepared under acceptable standards of sanitation, and pleasingly served at the allotted cost.* Among the essentials in the attainment of this goal are *knowledge of meal planning, food selection, preparation and service, coherent thinking, clear-cut organization, successful personnel direction, including delegation and supervision, sanitation, an adequate system of cost control, and wise planning of the physical layout with selection of proper equipment.* Since these phases of management are the responsibility of the foodservice director, either directly or indirectly, they will be given detailed consideration in the following chapters.

Complete coverage of subject matter relating to foodservice in institutions is impossible in one volume. Therefore, references for supplementary reading are listed at the end of each chapter. Also, it is expected that readers will keep themselves informed of new developments in this area through current issues of professional and technical journals and trade magazines, new books, and educational literature from food production and food equipment manufacturing companies, research laboratories, and commercial organizations. Particularly helpful to the student and the foodservice director and staff are publications such as *Administrative Management, Cornell Hotel and Restaurant Quarterly, Food Service, Food Technology, Hospitals, Institutions/Volume Feeding Management, Journal of the American Dietetic Association, Management Review, Modern Hospital, Personnel, Personnel Journal, Restaurant Business, School Foodservice Journal, Supervisory Management,* and *Training and Development Journal.*

SELECTED REFERENCES

Abram, A., *English Life and Manners in the Later Middle Ages,* George Routledge, London, 1912.

A Look at Business in 1990, A summary of the White House Conference on the Industrial World Ahead. U.S. Government Printing Office, Washington, D.C. 1972.

The American Heritage Cookbook and Illustrated History of American Eating and Drinking, American Heritage, Marion, Ohio, 1964.

Barber, Mary I., *History of The American Dietetic Association,* J. B. Lippincott, Philadelphia, 1959.

Byran, Mary deGarmo, *The School Cafeteria,* Second Edition, F. S. Crofts, New York, 1946.

Cronan, Marion, *The School Lunch,* Charles A. Bennett, Peoria, Illinois, 1962.

Cummings, Richard Osborn, *The American and His Food,* University of Chicago Press, Chicago, 1940.

Dahl, J. O., *Restaurant Management,* Fourth Revised Edition, Harper and Brothers, New York, 1944.

Furnas, Clifford Cook, *Man, Food and Destiny,* Reynal and Hitchcock, New York, 1937.

Hunt, Gaillard, editor, *The First Forty Years of Washington Society,* Scribner's, New York, 1906.

Lathrop, Elsie, *Early American Inns and Taverns,* Tudor, New York, 1935.

Long Term Care Facts, American Health Care Association, Washington, D.C., 1975.

Mead, William Edward, *The English Medieval Feast,* Houghton Mifflin, Boston, 1931.

Montague, Prosper, *Larousse Gastronomique,* Crown, New York, 1961.

Paddleford, Clementine, *How America Eats,* Scribner's, New York, 1960.

The Relation of Nutrition to Health, Agriculture, and Economic Policy, Final Report of Mixed Committee, League of Nations, 1937.

Report of the Commission on the Renovation of the Executive Mansion, complied under the direction of the Commission by Edwin Bateman Morris, U.S. Government Printing Office, Washington, D.C., 1952.

Soyer, Alexis, *The Gastronomic Regenerator,* Simpkins Marshal, London, 1852.

Stokes, John W., *Food Service in Industry and Institutions,* Wm. C. Brown, Dubuque, Iowa, 1960.

Strachey, Lytton, *Eminent Victorians,* G. P. Putnam's Sons, New York, 1918.

Watson, Betty, *Cooks, Gluttons and Gourmets,* Doubleday, Garden City, New York, 1962.

The White House, An Historic Guide, White House Historic Association, Washington, D.C., 1962.

Williamson, Jefferson, *The American Hotel,* Knopf, New York, 1930.

Wright, Thomas, *Homes of Other Days,* Trübner, London, 1871.

2.
MEAL PLANNING AND FOOD STANDARDS

The American public consumes approximately one-fourth to one-third of all its meals outside the home in establishments that provide a variety of meal services. The task of planning meals for these institutions that provide so large a share of the total food consumed is the responsibility of management. It is the "heart" of the entire establishment on which all activity is centered. The menu determines the foods to be purchased, the equipment and personnel needed, the work schedules, and the supervision required, and it is the basis for precosting food to be served. Success or failure of a foodservice often can be traced to the menu. The well-planned menu reflects careful thought and represents three points of view: *the customer or guest* who desires and expects variety and ample amounts of food to satisfy his appetite and bring him pleasure; *the employees* on whom falls the burden of work in translating the written word into attractive, palatable, and nourishing food; and the *mangagement* who derives satisfaction from work well done in the tangible form of profits and a satisfied, happy clientele.

The menu planner must be cognizant of all the problems common in home meal planning plus numerous others arising in situations uniquely characteristic of diverse types of institutions. This person must have a wide knowledge of foods, their nutritive value, availability, cost, and the many different methods and procedures for preparing and serving them. The ability to interpret the written meal plan to those who will prepare and serve the food also is basic to the achievement of excellence.

CONSIDERATIONS BASIC TO GOOD PLANNING

Before actually writing the menus, certain factors basic to the situation must be known in order to ensure a successful meal plan. They include a knowledge of the people to be served: their nutritional needs as based on age, sex, and occupation; the food habits of the group as determined by their racial, regional, and religious custom; and the number of people to be served. The menu planner should be aware of the conditions under which food is to be prepared and served, such as the arrangement of the kitchen and serving areas, and the equipment available; the personnel, their schedules, abilities, and skills; the amount of money provided in the budget; and the style of service.

An appreciation of outside influences on meal planning such as the season of the year, the climate, and the availability of foods also is essential. A knowledge of pleasing combinations based on variety in texture, color, flavor, form or shape, consistency, temperature, satiety value, and the method of preparation is necessary to yield quality foods.

KNOWLEDGE OF PEOPLE TO BE SERVED

Nutritional Needs. The nutritional requirements of the members of the group to be served are an important consideration in meal planning. This is a major concern, especially in institutions that provide all meals for the group such as in residence halls, hospitals, and homes for adults and children. Table 2.1 lists the recommended daily dietary allowances for different age and sex groups.

A simple guide for planning meals to meet the daily nutritional needs of normal groups has been prepared by the Institute of Home Economics.[1] This guide classifies food into four categories with suggested amounts of specific items within each group. These are: (1) Milk Group—some milk for everyone: children, 3 to 4 cups; teen-

[1] Food for Fitness—A Daily Guide, *Leaflet No 424, U.S. Department of Agriculture, U.S. Government Printing Office, Washington, D.C., 20250, revised 1971.*

agers, 4 or more cups; adults, 2 or more cups; (2) Meat Group—2 or more servings: beef, veal, pork, lamb, poultry, fish, eggs, or alternates of dried beans, dry peas, or nuts; (3) Vegetables and Fruit Group—4 or more servings to include a citrus fruit or vegetable important for vitamin C, a dark green or deep yellow vegetable at least every other day, other fruits and vegetables including potatoes; (4) Bread and Cereal Group—4 or more servings: use whole grain, enriched, or restored products. Each group contributes nutrients to provide an adequate diet. The pattern of choices suggested is based on what is known about individuals' needs for protein, vitamins, minerals, and other nutrients.

To complete the meals and to supply adequate calories and acceptable variety, other foods not listed will need to be used. These include butter or fortified margarine, other fats and oils, and sugars and sweets. Checking the menus to make certain that each food group is represented by the number of servings suggested for each day is a relatively simple procedure. Choices from the four groups allow for ample variety from day to day and should safeguard nutritional quality of meals offered.

Planning meals for groups of *children* involves consideration of their nutritional needs and much more. Eating together as a group is for them a significant social and educational experience. It is important that they have the food served attractively and that the mealtime be pleasant and free from undue stress and resentment. Plain, well-cooked food, prepared for easy mastication, free from strong flavors and odors, and well seasoned is usually more acceptable to them than highly seasoned or not readily identifiable foods. Foods that are easily eaten, such as meat cut into pieces before cooking, or that can be cut easily with a fork, shredded lettuce instead of a wedge, and the use of "finger foods," such as raw vegetable strips or sectioned raw fruits will encourage young children to eat the foods offered. Interesting variety in color, flavor, and texture should help the child to extend his list of acceptable foods and free him from taboos against the unknown.

A nutritional pattern for the Type A school foodservice menu is planned to provide approximately one-third of the daily dietary allowances recommended by the National Research Council for children 10 to 12 years of age. This pattern includes 2 ounces edible portion of lean meat, poultry, or fish, *or* 2 ounces of cheese, *or* 1 egg, *or* 1/2 cup of cooked dry beans or dry peas, *or* 4 tablespoons of peanut butter, or an equivalent quantity of any combination of the above listed foods; 3/4 cup serving of 2 or more vegetables or fruits,

TABLE 2.1 RECOMMENDED DAILY DIETARY ALLOWANCES,[a] NATIONAL RESEARCH COUNCIL

Designed for the maintenance of good nutrition of

	Age	Weight		Height		Energy	Protein	Fat-Soluble Vitamins			
								Vita-min A Activity		Vita-min D	Vita-min E Activity [e]
	(yr)	(kg)	(lb)	(cm)	(in)	(kcal) [b]	(g)	(RE) [c]	(IU)	(IU)	(IU)
Infants	0.0–0.5	6	14	60	24	kg × 117	kg × 2.2	420 [d]	1400	400	4
	0.5–1.0	9	20	71	28	kg × 108	kg × 2.0	400	2000	400	5
Children	1–3	13	28	86	34	1300	23	400	2000	400	7
	4–6	20	44	110	44	1800	30	500	2500	400	9
	7–10	30	66	135	54	2400	36	700	3300	400	10
Males	11–14	44	97	158	63	2800	44	1000	5000	400	12
	15–18	61	134	172	69	3000	54	1000	5000	400	15
	19–22	67	147	172	69	3000	54	1000	5000	400	15
	23–50	70	154	172	69	2700	56	1000	5000		15
	51+	70	154	172	69	2400	56	1000	5000		15
Females	11–14	44	97	155	62	2400	44	800	4000	400	12
	15–18	54	119	162	65	2100	48	800	4000	400	12
	19–22	58	128	162	65	2100	46	800	4000	400	12
	23–50	58	128	162	65	2000	46	800	4000		12
	51+	58	128	162	65	1800	46	800	4000		12
Pregnant						+300	+30	1000	5000	400	15
Lactating						+500	+20	1200	6000	400	15

Source. Recommended Dietary Allowances, *Eighth Edition*, National Academy of Sciences, Washington, D.C., 1974.

[a] The allowances are intended to provide for individual variations among most normal persons as they live in the United States under usual environmental stresses. Diets should be based on a variety of common foods in order to provide other nutrients for which human requirements have been less well defined. See text for more detailed discussion of allowances and of nutrients not tabulated. See Table I (p. 6) for weights and heights by individual year of age.

[b] Kilojoules (kJ) = 4.2 × kcal.

[c] Retinol equivalents.

[d] Assumed to be all as retinol in milk during the first six months of life. All subsequent intakes are assumed to be half as retinol and half as β-carotene when calculated from international units. As retinol equivalents, three fourths are as retinol and one fourth as β-carotene.

FOOD AND NUTRITION BOARD. NATIONAL ACADEMY OF SCIENCES WASHINGTON, D.C. 1974

practically all healthy people in the U.S.A.

Water-Soluble Vitamins							Minerals					
Ascor-bic Acid (mg)	Fola-cin [f] (µg)	Nia-cin [g] (mg)	Ribo-flavin (mg)	Thia-min (mg)	Vita-min B_6 (mg)	Vita-min B_{12} (µg)	Cal-cium (mg)	Phos-phorus (mg)	Io-dine (µg)	Iron (mg)	Mag-nesium (mg)	Zinc (mg)
35	50	5	0.4	0.3	0.3	0.3	360	240	35	10	60	3
35	50	8	0.6	0.5	0.4	0.3	540	400	45	15	70	5
40	100	9	0.8	0.7	0.6	1.0	800	800	60	15	150	10
40	200	12	1.1	0.9	0.9	1.5	800	800	80	10	200	10
40	300	16	1.2	1.2	1.2	2.0	800	800	110	10	250	10
45	400	18	1.5	1.4	1.6	3.0	1200	1200	130	18	350	15
45	400	20	1.8	1.5	2.0	3.0	1200	1200	150	18	400	15
45	400	20	1.8	1.5	2.0	3.0	800	800	140	10	350	15
45	400	18	1.6	1.4	2.0	3.0	800	800	130	10	350	15
45	400	16	1.5	1.2	2.0	3.0	800	800	110	10	350	15
45	400	16	1.3	1.2	1.6	3.0	1200	1200	115	18	300	15
45	400	14	1.4	1.1	2.0	3.0	1200	1200	115	18	300	15
45	400	14	1.4	1.1	2.0	3.0	800	800	100	18	300	15
45	400	13	1.2	1.0	2.0	3.0	800	800	100	18	300	15
45	400	12	1.1	1.0	2.0	3.0	800	800	80	10	300	15
60	800	+2	+0.3	+0.3	2.5	4.0	1200	1200	125	18+[h]	450	20
80	600	+4	+0.5	+0.3	2.5	4.0	1200	1200	150	18	450	25

[e] *Total vitamin E activity, estimated to be 80 percent as α-tocopherol and 20 percent other tocopherols. See text for variation in allowances.*

[f] *The folacin allowances refer to dietary sources as determined by* Lactobacillus casei *assay. Pure forms of folacin may be effective in doses less than one fourth of the recommended dietary allowance.*

[g] *Although allowances are expressed as niacin, it is recognized that on the average 1 mg of niacin is derived from each 60 mg of dietary tryptophan.*

[h] *This increased requirement cannot be met by ordinary diets; therefore, the use of supplemental iron is recommended.*

or both; 1 serving of whole-grain or enriched bread; 2 teaspoons of butter or fortified margarine; and 1/2 pint of fluid whole milk as a beverage. Schools participating in the National School Foodservice Program under the authority of the National School Lunch Act of June 1946, are playing a major role in developing good food habits among our nation's children and helping to build a strong, healthy population.

The USDA realized, however, that consumption of food classified into four basic groups (p. 36), which is followed in the Type A meal pattern, does not necessarily insure consumption of all required nutrients. Therefore, in 1972, the USDA sponsored a study [2] to examine alternatives to the Type A meal planning. Results were a new technique known as nutrient standard menu planning. "With this method, menu planners no longer adhere to the four groups in their menu selections. Rather, menus are planned for their nutritional content, based on the Recommended Dietary Allowances of the Food and Nutrition Board of the National Research Council."

Two methods using this technique have been developed and are used with success in some schools throughout the country. One method is visual and uses an abacus-like device for an individual to "total up" the amounts of nutrients in each menu. To use this method, nutrient values of recipes for computerization must be obtained and shown on the recipe in terms of 11 nutrients—protein, calcium, phosphorus, iron, vitamin A, vitamin C, riboflavin, thiamin, niacin, calories, and fat. Computer data are designated in "bead units," each bead representing about 6 percent of the USDA nutrient standard requirement for each meal—or about 2 percent of the RDA.

The abacus device has 12 rows of 15 to 17 beads, each representing a part of the daily requirements. In addition to the 11 rows representing nutrients, a twelfth row is adding for cost calculations.

The person who is planning menus selects a desirable combination of foods to make up the meal, and then calculates on the abacus the amounts of various nutrients contained in each item. If the combination of foods is too low or too high in a particular nutrient, another food with the appropriate amount can be substituted. A handbook with a printed list of nutrients in each recipe is available to the planner.

A second method utilizing the nutrient standard menu planning

[2] *"Nutrient Standards Compete with Type A,"* School Foodservice Journal, *27, 47 (May 1973). Copyright © American School Food Service Association (1973).*

technique is by computer instead of "by hand." This method relies on computerized menus that group together recipes based on required nutrients. With these groupings, the computer can select from among several choices to plan a menu within the constraints established by the USDA for nutritional values.

Although it is likely that the Type A meal will continue to be used as a guide in planning school foodservice menus, no doubt this alternative method will gain acceptance as menu planners learn more about it and how it is applied. Nutrient standard planning appears to offer greater flexibility, since any food that meets nutrient standards is acceptable. For example, traditional whole milk could be substituted with some other beverage if it meets the nutrient standard. Also:

. . . with this method many times a menu planner will not meet the RDA for each nutrient every day. However, a standard set forth by the Food and Nutrition Service division of USDA states that all nutrients, except calories, may be met on a weekly instead of on a daily basis. Therefore, if a meal is deficient in or has an excess of a particular nutrient, the menu planner simply compensates for this later in the week.[3]

Older persons are receiving increased and deserved attention to their special nutritional needs. Many are living in retirement residences or extended care facilities where regular meal service is a part of the living cost. Individual consideration for the likes and requirements of each person in this age group must be given, because:

Food habits are closely associated with the individual's sense of security, and any modification, particularly as he grows older, will require strong motivation.[4]

The same nutritional principles used in meal planning for earlier periods of life apply to later periods. Some metabolic processes are slowed down, however, and the amount of activity of older persons

[3] *"Nutrient Standards Compete with Type A."* School Foodservice Journal, 27, 50 (May 1973). Copyright © American School Food Service Association (1973).
[4] Mary M. Hill, *"Creating Good Food Habits—Start Young, Never Quit."* Food for Us All, Yearbook of Agriculture 1969, p. 265, U.S. Government Printing Office, Washington, D.C. 20402.

usually is reduced, thus decreasing their caloric needs. Such reduction in calories places an arbitrary limit on sugar- and fat-rich foods in their meals. Nevertheless, the diet must be varied and contain protein-rich foods with emphasis on protective foods, rich in vitamins and minerals.

Mechanical impairments, such as palsied hands or the loss of teeth, may necessitate the use of easily handled and masticated foods. Frequent inclusion of semisolid, chopped, grated, and ground foods in the menu will be appreciated by those experiencing these difficulties.

Nutrition programs for the elderly reflect the nation's concern for the well-being of the older segment of our population who are isolated or alone. Community meals, funded by the Administration on Aging, U.S. Department of Health, Education and Welfare, have been initiated in every section of the United States in recent years. Elderly persons do not always take the time or have the energy to prepare meals adequate to maintain their nutritional health. Therefore, nutritious meals served to older persons in groups can contribute to their better health and nutrition. The stimulation of being with others and eating a well-balanced meal 5 days a week has proved a boon to this age group in meeting their nutritional needs.

The differences in nutritional requirements based on *sex* are less significant than those of age. Men and women may be served the same kinds of foods, although the acceptability of any given item may not be the same nor are their caloric needs comparable. Women may prefer lighter foods with fewer calories, less pungent and, perhaps, less highly spiced. Also, women appreciate more the interesting combinations, the unusual foods, and the niceties of service. Men commonly like ample portions of hearty foods in their natural forms, simply prepared, and readily identifiable.

The meals served in restaurants, school and industrial lunchrooms, and hotel and motel dining rooms, among others, may constitute only a part of the daily food consumption of the individual patrons. The adequacy of the total daily diet is then the responsibility of the individual. However, such foodservice operations should so plan their meals that the patron will be able to select readily the foods necessary for his body needs. Also, sufficient variety should be offered to satisfy the desires of those preferring a relatively light lunch and those wishing a heavier meal.

Planning meals for individuals who are hospitalized for physical disorders requires special knowledge of the modification of the normal diet to meet the patients' specific needs. Such diets are planned by a qualified dietitian who ensures their nutritional adequacy and so helps to restore the patient to full health as quickly as possible. The nutritional aspects of menu planning deserve major consideration by all those responsible for the foodservice in institutions.

Food Habits. The habits of individuals and groups play a much larger part in food practices and, indirectly, in the determination of nutritional standards than is commonly recognized. It has been said that:

Probably everyone has a unique pattern of food behavior which is shared with only a few others. Individual differences may even obscure the common food habits and attitudes of a shared culture which are brought about in a group by similar physiological makeup and environment.[5]

Anthropologists point out that our food habits are instilled in us as children and that the way these habits are acquired may be studied. Even so, it is difficult always to understand why people eat what they do. A research nutritionist [6] has said that:

The most direct influence, however, is the parents, themselves—their food preferences, attitudes toward food, and their information about the nutritive value of foods.

Psychological factors play an important role in the development of habits and attitudes toward food. Pleasant or unpleasant experiences that have centered around food often affect a person's acceptance or rejection of a certain item. Traditional food served for holidays or special occasions brings a happy response to those foods. Conversely, overeating of a particular food or an argument at mealtime could well create a dislike that may last a lifetime.

Within the last 2 or 3 decades, rapid developments relating to food have come into American life and have affected our food habits to the point of being almost revolutionary. One such development is the *technological advance* in the form and kind of food available,

[5] *Miriam E. Lowenberg, E. Neige Todhunter, Eva D. Wilson, Moira Feeney, and Jane Savage,* Food and Man, *Wiley, New York, 1968, p. 97.*
[6] *Mary M. Hill, "Creating Good Food Habits—Start Young, Never Quit."* Food for Us All, *Yearbook of Agriculture 1969, p. 260, U.S. Government Printing Office, Washington, D.C. 20402.*

making thousands of new products accessible. Another development is the constantly increasing growth in scientific knowledge about the nutritional needs of individuals and their desire to select and consume the foods that will build and maintain strong and healthy bodies. The desire to achieve the marks of a properly nourished person has become another factor affecting choices of food and hence develops food habits.

The *racial, regional,* and *religious* preferences of the group to be served are additional cultural factors of significance in the planning of group menus. It is recognized that habits arising from foreign backgrounds persist within certain communities. However, with our mobile population, the assimilation of foreign born proceeds rapidly so that today there is little concentration of racial food habits in the United States.

The many students of diversified *nationalities* now attending our colleges and universities have made dietitians in this type of foodservice aware of the need to satisfy the desires of those people to whom our foods seem strange. Rice is seldom served often enough for those from the Orient, whereas a craving for more highly seasoned foods is noted among the students from the southeastern countries.

Regional food habits within the United States are distinctive and perhaps more marked than those relating to foreign habits. Hominy grits, black-eyed peas, mustard and turnip greens, kale, and sweet-potato pie might be essential items on a successful menu in a southern restaurant and fail absolutely to please the clientele of a New England village inn. The popularity of Boston baked beans and brown bread is basically regional, although it now extends beyond the section of its origin. The dietitian newly arrived in a section of the country strange to her should study its habits and cultivate an appreciation of foods popular in that area. Care is necessary to ensure that there will be no obvious effort to force the food habits of the food manager on the clientele.

Religious restrictions and taboos affect the acceptance or rejection of certain foods. The wise foodservice manager will learn all she can about food requirements of various religious groups having basic tenets regarding the use of food, in order to cater to their needs and provide an adequate, varied menu for them.

That the food habits of the American people as a whole have been changed over the last few decades is well shown by the statistics of the average annual per capita consumption of certain foods in this country. The data on this subject are presented in Fig. 2.1.

Per capita consumption:
Meat and total livestock products*

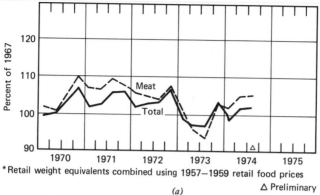

*Retail weight equivalents combined using 1957–1959 retail food prices

(a)   △ Preliminary

Per capita food consumption*

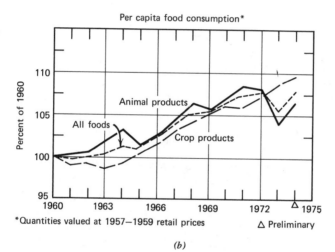

*Quantities valued at 1957–1959 retail prices   △ Preliminary

(b)

FIGURE   2.1   *Per Capita Consumption of Certain Foods reflects changing trends in eating habits. Courtesy, Economic Research Service, U.S. Department of Agriculture.*

CONDITIONS INFLUENCING PREPARATION AND SERVICE

Physical Facilities. The physical facilities including the equipment arranged in units for food storage, preparation, cooking, and service influence directly the meal planning. If the physical plant facilitates the dispatch of various activities, the employees tend to produce at nearly peak capacity. If the kitchen is too large or poorly arranged, time is lost in unproductive travel; if it is too small, the workers interfere with each other. The space should provide adequate housing for the necessary equipment and for the traffic flow, which includes the passage of workers, the movement of consumable supplies, and the transport of needed small equipment.

Diversified types of preparation of menu items will tend to utilize available equipment and not overburden any one piece. If the menu plan distributes the work load evenly for oven, top of range, and steam equipment, there is reasonable hope that the work can be accomplished smoothly and successfully. If some of the equipment is unused or expected to do double duty, inefficiency has been introduced by the menu plan. An accident hazard may be created by requiring a convergence of activity in any one area.

The present trend toward the use of many preprepared foods by institutions demands adequate equipment for the finishing processes and accessible refrigerator and freezer space. Without these, the frequency of perishable food deliveries becomes a determining factor in the planning of the menu.

The distance between the point of preparation and the point of distribution should be considered as definitely as the type of service to be offered. The time elapsing between the completion of the preparation of the food and its service is an influential if not a determining factor in its quality. Foods that will not change too markedly during their transportation must be selected if a central kitchen is remote from service areas.

Shortages of certain items of glassware, china, or silver may reflect the omission of interesting foods from the menu such as fish cocktails or parfaits.

The menu pattern should be determined prior to the selection of the equipment and its arrangement if the food manager has the opportunity to plan a new kitchen instead of taking over the management of an old one. Discussion of menu analysis to determine equipment needs is presented in Chapters 11 and 12.

Personnel. The number of workers available and their skills and abilities, as well as efficiency and productivity, affect greatly what may be achieved in the diversity of foods offered. In some situations, such as small school foodservices where the labor budget is limited, the employees chosen usually are, of necessity, those with limited skill in quantity food production. Even with on-the-job training there may not be time for them to develop the kinds of skills required of highly paid chefs in exclusive restaurants, who may be expected to create elaborate salads, pastries, or ice carvings, and to bring this ability to the job. In schools the simple, easily prepared and served foods found on the menu usually can be prepared well by the type of employee available.

In addition to the skills and abilities of the personnel, the total man-hours available and the number of employees on duty at any given time will be limiting factors in selecting foods and food combinations that can be included on the menu. Therefore the food manager is expected to know what constitutes a reasonable rate of production for each of the various activities and to be able to plan a time schedule compatible with the work to be accomplished. Or, conversely, he must be able to plan a suitable menu within the time and ability limitations of the employees.

The skillful menu planner will not overlook the limitations of the relief worker who fills in 1 or 2 days a week for the regular employees. Whereas the regular baker, for example, may make wonderful pies, the relief baker may not be so successful with them, but "loves to make gingerbread." Results sometimes can be disastrous if the planner neglects to consider the employees' days off when planning the menu. Thus the schedule of employees plays an important role in menu planning, whether it be a cycle menu or one planned week by week.

Careful planning will provide a balance of work in each production unit each day. It is easy to overwork one employee or one unit and give too little to another by the choice of menu items. Overloads resulting from the inclusion of numerous foods requiring lengthy last-minute preparation and time-consuming elaboration endanger the morale of the staff, disrupt organization, and may prove expensive in other respects. For example, a menu involving a great deal of last-minute preparation, such as one including cream of tomato soup, broiled steak, fresh asparagus with hollandaise sauce, individually arranged salads, and baked Alaska, presents difficulties all too evident to the wise manager whose personnel is limited in time or skill or both.

Planning for several days at a time makes possible an efficient interrelation of food preparation duties for the period, and thus prevents overloads that might accompany a particular menu or relieves the stress of unusually large crowds. Homecoming Day, which may bring hundreds of additional patrons to a college foodservice, or a convention in town, which may overtax the facilities of the nearby restaurant, are examples of this situation. The ability to plan for the utilization of manpower at slack times in order to produce for peak periods is an example of good management. Certain foods may be prepared during slow periods for use at some later time, if they can be stored at proper low temperatures. Some organizations have a carry-out sale of such items to supplement incomes from sales in their regular operations.

Rising labor costs and the concurrent technical developments in the food industry have greatly changed foodservice operations. Preportioned meats, peeled vegetables, mixes, and frozen foods of all kinds make food preparation a relatively simple process. Fewer workers than before are needed in most foodservices, since much of the prepreparation has been taken out of the kitchen.

Amount of Money Available. Before any meal can be planned intelligently, a knowledge of the amount of money to be spent for the food must be known. The determination of the expected income is not always an easy process, because there is no known formula applicable to every organization. The type of foodservice and its location, both as to region of the country and given area, will influence the class of patrons who eat there. The economic level of this clientele will determine to a large extent the amount of money that they will spend when dining out. The volume of business will affect the amount of the income also.

The amount of money available from food sales constitutes the potential income to be budgeted for the foodservice department. This income must give adequate revenue to cover not only the cost of the raw food used, but also the cost of labor and operating expenses. Management determines the percent of the income to be spent for each of these items. Food, usually the most costly and most variable expense, has to be subject to close control. In fact, much of the financial success of the operation depends on effective control of food cost. The person planning meals must know both raw food costs and portion cost of prepared foods in relation to the budgeted allotment. With the rapid rise in food costs over the last few years, the menu planner must be ever alert to current food prices and items available that can profitably be put on the menu.

Some foodservices, as in residence halls, homes for adults or children, and certain hospitals, operate on a fixed income and number of people to be served. The budget then is determined by multiplying the board rate by the number of residents, or from a per capita allowance multiplied by the number of patients. Menu planning is relatively simple when the food budget is predetermined and serves as a known guide. In other institutions like hotels, restaurants, and industrial units, the income varies with the volume of business. Once established, the food percentage figure serves as a budgeted figure and should be used as a basic guide to every aspect of menu planning.

Type and Style of Service. The type and style of service used in an institution will influence the food items to be included on the menu. The method of serving the food to the patron, patient, student, or guest will vary according to the kind of institution. The college residence hall with all cafeteria service will present different problems in menu planning than the one using family-style service with little if any choice of foods.

A restaurant using waiter service will have a different menu plan than a do-it-yourself vending cafeteria or a buffet service in a department store. Obviously some food will "hold up" under certain conditions better than others and therefore will be appealing and appetizing when served. This is especially important when planning for the hospital patient who requires certain foods to regain his health and who must be tempted to eat. Also, the equipment available for the service of the food is a consideration for the menu planner.

Season and Climate. The weather exerts a definite influence on both appetites and body needs of people. That more and heavier foods are needed in cold weather than in hot is a well-known fact. A menu featuring roast pork and canned spinach on a hot summer day does nothing to inspire or refresh the weary traveler, whereas a crisp colorful salad, cool in temperature and appearance, has much more appeal. Usually each meal will include at least one hot food, even in warm weather.

Consideration of the season of the year includes attention to holidays, fast days, and special functions. Menu interest can be created by featuring goods appropriate for these occasions.

A season for specific foods has been eliminated for the most part with the advent of modern methods for food processing and distribution. However, certain foods are of better quality when fresh and are less expensive when in season locally. The use of such foods can give "lift" to an otherwise dull and routine menu. The first fresh strawberries and asparagus on the local market herald the arrival of spring, as does watermelon of summer or baking squash of fall.

Availability and Relation to Market. With the season of the year goes consideration of availability of foods. The location of the institution and its accessibility to the market has a limiting influence on the menu plan. The summer camp located on a mountain lake and reached only by boat, where shipments of food are received twice a week, presents quite a different problem in menu planning than a large city institution where deliveries can be received within an hour after placement of an order.

FOOD CHARACTERISTICS AND COMBINATIONS

A knowledge of foods and interesting methods of preparing and combining them to obtain variety is essential to successful menu planning. It is easy to talk about the need to consider color, texture, flavor, aroma, shape, temperature, consistency, and methods of preparation, but more difficult to translate them into a pleasing menu.

Color on the plate, tray, or cafeteria counter gives eye appeal and helps to merchandise the food. Even a touch of color in a garnish helps to "sell" a food to the patron.

Most foods combine well in *color* with the possible exception of some reds. The orange-red of tomatoes and the purple-red of beets is an example of an unpleasant color combination. A menu of baked whitefish, mashed potatoes, buttered cauliflower, pear salad, and rice pudding, or a cafeteria dessert counter with only a selection of apple pie, baked custard, and white cake are examples of dull combinations because of lack of color. How much more colorful is the menu of baked whitefish with lemon-parsley sauce, au gratin potatoes, buttered broccoli, raw vegetable salad, and a watermelon wedge.

Texture refers to the manner of structure of foods and can best be detected by the feel of foods in the mouth. Crisp, soft, grainy, smooth, hard, and chewy are adjectives describing food texture. A variety of textures within any one meal, such as soup and crisp crackers or a raw vegetable salad and a baked custard, is more pleasing than one in which each food requires much chewing.

Consistency is the way foods adhere together, their degree of firmness, density, or viscosity. Runny, gelatinous, and firm are words describing consistency, as are thin, medium, and thick when referring to sauces. A menu including baked ham with cherry sauce, creamed potatoes, and escalloped tomatoes would be undesirable. The three items with a "runny" consistency would make for intermingling of the foods and an unappetizing-looking plate.

Flavor combinations should be a major consideration of menu planning. In addition to the basic flavors of sweet, sour, bitter, and salty, we think of strong- and mild-flavored vegetables and spicy or highly seasoned foods such as chili or curried rice. Again, a variety of flavors within the meal is more enjoyable than duplications of any one flavor. The Pennsylvania Dutch have a custom of serving "seven sweets and seven sours" at their feasts, which gives a desirable balance to their menu.

Certain foods such as turkey and cranberries, roast beef and horseradish sauce, or pork and gooseberries seem to belong together because the flavors complement each other. Care must be exercised to avoid stereotyped combinations, however, as there are many other accompaniments that can be used to make menus more exciting. Red currant jelly instead of mint with lamb is an example. Also, foods with the same basic flavors, such as tomato soup, catsup, and sliced tomato salad, should be avoided in the same meal.

The shape of foods plays a big part in eye appeal, and much interest can be created through variety of the form in which foods are presented. How monotonous always to see carrots cut into strips when a variation of circles, cubes, or shreds would give interest to the menu. The shapes of a croquette, baked potato, and mashed squash are too similar, and the appearance could be improved by the use of broccoli spears and escalloped potatoes with the croquette. Modern dicing and cutting machines provide an easy method for obtaining different forms and sizes. The smart merchandiser will utilize various shapes to give variety and stimulate customer interest in the food.

Flair and drama in foodservice can be achieved through consideration of *arrangement* of the foods as they will be served.

The menu planner must be able to visualize how the foods will look, whether on a cafeteria counter, buffet table, or individual plate. Variation in the height of food to give a "three-dimensional" picture aids in eye appeal of foods to the customer. A fluffed-up baked potato, a whole broiled tomato, crisscrossed chops, or a mound of bread dressing on top of a baked pork chop are examples of ways to achieve this.

Method of preparation is another consideration in menu planning. It is helpful to compile a list of all the ways in which a particular food can be prepared to use as a reference when planning. Two foods prepared in the same manner should not be served in the same meal. Variety may be gained by serving some items fried, broiled, baked, braised, steamed, or boiled. Foods thus cooked can be further varied if served creamed, buttered, escalloped, or by adding a variety of sauces.

The person with a wide range of food likes, a knowledge of all factors that make for quality food, considerable imagination, and a sincere interest in pleasing the clientele should become a successful menu planner.

MECHANICS OF PLANNING

All menu planning should proceed from the premise that the primary purpose of any food organization is to plan, prepare, and serve attractive, flavorful, and nourishing meals at a cost consistent with the policy of the operation. This is true whether menus are planned by an individual or by a computer; computers are used in an increasing number of foodservices with tremendous savings in time and effort. Whichever system used requires that certain decisions be made in advance and procedures established for planning the menus in an orderly fashion. The number of days to be planned at one time, the number of choices, if any, to be offered, the use of cycle menus or not, and the form for writing or printout of the menus are decisions to be made. Procedures to be followed are outlined below.

PRELIMINARY CONSIDERATIONS

1. Planning Cycle. The number of days for which menus are planned at one time is considered the *menu cycle.* Many administrative dietitians and food production managers use a 5- or 7-day week as the cycle. Others prefer an 8- or 12-day period. The advantage of 8 to 12 days is that it helps to eliminate the possibility of serving the same food item on the same day each week, as may happen on a weekly cycle. Also, it decreases the number of planning times during the year and facilitates buying food in advance. If a 7-day period is used, it is suggested that the beginning day be a midweek day instead of Sunday or Monday. Thus, if one should inadvertently "run out of menus," it would not be on a weekend, when it may be difficult to obtain foods at the last minute for a newly planned menu.

2. Cycle Menus. One popular system for the use of menus, particularly with foodservices having a frequent change of clientele, is the *cycle menu.* This is defined as a carefully planned set or sets of menus that are rotated at definite intervals. Menus are planned for 3 or 4 weeks or more, at the end of which time the same menus are repeated. Most foodservices would recognize the seasonal variations in foods and so plan 4 sets of menus, 1 each for spring, summer, autumn, and winter. Within each season, the 3-week menu would be repeated 4 times, as an example.

The type of organization has a bearing on the length of any one set of cycle menus. For example, a 3-week plan would be appropriate for a hospital, where the average patient stay is 6 to 8 days. In a university residence hall or other organization where patrons "live in" and are a "captive" clientele, a longer cycle is desirable to avoid monotony and any recognition of repetition.

Foodservice managers find that the use of cycle menus has many advantages. After the initial planning has been completed, time is freed for the planner to review and revise to meet changing needs such as holidays, vacations, change in personnel, unavailability of a food item, or the use of new ones. Repetition of the same or nearly the same menu aids in standardizing preparation procedures, giving the cooks an opportunity to become more efficient in their plan of work, coordination, and utilization of time. Also, work loads tend to become constant and fairly distributed, available equipment is used to good advantage, purchasing is simplified, and inventories are easily controlled.

The use of the cycle menu presents some disadvantages and should not be considered to be applicable in every situation. Menu repetition may become monotonous if the cycle is too short or it if presents the same food on the same day each week. If a selective menu is rotated, the choices made by the patient or guest could result in undue repetition within a short period. Cycle menu changes become necessary to take advantage of seasonal foods that come onto the market at varying times each year; otherwise the cost of this menu could become unduly high. If these disadvantages can be resolved and the menu properly developed to meet the needs of a particular foodservice organization, the cycle menu can become an effective management tool. The cycle menu is of little value unless evaluated after each use.

3. Menu Pattern. The menu pattern is the outline of food items to be included in each meal, and the extent of this choice must be decided on before menus are planned. The *set menu* with a single item in each course is a pattern that may be used in a school foodservice for the Type A lunch. The no-choice menu pattern also may be followed in hospitals and in homes for adults and children.

A *selective menu* or one with choices within each course is used in order to better please the food likes and habits of the clientele served. Hospital dietary departments use it extensively, as do most commercial foodservices. In a restaurant, the pattern for one meal could be: 2 soups, 1 cream and 1 broth; 6 entrees, 1 each of a chop or a steak, roast, seafood or fish, poultry, meat extender, and 1 other high-protein food; 2 potatoes and 5 other vegetables; 4 salads, gelatin, protein type, vegetable, fruit; and 6 desserts, 2 pies, 1 cake, a pudding, frozen dessert, and fruit. Thus it is seen that meal patterns may vary from a single set meal without choice to a more complex one offering a large selection of items. Using the established pattern, specific food items for the day are planned.

Adequate records of the number of each item chosen from a selective menu are essential. Such a popularity index is a guide for determining the percentage of diners who will select Swiss steak instead of lamb stew or baked ham. The ability to predict the portions needed with some degree of accuracy is essential to good cost control and to avoid overspending the prescribed food budget.

4. Menu Form. The recording of the menus on a form designed for that purpose and suited to the needs of the particular foodservice is recommended (see Forms 2.1 and 2.2). These forms should be large enough to record all menu items for the period for which menus are planned.

Forms for use in planning menus are designed by dividing a sheet of paper into the number of days to be planned at one time and the number of meals to be served each day. The "pattern" is often typed on the form as a ready guide. Such forms facilitate the building of menus step by step and also simplify evaluating them. Errors are easily made and should be corrected before the final typing of the menus. The forms may be printed or mimeographed and made into a pad for uniformity and orderly use.

Forms for menu printout by computer will be designed by the programmer to include information desired by the dietitian or foodservice manager.

5. Aids to Menu Planning by an Individual. The wise manager will schedule a definite time each week for menu planning and will permit no interruptions. Employees soon learn to respect this schedule and will not disturb the manager needlessly. The time set aside for menu planning should be before, not directly after, a meal. It is much easier to think of appealing food when one is hungry.

Planning well in advance of the time menus are to be used tends to ensure a minimum amount of repetition of foods and food combinations; it facilitates the purchase of supplies and provides a basis for the wise use of employees' time. In some institutions it is

SCHOOL LUNCH PROGRAM—MENU FORM

Name of School _____ Week of _____

Type A Lunch Requirements		Monday	Tuesday	Wednesday	Thursday	Friday
1/2 pt fluid whole milk—3.5% B.F.						
Protein-rich foods (edible portion as served): 2 oz cooked meat, fish, poultry *or* 2 oz cheese *or* 1 egg *or* 1/2 c (cooked measure) dried peas, beans *or* 4 T peanut butter						
Vegetables and fruits: 3/4 c or 6 oz veg. and/or fruit, raw, cooked canned, frozen. Two or more to be included in each meal Full-strength veg. or fruit juice will contribute 1/4 c of veg. and/or fruit requirement	Vitamin A foods twice a week					
	Vitamin C foods each day					
	Other foods as needed to total 3/4 c					
One slice whole grain or enriched bread; or serving of cornbread, biscuits, rolls, muffins, hot bread, made from whole grain or enriched meal or flour						
2 t butter or fortified margarine (1 lb will serve 48 lunches)						
Dessert—optional. Pastries, puddings, ice cream *Do Not* take place of above						

FORM 2.1   *Suggested form for Type A lunch menu.*

feasible to plan menus as far ahead as 8 weeks or more; in others, 3 weeks; and in still others, 1 week or less. In determining how far in advance meals should be planned, consideration is given to both the size of the institution and the multiplicity of units represented in it. For example, the dietitian in a large hospital with a dietary department including 4 to 8 service units and a large staff must plan further ahead than would be necessary in a school foodservice serving one meal a day for 5 days and staffed by a cook-manager and an as-

Week of _____

Smith Hall
_____ University

	Monday	Tuesday	Wednesday	Thursday
Breakfast Fruit	1. 2.			
Cereal	1. Assorted dry 2.	Assorted dry	Assorted dry	Assorted dry
Entree	1.			
Bread	1. Toast, buttered 2.	Toast, buttered	Toast, buttered	Toast, buttered
Beverages	1. C. T. M.	C. T. M.	C. T. M.	C. T. M.
Lunch Soup				
High Protein	1. 2.			
Vegetables	1. 2. 3.			
Breads	1. Assorted	Assorted	Assorted	Assorted
Salads	1. 2.			
Dessert				
Fruit				
Beverages	C. T. M.	C. T. M.	C. T. M.	C. T. M.
Dinner Meat	1. 2.			
Vegetables	1. 2.			
Breads	1. Assorted	Assorted	Assorted	Assorted
Salads	1. 2.			
Dessert				
Fruit				
Beverages	C. T. M.	C. T. M.	C. T. M.	C. T. M.

FORM 2.2   *Suggested menu form for a university dining hall.*

sistant. Failure to plan ahead results in unnecessary expenditure of time and money and introduces into the management haphazard methods that have no place in modern business.

A work center for menu planning, away from the telephone and other disturbances, is desirable. This center should be equipped with aids for the menu planner such as files of standardized recipes with portion size and cost; previous menu files; market quotations; lists of suggestions given by patrons and ideas obtained from dining out or from friends; lists of food items classified for easy reference; women's magazines; trade publications; and cookbooks, can all provide inspiration and new ideas.

Information on consumer preference in any foodservice can be helpful to the manager concerned with planning menus. The relative popularity of a food or food group may serve as a guide to the frequency that a given group or any one item within the group appears on the menu.

A file of previous menus with comments concerning the reactions of guests, the difficulty or ease of preparation, and the cost will help in preventing repetition and serve to indicate combinations found satisfactory and profitable. Thus equipped, the planner should find it easy to concentrate and build a successful menu.

PLANNING PROCEDURE

Menus Planned by an Individual. Provision should be made for flexibility in the meal plans. The menus for each day must be adjusted and interrelated to those of both preceding and succeeding days to use effectively the supplies on hand in the storeroom and refrigerator, and also to take advantage of the daily food market. The first of these objectives must be accomplished without lowering the standards of either preparation or palatability. The serving of leftover food in unpalatable forms may result in loss of reputation of the foodservice. The freezing of leftover foods until the same items reappear on the menu or until they can be incorporated into other dishes is now a common practice in institution foodservices.

A step-by-step procedure that has been used successfully by many people for planning menus for three meals a day involves:

1. Plan first the dinner meats or main dish items for the entire cycle. These are the most expensive items in the menu, and costs can be controlled to a great extent through careful planning at this point. Good balance

among items selected will average out the cost between high- and low-priced items throughout the period. The entree is the main item around which the remainder of the meal is planned, and the main dish must be decided before the complementary foods are selected.

If the menu pattern provides entree choices, the selection should include a choice of a roast or portion cuts of meat, chicken or other fowl, a fish item, a meat alternate, and a meat extender such as croquettes, meat loaf, or stew. In making an entree list for the day or a meal, duplication of any one of the suggested meats is to be avoided; that is, fresh pork roast, pork chops, and baked ham would not appear as choices. A similar check of the menus of the preceding and succeeding days is necessary to prevent repetition in the choices offered.

2.   Select the luncheon entree or main dish. Note the dinner meat planned for that day and avoid using the same kind (pork, beef, lamb, and poultry). Give variety in method of preparation. Here again, a cost balance can be attained by serving a less expensive item one meal of the day when a more expensive food has been planned for the other meal.

3.   Decide on the vegetables appropriate to serve with the dinner meats. Usually, if the meat is one that will have drippings or juices for gravy, a plain potato, mashed, steamed, or baked, is best in order to use the gravy available. Escalloped, creamed, or au gratin potatoes are most appropriate with meats having no gravy.

Variations in vegetables are obtained by serving them raw or cooked, peeled or unpeeled, or cut into different shapes and sizes. For example, carrots may be served raw as relishes; cut into sticks, curls, or latticed; shredded, grated, or diced in salads; or they may be cooked and served whole, quartered, sliced, diced, or julienne. They may be combined with other vegetables such as peas or celery or made into combination dishes to produce different form, color, texture, and flavor results. Other vegetables may be baked, buttered, creamed, and scalloped, or prepared with various sauces and seasonings to produce widely different effects.

4. Select the appropriate salads and accompaniments next. The planner works back and forth between the two meals to avoid repetition, to introduce texture and color contrast into the meal, and to provide interesting flavor combinations. A protein-type salad such as chicken, tuna, deviled egg, or cheese often is used as the main course of a luncheon or supper.

5. Finally, plan desserts for both lunch and dinner. They may be selected from the following main groups: fruits, hot or cold puddings, ice creams, sherbets, gelatins, cakes, pies, and cheeses. If choice is to be offered, each dessert group should be represented by one or more items, depending on known customer demand. A recent survey [7] revealed that of the people dining out, 42 percent rated apple pie as their favorite dessert, 41 percent preferred ice cream, and 37 percent named fruit desserts such as cherry cobbler, prune whip, and strawberry shortcake. Next in order came pumpkin pie, chocolate cake, cheese cake, cherry pie, lemon pie, and fresh fruits in season. On the basis of this, the menu planner should make a determined effort to include a variety of these favorites and to break the chocolate, strawberry, vanilla ice cream "rut" that is all too common in many foodservices. Many other interesting ice cream flavors as well as other frozen desserts are available to "spark" the meal and help develop the unadventurous public taste.

6. After the luncheon and dinner menus have been planned, breakfast and other meals are added. Duplication of fruits used elsewhere during the day is to be avoided in the breakfast menu.

The menu planner considers the entire day as a unit and checks vertically on the menu form for adequacy in all respects for each day, and horizontally for duplication and repetition from day to day. The use of a *checklist* aids in making certain that all factors of good menu planning have been met.

---

[7] *Gallup Survey: National Poll of Patron Preferences. Reprints from* Food Service Magazine (*now* Food Service Marketing), *1969. Box 1648, Madison, Wisconsin, 53701.*

CHECKLIST FOR MENU EVALUATION

1. Does it meet Basic 4 for nutritional adequacy?

2. Are the foods offered in season, available, and within price range?

3. What foods in each menu offer contrasts of color? texture? flavor? consistency? shape or form? type of preparation? temperature?

4. Can these foods be prepared with the personnel and equipment available?

5. Are the work loads balanced for personnel and equipment?

6. Is any one food item or flavor repeated too frequently during this menu period?

7. Are the meals made attractive with suitable garnishes and accompaniments?

8. Do the combinations make a pleasing whole, and will they be acceptable to the clientele?

Planning Menus by Computer. If the foodservice department has access to a computer, the dietitian or foodservice manager may wish to develop a computer-assisted menu planning program. By doing so, accurate menus within the constraints of budget allocations, nutritional standards, and desired food characteristics can be assured. In addition, there will be real savings in time, money, and effort in the menu planning function in the future. This electronic data processing (EDP) application may be used in any foodservice organization. Hospitals were the first to use it, however, for their nonselective regular diets and general menus. Programs have been developed for planning modified diets, also. Whatever the situation, menu planning by computer is the process of finding the optimum combination of menu items within given constraints that meet predetermined objectives for a sequence of days.

The process of gathering the information needed for a computer program may seem time-consuming. Remember, however, that any data collected for computer-planned menus is the same as that needed for planning by an individual, but in more specific detail. The more efficiently the foodservice department is organized and managed, the easier it will be to make ready the information required.

In order to utilize computer assisted menu planning, each institution must establish constraints (limitations) which satisfy its clientele and institutional objectives. Prominent among these are the menu pattern, nutrient requirements, separation ratings, dominant food characteristics, and cost.[8]

"Separation rating" means the number of days between times of serving a menu item. This time interval is often determined within the foodservice by making customer or patient food preference surveys. "Dominant food characteristics" are the outstanding color, texture, and flavor of each menu item.

To give some idea of the process required for menu planning by computer, the following outline adapted from Balintfy[9] is presented. Further details may be obtained by reading this reference.

Steps required in order to prepare data for menu planning by computer are:

1. Recipes to be used to produce menus must be standardized for total yields, cooked weight or volume, portion size and number of portions as well as ingredient amounts and preparation procedures.

2. All recipes to be used in the meal planning must be coded according to place in the meal (course, as appetizer, soup, dessert) and for what meal it would be an appropriate item. The dominant flavor, color, and texture must be given by code designations as must the number of days separation between times of serving them.

[8] *Aimee N. Moore and Byrdine H. Tuthill, editors, "Computer Assisted Food Management Systems," University of Missouri Medical Center, Technical Education Services, Columbia, Missouri, p. 63, 1971.*
[9] *Joseph L. Balintfy, "Computerized Dietary Information System, Data Organization and Collection Procedures." Research Paper 14, Vol. I, Computer System Research, School of Business Administration, Tulane University, New Orleans, Louisiana.*

Codes are not "sacred" and may be made up for any foodservice. However, a code developed by Balintfy et al.[10] at Tulane University is available for those who may wish to follow one already developed.

3. Nutrient values and costs may be computed for all recipes and are then available for selection by the computer in finding the menu item (recipe) that will fulfill the requirements, yet be within the constraints predetermined by the foodservice.

Recipe information should be collected on forms designed for the purpose, usually one that matches the 80-column punch card, so that information can be abbreviated in advance to comply with spaces available. The recipe must have a code number matching the menu item code number. Each ingredient is listed with its code number from the inventory list. Other data to be provided are: *purchase* unit and *purchase* cost, and the conversion factor codes used to change them to *issue* unit and *issue* cost. A study of the edible portion (EP) yield of the food from the as purchased (AP) form during production stages and expressed in percent yield is desirable. However, such information is available from the USDA Handbook No. 102.[11] The total yield of the recipe in volume or weight, total cost, portion size, and portion cost complete the recipe data necessary for basic menu planning. Nutrient values are usually an important component of the menu plan. USDA Handbook No. 8 [12] provides this nutritional data and is available on punched cards ready for computer use.

Consultation with a computer programmer who will develop a program to be used in conjunction with data provided by the foodservice manager should be carried on while recipes are being standardized and coded.

One decision to be made is the type of computer planning to be used—linear or random programming. The first approach, linear

[10] *Ibid.*

[11] *Food Yields Summarized by Different Stages of Preparation, Agriculture Handbook No. 102, Agriculture Research Service, USDA, 1970. U.S. Government Printing Office, Washington, D.C. 20402.*

[12] *Composition of Foods, Agriculture Handbook No. 8, Agriculture Research Service, USDA, 1963. U.S. Government Printing Office, Washington, D.C. 20402.*

programming, is a mathematical method based on the optimization technique; that is, choosing from a group of alternatives. The dietitian decides on the restraints and must observe the results to obtain optimum value of the objective desired, the least expensive combination of choices, for example. A linear program may be used in situations where data can be quantified, some restrictions on feasible choices are involved, alternative courses of action are permitted, and optimization in respect to certain appropriate criteria is required. In menu planning by linear programming the problem is to find the optimum combinations of menu items within given constraints that meet a predetermined set of objectives for a sequence of days.

In the second approach, random programming, the computer selects an item at random and tests its acceptability when put into combination with other menu items. This method simulates the judgment process of the dietitian in planning dinner menus; that is, a decision is reached without knowing all of the alternatives. In other words, solutions are produced when the *first* item that satisfies the criteria is found. The linear method, on the other hand, tests all possible choices and selects the one with the optimum value.

THE COMMERCIAL MENU CARD

Any foodservice presenting the menu to its customers through the printed word is confronted with an additional menu planning consideration not previously discussed. A menu card must be designed and worded to appeal to the guest and to stimulate sales.

The card serves as an introduction of the food to the public. It should be of a size easily handled at the table, spotlessly clean, simple in format with ample margin space, highly legible, and interesting in color and design to harmonize with the decor of the restaurant. The card should bear the name and address of the organization, the days and hours of service, and other information that will be of interest and elicit a favorable and friendly response.

An attempt should be made to paint an accurate word picture of the foods available on the menu card, so that the patron can visualize what you are selling. It is disappointing for the guest to anticipate one thing and be served something entirely different; for example, fruit cup envisioned as fresh fruit but proving to be canned fruit cocktail fails to create good will or build patronage.

Menu merchandising can be effected through descriptive words that have an interesting connotation; new potatoes, fresh green beans, imported sardines, and Prime beef indicate desirable quality characteristics. Adjectives denoting temperature are: chilled apple juice, iced melon, steaming plum pudding, and sizzling lamb chops. Words describing texture might be crisp ginger cookies and toasted coconut ice cream ball; words for color are black bean soup and golden brown chicken. The name of the place of origin of the food makes for interest on the menu, such as Maine lobster, Lake Erie whitefish, or Columbia River salmon. Naming the method of preparation, such as broiled, baked, or stewed or describing the form as whole, diced, or quartered may further influence the customer selection. Listing sauces and accompaniments creates a good feeling of "getting more for one's money."

The trend of menus in the United States is away from the use of French terms unless they are well understood by the public or an explanation is given. Sometimes the American wording is not understood, so the food does not sell. Veal Birds on one restaurant menu brought few sales, but when the name was changed to Baked Stuffed Veal Steak, the sales zoomed.

Specials on the menu may be placed in a box on the menu card, underlined, starred, or used as a rider attached to the card to call attention to them and stimulate sales.

It is important that the customer reading the menu understands what food items he will receive for the money he pays. Menus are presented either *a la carte,* where every item is priced individually; *table d'hôte* (sometimes called club), where the complete meal is given at a set price; *selective,* where the price of the entree determines the price of the complete meal and choices are allowed among the appetizers, vegetables, salads, and desserts, or *elective,* in which the entree and accompaniments (usually the vegetables and sometimes salad) are priced as one and other courses are available at additional cost.

Menus will have to be carefully edited to avoid misspelled words, incorrect prices, and incomplete listings. The menu card should not be thought of as a price sheet alone, but as a selling device and an instrument for creating good will and good public relations. If so used, the time, effort, and money spent on it will be well justified, and a marked increase in business and patron satisfaction may be expected.

QUALITY FOOD STANDARDS

Translating the well-planned menu into high-quality foods is a prime responsibility of the administrative dietitian or foodservice manager. Food quality varies widely from place to place and often from time to time at the same place. This is attributable to two major factors: the standards of the food manager and the degree and amount of supervision given to those who prepare and serve it. Each person has his own perception of what constitutes "quality" food and each considers himself an expert, based on his own likes and dislikes.

The wise foodservice manager is well aware of the several factors that tend to influence individual opinion about food quality; age, cultural and socio-economic backgrounds, past experiences relating to foods, education and scientific knowledge, and emotions. Using this information, the foodservice manager is better prepared to satisfy the many people who make up the clientele than would be true if such factors were unknown or ignored when planning menus. However, the desired result of food production is palatability, the factors of which may be diagrammed as follows.

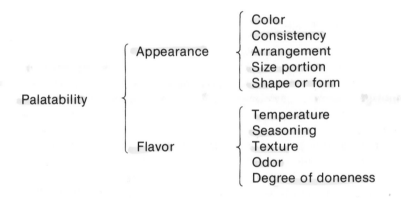

Palatability
- Appearance
  - Color
  - Consistency
  - Arrangement
  - Size portion
  - Shape or form
- Flavor
  - Temperature
  - Seasoning
  - Texture
  - Odor
  - Degree of doneness

Flavor of food is determined by the methods of prepreparation and cooking used, suitable seasonings to supplement natural flavors, and proper temperature when served. All of these greatly influence the acceptability of all food items.

The appearance of the food when served also influences its acceptability to the consumer and his enjoyment of it. Eye appeal is gained through contrasting and interesting combinations of foods differing in type, color, and form, as well as the arrangement on the plate. Properly prepared and attractively served meals are stimulating to even the most jaded appetites. Since quality of most food deteriorates rapidly, especially in heated holding units, foods should be prepared as near to the serving time as possible.

Added to palatability must be wholesomeness of the product, and the assurance that foods are safe for human consumption. No food, no matter how beautiful in appearance, can be considered good quality if it has been mishandled and become contaminated during preparation or holding.

Quality assurance programs have been instigated in many food-service organizations to make certain that the customers receive the very best. One group of writers state:

The establishment of an effective Quality Assurance (QA) program in any food operation requires, in part, that the program

1. *Be well defined and supported by management and communicated to all in the organization.*
2. *Standardize and clearly specify all formulas.*
3. *Involve on-going testing and monitoring of chemical, physical, microbiological, and sensory qualities.*[13]

STANDARDIZED RECIPES

One of the tools for quality assurance control is the standardized recipe, or formula. A recipe is considered "standardized" only when it has been tried and adapted for use by a given foodservice operation. *Tested* quantity recipes are available from many sources, such as cookbooks, magazines, materials distributed by commercial food companies from their own experimental kitchens, and from other foodservice managers. Regardless of the source, all must be adapted and standardized for use in a particular situation. Each recipe must be tried in one's own institution kitchen with its particular equipment, available ingredients, and skills and abilities of its personnel, and then adjusted for the quantities required, based on the number of people to be served and the portion size desired. Only then is standardization possible. Accuracy in the use of standardized recipes and in weighing and measuring ingredients, as shown in Fig. 2.2 takes the guesswork out of quantity food production. Customers and guests expect and should be able to depend on having a food item the same each time it is selected. This is not possible if the recipe is kept in the "head of the cook" and is not written for use by the relief or substitute cook.

[13] *Andre Bolaffi, E. A. Tillinghast Jr., K. J. Hoyt, and V. D. Mallary, "Quality Assurance in A Franchised Food Industry,"* Food Technology, *27, 24 (August 1973).*

FIGURE 2.2   *Accuracy in weights and measures of ingredients is necessary to obtain quality products.*

Large foodservice systems such as universities with many residence halls or restaurant chains now have product standardization laboratories. (Fig. 2.3) Under the supervision of an experienced dietitian, recipes are developed, tested, and standardized for acceptance by all units before the recipes are put into use. A product evaluation form to be used by the unit managers (Form 2.3) assists the dietitian in the production of a recipe that will be acceptable by all who will be using it.

Household recipes cannot be depended on to give satisfactory results if simply multiplied to give a larger quantity. The relative proportions may be wrong in larger volume, the mixing time too brief, the size of the batch too large or too small for the size of pans available, or the yield inconsistent with established standards for portion size. Also, there are so many variables in the varieties of flour milled, the kind of shortening and sugar manufactured, and the formulas for leavening powders used that we cannot treat recipe changes in generalities.

FIGURE   2.3   Product standardization laboratory. Courtesy, Stouffer Foods Corporation.

Lacking any kind of conversion factor for recipe adjustment, it is best to proceed systematically, increasing the recipe gradually and evaluating results at each step, Firsthand knowledge of the desired results and information about the quality of the ingredients in the original recipe are essential at the start. These are obtained by making the recipe in the original amount before attempting to enlarge it, then doubling it and, if results are satisfactory, doubling it again.

Special attention should be given to the yield of the first quantity trial, because this is the level at which yield is most likely to deviate. If the yield is more than 10 percent over or under that anticipated or if the quality is unacceptable, adjustments should be made and another trial performed. Adjustments may be needed in the speed of the mixer and the time of mixing to give the same results as were obtained using the smaller recipe.

Another procedure [14] for adjustment of recipe yield has been

[14] Grace A. Miller and Marguerite B. Goodenow, "Product Standardization for Quality and Profit Control," paper presented at the 44th Annual Meeting, American Dietetic Association, St. Louis, Missouri, 1961.

Recipe Evaluation Card—Please Return This Card to the Test Kitchen as Promptly as Possible.

Product _____   Residence Hall _____
                                      Date _____

Quantity prepared _____

Did you obtain yield as stated in recipe?_____

If not, what quantity was obtained? _____

Do you consider size of portion adequate? _____

If not, what change would you suggest? _____

Was product generally well accepted? _____

Further comments on recipe—for example—ease of using recipe; problems encountered; suggestions for changes in procedure, kind and/or amount of ingredients, etc.:
(Consult cooks for suggestions) _____

_____
_____
_____
_____
_____

_____
Reporting Supervisor

FORM 2.3   Recipe Evaluation card. Courtesy, Central Food Stores, University of Illinois.

developed and is especially helpful for use with those recipes with yields not divisible by 25. This method, known as the "factor method," requires calculation and concentration to ensure accuracy. The steps of the procedure are the following:

STEP 1. Convert any measured ingredients to weight. For any you may not know, consult an equivalent weight-measure table in a quantity cookbook or file.

STEP 2. Change the weight of each ingredient to ounces or parts of ounces. *Add* together the weights of all ingredients.

STEP 3. To decrease or increase the original recipe, *divide the new yield by the original yield.* Your answer is the FACTOR, which you use to adjust your recipe yield. Remember, if you are increasing a recipe, the FACTOR will always be *greater* than 1.0; if you are decreasing a recipe, the FACTOR will always be *less* than 1.0.

STEP 4. Multiply the amount of each ingredient in the original recipe (Step 2) by the FACTOR. Also, *multiply* the *total weight* of the original recipe by this SAME FACTOR. *Add* together the *new weights* of each ingredient calculated above. Compare this answer with the one that you got when you multiplied the total weight of the original recipe by the FACTOR. IF THESE TWO ANSWERS DO NOT MATCH, SOMETHING IS WRONG! Go back and check the calculation until these two figures agree. Even a slight error is not safe to let pass, or you may have a product failure—not to mention the cost of materials and the manpower involved in producing an item that failed because of faulty calculation.

STEP 5. Carefully change the new calculated weight of each ingredient back to pounds and ounces (or, in a few cases, back to *logical* measurements).

The following chart is an illustration of this method for converting a recipe.

PASTRY   ADJUSTING YIELD *FROM* 12 2-CRUST PIES *TO* 66 2-CRUST PIES

Ingredients	Original Recipe 12 2-Crust Pies	Step 1 Original Recipe in Weight	Step 2 Original Recipe in Ounces	Step 4 Each Amount in Step 2 Multiplied by Factor	New Recipe in Weight	Step 5 New Recipe Rounded Weight and Measure
Pastry flour	5 lb	5 lb	80	440.0	27 lb 8 oz	27 lb 8 oz
Salt	1 1/4 oz	1 1/4 oz	1 1/4	6.9	6.9 oz	7 oz
Shortening	3 lb	3 lb	48	264.0	16 lb 8 oz	16 lb 8 oz
Water	3 c	1 lb 8 oz	24	132.0	8 lb 4 oz	1 gal 1/2 c
Total weight		9 lb 9 1/4 oz	153 1/4	842.9	52 lb 9 oz	52 lb 11 oz

Step 3: Conversion Factor

$$\frac{66 \text{ (new)}}{12 \text{ (original)}} = \frac{11}{2} = 5 \ 1/2 = 5.5$$

Total Weight in Step 2 × Factor
153 1/4 oz × 5.5 =
    153.25 × 5.5 = 842.875 = 842.9 oz

Essential information needed:
Water: 1 c = 8 oz
        4 c = 1 qt = 2 lb
        4 qt = 1 gal = 8 lb

1 lb = 16 oz

Source. *Procedure for Adjusting Recipe Yield, Department of Institution Administration, Michigan State University, East Lansing.*

A word of warning is given for the use of this method.

For small amounts of ingredients (less than 1 oz) for which you may wish to use measure instead of weight, round fractions to the nearest measurable amount. *In measuring use the standard cup with fractions limited to 1/4, 1/3, 1/2, 2/3, and 3/4 c; for measuring amounts in tablespoons, use the fraction 1/2 T only for materials which will pack, level, and cut accurately. In measuring by teaspoons use only 1/4, 1/2, and 3/4 t for fractions. Including such fractions as 13/16 c, and 1/6 T, and 3/8 t invites guessing and may increase the possibility of product failure. Keep weights and measurements for ingredients in* realistic *terms, with the available equipment always in mind.*[15]

Recipe File. A *file* of recipes should be developed and maintained for each foodservice to include the foods acceptable to its patrons and consistent with the food-cost level of the organization. A suitable form or *format* for writing the recipes should be decided on according to the preference of a particular organization. Figures 2.4*a*, 2.4*b*, and 2.4*c* illustrate three different formats that may be used.

The size and form of the recipe sheet or card, as well as the format to be followed and the manner of filing the recipes, are optional. Cards, 4″ × 6″ or 5″ × 8″, are popular sizes, and recipes are more often typed than printed. Sheets, 8″ × 11″, on which the recipes are duplicated, have been found desirable if they can be hung above the work table or placed on a stand to keep them off the work surface. Recipes, set up on cards, can be located easily if classified, numbered, and filed alphabetically under headings such as Meats, Vegetables, Pies, and Cakes.

Whatever the system, certain points deserve consideration in recording recipes.

The card should have a neat, uncluttered appearance with ample margin space to make it more readable.

Guide lines to direct the eye across or down the sheet are helpful.

The name of the recipe and classification code are given in boldface type at the top of the card.

The yield, portion size, number of portions, pan size (if necessary) or equipment to be used, and how portioned, should appear at the top of the card.

[15] *Grace A. Miller and Marguerite B. Goodenow, "Product Standardization for Quality and Profit Control," paper presented at the 44th Annual Meeting, American Dietetic Association, St. Louis, Missouri, 1961.*

(a)

Cakes-19
WHITE CAKE

Portions: 60   Size of pans: 9″ × 9″
How portion: Cut each cake   Yield: 4 pans or 2
     3 × 10   2-layer cakes

Mixing Machine Method:
1. *Set oven for 350°* F. Take milk and eggs from refrigerator. Oil pans.
2. Sift flour and baking powder together into mixing bowl.
3. Add shortening, mix together at low speed for 2 min.
4. Mix sugar, salt, and first amount of milk. Add to flour mix, and mix 2 min at low speed. Scrape and mix 3 min more.

Ingredients	Wt. or Amt.	Measure
Flour, cake	2 lb	2 qt 1 1/2 c
Baking powder	1 2/3 oz	3 1/3 T
Fat	1 lb	2 1/4 c
Sugar	2 lb	1 qt
Salt	2 t	2 t
Milk	1 1/3 c	1 1/3 c
Egg whites	14 oz	1 3/4 c (14–16)
Milk	2 c	2 c
Vanilla	1 1/3 T	1 1/3 T

5. Combine whites, milk, and vanilla. Add 1/2 this mixture to flour, etc. Mix 30 sec. Scrape. Mix 2 1/2 min. Add other 1/2 mixture and mix 2 1/2 min.
6. Pour in oiled pans, bake 30–35 min at 350° F. **Note:** 2 2/3 oz melted baking chocolate may be added to 1/3 batter to make a marble cake.

(b)

WHITE CAKE

Bake: 40–45 min.   Yield: 1 pan 12 x 20 x 2 in.
Oven: 350° F.   40 portions 2 1/4 x 2 1/2 in.
                                       48 portions 2 x 2 1/2 in.

Amount	Ingredients	Method
1 lb 8 oz	Cake flour	Mix flour, baking powder, and fat (low speed) 2 min.
1 oz	Baking powder	
12 oz	Fat	Scrape down bowl; mix 3 min more.
1 lb 8 oz	Sugar	Add combined sugar, salt, and milk. Mix (low speed) 2 min.
1 1/2 t	Salt	
1 c	Milk	Scrape down bowl; mix 3 min more
8	Egg whites	Add half of combined egg whites, milk, and vanilla. Mix (low speed) 30 sec.
1 1/4 c	Milk	
1 T	Vanilla	Scrape down bowl; mix 1 min.
		Add remaining egg–milk mixture. Mix (low speed) 1 min.
		Scrape down bowl; mix 2 1/2 min.
		Pour into greased baking pan. Bake.

Notes:
1. For 6 9-in. layer pans, use 1 1/2 recipe; scale 1 lb 6 oz per pan.
2. For cup cakes, increase flour to 1 lb 14 oz. Use No. 20 dipper to portion.
Variations:
1. *Chocolate Chip Cake.* Add 4 oz chocolate chips.
2. *Poppy Seed Cake.* Add 4 oz poppy seed.

(*c*)

| **WHITE CAKE** | | V. Desserts-20 |

Yield: 4 9-in. square cake pans
  2 two-layer cakes
Portion size: One slice, 4 1/2 x 4 x 1/2 in.

Baking temperature: 350° F.
Baking time: 30–35 min.

Amount	Ingredients	Amount	Procedure
	Cake flour, sifted	2 lb	1. Set oven. Take eggs and milk from refrigerator.
	Baking powder	3 1/3 T	2. Sift flour and baking powder together into a mixing bowl.
	Shortening	1 lb	3. Add shortening. Mix at low speed for 2 min.
	Sugar	2 lb	4. Mix 2 min (low speed). Scrape bowl; mix 3 min more.
	Salt	2 t	
	Milk	1 1/3 c	
	Egg whites	1 3/4 c	5. Add 1/2 this mixture; mix 30 sec. Scrape down bowl; mix 1 min. Add remainder of mixture. Mix 1 min. Scrape down; mix 2 1/2 min.
	Milk	2 c	
	Vanilla	1 1/3 T	6. Pour into 4 oiled pans 9″ x 9″. Bake 30–35 min at 350° F.

FIGURE 2.4   *Suggested recipe formats.* (a) *Form desirable when there is a central ingredient room.* (b) *From Fowler, West, and Shugart,* Food for Fifty, *Fifth Edition, Wiley, New York.* (c) *Form easy to use in most production kitchens. Format from Iowa State University Quantity Recipe File.*

Ingredients are listed in order of combining, with amounts for the dry given by weight and for the liquids by measure; ingredients to be added together can be bracketed or separated by lines.

Awkward fractions like 7/16 ounce are to be avoided, as they cannot be weighed on most kitchen scales.

Abbreviations should be consistent so they will always be understood.

Directions for combining the product must be clear, complete, and concise, leaving nothing to the imagination of the person using the recipe.

Time and temperature for cooking must be included.

Serving suggestions or special handling precautions may be included also.

Triplicate copies of every standardized recipe are essential to insure against loss, which would result in having to restandardize the recipe. A copy in the manager's office serves as a basis for purchasing and costing and assures that one copy is always available.

Another procedure for quality control used in many foodservice organizations is a central ingredient room, generally located near the storage areas. Here all ingredients for recipes and menu items for the day are weighed, measured and, in some cases, prepreparation of produce items is completed. Personnel especially trained in accuracy are employed to work in this unit. Only the quantities actually needed for the production of the day are sent to the kitchen; there can be no deviation from the standardized recipes, because extra food supplies are not available to the cooks. The time of the highly paid cooks is not required for measuring and weighing ingredients, thus enabling these highly skilled employees to engage in more productive work.

EVALUATION OF FOOD PRODUCTS

Evaluation of products made from standardized recipes should be a continuing process to make certain that the original high quality is maintained. Score cards suitable for evaluation are illustrated in Figs. 2.5, 2.6 and 2.7. Evaluation of food products is an essential part of assuring the desired food quality. It should be an ongoing regularly scheduled part of every institution foodservice regime.

Techniques used for evaluation include the *subjective, or test panels* of people, the *objective or instrument measurement,* and *chemical tests.* Nutritive value, color, texture, and flavor can be evaluated by various positive methods, and help to give meaning to the words "quality foods." For *subjective testing,* panels should be composed of several persons so as to average out some errors of human judgment. Those selected must have sensitivity to flavor and a knowledge of standards of a desirable product. A special room for testing is advisable. It should be quiet and free from distractions, well lighted and ventilated, and have an individual booth or table for each panel member. Samples to be tested are coded, and score sheets such as those illustrated in Figs. 2.5, 2.6, and 2.7 are provided on which to record evaluations. In institution foodservice departments, panel testing may be used to evaluate products prepared from recipes being developed, or to judge samples of products under consideration for purchase.

SCORE CARD FOR COOKED VEGETABLES

Name of Product:	1	2	3	Score
Color	1. Discolored or burned	Original color retained		1.
Moisture Content	2. Watery or dry	No excess water		2.
Texture	3. Hard or mushy	Hold shape; tender but firm		3.
Taste and Flavor	4. Flat or overseasoned	Well seasoned		4.
	5. Raw or strong	Natural flavor well developed		5. _____
			Total	

SCORE CARD FOR MEAT

Sample No.: _____   Judge _____

Factor	10	9	8	7	6	5	4	3	2	1
Aroma	Extremely good	Very good	Good	Plus	Medium	Minus	Fair	Poor	Very poor	Extremely poor
Flavor of lean	Extremely good	Very good	Good	Plus	Medium	Minus	Fair	Poor	Very poor	Extremely poor
Tenderness	Extremely tender	Very tender	Tender	Plus	Medium	Minus	Fair	Tough	Very tough	Extremely tough
Juiciness	Extremely juicy	Very juicy	Juicy	Plus	Medium	Minus	Fair	Dry	Very dry	Extremely dry
Flavor of fat	Extremely good	Very good	Good	Plus	Medium	Minus	Fair	Poor	Very poor	Extremely poor

Date: Total Score _____
Remarks:

FIGURE 2.5   Suggested score cards for prepared foods.

Score Card for Plain Cake

Date _____

Experiment No. _____

Factor	Qualities	Stand-ard	Sample No. 1	2	3	Comments
I. External appearance	Shape, symmetrical, slightly rounded top, free from cracks or peaks	10				
	Volume, light in weight in proportion to size	10				
	Crust, smooth uniform golden brown	10				
II. Internal appearance	Texture, tender, slightly moist, velvety feel to tongue and finger	10				
	Grain, fine, round, evenly distributed cells with thin cell walls, free from tunnels	10				
	Color, crumb even and rich looking	10				
III. Flavor	Delicate, well-blended flavor of ingredients. Free from unpleasant odors or taste	10				

Directions for use of score card for plain cake:

Standard	10	No detectable fault, highest possible score
Excellent	8–9	Of unusual excellence but not perfect
Good	6–7	Average good quality
Fair	4–5	Below average, slightly objectionable
Poor	2–3	Objectionable, but edible
Bad	0–1	Highly objectionable, inedible

Signature of judge

FIGURE 2.6   Suggested rating sheet for evaluation of muffins or cake.

Preference

Name	Division	Date

Code	Code	Code	Code

__ Like Extremely	__ Like Extremely	__ Like Extremely	__ Like Extremely
__ Like Very Much	__ Like Very Much	__ Like Very Much	__ Like Very Much
__ Like Moderately	__ Like Moderately	__ Like Moderately	__ Like Moderately
__ Like Slightly	__ Like Slightly	__ Like Slightly	__ Like Slightly
__ Neither Like Nor Dislike	__ Neither Like Nor Dislike	__ Neither Like Nor Dislike	__ Neither Like Nor Dislike
__ Dislike Slightly	__ Dislike Slightly	__ Dislike Slightly	__ Dislike Slightly
__ Dislike Moderately	__ Dislike Moderately	__ Dislike Moderately	__ Dislike Moderately
__ Dislike Very Much	__ Dislike Very Much	__ Dislike Very Much	__ Dislike Very Much
__ Dislike Extremely	__ Dislike Extremely	__ Dislike Extremely	__ Dislike Extremely
Comments:	Comments:	Comments:	Comments:

FIGURE 2.7   Hedonic rating scale may be used for judging any food product.

Most foodservices do not possess instruments for *objective testing* of foods. However, occasions do arise in regard to food standards when an objective test would aid in its solution. In such cases the food administrator may arrange with a research laboratory nearby to conduct certain tests for him. A knowledge of some of the kinds of tests available is of value.

The determination of nutritive value of foods is an exhaustive laboratory procedure. Much is already known about nutrients in most foods and about the effects of various processing and cookery procedures on them. Additional research will provide new information, however, that should be used to supplement that which is now known.

Control of color in food products deserves much attention, and a variety of instruments has been developed to measure food color accurately. The spectrophotometer, which determines intensity, various colorimeters used for specific foods, and the newer chromatography methods are among them. These objective methods of color testing are used to good advantage by food processing companies as well as by research workers to help develop products of greatest eye acceptability to the consumer. There is a definite art and psychology involved in food color, and a wise production manager and food merchandiser will capitalize on it to please the patrons and increase business.

Texture has many definitions but, as a quality attribute of food, it requires its own definition. Texture, from the sensory standpoint, refers to the sense of feel of the food in the mouth. Words of texture are crisp, hard, soft, and chewy.

Instruments for measuring texture include those that compress, for testing freshness in bakery products; those that pull apart, known as tensile-strength testing, used less often for food than for textiles; those that cut without changing the shape of the sample, such as testing for "fork cutting" quality in vegetables; and those that shear or cut and move the sample to resemble chewing action, as needed to test tenderness of meats.

Several factors often are involved in quality that are interrelated with texture, such as degree of maturity and ripeness in fresh produce and volume size, or color in bakery products. Measurements of the latter factors are easily accomplished without elaborate instruments.

Flavor is more elusive to judge accurately than either texture or color, since it may be influenced by factors such as temperature, the state of physical well-being, and the sensitivity of taste of the person who is testing. Flavor in food usually is tested subjectively; however, certain instruments can be used to measure the interrelated factors such as texture and color. For example, color in tomatoes is an indication of maturity that is related to optimum flavor development.

Attention is given by certain researchers to the development of flavor enhancers, the chemical compounds used with food to intensify flavor. Monosodium glutamate, which has been used for many years, is an example. Some other enhancers, specific to a structure of 5-ribo-nucleotides, are much stronger than MSG. For the most part, their use appears to be with food processors who hope to improve flavor defects and monotony found in certain of the new forms of food.

An understanding of these attributes of food that together make up measurable quality is the first step toward producing quality food. In most foodservices more emphasis is placed on acceptance of a food product as "standard" by persons preparing it and persons consuming it then by measurement through other means. For this reason, the practice of tasting a product before it is served to check on flavor, the use of a thermometer to check for desired temperature, and the visual judging of the appearance of the food, all in relation to acceptable standards, should be routine in every foodservice.

Final responsibility for preparation of palatable, safe, nutritious, and attractive food rests with the administrative dietitian or food production manager. Unless this person has high standards as well as the desire and know-how to transmit them to the staff and to build enthusiasm for "quality production," there is little hope that superior food will result.

SELECTED REFERENCES

Arnold, R., C. Hill, and A. Nichols, *Introduction to Data Processing,* Wiley, New York, 1967.

Cronan, Marion L., *The School Lunch,* Charles A. Bennett, Peoria, Illinois, 1962.

Establishing and Operating a Restaurant, U.S. Department of Commerce, U.S. Government Printing Office, Washington, D.C., 1957.

Food and Nutrition Board: *Recommended Dietary Allowances,* Eighth Revised Edition, 1974, Washington, D.C., National Academy of Sciences, 1974.

Food Selection for Good Nutrition in Group Feeding, Home Economics Research Report No. 35, U.S. Department of Agriculture, U.S. Government Printing Office, Washington, D.C., 1971.

Fowler, Sina Faye, Bessie Brooks West, and Grace Severance Shugart, *Food for Fifty,* Fifth Edition, Wiley, New York, 1971.

Hoke, Ann, *Restaurant Menu Planning,* Revised Edition, copyright the Hotel Monthly Press, John Willey, Evanston, Illinois, 1954.

Institution Management Department, Iowa State University, *Standardized Quantity Recipe File for Quality and Cost Control,* Iowa State University Press, Ames, Iowa.

Seaberg, Albin C., *Menu Design,* Second Edition, Cahners, Boston, 1973.

Terrell, Margaret E., *Large Quantity Recipes,* Third Edition, Lippincott, Philadelphia, 1975.

Treat, Nola, and Lenore M. Richards, *Quantity Cookery,* Revised Edition, Little, Brown, Boston, 1951.

Vail, Gladys, Jean Phillips, Lucile Rust, Ruth Griswold, and Margaret Justin, *Foods,* Sixth Edition, Houghton Mifflin, Boston, 1973.

Visick, Hubert E., and Peter E. VanKleek, *Menu Planning: A Blueprint for Better Profits,* McGraw-Hill, New York, 1974.

3.
FOOD SELECTION AND STORAGE

The procurement of food has been a challenging process since primitive times when man depended on the resources of nature and his ingenuity for survival. Today, less physical effort is required of the food buyer, but the problems are compounded by the many kinds and forms of foods from which selections must be made to meet the needs of the particular foodservice and to satisfy the clientele, yet keep within the limits of the economic structure.

THE FOOD BUYER

The buyer of food for an institution represents a large segment of the consumer population to the wholesale market, as does the homemaker to the retail trade. He may buy the food for a small operation as only one of his responsibilities, or perhaps he may be the purchasing agent with one or more assistants in a large restaurant chain or on a university campus. In any case he must be an astute business person well qualified for the position.

Maintenance of a high standard of ethics is a requirement of a buyer. He is entrusted with high buying power and cannot afford to compromise either money or position. Judgment must be exercised, and no gifts, meals, or other favors can be accepted that might easily obligate him. Courtesy and fair treatment of all sales representatives with no playing of one firm against another, selection of products on an objective evaluation of quality, price, and service, and keeping regular office hours for salesmen to call are examples of other ethical standards for the good buyer to observe.

The food buyer must be a well-informed person. To purchase the amount and quality of food required for the institution within the limitations imposed by the budget and the financial policies requires thorough knowledge of the marketing system, the quantities of food needed, the standards for foods, what is available in the market, the possible methods of purchase, and storage requirements. In addition, he should have some knowledge and understanding of legal requirements, especially as they relate to orders and contracts.

The sales representative can be a valuable source of information on new products and availability of foods on the market. An interested buyer or dietitian who establishes good communications with the sales representative benefits not only from market information but can, in turn, express his needs and quality standards to the sales representative and to the manufacturer when necessary.

THE MARKET

Food marketing includes the processes and transactions from production on the farm to the consumer's table. The raw agricultural product is delivered to a food processor or middleman where it is processed, divided into smaller lots, and delivered by middlemen to distribution centers in marketing areas throughout the country. The middlemen may be wholesalers who take ownership of food materials and arrange for final distribution from their own warehouses, or they may be brokers who act only as agents between buyers and sellers without assuming ownership of the commodity.

Thus, involved in the system are the growing, harvesting, transporting, processing, packaging, storing, selling, financing, and supplying of market information for the many foods and food products available. Each process and transfer of ownership adds to the cost of the end product so that the ultimate consumer cost is far in excess of the amount paid to the original producer of the commodity.

The market is dynamic and ever changing, and the food buyer must keep alert to trends and conditions that affect it. Foods in plentiful supply, new market forms of food, and fluctuations in price are but a few of the factors that demand his attention.

Adverse growing conditions can affect food prices, as can unusual consumer demands and seasonal variations. Some foods are relatively stable in price and follow general economic conditions. Others are more perishable and have greater price fluctuations during the year. Most fresh fruits and vegetables are considered best at the height of the production season, particularly those grown within a given market area. However, modern treatments of fresh foods and improved transportation, refrigeration, and storage facilities have reduced greatly the so-called seasonability of foods. Stocks of processed foods may be high or depleted at times, which will affect both price and availability. The USDA tries to keep the public informed of foods in plentiful supply through newsletters, circulars, and the press.

Market information is accumulated from sources such as local and federal market reports, newspapers, technical and trade association meetings and magazines, research reports, talks with sales representatives, and visits to the produce markets and wholesale firms.

Today's market offers a wide variety of food items and also reflects the rapid advancement in technology of food production, processing, and packaging. An understanding of the various forms of food available will aid the buyer to know the full potential of the market.

MARKET FORMS OF FOOD

Food is available in fresh or processed forms. Basic processing methods include canning, drying, freezing, dehydrofreezing, and freeze drying; and salting and brining, smoking, and adding of condiments, spices, and flavorings for foods such as meat, fish, and pickles. Specifications for fresh and natural forms of food are included under each grouping in "Selection of Foods" (pp. 96–193).

Enrichment and fortification have been used for some time for nutritional improvement of existing foods, but advances in technology have made possible the formulation of new foods. Textured vegetable proteins, presently made from soybeans, retain their structural integrity when hydrated and cooked, and meat analogs, which are textured protein products fabricated to simulate muscle tissue foods from various animal sources, are examples. Alterations may be made in the composition of common foods to improve nutritional content; for example, macaroni and other pasta are being manufactured with as high as 20 to 25 percent protein, and food components are being combined that will satisfy nutritional requirements for a complete meal. As yet, few purchasing standards have been established for these formulated and engineered foods, but their use in the future appears to have merit if they are acceptable to the consumer and if appropriate controls in their use are exercised.

More and more important to the food buyer is the availability of convenience foods. These are foods that have services "built in" to the basic ingredients to reduce the amount of preparation required in the foodservice.

Convenience foods may be purchased fresh, frozen, dried, freeze-dried, dehydrofrozen, or canned; as individual ingredients, mixtures of ingredients, or as finished products ready for heat reconstitution. The list of convenience foods is almost endless. It includes everything from baking mixes to complete frozen meals, and the many gourmet, special diet, and kosher foods now available in frozen form. Assorted vegetables, prepeeled and ready for incorporation in a stew, and freeze-dried shrimp are other popular convenience items.

Foods processed by any of the methods mentioned have some preparation services built into them. The advantages to the user are obvious: labor-cost savings, reduced preparation losses, a lower inventory required and perhaps less storage space, and a high degree of uniformity. Disadvantages vary with the product, but the primary one appears to be poor quality caused by lack of following specific directions accurately for final preparation and from improper storage, especially with frozen foods. Also, there is much to learn about the nutritive value of many of these foods. Convenience foods are gaining acceptance and popularity with improved techniques in production.

The decision as to the form of food to purchase and use in any given situation requires careful study. Several different products may be available, all of which will produce an acceptable menu item. Costs involved in purchase and use of fresh or natural forms of food versus partially prepared or ready-to-eat foods and the acceptability of such items by the consumer are major factors to consider. Certain fresh items that are inexpensive and plentiful when in season may be prohibitive in cost when that season is over.

As the amount of processing and preparation increases, cost of the product usually increases proportionally. However, for some items, because of volume production, the manufacturer or processor may be able to offer the product at a lower combined food and labor cost than if preparation took place in the foodservice.

REGULATORY AGENCIES

Quality in food as purchased is assured to a large extent by the standards that have been established by governmental agencies to protect consumers. Such standards give definitions and descriptions of the food product including its appearance, quality factors and, in some cases, its composition.

Federal agencies establish quality standards and provide the regulatory control over these standards. All food shipped in interstate commerce must meet the requirements of one or more federal laws and regulations. Food sold locally or within the state where it is produced or processed may be regulated by state and local laws. Less control exists over these products, and great variation and rapid change occurs within the state and from state to state. The food buyer should not only be knowledgeable about federal laws, but should be informed of the current situation in the state involved.

A brief summary of the federal agencies responsible for standard setting and control follows.

Food and Drug Administration. The FDA, in the Department of Health, Education and Welfare, is responsible for enforcement of the Federal Food, Drug and Cosmetic Act covering production, manufacture, and distribution of all food involved in interstate commerce except meat and poultry, which are regulated by the U.S. Department of Agriculture. This act defines adulteration and misbranding and clarifies certain definitions and standards. *Standards of identity* define what a food must be to be called by a particular name, such as preserves, salad dressing, and mayonnaise. *Standards of quality* are minimum standards only and specify factors such as flavor, color, size, and freedom from defects. *Standards of fill of container* tell the packer how full the container must be to avoid deceiving the consumer. All are mandatory for foods in interstate commerce and may be used voluntarily for others. Most states have similar standards, and some require grade labeling of canned products.

The Federal Food, Drug, and Cosmetic Act requires that labels on packaged food shipped from one state to another identify appropriately each particular product. Included must be name of the item, name and address of the manufacturer, packer, or distributor, net contents by weight or count, list of ingredients with foods in order of decreasing quantities, full information of claimed dietary properties, statement of use of artificial coloring or flavoring, or chemical preservatives, and a statement of substandard quality of product or fill of container; all must be clearly stated and easily understood. Some manufacturers or distributors make the labels more informative or "descriptive" by adding accurate reproductions of the items in color, size, and appearance by listing the number of portions, pieces, or cups, with a description of the raw product and method of processing, and with directions for preparation and suggestions for use.

The FDA recently established regulations concerning nutritional quality and nutrition labeling of foods. Nutritional quality guidelines prescribe the minimum level or range of nutrient composition appropriate for a given class of food. Nutrition labeling provides the consumer with information concerning the nutritional quality of a defined serving of the food. Nutritional labeling is voluntary for most foods, but it is mandatory for foods to which nutrients are added; foods to which reference is made on the label or in advertising to the caloric value or to the content of any nutrient other than sodium; and foods for which any nutritional claim is made on the label or in advertising.

U.S. Department of Agriculture. The Agricultural Marketing Service, USDA, has grading and inspection programs designed to certify quality and condition of agricultural commodities and food products. This agency develops standards on which grades are based. For most agricultural products, grading is voluntary. However, inspection of commodities for wholesomeness is mandatory for meats, poultry, and other processed foods distributed through interstate commerce. An inspector from the appropriate federal or other agency must give approval that the product is of high quality and processed under sanitary conditions before the official inspection stamp can be affixed.

The Wholesome Meat Act, passed in 1967, is an extension of the Federal Meat Inspection Act of 1906, and provides for establishing a uniform standard for state and federally inspected meats. Under this law, meats that do not cross state lines are required to be inspected in programs "at least equal to" federal inspection. The USDA is authorized to pay up to half the cost of the state inspection program, and provides technical assistance as needed. The Meat Inspection Division guards against use of harmful preservatives and residues from pesticides and from growth promotion substances such as drugs. This division also has established standards for minimum meat contents for meat products such as hash, stew, and chili con carne.

The Wholesome Poultry Products Act, effective in 1968, made similar provision for poultry inspection that the Wholesome Meat Act made for meat inspection. State inspection is encouraged but, if a state does not develop an adequate inspection program, all poultry processing plants within that state will come under mandatory federal inspection. The Egg Products Inspection Act, passed in 1970, provides for mandatory inspection of egg processing plants and requires that all liquid egg for freezing and drying be pasteurized. Standards of quality for poultry, eggs, and egg products have been set by the USDA. Minimum requirements for content of poultry have been specified also for processed poultry products defining percent of meat in items such as chicken or turkey pie, chicken á la king, chicken dinners, and chicken and noodles.

The USDA has an Acceptance Service for meat and poultry products available to large-scale purchasers. Large-scale meat purchasers are able to buy meat according to detailed specifications called Institutional Meat Purchase Specifications. For poultry and egg products, specifications are developed by the buyer. The product is "accepted" for the foodservice buyer by a qualified USDA trained grader at the processing plant. The product bears the stamp of the Acceptance Service, indicating that it does, indeed, meet the buyer's specifications and has been accepted.

U.S. Department of Commerce. A voluntary inspection system for fish and fish products and standard of grades for some products are controlled by the National Marine and Fisheries Service, U.S. Department of Commerce. If the product carries a U.S. grade designation, the purchaser is assured of continuous inplant inspection during processing by federal inspectors. An ungraded product may or may not have been inspected during processing.

The Public Health Service. This agency of the Department of Health, Education and Welfare is concerned primarily with control of infectious and contagious disease. The PHS assists states and municipalities with preparation of laws for prevention and control of diseases, especially those that may be transmitted through milk, shellfish, and foods served to the public in restaurants and vending machines. The Milk Ordinance Code, recommended by PHS, has been widely adopted.

QUALITY STANDARDS

Quality may refer to wholesomeness, cleanliness, or freedom from undesirable substances. It may denote a degree of perfection in shape, uniformity of size, or freedom from blemishes. It may also describe the extent of its desirable characteristics of color, flavor, aroma, texture, tenderness, and maturity. Assessment of quality may be denoted by grade, brand, and condition.

Grades. Grades are market classifications of quality. They reflect the relationship of the quality of the product to the standard established for the product, and they indicate the degree of variation from that standard.

There are established standards for most agricultural products and many fish items. Most of these standards are voluntarily used by growers, canners, and processors. The usual designations of quality grades are by:

Numbers: like U.S. No. 1, U.S. No. 2, U.S. No. 3, or as scores (87-93).

Letters: like Grade A, B, C.

Adjectives: like Prime, Choice, Good.

Mixed numbers, letters, and adjectives: like Extra Fancy, Fancy, No. 1, Utility.

Grade marking in the form of a shield is permitted only on foods officially graded under the supervision of the Agricultural Marketing Service of the U.S. Department of Agriculture. Figure 3.1 is an example of meat inspection and grade stamps.

(a)   (b)   (c)

FIGURE   3.1   *Federal meat stamps.* (a) *Round stamp shows that meat was federally inspected and passed as wholesome food; the number identifies the establishment in which meat was inspected.* (b) *Shield-shaped stamp shows that meat was federally graded.* (c) *Yield stamp denotes amount of usable meat in carcass.*

Brands. Brands are assigned by private organizations. Producers, processors, or distributors attempt to establish a commodity as a standard product and to develop demand specifically for their own brands. The reliability of brand depends on the reliability of the company. Brand names may represent products that are higher quality than the corresponding government grade, but some brand name products are not consistent in quality. Private companies may set up their own grading system, but such ranking may show variation from season to season. Some knowledge of brand names is essential in identifying food products and food quality in today's marketing system.

Condition. The condition of food products is concerned with factors that may change, resulting in loss of quality. Foods have varying degrees of perishability, from the comparatively stable canned and dried foods to the highly perishable fresh fish, poultry, dairy products, and produce. Although products may be the quality or grade specified at time of grading, the condition of the product may change rapidly because of poor environmental factors.

Changes in condition resulting in impaired quality can be avoided in part by careful inspection at delivery and by defining in the specifications where appropriate the interval of time that may elapse between grading and delivery; for example, for eggs it may be specified that not more than 72 hours elapse between grading and delivery.

PURCHASING PROCEDURES
DETERMINING FOOD NEEDS

Determination of food needs is a major phase of the total purchasing responsibility. "Needs" refer to quality as well as quantity, both of which are closely interrelated with cost control. The person who buys the food, whether he be the owner, dietitian, manager, or full-time purchasing agent, must make his selection to obtain the best quality possible for the money spent and at a suitable price for the particular foodservice. Where the food is bought by a purchasing agent, it is important that the dietitian or food manager be able to express in specific terms his needs for quantity and quality so the buyer has no doubt as to what and how much to purchase from the many grades, styles, varieties, and forms of food available.

If convenience foods are to be purchased, the dietitian or manager should determine whether to buy individual ingredients, mixes, or finished products. Because of lack of space, equipment, or personnel, some institutions are faced with a decision to convert to an all-convenience system in which all prepared foods are purchased. Once this decision is made, the dietitian and buyer must establish quality standards for these foods. Standards of identity are being developed for some of them, but there is wide variation in quality.

For the foodservice preferring onsite preparation, there are alternatives in purchasing that may be beneficial in terms of saving preparation time. Processed ingredients, such as dehydrated chopped onions or frozen lemon juice, have become commonplace in foodservices, as have the various baking, sauce, and pudding mixes. Casserole-type entrees, often requiring time-consuming processes, may be made by combining several convenience items such as freeze-dried or frozen diced chicken, meat or fish, sauce made from a mix or from canned soups, and pasta or vegetables. Keeping in mind the quality standard established for the finished product, the dietitian or manager must find the right combination of available foods in a form that will keep preparation time to a minimum, yet yield a high-quality product.

Quantities of food needed are based on the number of persons to be served, the size portion to be given, and the amount of waste and shrinkage loss involved in the preparation of foods. This general procedure may be used in determining amounts of meats, poultry, fruits, and vegetables for specific menu items.

1. Determine portion size.

2. Multiply portion size by the number to be served and convert to pounds. This determines edible portion (EP) required. EP may also be given in the standardized recipe.

3. To determine amount to purchase, EP will be divided by the percent yield (or the amount provided by 1 pound of the commodity).

$$EP \div yield = amount\ to\ purchase$$

4. The amount to purchase is converted to the most appropriate purchase unit (e.g., case, crate, roast, or carton). If the food is needed for other menu items, amounts may be combined prior to conversion to purchase unit, if timing according to the menu is suitable. When only a portion of a purchase unit is needed, the full unit must be

purchased as a rule. Care must be taken to utilize the remainder of the unit, especially with perishable products.

Records of meal census may be used to good advantage to determine present numbers to be served. Standardized recipes give portion sizes and quantities required for prepared foods. A knowledge of wholesale weights and sizes for various commodities helps the buyer to translate his quantity needs into appropriate units of purchase.

SYSTEMATIC ORDERING PROCEDURES

The complexity of the purchasing system will depend on the size and type of organization, whether the buying is centralized or decentralized, and established management policies. Procedures should be as simple as possible, with record keeping and paper work limited to those essential for control and communication. Good purchasing procedures include the use of specifications and appropriate buying method, a systematic ordering schedule, and maintenance of an adequate flow of goods to meet production requirements. A system of communicating needs from the production areas and the storeroom to the buyer is essential. Establishing a minimum and maximum stock level provides a means of alerting the buyer to needs, particularly regarding canned and frozen foods and staples.

Frequency of purchase and the amount of food purchased at one time is fairly dependent on the amount of money at hand, the method of buying, frequency of deliveries, and space for inventory stock. With adequate and suitable storage, the purchase of staples may vary from a 2- to 6-month supply, with perishables weekly and/or daily.

A well-organized purchasing routine will save time, eliminate error, and give assurance that the right food will be at the right place when needed.

METHODS OF BUYING

Buying food is a management function and, as such, the food service administrator will have policies and procedures to guide him in setting up a course of buying action. Overall policies may decree, for example, that the manager shall buy only from certain vendors, as might be true in a private or religious organization, or that purchases shall be distributed to vendors in the locality, perhaps in rotation for a certain period of time or volume of business for each. State and municipal institutions often follow this policy. In addition, the buyer will be guided by the customs and traditions of wholesale buying that are practiced in this country and that vary according to the size and location of the organization. They may be quite informal, known as "open-market" buying, or on a formal basis, known as "competitive-bid" buying. Food managers may use both methods at various times for different commodities.

Informal or the *open-market* buying is used by a majority of institutions. The buyer requests quotations on the specific food items he needs and for specific amounts and quality from one or more sources of supply. The order is placed after consideration of price in relation to quality, delivery, and other services offered. Contact between the buyer and vendor is made by telephone, a visit to the market, or through salesmen who call on the buyer.

The use of "price quotation and order sheets" on which to record the prices given by each seller is an aid to the buyer. Examples of such sheets are Forms 3.1 and 3.2. When the order is placed, the price quoted by the vendor selected is circled. This type of buying is used for most perishables particularly fruits, vegetables, and meat.

Multiple-unit and other large foodservice organizations sometimes employ methods of informal buying, such as *blank-check* buying. In this procedure buyers entrust the purchase of specific foods that may be in critical supply to reputable sellers, and give them a "blank-check" privilege of shipping to the institution when, if, and as a commodity is available within a given price range and period of time.

Formal competitive-bid buying is the procedure of submitting written specifications and quantity needs to vendors with an invitation for them to submit prices for the items listed. The request for bids may be quite formal and advertised in the newspaper, printed or mimeographed and copies widely distributed, or less formal with single copies supplied to interested sellers. In addition to definite specifications for each item of food, the requests for bid must include the general conditions of acceptance as date and method of delivery, terms of payment, willingness to accept all or part of the bid, discounts, and other terms of the negotiations, as well as the date of closing bids. The bids received remain sealed until a specified time and are opened in public for governmental and other large organization bidding or, more often, in private for the smaller insti-

Name of Food Service

Fruit and Vegetable Quotation and Order Sheet

For Use on _____   Delivery Date _____

	Specs	Amount Needed	Amount on Hand	Amount to Order	Price Quotes Vendors A	B	C	D
Fruits:								
Vegetables:								

FORM   3.1   *A suggested form for recording telephoned price quotations for fresh produce. Combines a listing of total needs, the inventory on hand, and the resulting quantities to order. When order is placed, price quote from vendor from whom it is to be purchased is circled.*

_____ **University**
FOOD STORES DEPARTMENT

	INQUIRY NO.

_____
(Date)

To: ⌐　　　　　　　　　　　　¬　Quote on this sheet your net price f.o.b.
　　　　　　　　　　　　　　　　for the items specified below. We re-
　　　　　　　　　　　　　　　　serve the right to accept or reject all
　　　　　　　　　　　　　　　　or part of this proposal.
　　　　　　　　　　　　　　　　Quotations received
　　└　　　　　　　┘　　　　　until 4:00 P.M. _____

Important: Read instructions on reverse side before preparing bid.

Quantity	Unit	REQUEST FOR QUOTATIONS—This is NOT an order	Price Unit	Total Price
		Return—TWO COPIES—To: Food Stores		
		Department		

We quote you f.o.b._____ Delivery can be made ⎰immediately
　　　　　　　　　　　　　　　　　　　　　　　　　　　⎱_____ days.

_____
　　Sign Firm Name Here
　　　　　　　　　　　　　　　Cash Discount: _____
_____ Per _____
　　Date

FORM   3.2   Suggested form for requesting price quotations by mail.

tutions. Generally, the order must be placed with the company submitting the lowest bid unless the product fails to meet specification.

Negotiated buying, a *semiformal* method, is the practice of purchasing in times of seasonal, limited, or restricted production. It is a method that provides a flexible means of obtaining quick, decisive action in a fluctuating market. Buyers contact vendors directly and request bids that are then submitted in writing as soon as possible. There are less strict regulations on this type of bidding and acceptance than with the competitive-bid buying.

Food buyers for large institutions may purchase at *auction* certain commodities, such as eggs or produce. They often buy direct from a packer or canner, also. This requires a contract of one of two types: an "unsigned" or FAOP (Firm at Opening Price) contract in which the buyer agrees to take the supplies at a price established at a future time when crop yield is known instead of preseason when the contract is signed. Or, a contract may be SAP (Subject Approval of Price), in which case the buyer has the privilege of rejecting the order if the price is not suitable to him.

Future contracts, another term used on the wholesale market, means the purchase of goods at a specific price but shipped later at specified intervals. Other intricacies of buying are possible for large-volume purchasing; however, the terms included here are the more generally used ones and should suffice for a fair understanding of the procedures used by less complex foodservice organizations.

SPECIFICATIONS

Knowledge of how to write specifications for the desired quality is essential. If adequate communications are not established between the buyer and seller, there is no recourse if the food received is not what was expected. Before specifications are written, however, the production manager must decide on the form and quality of food suitable for the specific needs. For example, over a period of time the menu may call for pineapple salad, pineapple cream pie, pineapple sauce for ham, and a molded fruit salad with pineapple in it. Should the manager buy fresh pineapple or frozen sections? Is canned best suited for all purposes? If so, should he buy whole rings, broken slices, crushed, diced, tidbits, or spears? Should it be packed in a heavy or light syrup? What size pieces of fruit will give the best portion yield? These are but a few of the questions that the buyer must answer.

After the use has been determined, the food buyer must determine the specifications for each quality of food desired, define in detail the specifications of each standard, and proceed to locate a product that will meet these standards. A specification may be considered an accurate word picture or a definition of a product. It must be definite enough so that there will be no misunderstanding as to the item required. Such a precise specification not only makes it possible to obtain the quality wanted, but it makes competitive bidding effective.

Specifications should be brief and simple but complete. Always included are: name of the product, quantity, size or type of unit or container, federal grade or brand, unit on which price will be quoted, and additional information appropriate for each item. Examples of a few specifics follow: count and density (brix) of syrup for peach halves; production area and variety of citrus fruit; style of canned corn; variety of frozen apples; sieve size of canned peas; cut, weight, and style of beef roast; packing medium; and maturity, as in tree-ripened apricots. Specifications for food purchasing are not easily developed but, with federal standards available as a guide and with the assistance of manufacturers, processors, researchers, and salesmen, the institution food buyer can readily identify grades that will meet his needs and describe to the seller precisely what is wanted. Familiarity with grade standards for each commodity is essential to an understanding of the levels of quality in foods. These are discussed for each food group on the pages that follow.

Inspection of the products at the time they are received is an important function in food purchasing. A check with the purchase order and delivery sheet should be made before the latter is signed for the deliveryman, unless it has been agreed that the driver need not be detained for a check of weight, count, and condition, and that discrepancies may be reported later.

SELECTION OF FOODS

Familiarity with grade standards for each commodity is essential to the understanding of the levels of quality in foods. Also, the buyer must know the market forms available and the corresponding units of purchase, including size, count, and weight. Some knowledge of the bases for making estimates of quantities of each food needed and of how they will be stored and used are other requirements of the person who purchases food in quantity for a given foodservice.

A condensed compilation of certain pertinent facts about food groups follows. It should be supplemented with detailed reference materials on each item, current research findings, and local market information.

MEAT

The amount of money spent for meat in the average foodservice represents 40 to 50 percent of the total food costs; therefore selection demands more than casual attention of the buyer.

Style. Meat may be purchased for institutions in any one of several forms—in the carcass, by the quarter, wholesale cut, or in ready-to-serve portions. The method of purchase best suited to any particular institution depends on several factors, including delivery service, storage and breakdown facilities, labor costs, and ability to utilize all parts of the edible meat. Inefficiency in any one of these steps can result in an increase in waste and a higher servicing cost per unit.

Carcass and Cuts. When carcass meat is purchased, increased storage and breakdown facilities are necessary. Breakdown calls for additional high-priced labor if it is to be done efficiently. Also, there is always the additional problem of disposing of bones, excess fat, and other waste. Meat purchased by the carcass also demands efficient management within the institution; otherwise this type of purchase can result in high inventories. Menus must provide for a complete utilization of the carcass and a quick turnover of all parts. Inferior cuts should never be substituted for luxury cuts, and potential steaks and roasts should not be sacrificed as ground beef or stew if the unit cost is to be held within reasonable limits.

Selection of wholesale cuts of meat, chiefly ribs, loins, and rounds, is preferred by some operators. Further breakdown is necessary to obtain steaks, chops, or small roasts (see Fig. 3.2). This requires precision cutting in order to eliminate waste and to control the cost per portion. Wholesalers or jobbers cater to this type of trade by buying carcass meat, breaking out the cut, and disposing of the balance of the carcass through other channels. When purchasing is done in this manner, rigid specifications of weight, quality, and trim must be designated.

"Meat Buyers Guides," one for carcass, wholesale, and subprimal cuts and one for portion control cuts, are available from the National Association of Meat Purveyors. These guides contain suggested specifications and a cut numbering system that is in wide use today and that has been adopted by USDA specifications.

Prefabricated Meat. The purchase of meat in prefabricated or portion-ready form offers a maximum of control. This type of service is readily available today and offers a real opportunity to lighten the load of management and make control possible. A wide variety of cuts may be purchased and stored ready for use. The fact that these cuts may be purchased either fresh or frozen aids in making it possible to

BEEF CHART
Wholesale and Retail Cuts

Numerals in circles ◯ refer
to wholesale cuts and major
subdivisions of such cuts.
Letters refer to retail cuts.

①HIND SHANK
a. Soup bones
b. Heel of Round

⑥FLANK
a. Flank steak
b. Stew or ground
   beef

⑨PLATE
a. Stew, ground beef,
   or boned and rolled
   pot roasts
b. Short ribs

⑩BRISKET
Stew or boned and
rolled pot roasts

⑪FORE SHANK
Soup bones or
ground beef

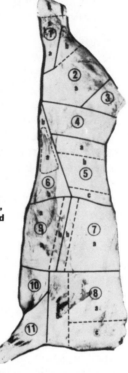

②ROUND
a. Round steaks or roasts
b. Pot roast

③RUMP
Roasts or steaks

④SIRLOIN
Sirloin steaks or
roasts

⑤SHORT LOIN
a. Porterhouse steaks
b. T-bone steaks
c. Club or Top Loin
   steaks

⑦RIB
a. Rib roasts or
   steaks
b. Short ribs

⑧CHUCK
a. Chuck blade roasts
   or steaks
b. Arm pot roasts or
   steaks
c. Stew or ground beef

YIELDS OF WHOLESALE CUTS AND SUBDIVISIONS
Percentage of Carcass Weight

① to ⑥ HINDQUARTER 48.0%	⑦ to ⑪ FOREQUARTER . . 52.0%
① to ③ Round and Rump . 24.0%	⑦ Rib 9.5%
① Hind shank . 4.0%	⑧ Chuck 24.5
② Buttock . . . 15.5	⑨ Plate 8.0
③ Rump 4.5	⑩ Brisket . . . 6.0
④ and ⑤ Full loin inc. suet. 20.5	⑪ Fore shank . 4.0
④ Sirloin . . . 9.0	
⑤ Short loin . . 8.0	
Kidney knob . 3.5	
⑥ Flank 3.5	

FIGURE 3.2. A buyers' guide identifying wholesale and retail cuts of
beef.

carry a large inventory of any one item with limited storage space and small risk of deterioration.

Ready-to-serve portions can be purchased according to quality, size, and trim to meet the needs of any institution. This means elimination of waste, an established cost for each serving, and equal portions for all customers. This type of purchasing is unusually well adapted to steaks, lamb, veal, and pork chops, pork tenderloin, chicken, and turkey, but is applicable to all meat cuts. Even ground meat and stew meat will be more uniform and more satisfactory when purchased in this manner than if assembled from accumulated leftover cuts in the refrigerator.

Advantages of purchasing prefabricated cuts may be summarized as follows: each portion is cut, trimmed, and ready to be cooked with no trimming waste to be absorbed; each steak, chop, cutlet is cut to specification as to quality, weight, age, and cost; and each person served receives the same size portion; the cuts are packaged with wax-paper separators in cartons or boxes with nonabsorbent linings, and shipped by refrigerated truck if distance is a factor. When unpacked, the meat is ready to use, and there is no refuse to soil the preparation area; refrigeration space required is far less than for carcasses or wholesale cuts; less equipment, such as electric saws and grinders, is required; high-priced personnel skilled in the art of meat cutting are unnecessary; and, most important, as a control measure, the cost of each portion of meat, the most expensive part of a meal, is known when the menu is planned.

Prefabricated meats are sold by packers (usually frozen) and by jobbers (fresh or frozen). The usual package is a 10-pound carton, as illustrated in Fig. 3.3. Cuts are sized according to specifications, such as "medium-weight, center-loin pork chops, cut 3/1 pound," and are packaged individually wrapped or layer style.

The quality of meat is highly variable and, for the convenience of the consumer and seller, beef, veal, lamb, mutton, and some meat products are classified into groups based on age, into classes based on sex, and into grades based on quality. The bovine animals are classified, because of age characteristics, into beef, calves, and veal. Ovine animals are divided into mutton, yearlings, and lamb. There are no standards for the age group of pork.

Classes and Grades of Meat. The classes of beef are steer, heifer, bullock (young bull up to 24 months of age), cow, stag, and bull. The classes for sheep are ewe, wether, and ram; the pork classes are barrow, gilt, sow, stag, and boar. Standards indicating quality

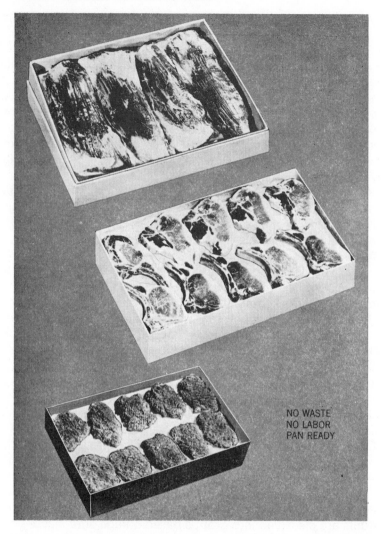

NO WASTE
NO LABOR
PAN READY

FIGURE   3.3   *Ten-pound cartons of portion-ready meat cuts. Top: flank steaks; middle: pork chops; lower: veal cutlets. Courtesy, Armour and Company.*

have been set by the U.S. government for the grading of meat and meat products.

Beef. The grade of beef is determined by (1) maturity or approximate age of animal from which carcass was derived, determined from skeleton and color of muscle, and (2) the quality of the flesh. Quality refers to marbling or amount of fat deposited within the lean, muscle texture or the fineness of grain, and firmness and color of the flesh. Carcasses must be ribbed for grading, as ribeye muscle cross section exposed between front and hind quarter. The gradation from white through pink, to a brilliant red, exemplified by veal, calf, and mature beef is produced merely by increased amounts of muscle pigmentation or muscle hemoglobin.

Grades of fresh beef that may be specified by the buyer are USDA Prime, Choice, Good, Standard, Commercial, Utility, Cutter, and Canner. Grades are based on definite federal grade standards that are applied by skilled impartial federal meat graders in the same uniform manner throughout the year, without regard to supply and demand or other economic conditions. Brief descriptions for each grade of beef follow:

USDA Prime. Prime beef is produced from young well-fed beef cattle. Liberal quantities of fat are interspersed within the lean. Because of its high quality, more cuts are suitable to roasting or broiling than in any of the other grades. Only about 3 to 4 percent of the beef graded qualifies for the Prime grade.

USDA Choice. This is the grade produced in greatest abundance (80 percent of graded beef) and is available in good supply throughout the year. It has less fat than the Prime grade. Roasts and steaks from the grade are normally tender, juicy, and well-flavored.

USDA Good. An acceptable quality especially to thrifty buyers who seek beef with little fat. Cuts of this grade may lack the juiciness associated with a high degree of intramuscular fat.

USDA Standard. Standard beef is from young animals and has a thin covering of fat and little mixture of fat within the lean. It will appeal to food buyers whose first concern is a high proportion of lean. It is mild in flavor but lacks juiciness and tenderness usually found in beef with more marbling.

USDA Commercial. Commercial beef is produced from mature animals, and therefore lacks natural tenderness. It has a characteristic beef flavor that is associated with its maturity; requires long slow cooking with moist heat.

USDA Utility. Usually this grade is produced from animals advanced in age and lacks natural tenderness and juiciness. However, it is usable in dishes such as meat loaves, spaghetti sauce, and chili, when ground beef is the basis of the recipe.

USDA Cutter and Canner. These grades are ordinarily used in processed meat products.

The institution buyer usually purchases from the first 3 grades. Steers, heifers, bullocks, and young cows may be placed in any one of the top 4 grades, except cow does not qualify as Prime. An extremely small percentage of young cattle, up to 42 months of age, could grade Utility. Mature cows, bulls, and stags grade Commercial or lower. Packers also may grade meat and use their individual brand names to designate grades.

The specifications for each grade are so clearly defined that it is possible to purchase satisfactorily large quantities of meat entirely by grade. This is the only method that will ensure the average buyer the quality he desires, other than by personal selection. Also, he can be certain that the quality delivered is the same as that ordered.

Beef carcasses are also yield graded to identify "quantity" or "cutability" differences among carcasses. The yield grade is an estimate of the percentage yield of boneless, closely trimmed retail cuts from a carcass, with highest percentage in Yield Grade 1 and lowest in Yield Grade 5. Factors considered in yield grade are amount of external fat, as measured by the fat over the ribeye muscle; size of the ribeye; quantity of kidney, pelvic, and heart fat; and weight of carcass before chilling.

New grading standards for beef, effective in February, 1976, reduce the amount of marbling required for the Prime and Choice grades, especially in cattle from 18 to 30 months of age. In addition, conformation will no longer be considered in quality grading, and yield grade is mandatory for all carcasses that are quality graded. The new grading has had the effect of narrowing the quality standards for the Good grade, making it a more reliable index of quality.

An acceptance type of grading service for meat is available to quantity buyers through the USDA grading stations. For a nominal fee the shipment is inspected and each carton stamped to assure the buyer that the products meet contract specifications. Most institutions now use Institutional Purchase Specifications (IMPS) developed by the USDA Livestock Division as guides for establishing their own specifications. The federal grade stamp on the meat is a reliable guide to quality and may be recognized easily, since the grade name appears on each wholesale cut (see Fig. 3.4).

Since the inauguration of the U.S. grading system in 1927, some timely revisions have been made to meet changes in the meat industry. At the present time the grading of beef and lamb is based on subjective standards and, until such time as reliable objective measurements are perfected, some variation may enter into the grading system. However, the training and supervision of those persons responsible for federal grading is such that the personal element is reduced to a minimum. Federal grading is optional and is only per-

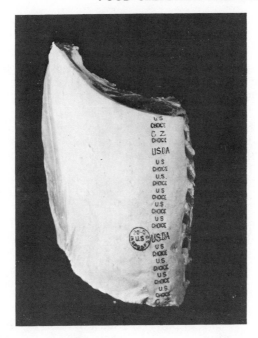

FIGURE   3.4   *The round stamp indicates that the meat has passed federal inspection for wholesomeness; the ribbon stamp indicates quality. Courtesy, U.S. Department of Agriculture.*

formed on request. The cost of this service is paid by fees charged to the packer. The demand for graded meat has increased in recent years.

Amount To Buy. The menu item, such as roast, steak, Swedish meatballs, and the cost level of operation determine to a great extent the quality and cut of beef to purchase. A guide for suggested suitable cookery methods for various cuts of different qualities of beef is found in Table 3.1.

The quantity to buy is based on the number and size of portions needed, although the quality of beef, the cut, and method of preparation are important factors, also, because they all affect the amount of shrinkage, evaporation, dripping, and cutting losses.

The amount of bone in the cut of meat also is an important factor in determining the amount to buy. Many foodservices purchase boneless cuts for ease of portioning and serving. Where a standing rib roast, T-bone steak, or short ribs would yield only 2 servings per

TABLE 3.1   SUGGESTED COOKING GUIDE FOR BEEF

The use of an appropriate method of cooking is essential to bring out the desirable eating qualities of the specific cut and grade selected. Below is a guide suggesting the most generally accepted method of cooking retail cuts of beef of each grade.

Flank, plate, brisket, foreshank, and the heel of the round should be prepared in the same manner for all grades of beef. These less tender cuts are used for stewing, braising, pot roasting, or boiling, or are ground for use in meat loaves and similar dishes.

Cut	Prime	Choice	Good
Top round and sirloin tip (steaks and roasts)	Braise, broil, pan fry, pot roast, or roast	Braise, broil, pan fry, pot roast, or roast	Braise, pan fry, pot roast, or roast
Bottom round (steaks and roasts)	Braise, pan fry, pot roast, or roast	Braise, pan fry, pot roast, or roast	Braise, pot roast, or roast
Rump roast	Roast or pot roast	Roast or pot roast	Roast or pot roast
Sirloin (steaks and roasts)	Broil, pan fry, or roast	Broil, pan fry, or roast	Broil, pan fry, or roast
Porterhouse, T-bone, club and rib steaks	Broil	Broil	Broil
Rib roast	Roast	Roast	Roast
Chuck, round bone and blade (roasts and steaks)	Roast, pot roast, or braise	Roast, pot roast, or braise	Roast, pot roast, or braise

Source. *"U.S. Grades for Beef,"* Marketing Bulletin No. 15, *U.S. Department of Agriculture, Washington, D.C., 1960.*

pound, 3 to 5 servings per pound of boneless roasts, steaks, or stew meat could be planned. When meat is portioned prior to cooking, as in swiss steak or cubed steak, an exact number of portions can be ordered. In purchasing roasts, an allowance should be made for slicing losses—meat that is unsuitable for serving as slices but that is usable for sandwiches or prepared entrees. In addition, the amount of meat needed must be translated into uniform size roasts, which may result in slightly more than the amount needed for slicing but for which usage should be planned.

Stew meat and ground beef generally are used with extenders so less meat per portion is needed. However, if a manager must meet USDA protein requirements for school foodservice or Medicare and Medicaid requirements for extended care facilities, an adequate amount of meat should be purchased to yield 2 to 3 ounces of cooked meat per person. Yield information based on controlled research is available. One source is the USDA's publication PA-270, "Food Buying Guide for Type A Lunches."

Lists of amounts of food required to serve 100 or more and the average weights of wholesale cuts are found in most quantity cookbooks and in meat manuals available from salesmen, or from organizations such as the National Live Stock and Meat Board. A few typical examples follow: if the estimated quantity for 100 3-ounce portions (cooked weight) of standing rib roast is 50 pounds, or 2 servings per pound raw weight, similarly, the buyer would order 42 pounds for 100 2.5-ounce portions. Another basic estimate is approximately 3 portions per pound raw weight for top round roast, and the order might read 3 10-pound inside top round roasts, USDA Choice. Likewise, on the basis of 3, 4, or 5 servings per pound raw weight for Swedish meatballs, the order would be 34, 25, or 20 pounds of fine ground beef (3/16 inches grinder plate), U.S. Good chuck with 20 percent fat. An order for steaks would give the number, weight of each steak, the cut, grade, packed ____ to the carton, and whether fresh or frozen. Calves liver might be requested thus: 2 10-pound boxes, skinned calves liver, sliced 1/4 inch thick, portioned 5/1 pound, layer style.

Orders should be given to the salesman or jobber several days in advance of the time specified for delivery and copies kept to check on items received.

Other Kinds of Meat. Important kinds of meat other than beef are veal, calf, pork, lamb, and mutton.

Veal. Veal is defined as the flesh of bovine animals, usually not over 12 weeks of age at the time of killing, the largest number being slaughtered between the ages of 3 and 6 weeks. Calf carcasses are from more mature animals of the bovine species that have passed beyond the veal stage but have not yet taken on beef characteristics. Veal carcasses usually weigh between 50 and 150 pounds; calf carcasses, between 100 to 350 pounds.

The musculature of veal carcass resembles that of beef, the immaturity expressed not in muscle pattern but in character of flesh. The ruddy color of beef is lacking, the flesh being a light pinkish gray-brown. The flesh is fine grained, soft or flabby in texture, and contains little intramuscular fat. The coat of exterior fat is thin and pinkish white.

The grades of veal most commonly used in institutions are USDA Prime, USDA Choice, and USDA Good. The meat of good veal is light pink in color, fine in grain, and firm and velvety in texture. The small quantity of fat is clear, firm, and pinkish white. There is no marbling of fat in the meat. The bones are porous, soft, and red.

Veal is used less often than beef or pork in the institution menu. Ordinarily legs, shoulder, and breast are used for roasts; loin, ribs, and shoulder for chops; and shoulder, shank, and neck for stew. Shrinkage is high in veal because of its immaturity and high moisture content.

Pork. Pork is the flesh of swine. Government grades are USDA 1, 2, 3, or 4 and Utility. A USDA 1 carcass is well muscled and with a minimum of fat, and a 3 would be heavier and fatter in appearance. Currently, many packers are grading both carcasses and wholesale cuts on the basis of their own standards, which estimate cut-out yield. Cuts are not graded.

The best quality of pork has muscle that is grayish white to pink in young and deep rose in older animals. The flesh is firm and fine grained, and the bones are soft and red. With the marketing of hogs at an earlier age (5 months instead of the previous 8 months) the flesh is often relatively soft and high in moisture, because of immaturity, and the amount of fat in relation to lean is reduced.

Fresh ham and loin cuts, both regular and boned, are used extensively for roasts, and loins for chops. Shoulders and other cuts are utilized in processed meats such as cold cuts and sausage; sides are cured for bacon. A high percentage of hams and shoulders are cured, as are an increasing quantity of loins. Fresh spareribs are popular, often in barbecue form.

Lamb and Mutton. Lamb is a term commonly used to designate the flesh of young animals of the ovine species, usually limited to those under 12 or 14 months of age and yielding a carcass weighing between 35 and 65 pounds. Mutton is the flesh of the mature sheep more than 20 months of age. Lamb carcasses differ from mutton in that they are usually lighter in weight, have a smaller, softer bone, lighter-colored flesh, softer and whiter internal fat, and the break joint is always in evidence. The grades in which the institution buyer would be interested are Prime and Choice. Standards for these grades are much like those of beef and are based on shape or conformation, color, and fineness of bone, feathering (fat streaks between ribs), flank fat lacing and thickness, and firmness of flank. The last three standards presumably estimate marbling. USDA also grades lamb for yield, No. 1 representing the highest yield. Yield grade considers fat thickness over the ribeye, percent kidney-pelvic-heart fat, and leg conformation.

Amount To Buy. Determinations of the quantities of the various cuts and qualities of veal, pork, and lamb are made in similar manner as those suggested for beef. Tables of cooking losses and yields from reports of controlled research and experimentation, pertinent records within the particular foodservice, and a study of up-to-date market information are helpful aids to buying. Influencing factors for each item will need to be considered by the dietitian or food manager in cooperation with the buyer, if he is a different person.

Variety Meats. Liver is incorporated into menus regularly in many institution foodservices. Calf and beef liver are more generally accepted than that from other sources. Usually it is purchased skinned and sliced to specification, either fresh or frozen. Since liver is solid but light, 1/4 to 1/5 pound per serving is a standard that can be used in estimating quantities needed. Heart, sweetbreads, and brains are purchased fresh. Tongue may be obtained fresh, smoked, or pickled. Generally, the amount needed would be comparable to liver.

Processed Meats. New meat products appear on the market almost daily. Among them are a variety of forms of cured meats, cooked or partially cooked, frozen, dehydrated, or freeze-dried items.

Ham and Bacon. Years ago most commercially cured meat products, particularly ham and bacon, represented a product that was so preserved that it could be stored without refrigeration. Such full-cured or country-style hams are still available, particularly in the southern part of the United States. Most imported hams, other than canned, are of this variety. The modern American ham is, however, a quick-cured product low in salt level, mild in flavor, and highly perishable. The process involves color fixation and a light smoke applied in the smokehouse, which cooks the ham. The resulting product may be partially cooked ham, or a fully cooked ham that is ready to serve. These hams are fragile and must be stored under refrigeration.

Many users prefer cured hams (bone in) ranging from 12 to 16 pounds in weight. Popular weights of boned hams, compressed into viscose casings or pressed into the popular flat ham shape, are 10 to 14 pounds. Fully cooked hams in artificial casings or pear-shaped tins usually weigh 8 1/2 to 10 pounds and may be served without reheating. The actual nature of the ham and the recommended preparation should be stated on the wrapper. The cost of sliceable meat obtainable from each type of ham and its acceptability are factors of sufficient importance to the manager to encourage a study of the relative value of each type in the foodservice for which he is responsible.

Bacon is given a short cure that aids in fixing the color and developing the flavor. It should be well streaked with lean, with strips not longer than 8 to 10 inches. Refrigerated storage is necessary as it is not a cooked product. Most institutions purchase sliced bacon as regular—20 to 22 slices per pound—or hotel—28 to 30 slices per pound, layered in 6- or 12-pound cartons. Bacon may be purchased in regular or shingle pack, in which bacon slices adhering to each other are arranged in layers. A more convenient choice may be the layout or flat pack where single layers of bacon are placed on parchment paper. The bacon is panned on the parchment paper, eliminating the time-consuming task of separating each strip. Slab bacon may be purchased with rind on or off and cut 18 to 20 slices per pound.

Sausage Products. Only meat and spices of high quality should be incorporated in sausage, and the inspection stamp for wholesomeness should be on all products or their containers. Fresh sausage is prepared mainly from fresh pork trimmings, whereas frankfurters or wieners may run 30 to 100 percent beef and usually are 30 to 70 percent pork plus extenders such as cereal or dry milk. Bologna is a mixture similar to frankfurters except the sausage is large in diameter and often presliced. Sausage may be purchased in natural and artificial casings from fingerlike links, 4, 8, 12, or 16 per pound to those 20 inches or more in length and 3 to 4 inches in diameter or sliced. Fresh sausage is also available in bulk. Frankfurters, wieners, Vienna, and bologna and some others are given a light smoke. Numerous varieties and types of sausages are available on the market. Some are fresh, smoked, fully cooked, or partially cooked, such as the brown-and-serve style. Directions on the package must be followed for the best utilization of the particular product, and storage should be for a short time only at no higher than 38°F.

Cured Beef. Corned beef may be made from the round, brisket, or plate as specified, and in appropriate weight for the cut, for example, 6 to 12 pounds for brisket. Range in color is from grayish to light pink to medium red. The fat should be fairly firm and waxy, not soft and oily.

Usually, *dried beef* is prepared from inside round and knuckle cuts from very lean carcasses and sliced thin across the grain of the main muscles. Institution users purchase 5- or 10-pound cartons, although the 1-pound package may be more adapted to the needs of the small foodservice.

Frozen Entree Items. A wide variety of meat and prepared meat entrees are now available from commercial processors. Packaged in individual servings or in bulk in the frozen or chilled state, these foods are ready for reheating by immersion in hot water, in a conventional or convection oven, in the steamer, or electronically. Because these products have been on the market a relatively short time and the numbers and variety are increasing so rapidly, very few specifications have been established for their purchase. Until standards do exist, the buyer may need to purchase by brand after sampling and comparing brands against each other and with onsite prepared entrees. In comparing products, the ratio of meat to other ingredients should be noted, as well as flavor, consistency, appearance, and cost.

Preservation of meat and *meat products by freezing* has become more and more important to the institution food buyer. Practically all meat items are available in frozen form, which means dependability of the supply throughout the year, reasonable assurance of good quality and, frequently, economy. In this method of processing meat, it is first chilled by reducing the temperature from approximately 180° to 38° or 40°F. Beef and lamb may then be aged, but veal and pork should be further processed as rapidly as possible. When meat is to be frozen it is usually broken down into wholesale or retail cuts, packaged, and frozen. For best results freezing should be rapid at temperatures well below 0°F, and the storage temperatures maintained not above 0°F. For long-term storage lower temperatures are more desirable. Freezing protects the natural flavor, texture, color, and palatability as well as nutritional value of meat to a higher degree than any other method of preservation in general use at the present time.

Although few institutions freeze meat for their own use, they often store it in the freezer unit that is standard equipment for all foodservices. It has been said that the storage unit should not be used as a safe deposit box but, instead, as a checking account. . . . Deterioration progresses even when food is frozen, though at a very slow rate. Zero degree Fahrenheit has been suggested as a desirable storage temperature, provided the period of storage is not too long.

The two greatest difficulties encountered with frozen meat are dehydration and rancidity, both of which can be avoided by proper packaging, rapid freezing, and storage at 0°F or lower. Pork fat becomes rancid more readily than that of beef, veal, or lamb; therefore, the storage life of frozen fresh pork should be relatively short. Salt and slicing or grinding encourage and speed up rancidity.

Freezer storage time should be limited to not over 12 months for beef and lamb cuts, 6 months for ground beef, 9 months for fresh pork, 6 months for cured pork, 1 month for sliced bacon, and 3 months for sausage.

Care of Meat. Meat for institution foodservices, other than that sold by the carcass or wholesale cuts, is usually delivered in refrigerated trucks. The first step after unpacking is the checking of the weight delivered with that called for by the invoice. Thaw indicators are now available that can be placed in boxes at point of shipment and, in a general way, show temperature abuse. Chilled products should be at 40°F or colder at delivery and should not be accepted if the temperature is above 45°F. A thermometer is a good investment, and taking two pictures of substandard products at receipt will help settle claims. One picture is sent to the supplier with the claim and one is retained.

If the meat is not to be used at once, it is unwrapped and stored in the meat refrigerator. For fresh meat the temperature should be held close to 32°F and the relative humidity from 80 to 90 percent. Temperatures below this level cause the surface of meat to darken because of slow freezing action; above this level bacterial spoilage develops. Even when stored at this temperature, fresh meat should not be kept unfrozen for longer than 3 to 4 days. If any section of the refrigerator is colder than the average temperature of 33 to 36°F it should be reserved for fresh pork cuts. Meat should be stored away from other foods. Foreign flavors in meats may be traced to fresh fruits and vegetables stored in the same refrigerator.

The present-day light-cured meats and "tenderized" hams *must* be stored under refrigeration but, unlike fresh meats, they are stored wrapped or covered to prevent the odor from permeating throughout the refrigerator. Full-cured hams may be stored in a cool room. Ground meat should be used within 24 hours; otherwise it should be precooked, or frozen. *Frozen meat that has been allowed to thaw should be cooked at once.* Cooked meat should be well covered when stored.

Textured Vegetable Protein Products. Simulated meat products made from soy protein are becoming increasingly well accepted, and their use in foodservices undoubtedly will increase as meat costs rise and as new uses for these products are found. In the current National School Foodservice Program, textured vegetable proteins may be mixed with meat, poultry, or fish in an amount not to exceed 30 percent. Although its main use so far has been to mix with ground beef, TVP also is available in other forms, such as cubed "beef, veal, ham, or chicken."

FISH

Edible fish and shellfish are readily available in today's market as fresh, frozen, canned, and cured; a few items are available in the freeze-dried form.

The Agricultural Marketing Act was extended to include fish in 1956. Standards of identity and quality were established, although inspection of products was not required for interstate shipping. The National Marine and Fisheries Service of the U.S. Department of Commerce provides grade standards and voluntary grading services for fishery products. Such products, when produced and graded under the USDC inspection program, may carry the USDC "Federally Inspected" mark and the United States grade shield.

Fresh and Frozen Fish. The number of varieties of fresh fish in the local markets varies considerably with the location and the season, although improved freezing methods and cold storage facilities make it possible to obtain fish in frozen form the year round, inland as well as in areas adjacent to the source of supply. Frozen fish retain most of the characteristics of fresh fish.

Sanitary inspection, which is a routine requirement in the processing of meat for interstate commerce, has been less extensively applied to fish, so the buyer must assume the major responsibility for the condition of the fish purchased for a public foodservice. An important aid to wise selection of fish is the choice of a sanitary market with known dependable standards in its merchandise. It is well, however, to examine carefully at the time of purchase fish bought from even the most reliable market. Characteristics of a fresh fish in satisfactory condition are: freedom from objectionable odor; eyes, bright, clear, and full; flesh, firm, elastic, and not separating from the bones; gills, reddish-pink and with no slime or odor; scales, bright colored, glossy, and adhering to the skin.

Style. Fresh and frozen fish may be purchased as whole or round, drawn, dressed, steaks, single and butterfly fillets, and sticks (see

Fig. 3.5). Whole drawn fish are marketed by weight. Cut frozen fish are commonly marketed in packages of 5, 10, 15, and 20 pounds, and may be raw or precooked, breaded or unbreaded. Breaded fish portions, each weighing 1, 2, 3 or 4 ounces, are packed 72, 36, 24, or 18 pieces, respectively, in a 4 1/2-pound carton.

U.S. grade standards have been developed for products such as semiprocessed raw whole fish, fish blocks, cut fish portions, steaks and fillets, breaded raw and precooked fish portions and sticks. For example, Grade A frozen fried fish sticks [1] must possess a good flavor and odor when cooked and score not less than 85 points on the following:

Appearance—uniformity of size and shape, color of heated sticks, continuity of coating after heating	30–35
Defects—freedom from bones, broken, or damaged sticks	34–40
Character—presence or absence of free oil in the package and effect on package, ease of separation of sticks, tendency of sticks to remain whole when heated, tenderness and moistness of flesh, consistency of breading and adherence to heated product	21–25

Breading standards have been developed by the Department of Commerce for frozen portions and sticks. For uncooked portions, not more than 25 percent of the weight may be breading, for frozen fried portions, not more than 35 percent. Uncooked frozen sticks may have 28 percent breading and fried not more than 40 percent. When purchasing seafood, the amount of breading should be carefully considered. Lower prices may reflect increased amounts of breading. Ungraded products have no standards to meet and may contain excessive breading.

Care of Fish. Fish deteriorates rapidly if it is improperly handled. Fresh fish should always be packed in ice for delivery and stored immediately at low temperature, preferably in a refrigerator unit used for this food only.

---

[1] *United States Standards for Grades of Frozen Fried Fish Sticks, National Marine Fisheries Service, U.S. Department of Commerce.*

a. Whole or round marketed as brought from the water. All details of preparation such as scaling, eviscerating, and removing head, tail, and fins remain to be done by the purchaser.

b. Drawn whole fish, eviscerated only.

c. Dressed whole fish, scaled and eviscerated; usually head, tail, and fins are removed. Small sizes are ready for the pan, and large sizes may be baked whole or cut into individual portions before cooking.

d. Steaks: cross-section slices of large dressed fish; ready to cook. A cross section of the backbone is usually the only bone in a steak.

e. Fillets: sides of fish, cut lengthwise away from backbone; may be skinned. *Single* fillet is cut from one side of a fish; *butterfly* fillet is cut from two sides of the fish and skin of the belly.

f. Sticks: lengthwise or crosswise pieces cut from fillets or steaks for individual portions.

FIGURE 3.5 *Market forms in which fish may be purchased. Courtesy, National Marine Fisheries Service, U.S. Department of Commerce.*

Frozen fish should be delivered still frozen and kept in this condition until time for cooking. If frozen fish has been allowed to thaw, it must be cooked immediately. Frozen fish requires a longer cooking time than fresh if the process is started while the fish is still in the frozen form. Preliminary thawing is advisable for convenience of breading, frying, or stuffing of fish. Thawing at refrigerator temperature (36 to 40°F) is recommended rather than at room temperature or under water, except for large whole drawn fish. For them, much time may be saved by immersing the fish in cold running water for a short time.

Amount To Buy. The edible part of whole fish may be as low as 20 percent or as high as 60 percent of its total weight. Fish weighing 1/2 to 1 1/2 pounds each may be used for individual service, the size selected depending on the expected money return. The estimated yield in servings from larger fish bought with bones, head, and tail is based on an allowance of 1/3 to 1/2 pound per portion. Fillets, steaks, and boned fish minus heads and tails usually yield 3 to 5 portions per pound, the number depending on the method of preparation. The smaller per capita allowance in the use of fillets and steaks is based on the fact that they are 100 percent edible.

Table 3.2 suggests varieties of fish suitable for institution foodservice and indicates their usual market forms and preparation methods.

Canned Fish. Canned fish is used in many recipes calling for cooked fish, such as cutlets, loaves, and casseroles. Salmon, tuna, shrimp, and crab are popular for such use.

Five main species of salmon are canned, each different from the other in color, texture, and flavor, the more highly colored and flavorful being most costly and rated as superior. The flesh of Red or Sockeye salmon is the deepest red, followed by Silver or Coho, Chinook, Pink or Humpback, and Chum, which is quite light colored and is not accepted by some foodservices. Salmon is available in 3 3/4-, 7 1/2-, 15 1/2-ounce and 4-pound cans. The last two sizes are commonly bought by the institution purchaser. The 15 1/2-ounce or No. 1 cans are packed 48 to the case, and the 4-pound cans are packed 12 to the case.

There are two broad classifications of canned tuna—white meat which, in the United States, may be canned only from albacore, and light meat, which is canned primarily from yellowfin, bluefin, and skipjack species.

TABLE 3.2   FISH PURCHASE GUIDE

Name	Type	Usual Market Forms	Preparation Methods
Catfish	Lean	Whole, dressed; fresh or frozen	Deep fat fry
Cod	Lean	Breaded, raw and pre-cooked in sticks or por-tions; drawn, dressed, steaks, fillets; fresh or frozen	Deep fat fry, broil, poach, or bake Use salt cod in creamed dishes and fish cakes
Haddock	Lean	Whole, drawn, fillets; fresh, frozen, salted, or smoked; breaded and precooked sticks and portions	Deep fat fry or bake
Halibut	Lean	Drawn, dressed, steaks, fillets; fresh or frozen; breaded portions	Broil or bake Stuff and broil or bake Use cooked flakes in casseroles
Perch	Lean	Whole, pan-dressed; fresh or frozen	Pan fry, deep fat fry, or bake in sauce
Pollock	Lean	Drawn, dressed as fillets or steaks; fresh or fro-zen; raw and precooked breaded sticks and portions	Deep fat fry, broil, or bake
Red snapper	Lean	Drawn, dressed, steaks, fillets; fresh or frozen	Deep fat fry, broil, or bake Stuff and bake
Salmon	Fat	Dressed, steaks or fillets; fresh or frozen; smoked and canned	Poach, bake, broil, or pan fry Use cooked flakes for patties, cakes, loaf, salads
Sole	Lean	Whole, fillets; breaded portions; fresh or frozen	Deep fat fry, broil, or pan fry Stuff and bake
Trout	Fat	Whole, dressed; frozen 6–12 oz brook or rain-bow most popular	Broil, bake, pan fry Stuff and bake
Whitefish	Fat	Whole, drawn, dressed, fillets; fresh or frozen	Bake, broil, or poach

Source. *Adapted from "How to Eye and Buy Seafood", National Marine Fisheries Service, U.S. Department of Commerce, 1970.*

Oil-packed tuna is available in the following grades: *Fancy,* choice cuts, large pieces of solid flesh; *Standard,* 75 percent large pieces and 25 percent flakes; *Shredded* or *Grated,* small uniform pieces; and *Tuna Flakes.* Brine-packed tuna has a low import duty, which is reflected in a lower selling price than the oil-packed tuna. Tuna is available also in a salt-free pack for modified diets. Can sizes for tuna are 3 1/2, 7, and 13 ounces. In addition, shredded and flaked tuna are packed in 3-, 6-, 12-ounce and 4-pound cans.

Cured Fish. Fish may be preserved by salting, smoking, pickling, or a combination of two or more of these methods. Kippered salmon or herring are split, salted, and then dried or smoked. Often these items are purchased in bulk by the pound. Sardines are prepared by soaking the pilchard or small herring in salt water for an hour, drying, immersing in boiling oil for approximately 2 minutes, draining, and packing in cans with oil or sauces.

The removal of salt from salted fish, commonly termed freshening, may be accomplished by placing the fish on a rack, skin side up, in a pan of water. Such an arrangement provides for the passage of the salt from the meat. Another means quite commonly used is placing the salted fish in cold water, bringing to a boil, draining and repeating the process until the salt is removed. Usually three times is sufficient.

Shellfish. Shellfish are divided into two classifications: mollusks, which include oysters, clams, and scallops; and crustaceans, which include crabs, lobsters, and shrimp.

Oysters. Oysters vary in size, texture, and flavor according to where they are harvested. Approximately 89 percent of the oyster production comes from the Atlantic coast and 11 percent from the Pacific. Those taken from the waters of the Atlantic are known as Eastern oysters. The Olympia, a small, delicately flavored oyster, is found in Puget Sound in the western United States.

Since 2 to 4 years are required for the seed to mature to a marketable oyster, planning and conservation are necessary to provide for a continuing and expanding market. Oyster beds are subject to strict sanitary inspection by the health authorities of various producing states, who act on carefully framed regulations. Only beds meeting the established standards are certified for production.

Oysters are marketed alive in the shell, fresh and frozen, shucked, and canned. Shell oysters must be alive when purchased and have tightly closed shells. They are purchased by the dozen or bushel and may be held only for a short time in the refrigerator at

40°F. Fresh oysters may be served raw on the half shell, or as oyster cocktail. In either of these methods of service it is most important that the oysters be thoroughly chilled.

Shucked or opened oysters have been removed from the shell and are in far greater demand than those in the shell. Shucked oysters are subjected to rigid bacteriological examination and may not be sold if pollution is evident. Shucked oysters should be plump, creamy in color, and free from shell particles.

Fresh shucked oysters are commonly marketed in gallon cans, solid packed and free from excess liquid. Because of the high liquid content of oysters, a small amount oozes out and collects at the top of the can. This exudate should be clear. It is highly palatable and should be used in stews or other oyster dishes. Shucked oysters can be held at freezing temperature for a week or 10 days without marked deterioration. If storage conditions are not right, a sour taste and odor develop in oysters, indicating that they are no longer edible. At this point, the exudate becomes cloudy in appearance.

Shucked Eastern oysters are usually marketed as *Straights,* ungraded, and perhaps including the entire output; *Counts,* perfect in shape and color, large in size, and not bruised in opening, used for frying and baking; *Selects,* in perfect condition but smaller than Counts, usually used on the shell or for frying; *Standards,* ordinarily the quality that remains after Counts and Selects have been removed, and that is used for stews and cocktails. These commercial grades and the corresponding numbers of oysters in a gallon are:

Grade	Oysters per Gallon
Counts or *extra large*	Not more than 160
Extra Selects or *large*	Not more than 161 to 210
Selects or *medium*	Not more than 211 to 300
Standards or *small*	Not more than 301 to 500
Very small	Over 500

Shucked oysters are now available throughout the year as a quickfrozen product. If it is necessary to thaw them for preliminary preparation, refrigerator thawing is advised.

Clams. The market forms of clams are: alive in the shell, shucked, and canned. Factors to consider in selecting fresh clams are similar to those for oysters, as are the purchase units (bushel, peck, pound).

Shucked clams are marketed fresh or frozen in gallon and No. 10 cans. Canned clams are minced, whole, or processed into chowder. Since the demand for canned clams is limited in institutions, the small retail size is the common unit of purchase.

Scallops. The adductor muscle or "eye" that holds together the shells of the scallops is removed, cut into pieces, and marketed commercially as scallops. Bay scallops, taken from inshore waters, are small and are considered a delicacy, but the supply is very limited. The large sea scallop, an inhabitant of offshore banks and deep waters, is the one used extensively in quantity food operations. Both species have sweet, firm, white meat. Scallops can be purchased fresh or frozen in gallon containers. Count: small (Cape) 500 to 850 per gallon, large (deep sea) 110 to 170 per gallon, or packaged breaded and ready to cook.

Crabs. The geographical sources of crabs are the Gulf and the Atlantic and Pacific coasts. The blue crabs of the Gulf and the Atlantic coast, when caught just after they have shed their old shells and before their new ones have hardened, are designated as *soft-shell* crabs. These crabs pass through this phase of their life cycle from May to October. Hard-shell crabs are on the market throughout the year. Crabs may be purchased alive, cooked in the shell, or as chilled, frozen, canned, or freeze-dried crabmeat.

The meat from the blue crab is sorted as (1) *lump meat,* which includes the white, large propelling muscles of the back fin, sometimes designated as "special" grade, (2) *flake meat,* including the edible portion of the rest of the body, and (3) *claw meat,* which is that removed from the claws and is brownish in color. Sometimes the lump meat and the flake meat are combined in a pack, and sometimes each is packed by itself. The claw meat is regarded as less choice and is infrequently combined with the others. The pinkish meat of the Dungeness crab from the Pacific coast is given a common single pack. The chilled or frozen meat is sold in pound cartons. Canned crab meat is marketed in No. 1/2 flat cans containing approximately 6 1/2 ounces net weight and packed 24 or 48 in a case. One No. 2 1/2 can of freeze-dried crab reconstitutes to 1 quart of cooked meat.

Lobster. Most of the lobster on the market comes from the Atlantic coast, from Labrador to North Carolina, although many people prefer the spiny lobster or crawfish found on the Pacific coast from Santa Barbara south. Lobsters as caught are approximately 11 inches long, dark green in color, with red flecks, weighing 1 1/2 to 3 pounds. If the lobster is larger, the flesh is likely to be tough and stringy. Opinions differ as to the effect of sex on the desirability of lobster flesh. Some prefer male lobster, believing the flesh to be firmer and liking the brighter hue to which the male turns in cooking. Others prefer the female because of its roe or coral. The female lobster has a broader, flatter tail than the male, and her upper fin-like appendages are softer and nearer the main part of the body. Lobster may be purchased in the following forms: alive, cooked in the shell, cooked lobster meat, chilled or frozen, frozen spiny lobster tails, and canned.

One-half to 3/4 pound of lobster in the shell or one spiny lobster tail is estimated as an adequate portion allowance. If cooked lobster meat, chilled or frozen, is bought, the portion allotment is usually estimated as 2 1/2 ounces for most purposes. The high cost of lobster meat prevents its common use in most institution foodservices. Its importance lies in highly specialized foodservices and a limited catering trade.

Shrimp. Shrimp may be purchased in the following forms: fresh or frozen, cooked and then chilled or frozen, canned, either as a wet or dry pack, and freeze-fried. Shrimp that is marketed fresh is known as *green* shrimp, the heads and thorax being removed and the bodies packed in ice or frozen. The shell-like gray-green covering affords protection to the curl of meat inside. The term prawns refers to large shrimp from the Gulf area. Fresh shrimp are graded according to the number per pound, ranging from the *Jumbo,* under 25 shrimp per pound, to *Large,* 25 to 35 per pound, to *Medium,* 30 to 42 per pound, and to *Small,* 42 and over per pound. Shrimp also may be purchased breaded. Standards for breading for uncooked shrimp permit 50 percent breading and 50 percent shrimp.

Cooked shrimp, shells removed, are sold by the pound, chilled or frozen. The usual portion of cooked or canned shrimp is 2 1/2 ounces per person. Canned shrimp may be purchased in 8- and 16-ounce cans, each packed 24 to the case. Inspection of canned shrimp is necessary to insure that removal of the vein or tract has been complete.

Many managers find freeze-dried shrimp a real convenience item in quantity food production, since much time-consuming hand labor is eliminated. In this process the shrimp are cooked, cleaned, blast-frozen, then vacuum-dried, and sealed in No. 2 1/2 or No. 10 cans. One No. 10 can weighs 13 1/4 ounces and is the equivalent of 7 pounds of raw green headless shrimp. This product may be stored at room temperature for several months without deterioration. Rehydration requires only 20 minutes in lukewarm water to which lemon juice and salt are added. Flavor and color retention are good, the quality is uniform, and the cost is nominal.

POULTRY

Poultry is a well-liked menu item and lends itself to many types of preparation and adaptation to dietary needs. Usually the price is reasonable and availability is no longer a seasonal factor, since modern processing, grading, packaging, and freezing procedures make it possible to buy any quality, size, or quantity at any time of the year.

Mandatory federal inspection of all poultry shipped interstate became effective January 1, 1959 and, since 1968, poultry not crossing state lines must be inspected in programs at least equal to federal inspection.

The kinds and classes of poultry and the quantity of any one type available depend somewhat on the size and geographic location of the market. In any large market poultry will be classified by weight, so that purchases in dozen lots may be made without a difference in weight of more than 1/8 pound among the birds. Usually there are available quantities of the various categories of either fresh-killed or frozen poultry to meet demands for any one type.

Kinds and Classes of Poultry. The kind of poultry refers to different species, such as chickens, turkeys, ducks, geese, and guineas. Class indicates the physical characteristics due to age and sex, described in brief on the following page.

The classes of other kinds of poultry are: ducks, *broiler* or *fryer duckling* (under 8 weeks of age), *roaster duckling* (under 16 weeks of age), *mature* or *old duck* (over 6 months of age); and geese and guinea, *young* and *mature.*

Grades. Poultry must be inspected for wholesomeness before it can be graded for quality. The top grade for poultry, and the one commonly found in the retail market, is U.S. Grade A. Grade A birds have good overall shape and appearance, are meaty, have a well-developed layer of fat in the skin, and are practically free from defects such as cuts and bruises. The grade does not indicate the tenderness of the bird—the age (class) is the determining factor. Official standards also provide for U.S. Grade B and U.S. Grade C. These birds are not as attractive as Grade A, may have defects and faulty conformation, and could be lacking in fleshing and fat cover. Figure 3.6 shows examples of these grades. U.S. Grades and stan-

Class	Characteristics
Chicken	
Rock Cornish game hen or Cornish game hen	Young immature chicken usually 5 to 6 wk of age, weigh not more than 2 lb ready-to-cook, prepared from a Cornish chicken or progeny of a Cornish chicken with another breed.
Broiler or fryer	Young chicken usually 9 to 12 wk of age, either sex, tender-meated with soft, pliable, smooth-textured skin, flexible breastbone cartilage.
Roaster	Young chicken usually 3 to 5 months of age, either sex, tender-meated with soft, pliable, smooth-textured skin, breastbone cartilage somewhat less flexible than broiler or fryer.
Capon	Surgically unsexed male chicken usually under 8 months of age, tender-meated with soft, pliable, smooth-textured skin.
Stag	Male chicken usually under 10 months of age, coarse skin, somewhat toughened and darkened flesh, considerable hardening of breastbone cartilage.
Hen or stewing chicken or fowl	Mature female chicken usually more than 10 months of age, meat less tender than roaster, nonflexible breastbone.
Cock or rooster	Mature male chicken with coarse skin, tough and darkened meat, hardened breastbone tip.
Turkey	
Fryer-roaster	Young turkey usually under 16 wk of age, either sex, tender-meated with soft, pliable, smooth-textured skin, flexible breastbone cartilage.
Young hen or young tom turkey	Young female (or male) turkey usually 5 to 7 months of age, tender-meated, with soft, pliable, smooth-textured skin, breastbone cartilage somewhat less flexible than in a turkey fryer.
Yearling hen or tom	Fully matured female (or male), usually under 15 months of age, reasonably tender-meated, reasonably smooth-textured skin.
Mature or old hen or tom turkey	Mature female (or male) turkey usually over 15 months of age with coarse skin, toughened flesh.

Grade A

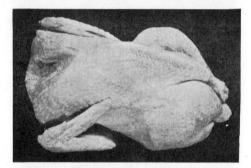

Grade B

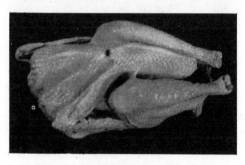

Grade C

*FIGURE 3.6   Examples of Grades A, B, and C ready-to-cook stewing chickens.
Courtesy, Poultry Branch, Production and Marketing Administration.
U.S. Department of Agriculture.*

dards also have been established for poultry parts and for raw and
ready-to-cook poultry rolls and roasts.

Table 3.3 summarizes the standards of quality for ready-to-cook
carcass turkey and geese. Letter grading (A, B, and C) is restricted
to individually graded, ready-to-cook poultry. The wholesale grades
(U.S. Extras, U.S. Standards, and U.S. Trades) and procurement

grades (U.S. Procurement Grades I and II) are comparable to the A, B, and C grades but permit some allowance for lower-quality birds. For example, a food buyer is interested in wholesomeness and yield rather than appearance if the poultry meat is to be cut up and used in a creamed entree or a salad. Crooked breast bones or broken wing tips would not be an important factor to him, and the lesser amount of fat on an otherwise Grade B bird might be to his advantage.

Poultry to be processed into parts is graded for fleshing before it is cut up, and each piece is examined after cutting. The grading regulations authorize the elimination of any parts that are below the standards for the grade, with lesser defects permitted on an individual part than when the carcass is graded. Supervision of packaging is included in the regulation.

The shield design is the official grade mark. It contains the letters "USDA" and the letter grade printed in a light color on a dark field. Grade labels in cooperating states may use the phrase "Federal-State Graded" near but not in the shield. Inspected and graded ready-to-cook poultry may have the grade shield and inspection circle side by side on the label—or on paper inserts, wing tags, or giblet bags. Each container of poultry bought on contract specification and inspected by the Poultry and Egg Acceptance Service bears the stamp shown in Fig. 3.7(b).

Processed Poultry. Most of the poultry supply is marketed in a *ready-to-cook style* or *form*, either fresh chilled or frozen, and as whole carcass or cut-up pieces. The whole birds have been cleaned

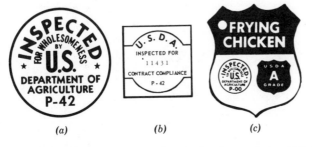

(a)   (b)   (c)

FIGURE 3.7   *Federal grade and inspection stamps for ready-to-cook poultry. (a) Inspected for wholesomeness. (b) Acceptance stamp on package assures buyer that contents have been examined and meet specifications; graded and inspected. (c) Label indicating class name, inspection mark, and grade mark. Courtesy, Production and Marketing Administration, U.S. Department of Agriculture.*

TABLE 3.3 SUMMARY OF SPECIFICATIONS FOR STANDARDS OF QUALITY FOR INDIVIDUAL CARCASSES OF READY-TO-COOK TURKEYS AND GEESE (MINIMUM REQUIREMENTS AND MAXIMUM DEFECTS PERMITTED)

Factor	A Quality	B Quality	C Quality
Conformation:			
Breastbone	Normal	Practically normal	Abnormal
	Slight curve or dent	Moderately dented, curved, or crooked	Seriously curved or crooked
Back	Normal (except slight curve)	Slightly crooked	Seriously crooked
Legs and wings	Normal	Slightly misshapen	Misshapen
Fleshing:	Well fleshed, moderately long, deep and rounded breast	Moderate covering of flesh considering class and part—substantial covering on breast	Poorly fleshed
Fat Covering:	Well covered—considering class and part	Sufficient fat over carcass, especially on the breast and legs, to prevent distinct appearance of flesh through skin	Lacking in fat covering over all parts of carcass
Pinfeathers:			
Nonprotruding pins and hair	Free	Few scattered	Scattering
Protruding pins	Free	Occasional on close examination	Occasional on close examination

	Breast and Legs	Elsewhere	Breast and Legs	Elsewhere	
Cuts, Tears and Missing Skin:[a]	Free	3 in.	3 in.[b]	6 in.[b]	No limit
Discolorations[c]	2 in.	3 in.	3 in.	6 in.	No limit[d]
Disjointed bones	1		2 disjointed and no broken or		No limit
Broken bones	None		1 disjointed and 1 nonprotruding broken		No limit
Missing parts	Wing tips and tail[e]		Wing tips, second wing joint and tail		Wing tips, wings and tail
Freezing Defects: (When consumer packaged)	Slight darkening over back and drumsticks	Few small (1/4 in. diameter) pockmarks	Occasional small areas showing layer of clear or pinkish ice	Moderate-dried areas not in excess of 1/2 in. in diameter; May lack brightness; Moderate areas showing layer of clear, pinkish or reddish colored ice	Numerous pockmarks and large dried areas

Source. Regulations Governing the Grading and Inspection of Poultry and Edible Products Thereof and U.S. Classes, Standards, and Grades with Respect Thereto, USDA Agricultural Marketing Service, Poultry Division, p. 22, July 1964.
[a] Total aggregate area of flesh exposed by all cuts and tears and missing skin.
[b] A carcass meeting the requirements of A quality for fleshing may be trimmed to remove skin and flesh defects, provided that no more than one third of the flesh is exposed on any part and the meat yield is not appreciably affected.
[c] Flesh bruises and discolorations such as "blue back" are not permitted on breast and legs of A Quality birds. Not more than one half of total aggregate area of discoloration may be due to flesh bruises or "blue back" (when permitted), and skin bruises in any combination.
[d] No limit on size and number of areas of discoloration and flesh bruises if such areas do not render any part of the carcass unfit for food.
[e] In geese, the parts of the wing beyond the second joint may be removed, if removed at the joint and both wings are so treated.

thoroughly inside and out with the neck, giblets, and any abdominal fat wrapped and placed in the body cavity. The weight of a ready-to-cook chicken generally is 65 percent of the live weight; that of a turkey is about 75 percent. Ready-to-cook poultry is usually packed 12 or 24 birds to a box.

Whole birds cut into pieces ready for frying is a popular style of purchasing poultry for quantity preparation. Disjointed fryers are commonly cut into 11 pieces for packaging. Purchasing an exact number of certain pieces, cut to specification, ensures that each person will be served the same cut and size portion, and at a predetermined cost.

Common cuts are chicken and turkey halves and quarters, breasts, drumsticks, thighs, and livers. Figure 3.8 shows how frozen chicken breasts are packaged. The decision whether to purchase fresh or frozen poultry is largely a matter of individual preference, since both types are usually available in most markets. Some institution food managers prefer to purchase whole birds and make their own boneless roasts instead of purchasing the processed product. The method is fairly simple and makes it possible to reduce the amount of oven space and cooking time needed, and the boneless cooked meat can be sliced on a machine with minimum waste.

Poultry products are available in many forms other than the

FIGURE   3.8   *A 10-pound carton of identical-weight chicken breasts. Other cuts of poultry to meet the menu needs may be purchased in similar units. Courtesy, Ocoma Foods Company, Omaha.*

ready-to-cook birds or pieces. Turkey rolls are economical and convenient for use in institutions and may be either cooked or ready to cook. Although the usual combination is 60 percent white meat and 40 percent dark meat, rolls are available as all white and all dark meat. Precooked turkey rolls yield more than twice as much meat as the ready-to-cook whole bird per purchased pound, are convenient to store, and slice efficiently. Also included in an evergrowing list are: frozen chicken and turkey pie, frozen fried chicken and roast turkey dinners, freeze-dried chicken cubes, canned boneless chicken and turkey meat, chicken soup, and mixtures with other foods such as noodles or vegetables.

USDA has specified minimum meat requirements for many of these processed poultry products. For example, if a product is labeled "Turkey Pie," it must contain at least 14 percent cooked, deboned turkey meat.[2] Chicken dinners must contain at least 18 percent cooked, deboned chicken meat; chicken a la king must contain at least 20 percent meat; and chicken noodles or dumplings must contain at least 15 percent meat.

Amount to Buy. The quality, style, portion size, and method of preparation are important factors in determining the quantity of poultry needed. Table 3.4 suggests an average per capita allowance for various types of poultry and their usual methods of preparation.

Table 3.5 indicates an estimated yield in weight of cooked meat, and the number of 2-, 3-, and 5-ounce portions one might expect from different sizes of turkeys when cooked. Many foodservice buyers prefer the heavy young toms, weighing 18 to 22 pounds and up. This size turkey gives a better yield than small turkeys and is usually priced a few cents under hens or smaller toms. Large turkeys are excellent for roasting whole or in halves or quarters. The halves and quarters are easier to handle and require shorter cooking times, less oven space, and less refrigerator space when being thawed.

When purchasing chicken to fry, consideration should be given to cost and standardization of portions. Halves or quarters of fryers make adequate, uniform servings. If buying whole chickens cut up, a "meaty" piece and a "bony" piece could be combined for a serving. Purchase of individual pieces, such as drumsticks, thighs, drumsticks and thighs combined, or breast gives standardized portions and simplifies serving.

[2] *U.S. Department of Agriculture, "Food for us All,"* Yearbook of Agriculture, *1969.*

TABLE 3.4 QUANTITY GUIDE FOR PURCHASING SELECTED POULTRY MEAT

Type of Poultry	Most Frequently Purchased Form	Most Frequently Used Preparation Method(s)	Size Ranges (Ready-to-Cook Style) (lb)	Usual Serving Size (oz)	Approximate Amount to Buy per Serving (lb)
Chicken					
Broiler-fryer	Ready-to-cook, fresh, iced	Broil, barbeque, fry	1–3	1/4–1/2 bird	1/4–1/2 bird
Quarters or halves					
Cut in pieces	Ready-to-cook, fresh, iced or frozen	Fry, oven fry	2 1/2–2 3/4	2–3 pieces	4–6 servings per bird
Roaster		Roast	3–5	3	3/4–1
Capon, caponette	Ready-to-cook, fresh, iced or frozen	Roast	5–8	3	1/2–3/4
Hens, stewing hen, fowl	Ready-to-cook, fresh, iced or frozen	Stew, braise	2–5 1/2	3	1/4–3/4
Turkey					
Fryer-roaster	Ready-to-cook, frozen	Broil, fry, roast	4–10	3	3/4
Roaster (heavy breed)	Ready-to-cook, frozen	Roast	12–28	3	1/2–3/4
Turkey roll	Ready-to-cook, frozen	Roast	10–12	3	1/3
Turkey roll	Cooked, frozen	Heat or serve cold	8–10	3	1/4
Ducks and geese					
Roaster duckling	Ready-to-cook, frozen	Roast	3–4	3	1
Mature goose	Ready-to-cook, frozen	Roast	10–20	3	1

TABLE 3.5 YIELDS OF STANDARD PORTIONS OBTAINABLE FROM VARIOUS SIZES OF TURKEYS

Ready-to-Cook Weight (lb)	Cooked Yield (lb)	Number of Portions		
		2 oz	3 oz	5 oz
10/12	4 1/2	36	22	12
12/14	4 1/2	42	26	15
14/16	6	48	30	18
16/17	6 2/3	54	32	20
17/18	7 1/3	59	37	23
18/20	8	64	40	25
26/30	13 1/2	108	67	40

Source. "Turkey Handbook," *Revised Edition, National Turkey Federation, Mount Morris, Illinois, p. 31.*

Many entree recipes specify cooked chicken or turkey meat by weight or measure. The following information is useful in calculating the amount to purchase.

YIELD IN COOKED EDIBLE MEAT

Weight as Purchased	Cooked Meat Weight		Measure
	(lb)	(oz)	
1 lb ready-to-cook chicken, as purchased	0.34	5	1 c
1 lb ready-to-cook turkey, as purchased	0.44	7	1 1/3 c
1 lb ready-to-cook turkey roll	0.61	10	1 3/4 c
1 lb cooked turkey roll	0.92	15	

Source. *Adapted from U.S. Department of Agriculture.* Food Buying Guide for Type A School Lunches, PA-270 (*rev.*), 1972.

In general, the larger the bird, the higher the proportion of meat to bone, so the yield of turkey is proportionally greater than chicken.

Storage. The deterioration of poultry is rapid unless the poultry is handled carefully and stored under properly controlled conditions.

Ready-to-cook poultry can be kept 2 or 3 days in a refrigerator at 38°F or less. Frozen poultry should be stored at 0°F and cooked soon after defrosting. Under normal conditions it is advisable to use frozen poultry within 6 months after it has been processed to get the most satisfactory results. Freezer burns may develop if poultry has been poorly packaged or stored at too high a temperature for too long a time. The skin becomes dry and discolored, and the meat develops a strong flavor in the case of excessive burning. The darkened bones of many cooked frozen broilers and fryers affect the appearance but not the quality of the meat. The heat of cooking oxidizes the bone-marrow hemoglobin that has filtered through the porous bone wall during the freezing and thawing processes. Freeze-dried poultry may be stored at room temperature until it is reconstituted, then chilled and used as fresh cooked meat. Cooked poultry meat should be served or covered lightly and refrigerated as soon as possible after preparation to prevent contamination.

EGGS

The production and marketing of quality eggs is a highly scientific business. It begins at the farm with the selection or breeding of stock with potential for good laying. Nutritionally balanced rations, well-engineered and sanitary housing, eggs gathered often, and cooled and sent to egg-handling plants as soon as possible, further contribute to the successful production of quality products. At the plants, the fresh shell eggs are separated by size and graded for quality, usually on the basis of federal or state standards.

Grades. The first tentative standards for the quality of eggs were proposed in 1925 and have undergone several revisions since that time. Cooperative agreements are maintained between the U.S. Department of Agriculture and each of the states for the official grading of eggs, and most states now designate grades by the same terminology as set up by the USDA. Practically all states have legislation for egg standards, but grading is on a voluntary basis. There is wide agreement in details of regulations, such as weight designations, candling requirements, marking of storage eggs, and indication of grade of eggs to the consumer, where USDA standards are followed. The Egg Products Inspection Act, effective for egg products in 1971 and for shell eggs in 1972, assures the consumer that eggs and egg products distributed to them and used in products consumed by them are wholesome and properly labeled and packaged.

Federal consumer grades are U.S. Grade AA (Fresh Fancy), U.S. Grade A, and U.S. Grade B. Eggs also are classified according to size, but size and quality are not related. Large eggs may be high or low quality; high-quality eggs may be either large or small.

Quality in shell eggs is based on exterior and interior factors. The first is by observation of the cleanliness, soundness, shape of shell, and texture. The interior quality is based on condition of the yolk and white and the size and condition of the air cell. It is determined by candling, the process of passing each unbroken egg in front of a light and observing the condition of the yolk and white and the size of the air cell. Blood spots on the yolk and meat spots in the albumin can usually be detected and such eggs removed so they do not reach the consumer. New automatic methods with electronic candling devices are replacing the slow hand operation. Breakout tests give a more exact evaluation of the quality of eggs. The outstanding quality characteristics for each grade of broken-out eggs by subjective examination are noted in Fig. 3.9.

An accurate objective test of egg quality is based on Haugh Units, which are determined by using the weight of the egg and height of the thick albumin, as measured by a tripod micrometer after the egg has been broken out on a flat surface (see Fig. 3.10). Haugh Units correspond to U.S. grades as follows: AA—72 and above, A—55 to 72, and B—31 to 55.

Fresh Fancy Quality corresponds to AA, except that the eggs have been produced and marketed under USDA's Quality Control Program. These eggs reach the market quickly under strictly controlled conditions. Eggs from each flock are packed separately and

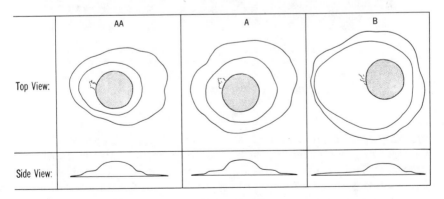

FIGURE 3.9   Visible qualities for consumer grades of broken-out eggs. Courtesy, American Egg Board, Park Ridge, Ill.

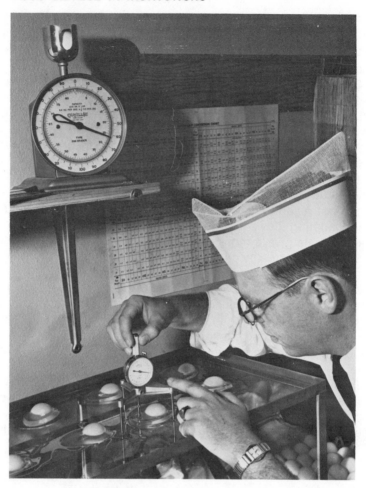

FIGURE 3.10   *Haugh units are determined by mathematical calculation using weight of egg and measurement of height of albumin (thick white). Courtesy, Poultry Division, Agricultural Marketing Service, U.S. Department of Agriculture.*

are not hand candled individually. Abnormalities are removed either by flash or mass candling, or by the use of an electronic bloodspot detector. The quality of the eggs is determined by a biweekly or weekly breakout of a sample of eggs. The basis for the program that permits automation in handling and marketing the eggs is that a flock of hens of a given age and on the same management and feeding program will lay eggs of uniform quality. Certain specifications or conditions regarding handling and marketing of the eggs are set down by regulation. Each carton or case of eggs will have, in addition to the grade label, which may be either Fresh Fancy Quality or U.S. AA, the following wording: "Produced and Marketed under Federal-State Quality Control Program."

Eggs graded by an approved grader and meeting federal standards may carry the shield-shaped stamp on the container for the appropriate grade, although eggs scoring less than Grade A cannot carry the notation that the eggs were produced and marketed under the federal-state quality control program. Sample grade labels are shown in Fig 3.11. Either the date the eggs were graded or an expiration date not to exceed 10 days from the date of grading is stamped on the package or sealing tape.

Eggs classified by weight (and size) are Jumbo, Extra Large, Large, Medium, Small, and Peewee. The three sizes below Jumbo have the highest usage in quantity foodservices. (Note weights and tolerances under "Wholesale Grades" in Table 3.6.)

Amount to buy. Institution buyers should always purchase eggs from distributors who handle eggs that are properly graded and labeled as to quality and size in order to maintain high quality food products in their foodservices. The quality of shell eggs selected will be determined by their intended use, and the price. High-quality eggs are necessary for cooking in the shell and for poaching and frying. Lower qualities may be used economically for other cooking where the delicate flavor of eggs may not be the predominant one. The color of shell depends on breed of the stock and has no bearing on the flavor, color, nutritive value, or cooking qualities of the broken-out egg. Hereditary and nutritional differences in the hens have

PRODUCED and MARKETED
under FEDERAL - STATE
QUALITY CONTROL PROGRAM

FIGURE   3.11   Sample grade labels for shell eggs. Courtesy, U.S. Department of Agriculture.

TABLE 3.6 MINIMUM WEIGHTS OF CONSUMER AND WHOLESALE GRADES OF EGGS IN THE U.S. WEIGHT CLASSES FOR SHELL EGGS, BY SIZE OR WEIGHT CLASS

For Consumer Grades

Size or Weight Class	Minimum Net Weight per Dozen (oz)	Minimum Net Weight per 30-Dozen Case (lb)	Minimum Weight for Individual Eggs at Rate per Dozen [a] (oz)
Jumbo	30	56	29
Extra large	27	50 1/2	26
Large	24	45	23
Medium	21	39 1/2	20
Small	18	34	17
Peewee	15	28	—

For Wholesale Grades

Size or Weight Class	Average Net Weight per 30-Dozen Case (lb)	Minimum Net Weight per 30-Dozen Case (lb)	Basic Minimum Weight for Individual Eggs (oz per dozen)	Permitted Tolerance 10% of Individual Eggs (Minimum Weight) (oz per dozen)
Extra large	50 1/2	50	26	Under 26, but not under 24
Large	45	44	23	Under 23, but not under 21
Medium	39 1/2	39	20	Under 20, but not under 18
Small	34	33 1/2	17	No limit

[a] *Minimum weights listed for individual eggs at the rate per dozen are permitted in various size classes only to the extent that they will not reduce the net weight per dozen below the required minimum, consideration being given to variable weight of individual eggs and variable efficiency of graders and scales that should be maintained on a uniform and accurate basis.*

some effect on the yolk color influencing acceptability for some uses.

The price of eggs varies slightly at different seasons of the year but, with the improved standards of production and storage facilities, the market remains fairly stable. However, the quality grade, and size or weight are important factors of price. The table on p. 136 compares the cost per pound of eggs of various sizes and serves as a guide in determining the most economical size to buy.

Always compare prices of eggs of the same quality grade. For example, when Large Grade A are 80¢ per dozen, any price below 69¢ for Grade A Medium, below 88¢ for Grade Extra Large, or below 60¢ for Grade A Small would probably be more economical to buy. Large eggs at 80¢ are equivalent to 52¢ per pound. It is important to remember, however, that a high degree of uniformity in size and appearance is essential when eggs are served in counter, tray, or table d'hote service. If fresh shell eggs are used in baking and for other prepared foods, a change in size of eggs would necessitate recipe adjustment unless amounts were given in weight. The 30-dozen case is the usual purchase unit for shell eggs.

Processed Eggs. Institution foodservices make extensive use of processed eggs, especially liquid-bulk, frozen, or dry egg solids. Food processors make use of these products in the preparation of many convenience foods as do commercial bakeries.

Eggs are available as *liquid-bulk* and *frozen* whole eggs, yolks, or whites. Inspection for quality is made at the breaking machine after which the eggs, yolks, or whites are thoroughly agitated and pasteurized. For the frozen product the cans are passed through sharp-freezing rooms at 0 to $-50°$ F, and stored at 0 to $-5°$ pending sale. The addition of sugar or salt to the yolks, before freezing, yields a thawed product with normal viscosity. Without this addition, thawed yolks are thick and leathery and do not combine easily with other ingredients. The choice of additive depends on the intended use. The facts that the use of frozen eggs eliminates the time-consuming tasks of breaking and separating fresh eggs, little storage space is required, no spoilage and practically no decline in quality occur during storage, and a uniform product is assured at usually a lower cost than that of fresh eggs contribute to the increased use of frozen eggs in institution cookery. Also, the wide variation in sizes of containers makes them adapted to different size and type food units. The most popular purchase units are 30- and 10-pound cans. A pint (or pound) container of frozen eggs is equivalent to 10 or 11

COST OF EGGS PER POUND [a]

The following table shows you how to get the most eggs for your money. To use it, find the current price for a dozen eggs in any size and then follow that column across to the one on the far right. There you will find the price per pound for that size. For example, if large eggs are being sold at the supermarket for 80 cents a dozen, they cost you 52 cents a pound. If medium eggs are being sold for 59 cents a dozen, they cost you 45 cents a pound. Obviously, then, the medium eggs are a better buy per pound of protein food. Be sure the eggs are the same quality grade when you compare cost of different sizes. Higher grades usually sell for more per dozen than lower grades.

Here's a general rule you can remember at the supermarket: if there is less than a 7-cent difference between the cost of a dozen eggs of one size and the cost of the next smaller size, you get more for your money by buying the larger size. If the difference is more than 7 cents, the smaller size would be the best buy. (Remember to compare eggs of the same grade.)

| | Price per Dozen by Size | | | Price per Pound |
X Large	Large	Medium	Small	¢ / lb
52	46	41	35	31
54	48	42	36	32
56	50	43	37	33
59	52	46	39	35
61	54	47	41	36
62	56	49	42	37
65	58	50 1/2	43 1/2	38 1/2
68	60	53	45	40
69	62	54	46	41
72	64	55 1/2	47 1/2	42 1/2
74	66	58	50	44
76	68	59	51	45
78 1/2	70	61	52 1/2	46 1/2
81	72	63	54	48
83	74	64	56	49
85	76	66	59	50 1/2
88	80	69	60	52
90	82	72	63	53 1/2
93	84	73	64	56

Source. *Reprinted courtesy of American Egg Board, Park Ridge, Ill.*
[a] *Based on the following weights: Extra Large Eggs—27 ounces; Large eggs—24 ounces; Medium eggs—21 ounces; Small eggs—18 ounces.*

eggs, and a 30-pound tin will hold about 25 dozen eggs. A 30-pound tin of egg whites or yolks is equivalent to approximately 45 dozen eggs.

Frozen eggs should be defrosted rather quickly. The cans of frozen eggs may be left in a refrigerator, which would take at least overnight, set in a vat of running cold water 4 to 6 hours or exposed to a strong current of air. Defrosting at higher temperatures tends to produce curdling and off-flavors. Defrosted eggs should be used promptly, because they are highly perishable. Any unused portion of containers should be refrigerated and used within a few days.

Frozen, chopped, hard-cooked eggs are available on the market. Packaged in plastic bags, this product is individually quick frozen so that any part of a bag may be used without thawing the remainder. A new convenience item is the frozen egg roll or long egg used for slicing, dicing, or chopping. The hard-cooked egg roll is equal in weight and volume to 12 medium eggs and will yield as many center slices as 17 medium eggs.

Freeze-dried scrambled egg mix, packed in No. 10 cans, is now available. Low-fat milk solids, salt, and butter are included in the ingredients.

Dry egg solids are processed by spray drying for the most part, with some pan-dried or fluff-dried to meet special bakery needs. As with frozen eggs, all liquid eggs used in federally inspected plants must be pasteurized before they are dried, and it is recommended that dried eggs that have been processed under government supervision be purchased. The finished product should not have more than 3 to 5 percent moisture. Dry egg solids are available as whole egg solids, egg white solids, and egg yolk solids with occasionally specified variations as fortified, or glucose-free whole egg solids. They are used extensively in bakery product mixes in the dry form, or they may be reconstituted and used as fresh eggs in recipes where cooking is thorough and prolonged. The acceptance of dehydrated eggs in dishes where their characteristic flavor is predominant is limited. The common purchase unit is 6 3-pound cans per case or 50-pound drums. Table 3.7 may be used as a guide in estimating quantities to buy in relation to use.

Storage. The high water content of eggs and the nutrients present make rapid spoilage probable. The mode of handling, more than the age of the egg, affects its condition. Apart from complete spoilage, the deterioration of eggs may affect their appearance and use and the salability of products prepared from them. Eggs with liquefied or

TABLE 3.7   WEIGHTS OF EGG SOLIDS AND FROZEN EGGS AND THEIR EQUIVALENTS IN MEASURE

	Egg Solids		Frozen Eggs	
Number of Eggs	*Weight of Fresh Eggs (lb)*	*Dried Weight (lb)*	*Number of Eggs Fresh or Frozen*	*Liquid (lb or pt)*
39 (whole)	3 1/3	1	9–11 (whole)	1
70 (whites)	7	1	17–20 (whites)	1
48 (yolks)	2	1	19–22 (yolks)	1

Egg solids are easily reconstituted by the addition of water as follows:
Whole egg solids. Use 1 part of egg solids to 3 parts of water. Allow to stand 4 to 5 hr or until normal liquid egg consistency is obtained.
Egg yolk solids. Theoretically the ratio of 1 part of yolk to 1 part of water should be used, but practically 2 to 3 parts of water are required for 1 part of yolk. Allow to stand 1 hr.
Egg white solids. Use 1 part of dried albumen to 10 parts of water. Allow to stand 3 hr.

watery whites, flattened yolks, and stretched membranes may be unacceptable poached or fried, and may not beat up well to combine in made dishes. However, they may be successfully used in batters and doughs.

Eggs are highly perishable, and varied handling and storage methods will produce wide changes and different degrees of deterioration, even in eggs originally identical. Among the physical changes found as deterioration advances are loss of viscosity by the thick layer of the white, passage of water from the white to the yolk attended by an increase in size and fluidity of the yolk, weakening of the vitelline membrane so that the yolk may break when the shell is opened, increase in size of the air space, and absorption of odors. Among the chemical changes are a loss of carbon dioxide, a loss of water, a change in the pH, the hydrolysis of protein, an increase in ammonia in the yolk, and an increase in water-soluble phosphorous. If stored at 45 to 60°F, the loss of carbon dioxide is slowed considerably; at a temperature from 33 to 45°F, the rate of loss is extremely slow. The proper handling and storage of eggs are so important to the institution buyer that he should be informed of the conditions under which they have been kept before they are delivered to the storerooms. Eggs removed from storage "sweat." The moisture that collects around each egg dissolves the bloom and collects dust and bacteria. Hence, eggs should be used promptly after removal from storage if they are held at room temperature. All eggs at the time of storage should be clean and sound, and cases, flats, and cushions should be odorless and in good condition. Eggs absorb odors; therefore foods that give off strong odors, such as onions, cabbage, and turnips, should not be stored near eggs. The relative humidity of rooms in which eggs are left for long periods must not be too low, as this causes excessive shrinkage; on the other hand, if the humidity is too high, the eggs will mold. The recommended temperature for long inventory is 29°F with not more than 1° variation, and a relative humidity of 80 to 85 percent. Eggs freeze at 28°F. Under proper storage conditions, eggs may be held as long as 9 to 10 months. Frozen eggs should be held at about 0 to 20°F, and egg solids in cool dry areas but not necessarily in refrigerated storage.

MILK AND RELATED FOODS

Sanitary laws regulating the composition of milk and its production, when properly enforced, afford protection to the consumer. Most state and local regulations for milk products are based on the U.S. Public Health Service Grade A Pasteurized Milk Ordinance. Standards for manufactured dairy products have been developed by the Dairy Division of the U.S. Department of Agriculture. Because milk and milk products are highly perishable and are subject to contamination, adulteration, and development of off flavors, it is important that the foodservice manager purchase only the highest-quality products available. The buyer should be informed concerning the legal specifications in his vicinity and should know the ratings given the various agencies that contribute to the local milk supply. All milk products purchased for foodservices should come from milk that has been pasteurized and that has been produced and handled in accordance with the best sanitary practices.

Fresh Fluid Whole Milk. Fresh whole milk usually is homogenized and must meet the requirements for minimum milk fat content set by the state or municipality where it is sold. The milkfat content generally is about 3.25 percent, the minimum recommended by the Public Health Service Grade A Pasteurized Milk Ordinance.

All Grade A milk and milk products sold today are pasteurized to kill harmful bacteria. Milk is heated to a temperature of not less than

145°F for 30 minutes or a temperature of not less than 161°F for 15 seconds, then cooled as quickly as possible to 50°F. After pasteurization, the bacterial count may not exceed 20,000 per milliliter for Grade A milk. Grade A pasteurized milk, according to the standards recommended in the Pasteurized Milk Ordinance, must come from healthy cows and be produced, pasteurized, and handled under strict sanitary control enforced by state and local milk sanitation officials. Requirements may vary in different localities. The Grade A rating designates wholesomeness rather than a level of quality.

Homogenized milk has been treated to reduce the size of the milkfat globules. Milk is forced under pressure through tiny orifices to divide fat globules so finely that they remain in permanent suspension.

In Vitamin D milk, the vitamin D content has been increased to at least 400 U.S. Pharmacopoeia units per quart.

Milk as a beverage should be served in the original container as far as is possible. This practice is required by law in many places. Table milk is packaged in paper 1/2-pint containers, 48 per case, for delivery to institutions. Bulk milk, whole or skimmed, to be used for cooking purposes is purchased in 5- or 10-gallon containers that should be kept covered and refrigerated at all times. Where legislation permits, refrigerated milk dispensers may be used in the service of milk, thus eliminating the individual containers. Filled dispenser inserts are sealed at the dairy and delivered directly to the dispenser. Such a method of service conforms to the requirement that milk be served to the consumer from the original container. Most dispensers are designed to accommodate 2 1/2- or 5-gallon stainless steel, or plastic disposable inserts.

Chocolate Milk. Chocolate-flavored milk is made from pasteurized whole milk with sugar and chocolate syrup or cocoa added. In most states, regulations require that to be labeled chocolate-flavored milk, the product must be made from whole milk; to be labeled chocolate-flavored milk drink, it must be made from skim or partially skimmed milk. The foodservice buyer should demand the same standards for this product as for plain milk. It is desirable also to limit the amount of chocolate to 1 percent.

Skim and Low Fat Milks. Skim or nonfat milk differs from the whole milk only in that its fat content has been greatly reduced, the exact amount depending on state requirements. The Pasteurized Milk Ordinance recommends a milkfat content of less than 0.5 percent. Otherwise its nutrients are the same as those of whole milk. Institutions in which the cost of food is an important factor and where an adequate supply of butter or fortified margarine is provided may well include skim milk in the preparation of many dishes. Low fat milk has had the content of milkfat lowered, generally to 1 or 2 percent.

Cultured Buttermilk. Buttermilk may be either a churned or cultured product, although almost all commercially marketed buttermilk is cultured. A lactic acid-producing bacterial culture is added to fresh pasteurized skim or partially skimmed milk to produce cultured buttermilk. The resulting product is much thicker than skim milk with the same nutritive value. Another fermented milk product that is gaining in popularity and use is yogurt, a custardlike product made by fermenting milk with a special culture. It usually is made from homogenized, pasteurized whole milk, but may be made from skim or partly skimmed milk. Yogurt has the same nutritive value as the milk from which it is made. Often yogurt is sweetened and fruit flavored.

Processed Milks. The processed milks most used in institutions are evaporated, condensed, and dry. These products are of special value in food preparation where fresh milk is unavailable or where storage and refrigeration space is limited. Also, they usually cost less per unit volume than fresh fluid milk.

Evaporated Milk. Evaporated milk is whole milk from which about 60 percent of the water has been removed. After evaporation of the water the milk is sealed in cans and sterilized. The final product contains about 26 percent total milk solids and 8 percent milkfat. An 8-pound or No. 10 can is convenient for the institution using large quantities of evaporated milk.

Condensed Milk. Condensed milk is whole or skim milk from which part of the water has been removed and to which sugar has been added. The final product contains about 40 percent sugar, 30 percent water, and 28 percent milk solids. If purchased near the source of supply, it may be obtained in 5- or 10-gallon cans, otherwise the usual purchase unit is a 14-ounce can.

Dry Milk. Whole and nonfat dry milk are made from fluid whole and skim milk with only the water removed. Of the two, nonfat dry milk is more widely used, doubtless because of its superior keeping qualities. Federal grades for nonfat dry milk solids are U.S. Extra and U.S. Standard. *Instant* dry milk has been processed so that it is readily reconstituted into liquid form. Dry buttermilk is available also and is convenient for preparation of many baked products.

The quality of dry milk depends on that of the fresh milk from which it is made, on the method of drying, and on the care taken in the manufacturing process. Dry milk from first-class creameries is prepared from milk of exceptionally high quality. Most of the dry milk for human consumption is made by the spray process, which produces fine particles readily dispersed in water. The usual purchase units of dry milk are 5-, 50-, or 100-pound plastic innerlined bags. It should be kept in cool, dry storage away from foods with strong odors. Table 3.8 serves as a guide for substituting dry milk for fluid milk.

Cream. Pasteurized cream, produced under the same sanitary conditions as milk, should be purchased by institution foodservices. The U.S. Food and Drug Administration has standards of identity for many of the different types of cream if they are shipped in interstate commerce. These standards give minimum milkfat requirements for each type of cream. Light cream must have at least 18 percent milkfat, according to federal standards of identity and most state standards. Half-and-half is a mixture of milk and cream, homogenized. Under state requirements, it must have between 10 and 12 percent milkfat. Light whipping cream contains at least 30 percent milkfat, and heavy whipping cream must have at least 36 percent milkfat.

The whipping quality of cream depends on: fat content, aging at a low temperature (40°F or less) for 15 to 24 hours, temperature of 40°F or lower desirable for cream and container while whipping, type of whipper, volume or amount of cream whipped. It is better to whip several portions of cream than one large quantity. If pasteurization has been properly carried out, the whipping quality of cream will be only slightly altered.

Sour cream is made by adding lactic acid bacteria culture to light cream. It is smooth and thick and contains at least 18 percent milkfat. Sour half-and-half is available also in some markets.

Cream for institutions is purchased by the quart or the gallon. Cream should be kept covered and refrigerated.

A variety of coffee whiteners, whipped toppings, and other nondairy products are available to the consumer today. Most contain vegetable fats and oils, emulsifiers, and stabilizers. Available in both dehydrated and ready-to-use forms, their convenience, shelf life, and economy has led to wide acceptance in institution foodservices.

Butter. Butter is commonly defined as a "food product made exclusively from milk or cream or both, with or without common salt, and with or without additional coloring and contains not less than 80 percent by weight of milkfat, all tolerances having been allowed

TABLE 3.8 EQUIVALENT AMOUNTS OF DRY MILKS TO FLUID WHOLE MILK

To Equal the Amount of Fluid Whole Milk Listed Below	Substituting Dry Whole Milk Use This Amount of		Substituting Nonfat Dry Milk Use This Amount of		
	Warm Water	Dry Whole Milk	Warm Water	Nonfat Dry Milk	Butter or Shortening
1 qt	3 3/4 c	4 1/2 oz	3 3/4 c	3 1/4 oz	1 1/4 oz
2 qt	1 qt 3 1/2 c	9 oz	1 qt 3 1/2 c	6 1/2 oz	2 1/2 oz
3 qt	2 qt 3 1/4 c	13 1/2 oz	2 qt 3 1/4 c	9 3/4 oz	3 3/4 oz
1 gal	3 3/4 qt	1 lb 2 oz	3 3/4 qt	13 oz	5 oz
2 gal	1 gal 3 1/2 qt	2 lb 4 oz	1 gal 3 1/2 qt	1 lb 10 oz	10 oz
3 gal	2 gal 3 1/4 qt	3 lb 6 oz	2 gal 3 1/4 qt	2 lb 7 oz	15 oz
4 gal	3 3/4 gal	4 lb 8 oz	3 3/4 gal	3 lb 4 oz	1 lb 4 oz
5 gal	4 gal 2 3/4 qt	5 lb 10 oz	4 gal 2 3/4 qt	4 lb 1 oz	1 lb 9 oz
6 gal	5 gal 2 1/2 qt	6 lb 12 oz	5 gal 2 1/2 qt	4 lb 14 oz	1 lb 14 oz
7 gal	6 gal 2 1/4 qt	7 lb 14 oz	6 gal 2 1/4 qt	5 lb 11 oz	2 lb 3 oz
8 gal	7 1/2 gal	9 lb	7 1/2 gal	6 lb 8 oz	2 lb 8 oz
9 gal	8 gal 1 3/4 qt	10 lb 2 oz	8 gal 1 3/4 qt	7 lb 5 oz	2 lb 13 oz
10 gal	9 gal 1 1/2 qt	11 lb 4 oz	9 gal 1 1/2 qt	8 lb 2 oz	3 lb 2 oz

Source. Adapted from "A New Milky Way—Whole and Nonfat Dry Milk," Circular Bulletin 225, Agricultural Experiment Station and College of Home Economics, Michigan State University, 1958.

Different brands of dry milk vary greatly in crystal size and shape. Various forms of spray-process and "instant" nonfat dry milk differ in the number of cups of dry crystals per pound. Thus, for accurate substitution in recipes, weigh the amount required. If you do not have a scale, follow with special care the package directions for measuring to reconstitute the brand of dry milk you are using.

for." The butter that scores highest on the present market is made from pasteurized sweet cream.

Federal grading of butter is not compulsory, and only butter that carries the U.S. grade label on carton or wrapper has been inspected and rated by an authorized grader of the U.S. Department of Agriculture at the request of the butter maker or dealer. A grade designation without the federal stamp is the manufacturer's or packer's statement that in his opinion the butter meets the federal standards for the grade indicated.

The United States standards for grades of butter are on a numerical basis. Points are allocated to flavor (45), body and texture (25), color (15), salt (10), and package (5): The highest flavor score given for commercial butter is 38, so that the highest total score possible is 93. Federal grades and scores are as given in the accompanying table.

Butter Grades

U.S. Grade AA or U.S., 93 score
U.S. Grade A or U.S., 92 score ⎫
U.S. Grade B or U.S., 90 score ⎬ standard
⎭
U.S. Grade C or U.S., 89 score
U.S. Cooking Grade
No grade

Butter of less than standard grade is no longer purchased by institutions, since other fats are substituted when the price prohibits the purchase of an acceptable grade of butter.

Most institutions now purchase ready-cut table butter. It is available cut 48, 60, 72, or 90 pieces per pound, packaged with parchment paper between layers or each cut on individual paper server in trays, in 5-pound boxes, and packed 3 or 6 to the carton (15 or 30 pounds). Pound prints are packed 30 in a carton.

Butter absorbs odors readily, so it should be stored in cartons or containers away from food having pronounced odors. Freezing does not injure it, and if it is to be left for a long period, it should be stored wrapped, at a temperature not higher than 0°F. The temperature for a short storage period, however, may be as high as 35°F.

Ice Cream. Among the most popular desserts in any foodservice are ice cream and other frozen desserts. Ice cream is not only palatable but also nourishing. The usual basic mix contains over 80 percent cream and milk products, 15 percent sugar, 4.5 percent flavoring, and 0.3 to 0.5 percent stabilizer (often food gelatin).

Ice milk is made from milk, stabilizers, sugar, and flavorings. It must contain between 2 and 7 percent milkfat if it is sold in interstate commerce.

In the majority of foodservices ice cream and other frozen desserts are purchased instead of being made within the institution. Specifications for ice cream include the following: ice cream must be made from clean sweet cream, milk and milk products, and sugar; the mix should be pasteurized at 160 to 165° F for 30 minutes; any coloring and flavoring added to the mix should be from natural sources; the finished product should contain an average of not less than 10 percent milkfat, and not less than 38 percent total solids; it must weigh at least 4 1/2 pounds per gallon and have not more than 100 percent overrun; individual wrapped bricks must be machine cut, the size per gallon to be as designated. It shall be produced and handled in accordance with the best sanitary practice and shall be furnished by dealers who can certify that all persons employed in the plant where the ice cream is manufactured have passed a satisfactory health examination. Ice cream shall be packed and delivered in clean, sound, standard, sanitary, commercial containers. The finished product must be in well-frozen and otherwise prime condition when delivered. The usual purchase units for ice cream are 1-, 2 1/2, and 5-gallon paraffined paper or plastic-covered containers, individually wrapped portions, or individual cups. Specialty items such as ice-cream cakes, pies, and individual forms are used extensively in catering services. Ice cream is delivered directly from the manufacturing plant to the holding units of the purchaser, in refrigerated trucks so that only occasionally is packing with dry ice made necessary. Less rich frozen desserts made of animal or vegetable fats combined with milk are prepared under similar conditions to those found in the manufacture of ice cream. Some units find it advantageous to produce their own frozen products on the premises, even though it requires extra equipment.

Cheese. The purchase list of the institution buyer usually includes only a limited number of the numerous varieties of cheese. Always buy the type of cheese that will best fit the use. Table 3.9 provides a list of cheeses most often used in institution foodservices. In selecting cheese, the fat and moisture contents are important considerations, because cheese may be adulterated by reducing the butterfat

TABLE 3.9   CHEESES MOST OFTEN USED IN INSTITUTION FOODSERVICES

Name	Ripened	Characteristics	Chief Uses	Place of Origin [a]
Hard				
Cheddar	Bacteria, 3–12 months	Smooth, light yellow to orange, mild (whole cow's milk)	Cookery, spread	England
Edam	Bacteria, 3–12 months	Round, red-coated, 2–4 lb, smooth, mild Cheddar nutlike flavor (partly defatted cow's milk)	Spread, dessert	Holland
Parmesan	Bacteria, 12–18 months	Granular, light yellow, sharp flavor, usually grated (partly defatted cow's milk)	Cookery, seasoning	Italy
Swiss	Bacteria, 3–12 months	Smooth, many gas holes, nutlike sweet flavor (partly defatted cow's milk)	Spread, salads	Switzerland
Semihard				
Bleu	Mold, 2–3 months	Roquefort-type, white with blue-green mold, crumbly, rich tangy flavor (whole cow's milk)	Salads, dessert	France
Brick	Bacteria, 1–8 months	Smooth, clean sharp flavor (whole cow's milk)	Spread, salads	United States
Gorgonzola	Mold, 2–12 months	Marbled with blue-green mold, spicy flavor (whole cow's milk)	Salads	Italy
Gouda	Bacteria, 1–8 months	Flattened sphere shape, about 1 lb, smooth, mild nutlike flavor (partly defatted cow's milk)	Spread, dessert	Holland
Roquefort	Mold, 2–12 months	White with blue-green mold, sweet, sharp flavor (whole sheep's milk)	Salads, dessert	France
Stilton	Mold, 2–12 months (best at 2 yr)	White with blue-green mold, spicy (whole cow's milk, cream added)	Salads, dessert	England
Soft				
Brie	Mold, 2–5 months	Creamy, full flavor (whole cow's milk)	Spread, dessert	France
Camembert	Mold, 2–5 months	Creamy, rich full flavor (whole cow's milk)	Dessert, spread	France
Cottage	Unripened	Separate white curds, mildly sour (defatted cow's milk)	Salads	Not known
Cream	Unripened	Smooth, buttery, slightly sour (whole cow's milk, cream added)	Dessert, spread	Not known
Limburger	Bacteria, 1–2 months	Smooth, full sharp flavor, aromatic (whole or partly defatted cow's milk)	Spread	Belgium
Neufchâtel	Unripened	Creamy, mild (whole cow's milk)	Spread, dessert, salads	France

Source. *Adapted from* Origin, Characteristics, and Mode of Serving Commonly Used Cheeses, *National Dairy Council, Chicago.*
[a] *Varieties with similar characteristics now produced in the United States.*

or substituting for part of it and by retaining an excess amount of moisture. Soft cheese will contain 40 to 70 percent moisture, hard cheese 30 to 40 percent. Cheese may be ripened by molds or by bacteria, the agent employed determining to a large extent the characteristic odor and flavor obtained. The method of manufacture, the degree of ripening, and the acidity of a given cheese affect the ease and completeness with which it can be blended with other ingredients. A "green" or uncured cheese is rubbery and resistant to blending. Ripening is accompanied by the development of volatile acids and proteolytic-decomposition products that give the cheese its distinctive flavor, as well as by changes in form that make for ease in blending during cookery.

Cheddar cheese leads all other types in amounts used in quantity food operations. It is adaptable to many preparations or to service in the natural form as slices, cubes, or grated. Qualities available are U.S. Grades AA, A, B, and C. Scores for the standards are on the basis of flavor, aroma, body and texture, finish and appearance, and color. Regulations require that pasteurized milk be used. The curing process changes the texture from a soft waxy form to a solid, compact, close grain, almost translucent consistency, and the intensity of flavor is increased from mild to strong as the cheese ages. Consequently, a lesser quantity of "ripened" than "green" cheese is needed to give the characteristic cheese taste in menu items in which it is incorporated. Cheddar cheese is pressed into many shapes or styles of varying weights for curing; for example, large thick rounds called "Cheddars" weigh 30 to 60 pounds; thin rounds—"flats" or "daisies"—weigh 20 to 35 pounds; long cylinders—"longhorns"—weigh 12 to 13 pounds; "bricks" weigh 5 or 10 pounds. Some users prefer prepackaged 1-, 5-, or 10-pound cuts for convenience in handling.

The variety and volume of other types of cheeses purchased for institution foodservices depends considerably on the locale, ethnic clientele, and the budget for protein-high foods. *Process* cheese is popular for use as luncheon slices and for sandwiches. It is a mixture of cheeses in which the curing is stopped by pasteurization at the desired stage, so it is available from strong to mild flavor. Through controlled conditions, consistent products and qualities are obtained repeatedly. Ordinarily this blended cheese is purchased in 5- or 10-pound plastic-covered bricks or as packaged individually wrapped slices. *Swiss* cheese in 10 pound cuts is purchased by some buyers instead of the 30- to 60-pound or larger rounds. This type of cheese is easily identified by the characteristic holes or "windows" produced during the fermentation process, rubbery glossy texture, odor, light color, and nutty flavor.

The soft acid-coagulated products such as cream, cottage, and Neufchâtel cheese are not aged. *Cream* cheese is a soft unripened cheese made from fresh sweet milk enriched with cream. Coagulation is aided by the addition of a starter to the pasteurized mixture, after which the mass is stored in covered vats under controlled temperature for 18 hours. The whey is drained from the soft fine curd; salt is added; and as the temperature is lowered, the product becomes a creamy or spreadable semisolid. *Cream* cheese should be purchased often as it deteriorates rapidly. The usual institution purchase unit is a 1-, 2-, 3-, or 5-pound brick, foil wrapped to exclude the air. *Cottage* cheese is either the cultured large-soft or the small-hard curd variety. Cream may be added to produce a more appetizing flavor and appearance. It is commonly in 5- or 10-pound plasticized and covered containers.

Many other cheeses are used in specialty cookery or in catering. For example, any of the blue cheeses are popular in either oil and vinegar or cream salad dressings, grated Parmesan-style cheese is served with many Italian dishes, and cream cheese or sour cream are good bases for "dip" mixtures. Practically all of the once-imported cheeses now have American-made counterparts and must be so labeled, as American-made Roquefort cheese is labeled American blue cheese.

Storage. The storage of all dairy products is an important factor in the sanitation, safety, and acceptability of this group of foods. Clean refrigerated storage space, covered containers, and proper temperature controls are necessary. Suggested temperatures for a few are: butter, 45 to 50°F; Cheddar cheese, 36 to 38°F; cream, 40 to 45°F; ice cream 0 to 10°F; and fresh milk, 40 to 45°F. Dry milk solids may be stored in a cool (50 to 70°F) storeroom in unopened packages or in tightly covered metal containers. Storage of perishables such as butter, cream, fresh milk, and cottage and cream cheese should be of short duration.

FRUITS AND VEGETABLES

The introduction of new fruits and vegetables from other countries and distant areas through improved means of refrigeration and transportation, and new technologies in growing, processing, and packaging have contributed to the rapid increase in availability of more products with almost year-round seasonability. Simultaneous with this increase in availability has been wide scientific study of the contributions of fruits and vegetables to the health and well-being of individuals.

Greater variation and interest in menus is possible through the inclusion of fruits and vegetables than by any other food group. Not only is there a wide range in type, color, texture, flavor, and cost from which to choose, but they are readily available in many forms, such as fresh, frozen, canned, dehydrated, or juice. Most fruits and vegetables also lend themselves to many methods of preparation. The popularity of fresh produce is high but, with the improved and new forms of preprepared products and high labor costs, most food-service managers are rapidly increasing the selection of certain processed foods to help meet the needs of their institutions.

The quality characteristics that determine the standards for selection of each item vary considerably with the type of product. Uniformity in variety, size, and pack, the degree of maturity, freedom from defects, and condition of the product are bases for such determinations. Generally, fruits or vegetables of high quality, either fresh or processed, are considered economical because of high acceptability and minimum preparation losses. Standards for grades have been established for most products by USDA, but grading is not compulsory in all states or local markets.

Each foodservice must determine its own policy regarding the selection of fresh or processed fruits and vegetables. Factors to be considered include the food habits and needs of the group, how the food is to be used in the menu, the location of the institution in relation to market, storage facilities within the institution, the amount and skill of available labor, the relative cost of the forms in which the foods are available, and the amount of money to be spent. The inclusion of one or more servings of fresh fruits or vegetables in each day's menu for each person is a common pattern, although there are those few people who can eat them only in the cooked form. An appetizer or dessert of fresh fruit sections is usually far more acceptable than the canned cut-up fruit cup so often served. However, canned pineapple slices for a salad would be preferred to fresh pineapple by most people. Whether the fruit is to be served in a fresh fruit salad or cooked in a cobbler also would influence one's choice, both of quality and form. Should the institution be located in some isolated section where daily deliveries of fresh produce might be difficult, the institution would have to depend on the extensive use of canned, frozen, and dehydrated items. If the labor hours are limited, the use of frozen or preprepared items would be economical, since most fresh fruits and vegetables require considerable hand labor for preparation. The foodservice on a limited cost plan may need to substitute canned or frozen beans or a less expensive fresh vegetable when the individual portion cost of fresh beans reaches a certain level. Such information must be worked out by the person in charge of food production, and frequent checks must be made to keep it up to date, because of fluctuation in market prices. Some buyers find it a convenience to work out a handy reference chart on the portion costs of all items showing a range of raw-food prices.

Fresh Fruits and Vegetables. Wholesale markets offer an abundance of garden-fresh produce the year round. Peak production seasons for either locally grown or shipped-in produce is still a big factor in selection and sometimes in the price of many items, but we are no longer limited to the use of particular fruits and vegetables at particular times. Abundance of each item depends largely on the crop conditions in the large producing areas.

Rapid chilling and improved methods of handling leafy, stalk, pod, and some root vegetables harvested at their proper stage of maturity contribute much to the condition and acceptability of this type of produce upon delivery. Many of these vegetables are chilled, washed, graded, iced, or dry-vacuum packed in nonabsorbent paper-lined containers, and are in transit in temperature- and humidity-controlled mechanically refrigerated trucks or express cars within a few hours from the field. Others, such as potatoes and dry onions, are harvested at full maturity, cleaned, graded, and stored under controlled conditions for later shipment. Unfortunately, for the best flavor development, most fruits are harvested before they reach full maturity because of the high perishability of fully matured and ripened fruits. Apples, pears, and citrus fruits are cleaned and sometimes waxed, and packed in their respective types of containers for continued storage or are placed in controlled atmosphere storage (CO_2). Most other fruits are highly perishable and ripen rapidly after harvesting and therefore require a minimum of handling and quick delivery to the markets under well-controlled conditions.

Grades. Standards for grades of fresh produce as established by the Department of Agriculture designate minimum quality characteristics of maturity, firmness, color, freedom from defects, uniformity of shape, size, which may include measure, weight, or count per container, and tolerances for the above as permitted for each grade.

The names of the grades vary with the product; for example, the top quality for some items may be U.S. No. 1 and for others U.S. Fancy, U.S. Grade A, or U.S. Extra Fancy.

The grade standards are used as the bases for state regulations and for much of the trading done in the wholesale market. Also, growers' and packers' associations use them in establishing grades for their products. These grades are often designated by trade names and indicated on box labels, wrapping papers, or stamped on each fruit, as is often seen on oranges. Some states require that these brand names be registered with the Department of Agriculture in the state where produced, with a statement of the grade represented.

Space does not permit inclusion of the details of "minimum standards" for each of the 60 or more items for which standards have been listed but it is highly advisable for each food buyer and foodservice director to keep on file for ready reference the current regulations for the grading of fresh products in the state in which he lives. This information is available from the Director of Agriculture in each state, as is the information regarding shipping-point inspection for various commodities.

Containers. Variation in containers and styles of packing for the different fruits and vegetables in the wholesale market is most confusing to the inexperienced buyer. There are many size of crates, boxes, cartons, baskets, and sacks. Some are used interchangeably for the same item in local markets. Crates and boxes are used mainly for produce shipped from west of the Rocky Mountains, (Fig. 3.12) whereas baskets and sacks are generally used in the Middle West and East.

Federal standards for barrels and baskets have been established, although barrels now have limited usage. The Standard Container Act of 1916 established 2-, 4-, and 12-quart size baskets and prescribed definite dimensions for Climax baskets for grapes and other items. An amendment in 1934 standardized the 1-pound Climax basket for mushrooms, and the 1/2-pint, 1-pint, and 1-quart capacity containers for berries and other small fruits and vegetables. The Standard Container Act of 1928 fixed the standard sizes of hampers, round stave baskets, and splint or market baskets, which apply in both intrastate and interstate transactions. Nine standard sizes each for hampers and round stave baskets have been provided, but only the 1/2-, and 1-bushel sizes are used to any great extent. Continuous stave baskets with 1 or 2 hoops are known as *round-bottom* baskets, all others as *tubs* (Fig. 3.13). Standard sizes for splint or

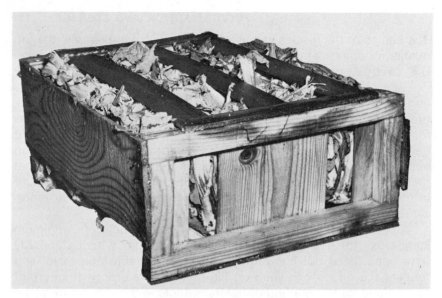

FIGURE 3.12   Western Pony crate for cauliflower and broccoli. Many wood crates have been replaced by impregnated heavy cardboard cartons that protect produce from moisture and bacterial growth. Courtesy, U.S. Department of Agriculture.

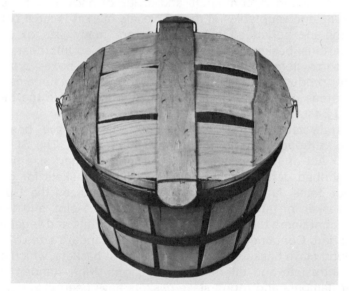

FIGURE 3.13   One-bushel round-stave tub basket showing desirable four point fastening of cover, with ends of cover slat under the handles and wire loops midway between the handles. Courtesy, U.S. Department of Agriculture.

market baskets are 4-, 8-, 12-, 16-, 24-, and 32-quarts and often are made of paperboard. Their use is general for all types of produce. Many states have adopted the federal standards for berry and grape baskets and tills, hampers, and round stave and splint baskets, usually of the 1- and 1/2-bushel capacities.

Other containers, such as boxes, crates, cartons, and sacks, have become fairly well standardized through usage in the various producing areas and according to content, for example, Western vegetable crate, citrus box, and tomato lug. Many of the containers are used for several items that have different weights per unit volume, so that constant attention to weights is necessary when buying. Also, the fill of containers varies in different areas, which means a variation in the net weight of the contents. Most weights are based on the *struck* or *level* fill instead of the *heaped* fill.

The styles of packing vary with the product and the geographic location. Those from the Pacific coast area are usually uniform in size and are *row packed* in layers, whereas those from other areas are *filled and faced,* which means that the contents of the bottom of the container are *jumbled* or *poured in* with a top layer of like-size fruit arranged in orderly manner. Local-grown produce is usually not arranged in the containers. With the possibility of so many different size and type containers for produce in a local market, no attempt is made to name more than a few of the most common sales units for various items, with approximate weights, in Table 3.10. The listing is far from complete, and each food buyer must become well acquainted with the package units in his area.

Know the Market. A daily or even semiweekly visit of the buyer to the wholesale market to inspect and select fresh produce is not always possible or feasible, although it is highly desirable. The produce may have more than met the grade standards when packed, but may have deteriorated beyond acceptance before reaching the foodservice, and certain items may have reached the market in exceptionally good condition, which would make them a most satisfactory purchase. The buyer would not have been aware of either situation until too late if he had ordered by telephone. Usually adjustments can be made in planning the needs to avoid wasteful buying and take advantage of the opportunities for "good buys." Most buyers who go to market regularly and select their produce believe that they save much money for the organization and also have the feeling of satisfaction that they obtained the best available for their particular purpose and for the price. Specification buying by grade does insure certain minimum quality characteristics and is possible

TABLE 3.10 CONTAINER NET WEIGHTS

A wide variety of packages, often varying only slightly in dimensions are used to ship fresh fruits and vegetables. Probably in the future there will be fewer and more standardized packages to meet the requirements of palletized and other unitized shipping. A comprehensive list of present packages would be bulky and impractical and would consist largely of packages not often used. Instead, the following is a list of what are believed to be the main packages in which each of 99 commodities are shipped and their net weight so far as known. Where two net weights are given, this is the general range. It is characteristic of fresh commodities that their weights vary between packages of the same volume and even in the same package with time. Consequently, weights can only be approximate. (See page 159 for list of abbreviations).

Commodity	Containers	Net Weight (lb) (Approximate)
Anise	Sturdee crt and wbd	40–50
	Crt 24	35–40
Apples	Ctn tray pk or cell pk	40–45
	Ctn bulk	36–42
Apricots	Brentwood lug	24–26
	L A lug tight fill	27–30
Artichokes	7 in. deep ctn	20–25
Asparagus	Pyramid crt	32
	Ctn 16 1 1/2 lb-pkgs	24
	2-lyr ctn	28–30
	1-lyr flat	14–18
Bananas	Ctn	40
	Ctn	20
Beans, snap	Wbd crt	28–30
	Ctn	28–30
	Bu hmpr	28–30
Beets, bchd	Wbd crt 24 bchs	36–40
Beets, topped	Film or mesh bag	50
	1-lb bags in master	24
Berries (misc) Raspberries, Blackberries	12 1/2-pt on tray	5 1/2–7 1/2
Blueberries	12-pt tray	11–12
Broccoli	Pony crt	40–42
	Ctn or crt 14 bch	20–23
Brussels sprouts	Drum	25
	Flat 12 10-oz c	7 1/2–8
	Ctn	25
Cabbage	Crt or ctn	50–55
	Bag, mesh or paper	50–60
	Wbd crt	50

154

Commodity	Containers	Net Weight (lb) (Approximate)
Cantaloupes	Jumbo crt 18–45	80–85
	Std crt	70–80
	Ctn 9, 12, 18, 23	38–41
Carrots, bchd	Ctn 2-doz bch	23–27
Carrots, topped	48 1-lb film bags in ctn or wbd crt	50
	Bulk in mesh film lined bag	50
Casabas	Ctn 4, 5, 6	32–34
	Flat crt 5, 6	48–51
Cauliflower	Ctn 12–16 trimmed, wrpd	18–24
	Catskill or Ll wbd crt	45–50
Celeriac	24 1-lb bags in master	24
	L A lug	30
	Sack	50
Celery, bchd	Fla wbd crt	55–60
	Calif wbd crate	60–65
Celery, hearts	12 film bags in ctn	24–28
	Wbd crts 24	30
Cherries	Calex lug	18–20
	Campbell lug	15–16
	Lug, loose pack	12–14
Chinese cabbage	Wbd crt	50
Coconuts	Burlap bag 40, 50	75–80
Sweet corn	Wbd crt	40–60
	Mesh or multiwall bag	45–50
Cranberries	Ctn 24 1-lb bags or boxes	24
Cranshaws	Ctn 4, 5, 6, 8	30–33
Cucumbers	1-1/9 bu wbd crt	55
	Bu bskt or ctn	47–55
	L A lug	28–32
	Ctn	26–30
Cucumbers, Greenhouse	Ctn	8–10
Eggplant	Bu bskt or crt	30–34
	1-1/9 bu wbd crt	35
	L A lug 18–24	20–22
Endive-escarole	Sturdee crt	30–36
	Wbd crt and ctn	30–36
	1-1/9 bu wbd crt	25–30
Figs	1-lyr tray	5–6
	2-lyr tray	10–15
Garlic	Crt and ctn	30
	Sack	50
	L A lug	20–22
Grapefruit, Florida	4/5 bu ctn or wbd crt	42 1/2
	Bags 4, 5, 8, 20 lb	
Grapefruit, West	Ctn	32–33 1/2
	6 8-lb bags in master	48

TABLE 3.10 CONTAINER NET WEIGHTS (Continued)

Commodity	Containers	Net Weight (lb) (Approximate)
Grapes, table	Lug or ctn	24–28
	Lug 16, 22, 24 wrpd bchs	22
Grapes, juice	Lug	36–44
Greens	Bu bskt or crt	20–25
Mustard	Bu bskt or crt	25
Turnip tops	Bu bskt or crt	25
Greens	1 1/2 bu wbd crt	30–35
Honeydews	Ctn 4 or 5	29–32
	Flat crt	40–45
	Jumbo flat crt 6–8	45–50
Leeks	4/5 bu wbd crt	25–30
Lemons	Ctn	38
Lettuce, Iceberg	Ctn	40–45
Lettuce, Boston	Eastern crt 1-1/9 bu wbd	20–25
Lettuce, Romaine	1-1/9 bu wbd crt	30
	Ctn 2-doz	35
	Bu bskt	25–28
Lettuce, looseleaf	Var contrs 2-doz	20–25
Lettuce, Bibb	12-qt bskt	5
Lettuce, hothouse	Bskt (2 sizes)	5–10
Limes	Flat or ctn	10–11
	Box or ctn	40–41
Mangoes	Flats var sizes	12–17
	Box or ctn	32–36
Mushrooms	Flat 12 4 1/2-oz c	4 1/2–5
	Ctn 4 2 1/2-lb bskts	10
	Ctn 8 2 1/2-lb contrs	20–21
	4-qt bskt	3
	Var contrs of 1-lb ctns	*
Nectarines	Sanger lug or ctn 2-lyr tray pk	19–22
	L A lug 2-lyr	22–29
	4-bskt crt	28–32
Okra	Bu bskt or crt	30
	L A lug	18
	5/9 bu wbd flat	18
Onions, dry	Sack	50
	Ctn	48–50
	Film bags 1 1/2, 2, 3, 5, 10-lb in master contr	*
Onions, green	Ctns 4-doz bchs	15–18
	Wbd crt 8-doz bchs	35–40

156

Commodity	Containers	Net Weight (*lb*) (*Approximate*)
Oranges, Florida	4/5 bu ctn	45
	4/5 bu wbd box	45
	Also consumer bags	
	4, 5, 8, 20-lb	
Oranges, West	Ctn	37 1/2
	8 5-lb film bags in	
	master contr	40
Oriental vegetables	L A lug	26–28
	Wbd crt	20–22
Papayas	Ctn	10
Parsley	Bu bskt	21
	Ctn 5-doz bchs	21
	1-1/9 bu wbd crt 5-doz	21
Parsley root	Sack, film or mesh	50
	L A lug	30
	Film bag	25
Parsnips	Sack, film or mesh	50
	L A lug	30
	Bu bskt	50
	Film bag	25
Peaches	1/2 bu wbd crt or ctn	23–28
	LA lug 2-lyr	22–29
	3/4 bu ctn, wbd crt or bskt	35–42
	Sanger lug 2-lyr	19–22
Pears	Western box, lug and	
	tight-fill ctn	45–48
	Ctn tight-fill	36
	L A lug or 2-lyr ctn	21–26
Peas, green	Bu bskt or hmpr	28–30
	Wbd bu crt	28–30
Peppers, sweet	Ctn	28–34
	1-1/9 bu crt	28–33
	Bu bskt or crt	28–30
Peppers, chili	L A lug or ctn, loose pk	16–25
Persians	Ctn 4, 5, 6	*
	Flat crt	35–50
Persimmons	Lug 2-lyr tray pk	20–25
	Flat 1-lyr tray pk	9–12
Pineapples	Crt or ctn	35
	1-lyr flat 4, 5, 6	18–20
	2-lyr flat 8, 10, 12	36–40
Plums	4-bskt crt	24–32
	Sanger 2-lyr lug tray pk	18–22
	L A lug	27–30
	Ctn loose	26–30

TABLE 3.10 CONTAINER NET WEIGHTS *(Continued)*

Commodity	Containers	Net Weight (lb) (Approximate)
prunes, fresh	NW prune lug	15
	NW prune lug	12
	1/2 bu bskt	28–30
Pomegranates	Lug 2-lyr place pk	23–26
Potatoes	Sack	100
	Sack or ctn	50
	5 10-lb sks baled	50
	10 5-lb sks baled	50
Radishes,	Ctn of 30 6-oz bags	11 1/4–11 1/2
topped	Film bag, bulk	25
	12-qt bskt 30 6-oz bags	11 1/4–11 1/2
	Film bag, bulk	40
bchd	Ctn or crt 4–5 doz bchs	30–40
Rhubarb	Case 10 5-lb ctns	50
	Ctn	20
	Western apple box	35
Rutabagas	Sack	50
Spinach	Bu bskt or crt	18–25
	Ctn 2-doz bchs	20–22
	Wbd crt	20–22
Squash, small	Bu bskt or crt	40–45
	1-1/9 bu wbd crt	44
	1/2 bu wbd crt	21
	Ctn or L A lug	24
Squash, large	Bulk bins, var sizes	900–2000
Strawberries	12 pt cups in tray	11–12
Sweet potatoes	Ctn	40
	Bu bskt or crt	50
Tangelos	Fla 4/5 bu ctn or wbd crt	45
	Calif ctn	30
Tangerines	Fla 4/5 bu wbd crt	45
	Calif ctn and lug	23–30
	Fla ctn	30
Tomatoes	Ctn or wbd crt	40
	L A lug	30–34
	Flats, ctns, 2-lyr	20–23
	Lugs and ctns, 3-lyr	30–33
	8-qt bskt	9–11
	12-qt bskt	18–20
cherry	12 bskt tray	16–18
Topped root vegetables	Sack or bu bskt	50
	Film or mesh bag	25

Commodity	Containers	Net Weight (lb) (Approximate)
	L A lug	30
	1-lb bags, 24 per master	24
Turnips,	Sack	50
topped	Mesh or film bag	24
	L A lug	30
bchd	Bu bskt or crt	29
Watercress	Ctn 2-doz bchs	*
Watermelons	Var bulk bins	800–2000
	Ctns 3, 4, 5	55–80

Source. *The Market News Service of the Fruit & Vegetable Division, Consumer and Marketing Service, U.S. Department of Agriculture; California Department of Agriculture; Florida Department of Agriculture; Package Research Laboratory; and Fruit and Vegetable Facts and Pointers series, United Fresh Fruit & Vegetable Association. Prepared by R. A. Seelig, Information Consultant, United Fresh Fruit & Vegetable Association, Washington, D.C.*
Abbreviations: * *weight not available; bchd bunched; bskt basket; bu bushel; crt crate; ctn carton; contr container; hmpr hamper; L A Los Angeles; lb pound; lyr layer; oz ounce; pk pack; pkg package; pt pint; sk sack; std standard; var various; wbd wirebound; wrpd wrapped.*

in most wholesale markets today; however, the effect of weather conditions on production, the high perishability of produce, and the variation in reliability of the wholesalers continue to present problems to the buyer. A study of daily market reports in the newspaper, on quotation sheets compiled by the Consumer and Marketing Service of the Department of Agriculture, and in weekly or monthly publications of governmental agencies or trade associations helps to keep one informed regarding the ever changing market conditions.

The buyer must be watchful of the varietal differences in the products and select the kind that will be most satisfactory for the use. A Ben Davis apple may be large, firm, red, and entirely satisfactory as to appearance, but it lacks the eating and cooking qualities necessary to make it an acceptable apple. Potatoes for French frying need to have a low sugar content (under 2 percent) to avoid production of a dark color by caramelization during cooking. In any discussion of the relation of appearance to desirability in a fruit, it should be stressed that surface blemishes that are not the result of decay may affect appearance without affecting eating quality. If such spots can be removed from the fruit in the normal course of preparation without undue waste, the purchase of blemished fruit of good eating quality at the price of a lower grade may present certain advantages.

Another point that should be considered in the purchase of fresh produce is the choice of the size best suited to the purpose. For example, apples to be used in pies may be much smaller than those selected for baking. Some consideration should also be given to the seasonability and availability of various fruits. Strawberries out of season may be available as frosted fruit, but the price may prohibit their use in many services. On the other hand, pears lend themselves to long-time storage without treatment and under conditions that may be readily established in even relatively small cities. Their use out of season is favored by the fact that the cost of pears varies little throughout an extended season.

Consideration should also be given to the containers in which the fruit is marketed to see that facing or plating with superior specimens has not occurred. The pack should be uniform throughout. Frequently the container is found to be loosely packed so that the quantity of fruit is far less than it is supposed to be. A demand for a sound pack is reasonable and just. Purchase by weight is an advisable approach to this marketing problem.

Preprepared items such as pared and cut apples, potatoes, and carrots, and washed spinach are now available in many markets. The apples and root vegetables are treated so that they may be kept at refrigerator temperature for several hours without deterioration. The purchase units for this type of merchandise vary with the locality, although the 30-pound bag is a common unit for prepared potatoes. Chopped cabbage for slaw, mixed salad greens in sealed bags, and fresh citrus sections in gallon glass jars are other examples of preprepared fresh foods. The selection of such items eliminates much labor and equipment formerly needed in most kitchens for these time-consuming preparations.

Amount To Buy. The amounts of fresh fruits and vegetables to buy at a given time for any one foodservice are determined by the type of menu served, the method of preparation, the numbers of persons to be fed, the availability of the market, storage facilities, the amount of money available, and the keeping qualities of the particular item in question. The average-size portion of most vegetables is 2 1/2 or 3 ounces cooked weight. From the standardized recipe card the buyer can determine the amount of each item needed. Tables of estimated quantities needed for 100 average-size portions are found in buying guides and quantity cookbooks.

Most institutions keep in their refrigerators a 2-day to 1-week supply of items such as lettuce, celery, tomatoes, oranges, lemons, and grapefruit and supplies of apples, potatoes, and dry onions according to storage facilities. Other less frequently used foods are purchased usually not earlier than the day preceding their use.

The initial price of fresh produce is by no means the ultimate cost, as there is usually a wide margin between the cost as purchased and the edible-portion cost. Because of waste in preparation and storage and losses in cooking, a highly perishable product such as cauliflower may cost 6 cents per pound as purchased and 30 cents per pound edible portion. The matter of immediate and proper storage after delivery is important, and most fresh produce should be removed from storage only in time for preparation (see Fig. 3.14).

FIGURE 3.14   *Fresh fruits and vegetables retain maximum freshness when stored in their original containers in a refrigerator unit with proper temperature and humidity controls. Skids or dollies and mobile shelf sections keep food containers off the floor and make for easy cleanability and flexibility of arrangement in the area. Courtesy, Metropolitan Wire Goods Corporation.*

Factors of Selection. The condition of the produce when delivered exerts a great influence on the probable acceptability and yield of the different items. It is to the advantage of the buyer to check in and weigh the delivered produce to see that it meets his specifications or is what he selected at the market, and to accept no other. Spot cutting is advisable to check quality, but even then some defects in produce may be hidden that will not show up until the preparation stage. A good buyer is alert to shifts in market conditions and when so-called "specials" are good investments.

Space does not permit the listing of quality characteristics of individual fresh fruits and vegetables, so only summaries by categories will be included in this text. Publications with emphasis on the selection of fresh produce, such as the USDA Home and Garden bulletins 141, "How to Buy Fresh Fruits," 143, "How to Buy Fresh Vegetables," and 198, "How to Buy Potatoes," materials from the United Fresh Fruit and Vegetable Association, and other texts provide excellent detailed information on varietal differences, quality standards, production areas, and storage that would be of help to the food buyer. Since so much of the fresh produce in a wholesale market is graded, the buyer is assured of weights and uniformity of size and quality within the tolerances permitted for the grade. All fresh fruits and vegetables should be clean, crisp or firm, in sound condition, and free from damage by decay, insects, or disease.

Apples have been a favorite fresh fruit for years. Many foodservices, however, now use canned and frozen apples for cooking, restricting fresh apples mainly to salads and eating raw. Some varieties of apples used quite generally in institution foodservices are shown on p. 163.

Apples may be purchased by size according to count per box or by diameter. For baking or serving raw, a uniform serving is possible if size is specified. A size 113 count (2 1/2 inches) is a medium-sized apple. A larger size 88 (3 inches) is good for baking. Apples should be refrigerated for long keeping and for maintaining high quality; best temperature for all varieties is between 32 and 34°F; controlled atmosphere storage (CO_2) keeps apples fresh, crisp, and juicy for a prolonged period of time.

A few characteristics for other fruits commonly purchased for foodservices follow.

> *Apricots*—best if tree-ripened. They should be mature, plump, juicy, and be a uniform golden color. Top quality: U.S. No. 1.

Variety	In Season and at Their Best	Eat-ing	Bak-ing	Freez-ing Slices	Freez-ing Sauce	Pies	Salad	Sauce
Transparent	July to Sept.				X	X		X
Wealthy	July to Nov.	X	X	X	X	X	X	X
Grimes Golden	Sept. to Dec.	X		X		X	X	X
Cortland	Sept. to Jan.	X	X		X	X	X	X
Jonathan	Sept. to Jan.	X	X	X		X	X	X
McIntosh	Sept. to Mar.	X	X		X	X	X	X
Delicious	Oct. to Apr.	X					X	
Golden-Delicious	Oct. to Mar.	X	X	X	X	X	X	X
Northern Spy	Oct. to Mar.	X	X	X	X	X	X	X
Baldwin	Oct. to Mar.	X	X	X	X	X	X	X
Stayman	Nov. to Apr.	X	X	X		X	X	X
Rome Beauty	Nov. to Apr.	X	X	X		X	X	X

Each variety of apple matures and reaches its highest quality at or near a definite time or season. When used in its proper season, a variety will best serve the uses for which it is intended. Desirable characteristics of apples: fresh, firm, well-shaped and well-colored for the variety, mature but not overripe fruit with juicy, fine-textured, and fine-flavored flesh. Top federal grades for apples are U.S. Extra Fancy, U.S. Fancy, and U.S. No. 1.

Avocados—should be fresh and bright appearing with flesh just beginning to be soft when pressed. Store at 50°F. If hard, avocados can be ripened in 2 to 5 days at room temperature. California grades No. 1 and 2; Florida No. 1, 2, and 3; no federal grades. Purchase firm, break-ing, or ready to eat.

Bananas—have no official grade. They should be plump, free from bruises, and ripened under controlled condi-tions. Select partly ripe (yellow ripe or green tip) for use within a few days and full-ripe for immediate use; hold at normal room temperature.

Berries—desirable characteristics: bright, clean, fresh ap-pearance, firm, plump, dry, and free from trash, sticky juice, molds, and over- or underripe fruit. Top qualities: U.S. No. 1 except cranberries, U.S. Grade A; blueberries no grade.

Citrus fruits—popular in all types of foodservices, although the trend is toward the use of more and more frozen concentrated and canned juices and refrigerated orange and grapefruit sections processed near the area of origin instead of whole fruit. Citrus fruits should be firm but springy to the touch, well-shaped, heavy for size, thin-skinned, and juicy, and should have few seeds. Some varieties have more skin color than others. Keeping quality is good at 36 to 45° F and relative humidity from 85 to 90 percent. Top qualities are U.S. Fancy and U.S. No. 1. Oranges: specify size (count per box), variety (Valencia, summer orange; or Navel, winter orange, for example). Grapefruit: specify white or pink flesh, size (count per box), growing area (Florida and Texas fruit are heavy, juicy and full flavored, thin skin; California and Arizona fruit have thicker skin, less juicy).

Grapes—these are berries with tough skin; they grow in bunches; they should be plump, fresh, highly colored for the variety, firmly attached to stems; and they do not improve in color, sugar, or quality after harvesting. Top qualities: U.S. Fancy, U.S. No. 1.

Melons—Cantaloupes: "full-slip" separation from stem as shallow scar indicates melon was mature when picked; grayish netted outer rind, light ground color, and distinctive aroma. *Casabas, Honeydews, Persians:* maturity difficult to determine, usually ripen off the vine; not all graded. *Watermelons:* should have bloom or gloss on rind surface; light ground color. Top quality: U.S. No. 1.

Peaches—quality depends on ripeness and soundness, but tree-ripe fruit cannot be shipped; precooled firm-ripe fruit satisfactory; taste for sweetness. Top qualities: U.S. Fancy, U.S. Extra No. 1, U.S. No. 1.

Pears—picked at mature green stage, fairly firm, and free from blemishes. They may be ripened at room temperature or stored under controlled refrigeration for future sale; flesh becomes delicately smooth, fine-grained, sweet, and juicy. Top quality fall pears: U.S. No, 1; winter pears: U.S. Extra No. 1.

Pineapples—quality determined much by color and odor; they should have fresh clean appearance and almost hollow eyes. Fruit should mature before harvest to develop the sugar. Top quality: U.S. Fancy.

Plums—must be well matured when harvested; softening at the tip indicates maturity; taste for sweetness. Top quality: U.S. Fancy.

Rhubarb—crisp, shiny stalks, uniform size. Forced: tender, light pink to pale red; field grown: sturdy, bright red.

Some outstanding desirable qualities to consider in selecting fresh vegetables follow.

Asparagus—fresh, moist, and cool, since edibility decreases rapidly in dry heat; tender stem, deep green or bluish green tips; whitish stem indicates age. Top quality: U.S. No. 1.

Beans—oval or semioval cross-section pod preferred; firm, crisp, snap readily when broken, stringless; immature seeds; avoid spots and russeting. Top qualities: U.S. Fancy, U.S. No.1.

Broccoli—firm, bright, tender young stalks and compact bud clusters; dark to purplish green; yellowed or wilted leaves indicate aging. Top quality: U.S. Fancy.

Brussels sprouts—similar to cabbage; consumer Grade A.

Cabbage—bright, fresh, firm to hard; free from yellowing or cracks. Top quality: U.S. No. 1.

Carrots—firm, fresh, crisp, well-shaped; good color, usually topped. Top quality: U.S. Extra No. 1. Other root vegetables: *beets, radishes, turnips, sweet potatoes*— fresh, crisp, smooth.

Cauliflower—compact, heavy, firm, curdlike heads; fresh crisp green leaves; avoid black-spotted curd and yellow leaves. Top quality: U.S. No. 1.

Celery—white or green (Pascal); medium length, crisp, solid, brittle stalks. Top qualities: U.S. Extra No. 1, U.S. No. 1.

Chickory, endive, escarole—fresh, crisp, narrow curly to broad leaf.

Eggplant—uniform dark color, smooth, heavy for size. Top quality: U.S. Fancy.

Globe artichokes—compact, firm, olive green head; free from dark spots or yellowish color.

Greens—spinach, beet tops, kale, turnip tops, chard, collards, mustard, endive, and others—fresh, clean, tender leaves.

Lettuce—crisp-head or iceberg: fresh, bright, crisp, tender, solid heads with large medium green outer leaves; butterhead or Bibb, Boston: rosette head, fairly light colored, soft, tender, succulent; cos or romaine: long cylindrical folded dark leaves. Top qualities: U.S. Fancy, U.S. No. 1.

Onions—green (shallots) and dry; bright, hard, well-shaped.

Green peas—young, fresh, tender, sweet; fresh, bright green velvety appearing pod; swollen, flecked, yellowish pods indicate overmaturity. Top quality: U.S. Fancy.

Peppers—tapered or semipointed; shiny bright green surface. Top quality: U.S. Fancy.

Potatoes—proper variety for use as high-starch, mealy potato for baking, mashing, French frying; moist, slightly waxy potato for boiling, hash browns or potato salad (See Table 3.11). New potatoes have high moisture and sugar

TABLE 3.11   THE CHARACTERISTICS OF COMMONLY USED POTATOES [a]

Variety	Characteristics	Preferred Method of Cooking (All may be buttered)
Early		
Burbank (West)	Large size; long, cylindrical or slightly flattened shape; smooth white skin; few shallow eyes; firm fine-grained white flesh.	Mash, bake, fry
Early Ohio	Medium size; round-oblong shape, round ends; smooth pink skin; numerous shallow to medium deep eyes; white flesh.	Cream, scallop
Triumph	Medium to large size; round shape, thick; smooth light-red to pink skin; medium-deep eyes; creamy-white fine-grained flesh.	Salad, mash, fry
Irish Cobbler	Medium to large size; roundish shape with blunt ends; smooth creamy-white skin; deep eyes; white flesh, frequently afflicted with hollow heart.	Cream, scallop
Intermediate to late		
Chippewa	Large size; elliptical to oblong shape, medium in thickness; smooth white skin; shallow eyes; white flesh.	Mash, fry, bake
Katahdin	Large size; short, roundish to elliptical shape; medium thickness; smooth dark creamy-buff skin; shallow eyes; white flesh.	Mash, scallop, fry, bake
Late		
Green Mountain	Large size; roundish-flattened or oblong-flattened shape; creamy-white somewhat netted skin; medium deep eyes; white flesh.	Mash, fry, bake
Red McClure	Medium size; round, flattened shape; red somewhat netted skin; few very shallow eyes; white flesh.	Mash, bake, fry
Russet Burbank	Large size; long, cylindrical or slightly flattened shape; heavily netted and russeted skin; shallow eyes; white mealy textured flesh.	Bake, mash, fry
Sebago	Large size; elliptical shape, medium thick; smooth ivory yellow skin; shallow eyes; white flesh.	Mash, fry, bake

[a] Classified according to time of harvest and storage characteristics. Late varieties are usually more mature and heavier skinned than early potatoes. (Also classified according to shape, long or round.) Potatoes should be kept in well-ventilated storage room at temperature of 35–40° F with relatively high humidity to keep conversion of starch to sugar at a minimum.

167

content and lower starch, giving a waxy moist texture when cooked. Select sound, firm, fairly smooth skin. Top quality: U.S. Fancy; most common grade is U.S. No. 1 (minimum diameter, 1 7/8 inches). Objective measurements of quality and specific gravity are possible with special equipment. A specific gravity of 1.08 or more indicates a dry, mealy potato; 1.07 to 1.08 indicates a moderately dry potato; and below 1.07 indicates a moist potato. A simple indicator test is to immerse potatoes in brine (1 cup salt to 11 cups water) at room temperature. If potatoes float they have a low solids content, and their best preparation is boiling, whereas potatoes that sink would be adaptable for baking. Fresh prepeeled, dehydrofrozen, and dehydrated potatoes are often used by institutions.

Squash—soft- and hard-skin; heavy for size; great varietal differences. Top quality: U.S. No. 1.

Tomatoes—mature, firm but not overripe, plump, smooth; good color, free from blemish, heavy for size. Top quality: Field—U.S. No. 1, greenhouse—U.S. Fancy.

Frozen Fruits and Vegetables. Fruits and vegetables prepared by a quick-freezing process are used extensively in institution foodservices. The improved standard practices of the selection of high-quality produce at its best stage of maturity, the immediate processing, packaging, and freezing under well-controlled conditions, and the convenience in preparation and storage have contributed much to the wide acceptance of these products. The original nutritive value, flavor, and color of foods are better preserved by freezing than by any other practical method of holding, and spoilage and storage space are reduced to a minimum. Since preliminary food preparation has been completed, the number of servings per sales unit is predictable with only slight error, and the labor costs are in the main comparable with those for canned foods. The cost per serving is usually on a level with that of fresh foods.

Grades. Grade standards for frozen fruits and vegetables that parallel in most regards those set up for canned products have been established by the USDA. They are: Grade A or Fancy, Grade B or Choice (for fruits), Extra Standard (for vegetables), and Grade C or Standard.

Grades are based on factors that reflect the quality characteristics of the finished product, such as color, size, excellence of workmanship, succulency in vegetables, ripeness and shape in fruit, and flavor.

Most frozen fruit and vegetable products are graded, although it is advisable to try out various brands to find the most satisfactory product for the purpose. The 40-ounce carton, packed 12 to a case, is the institution-size package for most vegetables. Broccoli, Brussels sprouts, and cauliflower are currently packaged in 32-ounce cartons. Also, dry-frozen corn, cut green beans, and peas are available in bulk 20-pound polyethylene bag-lined cartons. Some fruit juice concentrates are to be reconstituted 3–1, 4–1, or 5–1, in which case the weight of the can of concentrate is proportionately less to make a comparable amount of beverage. The usual unit of purchase of frozen apples, cherries, strawberries, and rhubarb is a 30-pound can. Some berries are available in 20-, 25-, and 30-pound cans or in polyethylene bag-lined cartons. An example of another size unit is 6 8 1/2-pound tins per case for frozen peaches. Packs with sugar may contain different ratios of fruit to sugar; that is 4:1 or 5:1, meaning 4 or 5 parts of fruit to 1 part of sugar.

Most users of frozen vegetables rely on obtaining a yield of 12 to 16 portions per 40-ounce carton, depending on the standard portion for the particular organization.

Frozen fruits and vegetables should be kept in solid form at low temperatures (0° to −10°F) until preparation time. Fruits are thawed, preferably in the refrigerator, and should be used at once. Vegetables are always cooked but need not be thawed in advance. Less cooking time is required than for fresh vegetables, since blanching is a part of the freezing process. Thawed fruits or vegetables should never be refrozen.

Canned Fruits and Vegetables. The extensive use of canned foods in institution foodservices of all types makes their selection of particular importance to the buyer. The choice between fresh, frozen, and canned fruits and vegetables depends largely on the fresh foods available and the prevailing labor costs. In localities where many fresh vegetables are available at a reasonable price and labor costs are not prohibitive, the consumption of canned foods is usually low. Under average conditions, however, when food costs must be held at the lowest level compatible with satisfactory standards, canned fruits and vegetables have an important place in the diet. The quality of the foods put into cans is often better than that of fresh foods available during out-of-season months, the nutritive value is comparable with that of the fresh fruit or vegetable, the waste is negligible, and the cost per serving is known.

Grades. Definitions and standards for various processed foods have been established by the Federal Food and Drug Administration, current issues of which are available on request.

The wide variance in quality and price among the same kinds of canned foods makes it necessary for the buyer to base selection on the use, the preference of the patrons, and the money return or the amount that may be spent for each serving.

Standards have been set for different grades of canned food, and their purchase by grade is common practice. However, some of the packs are still marketed under trade names that indicate to only the informed the placement of the product within the quality range represented by the company brands. The USDA has made available to the canning industry inspection and grading services that have fostered the development and wide use of official-grade standards for canned fruits and vegetables.

Form 3.3 is the score sheet for checking the quality of canned tomatoes.

Each product has its own set of standards and interpretations and a numerical rating or score sheet. The general characteristics for each grade of canned fruits and vegetables are summarized in Table 3.12. All products labeled Grade A, B, C, or D must meet the U.S. standard for the grade, but the letters "U.S." as a prefix may be used only when the processing has been done under continuous inspection and when the grading is done by an approved government agent. Foods so handled have a shield-shaped stamp on the label and an embossed shield on the end of each can. The U.S. Grade "Not Certified" designates all products that do not meet the minimum quality standards of the respective grades. It is based on the possible presence of a high mold count or extraneous material, a low fill, fermentation, or improper processing conditions of an otherwise high-quality-product.

Quality Control. Preventive measures for quality control of foods for processing have received much attention in recent years. The development of improved varieties of fruits and vegetables, grown and processed under controlled conditions, as well as the recognition of and demand for quality standards, have been effective.

Much is being accomplished through the development of improved techniques of processing to retain the natural color, texture, flavor, and nutritional qualities of the raw products. Subjection to

Score Sheet for Canned Tomatoes

Number, Size, and Kind of Container

Label

Container Mark or Identification	Cans/Glass		
	Cases		

Net Weight (oz)			

Vacuum (in.)			

Drained Weight (oz)			

Factors		*Score Points*		
I. DRAINED WEIGHT	20	(A) 18–20 (B) 15–17 (C) 12–14 (SStd) 0–11		
II. WHOLENESS	20	(A) 18–20 (B) 15–17 (C) 12–14		
III. COLOR	30	(A) 27–30 (B) 23–36 (C) 19–22 (SStd) 0–18		
IV. ABSENCE OF DEFECTS	30	(A) 27–30 (B) 22–26 (C) 17–21 (SStd) 0–16		
TOTAL SCORE	100			

NORMAL FLAVOR AND ODOR

GRADE

FORM 3.3   *Government score sheet for grading canned tomatoes.*

171

TABLE 3.12 SUGGESTED STANDARDS FOR CANNED FOODS

Fruits

Grade	Quality of Fruit	Syrup
U.S. Grade A or Fancy	Excellent quality, high color, ripe, firm, free from blemishes, uniform in size, and very symmetrical	Heavy, about 55%. May vary from 40 to 70%, depending on acidity of fruit
U.S. Grade B or Choice or Extra-Standard	Fine quality, high color, ripe, firm, free from serious blemishes, uniform in size, and symmetrical	About 40%. Usually contains 10 to 15% less sugar than in Fancy grade.
U.S. Grade C or Standard	Good quality, reasonably good color, reasonably free from blemishes, reasonably uniform in size, color, and degree of ripeness, and reasonably symmetrical	About 25%. Contains 10 to 15% less sugar than in Choice grades
Substandard	Lower than the minimum grade for Standard.	Often water-packed. If packed in syrup, it is not over 10%.

Vegetables

Grade	Quality of Vegetable
U.S. Grade A or Fancy	Best flavored, most tender and succulent, uniform in size, shape, color, tenderness; represents choice of crop.
U.S. Grade B or Extra-Standard (sometimes called Choice)	Flavor fine; tender and succulent; may be slightly more mature, more firm in texture, and sometimes less uniform than Fancy grade.
U.S. Grade C or Standard	Flavor less delicate; more firm in texture, often less uniform in size, shape, color; more mature.
Substandard	Lower than the minimum grade for Standard.

high heat for a short period is favored over low heat for a long period of time to insure a commercially sterile product. The short, high-heat treatment has been found to be relatively more destructive to microorganisms than to food quality. The agitating retort method where cans are rolled or turned end over end produces products of higher quality and in much less time than by the common still retort method. The agitating movement causes air bubbles to be forced through the contents of the cans, thereby producing currents and rapid even heating. The products must be of a fluidlike consistency such as cream-style corn to enable the stirring action to take place. Another noteworthy development is processing in a pressurized room for fragile foods such as bean sprouts.

How to Buy. The method of purchasing canned foods varies with the size and policies of the institution. Buyers for large concerns often deal directly with the packers on a specification-and-contract basis, and the foods are shipped in carload lots. Contracts may be signed without a specified price, the buyer agreeing to take his foods, when ready for shipment, at the price named by the packer or with an estimated price, the buyer having an option to buy a specified amount when the price is known; or future contracts may be made, with a maximum price and times of delivery named, the packer free to make adjustments downward but not upward. Usually 1/4 to 1/2 of 1 percent is deducted from the invoice as a "swell" allowance on large contracts. A reduction of several cents a can would be affected in most cases by dealing direct with the packer.

Smaller users may pool their orders for direct shipment or more often will purchase canned products through a wholesale dealer who warehouses and delivers the foods as ordered. The steps in the purchase of an order of canned goods by the latter method follow.

> *List the foods to be purchased.* A list of canned foods needed should be made; that is, apples, apricots, carrots, peas, salmon, and so forth.

> *Determine the grade or quality.* An institution in which different types of menus are served will obviously have to purchase several grades of the same food. For example, a Fancy Grade of peach may be required for a dessert fruit, a Choice Grade for a salad, and a Standard Grade for peach cobbler.

> *Determine the approximate amount to be purchased at one time.* If proper storage facilities are available, enough canned foods of each grade for 6 months to 1 year may be purchased at one time. This amount may be based on the quantity used in the same period of other years or may be determined by estimating the number of times that this food will be served during the given time and the amount

necessary for each serving period. It is usually wise to underbuy instead of overbuy, because canned foods should not be held longer than 1 year.

Submit specifications. A list of foods giving the approximate grade and quantity of each to be purchased should be submitted to not fewer than three or more than four or five well-known and reliable packers or distributors of canned foods. Specifications should include size of can, style of pack, syrup density, variety, size, and count or sieve, where appropriate.

The procedure from this point will vary, depending on the policy of the buyer and the seller. The bidders usually return the list with the brand name and the selling price of each article and, from this list, the buyer eliminates on the basis of brand or cost. The revised lists are then sent to each seller and samples are called for. If the desired quantity is large, free samples are often offered for inspection; if it is small, the samples may have to be purchased.

Select desired food. When the coded samples have been delivered and each can and label has been carefully numbered for purposes of identification, all labels are removed. All cans of one food, such as peaches, are opened, left in the original container, and scored by at least three persons who are directly responsible for the purchase and use of the foods. This inspection group should include the dietitians and the buyer, if there is a special purchasing agent. Form 3.4 suggests a form for recording pertinent information about each sample. Quality and yield in individual servings are highly important to

Kind	Code	Label Net Weight	Actual Weight	Sp. Gr. or Drained Weight	Brix	Count	Remarks and Ratings (Defects, Color, etc.)	Price Per Dozen	Price Per Can	Price Per Piece

FORM   3.4   *Suggested form for recording data on samples of canned products.*

those responsible for the satisfaction of the guest and to the efficient business management of the food unit. Special attention must be given to price quotations to be sure that the rate is per dozen or per case. If doubtful that specifications have been met, official sampling may be requested of the area laboratory maintained by the Consumer and Marketing Service, USDA, for testing. A reasonable sum is charged for this service.

Fruits and vegetables are available in many can sizes, but those used most by institutions are Nos. 10, 3 cylinder, and some 2 1/2 and 2. Small units find it advantageous to have a few of the small-size cans to fill in at the end of a serving period when a No. 10 can might be more than is needed. Juice is purchased in both No. 3 cylinder and No. 10 cans. The net contents and weights vary with the density of the commodity and the solidness of the pack. Usual capacities and yields of cans are given in the accompanying tabulation.

Size of Can	Number per Case	Net Weight	Measure	Number of Servings
No. 10	6	6 lb, 9 oz	12–13 c	20–25
No. 3 cyl	12	46 oz	5 3/4 c	12–15
No. 2 1/2	24	1 lb, 13 oz	3 1/2 c	6–8
No. 2	24	1 lb, 4 oz	2 1/2 c	4–6

Careful checking for condition of cans should be made at the time the order is received, and "swells" or bulged cans rejected. Cans may be dented or have evidence of rust on the outside without injury to the contents, unless leakage has occurred. All canned foods are coded, identifying the packer, date and time of pack, and name and style of an item. Code markings found on the bottom of the can are used to trace defective foods. Canned foods should be kept in a moderately cool dry storage room away from steam pipes or heating units. Freezing does not harm canned foods, although it may cause breakdown of texture and curdling of some foods of creamy consistency. The normal appearance is usually restored by heating. Care should always be used to keep canned food covered after it has been opened and to store it in a cool place.

Fruit and Vegetable Juices. Fruit and vegetable juices are served as a first course for breakfast, as appetizers for luncheons and dinners, and as refreshing afternoon drinks. They are most satisfying when chilled or iced. A 4- or 5-ounce glass is considered a serving. Fresh, frozen, concentrated, or powdered orange juice is available. Grape, sauerkraut, rhubarb, pineapple, lime, and lemon juices also form the basis for many refreshing drinks. Cider makes a satisfying drink when chilled and is equally palatable served spiced and hot. Juices for institution use are usually purchased in 46-ounce or individual-size cans, or as a frozen concentrate in 32-ounce containers and larger units such as the polyethylene bag that yields 20 gallons of juice.

Dried and Dehydrated Fruits and Vegetables. The preservation of food by drying is not new, but procedures have changed. Sun drying has given way for the most part to the faster, more sanitary, and better controlled artificial drying processes. Vacuum drying is a comparatively new method that results in fruits of very low moisture content, about 2 1/2 to 5 percent, with excellent keeping qualities. Federal regulations refer to these foods as "dehydrated" and to fruits that have been prepared by conventional drying methods and have had only 75 percent of the moisture removed, as "dried" fruits. Freeze drying, a type of dehydration, produces foods that are superior in flavor and texture to other types of low moisture foods. The product is flash frozen and then, in the frozen state, the water is evaporated out by sublimation, wherein the water molecules pass from the solid to the gaseous state without going through the liquid state. Evaporation takes place in a vacuum, and the resultant product is soft and spongy, but the cell structure is undamaged. About 98 percent of the water is removed; the weight is about 1/10 of the original, and products can be stored at room temperature. When rehydrated in warm water for a few minutes, the original flavor, form, and color are restored to a high degree.

Some of the commonly used dried fruits in foodservice operations are apples, apricots, dates, figs, peaches, prunes, and raisins. These fruits may be purchased with regular moisture content of 18 to 25 percent, but some also are available as low-moisture or dehydrated fruits, with a 2 1/2 to 5 percent moisture content. An example is apples, which may be purchased as low-moisture slices, wedges, or nuggets for applesauce, or as regular-moisture slices. Instant fruit powders, made by dehydrating fresh juice and reconstituting by adding cold water, also are used to some extent in foodservices.

Some dried and dehydrated fruits may be purchased in convenience forms, such as high-moisture pitted prunes ready for immediate use or dates in pitted, cut, or chopped form or as low-moisture nuggets.

Dried prunes and apricots are graded by size; for example, size 40/50 in prunes means not more than 50 nor less than 40 prunes to the pound. Cost generally increases with size. Most fruits are available in 5-, 10-, and 25-pound boxes and in 1- and 2-pound cartons or bags.

Dehydrated vegetables such as onions, celery, green peppers, and parsley are readily adaptable to institution cookery and have gained wide acceptance. One pound of dehydrated onions is the equivalent of 8 pounds of freshly prepared onions. Three No. 10 cans or three 1 3/4-pound bags of dehydrated onions will give the same onion flavor and bulk after cooking as onions prepared from a 50-pound bag. Dehydrated potato products are widely used, with the most commonly purchased being instant flakes or granules for mashed potatoes. Some brands include nonfat dry milk solids. Diced, sliced, and other forms of potatoes also are available, as are dehydrated sweet potato flakes. Common containers are No. 10 cans and sealed polyethylene bags. One No. 10 can of flakes yields approximately 60 servings of mashed potato. Cool dry storage is recommended.

Foods such as legumes are marketed in dried form. Among the common dried legumes are peas, black-eyed peas, crowder peas, soybeans, and navy, pinto, kidney, and lima beans, as well as a limited quantity of lentils. In foodservices operated on a low-cost basis, legumes are so important that it would be difficult to plan without them.

Legumes are graded according to size, uniformity of color, and freedom from insects. Mature beans should be smooth and shiny. The size and color are relatively unimportant except that beans of the same size soften uniformly when cooked. There should be no prejudice against beans that darken during cooking, since they usually have a good flavor and often are more tender when prepared than the white beans. Legumes are usually purchased by institutions in 100-pound sacks. They should be stored in a dry, cool place away from insects.

FAT

Fats and oils may have one or more of five principal uses in the average institution foodservice. The first is as a spread on bread, hot biscuits, or toast. The second is as flavoring for a cooked vegetable or other food, thus increasing its palatability, such as butter or bacon fat when added to freshly cooked beans or turnips. The third is as an ingredient of a sauce or dressing for raw or cooked foods, such as white sauce, mayonnaise, French dressing, and tartar sauce. The fourth is in frying, basting, and other methods of cooking food. The fifth is for shortening, as in the making of batters and doughs. In each case flavor, form, and other physical and chemical characteristics, as well as the food habits to which we are accustomed, influence the choice of fat and its use.

Butter and margarine are equally acceptable as a spread or for the seasoning of vegetables, depending on the preference of the user. Color, flavor, odor, consistency, keeping quality, and nutritive value are important factors to keep in mind when selecting fat for these purposes. Added to the above would be the emulsifying property and stability under heat for fats to be included in sauces and cooked foods. Grades and purchase forms for butter are found on p. 144. Margarine is purchased in 1-pound prints packed 30 in a carton or individual pats cut as designated, layer- or tray-packed in 5-, 10-, 12-, or 15-pound cartons. Individual pats of margarine must be stamped as such.

Fats are available in liquid or solidified form. *Oils* are liquid at room temperature. They are extracted from seeds or fruit of certain plants. The most commonly used oils are olive, cottonseed, corn, soybean, peanut, and coconut. Of these, olive oil is the most highly prized and the most expensive. Oils are used in salad dressings and in browning and frying. Most cooking and salad oils are purchased in 5-gallon tins, each packed in an individual carton. All solid fats have not been subjected to the hydrogenation process, although most of those used in cookery including lard have been so treated. *Hydrogenated* fats have had hydrogen added to the unsaturated carbon bonds of the glycerides during the processing of a natural fat, either animal or vegetable, which improves the texture and firmness or plasticity of the fat, raises the melting point, increases the keeping qualities, and makes the fat odorless and tasteless.

Fat-frying shortening should be bland and impart no flavor of its own to the fried food; it should resist rancidity and have a high smoking point, long frying life, and low turnover or absorption by the food. Oils, lard, and shortenings are adaptable for use in frying, but care must be taken to select one with a smoke point of well over 400°F. Commercial shortenings are mixtures, for the most part, of unsaturated and saturated fatty acids combined with glycerol. Natural fats and oils most economical to use for shortenings include beef and pork fats and cottonseed and soybean oil. Peanut and corn oil are used to a lesser extent.

The characteristics of *shortening* agents in the preparation of flour mixtures vary with the products to be produced. In general, bland-flavored, colorless, odorless fats with high plasticity are used for cake and pie making, whereas oils and melted fats may be used in muffins and biscuits. The liquid fats yield a less flaky product, because of the tendency of the oil to spread into layers of extreme thinness; however, for many of the mixtures, the convenience of combining them in the liquid state far outweighs the disadvantages of nonplasticity. Emulsifying agents incorporated in the fats selected for use in flour mixtures tend to improve the moisture retention in the baked product.

Deterioration of cooking fats is due primarily to oxidation, hydrolysis, and the absorption of odors. The addition of an antioxidant agent to the shortening in the manufacturing process acts as an inhibitor of oxidation and improves the stability of the fat. Most foodservice managers find 50- and 100-pound containers the most convenient size for them to buy.

Nuts and *nut butters* have many uses in quantity food production and service. Nuts are usually purchased as whole, half, or broken nut meats in 5-, 10-, or 15-pound packages or cartons. Peanut butter is the most generally used of this group. Quart jars, No. 10 cans, and 25-pound tins are purchase units.

Storage. Careful storage is necessary to prevent the development of rancidity in these foods. The strong unpleasant odor and flavor that rancid fat imparts to food in which it is used are familiar to all. If fats and fat-rich foods are to be safeguarded from rancidity, they should be stored in closed containers that exclude air and light and the possibility of gross contamination by microorganisms, and they should be kept at low temperatures that will deter enzymatic and bacterial action.

In general hydrogenated fats present a less acute storage problem than other fats. Because of their excellent keeping qualities, these fats are often purchased in larger units than the natural fats are.

FOOD GRAINS

Grains are the seeds or seedlike products of any grass and those used for food are known as cereals. Cereals and cereal products include wheat, corn, oats, and rice in their various forms, and products such as prepared breakfast foods, macaroni, spaghetti, and noodles. For convenience, flours manufactured from soybeans, potatoes, bananas, and tapioca, none of which are cereal in source but which are closely allied to cereal products in use, may also be grouped under this heading.

The kernels of cereal grains are the dried fruits of the grasses and, although the seed structure varies characteristically with each kind, there are certain basic similarities among all of them. The first is the likeness of the kernel to a well-wrapped, sealed parcel. The bran or outer covering is comprised of several layers. It is high in cellulose and minerals and contains some protein and thiamine. Beneath it lie the endosperm and the starchy central portion that make up approximately 75 percent of the grain. At one end of it is found the germ or embryonic plant, which is relatively high in protein, minerals, vitamins, and fat. The endosperm seals the germ from air, thus protecting its fat content from oxidation. As the natural packaging is broken, the possibilities of rancidity increase. Early measures taken to prevent or reduce rancidity in milled products included removal of the germ in the process of refining the cereal. This simplified storage problems and hazards, but reduced sharply the natural nutritive value of the product.

The purchasing of food grains and the products in which they are incorporated varies with the size and type of unit. For example, in one bakery most items may be made on the premises, while another will purchase the finished products or perhaps bake prepared rolls and frozen fruit pies just previous to serving time.

Guides for the purchase of selected items follow.

Flour. The grades of wheat flour are designated as straight, patent, clear, and low. These grades, however, mean little to the buyer, since they are not sufficiently standardized to be interpreted the same by all millers. The ash and protein content of any flour furnish only an indication of grade; therefore, no large quantity should be purchased without a standardized baking test that will make evident the difference in absorption, stability, fermentation time, and quality of the finished product made from the flours being tested. The characteristic qualities of flour are determined by the variety of wheat, the soil composition, the milling process, and the amount of moisture available especially during the ripening season.

Hard wheat has a high protein (11 to 13 percent) content, and the flour milled from it is known as *bread flour. Cake flour* is milled from soft wheat and has a gluten content of 7 to 7 1/2 percent. It may be as much as 27 times finer than bread flour. *All purpose flour* is a blend of flour from soft and hard wheat, and its protein content varies according to varieties of wheat used and area where grown. *Self-rising flour* contains the constituents of baking powder as well as salt and is popular in the South, particularly for use in making quick breads. *"Instantized"* flours are forms of white flours that disperse rapidly in hot or cold liquids, do not pack, and pour like salt. Other properties seem to be unchanged from regularly milled flour, but more research is necessary to make known its full potential for use in various types of cookery. The usual purchase units are 50- and 100-pound bags for flour.

Storage. Storage conditions of flour should be carefully watched, since temperature, humidity, and length of storage period have an important effect on the baking qualities. The storage room should be maintained at an average temperature of 70°F and a relative humidity of 65 to 70 percent and should be well ventilated, as flour readily absorbs objectionable odors.

Other Grains and Grain Products. Many kinds and types of processed cereal products are available to the institution buyer to be consumed as purchased or incorporated into cooked products. No attempt will be made to discuss prepared cereals other than to mention that they may be purchased in individual or large-size packages, the weight and number of packages to a case depending on the product and, since keeping qualities are limited, such items should be purchased often and stored in a cool dry place.

Rice. A number of varieties of rice are grown commercially in the United States with Texas, Louisiana, and Arkansas as the leading production areas. Rexoro, Fortuna, and Blue Rose are the important varieties, each kind varying in size and texture of grain and maturing at different seasons. All varieties are available as brown, unpolished, and polished forms. Brown rice has not been subjected to the complete milling process and so has a higher fat content and nutritive value. The flavor is enjoyed by persons accustomed to it, but it has had limited acceptance for use in institutions. Polished rice may be coated or uncoated. Coating rice with a talc, removable by washing, gives it a luster that is desired in certain trade areas.

Standards for grading rice are based on wholeness of the kernel and cleanness. All classes of rice are sorted and sold according to the number of whole grains and the cleanness of the test sample. All varieties may be purchased in brown, unpolished, and polished form in 100-pound bags, or 24 1-pound boxes to the carton.

Many new processes are used in preparing rice for the market today. As with wheat, the milling process removes much of the nutritive value of rice, and so it, too, is *enriched* or *fortified.* Definitions and standards of identity have been established by the federal government for the enrichment of milled rice with thiamine, riboflavin, niacin and iron, vitamin D, and calcium. Enriched rice is available under various trade names.

Converted rice is that which is subjected to treatment in a vacuum, followed by hot-water pressure, steaming, and vacuum drying so that the minerals and water-soluble vitamins from the outer layers are diffused into the inner layers of the rice grains in such manner that most of these nutrients are retained after the milling process. This rice is a highly desirable product nutritionally.

"Instant rice" is that which has been precooked and dried and needs only rehydration and short cooking to take on properties of cooked rice. Instant rice is usually enriched.

Wild rice is not a grain but, instead, a seed of tall water grass that grows in swampy districts near the Great Lakes region, particularly in Minnesota. It must be hand harvested by workers who go through the swamps by boat or canoe, thus making the cost of wild rice excessively high compared to cultivated rice. The grains are long, thin, and a greenish brown. Although not a real rice, it is considered a delicacy by many and is popular as a stuffing for wild game or as an accompaniment of fowl.

Oats. The outer coat of this grain is removed, exposing the inner kernel, which is known as the groat. It is then ground or cut to various degrees of fineness as *oatmeal* and *rolled oats;* uncooked and partially cooked are the usual forms in which this cereal is marketed. In the preparation of rolled oats the coarse groats are brushed, steamed, flaked, and aspirated so that they are cool when put into packages. The quick oats are partially cooked through a greater application of steam than is used for the regular rolled oats. Both types may be purchased in bulk or in 3-pound round cartons, packed 12 to the case.

Corn. This is an important cereal product of the new world that has served an important place in the diet from earliest pioneer days. Today the mature grain is processed into breakfast cereals, meal, flour, oil, and starch, as well as several forms of hominy, some of which are enriched and quick cooking. Both yellow and white varieties of corn are used to make meal, and choice depends on the preference of the clientele to be served. The use of cornmeal has declined steadily over the last several years; however, sales of prepared cereals made of corn have increased. Like whole wheat flour, cornmeal has poor keeping qualities, and quantities to last only a short time should be purchased. Bags holding 9 or 24 pounds are the usual purchase units.

Barley. This is one of the oldest of cereal grains, but it has only limited use in this country. Barley does not contain gluten, so its flour is less well suited to bread making than wheat. Pearl barley is the polished grain with the bran removed and may be used to thicken soups or as a cereal substitute for potatoes to give variety in the menu. More barley is used for malt making than as a cereal; malt is important in the making of yeast, malted milk beverages, and malt syrups used in bakeries.

Alimentary Pastes or Macaroni Products. These products are made from durum wheat flour, a variety with an especially high gluten content, important for yielding macaroni products that will hold their shapes well when cooked. Durum wheat contains a yellow pigment that gives the products made from it a yellowish tinge. This natural color is an indication of good quality since no artificial coloring may be used. Pastes made from the coarse flour, called semolina, are shaped and dried. Many shapes are available, the most common being rods, tubes, ribbons, and small pieces in cut lengths, stars, bows, shells, and alphabets. The usual purchase units for *macaroni* and *spaghetti* are 20-pound cartons, and for *noodles* the units are 10-pound cartons.

Mixes. Both fully prepared and base mixes are great time and labor savers. They may be purchased in many varieties and, if properly handled, make excellent products. Some cake mixes are packaged in 4 1/2- to 5-pound cartons, 4 to the case. Large foodservices may contract for mixes made to their specifications.

Bread and Bakery Products. In many of the smaller foodservices that lack bakeshop facilities, bread and certain other bakery products are obtained daily from commercial bakeries. Standards for certain types of bread have been established that insure consumers of the content of the loaf.

Items specified in the standards are: name under which the type must be sold, such as white bread, enriched bread, milk bread, raisin bread, and whole wheat bread; required ingredients, which are flour, a moistening agent like water or milk, yeast, and salt; optional ingredients such as shortening, eggs, milk, and milk products, sugars, enzyme preparations, and certain salts; and labeling.

White bread is prepared by baking a kneaded yeast-leavened dough, made by moistening flour with water or one or more of the optional liquid ingredients specified in the standards, and seasoning with salt. *Enriched* bread, rolls, and buns must meet the standards for white bread and the nutrient requirements for enrichment. If nonenriched flour has been used, specified quantities of nutrients must be added to the mix at the bakery to provide bread of standard nutritive quality. Vitamin D is an optional ingredient that may be added to enriched bread in quantity to provide a minimum of 150 and a maximum of 750 U.S. Pharmacopoeia units for each pound of finished bread. Not less than 300 or more than 500 milligrams of calcium salts may be added, and the addition of wheat germ is permitted to further fortify this type of bread. Likewise, definite specifications are set up for milk, raisin, and whole wheat breads. *Raisin bread,* rolls, or buns must meet the standards for white bread plus 50 parts by weight of seeded or seedless raisins to 100 parts by weight of flour. Whole wheat, graham, entire wheat bread, rolls, or buns must be made with whole wheat flour and no other flour combined with it. The nonstandardized types of bread must carry complete ingredient listings on the labels.

Care should be taken to have bread and other bakery products fresh daily, if this is possible. Staling, with an attendant loss in palatability, takes place in a short time. Changes are evident in the crust, which becomes soft and leathery, and in the crumb, which becomes tough, crumbly, and somewhat hard. Staling is accompanied by loss of water and certain other substances responsible for the pleasant aroma of fresh bread. Bread purchased wrapped is protected from moisture loss, and hence staling may be delayed. High storage temperature delays staling but favors spoilage through molding, a common cause of deterioration of bread and other bakery products held for several days.

Bread is made into many size loaves and can be sliced according to specification. More or less standard are: 1-pound loaf (16 5/8-inch slices), 1 1/4 pound loaf (19 5/8-inch slices), 1 1/2-pound loaf (24 5/8-inch slices), and 2-pound sandwich loaf (38 1/2-inch slices). Rolls of varying sizes and styles are available to meet the particular needs. Other bakery products like sweet rolls, doughnuts, and cookies may be specified as to size and type. Bakery orders are usually placed the day before for early morning delivery.

BEVERAGES AND FOOD ADJUNCTS

Beverages. The beverages coffee, tea, and chocolate play important roles in the success of a foodservice. The relative importance to be attached to each is largely determined by the geographic section in which a foodservice is located, as well as by the food habits of its clientele.

Important production areas of coffee have been the Latin American countries, with Brazil the largest supplier and Colombia second largest. Today these countries continue as important sources, but Central America and Africa, especially the Ivory Coast, Angola, and Uganda, are gaining recognition as exporters of coffee. Africa produces approximately 20 percent of the total world supply. Tea imports to this country come from India and Ceylon, with small amounts from Indonesia and other countries in that general geographical area. Green tea comes primarily from Japan. Chocolate and cocoa are produced from the bean of the cacao tree grown in most countries in the tropical belt, near the equator. Largest imports of cacao beans are made from Africa and Brazil.

Coffee. Coffee is imported into the United States as unroasted green beans. Coffee shrubs or trees begin to bear fruit from 3 to 6 years after the seeds are planted. Usually they are kept pruned to about 8 feet in height to facilitate picking of the berries. A temperate climate of 60 to 70°F in a tropical area with 40 to 70 inches annual rainfall, well distributed throughout the year, protection from long exposure to the sun by natural cloudiness or interplanting of larger trees, and an altitude of more than 2000 feet are conducive to the production of a high-quality product. Often the bushes grown at sea level produce large, soft, misshapen beans with undesirable pungent flavor. The ripened deep reddish-black berries are ready to be harvested 6 to 8 months after the appearance of white fragrant blossoms. Picking of the berries extends over a period of several months, since a single tree may produce blossoms and ripe fruit simultaneously. Harvested berries are processed for market by washing and mechanically removing the pulp before drying and hulling (wet method) or by fermentation while drying (dry method). Usually high-quality mild coffees have been processed by the wet method and then sun or machine-hot-air dried. The yield of an average tree is 10 pounds of berries, which approximates 2 pounds of clean green coffee beans or 1.7 pounds of roasted coffee.

A common classification of coffees is by production area or port from which exported, such as Rio, Santos, and Bourbon Santos from Brazil, Bogota from Colombia, Mocha from Arabia, Java from the Dutch East Indies, and Kenya from Africa. Coffee grown in the western hemisphere usually is of the *Arabica* species, which is considered superior in quality to the *Robusta,* grown mostly in Africa. The latter is a rugged variety, resistant to pests and diseases, especially the fungi, and is grown mainly in low, humid, and hot regions.

All coffee beans, regardless of their geographic source, are roasted to develop the caffeol, a volatile oily substance capable of entering into solution with water and largely responsible for the aroma and flavor of coffee. Roasting coffee also brings out a "fixed" oil, which does not evaporate. Carbon dioxide gas is another product formed in the roasting coffee berry. About 65 percent of this gas is liberated within 24 hours after the coffee is ground. If the roasted and ground coffee is exposed to the air, oxygen reacts on the carbon dioxide so that in 9 days practically all this gas has disappeared and carried with it most of the volatile oil. On the tenth day a disagreeable flavor appears that develops rapidly within the next 10 to 15 days. The color of the coffee berry is changed to the characteristic dark brown in the roasting process. The time of roasting varies, depending on whether a light, medium, or dark roast is desired. The medium roast is most popular for the average service.

Green coffee beans from various areas are combined to produce the desired blend of flavor, color, and body. Inspection of the blended beans does not afford the average buyer any clue as to what characteristics the beverage made from them will have. Decision is usually based on cup tests of a number of blends furnished by the wholesaler, the test being run under the conditions of equipment and water supply prevailing in the given service. Three or more people who really enjoy coffee and are discriminating about it should participate in a cup test to make the choice decisive. Qualities checked by professional coffee tasters to judge aroma and flavor may well be used by such a taste panel. Ratings may be based on intensity, ranging from none to slight, moderate, strong, and extreme, and may be used to evaluate characteristics of aroma and flavor such as fragrance, dryness, pungency, sweetness, density, acidity, and retentivity.

A more positive means for determining coffee quality is by the use of a hydrometer. This instrument measures the buoyancy, density, or strength of the beverage, based on the amount of soluble solids extracted in the brewing process. However, to be meaningful, the hydrometer readings must be converted into percent of beverage solids by means of a conversion table or chart and allowances made if the temperature of the brew is above or below the standard (usually 140°F).

Instant or soluble coffee powder is available in a number of blends. Some are freeze dried, while others are prepared by various extraction, evaporation, and drying processes. Also available now is a frozen concentrated coffee. A dispenser carefully proportions a mixture of coffee concentrate and hot water as each cup or decanter is drawn. Instant coffee is not greatly affected by ordinary storage methods, and the convenience of use with no expensive coffee-making equipment needed, no grounds to be discarded, and no delay in service for remaking during peak periods make this a preferred product by some institution managers.

Coffee from which a large percentage of the caffeine has been removed is known as *decaffeinated* coffee. It is used by persons who enjoy the flavor but do not desire the stimulating effect of coffee. The brew is made in exactly the same manner as untreated coffee.

Orders for coffee may be placed for the roasted whole beans, or ground according to specification to be delivered daily, weekly, or as preferred. The grind must be appropriate for the coffee maker, for example, medium-fine or drip grind for a dripolator-type urn. Also the coffee should be packaged so that the contents of one unit (3-, 14-, 16-, 32-ounce) will be used each time coffee is made. This eliminates weighing or measuring or having some amount left in the container. Ground coffee once exposed to the air deteriorates rapidly. Users may find the standard vacuum-pack coffee entirely satisfactory, although moisture-proof, sealed paper bags are the usual form for packaging coffee for institutions. Various brands of soluble coffees that readily dissolve in hot or cold water are available in institution-size units. Most of these are the dehydrated brews of the coffee blends with the same brand names.

Tea. The quality of tea depends on locality, mineral content of the soil, and weather. Tea grown on the cool high slopes of the Himalaya Mountains is rated superior to that grown in the lowlands, the finest quality being produced at around 10,000 feet elevation. The quality of tea also depends largely on size of leaf, time of picking, selection and preparation of the leaves. The smaller the leaf, the better the quality, other factors being equal.

The three types of tea are known as *black, green,* and *oolong,* or semifermented. The difference among them lies in the method of preparation. Leaves from a single shrub may yield black, green, or oolong tea, depending on the processing employed. Black tea is fermented or oxidized and then dried, which darkens the leaves to almost black; green tea is unfermented and fired or dried while green, which preserves the original color; oolong is semifermented before drying so that it has some of the characteristics of both the black and green teas.

The grades of black teas are determined by the size of leaves and the relative positions on the plants on which grown. The young, tender, orange-tinted leaves from the tip ends of the stems or branches are known as *orange pekoe,* those from the middle as *pekoe,* and the larger leaves from the base of the stems as *souchong.* Orange pekoe is usually considered the highest quality of black tea. However, souchong produced at a high elevation would be superior to orange pekoe produced at sea level. A blend of orange pekoe and pekoe is preferred by many people. The delicate flavor of the one combined with the greater strength of the larger leaves produces what is regarded as a most satisfying beverage. The finest quality of black tea produced in India is known as *Darjeeling.* Black teas are sometimes scented and made more of a specialty product by the inclusion of dried blossoms such as jasmine.

Green tea is classified also according to the relative size and position of leaves on the stems. The smallest end leaves are rolled tightly into balls during the curing process and are known as *gunpowder;* the next larger leaves are rolled lengthwise and are known as *young hyson;* and the largest leaves are rolled into balls and designated as *imperial.*

Both green and black tea for institution use are commonly purchased in cartons containing 100 or 500 individual bags, usually packaged 250 to 300 per pound, each bag holding enough to brew 1 cup of strong or 2 cups of weaker infusion. High qualities of tea will produce greater amounts of a more satisfactory beverage than the less expensive and poorer qualities of leaves. The blend found most desirable for iced tea is put into bags containing an ounce or an amount sufficient to make 1 gallon of tea. The higher cost of tea so packaged is compensated for by the ease of handling, the removal of chance from the amount of tea used per unit desired, the uniform quality of the beverage, and the higher sanitary standards that prevail. Instant tea is adaptable to use for either hot or iced tea.

Cocoa and Chocolate. Cocoa and chocolate are produced from the beans or seeds of cacao trees, which grow in countries near the equator, especially in Central and South America and near the west coast of Africa. The latter produces approximately 70 percent of the world's supply of cacao. The trees grow best when protected from heavy winds and direct sunlight, although they require heavy rainfall, high humidity, and a mean shade temperature of about 80°F. The fruit develops from flowers that appear on the trunk and branches of mature trees after about the third year until 60 years or more. From 20 to 50 seeds are encased in each melonlike fruit, which grows 6 to 14 inches long. The beans are removed from the pods, fermented in tanks, dried, and shipped to the manufacturer. There they are cleaned, roasted, and broken to remove the shells, leaving the heavier part of the bean or "nibs." The nibs are crushed, exposed to a moderate heat, and reduced to a paste from which various forms of the finished product are made. Cocoa is chocolate with a high percentage of the fat removed and is sold in powder form, whereas chocolate contains approximately 50 percent fat and is sold in a solid cake or bar. The brown color of cocoa and chocolate is said to be largely due to the presence of oxidized tannins.

Cocoa and chocolate most commonly used in institutions are: plain, bitter, sweet, and milk chocolate; and breakfast, sweet, milk, and Dutch-process cocoa. The latter has been treated with an alkali that produces a cocoa of darker color and milder flavor than an untreated cocoa. Dutch-process cocoa also enters and remains in suspension more readily than other types.

Cake chocolate of various kinds may be purchased in 1- and 10-pound cakes. Cocoa is packed in fiber drums, shellac coated, containing 25 to 100 pounds net weight. Larger quantities are packed in paper-lined bags, in steel drums, and in 3-ply kraft paper bags. Smaller quantities are marketed in glass jars, tin cans, or cardboard boxes.

In choosing cocoa or chocolate the definition of terms established by the government affords an index as to the composition of the product. Breakfast cocoa, containing "not less than 22 percent cocoa fat," is commonly used for making beverages and may be successfully employed in baked products. Chocolate contains "not less than 50 percent of cacao fat." Formulas in which breakfast cocoa has been successfully used may not prove satisfactory if a cocoa or chocolate containing a different amount of fat and producing a different color is substituted. In the selection of a cocoa for beverages the cup test may well be made, and any knowledge the buyer may have of the chemical composition should influence his choice. Individual packets of instant cocoa are convenient for use in foodservices where the demand for cocoa is irregular.

Coffee, tea, cocoa, and chocolate should be stored in a clean, cool, dry place.

Food Adjuncts. Products like salt that add zest, flavor, and interest to another product are known as food adjuncts. They include flavorings, salt, spices and herbs, condiments, vinegar, and concentrates. These are considered among the staple items in a foodservice, and a reasonable supply is maintained.

Flavorings. Nature provides a limited botanical source of flavorings that come from roots, leaves, seeds, flowers, and other portions of plants, trees, and shrubs. The flavor is extracted from these botanicals either by maceration, digestion, percolation, or distillation, usually with alcohol or alcohol and water to draw the essential oils into solution. Commonly used natural extracts include vanilla from the vanilla bean, lemon from the oil or peel of the lemon, peppermint from the oil of peppermint, and almond from the oil of bitter almonds.

As demand for flavorings increased and natural supplies remained limited, the manufacture of chemical reproductions or imitations of the natural flavors was a necessary development. These aromatic chemical products closely resemble the natural flavors both in taste and aroma, and, as Merory [3] has stated, "the addition of from 5 to 25% of natural flavorings to flavor imitations increases the near likeness most effectively. Such combinations are often preferred to genuine products for their stability and resistance to high temperatures." Often they are more powerful in taste and less expensive than the natural extract and therefore more suitable for use in some institutions.

With synthetic as well as natural flavorings available on the market and each in several different forms, some confusion arises over the identity of various terms. The established integrity of certain food products becomes threatened as happened recently with vanilla. "Pure Vanilla Extract" was not always pure, and standards of identity became necessary. The Federal Food and Drug Administration, with the assistance of those in the food industry, consumers, and professional experts, established Federal Definitions and Standards of Identity for vanilla and vanilla products effective in December, 1963. These standards are:

Vanilla extract, *is the solution of vanilla constituent in ethyl alcohol. The content of alcohol must be no less than 35% by volume, and the content of the vanilla constituent not less than one unit per gallon. (A unit represents the flavoring equivalent of 13.35 ounces of vanilla beans, containing 25% moisture or less.) Vanilla extract may also contain glycerin or propylene glycol as additional solvents, and sugar, dextrose, or corn syrup to add sweetness.*

Concentrated vanilla extract *is the same as vanilla extract, except that each gallon contains two or more units of vanilla constituent.*

[3] *Joseph Merory,* Food Flavoring, Composition, Manufacture, and Use, *Avi Publishing Co. Westport, Connecticut, p. 159, 1960.*

Vanilla flavoring *has an ethyl alcohol content of less than 35% by volume, and one unit of vanilla constituent;* concentrated vanilla flavoring *contains two or more units of vanilla constituent.*

It will be noted that the difference between vanilla extract and vanilla flavoring is largely one of alcoholic content. The extract contains 35 percent or more alcohol, and flavorings contain less than that amount, but the *amount* of vanilla is the same.

Vanillin, *on the other hand, is an artificial flavor or flavoring, and if it is combined with vanilla that fact must be clearly stated on the label. Standards have also been set for vanilla-vanillin products, and these three highlights are of particular consumer interest. In any vanilla-vanillin product, the amount of flavor contributed by vanilla beans must be more than half the overall vanilla flavor; the flavoring strength must be printed on the label as must the statement "contains vanillin, an artificial flavor."*

Pure or synthetic flavorings like vanilla are usually purchased in quart or gallon glass jars by the case of 12 or 4, respectively. Lemon and other less used flavorings are usually in pints or quarts.

Salt. Salt is obtainable in different degrees of refinement and with certain elements added. The addition of carbonate of magnesia (1 percent) produces *free-running salt* by which caking by absorption of moisture from the air is prevented. Salt to which a small amount of potassium iodide has been added is now used extensively and aids in the prevention of goiter. *Iodized salt* is usable for all purposes with no detection of the iodine flavor. Ground celery seed or dehydrated garlic and onion are added to salt and sold commercially as *celery salt, garlic salt,* and *onion salt.* Most of the salt used in the United States is obtained from underground deposits of rock salt, although in some parts of the world sun evaporation of seawater must be depended on for the source. Salt deposits may be brought to the surface by regular mining methods, or water may be forced into the deposits through pipes with the resulting brine pumped up and evaporated.

Table and cooking salt is often purchased by institutions in 100-pound bags or in packaged units, such as 24 26-ounce boxes or cartons in a case. The price of the packaged salt may run approximately one fourth higher than the bulk product of comparable quality. The use of individual packets is particularly adaptable to hospital tray service, airlines, and certain types of catering. "Fine table grade" is a satisfactory quality for most purposes. Salt should have dry storage at moderate temperature.

Spices and Herbs. Spices and herbs are vegetable substances with pungent qualities peculiar to themselves. Many different parts of plants are represented. *Spices* are prepared from roots, buds, flowers, fruits, barks, or seeds, whereas *herbs* come from the leafy or soft portions of certain annual or biennial plants. The word "spice" has come to be accepted as an all-inclusive term for the group. Every spice or herb depends on delicate volatile oils for its ability to give off aroma and to impart flavor. In no two spices are these oils exactly the same, even in nutmeg and mace, where the aroma is almost identical. The root, bud, fruit, flower, bark, seed, or leaf is the part of the plant that holds the characteristic ingredient, as the root of ginger, the bud of clove, the fruit or seed of caraway, and the leaf of mint. Thirty or more different spices and herbs are available and may be employed in seasoning but, in many institution kitchens, the number in active use is limited to six or seven.

Spices are imported chiefly from the tropical regions of the Orient, the main countries of production being the East Indies, India, China, Japan, the Malay Peninsula, and certain islands off the coast of Africa, notably Madagascar, Pemba, and Zanzibar. Many of the herbs are found in local markets. The packers of spices face a difficult problem in providing safe and sanitary products, since the imported spices as delivered to them are usually heavily contaminated with bacteria. Mechanical screening facilitates the removal of dirt and helps in meeting the government standards for pure spice, but studies indicate that the bacterial count on many spices after screening is high enough to warrant sterilization of the packaged products as a sanitary measure.

Inasmuch as the value and effectiveness of spices lie in the presence of volatile oils, consideration of the problem of storage involves two warnings: first, buy only in quantities suitable for probable use within 6 months; and second, store in tightly covered, airtight containers in a cool place. Spices for institution use are usually packaged in 1- or 1/2-pound containers. Fresh or dried ginger root and fresh garden herbs are found in some markets.

Vinegar. Vinegar is produced by the action of acetic acid bacteria on dilute solutions of ethyl alcohol derived by fermentation from various sugary and starchy foods, such as cull apples, grapes, peaches, and sweet potatoes. The Pure Food and Drug Act by definition restricts the use of the terms *vinegar* (without qualifying term), *cider vinegar,* and *apple vinegar* to vinegar made from apples. The usual standard is "45 grain" vinegar, which contains 4.5 percent acetic acid and would require 45 grains of alkali to neutralize the acetic acid of the vinegar.

Other vinegars in use in the United States include *grape vinegar,* made from the alcoholic and subsequent fermentation of the juice of grapes by acetic acid bacteria; *grain vinegar,* also designated as *distilled vinegar;* and *spirit vinegar,* made by using sugars, syrups, or molasses for the carbohydrate material from which, through yeast fermentation, dilute alcohol is produced, distilled, and then subjected to acetous fermentation to produce vinegar. Vinegars are freed of sediment, extraneous material, and bacterial content by filtration, clarification, and pasteurization processes. Wines and herbs such as tarragon may be added to vinegar to give distinctive flavors.

After processing, vinegar is usually packed in 15- or 45-gallon wooden kegs or barrels or pint, quart, and gallon jugs or bottles. If stored for a few months before use, vinegar develops an improved flavor. The recommended temperatures for storage are between 40 and 50°F.

Condiments. This grouping includes items such as catsup, chili sauce, prepared mustard, and meat sauces, which are usually purchased in No. 10 cans, gallon jars, and individual packets. The usual retail-size unit is most advantageous for some items, such as meat sauces.

Soluble concentrates of chicken, beef, and other extracts to which tomato, spices, and other ingredients may have been added are now readily available. Such products may be used to intensify the flavor in a given food preparation or form the base for soups or other stocks. Although expensive, these items do have considerable merit as food adjuncts.

STORAGE

The proper storage of food immediately after it has been received and checked is an important factor in the prevention and control of loss or waste from pilferage, deterioration, or infestation. When food is left unguarded in the receiving area or exposed to the elements of extremes of temperature for even a short time, its safekeeping and quality are jeopardized.

Adequate space for suitable storage of the types of foods selected should be provided in locations convenient to receiving and preparation areas. With the rapid change in market forms of food and easier accessibility to markets has come the need for flexibility in planning the size and type of storage facilities. There is no standard formula applicable to all situations. However, both dry and refrigerated storage are necessary in any foodservice.

Storage areas must be kept clean and orderly. A few general procedures are: wash floors, walls, and shelves routinely; inspect in-

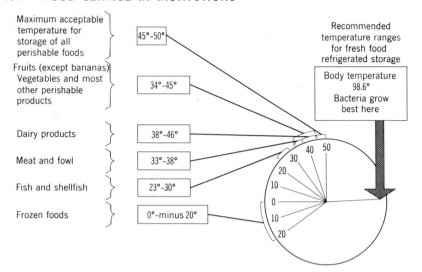

FIGURE 3.15   Recommended temperature ranges for storage of fresh food.

coming food for damage, spoilage, or infestation, as well as weight and count, before storing; store foods in an orderly and systematic arrangement, usually dated and left in the original package or in tightly covered containers if broken lots; group similar items together with the oldest stock in front; store items on racks or shelves instead of directly on the floor or against walls; and check often the condition of stored food and the temperature of the storage units.

Temperature and humidity controls and provision for circulation of air are necessary to retain the various quality factors and the nutritive values of the stored foods. A summary of recommended temperatures for the storage of various fresh food groups is found in Fig. 3.15. The Public Health Service reminds us:

All food, while being stored, prepared, displayed, served, or sold at food service establishments, shall be protected from contamination. All perishable food shall be stored at such temperatures as will protect against spoilage. All potentially hazardous food shall be maintained at safe temperatures (45°F or below, or 140°F or above), except during necessary periods of preparation and service.[4]

[4] *"Food Service Sanitation Manual,"* Public Health Service Publication No 934, *U.S. Government Printing Office, Washington D.C., p. 42, 1962.*

The length of time foods may be held satisfactorily and without appreciable deterioration depends much on the product and its quality when stored as well as the conditions of storage. Practical maximum temperatures and times for a few typical foods are given on p. 196.

Security protection for reserve food and supplies is obtained by enforcement of the "locked-door" policy. Daily stores and refrigerator areas are locked at night and during other closed hours when cooks and supervisors are not present.

DRY STORAGE

The main requisites of a food dry-storage area are that it be dry, cool, and dark, well-ventilated, free from insects and rodents, clean, and orderly. If possible it should be located convenient to the receiving and preparation areas and a separate room provided for the storage of cleaning supplies. Often, paper goods are included with food storage.

Dry storage means exactly that condition. A dark, damp atmosphere is conducive to the growth of certain organisms such as molds; to the deterioration of dry staples such as flour, sugar, rice, condiments, and the containers of processed foods; and to the development of unpleasant odors. The temperatures suggested for dry-storage areas range from 40 to 70°F, and frequent checks should be made to ensure their maintenance. The storeroom is more easily kept dry if located at or above ground level, although it need not have outside windows unless required by code. Any windows should be equipped with security-type sash and screens, and painted opaque to protect foods from direct sunlight. No more than 4 foot-candles of light at a height of 30 inches from the floor is recommended. Artificial lighting (15 foot-candles) should be adequate for checking inventories and the condition of food, and for cleaning.

Ventilation is one of the most important factors in dry storage. The use of wall vents is the most efficient method of obtaining circulation of air, but other methods are possible (see suggestions, Fig. 3.16). The circulation of air around bags and cartons of food is necessary to aid in the removal of moisture, reduction of temperature, and elimination of odors. Containers like cartons and bags may be stacked on slatted floor racks, dollies, or shelves, at least 10 inches above the floor and 2 inches away from the wall to permit a free flow of air; each layer of containers should be arranged in the opposite direction with air space between those in the same layer. Hand or

Food	Suggested Maximum Temperature (° F)	Recommended Maximum Storage
Canned products	70	12 months
Cooked dishes with eggs, meat, milk, fish, poultry	36	Serve day prepared
Cream filled pastries	36	Serve day prepared
Dairy products		
Milk (fluid)	40	3 days In original container, tightly covered
Milk (dried)	70	3 months In original container
Butter	40	2 weeks In waxed cartons
Cheese (hard)	40	6 months Tightly wrapped
Cheese (soft)	40	7 days In tightly covered container
Ice cream and ices	10	3 months In original container, covered
Eggs	45	7 days Unwashed, not in cardboard
Fish (fresh)	36	2 days Loosely wrapped
Shellfish	36	5 days In covered container
Frozen products	0 (to −20)	
Fruits and vegetables		1 growing season to another Original container
Beef, poultry, eggs		6–12 months Original container
Fresh pork (not ground)		3–6 months Original container
Lamb and veal		6–9 months Original container
Sausage, ground meat, fish		1–3 months Original container
Fruits		
Peaches, plums, berries	50	7 days Unwashed
Apples, pears, citrus	50 (to 70)	2 weeks Original container
Leftovers	36	2 days In covered container
Poultry	36	1–2 days Loosely wrapped
Meat		
Ground	38	2 days Loosely wrapped
Fresh meat cuts	38	3–5 days Loosely wrapped
Liver and variety meats	38	2 days Loosely wrapped
Cold cuts (sliced)	38	3–5 days Wrapped in semi-moisture-proof paper
Cured bacon	38	1–4 weeks May wrap tightly
Ham (tender cured)	38	1–6 weeks May wrap tightly
Ham (canned)	38	6 weeks Original container, unopened
Dried beef	38	6 weeks May wrap tightly
Vegetables		
Leafy	45	7 days Unwashed
Potatoes, onions, root vegetables	70	7–30 days Dry in ventilated container or bags

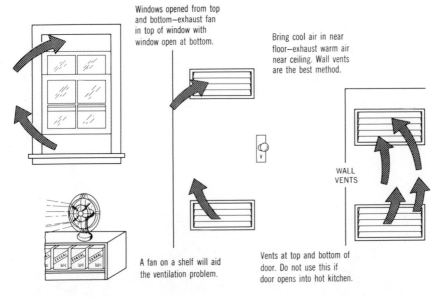

Windows opened from top and bottom—exhaust fan in top of window with window open at bottom.

Bring cool air in near floor—exhaust warm air near ceiling. Wall vents are the best method.

WALL VENTS

A fan on a shelf will aid the ventilation problem.

Vents at top and bottom of door. Do not use this if door opens into hot kitchen.

FIGURE 3.16   Suggestions of possible ways to provide circulation of air in a dry storage area. Courtesy, Ohio Department of Health.

motor-power lifts can move loaded skids or floor racks from one location to another without disturbing the load.

Food in dry storage must be protected from insects and rodents by preventive measures, such as good, tight construction and the use of proper insecticides and rodenticides, the latter under the direction of persons qualified for this type of work. Broken lots of dry foods like sugar, flour, and spaghetti should be stored in metal containers with tightly fitted lids.

Cleanliness and orderliness go hand in hand, and the importance and benefits of high standards of both cannot be overemphasized. No trash or spilled food should be left on the shelves or floor to harbor vermin or soil. A regular cleaning schedule will need to be designed according to the volume of traffic and other activity in this area. Suggestions for storeroom organization and control are discussed in Chapter 9.

REFRIGERATED STORAGE

Refrigeration affects markedly the quality and safety factors in perishable and some processed foods. For example, the retention of flavor and the fresh, crisp, colorful characteristics of fruits and vegetables adds to their appeal and reduces waste and loss of nutritive values. Many food-borne outbreaks of illness are attributed directly or indirectly to improper refrigeration in a food service. Low temperatures stop or slow down the growth of bacteria, yeasts, and molds; hence the recommendation that all potentially hazardous foods be stored at 45°F or lower. The recommended temperature for frozen products is 0 to −20°F.

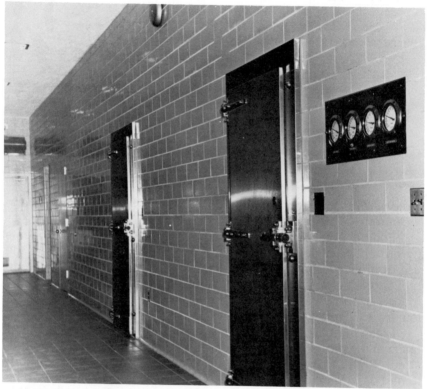

FIGURE 3.17   *Individual refrigerator units in a large foodservice are often grouped for convenience to receiving and preparation areas and for servicing. Separate cooling equipment makes it possible to control and maintain the proper temperature for the food stored in each unit. Floors on the same level as the corridor, easily visible temperature indicators outside the unit, and tight-fitting, well-hinged doors with locks that will release from the inside are only a few of the built-in features of a refrigerated walk-in storage area. Courtesy, Kent State University.*

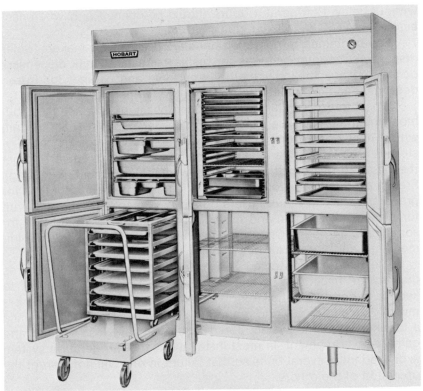

FIGURE   3.18   *Storage of made-up salads and other cold foods in a pass-through refrigerator, fitted with adjustable shelves or rod-type pan glides. Sliding glass doors on counter side facilitates rapid service. Product of Hobart Corporation.*

The trend is toward the use of more reach-in units near work stations for storage of daily perishables and foods in preparation, and walk-in units for general and long-term storage (see Figs.3.17 and 3.18). In either type, temperatures should be checked twice daily; every part should be kept clean with a thorough cleaning at least weekly and any spillage wiped up immediately; hot food should be placed in shallow pans to chill as soon as possible after preparation unless it is to be served immediately. Cooked foods and meats should be covered to reduce evaporation losses and to limit odor absorption and damage from possible overhead leakage or dripping. Daily checks on the contents of refrigerators is advisable so that left-over and broken package foods will be incorporated into the menu without delay. Refrigerator doors should be opened only when necessary.

Self-contained refrigeration units are used for ice makers, water dispensers, counter sections for display of salads, milk dispensers or storage box for individual milk cartons, and cabinet for frozen desserts; each is adjusted to maintain the temperature needed.

Small freezer units may be either chest or cabinet-style, but most institution foodservices need a larger capacity walk-in unit, which may open from a regular walk-in refrigerator or the dry-storage area. All refrigerated units must be defrosted regularly to get the best return from them (most new models are self-defrosting). Frozen products are stored in their original containers until time for preparation, except many users obtain best results by thawing fruit for pies, poultry, eggs, and meat in a refrigerator at 38 to 42°F for some 12 to 24 hours. Once thawed, the product should be used immediately and not refrozen.

The maintenance of modern refrigeration equipment requires the regular inspection by and services of a competent engineer to keep it in good working order. However, the manager and workers must be able to detect and report any noticeable irregularities, since a breakdown in the system could result in heavy loss of food and damage to equipment. In most installations the refrigeration system is divided into several units so that failure in one will not disrupt the operation of the others.

SELECTED REFERENCES

The Almanac of the Canning, Freezing, Preserving Industries, compiled by Edward E. Judge, Westminster, Maryland, published annually.

"Buying, Handling and Using Fresh Fruits," National Restaurant Association, Chicago.

"Buying, Handling and Using Fresh Vegetables," National Restaurant Association, Chicago.

Consumer and Marketing Service publications, U.S. Department of Agriculture, U.S. Government Printing Office, Washington, D.C.
A sample listing includes:
"Egg Grading Manual," Poultry Division, Handbook 75, Rev. 1969.
"Federal and State Standards for the Composition of Milk Products," Agriculture Handbook 51, 1971.
"How to Buy Food," Agriculture Handbook 443.
"Inspection, Labeling and Care of Meat and Poultry," Agriculture Handbook 416.
Institutional Meat Purchase Specifications, Livestock Division: Fresh Beef, Series 100; Fresh Lamb and Mutton, Series 200; Fresh Veal and Calf, Series 300; Fresh Pork, Series 400; Cured, Dried, and Smoked Beef Products, Series 600; Edible By-Products, Series 700; Sausage Products, Series 800; Portion-cut Meat Products, Series 1000; and General Requirements.
"Poultry Grading Manual," Handbook 31.
"USDA's Acceptance Service for Poultry and Eggs," Marketing Bulletin No. 46.
"USDA Yield Grades for Beef," Marketing Bulletin No. 45.

Cronan, Marion, The School Lunch, Charles A. Bennett, Peoria, Illinois, 1962.

"Food Buying Guide for Fresh Fruits, Vegetables, and Nuts," Blue Goose, Inc., Fullerton, California, 1971.

"Food Buying Guide for Type A School Lunches," U.S. Department of Agriculture, PA-270, rev., U.S. Government Printing Office, Washington, D.C., 1972.

Food for Us All, The Yearbook of Agriculture, U.S. Department of Agriculture, Washington, D.C., 1969.

Food Purchasing Guide, American Hospital Association, Chicago, 1966.

"Food Service Manual for Health Care Institutions," American Hospital Association, Chicago, 1972.

"Food Storage Guide for Schools and Institutions," Food and Nutrition Service, U.S. Department of Agriculture, PA-403, Washington, D.C. 1972.

Fowler, Sina Faye, Bessie Brooks West, and Grace Severance Shugart, *Food for Fifty,* Fifth Edition, Wiley, New York, 1971.

"Frozen Food Handbook," National Frozen Food Association, Hershey, Pennsylvania.

"Frozen Food Institutional Encyclopedia," Sixth Edition, National Frozen Food Association, Hershey, Pennsylvania, 1972.

"Fruit and Vegetable Facts and Pointers," United Fresh Fruit and Vegetable Association, Washington, D.C.

George, N. L., and Ruth D. Heckler, *School Food Centers,* Ronald Press, New York, 1961.

Kotschevar, Lendal H., *Quantity Food Purchasing,* Second Edition, Wiley, New York, 1975.

"Meat Buyer's Guide to Portion Control Meat Cuts," National Association of Meat Purveyors, Tucson, Arizona, 1967.

"Meat Buyer's Guide to Standardized Meat Cuts," National Association of Meat Purveyors, Tucson, Arizona, 1961.

Monthly Supply Letter, United Fresh Fruit and Vegetable Association, Washington, D.C.

"National Food Situation," Economic Research Service, U.S. Department of Agriculture, Washington, D.C., published quarterly.

"Net Weight of Fresh Fruits and Vegetables in Containers Delivered to Institutions," United Fresh Fruit and Vegetable Association, Washington, D.C.

Ross, Lynn and Roberta Mohr McHenry, *Food Purchasing Study Course,* The Iowa State University Press, Ames, Iowa, 1971.

"School Food Purchasing Guide, Research Bulletin 7, Association of School Business Officials and American School Food Service Association, Denver, 1968.

"Standard Guide to Spice Terminology," American Spice Trade Association, New York, 1964.

"Turkey Handbook," National Turkey Federation, Mount Morris, Illinois.

4.
QUANTITY FOOD PRODUCTION

Production of high-quality food involves a number of interrelated steps, each dependent on the other. The transformation of raw or processed foods into an acceptable finished product ready for service requires the purchase of high-quality food, initial storage and "holding" at optimum temperatures at various points in its production and, generally, one or more processing procedures under controlled conditions.

Traditionally, these procedures have been carried out in the individual foodservice. Today, however, there is a marked increase in the number of foodservice systems that are centralizing all or part of their food production in a location removed from the serving areas. Preparation in these facilities may range from controlled production of items such as desserts and baked goods; preparation of meats ready for cooking; prepreparation of fruits and vegetables for salads or for final cooking in the individual foodservice units; or complete preparation and cooking of menu items, packaged in individual or bulk containers, chilled or frozen for delivery to serving units. Many school systems, hospitals, and commercial foodservice companies with multiple units find that commissaries or "food factories" provide more efficient utilization of facilities, manpower, and equipment than onsite production and better quality control and a greater variety of foods at lower cost than the purchase of commercially prepared menu items.

In spite of this trend toward centralization, many foodservices prepare either all or part of the food in their own kitchens. Some purchase certain menu items in the ready-to-cook or ready-to-serve forms, and most use some type of convenience ingredients or components. Today's quantity food production has been simplified also through the use of automation and modern functional equipment.

FOOD PRODUCTION

PRODUCTION PLANNING

Production planning starts with the menu and the production forecast, which is based on numbers to be served and food selection prediction. An initial estimate at the time the major food orders are placed is later adjusted, one or two days prior to the day of production, for more accurate decisions on amounts of food to be prepared. The number to be served is based on a known population, such as a hospital patient census, number of paid residents in a college foodservice, number of students enrolled in a school, or estimate of potential customers; and on past records of meals served. Where the population is known, a pattern of meals served by day and by meal usually develops. For example, in a recent 17-week study in a residence hall food center, it was found that more students ate breakfast on Wednesday than on any other morning; the dinner count decreased on Friday, but was higher on Saturday.[1] Such information, along with knowledge of scheduled special events, holidays, weather conditions, and unusual circumstances, assists the planner in making a valid estimate. The food selection prediction is an estimate of the percentage of the total number to be served who will select each menu item. This information is based on past records and, in the case of a selective menu in a hospital, on prior selection by patients. Accurate forecasting not only is vital to cost control, but lessens the problem of leftover food to be reused or customer dissatisfaction when not enough food is prepared.

Recipes should be adjusted to the predicted number of servings required. Most quantity recipes are calculated in modules of 25, 50, or 100 or, in foods like cakes or casserole-type entrees, to pan sizes. Standardizing and calculating recipes for more than one quantity lessens the need for refiguring for each day's forecast. Where the

[1] *Mary Anne Shriwise, "Forecasting Production Demand in a Residence Hall Foodservice System," unpublished Master's thesis, Kansas State University, 1975.*

computer is used for calculating recipes, the daily printout can easily be based on the exact number of individual portions or on the number of pans or other modules needed.

Standardized recipes are essential to production of quality food, as are accurate weighing and measuring. The ingredient room, where all food is weighed or measured and delivered to the cooks for final preparation, assures the use of ingredients in the correct amounts and more efficient use of skilled cooks' time. Also helpful to the production planner are recipes that include mixer speeds and timing, detailed directions for combining ingredients, weight of food per pan, and any other pertinent information that would contribute to production of a high-quality product. Many foodservices also have developed recipe cards that explain procedures such as steaming vegetables, preparing lettuce, and deep fat frying fish.

PRODUCTION SCHEDULING

Careful planning and scheduling of food preparation assures the efficient use of employee time and a minimum of production problems. Foods that are ready for service at the scheduled time without undue holding will be superior in quality to those that are prepared early to avoid a last minute "panic."

Scheduling requires a knowledge of the steps through which a product must go and the time required for each, as well as the steps that can be completed early without affecting the quality of the food. Most menu items go through part or all of the following steps: storage (dry, refrigerated, freezer); assembly (weighing or measuring ingredients); prepreparation (vegetable cleaning, peeling, chopping, preparing pans); preparation (mixing, combining ingredients, panning); cooking (baking, frying, broiling, steaming, simmering); finishing (setting up salads, portioning desserts, slicing meat); and storage prior to serving (heated or refrigerated).

Up to the point of final cooking, many steps can and should be scheduled early, possibly the day before. For example, in preparing casserole-type entrees, preparation of the recipe components should be accomplished in time for cooking and chilling before final preparation if necessary, for example, simmering chicken for salad or pot pie or shaping croquettes prior to deep fat frying. Many times problems arise because time has not been allowed for refrigerator thawing of frozen foods.

In scheduling the cooking of foods, allowance must be made for the time required for heat to penetrate the large masses of food.

Final cooking should be scheduled so that only food needed for immediate service is cooked at one time. "Batch-cooking" of vegetables in small amounts, baking of pans of entrees at intervals, and continuous deep fat frying "to the line" are examples.

Because of the variation in complexity of menu items from day to day, production should be planned several days ahead to distribute the work load evenly. An increasing number of institutions are using advance production to equalize workloads and to prepare foods ahead so that kitchen production can be curtailed or shut down on weekends and holidays. Food preparation is scheduled during slack periods, and the food is frozen for later use. Such a program should not be attempted, however, without adequate freezing and refrigeration equipment and without some knowledge of foods that freeze well and the effect of length of storage on different foods. Proper cooling, packaging, and freezing are especially important to the quality and safety of the finished products, and the foods, of course, should be prepared under close supervision so that adequate sanitation and processing precautions are observed. If cooking to inventory and if foods will be stored for any length of time, a system of inventory control of the frozen prepared foods should be instituted.

Figure 4.1 is an example of a simple production schedule form that provides for assigning preparation to the different employees by hour of the day to assist them in planning their day's work. If cycle menus are used, time is saved by setting up orders and production schedules for each cycle as a "package" to be used with the cycle. Adjustments may need to be made if there are changes in menus or numbers to be served. In a large, more complex operation, schedules would be made for each department. Form 4.1 is an example of a production schedule that also serves as a production record.

FOOD PREPARATION

The principles of food preparation in large quantity are much the same as those for small quantity food preparation, but there are some differences in procedures because of the larger masses of food involved. Mechanized equipment is essential for heavy processes and for time-consuming procedures, especially in the larger operations. Steam-jacketed kettles with stirring paddles in which food can be chilled after cooking; timers on steam-cooking equipment; metering devices on steam-jacketed kettles for measuring water; and high-speed vegetable cutters are examples of labor-saving equipment in use. Convection ovens and high-pressure steamers

PRODUCTION SCHEDULE

Date _____
Menu Cycle: Week _____ Day _____

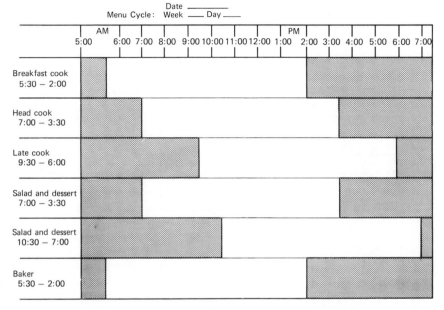

Figure 4.1   *Suggested form for scheduling food production in a small food service. Menu items are listed at approximate time preparation should be started. Courtesy, Dr. Marian Spears, Department of Institutional Management, Kansas State University.*

are used in many foodservices to reduce the time required for cooking, and no-transfer cooking equipment saves time and possible damage to the food quality through additional handling. For example, the steam-jacketed kettle and tilting frypan enable food to be browned, braised, and combined with other ingredients in the same kettle.

BASIC GUIDELINES FOR FOODSERVICE WORKERS

Also essential to attaining high standards in food production is the training of personnel to follow correct procedures of food preparation. Management is responsible for the development of the procedures written into standardized recipes and job break-downs. Supervision is the key word, however; if the manager allows even slight deviation from the established standards, all too soon they will be far below the desired level.

KANSAS
RESIDENC

DATE _____ AREA _____

Special Events _____		QUANTITY TO PREPARE	ACTUAL YIELD		DIRE
PERSON	MENU ITEM				

PRE·PREPARATION:

PERSON	MENU ITEM	QUANTITY	
Form 4.1			

FORM   4.1   *Production Schedule for a large residence hall food center. Informa-*
tion useful for production forecasting also is recorded on this form.
Courtesy Kansas State University.

ITY
RVICE

Meal Count _____
Weather _____

	TIME SCHEDULE	LEFT OVER AMOUNT	RUN OUT TIME	SUBSTITUTION	CLEANING ASSIGNMENT

PERSON	MENU ITEM	QUANTITY	
			F.S. Form 60

211

Observance of certain basic rules for foodservice workers will aid greatly in promoting efficient work habits for the beginner. The student learning quantity food production or the new foodservice employee should find the following suggestions helpful in the planning and carrying out of his duties.

1.   Check assignment to be sure that there is no question as to *what* is to be done or *how* it is to be accomplished.

2.   Plan work so that everything can be done within the time limit. Often several preparation procedures can be carried on simultaneously, but those that are preliminary or require the longest time should be started first.

3.   Assemble any equipment or ingredients not at hand and arrange them conveniently for use before beginning work. For example, the person who sets up the serving counter will save much time and energy if he assembles on a cart equipment such as towels, spoons, tongs, trays, spatulas, and certain foodstuffs and takes them to the counter in one trip; the person who makes a cake will save time and be able to concentrate on procedure if all ingredients have been weighed and assembled before preparation begins.

4.   Use proper equipment for the job. For example, an egg slicer will cut hard-cooked eggs faster, cleaner, and more uniformly than a knife on a board; a wire whip is many times more effective for stirring than a spoon because of the number of cutting surfaces of the whip; potatoes may be cooked in deep perforated baskets in the steam pressure cooker, whereas such treatment for green beans would render them unpalatable in appearance and flavor.

5.   Use power equipment whenever possible. Economy of effort and time can soon pay for additional conveniences.

6.   Arrange equipment and materials in the work area so that tasks can be accomplished in logical sequence with minimum movement of the worker. For example, for ef-

ficiency in breading chops, arrange pans containing the chops and dipping mixtures on the work table from left to right.

7. Use of smooth, continuous motions will keep fatigue to a minimum. Use both hands simultaneously whenever possible. Comfortable working heights and good lighting also reduce fatigue.

8. Carry through one step in a procedure before beginning the next for speed in accomplishing a task. For example, in preparing fresh grapes for a salad, all, in turn, should be washed, stemmed, cut in half and, finally, seeded.

9. Keep the working area clean and orderly. Cleaning the work area will be simplified by the use of a tray on which to work or to place soiled equipment. For example, place a cutting board on the tray when peeling citrus or other juicy fruits, or place soiled measuring cups and spoons on a tray as soon as the ingredients for a recipe have been weighed.

10. Accomplish something each time you pass one part of the kitchen to another. For example, when soiled dishes are taken to the pot and pan sink for washing, clean mixing bowls may be brought back on the return trip.

11. Attempt to make each motion rhythmic. For example, serve pudding by dipping and pouring into the dishes at regular intervals (count if necessary); stir mixtures evenly, taking each stroke in the same direction.

OBJECTIVES OF FOOD PREPARATION

The objectives of good food preparation are to: (1) conserve the nutritive value of the food, (2) improve the digestibility, (3) develop and enhance flavor and attractiveness of the original color, form, and texture, and (4) free it from injurious organisms and substances.

Conservation of Nutritive Value. The nutritive value of any food depends on its composition. If the preparation does not involve cooking or soaking, the original nutritive value may be regarded as largely conserved. When the preparation involves cooking, certain changes may occur, the most important of which are the destruction of the vitamin content and the loss of minerals. Investigations reveal that the conditions of preparation best suited to the retention of color, flavor, aroma, and texture tend to preserve also the nutritive value.

Improvement of Digestibility. In some foods cookery processes serve to bring about chemical changes identical with those of digestion. The transformation of starch into dextrin and sugars and the partial splitting of fats are examples of these changes. However, changes observed as the results of cookery processes are often mere differences in form. For example, egg white to which heat has been applied in the presence of moisture changes from its semifluid state to a gel. This alteration is not accompanied by any marked effect on the digestibility of the product unless high temperatures or long-continued low heat has been used.

Enhancement of Flavor and Attractiveness. The effect of cookery on the palatability of food may be to enhance and conserve the normal flavor, to develop a particular flavor, as by roasting meat, or to blend flavors, as in a casserole or cake. Conserving and enhancing the original flavor of foods such as mild-flavored vegetables is impossible if the heating continues over a long period or at a high temperature. The volatile substances that produce the flavor in a food may be largely driven off or may be changed to other compounds far less enjoyable. The undesirable effect on cabbage or cauliflower of long-continued cooking is well known to all.

The effects of cookery on color, form, and texture are also important factors in the palatability of food. Cookery may have as its goal the conservation of a color, such as the green of beans or the red of beets, or the development of a color, such as in the roasting of meats or the baking of cookies or cake.

Foods may be prepared so that the original form is maintained or some other form, at least as pleasing, is produced. Baked apples, boiled potatoes, and broiled steak are obvious examples of foods that, if well prepared, are not markedly changed from their original form. French fried potatoes, sliced beets, diced carrots, and all the pastries, batters, and doughs, as well as the various other "made" dishes, are characterized by changes in form from that of the original food or the ingredients used. The slices or other forms should be uniform in size, thickness, and contour and should be conducive to ease of service and eating. The form of slices or other shapes should be apparent as such instead of being submerged in a conglomerate mass.

Texture may be maintained in its natural state, softened, as in some fruits and vegetables, or hardened, as in pastries, batters, and doughs. It is closely associated with form, marked changes in texture usually being accompanied by changes in form. The food preparation should maintain or develop the texture regarded as desirable and characteristic of a given standard product.

Perhaps less frequently considered is the influence exerted by the form and hence the texture of food on the attractiveness and economy of its service. The salad ingredients too finely shredded, the creamed dish of a pasty consistency, and the cheese dish that "strings" present potential losses to the institution. Cookies too brittle for ease of handling may reach the consumer broken beyond acceptability, and meat that looks "scrappy" may be added to the long list of foods whose preparation often fails to increase their attractiveness.

Assurance of Safety for Human Consumption. The safety of food for human consumption often depends on destroying by cooking those microorganisms and parasites (1) that cause infectious diseases, (2) that are responsible for food poisoning, and (3) that cause off-flavors, discolorations, and similar spoilages that, although unpleasant and distasteful, are not important as causes of human illness. The effect of cooking on the food-borne microorganisms and their toxins is considered in detail in Chapter 10.

Foods must be handled properly from purchase until consumption. Remember that the slowness of heat penetration in solid and semisolid foods must be considered, because the temperature reached in the interior, not that on the surface, is the determining safety factor. Careful handling and rapid cooling of food after cooking are necessary to prevent bacterial contamination. If not served immediately, the hot food should be transferred from any original deep containers into shallow ones and placed at once in the refrigerator to chill. Healthy employees well trained in good sanitation practices contribute to the ensurance of safe food.

METHODS OF PREPARATION

The preparation of food may or may not include cookery, chilling, and freezing processes. Preparation influences chiefly the appearance and palatability of food and may determine the relation between the cost and the selling price or profit. The application of heat through one of the cookery processes or the exposure to low temperature, as in the freezing of food, is necessary, if the food is not to be served raw.

Cookery Processes. These methods may be summarized and classified according to the cooking medium as follows. (1) Methods in which air is the principal cooking medium, (2) methods in which water is the cooking medium, (3) methods in which steam is the cooking medium, (4) methods in which fat is the cooking medium, (5) methods in which there is no cooking medium but in which heat is transferred directly from the container, (6) methods in which more than one of the above are used, and the commercial adaptation of (7) methods in which electromagnetic energy is used as a means of cooking.

A brief discussion of the terms used to indicate various cookery methods follows.

1. *Air.* These are the methods included under the cookery medium, air. *Baking* is cooking by dry heat, usually in an oven, either conventional or convection. In the latter type of oven, circulation of air by fan speeds the baking process, resulting in decreased cooking time. The temperature for baking varies ordinarily from 250 to 500°F. *Roasting* is the term commonly applied to the baking of meats.

2. *Water.* The methods in which the cooking medium is water are well known. *Boiling* is cooking in moist heat with a boiling liquid as a surrounding medium. The temperature usually given is that of boiling water, 212°F. This point is raised by the presence of solids in the water and lowered by higher altitudes. *Simmering* is cooking in liquid at temperatures ranging from 185°F to a few degrees below the boiling point. *Stewing* is cooking in a small amount of water, which may be either boiling or simmering. *Poaching* is cooking by immersion in hot liquid maintained at simmering temperature.

The factors that determine the amount of heat and indirectly the amount of time required to raise the temperature of the kettle and the food in it to the desired degree are the mass of food, temperature of food, and specific heat of the food.

Since, in institution cookery, the food is cooked in greater quantities and in larger containers than in home cookery, more heat and time are needed to bring the food to the cooking temperature. The amount of heat required will also depend on whether the food is at room temperature when put into the cooker or has just been removed from the refrigerator, and whether the container (the kettle) has been preheated or not.

The specific heat of the food is determined to a large extent by its water content. The specific heat of water is 1.0. Milk, which contains more solid material, has a specific heat of about 0.9. Meat, potatoes, and eggs average about 0.8. In general, as the percentage of water decreases, the specific heat decreases.

Another factor that must be considered is the coefficient of conductivity of the food itself. Some foods will rapidly conduct heat from the walls of the kettle to the center portions of the food, but others are poor conductors. Regardless of whether the food is immersed in water, the size of the pieces and the manner in which they pack together, as well as the kind of food, all bear on its conductivity. For example, tomato bouillon is a better conductor of heat than Spanish rice. In large masses of food of poor conductivity the outer portions are commonly overdone by the time the center is cooked. When the food has reached the cooking temperature, only heat enough to keep the container and the food at cooking temperature need be supplied, that is, heat just sufficient to replace that lost by radiation, convection, and conduction. *Food will cook no faster in rapidly boiling than in slowly boiling water.*

Because the mass of substance to be heated is one of the factors determining the length of time required to raise the whole quantity to a given temperature, food cooked in large amounts is subjected to a greater extent to conditions that favor vitamin destruction and loss of attractiveness than food cooked at home. It has been suggested that vegetables and other foods of high vitamin content be cooked in small batches of 5 pounds or less to avoid overcooking.

Equipment for cooking by water medium in institutions includes stock pots on top of the range and steam-jacketed kettles. Some products such as eggs, macaroni, or noodles may be covered with water and heated by steam in the steamer.

3. Steam. Cookery methods in which steam is the means of transference of heat include *steaming,* or cooking (1) in water vapor above water, (2) in the so-called waterless cooker in which cooking is done in the presence of a small amount of liquid and the steam it produces, and (3) under pressure in a vessel that in institutions, is called a steam cooker, which is comparable to the pressure cooker found in many homes. The pressure steamer method is the only method classed under steaming in which a temperature higher than that of boiling water is reached.

Modern steamers provide for controlled cooking in constant temperatures that range from 185 to 240°F. The temperature depends on whether or not the cooker is pressure operated and on the altitude at which the cooking is done. Free-venting steam cookers operate without pressure in the cooking compartments and maintain the temperature of boiling water. Low-pressure steamers provide average temperatures up to 230°F. The pressure used in this type of steam cooker is usually 3 to 10 pounds per square inch with 4 to 6 pounds as the most desirable. The relation between the gauge pressure and temperature reached is indicated for water vapor:

Gauge Pressure (lb/sq in.)	Temperature in Degrees (F)	(C)
0	212.0	100.0
2	218.3	103.5
4	224.6	107.0
6	229.8	109.9
8	235.0	112.8
10	239.4	115.2
15	249.6	120.9

High-pressure steam cookers (15 psi) are used primarily for fast cookery of vegetables. The shortened cooking period possible in the pressure steamer is due partly to the quickly penetrating heat characteristic of live steam, but chiefly to the instantaneous start of the cookery process. Recently introduced on the market is the convection steam cooker. Faster heat transfer is accomplished by the steam interacting with the food through forced convection instead of by slower natural convection.

Food properly cooked in a pressure steamer is evenly cooked, retains a high vitamin content as well as its natural color and flavor, and suffers less of the usual cookery losses, such as shrinkage caused by prolonged cookery, boiling over, or burning. Overcooking results from reaching too high pressure or from holding the food at a given pressure for even a few minutes overtime. It is recommended that a timer and a thermostat provide stopwatch accuracy in steam cookery.

Steam is the source of heat in jacketed kettles. The heat is transferred through the walls of the inner lining of the kettle by conduction, but no contact between food and steam is possible. The temperature is higher than in a double boiler because the steam is under pressure. The temperature increases with increase in pressure.

4. Fat. The use of fat as the medium for heat transference is common in many foodservices. It browns food as well as cooks, adds richness of flavor, and serves an important role in introducing variety and interest into food preparation. The best temperature for the deep fat frying of cooked foods such as croquettes is 375 to 385°F and of uncooked foods, 350 to 375°F. A satisfactory fat for this method of cookery has a relatively high decomposition point, a smoking temperature well above the temperatures best for cooking, and no undesirable odor. In this type of cooking, the medium becomes part of the food during the cooking process. It is not unusual for foods to absorb 10 to 20 percent fat during frying.

5. Direct Transference or Conduction and Radiation Through the Container. Methods in which the transference of heat is *direct* from the container include the so-called baking of waffles and griddle-cakes and the pan-broiling or grilling of steak.

A recent application of this principle is in the integral heating system used for heating prepared frozen foods. Electrical energy is converted to heat through the use of thin-coat carbon composition resistors fused to the bottom of individual dishes that transmit the heat to the food they contain.

6. Combination Methods. Combinations of the methods listed above are most commonly applied to meats or fowl. *Braising* has for its first step browning in a small quantity of fat and then cooking slowly in liquid in a covered utensil. *Fricasseeing* is browning in fat and stewing in gravy. Steam-jacketed kettles and tilting frypans are used extensively for braising. Browning in the fryer and finishing in the oven is another combination method used in foodservices.

7. Electromagnetic Energy. Utilization of ultrahigh-frequency energy waves for institution cookery has been under experimentation for many years. These waves penetrate directly into the food and set up a rapid rate of molecular activity. This produces a high temperature within food at all points almost simultaneously because of the molecular friction. Waves with varying frequencies are used, each with its own particular characteristics. Infrared has been used extensively for cookery by direct exposure of the food to the infrared lights. Cooking of inner areas is continued as surface slices are served. Infrared ranges, broilers, and ovens are readily available.

Microwave ovens contain magnetron tubes to generate these waves, which are short in length and penetrate food to a depth of about 2 1/2 inches from all sides. Food must be cooked in glass, paper, or china utensils, since these materials are transparent to the waves. Metals reflect the waves and therefore cannot be used.

Foods in an electronic oven cook in 1/3 to 1/10 of the time required in a conventional oven. However, the capacity of microwave ovens is limited, and there is no browning of food unless the oven is equipped with a conventional high-speed broiler.

Microwave ovens for institution use are best adapted for cooking individual meals or servings and are especially useful in cooking foods rapidly from the frozen state and in reheating frozen cooked menu items.

Chilling and Freezing. Chilling, although a relatively simple process, is important in the preparation of many dishes. All fruits and vegetables to be served raw are far more palatable when properly chilled. Many cooked foods are chilled for service at a later time or as a preliminary step to freezing. Fruit and vegetable juices and iced bouillon are examples of first courses whose palatability depends on chilling. Not all chilling can be done at the same temperature. For example, orange juice may be delicious if chilled to the point where ice crystals just begin to form, but lettuce chilled to this degree is unfit for use. The old adage, "Serve hot foods hot and cold foods cold," cannot be ignored in successful food preparation, whether in institutions or in private homes. The freezing process is used extensively for frozen desserts, for preservation of fruits and vegetables and, more recently, for "holding" of prepared foods for later service.

Some prepared foods to be frozen require special treatment, and all should be properly packaged and quick frozen at −10°F or lower temperatures to maintain their quality during storage. According to Palmer,[2] "the main problems in frozen cooked foods are damage to texture or structure and the development of off flavors. Much of this damage can be reduced or eliminated by substituting more stable ingredients, adding stabilizers, and exercising greater control of storage time, temperature, and packaging." She recommends the substitution of at least 50 percent waxy rice flour for wheat flour in sauces and gravies to overcome the loss in smoothness after thawing. Substitution of waxy rice flour in custards and cream puddings also helps to solve the problem of separation and curdled appearance in these foods. A number of freeze-resistant starches made by modifying waxy corn or maize starches have been developed, but

[2] *Helen H. Palmer, "Preparing Foods for Freezing,"* Hospitals, JAHA, *103–106 (October 16, 1974).*

Palmer indicated that the waxy rice starch made a sauce more like that made with wheat flour.

The stability of souffles and soft pie meringues can be increased by an increase in sugar or flour content according to Palmer, who also recommends that souffles be baked before freezing, reheated from the frozen state, and covered during reheating to avoid loss of moisture.

Hard-cooked egg white does not freeze well, although the yolk can be frozen. Most meats freeze satisfactorily but lose freshness and develop stale or rancid flavors if improperly cooked or packaged and if stored too long.

Most types of bread, rolls, cake, cookies, and pies can be frozen, stored, and thawed without marked change if properly packaged, according to Tressler,[3] but most custard pies "weep" after thawing and, without a marked change in formula, are not very satisfactory. Moisture vapor-proof packaging is of great importance for baked goods to be frozen.

Reconstituting. This is a term frequently used to mean returning a food to its original form. The addition of water to dry milk or frozen orange juice are examples. The term is used also in institutional foodservices to indicate the use of heat to bring a product to serving temperature. Microwave, convection, conventional, or reconstituting ovens, or steamers are most often used.

Application of cookery principles to quantity production for ten classified groups of food follows. Coverage is far from complete; it is necessary and expected that this material be supplemented with basic food preparation and food science texts and current research. The ten groupings are:

Meat.

Fish.

Poultry.

Eggs.

Milk.

[3] *Donald K. Tressler, Wallace B. Van Arsdel, and Michael J. Copley,* The Freezing Preservation of Foods, *Fourth Edition, Volume IV, Avi Publishing Co., Westport, Connecticut, p. 41, 1968.*

Cheese.

Fruits and vegetables.

Fats.

Food grains.

Beverages and food adjuncts.

MEAT COOKERY

Selection of meat of suitable type, quality, cut, and cost for the purpose is an important responsibility of management. Once the meat has been purchased and delivered, proper cooking procedures are essential to the production of an acceptable cooked product. The methods of cooking meat and meat products will depend on the quality and cut of meat, the facilities available for its preparation and service, and the quantity that must be prepared at one time.

In general dry heat (broiling, roasting) is more satisfactory for tender cuts and moist heat cookery (braising, stewing, simmering) for the less tender cuts, the latter to provide additional moisture for breakdown of the large amount of collagen present. However, current research and practices show that safisfactory results can be obtained by using dry-heat methods for both tender and some of the less tender cuts, such as top round for roasts. Generally, moist heat is less suitable than dry for the tender cuts such as loin. Likewise, it has been found that the selection of a grade less than Choice or Prime can be utilized successfully and economically for many types of preparations.

Table 3.1, p. 104, suggests methods of cooking appropriate for various cuts and grades of beef. In veal, pork, and lamb practically any cut but the shank may be cooked by dry heat, although broiling is not as desirable for pork or veal as it is for lamb or beef. Veal, because of its delicate flavor and lack of fat in the tissues, combines well with sauces and other foods.

The quality of the cooked meat at the time of service influences to a marked degree its acceptability by the consumer, who is looking for palatability factors such as tenderness, flavor and aroma, juiciness, and color. Since meat represents a large part of the food dollar, the manager wants meat that is highly acceptable to the patron and that provides the largest possible number of servings.

FACTORS AFFECTING SHRINKAGE

The method of cookery has a direct bearing on shrinkage, or cooking losses. Use of proper methods will minimize these losses and produce the most palatable product. Meat shrinks during cooking, regardless of the method used, but the amount of shrinkage is determined to a large extent by the cooking temperature and degree of doneness.

Cooking Time and Temperature. It is obvious that the higher the cooking temperature, the more rapid the conduction of heat. The effect of higher temperatures on palatability and on the amount of shrinkage, however, is such as to make their use undesirable except perhaps in the case of broiling steaks "rare." The cooking temperature affects time required and shrinkage appreciably, as seen in Table 4.1.

TABLE 4.1   COMPARISON OF SHRINKAGE OF A PAIR OF BEEF RIBS COOKED AT DIFFERENT TEMPERATURES

				Length		Weight	
	Oven (°F)	Cooking Time (hr)	Internal (°F)	Before Cooking (in.)	After Cooking (in.)	Before Cooking (lb)	After Cooking (lb)
Roast I [a]	285	5.2	134	13	10.8	17.75	15.33
Roast II [a]	450	3.6	134	13	9.6	17.91	13.0

	Evaporation Loss		Drippings Loss		Total Loss		Weight of Sliceable Meat (lb)	Number of Servings	Weight of Serving (oz)
	(lb)	(%)	(lb)	(%)	(lb)	(%)			
Roast I [a]	1.25	7.04	1.15	6.48	2.40	13.52	9.05	62	2.34
Roast II [a]	2.61	14.57	2.29	12.78	4.90	27.35	7.45	55	2.17

Source. "Cooperative Meat Investigations," unpublished material, Kansas State University.
[a] U.S. government graded Choice. Full-rib cut.

According to the National Live Stock and Meat Board,[4] "high temperatures have little, if any, place in meat cookery. Low temperature not only produces more palatable meat but also more servings."

The cooking time is influenced by the size of the cut; normally the larger the cut, the longer the total cooking time required and the fewer the minutes per pound. However, the shape and style of the cut, the number of cuts in a pan, and the oven load also will affect the total cooking time. The more cuts there are in the oven at one time, the greater the total time required for cooking will be. A thin, wide roast will cook in less time than a thick compact one. Standing roasts will cook in less time than a boned and rolled roast because in boning and rolling the distance from the outside of the roast to its center has been increased. Most roasts, except standing ribs, are boned before cooking to conserve oven space and to make machine slicing possible. For ease in roasting and handling, it is advantageous to specify uniform size roasts (10 to 15 pounds, for example). Usually, it is recommended that frozen meat be refrigerator thawed before cooking to reduce both time and heavy drip losses during preparation.

Because of the length of cooking time required, especially for roasts, many institutions are searching for more effective ways to schedule meat cooking. Modifications of the conventional roasting method are not uncommon. Some managers cook roasts at low heat (250°F) for a long period of time, such as overnight, when ovens are not in use for regular meal preparation. However, it is difficult to predict the total cooking time required. "Extended-time roasting" or delayed-service method of cooking meat makes use of moderate oven temperatures for a period of time long enough to brown the meat and completes it at a temperature not higher than the final internal temperature desired. Interrupted cooking, in which pre-browned boneless steaks are refrigerated or frozen prior to final cooking, has potential for foodservice meat cookery.[5] Research [6] on cooking, refrigerator storing, and reheating beef roasts indicated

[4] *"Cooking Meat in Quantity."* National Live Stock and Meat Board, Chicago.

[5] Bernice M. Korschgen and Ruth E. Baldwin, *"Interrupted Cooking of Beef Rib Eye Steaks,"* Journal of the American Dietetic Association, 59, *116–119* (1971).

[6] Mary Ann Boyle and Kaye Funk, *"Holding Roast Beef by Three Methods,"* Journal of The American Dietetic Association, 56, *34–38 (1970).*

that refrigerating of unsliced cooked roasts was preferable to refrigerating and reheating of sliced meat, although recommendations from the study were that roast beef should be served immediately after cooking, if at all possible, to insure the highest quality.

Degree of Doneness. The degree of doneness to which meat is cooked may influence its shrinkage as much or even more than the temperature at which it is cooked. Greater total losses result from cooking meat to the well-done stage than to either medium or rare, as noted in much published data. However, some individuals prefer the appearance and flavor of well-done meat to either medium or rare, even though it may be less moist and somewhat toughened unless cooked in moist heat. When cooking a number of roasts for a cafeteria line, it is possible to offer meat at different stages of doneness by staggering the times that roasts are placed in the oven. The well-done roasts are started first and, when done, are removed from the oven, allowed to stand 10 minutes, sliced, and placed in pans in the warmer or in the oven at low heat. The rare meat is put in the oven last and, when the thermometer reaches 125°F, is removed from the oven, sliced, and sent directly to the line.

TABLE 4.2   INTERNAL TEMPERATURES OF LARGE BEEF ROASTS FOR THE DIFFERENT DEGREES OF DONENESS

Degree of Doneness	Color of Inside of Roast	Meat Thermometer Reading When Roast Comes from Oven [a] (°F)
Rare	Bright pink	120 to 125
Medium	Pinkish brown	135 to 145
Well done	Grayish to light brown	150 to 160

Source. From "Cooking Meat in Quantity," National Live Stock and Meat Board, Chicago.
[a] The temperature at which color changes take place in beef as it cooks is considerably higher than the temperatures above indicate; however, large roasts continue cooking for some time after they are removed from the oven. Therefore, to prevent overcooking, roasts should be removed from the oven when the thermometer shows several degrees lower than the temperature at which the actual color change takes place.

Cooking time-weight relationships expressed in minutes per pound are depended on by homemakers, but can be used only as guides in quantity preparation. The most accurate means of determining the doneness of a roast is by the use of a meat thermometer that registers the internal temperature. The thermometer is so placed in the roast that its bulb is in the center of the thickest part as the meat heats from the surface toward the center.

Table 4.2 shows recommended internal temperatures for large beef roasts. Pork should be cooked to the well-done stage, but even large pork roasts become dry and shrink unduly when overcooked. Recent findings indicate that pork is juicier and more palatable when cooked to an internal temperature of 170°F, lower than the previously recommended 185°F. The pink color disappears at between 165 and 170°F, and these temperatures are high enough to destroy any trichanae that might be present. Lamb usually is cooked to the medium or well-done stage (170 and 180°F), and veal to well-done (165°F).

EQUIPMENT FOR QUANTITY MEAT COOKERY

The equipment used in meat cookery in a foodservice usually includes ovens for roasting, broilers, tilting frypans, and steam-jacketed kettles. Utensils of the following types are commonly used: large rectangular roasting pans without covers, of aluminum, stainless steel, or black sheet iron; and covered roasters with racks (portable electrically heated roasters of this type are particularly well adapted to use in small operations). Small equipment of importance includes meat thermometers, to determine the internal temperatures of the meats, and oven thermometers. A frequent check is necessary to ascertain that the oven control is accurate, since faulty adjustments, leading to unanticipated high temperatures, occur frequently. Conventional types of ovens indicate comparable effects on the finished product. Meat can be cooked satisfactorily in the convection oven with less cooking time and a lower cooking temperature. The temperature should be reduced by at least 50°F from that used in the conventional oven. The electronic oven functions better for reheating prepared foods and for emergency cookery of short-order meats than for the cooking of roasts.

TENDERIZING OF MEAT

Pounding, scoring, cubing, grinding, and the addition of salt, vinegar, or enzymes are means of tenderizing meats of lower grades and the less tender cuts of higher-quality meat. The mechanical treatments are obvious and are used often in quantity food production. "Salt may, under certain conditions, tenderize meat since it increases the hydration of proteins even during heating." [7] However, the use of salt in amounts large enough to precipitate proteins in cookery would be distasteful and unlikely. Salting for flavor before cooking meat is questionable, especially for roasts, since the salt is believed to permeate into the roast no deeper than 1/2 inch from the surface. Increasing or decreasing the pH has some effect on tenderness of meat; this can be accomplished by adding tomatoes to a meat mixture or using vinegar in the preparation of sauerbraten.

Papain prepared from the green fruit of the papaya plant and bromelin from pineapple are two proteolytic enzymes used to tenderize meat. Reports indicate that they are effective for steaks but not for thick cuts such as roasts, other than they tend to decrease the juiciness of both.

METHODS OF COOKING

Roasting. Roasting is accomplished by placing the meat, fat side up, in an *uncovered* roasting pan *without* water. The meat is placed in an oven of low or moderate temperature and cooked at a constant temperature until it has reached the desired degree of doneness. Standards for doneness as stated by the Committee on Preparation Factors follow.

Roast beef
 Rare: Center a bright rose-red, shading into lighter pink toward the outer portions, changing into dark gray in layer underlying outer browned crust; juice a bright red; internal temperature 140°F.
 Medium rare: Center and most of slice a light pink; gray layer underlying crust extends a little toward the center; juice a light pink in color; internal temperature 160°F.
 Well done: Interior is brownish gray; juice is either colorless or slightly yellow; internal temperature 170°F.
Roast lamb
 Well done: Interior brownish gray; firm but not crumbly; tender; juicy; juice clear; internal temperature 175–180°F.
 Medium: Same as for well done except color is a light pink and the juice is pink.

[7] *Ruth M. Griswold,* The Experimental Study of Foods, *Houghton Mifflin, Boston, p. 133, 1962.*

Roast pork

Always *well done: Interior grayish white without a tinge of pink; firm, not dry or crumbly; tender; juicy (no pink tint); internal temperature 170°F.*

Roast Veal

Firm, not crumbly; tender; juicy; juice clear or faintly pink; internal temperature 165°F.

Broiling. In institution cookery broiling is usually done in a special broiler or salamander. The steaks or chops are placed on the rack in the broiling oven, the top of the meat being at least 3 inches from the source of heat. The steaks or chops when browned on one surface are turned, browned on the opposite side, and cooked to the desired degree of doneness, if rare, 130 to 135°F internal temperature. A steak 2 inches thick will require approximately 10 minutes of cooking on each side. However, many people prefer the application of higher temperature at the close of the cookery period to develop the rich brown color.

Panbroiling. The meat is put on a sizzling hot metal grill or frypan and turned at frequent intervals to provide for even cooking and to prevent scorching. Neither water nor fat is added, and excess fat is drained off. When the meat is satisfactorily browned on one side, it is turned, and the cooking process is continued until the desired degree of doneness is reached. In panbroiling a thick steak, it will be necessary to reduce the temperature after browning.

Braising. In braising meat, the first step is to brown it in a small quantity of fat. When this has been accomplished, moisture may or may not be added, the pan is covered tightly, and the cooking continued at a low temperature in the oven, in a tilting frypan, in a heavy kettle on top of the range, or in a steam-jacketed kettle. Cooking meat in a steam-jacketed kettle is common in institution kitchens, particularly those where large quantities of less tender cuts are prepared. Meat thermometers may be used effectively to indicate the degree of doneness in pot roasts. Their use in some types of cookers requires specially constructed covers to provide an opening through which the thermometer may be inserted. An internal temperature of 185°F is acceptable for pot roasts.

Stewing. Meat prepared for stewing is cut into small pieces. These pieces may or may not be browned. The meat is covered with hot liquid, the pan is covered tightly, and cooking is continued at a simmering temperature until the meat is tender. A steam-jacketed kettle or heavy kettle on top of the range is used.

Simmering. This method of cooking is advocated for less tender cuts. Meat cooked in a liquid should be at simmering (185°F) instead of boiling temperatures so that the meat may become tender and not shrink excessively.

COOKERY OF VARIETY MEATS

The preparation and cooking procedure for the various organs depend on the structure of the meat and the preference of the clientele. Brains and sweetbreads are often parboiled before inclusion in the creamed and escalloped dishes and croquettes in which they are commonly used. Heart and tongue both contain a high proportion of connective tissue; therefore long cooking at simmering temperatures is recommended for them. Boiling temperature should be avoided. Liver is popular if braised, fried, or combined as ground meat with other foods in a liver loaf. Kidney may be prepared by broiling, frying, or braising. Marinating kidney, from which the outer membrane has been removed, with French dressing for 1 hour before cooking is recommended as a means of improving the flavor.

COOKERY OF PORTIONED MEATS

Many foodservices use portioned meat, such as cube steaks, breaded pork or veal cutlets, and hamburger patties. The cutlets or patties may be placed on baking pans, which have been covered with a pan coating, and baked in a moderate oven. Cube steaks may be grilled to order or browned and then finished in the oven.

FISH COOKERY

The connective tissue of fish is small in quantity and is comprised largely of collagen, which readily softens during cookery. The high protein content indicates that low to moderate heat is desirable. It is important to remember that fish should be cooked only until the flesh may be easily separated from the bones. Fish too often is overcooked.

FRESH AND FROZEN FISH

The basic rules for cooking fish are few, although the flavor, texture, appearance, and size of the fish to be cooked vary according to the species. The variation in the fat content is the most important difference to be considered when choosing the best method of preparation for a specific fish. Fat fish such as salmon, trout, and whitefish are best for baking, broiling, and planking, because the fat content will tend to keep them from becoming dry. Lean fish such as haddock, halibut, and sea bass are considered best by many when poached, simmered, or steamed, although they may be successfully broiled or baked if basted frequently. All types of fish are suitable for frying. Whatever the method selected, fish should be served as quickly as possible after cooking for optimum quality.

Frozen fish may be completely thawed before cooking, but need not be unless it is to be breaded or stuffed. Fillets, steaks, and dressed whole frozen fish may be cooked as if they were in the fresh, chilled form, if additional cooking time is allowed. Frozen fish may be thawed at refrigerator temperature but only long enough to permit ease in preparation. Whole or drawn fish may be thawed quickly by immersion in cold running water. Thawing at room temperature is not recommended, since a large amount of drip usually results. Fish once thawed should be cooked immediately and never refrozen.

Frying. Much of the fish cooked in quantity food operations is deep fat fried. When properly fried, fish and seafoods have an attractive brown color, a crisp, nongreasy crust, a thoroughly cooked interior without being overcooked, and the characteristic flavor of the specific fish.

Quality of the frying fat and cooking temperature are important factors in the production of high-quality fried fish. Fish fried at too low a temperature absorbs a great deal of fat, while that cooked at too high a temperature tends to brown before it is cooked through. Uncooked fish should be fried at 350 to 375°F to assure cooking before browning. Precooked fish may be fried at a slightly higher temperature to brown and reheat. The frying kettle should not be overloaded. A ratio of 1:8, that is 1 pound of fish to 8 pounds of fat, is recommended. To prepare fish for frying, dip pieces in seasoned flour (2 tablespoons salt and other seasonings as desired to 1 pound flour), then in a liquid mixture of 2 eggs to 1 cup milk or water and, finally, in cornmeal, bread crumbs, or fine cracker meal.

Panfrying is a good method for preparing small, whole fish, steaks, or fillets and is feasible when a small quantity is prepared. Ovenfrying is an alternative method for preparing large quantities of fish. The fish portions are prepared with the desired coating and placed on baking sheets that have been covered with melted butter or other cooking fat. The tops may be dipped in the fat, or additional melted fat may be poured sparingly over the fish. Bake 10 to 15 minutes in a hot oven (400°F).

Broiling. Frozen fish usually is thawed before broiling. Fresh or thawed fillets and steaks are placed in a preheated broiler 3 to 4 inches from the broiling unit. The distance from the source of heat for split fish varies from 2 to 6 inches. Frozen fish or fish of a delicate texture is placed about 4 inches from the direct heat. The fish is brushed several times with oil, melted butter, or margarine. Steaks are turned once; fillets do not need to be turned.

Baking. Whole fish, steaks, and thick fillets may be baked successfully. Whole dressed fish is sprinkled with salt, pepper, and lemon juice before baking and may or may not be stuffed. For fish low in fat content, bacon strips may be laid across it to add moisture during cooking or it may be basted frequently as it bakes. Steaks and fillets are dipped in a mixture of melted butter or margarine and lemon juice, placed on greased baking pans, and seasoned with salt and pepper. Mayonnaise sometimes is brushed on the fish before cooking. Bake at 350°F until the fish flakes easily when tested with a fork.

Moist Heat Cooking Methods. Steaming, poaching, and simmering are closely related, the difference being in the amount of cooking liquid used. In steaming, the fish is placed on a rack over the liquid, covered tightly, and cooked. In poaching or simmering, the fish is covered with the liquid, usually lightly salted water, seasoned broth, or a specially prepared stock called court bouillon. Bring to a boil, reduce heat, and simmer gently until fish is cooked. Poaching is done in a flat pan on top of the range or in the oven. It may be necessary to wrap the fish in cheesecloth to prevent flaking or breaking apart during cooking and later handling. This is particularly true when cooking whole fish such as fresh salmon. Fish cooked in moist heat requires very little cooking time and usually is accompanied by a sauce (Table 4.3)

SHELLFISH

Oysters. Refrigerator thawing is advised if it is necessary to thaw for preliminary preparation. In the preparation of shucked oysters, washing is rarely regarded as necessary, since something of the flavor of the sea is believed to be lost in washing. Inspection of the pack enables one to remove any bits of shell that may be included.

TABLE 4.3 SUGGESTED METHODS OF COOKING FISH AND SHELLFISH

Species	Approximate Weight or Thickness	Baking Temperature (°F)	Baking Minutes	Broiling Distance From Heat (in.)	Broiling Minutes	Boiling, Poaching or Steaming Method	Boiling, Poaching or Steaming Minutes (per lb)	Deep-Fat Frying Temperature (°F)	Deep-Fat Frying Minutes	Pan Frying Temperature	Pan Frying Minutes
Fish											
Dressed	3 to 4 lb	350	40 to 60			Poach	10	325 to 350	4 to 6		
Pan dressed	1/2 to 1 lb	350	25 to 30	3	10 to 15	Poach	10	350 to 375	2 to 4	Moderate	10 to 15
Steaks	1/2 to 1 1/4 in	350	25 to 35	3	10 to 15	Poach	10	350 to 375	2 to 4	Moderate	10 to 15
Fillets		350	25 to 35	3	8 to 15	Poach	10	350 to 375	2 to 4	Moderate	8 to 10
Portions	1 to 6 oz	350	30 to 40					350	4	Moderate	8 to 10
Sticks	3/4 to 1 1/4 oz	400	15 to 20					350	3	Moderate	8 to 10
Shellfish											
Clams—live, shucked		450	12 to 15	4	5 to 8	Steam	5 to 10	350	2 to 3	Moderate	4 to 5
Crabs—live, soft-shell				4	8 to 10	Boil	10 to 15	375	2 to 4	Moderate	8 to 10
Lobsters—live	3/4 to 1 lb	400	15 to 20	4	12 to 15	Boil	15 to 20	375	2 to 4	Moderate	8 to 10
Spiny lobster tails—frozen	1/4 to 1/2 lb	450	20 to 30	4	8 to 12	Boil	10 to 15	350	3 to 5	Moderate	8 to 10
Oysters—live, shucked		450	12 to 15	4	5 to 8	Steam	5 to 10	350	2 to 3	Moderate	4 to 5
Scallops—shucked		350	25 to 30	3	6 to 8	Boil	3 to 4	350	2 to 3	Moderate	4 to 6
Shrimp—											
Headless, raw						Boil	3 to 5				
Headless, raw, peeled		350	20 to 25	3	8 to 10	Boil	3 to 5	350	2 to 3	Moderate	8 to 10

Source. "How to Eye and Buy Seafood," National Marine Fisheries Service, U.S. Department of Commerce, 1970.

Use of a fork should be discouraged, as should overhandling, to prevent a bruise or break in the membrane. If oysters are to be served cooked, care should be taken that they are heated through and the cooking continued only until the edges begin to curl. If the application of heat is continued beyond this point, the product will be tough. All oyster dishes should be served piping hot.

Clams. Perhaps clams are most widely used along the seashore, where they are served raw as cocktails, prepared as bouillon, steamed, roasted and dipped in butter, or made into chowder. If clams are purchased raw, care should be taken to obtain live ones, as indicated by the tightly clasped shell. To prepare the clams, scrub the shells and rinse well. To open, hold in the palm of the hand with the shell hinge outward and pry open the shell by inserting and slightly twisting a sharp, strong, slender knife. Cut the muscle free from the shell and remove the meat. In handling most varieties of clams the dark body mass is removed and the end of the siphon is snipped, after which the meat is washed. To cook clams in the shell, roast or steam 5 to 10 minutes until they open, remove the meat from the shells, and wash as directed above. Serve immediately or remove meats and cool in cold water; otherwise they will be tough.

Crustaceans. It is necessary that fresh crustaceans be alive at the time they are cooked. They cannot live at a temperature that exceeds 98.6°F. A usual method of preparation is to plunge them head down into boiling salted water and cook for approximately 20 minutes. A second recommended method is to place the crabs or lobsters into cold fresh water and gradually raise the water temperature to lukewarm (about 104°F) then simmer 15 to 20 minutes. Coagulation of crustacean protein occurs at about 126°F. Under such treatment crustaceans die quickly and easily and the flavor of the meat is reported superior to that when the former method is used.

Crabs. In the preparation for cooking, soft-shell crabs are placed face down, the taper points of the shell turned back about halfway, and the spongy substance found next to the shell is discarded. The tail or apron and face are removed, and the crab washed. Soft-shell crabs are usually parboiled and then fried in butter.

Cooked hard-shell crabs are chilled, the claws and apron removed, the shells broken apart, and the spongy substance removed from between the halves of the body and next to the shell. The meat is removed from the back and cracked claws, either in preparation for cooked dishes or salads, or at the table if the crab is served as an entree.

Lobster. The stomach, lungs, and intestinal tract of cooked lobster are removed before serving. If it is to be broiled, it may be boiled for 5 minutes, or it may be killed by cutting down between the body shell and the tail segment, severing the spinal column. It is then split from head to tail and the intestinal tract removed. The claws are cracked and the flesh brushed with melted butter and seasonings and spread out in the broiler pan, flesh side up. It is then broiled for 10 minutes and turned, after which the cooking is continued for another 10 minutes. The meat regarded as most delicate is that of the claws.

Shrimp. Usually the washed green shrimp are plunged into salted boiling water and cooked for 15 to 20 minutes, or they may be peeled and cooked as any fresh fish. If cooked first, the meat, now pinkish white, is removed from the shell, which has been opened on the underneath side. The intestinal tract, a black cord on the pink mass of the muscle, is removed, and the shrimp is ready for use. Canned, frozen, and reconstituted freeze-dried shrimp need examination and sometimes extra cleaning before final preparation.

POULTRY COOKERY

The losses in weight through processing, cookery, and boning are relatively high. These losses, reflected in the percentage of edible meat, should be known to the manager of a foodservice if food costs are to be controlled successfully. Chicken and turkey are used to a greater extent in foodservices than are other types of poultry because of the higher percentage of edible meat, the initial cost, and ease of portioning.

The development of a broad-breasted type of bird, more efficient methods of processing, and improved knowledge of poultry cookery have tended to increase the percentage of sliceable meat procurable from the cooked bird. Table 4.4 may be used as a guide in estimating the percentage loss caused by cooking.

METHODS OF COOKING

Two simple but important rules for cooking poultry are: first, *cook at moderate heat* so that the meat will be tender, juicy, and evenly done; second, *choose the cookery method best suited to the age and condition of the bird.* Usually young, tender, well-fatted birds are broiled, fried, or roasted; the mature or lean ones are braised in moist heat and the old birds are stewed or simmered in water or cooked in steam to tenderize them.

TABLE 4.4 THE PERCENTAGE OF PARTS, COOKING LOSS, AND EDIBLE MEAT OF CARCASSES AND PARTS OF DIFFERENT SPECIES AND CLASSES OF POULTRY

Observation (Average of 10 birds)	Chickens			Turkeys		Waterfowl	
	Broilers	Rock hens	Leghorn hens	Large	Small	Ducks	Geese
Ready-to-cook weight (lb)	3.1	4.9	2.8	22.6	6.7	4.9	7.4
Fat rendered out in cooking (%)	1.0	10.2	5.9	5.6 ·	1.6	21.4	6.2
Cooking loss including fat (%)	24.5	32.7	33.7	32.3	24.0	44.5	35.4
Cooked edible meat exclusive of fat (%)	51.0	46.1	46.2	56.7	54.0	38.4	41.4
Legs and thighs							
Weight (lb)	1.0	1.4	0.8	5.2	1.6	1.1	1.6
Percent of Carcass	32.0	28.4	27.7	23.0	23.9	22.4	21.6
Cooking loss (%)	24.5	37.0	38.0	33.7	26.0	45.1	34.0
Edible meat (%)	53.0	49.2	48.6	53.5	57.0	43.9	47.4
Breast							
Weight (lb)	0.8	1.1	0.7	8.3	1.6	1.5	1.8
Percent of Carcass	26.0	23.2	24.5	36.7	23.9	30.6	24.3
Cooking loss (%)	23.8	34.4	37.9	27.2	27.0	48.5	39.3
Edible meat (%)	63.2	59.1	55.7	67.7	65.0	43.3	47.7

Source. *Adapted from unpublished data from A. R. Winter, Department of Poultry Science, The Ohio State University.*

Broiling. Adjust rack to position bird about 4 inches under the heat. As chicken or turkey browns, brush with melted butter, turning about every 10 minutes. Cook until tender (35 to 60 minutes, depending on the size and thickness of the piece). Season and serve immediately.

Frying. Young poultry may be pan or oven fried successfully if special care and attention is given to time and temperature relationships. The meat may be brushed with melted butter or coated with a seasoned flour or crumb mixture, or dipped in a thin batter if it is to be fried in deep fat. Dipping poultry pieces in cold milk or water prior to dredging them aids the mixture in adhering closely to the meat.

To *pan fry,* brown poultry pieces in heavy skillets or tilting fry-pan containing 1/2 inch of hot fat. Turn until the pieces are well browned on all sides. Reduce heat and cook slowly until tender, usually 45 to 60 minutes, or place in counter inset pans and finish in the oven at 325 to 350°F.

Oven frying is a time-saving method of preparing chicken and is especially well suited to large quantities. Butter or cooking fat is melted to cover the bottom of each baking pan. Dredge chicken pieces in seasoned flour and roll in fat on the pan. Place pieces close together in one layer, skin side up. An alternative method is to place the chicken on a greased pan or a pan lined with silicone-coated paper. Brush top of chicken pieces with melted fat. Bake 1 to 1 1/4 hours at 350°F. For crisp baked chicken, coat with crushed potato chips or cornflakes.

Deep fat frying is preferred by many large foodservices because of ease of preparation and because of the uniform, golden brown color of the chicken. The pieces are dipped in a crumb mixture or a thin batter and allowed to drain for 10 to 15 minutes, then fried at 325°F for 12 to 15 minutes. Chicken may be browned in the deep fat fryer, placed in serving pans, and finished in the oven at 325°F for 20 to 30 minutes. Poultry may also be poached before dipping in the batter, then fried until golden brown and the batter fully cooked.

The process of cooking poultry pieces in deep fat under pressure is known as *broasting.* Special equipment has been developed for this process that reduces the cooking time to less than that for conventional frying.

Roasting. Rub skin of bird with softened or melted cooking fat, season inside and out, and place on rack in shallow roasting pan breast up. Bake at 325°F and maintain this temperature throughout the roasting process. The breast meat tends to be drier than the darker meat of the legs and thighs and is improved by some protection during roasting. The top and sides of the bird may be covered with a fat-moistened cloth and remoistened as needed or left uncovered and basted occasionally with a mixture of equal parts of water and melted fat. A foil "tent" that loosely covers the turkey but does not form a complete wrap may also be used. This method speeds up roasting time and eliminates the necessity for basting, but does not result in the disadvantages of a tight wrap. In poultry cooked in an aluminum foil wrap, the juice cooks out and the muscles tend to pull away from the bone. During the last half hour of cooking, remove cloth or foil tent if used. Fat birds, such as geese and ducks, need no basting, and the fat is poured off as it accumulates.

The importance of proper temperature in the cooking of poultry can hardly be overstressed. High temperatures inevitably result in stringy, tough, and unappetizing meat. The poultry is done when the leg joints move easily and the meat of the drumstick is soft when pressed. A meat thermometer is the surest test for doneness. It is placed in the heaviest part of the breast or the inner part of the thigh muscle and inserted to a point where the bulb will not be resting against a bone (Fig. 4.2). A thermometer placed in the thigh muscle should reach a point of 180 to 185°F; a thermometer placed in the breast should reach 170 to 180°F, depending on the degree of doneness

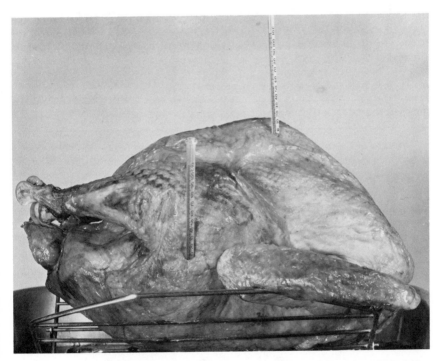

FIGURE 4.2 Thermometers should be inserted in the heaviest part of thigh and breast to determine when the turkey is cooked to the desired degree of doneness. Courtesy, College of Home Economics, Kansas State University.

desired. Poultry usually is cooked well done, but overcooking is undesirable because it results in loss of juiciness. Cooked turkey should stand 20 to 30 minutes before carving to allow the juices to be reabsorbed into the muscles, making the meat easier to slice (Table 4.5).

Sliceable roast meat is limited almost entirely to that on the breast and thighs, the remainder being removed from the carcass for use in "made dishes." Some cooks prefer to roast the boned, rolled, and tied breasts and thighs of large turkeys for slicing, and boil the bony parts, from which the meat may be utilized in items such as pies, croquettes, and salads. The roasting time for the smaller pieces is reduced to about half of that required for a whole bird of similar size, and the cutting yield is increased (Fig. 4.3). Also, it is possible to slice such roasts on a machine.

Many foodservices prefer to purchase boneless turkey roasts or rolls for convenience in roasting, slicing, and portion control. Cooking time for ready-to-cook rolls has been found to be longer in minutes per pound than for whole turkeys, but the total cooking time is less. The rolls compare favorably to whole turkeys in flavor and tenderness.

TABLE 4.5   TIME TABLE FOR ROASTING TURKEY

Form of Turkey	Weight of Turkey, Whole or Piece (lb)	Oven Temperature (° F)	Cooking [a] Time (hr)
Turkey, whole, ready-to-cook	12 to 16	325	3 1/2 to 4 1/2
	16 to 21	325	4 1/2 to 6
	21 to 26	325	6 to 7 1/2
Turkey parts			
Breast	8 to 12	325	3 to 4
Leg (drumstick and thigh)	3 to 8	325	1 3/4 to 3
Halves	8 to 12	325	2 1/4 to 4
Quarters	3 to 8	325	1 1/2 to 3 1/2
Turkey roasts, boneless			
Frozen	9 1/2 to 11 1/2	350	4 to 4 1/2
Thawed	9 1/2 to 11 1/2	350	2 3/4 to 3 1/2

Source. *Adapted from "Quantity Recipes for Type A School Lunches", PA-631, U.S. Department of Agriculture, revised 1971.*
[a] *Turkey is done when thermometer registers 180 to 185°F in inner thigh or 170 to 180°F in breast of whole turkeys; or 170°F in turkey roasts.*

FIGURE   4.3   *The roasting of boned turkey breasts and thighs reduces cooking time, oven space, and waste, and provides for easy slicing by machine. Courtesy, National Turkey Federation.*

It is recommended for large-quantity preparation that the stuffing or dressing be baked separately and served with the roasted sliced meat. This eliminates the possibility of bacterial contamination or growth in the dressing during any prolonged or inadequate heating or chilling of the mass when encased in the body cavity of the bird.

Other Methods. Mature but not old cut-up poultry may be *braised* in the oven or tilting frypan. The pieces are browned, a small amount of water added, covered, and cooked until tender. Larger compact and sliceable pieces may be *poached* by simmering in a steam-jacketed kettle, in a deep pan in the oven, or in a heavy kettle on top of the range. Usually older birds or bony parts are simmered or steamed and the meat separated from bones for various uses. The chicken or turkey may be cut in pieces or left whole. Poultry is *stewed* in a steam-jacketed kettle or stockpot. Cover with cold water and bring to simmering temperature if the purpose is to produce soup stock. If more flavor in the meat is desired, start with boiling water. Season with 1 tablespoon of salt per gallon of water; celery and onion may be added for flavor. Simmer until tender, about 2 1/2 to 3 hours. Poultry for *steaming* is placed in solid steamer pans, covered with water and seasonings, and cooked until tender, about 2 to 2 1/2 hours. Poultry should be removed from broth as soon as cooking is completed and placed on trays or sheet pans. When poultry is cool enough to handle, remove meat from bones. Uncooked chopped poultry may be incorporated satisfactorily in items such as croquettes, with considerable saving of time and labor.

Cooked poultry should be served as soon as possible after removal from the heat. However, if it has been cooked to be made into salad, croquettes, creamed, scalloped or à la king dishes, or sandwiches, or if it has been roasted in advance for later service, it must be handled as little as possible and refrigerated immediately to avoid contamination. Boning before storing saves much space, but care must be taken that the meat does not become packed solidly in the container. Clean, shallow, covered containers placed on the shelves so that the cold air can circulate freely about them are advised. Cooked poultry should be frozen if kept for more than a few days. Safe handling of poultry products is discussed in more detail in Chapter 10.

If frozen poultry is used for any of the above preparations, it is generally advised to thaw and then proceed as with freshly killed poultry. To defrost a turkey, leave it in its orginal moistureproof wrapping and place on an open rack in the refrigerator for 2 or 3 days, or place it in a pan under running cold water 4 to 6 hours. In either case the poultry should be cooked as soon as possible after defrosting and, at no time, should it be refrozen. Frozen cut-up poultry need not be defrosted, but a longer cooking time would need to be allowed than for that which had been defrosted or freshly killed.

ACCEPTED STANDARDS FOR COOKED POULTRY PRODUCTS.

Poultry products should be evenly cooked to a fairly well-done but not overcooked stage. Special attention is called to the following.

> *Broiled:* Crisp, brown surface; tender skin; juicy tender flesh; well-cooked to the bone; mild but characteristic flavor.

> *Fried:* Crisp, brown surface; tender skin; juicy tender flesh; well-cooked to the bone; low fat absorption; flavorsome.

> *Roasted:* Brown tender skin; meat firm enough to make a clean-cut slice; moist; no discoloration; flavorsome.

EGG COOKERY

The physical qualities of eggs such as thickening, binding, coating, leavening, emulsifying, and coloring determine their cookery functions. Egg proteins are coagulated by heat, thus making possible the thickening of custards, the binding together of particles of foods in croquettes, and the coating of foods. The temperature at which coagulation occurs depends on whether the whole egg, the white only, or the yolk only is used. The addition of sugar to egg protein in solution raises the temperature of coagulation, the effect being proportional to the amount used.

The addition of acid, such as vinegar or lemon juice, tends to produce a stiffer coagulation and likewise to lower the coagulation temperature. Beyond the point of coagulation, continued application of heat to a lemon juice or vinegar mixture with egg results in peptization of the protein and consequent thinning of the coagulation mass.

The amount of air beaten in and retained during preparation determines the effectiveness of egg as a leavening agent. The white forms a more stable and elastic foam than either the yolk or the whole egg. Overbeating causes loss of some elasticity, and addition of sugar retards the rate of coagulation. Egg yolk, a stable emulsion, is a more efficient emulsifying agent than either whole egg or egg white. Use is made of this quality in making mayonnaise. Egg yolks contribute color to such foods as mayonnaise, noodles, and some bakery products.

PROCESSED EGGS

Although fresh shell eggs are used extensively for table service, processed eggs are convenient for quantity food preparation and eliminate the time-consuming task of breaking the eggs. Great care must be exercised in the use of any type of processed eggs, however, beginning with the purchase of frozen or dried eggs that have been packed under USDA supervision. Salmonellae, bacteria responsible for numerous gastrointestinal disorders, are destroyed by pasteurization, which is now mandatory for all liquid eggs used for freezing or drying.

Processed eggs, although rendered free from salmonellae in pasteurization, may well become recontaminated, so certain precautionary measures are advised in the use of these products. Dried eggs should be used in the powdered form wherever possible because once reconstituted into a liquid, it is highly perishable. Likewise, frozen egg once defrosted is an excellent medium for bacterial growth and should be used within 1 to 2 days after thawing.

The USDA recommends [8] that dried eggs be used *only in thoroughly cooked products* such as baked breads, long-cooked casseroles, and baked custards or in cooked salad dressings for which short cooking is safe because of high acidity. They should not be used in egg-milk drinks, uncooked salad dressings, cream puddings, soft custards, ice creams, omelets, or scrambled eggs when cooked on top of the stove.

Frozen eggs may be obtained as white and yolks mixed, whites, or yolks. Freezing does not alter the egg white and, after defrosting, it is similar to the unfrozen white and can be used in the same way. The egg yolk on thawing tends to form a pasty, rubbery gel, and often does not mix well with other ingredients such as sugar and milk. The mixing of sugar or salt with the liquid yolk or whole egg prior to freezing helps to reduce the degree of gelation. Such additions to frozen eggs should be known to the user, who can make appropriate adjustments in recipes.

The recent increase in the demand for acceptable processed eggs for use in institution foodservices has focused attention on the need for products that meet desirable sanitary standards and other quality characteristics, especially flavor.

METHODS OF COOKING

Basic methods of preparing eggs for serving include cooking in the shell, either soft or hard, poaching, frying, and scrambling. When *poaching* in large quantity, a counter pan deep enough to permit 2 to 2 1/2 inches of water to amply cover the eggs is used. Eggs should be broken onto platters or saucers and slid into the water toward the side of the pan. The water should be simmering when the eggs are dropped in. The addition of 2 tablespoons of vinegar and 1 tablespoon of salt to 1 gallon of water prevents whites from spreading. Poaching may be done on the range top, in the oven, or in a steam cooker.

Eggs generally are *fried* to order and may be cooked in frypans or on a griddle. For large quantities, eggs may be oven fried. To prevent toughening, eggs should not be fried at a high temperature. *Scrambled* eggs are easily prepared in quantity in the steamer or

[8] *"Quantity Recipes for Type A School Lunches," U.S. Department of Agriculture, Food and Nutrition Service, PA-631, revised 1971.*

oven. The addition of milk to the eggs keeps them from drying, and medium white sauce added in place of milk prevents the eggs from separating and becoming watery when held on the serving counter.

Shell eggs may be cooked in a pan on top of the range, an automatic egg cooker, a wire basket in the steam-jacketed kettle, or in a compartment steamer at 5-pound pressure. If eggs are brought to room temperature, the shells will not crack when heat is applied. Eggs are covered with water and simmered approximately 3 to 6 minutes for soft-cooked eggs and 16 to 20 minutes for hard-cooked eggs. Cooling at once by plunging hard-cooked eggs into cold running water stops the cooking process. This helps eliminate the development of a ferrous sulfide (greenish) ring around the yolk.

Cooked eggs are also used in dishes such as egg cutlets, scalloped eggs, and meat and egg scallops. Acceptable standards may be maintained in these dishes when the component parts are well prepared before combining and further preparation processes do not alter the characteristics of the eggs from those given for hard-cooked eggs. Unless slices of hard-cooked eggs are a requirement, fresh eggs may be broken into an oiled counter pan (egg depth not to exceed 2 inches) and cooked uncovered in the steamer to the desired degree of doneness (usually about 20 minutes). The same procedure can be followed for baking in the oven except the pan should be covered and set into a larger pan containing boiling water. Approximately 40 minutes in a 400°F oven should be adequate for hard cooking the eggs, after which they can be chopped with the time-consuming task of shelling each egg eliminated.

STANDARDS

Accepted standards for cooked egg products are:

Soft-cooked eggs: white, set but jellylike and opaque; yolk, slightly set on outside but not firm.

Hard-cooked eggs: white, firm but tender; yolk, firm but not rubbery; no discoloration at juncture of yolk and white.

Poached eggs: white, set but jellylike and opaque; yolk, slightly set and well veiled with light albumin covering; generally round and compact.

Fried eggs: white, firm but not rubbery; free from browning or crisping and bubbles; yolk, set but not firm; generally round and compact.

Baked eggs: white, firm but not rubbery; free from crisping; yolk, set but not firm.

Scrambled eggs: loose, moist, tender rolls of yellow, free from traces of white or evidence of browning.

Omelet: light, delicately brown, tender.

Soft custard: smooth, homogenous; pours evenly; attractive yellow in color.

Baked custard: firm yet tender, jellylike mass; fine texture free from porosity or evidence of curdling.

Cooked salad dressing: smooth, homogenous, free from curdling or separation; pours easily, has glossy surface.

Souffles: light, fluffy, tender; free from layering; delicate brown.

Fondue: less delicate and fragile than souffles; delicate brown.

MILK COOKERY

Milk is a basic component of many prepared dishes, and the quality of the resulting product depends in large measure on the cookery procedures. The temperature to which milk is heated depends on the dish to be prepared. Fresh milk is seldom coagulated if the temperature is low or the cooking period short. To prevent coagulation or curdling of the casein, the use of the steamer or steam-jacketed kettle in foodservices is highly desirable. Whether the temperature required be lukewarm or just below the boiling point, it is important that the milk be used as soon as possible after reaching the desired temperature. If a lukewarm temperature is maintained for a long period, the possibility of curdling is increased; if high temperatures are maintained, a coating of coagulated albumin with calcium salts forms on the bottom of the utensil. Both the flavor and the odor of milk are affected adversely by the continued application of heat. The presence of steam while heating prevents the formation of a film, composed largely of calcium caseinate. Whether used in white sauce, in its various applications to creamed dishes, souffles, and croquettes, or as the basis for a custard, the cookery of milk requires a slow, low heat.

When other foods are present, coagulation may occur in a short period of heating. Lowe [9] reported that the factors bringing about this coagulation undoubtedly include the pH and the tannin content, as well as the salt content of the vegetable or other foods. Milk usually does not curdle when cabbage, spinach, or cauliflower is cooked in it, but it is likely to curdle when combined with asparagus, green beans, peas, or carrots. Curdling is more likely to occur when meat cooked in milk is salted and cured than when fresh meat is used. Evaporated milk has less tendency to curdle than fresh milk. Lowe further stated that if a portion of the milk is added to the cured meat when cooking is first started and the remainder of the cold milk added gradually during the cooking process, curdling is less likely to occur than when all milk is added at the beginning of the cooking process. Curdling is less likely to occur in tomato soup if the tomato is hot and added gradually to cold milk and the mixture heated together for as short a time as possible.

The keeping qualities, dispersibility, and flavor of instant nonfat dry milk have greatly increased the opportunities for its use as an ingredient of convenience foods or mixes used in institution food-services. Dry-milk solids may be combined with other dry ingredients and incorporated in a recipe, or reconstituted for use as fluid milk. To reconstitute, approximately 1 pound of dry-milk solid is sprinkled on 1 gallon of water in the bowl of the mixer and blended thoroughly on low speed. If whole milk is desired and nonfat dry milk is used, about 3 tablespoons of table fat for each quart of reconstituted milk may be added. For best results it is essential to follow the manufacturer's directions given on the label of the package.

CHEESE COOKERY

Careful preparation of cooked dishes in which cheese is used is necessary if desirable results are to be obtained. The degree of ripening, the acidity, and the method of manufacture affect the plasticity of cheese when heated for blending with liquid. In the process of ripening cheese loses its tough, rubbery qualities and becomes soft

[9] *Belle Lowe*, Experimental Cookery, *Fourth Edition, Wiley, New York, 1955.*

and mellow. During this change as much as 50 percent of the nitrogenous constituents may be converted to soluble form with the result that a well-aged or ripened cheese blends more readily than a green cheese does and results in a product of higher quality. These conditions influence its blending properties with other ingredients in dishes such as souffles and macaroni and cheese. In general cheese is added to other foods in a finely divided form by grinding or grating.

Cheese softens and finally melts as it is heated. Relatively high temperatures and long periods of heating cause it to curdle, string, or become hard and tough. Cheese melts at 324°F, and baked dishes containing cheese should be cooked at a temperature no higher than 350°F. Temperatures of 105 to 120°F are usually preferable for blending cheese with a sauce. When making souffle, the best results are obtained if the beaten egg yolks are added to the white sauce before the grated cheese is added. This procedure cooks the eggs and aids in emulsifying the fat of the cheese. The added moisture and the emulsification of the fat in process cheese causes it to combine readily with a sauce.

FRUITS AND VEGETABLES

Flavor, color, texture, and form of fruits and vegetables are the characteristics that make up quality. The basic physical and chemical attributes determine this to a large degree. The flavor is due to sugar, organic acids, mineral salts, and aromatic compounds and, in some instances, to pungent, astringent evidence of tannin content found in green or immature fruit. The colors of fruits and vegetables are due to the various pigments that they contain.

Among the substances responsible for certain strong flavors in foods are the volatile sulfur compounds found in the onion family, mustard, and in vegetables of the cabbage family. These may hydrolyze by enzymatic action or by long heating in the presence of acid to yield a product both unpleasant and strong smelling. It is important to choose a preparation process that will minimize as far as possible the undesirable development of these compounds.

The characteristic structure of fruits and vegetables is largely determined by the cellulose, which forms the walls of the plant cells, in combination with pectin and some other substances. The water content within the plant cells determines the crispness of the tissue. Lacking water, the structure wilts. The cellulose is altered by cooking, being partly broken down by steaming or long-continued boiling. This action is accelerated by the presence of alkalis and retarded by the addition of acids.

PREPREPARATION OF FRUITS AND VEGETABLES

More and more of the prepreparation of fruits and vegetables is taken out of individual institution kitchens and accomplished in centralized preparation units. Also, commercial prepreparation companies have found a ready market for their peeled potatoes and carrots, washed spinach and other leafy vegetables, cut vegetables ready for cooking, and peeled and sectioned citrus fruits and fresh pineapple, to name only a few. Modern processing of fruits and vegetables renders it virtually unnecessary for institutions to spend costly labor time for preliminary preparations. The need for purchase of expensive equipment for prepreparation has been eliminated in many foodservices by their use of convenience forms of fruits and vegetables.

On the other hand, many foodservice directors prefer to maintain control of standards of quality from the very beginning and to purchase produce in its natural state if they have ample supervisory staff to ensure good control throughout production. Therefore a brief review of some of these preliminary procedures is included in this text.

The time required for preparation of fresh fruits and vegetables will vary with the type of product, its quality, the equipment available, and any preparation beyond the preliminary that must be given, such as cutting potatoes for French frying, slicing apples for pie, or shredding cabbage for slaw. The relation of the weight of the vegetable as purchased to the edible portion obtained is important. Variations in waste are influenced by many factors, such as the skill of the worker, the condition, quality, maturity, size, and shape of the vegetable, the length and conditions of storage, the season, and the producing district. Because of the wide variations in the amount of waste, the cost of the edible portion rather than the cost as purchased should be the basis for determining the serving cost of vegetables. Representative figures on preparation losses may be found in various sources, but there is some variance among them. One such is given in Table 4.6.

Each food unit will find it necessary to make studies of its own and record actual preparation losses and costs under the particular conditions of operation and with varieties of foods used. Form 4.2 might be used for the collection of such data.

Major objectives in preliminary preparation of fruits and vegetables are to retain as much of the nutritive value as possible and to preserve the color, form, and quality to a high degree. The achievement of these objectives requires careful scheduling of the work to

TABLE   4.6   APPROXIMATE WASTE IN THE PREPARATION OF FRESH FRUITS AND VEGETABLES

Fruits	Average Percent Waste	Vegetables	Average Percent Waste
Apple	27	Asparagus	49
Avocado	40	Beans, green	16
Banana, peeled	42	Broccoli	38
Blueberries	16	Cabbage, green	21
Cranberries	3	Carrots	24
Cherries, pitted	21	Cauliflower	69
Cantaloupe, with rind	63	Celery	29
Cantaloupe, peeled,		Chicory	29
served without rind	39	Cucumber	28
Grapefruit, sections		Eggplant	22
and juice	52	Lettuce, head	31
Grapes, seedless	5	Onions, mature	11
Honeydew, served		Peas, green	63
without rind	46	Peppers, green	22
Orange sections	43	Potatoes	16
Peaches (average)	20	Potatoes, sweet	20
Pears	33	Radishes	40
Pineapple	52	Spinach	64
Plums	7	Squash, acorn	34
Strawberries	16	Squash, Hubbard	41
Watermelon	54	Squash, zucchini	2
		Tomatoes	14
		Turnips	20

Source. *Adapted from Elsie H. Dawson, Elsie F. Dochterman, and Ruth S. Vettel, "Food Yields in Institutional Food Service,"* Journal of the American Dietetic Association, 34, 267–272 (1958).

Note. *To change the prepared raw food weight to as purchased weight: (1) Subtract the percent waste from 100 to obtain percent yield. (2) Divide the known prepared raw food weight by the percent yield obtained in (1), then multiply by 100, to obtain the A.P. (as purchased) weight.*

reduce to a minimum the time lapse between preparation and cooking the food. The practice of preparing vegetables, particularly root vegetables, some hours before they are to be cooked and soaking them in cold water for a long period of time is undesirable. Investigations showed that the losses of nitrogenous matter in soaked potatoes were as high as 46 to 58 percent, and the losses of minerals

Product: Spinach
Amount: 1 bushel

Date	6/25/			Average
1. A.P. weight	18 lb			
2. E.P. weight	11 lb			
3. Weight of waste	7 lb			
4. Per cent waste	38.8			
5. Unit cost of ingredient	$6.00			
6. Cost of added ingredients	$0.60			
7. Total cost of product	$6.60			
8. Average weight of serving	3 oz			
9. Estimated servings	48			
10. Estimated cost per serving	$0.138			
11. Selling price (40% food cost)	$0.34			
12. Time of preparation	30 min			
13. Pay rate of worker	$2.25/hr			
14. Labor cost per serving	$0.023			

Comments: _____

FORM 4.2   *Fruit and vegetable preparation and cost study.*

about 38 percent. The size of the pieces and the length of the soaking period influence the losses, small pieces and long soaking causing the largest loss. It is therefore important from the standpoint of palatability and food value that the soaking be eliminated or sharply limited.

Some fresh fruits such as bananas, apples, and pears require special handling to prevent darkening and so should be peeled at the last possible moment before use.

Fruits and vegetables should be handled as little as possible. Convenient arrangement of the work area and its location close to the cooking unit help prevent undue loss of time. Suitable and adequate equipment conveniently arranged for efficient work should be provided for the employees.

Fruits. The following methods are desirable in the preliminary preparation of fruits.

1. All fruits should be washed to remove surface soil, sprays, and preservatives (such as wax on apples) before they are served raw or incorporated into made dishes.

2. Fruits are left whole or cut into segments of size or shape suitable for the purpose. For example, a fresh pear might be washed and served whole, whereas an orange might be peeled and sliced for a dessert.

3. Most raw fruits are prepared as late as possible before serving and returned to the refrigerator until mealtime.

Specific Preparation of a Few Selected Fruits. The preparation of *apples* usually includes peeling, removal of bruises and spots, coring, and dicing. Highly colored skins may make it preferable to leave them on at times. Peeling is sometimes done by hand, and removal of bruises and spots is included in the operation. If a mechanical peeler is used, bruises and spots must be removed by hand. The coring of apples is often done with a hand corer. A rapid and satisfactory procedure for dicing is to remove the core, peel if desired, slice into rings, stack on a slicing board, and complete the dicing with the use of the sectional cutter. To prevent discoloration caused by the action of an oxidase, the diced pieces are dropped into a bowl containing lemon juice and water, pineapple juice, other acid fruit juice, or salad dressing. Salted water is sometimes used for apples if they are to be made into salad or cooked within a short time. Do not allow them to soak in the solution. Crisp white apple segments are essential to the attractiveness of the salad in which they are an ingredient. When ready for combination with other fruits or with vegetables, the pieces should be well defined and uniform in size and shape.

Apples for baking are washed, cored, and placed in baking pans. The core is removed from the stem end. Care should be taken not to cut through the blossom, as the cavity will be filled with sugar, syrup, or honey, which should cook into the fruit, not fall through into the water. Buttered apples are most rapidly prepared by cutting the washed and unpeeled apples into quarters on a board, removing the cores, and dropping the pieces directly into the pans in which they will be steamed and baked.

Apricots, cherries, grapes, pears, and *plums* are most often washed in a colander, dried between two towels, and served whole without further preparation as desserts or cut and used in salads. Berries deteriorate rapidly after washing, so they should be prepared as close to serving time as is practical.

Bananas should be used at just the right degree of ripeness; when underripe, they are unpalatable and discolor rapidly, and when overripe, they are soft and unattractive. Their tendency to darken, because of action of an oxidase, makes it necessary that little time elapse between their preparation and service unless they are especially treated. Bananas may be prepared successfully in quantity for the institution menu if they are immersed in a solution of cream of tartar and Karo syrup, or cerelose. This solution prevents discoloration, preserves the firmness, and does not affect the flavor of the fruit. Pineapple, orange, grapefruit, or diluted lemon juice may be used effectively for this purpose, especially in the preparation of bananas for salads and fruit cup. Cut bananas treated in this way may be kept several hours without discoloring.

Oranges and *grapefruit* are used extensively in sections, cubes, or slices. All white membrane should be carefully removed when peeling the fruit, and the segments should emerge uniform in size and contour with no appearance of mushiness. The fruit is peeled by cutting a thick layer off both the top and the bottom to a depth great enough to expose the pulp. The fruit is then placed on end on the cutting board and cut down the sides from end to end. Care should be taken to follow the contour of the fruit and cut only deep enough to remove all white membrane. When the pulp is entirely exposed, a sharp fruit knife is used to cut along the membrane of a section to the center of the fruit, then turn the knife and force the blade along the membrane of the next section and out to the exterior of the fruit. This cutting is repeated for each section. See Fig. 4.4.

Peaches discolor rapidly when exposed to air so must be prepared as quickly and late as possible. Skins are easily removed by placing the peaches in a perforated basket or colander and lowering

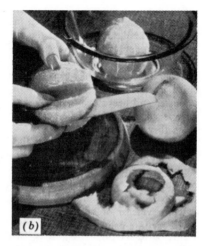

FIGURE 4.4   *Preparation of citrus fruit. (a) A fast way to peel fruit is to cut a slice off top and bottom, then cut away peel on sides. (b) Peeled fruit is easily sectioned by cutting on each side of dividing membrane and lifting out segments on knife. Courtesy, Sunkist Growers, Los Angeles, California.*

it into boiling water, or placing in the steamer for about 2 minutes or until skin will slip. Then plunge them into cold water. Skins should peel off easily and the fruit should be unharmed by the sudden heating and chilling. To slice rapidly, the peeled peach should be turned in the left hand while cutting to the pit with a heavy knife (stainless steel blade) and using a rapid chopping motion with the right hand. The cut wedges may be pushed off the pit with the thumb of the left hand while the right hand continues to hold the knife and picks up another peach.

Vegetables. The following methods are usually employed in the preliminary preparation of vegetables.

1.   All leafy and stem vegetables are washed thoroughly, drained, and crisped by placing them in covered containers in a refrigerator for at least 2 hours before use.

2.   Vegetables to be cooked unpeeled may be scrubbed well with a stiff brush or put into the vegetable peeler for a few seconds to remove the dirt.

3. Root and tuber vegetables put through a vegetable peeler need not be washed prior to peeling. Vegetables such as carrots, turnips, and potatoes are pared for approximately 1 to 2 minutes, the exact time depending on the size of the vegetables, the number put into the peeler at one time, and their condition. Uniformity of size aids in efficient peeling. Peeled vegetables are placed in containers of clean cold water and then trimmed or eyed as necessary. Cutting into desired shapes for cooking may be done with a French knife on a cutting board, or by machine.

Directions for Preparation of a Few Selected Vegetables. Asparagus and *broccoli* should be inspected, the wilted and decayed sections removed, the hard, tough parts of the stems cut off, and the remaining portions washed and soaked. The vegetable may be tied in bundles of 1 to 2 pounds each, each bundle being the equivalent of six servings, as a preparation for easy handling in cooking in water. This bunching permits placement of the stalks with the tender tips or heads up, so that they need not be submerged in the cooking water and hence overcooked.

In the preparation of *cauliflower,* any leaves are removed except for a few of the smallest, and dark spots are cut away. If the head is to be served whole no further cutting is necessary. If the head is to be used in pieces, the flowerets are separated from the core, a stem about 1 inch long left on each. In either method it is advisable to soak the cauliflower as well as broccoli and artichokes in water to which vinegar or salt has been added.

Greens require special care. In preparing *head lettuce* the heavy outside leaves are removed and discarded, the stem end or core is cut out about 1 inch, and the head is held with the cavity under running cold water until the leaves are loosened. The head is then turned right side up to drain and, in a short time, it is practically free from excess water. If lettuce cups are desired, the leaves are separated and stacked or nested, six or eight leaves to a pile. Each pile is inverted, packed in a container, and covered with a fitted lid or damp cloth. The container is placed in the refrigerator for 2 or more hours to complete the crisping.

Loose-leafed greens such as *leaf lettuce, watercress, endive, romaine, mint, spinach,* and *parsley* are sorted, washed in clear water, drained and packed in a container, covered with a fitted lid or damp cloth, and placed in the refrigerator for further crisping. Water cress and parsley are regarded as capable of remaining in prime condition through a longer period after crisping than the other greens. *Celery,* too, holds up well after crisping.

The preliminary preparation of celery includes separating the outer stalks from the heart of the bunch, washing with a brush, trimming, and removing the bruised and blemished parts. Further cutting may be done as desired. In the preparation of celery for use in shredded form, several stalks may be laid on a board across a tray, cut at once, and added to the salad mixture without further handling. Cutting by machine is common if uniformity of piece is not a factor.

The preparation of *cabbage* is far simpler than that of other leafy vegetables. The outer leaves are removed, and each head is then washed and cut into four or six pieces, depending on its size, by using a French knife and cutting board. The center stalk is removed from each piece in like manner. The edible portion remaining is then cut or shredded as desired, usually by running through the shredder attachment on the power mixer if a finely cut product is desired.

Spinach is prepared by removing the crown and all the petiole, if it is large and coarse. The leaves are carefully examined, and all dry, yellow, wilted, or slimy ones are discarded. The leaves and small tender stems regarded as forming the edible portion are cut or pulled from the stems and washed four or five times or even more, if necessary, to free them from bugs, sand, and other soil. The preparation of kale and other greens is similar to that of spinach.

Tomatoes to be used in salads should be peeled. They may be placed in a colander or wire basket, dipped in boiling water or placed in the steamer until the skins begin to loosen, then dipped in cold water to cool. The skins may be readily removed. In any method the procedure should be conducted as rapidly as possible to prevent cooking. After dipping in cold water the tomatoes may be placed in a covered container in the refrigerator and peeled later as needed. This will prevent the possibility of deterioration through long standing after peeling. Tomatoes are easily sliced on a power slicer.

Beets are usually washed and cooked, the skins removed, and blemishes or spots cut out. Alternatively, they may be prepared in the same manner as carrots and potatoes. *Turnips* are topped and then may be peeled by hand or in the vegetable peeler. The electric peeler removes the skins of turnips in about 4 minutes but tends to produce a soft, spongy product. Since *rutabagas* are usually waxed, they should be peeled by hand with a French knife and cutting board.

Onions are prepared somewhat differently, the layer structure of the bulb making the use of the electric peeler impossible. Hot water may be poured over the onions in lots of 5 pounds or whatever amount is easy to handle. Wilted leaves, the outer layer of the bulb, the firm root end, and all bruised or decayed parts are removed under water. The bulbs are then sliced or cut as desired. The worker should avoid bending directly over the onions while cutting them to prevent strong fumes from getting in the eyes and the resultant weeping.

FRUIT AND VEGETABLE COOKERY

The objectives of fruit and vegetable cookery are to conserve nutrients to a high degree, to retain the color and form of the food, and to develop a desirable texture and flavor. An understanding of the effects on fruits and vegetables of different conditions and cookery methods is essential. Many factors like color, form, and nutrients must be considered, and the best cooking method for one factor may not be suitable for another. Investigators are not always in agreement with all recommendations, which calls for continuing research on the interrelating factors that might determine optimum cooking procedures.

Fruits. It is generally agreed that there is little need for concern about fruit cookery. In institutions, methods are limited mainly to stewing or baking. The method used is determined by the character of the desired final product, although the selection of a variety of a fruit suitable for the specific use may be as important as the cooking method used.

When the shape of the fruit is to be retained, it may be baked whole with the skin on, or gently cooked in a sugar syrup without stirring. The concentration of sugar should be about the same as the concentration of soluble materials in the fruit for it to hold its shape; if too high, the water is drawn from the fruit by osmosis, leaving the fruit shrunken and tough. The optimum concentration varies for each fruit, so a standard recipe should be consulted for best results. If a sauce is desired, the fruit is cooked in water or steam until soft and mushy, and sugar to flavor is added at the end of cooking.

There is little loss of nutrients in fruit cookery, since fruits are cooked for a relatively short time and the juices are not discarded but served with the fruit. This promotes retention of both nutrients and flavor.

Vegetables. The problems involved in attaining good quality in cooked vegetables are more numerous and require more consideration than in fruits. Vegetables subjected to cookery processes inevitably suffer some loss because of escape of volatile substances, the solubility of other substances in cooking water, and the destruction by heat of certain important food constituents. The most significant losses are the nutrients: minerals, vitamins, and nitrogenous matter, and the essential oils and sugar that affect the flavor and palatability.

Effect of Cookery on Nutritive Value. Nutritive losses are those resulting from the solubility of nitrogenous compounds, sugars, mineral salts, and vitamins. In general, losses are less if the cooking of the vegetables is begun in boiling water and if the vegetable is cut into fairly large chunks.

Investigators sometime ago found that the greatest retention of both minerals and vitamins in vegetables was obtained when cooked without added water and the least retention was obtained when water to cover the vegetables was used, because of the "leaching" of these elements. Vitamin A is almost completely retained in vegetables cooked by most methods because the carotenoids are insoluble in water and resistant to oxidation. Destruction of vitamins A and C takes place more rapidly at high temperatures, and the greater the length of cooking time, the more loss. The higher temperature of steam at 5 or more pounds pressure over boiling water might be expected to cause greater loss of nutritive value. However, the short time required to cook vegetables in this manner may be less destructive than boiling for a long time. Ascorbic acid and the B vitamins are soluble in water and, since ascorbic acid is susceptible also to oxidation, they are not as well retained as the carotenoids in vegetable cookery.

Effect of Cookery on Color. Color is a major factor in customer acceptance of vegetables and some authorities place "eye appeal" at about 45 percent of the total quality score. Methods of cookery that give optimum color as well as nutritive value retention are to be sought.

Chlorophyll is the least stable of food pigments and considerable attention is given to ways and means of preserving this green color in vegetables. Carotenoids, the yellow and orange pigments, and flavones, pigments found in creamy white vegetables, are little affected by ordinary cooking methods. Vegetables owing their red color to anthocyanins may become more attractive in the presence of acids. Some vegetables, such as beets, have enough acid present to preserve their red color if cooked in a covered container. However, the addition of acid enhances the color of red cabbage. Anthocyanins are exceedingly soluble, so a vegetable such as beets may be cooked before peeling.

Chlorophyll is affected by acid to produce an unattractive olive-gray color. Vegetables are slightly acid in reaction and, when cooked, the acid is liberated from the cells into the cooking water. Fortunately, much of the acid is volatile and given off in the first few minutes of cooking. If an open kettle is used for cooking green vegetables the volatile acids may escape easily, aiding in the retention of the green pigment.

Length of cooking time probably has more effect on the color and flavor of vegetables than any other one factor. Overcooking of green vegetables particularly, or holding them too long before serving, will cause a change from the bright attractive color to one that is dull, drab, and unappealing.

The introduction of high-pressure (15 pounds per square inch) steamers has made possible the quick cooking of fresh and frozen vegetables with a resulting high-quality product. In this type of steamer, the steam is forced directly onto the food and, at the end of the cooking time, automatically exhausts from the heating chamber. This type of steamer is particularly successful in the cooking of chlorophyll-rich foods. For foodservices not having this type of equipment green vegetables such as beans, broccoli, and Brussels sprouts can be satisfactorily cooked in large quantities in a steam-jacketed kettle if the cooking period is brief and if a relatively small quantity of water is used.

Effect of Cookery on Flavor and Palatability. Flavor of vegetables is due primarily to sugar and essential oils present; some vegetables contain sulphur compounds and acids. Strong-flavored vegetables such as onions and cabbage will lose some of their undesirable flavor in the steam if cooked in an open kettle. These vegetables retain a good flavor, however, when cooked in a high-pressure steamer for the short time required.

Other factors that are believed to influence the effect of cooking on flavor and palatability are the hardness of the water and the presence of salt. The use of hard water in cooking may have an undesirable effect on the product. Calcium and magnesium dissolved in the water may combine with the cellulose, thus hardening the structure of the food. The addition of salt either at the beginning or at least early in the cooking period is regarded as important in developing and maintaining a good flavor, although it may have an effect on certain nutrients. Salt is usually added in proportion to the amount of water instead of directly to the quantity of vegetable being cooked. The use of 1 to 2 1/2 teaspoons of salt to each quart of water is a recommended allowance.

Many vegetables might be received with greater favor by the consumer if they were removed from the heat while still somewhat crisp instead of when completely tender. This procedure yields a product more desirable in shape, texture, and color than is possible when vegetables are cooked to the "completely done" stage. Canned vegetables need only to be heated, since they are cooked when canned. Overheating, as with overcooking of fresh and frozen vegetables, will result in further loss of nutrients and a soft-textured, poor-flavored, and unattractive product.

Close attention to preparation and cooking directions provided by the processor is necessary for attaining best possible quality results with the new forms of fruits and vegetables. The many different processes used and the variety of forms available, such as flaked, cubed, and granular, and dehydrated potatoes, require a different procedure for each. It is impossible to include directions for all in this text.

Cookery Procedures for Fresh and Frozen Vegetables. A summary of suggested cookery procedures for fresh and frozen vegetables in light of present knowledge follows.

1. Fresh or frozen vegetables may be cooked in a high-pressure steamer, a regular steamer, or in boiling water in an open kettle (steam-jacketed kettle or on top of the range).

2. Most vegetables can be cooked successfully in a high-pressure steamer (Fig. 4.5). If this type of equipment is not available, green or strong-flavored vegetables should be cooked in boiling water in an open kettle unless there would be a loss of shape, as with frozen broccoli.

3. Mild flavored, nongreen vegetables are best cooked in a steamer.

FIGURE 4.5   Rapid cooking of vegetables in small amounts is possible in high-pressure steam cooker. Courtesy, Market Forge Company.

4. For steamer cooking, best results are obtained when vegetables are arranged in thin layers, not over 2 inches in depth, in shallow pans. An advantage of using a steamer for vegetable preparation is that the vegetables can be cooked in the serving counter inset pans, thus eliminating the necessity of transferring food after cooking.

5. If vegetables are cooked in water, as small an amount as is practical should be used and it should be boiling before adding vegetables. Small steam-jacketed kettles are recommended for this type of cookery. Water can be brought to a second boil almost immediately after the addition of vegetables. Add no soda to cooking water. The use of insert baskets that fit inside the kettle facilitates removal and draining of cooked vegetables (Fig. 4.6).

6. The cooking time should be as short as possible, consistent with the type of vegetable. Cook until tender but slightly crisp for best color, texture, flavor, and nutritional

FIGURE   4.6   *Single- or multiple-unit wire basket inserts for steam-jacketed kettles make for fast and easy removal and draining of cooked vegetables. Courtesy, Groen Manufacturing Co.*

value. Avoid overcooking. Time of cooking should be controlled so vegetables will be ready just at serving time.

7.   Vegetables should be handled carefully to avoid mashing.

8.   Freshly cooked vegetables should go to the serving counter at frequent intervals and none held longer than 20 minutes for optimum quality. For most attractive service avoid mixing batches at the serving counter.

Production Scheduling. "Small-batch" or continuous cookery of vegetables throughout the meal service is the most satisfactory way to obtain high-quality products. Quantities of not more than 10-pound lots, and preferably less, should be cooked in one kettle or steamer at intervals as needed. This system reduces the need for the long holding periods after cooking that cause rapid loss of color and flavor. With a small load in one kettle or cooker there is uniformity of cooking and little chance of damaging the bottom layers of food. Dividing the vegetables into amounts equal to the size of a single cooking batch at time of prepreparation avoids the last minute rush to weigh out correct quantities. With small-batch cooking, fewer leftovers result and better waste control is effected and, with modern fast-cooking equipment, this can be accomplished in most institutions. Many foodservices locate their high-speed steamers close to the serving line so that small batches of vegetables can be cooked as needed. Some models are equipped with an automatic defrost control so that actual cooking time can be constant regardless of whether fresh, frozen, or thawed vegetables are used. In the larger conventional steamers, vegetables may be cooked from the frozen state also, but results are more satisfactory if the food is thawed before cooking. This is especially true of large masses of frozen vegetables in which the exterior may be overcooked before the heat has penetrated the center of the pan.

Scheduling of vegetable cookery does take good organization of the kitchen staff and close supervision, but the results are well worth the effort. Studies by the foodservice manager with written records of vegetable usage at frequent, stated intervals throughout the serving period will give a factual basis on which to determine production needs.

Dried Vegetables. Dried legumes such as navy, lima, pinto, soy, and kidney beans, and peas and lentils are soaked before cooking to restore the water content to that of the fresh legume and to shorten the cooking time. Legumes will absorb enough water to approximately double their dry weight, with an attendant increase in volume. The length of the soaking period depends on the temperature at which it is carried on; the use of warm water usually cuts the soaking time about half. The use of hard water containing calcium and magnesium salts is undesirable in cooking legumes, since such water has a hardening effect on the vegetable.

SALADS FROM FRUITS AND VEGETABLES

Fruits and vegetables used raw in salads receive the same preliminary preparation outlined for other fruits and vegetables. Cooked fruits and vegetables for use in salads should be free from any evidence of overcooking, each piece retaining fully the characteristics of its type. Vegetables may be slightly undercooked as a crispness of texture is desirable. Thorough chilling and marinating of vegetables particularly will enhance the flavor of the final product. Since leafy vegetables tend to wilt after being marinated, any dressing used should be added directly before serving.

Ingredients that go into a salad should be clean, crisp, chilled, and well drained. The pieces should be large enough to be distinguishable but not so large that they cannot be cut or eaten easily. Raw cauliflower, for example, is broken into small flowerets, because it is difficult to cut cauliflower with a salad fork at the table. A canned peach or pear could be served in halves or whole pieces, since they can be cut into bite sizes without any problem.

Proper seasoning, a simple arrangement on a prechilled plate or bowl, and selection of a dressing to complement its flavor add to the attractiveness of a salad. When a mixture is desired, the ingredients are tossed together as lightly as possible to avoid crushing or mashing them. If a dressing is used, all pieces should be coated with it before serving. Usually this is done just before serving time, except for potato and some protein types of salads where flavor is improved by standing 2 to 4 hours after mixing.

Emphasis should be placed on the creation of simple, palatable, colorful combinations. A conflict of strong flavors or colors or the production of an unpleasant blandness of taste, flatness of color, and sameness of texture must be avoided. The palatability of every food should be high and its use in the salad should enhance its natural flavor. Combinations of ingredients, garnish, and dressing should be made with this purpose in mind.

The undergarnish on salad plates forms a frame for the salad and adds to its appeal. Green leafy vegetables commonly used as undergarnish are leaf, Bibb, or head lettuce cups, romaine, endive, spinach, celery and beet tops, watercress, and parsley. Like other greens, they should be clean, crisp, chilled and dry, and be of a size to fit the plate without extending over the rim. Top garnishes add the final touch of color and flavor contrast. The list of such garnishes is almost endless, limited only by the ingenuity and imagination of the foodservice manager or salad worker.

Gelatin is used to give definite shape to fruit or vegetable juices and as a carrier for fruits and vegetables in finely subdivided form. It is available primarily in granulated and pulverized forms. The granulated (plain) must be soaked in cold water to disperse readily in hot water. Pulverized gelatin generally is in combination with sugar and flavoring and available under various trade names as flavored gelatins. This type of gelatin disperses readily in hot water without preliminary soaking in cold liquid. As the mixture cools, it changes from a liquid to a gel; this is known as "setting" of the gelatin. Hydrated gelatin goes into solution readily at 95°F.

The change from a liquid form to a gel depends on the concentration of gelatin, the character and temperature of the solvent, the temperature used for gelation, and certain interactions between these factors. The gelatin or solidification of the solution is largely determined by the concentration or the ratio existing between the gelatin and the liquid in the solution. With the other factors held constant, gelation occurs only at a given concentration. It is found that the dispersing medium also affects the concentration necessary for solidification. Acids, such as lemon juice and tomato juice, if included in the liquid, necessitate an increase in the concentration of gelatin in order to secure a gel of the desired firmness. An opposite effect is reported when milk is employed as the solvent. It is known that milk used with a lower percentage of gelatin makes as firm a gel as does a water solution of higher gelatin concentration. Sugar also affects the gel. A medium amount of sugar increases stiffness at a given concentration, whereas a large amount seems to retard the formation of a gel. Caution should be used when syrup from canned fruit is substituted for part or all of the liquid in a recipe that the added sugar will not weaken the gel, or else additional gelatin may have to be added. However, the common error of adding excess gelatin to insure stability does not yield a palatable, satisfactory product. A fruit or vegetable gelatin, to be satisfactory, must have clear-cut edges, firm and delicate but not rubbery texture, and definite but not rigid form.

Much time can be saved in the quantity preparation of gelatin salads by hydrating the gelatin in a small amount of cold liquid and then adding only enough boiling liquid to dissolve the moistened gelatin. The remainder of the liquid required in the formula is added cold. The amount of hot liquid used may be further decreased by placing the hydrated gelatin in the steamer for a short time until it is dissolved. The rest of the liquid needed may be added cold. Some quantity recipes call for ice to be substituted for part of the liquid, which further aids in rapid cooling of the mixture to gelatinization temperature.

The time element in gelation is definite for a solution having a given concentration of gelatin held at a definite temperature. Lower concentration, a higher temperature, or both result in the requirement of a longer time for gelation to occur. Lowering the temperature lessens the time needed for gelation and also the degree of concentration necessary. A solution having a concentration of 2 percent gelatin in water will set at 59°F, whereas at 32°F a solution having 1 percent concentration yields as firm a gel. If the gelation temperature is 50°F or less, or if it is cooled rapidly, the solidity of the gel may be so weak as to make serving at room temperature difficult.

A good practice in making gelatin dishes is to let the solution stand at room temperature for approximately 1 1/2 hours and then to put it in the refrigerator for the completion of the gelation process. This procedure produces a gelatin dish with a texture usually superior to that of one wholly refrigerator cooled.

The solidifying of gelatin dishes largely depends on reaching and maintaining certain temperatures; hence care should be taken that gelatin dishes are not planned when atmospheric conditions would make their solidification during the period of service doubtful. An enzyme found in fresh pineapple is known to destroy the solidifying power of gelatin; therefore only cooked and never fresh pineapple can be used in gelatin.

FAT COOKERY

The common uses of fats are as an ingredient in emulsions, as a medium for frying, and to give shortening power to batters and doughs.

EMULSIONS.

An emulsion is a dispersion of one liquid in a second liquid in which it is not soluble. Oil and water are most commonly named as typical immiscible substances. Although they are not soluble in each other, oil may be dispersed in water by mechanical agitation. The resulting emulsion breaks down rapidly, only a minute or so being required for the separation of the two substances; hence it is called a temporary emulsion. French dressing made of vinegar or lemon juice, oil, and condiments is a temporary emulsion also but, since an acid is used instead of water, the ease and completeness of dispersion are increased. The emulsion so formed is sustained also by the presence of some insoluble powders in the condiments that act as emulsifying agents. In the commercial preparation of French dressing, the larger use of condiments and other substances that serve as bases for emulsion and the process of homogenization alike serve to yield a relatively stable "temporary emulsion."

Mayonnaise is termed a permanent emulsion. The emulsifying agent in mayonnaise, the egg yolk or whole egg, lowers the surface tension of the liquids and, by forming films around the droplets of oil, makes the emulsion stable. Should demulsification take place, the emulsion may be reestablished by adding the demulsified dressing gradually to a few beaten eggs and continuing the beating until the mixture is complete.

FRYING.

Fat used as a frying medium should have a high smoking point and should, even at high temperatures, be as stable against deterioration as possible. Frying in fat with a low smoking point causes greater fat absorption by the food than occurs when fat of higher smoking temperature is used. Particles of food, such as flour or other cooking residue, lower the smoking point of fat. An increase in the surface of the fat exposed to heat is attended by a lowering of the decomposition point, which explains the use of a deep kettle with a relatively small surface. The smoke point varies with the type of fat. Ususally those with the highest smoke point are the vegetable oils or hydrogenated vegetable fats to which no emulsifier has been added. Emulsifiers that improve the quality of fats for baking lower their smoke points.

The frying life of fat is important to the foodservice that uses large quantities of this relatively high-cost food. The fat should be heated only to the temperature and for the time required for cooking. The heat should be turned off immediately after completion of the frying; in continuous operations the thermostat should be lowered to 200°F during slack periods. Table 4.7 gives suggested temperatures for deep fat frying of various foods, the exact temperature varying with the kind of equipment used, the size and temperature of food pieces, and the amount of food placed in the fryer at one time. Frying at too high a temperature browns the food before it is cooked, while too low a temperature results in excessive absorption of fat into the food. The fryer basket generally is filled half full, never more than two thirds of its capacity. Overloading results in an improperly cooked product.

The fryer should be cleaned daily and the fat strained to remove crumbs and food particles. The type of frying kettle now used in most foodservices is so constructed that the particles of food fall into the lower layer of relatively cool fat and are drawn off before decomposition takes place. In such kettles only the upper part of the fat is heated to the desired temperature, which is thermostatically controlled. Such a method cuts the cost of deep fat frying markedly. The fryer may be equipped with a strainer but, if it is not, the fat can be strained through several layers of cheesecloth. The fryer should be replenished with fresh fat to replace that lost during frying. Fat turnover is one of the most important factors in determining the life of the frying fat. The more rapid the turnover, the longer the life of the fat. In some foodservices that operate continuously, it may never

TABLE 4.7   DEEP FAT FRYING TEMPERATURES

Type of Product	Temperature (°F)	Frying Time [a] (min)
Bananas	375	1–3
Cauliflower, precooked	370	3–5
Cheese balls	350	2–3
Chicken, disjointed,		
1 1/2–2 lb fryers	325	10–12
2–2 1/2 lb fryers	325	12–15
Chicken, half,		
1 1/2–2 lb fryers	325	12–15
Croquettes (all previously cooked foods)	360–375	2–5
Cutlets, 1/4 in. thick	325–350	5–8
Doughnuts	360–375	3–5
Eggplant	370	5–7
Fish fillets	375	4–6
Fish sticks	375	3–4
French toast	360	3–4
Fritters	370–380	2–5
Onion rings	350	3–4
Oysters	375	2–4
Potatoes, 1/2 in.		
Complete fry	365	6–8
Blanching	360	3–5
Browning	375	2–3
Frozen, fat blanched	375	2–3
Sandwiches	350–360	3–4
Scallops	360–375	3–4
Shrimp	360–375	3–5
Timbale cases	350–365	2–3

[a] The exact frying time will vary with the equipment used, size and temperature of the food pieces, and the amount of food placed in the fryer at one time. If the kettle is overloaded, foods may become grease-soaked. If food is frozen, use lower temperatures listed and allow additional cooking time.

be necessary to discard the fat but, where maximum production is not maintained, the fat will need to be discarded at some point. If undesirable flavors develop in the fried food or if the fat foams excessively, the fat is no longer suitable for frying.

SHORTENING.

The shortening power of fat or oil in a batter or dough depends primarily on the surface area covered by the fat or oil. Factors affecting the surface area covered by a fat include: plasticity, degree of unsaturation, temperature, other ingredients used and their concentration, and the manipulation and extent of mixing.

The shortening value of a fat varies with a number of conditions and it is therefore absolutely essential in the comparison of two fats that a standard procedure be used. Factors other than the fat that influence the shortening power are (1) manipulation, (2) temperature, (3) ingredients other than flour and fat and their concentration, and (4) concentration of fat. . . . In general lard has a very high shortening value and butter a lower value, with hydrogenated shortenings intermediate. At least this is true in pastry made from water, flour, and fat. However, a fat that ranks high as a shortening agent for pastry is sometimes lower on the list when used in sweet cookie dough.[10]

Vail[11] states that current interest in the use of fats high in polyunsaturated fatty acids in the diet has raised the question of the use of fats such as corn, cottonseed, and peanut oil in recipes standardized to use either a liquid or a solid fat. As a result of such a study Vail concluded:

It would seem that oil could be used satisfactorily in any recipe calling for a liquid fat or for frying. On the other hand, there is every indication that corn oil margarine can be used satisfactorily in a wide variety of recipes in which a solid fat is specified. Doughs containing this fat are easily handled, and batters often appear more homogenous. It is probable that the corn oil margarine has its greatest advantage in batters mixed by "quick" methods, although pastry made with this fat scored consistently higher than that made with a hydrogenated shortening. As to flavor, the acceptability seems to depend somewhat on the individual.

[10] Lillian Hoagland Meyer, Food Chemistry, *Reinhold, New York, p. 62, 1960.*
[11] Gladys E. Vail, "Cooking with Fats High in Polyunsaturated Fatty Acids," Journal of the American Dietetic Association, 35, *119–121 (1959).*

The many variables in the complex stuctures of batters and doughs and the recent developments in the treatment of fats make it difficult to give information about their specific reactions in cookery. The dietitian or foodservice manager should try various types and brands of fats and oils and decide which are best suited for each particular product.

STANDARDS

Accepted standards for products in which fat is an important ingredient or medium of cookery follow.

Emulsions. *Temporary* as in French dressing. Oil and acid with condiments or finely chopped foodstuffs held in suspension; if emulsion breaks dressing is easily reemulsified by agitation. *Permanent* as in mayonnaise: smooth, creamy, semisolid emulsion, stiff enough to hold shape, no evidence of curdling or breaking, golden yellow in color. Mayonnaise with starch base, same as plain mayonnaise but may be lighter in color because of increase in bulk by use of starch gel.

Frying medium. *Pan frying.* All pieces of food evenly browned and fairly crisp, with no evidence of burning or of high grease absorption. *Deep fat frying.* All pieces of food evenly browned, fairly crisp but not hard, no evidence of burning or soaking, characteristic form retained.

Shortening. The standards for foods such as muffins, biscuits, cakes, and pastries which are prepared with fat as a shortening agent, are discussed under flour mixtures.

FOOD GRAINS
CEREAL COOKERY

The objectives of cereal cookery are to soften the cellulose and render it palatable, to retain the distinct form of the cereal, and to change the starch to a more digestible form. Moisture and heat are essential to accomplish these objectives. They soften the cellulose and cause the starch granules to swell and gelatinize. Flavor is thus improved also.

The extent of the mechanical subdivision of cereals will determine the relative amount of water and the length of time required for cooking. A fine, granular cereal may require only a few minutes to reach maximum gelatinization, whereas a whole grain may take several hours.

Cereals in quantity usually are cooked in a steam-jacketed kettle or pressure steam cooker, but they may be prepared in a heavy kettle on top of the range. Rice often is cooked in the oven. Table 4.8 indicates the proportions of cereals of various types to water and salt needed for cooking. Directions for cooking cereal follow.

DIRECTIONS FOR COOKING INCLUDE:

ACCEPTED STANDARDS

INSTITUTION METHOD OF PREPARATION

Breakfast cereals
  Cooked until pasty appearance and taste disappear.
  Just moist enough to retain shape when served into dishes and not flatten or pour.
  Free from lumps.
  Enough salt added to bring out full flavor of the otherwise bland product.
  Served hot.

1. Stir dry cereal into salted boiling water to prevent lumping. Continue stirring as needed to insure even cooking of the mass.
2. Use wire whip to stir, and cook in steam-jacketed kettle, double boiler, open kettle, or steam pressure cooker. Each starch granule must come in contact with the liquid so that swelling is uniform. The opaque suspension of starch must change to a gel before the cereal is cooked and palatable.

Because of the hydrolysis of starch, long-continued cooking of processed cereals further breaks down weakened cell structures of the already cooked grains and produces a sticky, gummy product.

Cereal products such as noodles, macaroni, and spaghetti are dropped into rapidly boiling salted water and cooked briskly until pieces are tender but firm. A small amount of vegetable oil added to the water will keep the product from sticking together. Remove products from container to colander and rinse under running water. Shake well to insure thorough rinsing to remove any excess starch and liquid. Either hot or cold water may be used for rinsing. The use of hot water shortens the time of oven cooking if combined into an item like macaroni and cheese.

Products thickened with flour or other starch such as gravies, white sauces, cream fillings and puddings require special consideration in quantity cooking to yield the desired viscosity and give a

TABLE 4.8　COOKERY OF CEREALS AND CEREAL PRODUCTS

Cereal or Cereal Product	Number of Portions	Amount of Cereal (lb)	Amount of Water (gal)	Amount of Salt (c)	Cooking Time Steam-Jacketed Kettle (min)	Cooking Time Pressure Steam Cooker (min)	Increase in Volume	Size of Portions (oz)
Breakfast cereals								
Corn meal	100	4	4	1/3	45	30	2	5
Cracked wheat— unprocessed	100	5	4	1/3	120	60	3	5
Cream of Wheat and Farina	100	4	4	1/4	20	15	1	5
Grits, hominy	100	5	4	1/4	20	15	1	5
Grits, wheat	100	4	4	1/4	20	15	1	5
Pettijohns	100	6	4	1/3	20	15	2 1/2	5
Rolled oats	100	5	4	1/3	20	15	2 1/2	5
Rice	100	7 1/2	4	1/3	50–60	30–40	3 1/2–4	5
Macaroni and spaghetti [a]	100	6	6	1/2	30	20	2	2 1/2–3
Noodles [a]	100	5	6	1/2	20	15	1	2–2 1/2

[a] Extended with other foods, i.e., sauces and meats.

smooth, homogeneous, opaque gel. A dispersing agent such as fat, sugar, or cold liquid mixed with the starch is necessary to prevent lumping unless instantized flour is used. For a firm gel most starches of ordinary concentrations need to be cooked to a minimum temperature of 90°C (194°F). Preheating the liquid will reduce time required for gelatinization.

Large amounts of sugar as used in certain puddings compete with the starch for the water present and so tend to inhibit the hydration of the starch granules. High concentrations of starch are necessary in such products to obtain the desired viscosity. An acid present in the mixture will weaken the gel also by reducing the size of the starch granules.

Viscosity decreases if the swollen starch granules are broken by continued heating or excessive stirring. Therefore the products should be heated quickly and stirred during the thickening process but discontinued, except to prevent sticking, after the particles are well disbursed. Cooking should be continued until the starch is fully swollen and transparent and the starchy taste is gone.

The size of the batch affects the viscosity of the food because it determines cooking time and amount of stirring necessary. Also, starch-thickened products that are refrigerated until used become stiffer as they cool. Continued storage brings about retrogradation, a change in which the starch becomes less soluble and appears to be precipitating out of the paste. This is due to the presence of amylose in the starch. Griswold [12] says:

Starch retrogradation is a serious problem in freezing certain foods because it causes sauces and gravies to separate and starch gels to be transformed to a pulpy sponge from which water can be squeezed. It can be avoided by the use of waxy starches which do not retrogade in ordinary concentrations because they contain no amylose. Gravies and sauces thickened with starch or flour from a waxy cereal have less tendency to separate on thawing than those made with wheat flour or cornstarch.

The basic proportions of ingredients and directions for making white sauce in quantity are as follows.

	Milk (gal)	Flour (lb)	(c)	Salt (T)	Fat [a] (lb)	Uses
Thin	1	1/4	1	1	1/2	Soup, scalloped potatoes
Medium	1	1/2	2	1	1/2	Creamed and scalloped dishes, gravies
Thick	1	3/4	3	1	1/2	Soufflés, creamed watery vegetables (i.e., celery and onions)
Heavy	1	1	4	1	1/2	Croquettes

Directions:
1. Scald the milk in covered container in a steamer or steam-jacketed kettle or on top of the range.
2. Make a roux of the fat and flour.[b]
3. Add to the heated milk while stirring briskly; continue to stir until mixture is thickened.
4. Continue to cook, stirring only occasionally, until the starch is thoroughly cooked and the desired thickness is obtained.

[a] *Often increased in thick and heavy sauces.*
[b] *An alternative method is to make a paste of the flour and 1/4 of the milk (cold). Add to remainder of hot milk, cook, then add fat. For quantities larger than 1 gallon, 1/4 of the milk may be added to the roux and stirred with a wire whip until smooth; then add this mixture to remainder of the hot milk.*

[12] Ruth M. Griswold, The Experimental Study of Foods, *Houghton Mifflin, Boston, p. 295, 1962.*

Savings in preparation time have been found in the use of a white sauce mix that has a shelf life of about 12 weeks when stored at refrigerator temperature. From the mix, sauces of various consistencies can be prepared.

WHITE SAUCE MIX

Amount	Ingredient	Method
3 lb	Flour	Blend flour and milk in 60-qt mixing bowl
9 lb	Milk, nonfat dry	
4 lb 8 oz	Fat, hydrogenated vegetable	Using pastry knife or flat beater,
4 lb 8 oz	Butter or margarine	blend fats with dry ingredients until mixture is crumbly, scraping down bowl occasionally Store in covered containers in refrigerator

To prepare 1 gal of white sauce, add to 1 gal hot water and 1 1/2 oz salt:
    2 lb 2 oz white sauce mix for thin white sauce
    2 lb 14 oz white sauce mix for medium white sauce
    3 lb 8 oz white sauce mix for thick white sauce

Source. *Sina Faye Fowler, Bessie Brooks West, and Grace S. Shugart,* Food for Fifty, *Fifth Edition, Wiley, New York, 1971.*

FLOUR MIXTURES

One of the criteria by which the success of any institution foodservice is judged is the type and quality of its hot breads, cakes, and pastries. Even today, when a high percentage of these products are prepared from mixes, a wide variety of each type contributes to an interesting menu and to the satisfaction of the guest.

In the preparation of hot breads, cakes, and pastries for institution foodservices, the goal may be said to be the production of foods that are nutritious, attractive in appearance, palatable, reasonable in cost, and so standardized that the quality does not vary from day to day. For those who prepare their own bakery products, the following discussion will be of interest.

Classification. The classification of formulas or recipes for batters and doughs is based on the ratio of flour to liquid.

PROPORTION OF FLOUR TO LIQUID (BY MEASURE)

	Flour	Liquid	Example of Product
Pour batter	1 part	1 part	Popovers, griddle cakes, waffles
Drop batter	2 parts	1 part	Muffins, cornbread, cake
Soft dough	3 parts	1 part	Cookies, biscuits
Stiff dough	4–8 parts	1 part	Yeast breads, pastry

The ratio of flour to liquid affects greatly the character of the mixture. Further variation is produced by the leavening agent, the combination and proportion of eggs, the shortening and sugar, and the kind of flour. A greater amount of baking powder is usually needed for thin batters than for stiffer ones, since the gas is not retained so well in the former and little or no air has been incorporated in the mixing or by the addition of beaten egg whites.

Ingredients. The type and quantity of ingredients affect the characteristics of the product. Basic ingredients in all flour mixtures are flour, a leavening agent, a liquid, flavorings like sugar and salt, and often fat and eggs.

Flour. The baking properties of any flour depend primarily on the grain from which it is milled, the fineness to which it is ground and the processing procedure, the aging to which it has been subjected, and the possible addition of so-called flour improvers. Wheat is usually classified as hard or strong and soft or weak, depending on the variety and protein content. *Bread flour,* with its high protein content, is milled from hard wheat and is suitable for bread making. The gluten that is formed from the protein when mixed with liquid gives strength to the cell structure of the dough, an important factor in making yeast bread and rolls. For muffins, cakes, and pastries the development of gluten strength in excess of that needed to carry the other ingredients is undesirable. *All purpose flour* is milled from a blend of wheats, usually both hard and soft, and is lower in protein content than bread flour. It is suitable for most products. *Cake flour* is made from soft wheat, has a low protein content, and has a fine uniform granulation. Cakes made with this type of flour generally have better volume and texture than those made with all purpose flour. *Pastry flour* generally is made from soft wheat and has properties between those of all purpose and cake flours and is designed for making pastries, cookies, and similar baked products.

Many foodservices, especially small operations, find it impractical to purchase and store more than one kind of flour; hence, all purpose may be the only flour used. Where cakes are baked on the premises and mixes are not used, however, cake flour often is purchased for this purpose.

Leavening. The leavening of flour mixtures is accomplished by the expansion of incorporated air, production of steam, or the generation of carbon dioxide. Air is incorporated by creaming, folding, and beating the mixture, or by the addition of air in beaten egg yolks or whites. Steam is produced when the ratio of liquid to flour is high, such as in thin batters, and when the oven temperature is high so that the liquid is heated quickly and the steam formed before the structure is set. Carbon dioxide, formed by the reaction of certain ingredients in the recipe, such as yeast and sugar, baking powder and the liquid, baking soda with an acid ingredient like chocolate, molasses, or sour milk, and on application of heat in some cases, causes the product to expand. By far the greater part of leavening is accomplished through baking powders.

Baking powders are composed of an acid, an alkali (sodium bicarbonate), and a starch filler. The classification of baking powders depends on the kind of acid employed to neutralize the sodium bicarbonate. A single acid such as cream of tartar, tartaric acid, or calcium acid phosphate or a double acid such as sodium aluminum sulfate are those commonly combined with the sodium bicarbonate. The three main types of baking powder are designated by these acids.

All baking powders have the capacity to liberate approximately the same amount of gas, but this process occurs at different rates. The tartrate powders liberate a large part of their available gas as soon as moistened, the phosphate somewhat less, and the combination powders very little. Quick mixing and immediate baking in a hot oven are necessary to obtain the best results from tartrate and phosphate baking powders. It is estimated that only 20 to 30 percent of the gas liberated from these baking powders during mixing is retained in the dough. In the combination powders the monocalcium phosphate alone is responsible for the liberation of carbon dioxide before baking, the sodium aluminum sulphate reacting slowly at low temperature. In the higher temperature of the oven the sodium aluminum sulfate liberates its portion of carbon dioxide. This delayed action of the combination powder makes it most satisfactory for institution cookery, since its use permits the making of muffin or cake batter sometime in advance of baking. Also, it is commonly stated that a smaller quantity of combination powder is necessary under ordinary conditions, approximately one third less being recommended. The temperature of the ovens into which the combination-leavened products are placed should be lower in order to obtain a complete expansion of the batter or dough before coagulation takes place. A baking powder containing sodium acid pyrophosphate is commonly used in mixes and by bakers.

Liquid. A liquid in the correct amount is essential for gelatinization of starch, development of gluten, and the reaction of the leavening agent. Milk is the most commonly used liquid, because it adds flavor and nutritive value. In quantity production, nonfat dry milk is often used, since it incorporates easily with the dry ingredients, is low in cost, and water is added as the liquid. Sour milk may be used with baking soda to neutralize it. Other liquids such as fruit juices are sometimes used to give variation in products, although substitution of one type of liquid for another is not possible without adjusting the whole recipe.

Fats. Fats play an important part in the characteristics of baked products, to give tenderness and flavor and improve keeping qualities. The shortening for flour mixtures should be a fat with a pleasing flavor and color and a wide range of plasticity. Fats commonly used for shortening may be of vegetable or animal origin or a combination of the two. Most hydrogenated fats lend themselves satisfactorily to this type of cookery.

The addition of emulsifiers to hydrogenated fats has improved the qualities of the fat for making of cakes. Vail[13] states:

> *The emulsifiers help in distributing the ingredients evenly throughout the batter and in retaining air by reducing the size and increasing the number of air cells in the batter. This helps to produce a cake with fine even grain. Butter and margarine are not quite so good as those of hydrogenated fats that contain emulsifiers. Neither lard nor vegetable oils hold air well in cake batters. They can, however, be used for cakes if air is incorporated by folding into the batter eggs or egg whites beaten with or without sugar. Before fats containing emulsifiers were available, the weights of flour and sugar in cakes were approximately equal. . . . The use of emulsifiers has made possible "high ratio" cakes that contain higher proportions of sugar than cakes made from shortenings without emulsifiers.*

[13] *Gladys E. Vail, Jean A. Phillips, Ruth M. Griswold, Margaret M. Justin, and Lucille Osborn Rust,* Foods, *Sixth Edition, Houghton Mifflin, Boston, p. 324, 1973.*

Eggs. Eggs are used in flour mixtures principally for color, shortening action, flavor, and nutritive value, although in thin batters they are also helpful in retaining the leavening agent. In cakes egg white acts as a binder of other ingredients and, when beaten, incorporates considerable air to the flour mixture. Egg yolk tends at act as an emulsifier, separating the mass into smaller particles that influence the texture favorably. Eggs break down the gluten strength of flour, causing cell walls in the mixture to become thinner and the baked product to become more tender.

Egg whites beaten at room temperature give a larger volume than those beaten at refrigerator temperature. Egg whites are stabilized by the addition of an acid such as cream of tartar, which is especially effective. The use of the acid improves quality and volume of cakes in which egg white is a major ingredient.

Frozen eggs are a satisfactory substitute for shell eggs in the making of bakery products, and they save much time and labor. However, time must be allowed for their complete thawing before incorporation into a mixture. It has been found that eggs defrosted fairly quickly under cold running water produce more satisfactory products than those defrosted for a longer period of time. Frozen egg whites defrost in approximately one half the time required for either yolks or whole eggs.

If dry egg powder is to be used it may be reconstituted by the addition of the stipulated amount of water, or it may be added to the mixture in the dry form. The dry powder is sifted either with the sugar or the flour, and enough water to provide the equivalent moisture content of fresh eggs is added to the liquid.

Ratio of Ingredients. The flour and its capacity to absorb moisture must be considered in determining the ratio of liquid to flour, and because of this variability of absorption of different flours, the consistency of the batter or dough must be left to the judgment of the baker. His problem is to take the flour furnished to him and, by regulating the ratios of other ingredients, balance them to give the best product. Richards [14] described a satisfactory ratio of the ingredients for cakes that is applicable today.

It is impossible to make positive statements on balance without careful consideration of variables in individual formulas. The flour must be close to an average soft flour, not too hard nor too soft. All ingredients must be con-

[14] *Paul Richards,* Cakes for Bakers, *Revised Fourth Edition, Bakers' Helper Company, Chicago, p. 12, 1932.*

sidered on an average basis. To consider just what is necessary for a properly balanced white layer formula (while there is no rule that does not have a few exceptions): (1) The weight of the sugar should not exceed the flour weight. (2) Liquid ingredients (milk and eggs) should equal the weight of flour. (3) Amount of egg whites should equal weight of shortening or slightly more. (4) Shortening should equal 50% of sugar weight. (5) Leavening. Since shortening will carry twice its own weight in sugar and eggs will carry their own weight in flour or sugar, for all ingredients added above this leavening agents must be supplied. Slight variations above or below these amounts are not harmful.

Sponge cakes differ markedly from cakes made with fat. In determining proportions it must be recognized that eggs are the foundation of sponge cakes and that fat is not added. The relationships established between the eggs, sugar, and flour are discussed later in this chapter.

Methods of Combining Ingredients. The methods used in combining constituents in all types of flour mixtures are important. Uniform distribution of all ingredients, particularly of the fat and liquid with the flour mixture, is essential in making batters and doughs. Also, the loss of carbon dioxide must be kept at a minimum. The poor emulsion formed by the combination of a fat and water increases the problem of obtaining a uniform distribution of the fat particles with the mixture. A melted fat added to the mixture may coat the particles with fairly large globules. Products so made are most satisfactory if consumed as soon as baked. Hard fats are more often mixed with the dry ingredients, as in the making of pastry, biscuits, or shortened cake.

Muffin Method. The muffin method of combining is ordinarily used for griddlecakes, waffles, muffins, and their variations. This method requires quick work and an avoidance of overmixing. In quantity production, exact timing and the use of low speed of the mixer is recommended to avoid overmixing. The batter may be lumpy, but such a condition is normal. This type of batter breaks, separates easily when lifted with a spoon. With as little agitation as possible muffin batter should be dipped into the muffin pans as soon as mixed. The use of an ice cream dipper for this purpose insures muffins of uniform size, prevents "stretching" the gluten strands in the batter by cutting it off, and is faster than dipping with a spoon.

Muffin batter swells to approximately twice its original volume in baking. A good muffin has a pebbly, rounded top, a tender golden-brown crust, and uniform medium fine texture, with no tunnels.

Muffins are baked at 375°F for 15 to 18 minutes or until golden brown.

Biscuit Method. In the biscuit method the dry ingredients are mixed in the bowl of the mixing machine; the fat is added and cut into the dry ingredients at low speed, using the pastry cutter or flat beater. Liquid is added all at once, and the mass is mixed until it adheres firmly together. The length of time of mixing is again important but, in this method, unlike the muffin procedure, undermixing must be avoided.

Biscuit dough should be light and soft but not sticky. The biscuits will tend to be smoother and finer in texture if kneaded lightly 10 to 20 times before they are rolled and cut. This kneading combines the ingredients more thoroughly than by stirring alone. After the mass of dough has been kneaded, it is rolled lightly to the desired thickness and cut with a floured cutter, and the biscuits are placed on an unoiled baking sheet. If biscuits with crusty sides are desired, they are placed far apart on the baking sheet; otherwise they are put close together. Biscuits are baked at a temperature of 425°F for 12 to 15 minutes or until the crust is evenly browned and the inside is flaky, light, and dry. The biscuits should be regular in shape with vertical sides and fairly smooth, level tops and should have tender golden-brown crusts. The thickness should be about twice that of the unbaked biscuit. The fine flaky texture is light and fluffy, and long, thin layers can be peeled off when the biscuit is broken open.

Cake Methods. The usual methods for combining ingredients for cakes containing fat are the conventional, or sugar-batter, dough-batter, and muffin methods. The *conventional* method of combining ingredients for shortened cakes consists of creaming the fat and sugar and adding the beaten eggs and then the sifted dry ingredients alternately with liquid. Best results are obtained when the fat and sugar are thoroughly creamed and the dry ingredients are well mixed before being added to the creamed fat and sugar.

The *dough-batter* method of making shortened cakes is used successfully in quantity production. This quick-mix or one-bowl method became popular with the common usage of hydrogenated fats to which an emulsifier had been added, thus eliminating the necessity for the creaming of the fat and sugar. Such fats could carry a high ratio of sugar to fat, producing a sweet, fine-textured cake. This method requires little time, few utensils, is easy to follow through, and yields a highly desirable product. The finished cake tends to be slightly smaller than those made by some other methods, but the uniformity of the cells is quite marked and the velvety texture is an outstanding characteristic.

A detailed procedure of this method follows:

Cream fat, flour, and baking powder 2 min, low speed.

Scrape the bowl.

Continue to mix 3 min.

Add sugar, salt, and 2/5 milk.

Mix 2 min, low speed.

Scrape the bowl.

Continue to mix 3 min.

Add egg and vanilla to remaining milk, and add 1/2 this mixture to bowl. Mix 30 sec.

Scrape the bowl.

Mix 1 min.

Add remaining milk-egg-vanilla.

Mix 1 min.

Scrape the bowl.

Mix 2 1/2 min.

A modification of this method, in which the baking powder is added after the flour and fat are creamed, is also satisfactory for use in quantity cake making. This method is widely used by commercial bakers. It yields a product similar to the dough-batter method.

Adding the baking powder to the beaten egg white and incorporating this in the final step of mixing gives cakes of high quality in both series. However, this method requires more time and effort in mixing, and there is greater chance for variation in manipulation than in the dough-batter method or the modified dough-batter method.

The more expensive cakes consistently score higher than the inexpensive cakes regardless of the method used. This seems to indicate that the problem of mixing, in order to obtain a satisfactory cake, is greater for an inexpensive cake than for a more expensive cake which contains a higher proportion of fat and egg.

The *muffin method* of combining ingredients may also be followed in making cakes. A detailed discussion of this procedure is found under muffins. This method is quick and most successful if the cake is to be used soon after baking.

Much of the success of the cake depends on the length of time of mixing. This time may vary with the quantity mixed but, for the usual institution formulas, 5 minutes is the common allowance. The amount of cake batter that can be mixed successfully at one time depends on the size of the mixer bowl, provided the formula is balanced and the correct mixing techniques are used. In addition, a suitable amount of batter in the pans, correct baking temperature, and even distritution of heat in the oven also contribute to the quality of the baked cake.

A good shortened cake is uniform in thickness and attractive in appearance. The crust is delicate brown, tender, thin, and daintily crisp with no cracks. The cake should be light, tender, and agreeably moist, but not sticky. It should have an even, fine-grained texture and a delicate, well-blended flavor. An excellent shortened cake has the characteristic commonly spoken of as "velvetiness," meaning that to the tongue or fingers it feels like soft velvet. A cake with this characteristic is always light and has a fine, even grain, but these qualities do not ensure the velvety feeling.

The methods used for mixing angel food and sponge cakes are essentially the same. The problem is to get the beaten egg whites well mixed with the other ingredients without liberating the air in the beaten whites. If the air is lost the cake will be heavy and compact, since leavening depends on the expansion of air. If the egg whites are not well blended with the other ingredients the cake will be coarse and uneven in texture. This thorough combining of ingredients without loss of air requires much mixing with gentle movements.

In combining the ingredients for angel food cake, good results are obtained if the salt and cream of tartar are added to the egg whites, which have been beaten until frothy and if the mixture is beaten until the egg whites are stiff but not dry. The best results will be obtained if egg whites are at room temperature at the time of beating instead of just out of the refrigerator. The sugar may be beaten in gradually and the flour folded in lightly. Sponge cakes may be made in similar manner with the addition of beaten egg yolks. This type of cake is baked in floured, ungreased pans in a slow to moderate oven for 45 to 60 minutes.

A good cake without fat is uniform in size and, in shape, has a flat or slightly rounded top. It is light, tender, and evenly fine grained. The crust is tender, thin, and delicately colored. The flavor is pleasing and well blended. Chiffon cake is a sponge type that includes oil. It is more open in texture than an all-egg sponge cake.

Pastry Method. The pastry method used for pie crust and other pastry is similar to the biscuit method. However, the proportion of fat to flour is much higher in pastry, which necessitates greater care in mixing. The fat must be divided into particles evenly distributed throughout the flour. Overmixing causes the fat to surround the flour and prevent it from taking up water necessary to bind the pastry together.

Pie crust is a relatively simple mixture, because the ingredients consist of only flour, shortening, salt, water, and sometimes sugar or baking powder, but the success or failure of the baker to meet the standards for good pie crust depends on the quality and temperature of these ingredients, their ratio to each other, and the method of mixing them.

The ingredients, in the proportion commonly used in large quantity preparation, are:

100 pounds of flour.

70–75 pounds of shortening.

30 pounds of (15 quarts of) water.

3 1/2 pounds of salt.

Some bakers prefer to use almost equal parts (by weight) of flour and shortening.

The all purpose flour is commonly used for pie crust, although there is on the market what is termed a "pastry flour," made from soft winter wheat, with low protein and ash content. Bread flour with the high gluten content important in making yeast bread is unsuited to making good pie dough.

The fat or shortening determines in part not only the character of the dough but also its flavor. A stable fat of a consistency to blend easily with the other ingredients and bland in flavor is preferred for this purpose. The choice between hydrogenated oils and lard is often based on the cost factor. Under certain conditions, local or national in scope, one fat or the other may be purchased for several cents a pound less than the other, equally good fat. Obviously, under such conditions, the less expensive product should be selected, and any changes necessary in the manipulations of the dough should be carefully checked by the baker. Butter and margarine are not often used for plain pastry because they are less plastic and produce less tender pastry than hydrogenated fats or lard.

The quantity of salt should be proportionate to the weight of the batch of dough instead of to the weight of flour used in the recipe. A satisfactory ratio of salt to dough is approximately 0.3 ounce of salt to each pound of dough. Best results are obtained when the salt is dissolved in the water instead of being mixed with the flour.

Water used in pie dough serves as a binder. The dough that has excess moisture is well bound, not tender; the dough that has too little water is too lightly bound and crumbles readily. The ability of water to bind dough is determined by both the quantity present and the method of mixing. If the flour and fat have been well mixed, the flour containing the gluten is sealed away from the water, and toughness cannot develop.

Strause [15] emphasizes the importance of the quantity of water and the method of mixing to get the best results.

The ingredient directly responsible for the tenderness of your pie crust is the water, for it is not the actual mixing of the shortening and flour which causes the toughness in our pie crust. It is when the water comes in contact with the flour that toughness starts to develop.

Of course, it goes without saying that your dough must contain the proper proportion of shortening, and I do not mean to infer that the mixing of the shortening and flour is not important. Quite the contrary—for if they are only partially mixed together, leaving live flour spots in the dough (that is, flour spots which are not entirely incorporated with the shortening), then development will start just as soon as the water and salt are added. The water immediately takes hold in these flour spots and develops the gluten in

[15] *Monroe Boston Strause,* Pie Marches On, *Second Edition, Ahrens, New York, pp. 13-15, 1951.*

that part of the dough. The more live flour spots, the more development takes place, and regardless of the amount of shortening used, a certain toughness will be evident. . . . .

The less the shortening and flour are mixed, the more water the dough will take, and many bakers in trying to obtain additional poundage, make this mistake, not realizing that too much moisture is the very reason their pie dough shrinks, does not bake well and is hard to brown. On the other hand, the more thoroughly the shortening and flour are blended, the less water the dough wil take up, and the shorter and more tender the crust will be. This is the reason why one pie dough may be tough and another almost too tender to handle, in spite of the fact that both utilize the same amount of shortening.

The method of mixing pie dough depends on the materials used, the quantity to be mixed at one time, the equipment available, and the type of crust desired. In any case, the usual procedure is to blend the fat and flour and add the water, in which the salt has been dissolved.

High-protein flour requires more thorough mixing than if the flour is soft. The temperature regarded as desirable for a fat during mixing depends on the type of fat. A soft-bodied fat is best used at a temperature of 60 to 65°F and a firm-bodied fat is best used at a temperature of 70 to 75°F. The baker who makes pie dough for a day's supply in a relatively small institution may prefer to mix the ingredients by hand; other bakers, because of the large quantity of dough made, must mix the ingredients in an electric mixer. An entirely satisfactory product may be made in a machine if a relatively weak flour is selected, if the special wire pastry-blender attachment is used, and if the machine is run at low speed and timed carefully to avoid overmixing.

The type of pie crust is determined by the method of combining the ingredients and modifying slightly the amount of water in a basic recipe. The types are known as *short flaky, mealy,* and *flaky* or *long flaky,* and are characteristic of their names.

Short flaky pie crust is produced when a dough is made by cutting or rubbing the fat into the flour until all flour spots are broken, but not until pasty. The full amount of water is added, and the mixing is continued until the mass holds together. The result will be a tender crust with small flakes, because of the coating of fat on the particles of starch which prevents the development of gluten. Also, the high water content will permit some oven expansion. Some bakers prefer to modify this method by combining half the fat with all the flour to a fine crumb, and then adding the remainder of fat and mixing only until it has been broken down to lumps about the size of a pea. This mass should be mixed only long enough to combine lightly after the water has been added.

Mealy pie crust is made by mixing the fat and flour quite thoroughly, then adding approximately 1/6 less water than listed in a basic recipe. A modification of this method is to combine all the fat with half the flour and then work in the remainder of the flour before adding the water.

Long flaky pie crust requires quick careful handling and chilling for several hours before using. The fat and flour are combined lightly, leaving chunks of fat 1/3 to 1/2 inch in diameter. Approximately twice as much water is needed for this type of crust as for the mealy crust, and it should be mixed only a few turns. It can be smoothed out on a flat pan for chilling. Overmixing after the water is added toughens this type of dough because much of the flour is free to combine with the water and thus form gluten. This type of crust is best suited for use as tops on fruit pies or as baked shells for cream pies.

Approximately 6 ounces of dough are necessary for each 9-inch pie shell or crust. Some bakers prefer to use 7 ounces of dough for the bottom crust and 5 or 5 1/2 ounces for the top crust. For hand rolling the scaled dough is worked slightly to shape it into a round mass, then rolled on a lightly floured board or pastry cloth to an even thickness. Roll from the center out in all directions without turning it over; or it may be given a few quick up and down strokes perpendicular to the edge of the table and the elongated piece of dough, just long enough for the pan, turned over and at right angles to the previous position. A few more up and down strokes will make it the exact shape and size for the pan. There should be few if any trimmings. Mechanical pie-crust rollers are used in most large institution kitchens with great saving of time and human effort (Fig. 4.7). The dough, scaled and shaped as for hand rolling, goes through two sets of rollers. The first elongates the piece of dough, which is rounded by the second set.

A shell for a one-crust pie, in which several very small holes have been made to release the steam, is baked either on the inside or outside of the pan for approximately 10 to 15 minutes at a temperature of about 450°F. Some bakers prefer to bake the shells between two pans at a temperature of 500°F. Care should be taken not to stretch the dough too tightly over the bottom of the pan, or the resulting crust will be smaller than desired. The cooked filling is poured into the baked crusts. If covered with a meringue, the pie is baked for 10 to 12 minutes at 375°F.

FIGURE 4.7   The use of mechanical pie-crust roller saves time and energy of employees. Note pastry table with special edge treatment to prevent flour falling onto the floor. Kuennings, Columbus. Courtesy, Ohio State Restaurant Association.

Two-crust pies are made by lining the pan with a layer of dough, usually filling with a sweetened raw, cooked, or frozen tart fruit, thickened slightly with corn or waxy maize starch, tapioca, or flour. The waxy maize thickens at a relatively low temperature and, on cooling, retains a consistency similar to that which it was when hot. Cover with a second crust and seal by moistening the edge of the bottom layer of crust and pressing the edges of the two layers together. If the top crust has been cut 1 inch larger than the pan, it can be folded over and under the edge of the lower crust. When the edge so prepared is pressed with a fork or fluted with fingers, the pie is completely sealed, so that the juices tend to be retained in it throughout the baking period. Pie tape, carefully placed to bind the two edges of the crusts, will seal them together to conserve the juice, also. However, this procedure is not feasible in institutions where preparation time is an important factor. A small fold across the center of the top crust allows for shrinkage, and several perforations permit the escape of steam from within the pie.

The temperature at which filled pies are baked depends on the filling. They may be placed in a hot oven so that the lower crust will begin to bake before the filling has soaked into it. The baking is then continued at a lower temperature; for example, to bake fresh apple and rhubarb pies, the temperature range might be 400 to 450°F for a 10-minute period, followed by a 40- to 50-minute baking period for apple and a 20- to 25-minute period for rhubarb at 300 to 350°F. A more common practice in quantity pie production is to bake fruit pies at a constant temperature of 425°F. This makes it possible for the crust to bake before the filling boils to cause sogginess of the bottom crust or spillage onto the oven floor. In all fresh-fruit pies the length of the baking period depends on the time necessary to insure tenderness of the fruit.

The following are given as possible causes for difficulties encountered in pie making.[16]

1. Shrinkage of crust.
   a. Not enough shortening used.
   b. Not coating all the flour with shortening.
   c. Hard shortening, hard to coat flour.
   d. Excess water used.
   e. Too strong a flour.
   f. Overmixing.
2. Soakage of bottom crust.
   a. Crust too rich or excess shortening.
   b. Lack of bottom heat.
   c. Too sweet a filling.
   d. Pies taken from oven before baked.
   e. Pies filled with hot filling.
3. Boiling out of fruit.
   a. Oven too cool.
   b. Excess acidity in filling.
   c. Hot filling used in making the pies.
   d. Not enough thickening agent used.
   e. Lack of holes in top crust for vapor to escape.
4. Sticking to pans.
   a. Dirty tins.
   b. Moisture on pans.
   c. Lack of bottom heat.
   d. Excess bottom heat.
   e. Boiling over.
   f. Break in bottom crust.

---

[16] *Information furnished by the Bakery Research Department, Wilson and Company, Chicago.*

5. Watery custard pies.
   a. Hot oven or excessive baking time.
   b. Excessive sugar in filling.
6. Watery meringue.
   a. Egg whites not whipped light enough.
   b. Not right percentage of sugar, 3 pounds per quart of whites.
   c. Watery whites.
   d. Baked in cool oven.

Individual tarts are made in a way similar to the single shells, being shaped and baked over the bottom or inside of muffin pans or ramekins. Cheese straws are made by sprinkling grated cheese and paprika over thinly rolled dough, which is folded over, sprinkled a second time with cheese, and rolled again until the desired amount of cheese is incorporated. The dough is cut into suitable shapes and baked. Puff paste is richer in fat than regular flaky pie paste because of the addition of butter or a substitute on each layer before it is folded and rolled.

Appearance, texture, and flavor are the qualities on which the finished products of batters and doughs are judged. These qualities are determined largely by the ingredients used and the amount of each, the method followed in combining them, the temperature at which they are combined, the length of time they are mixed, and the temperature at which they are cooked. Variations in the proportions of the ingredients will produce a proportionate number of variations in the finished products. Frequent evaluation of these products is necessary to ensure the maintenance of quality standards.

Preprepared Mixes. Although many foodservice managers purchase baking mixes, some prefer to make their own basic mix. The use of these preprepared mixes in quantity food production is conducive to the economical utilization of workers' time and effort and to the standardization of products. Ingredients for a basic mix can be weighed and assembled in slack work periods and made ready for scheduled and emergency use. Some managers find it advantageous to package the mix in labeled cellophane bags or covered metal containers in the quantity needed for one recipe of muffins, cake, cookies, or biscuits instead of storing it in bulk. Thus the time needed for the actual preparation of a given product is greatly reduced, since usually only the liquid ingredients need to be added. Also, one reliable person can be made responsible for the weighing of ingredients, which eliminates many of the human factors and inaccuracies. One formula for such a mix developed at Purdue University some time ago is shown in the following table.[17]

| Ingredients | Quantity | |
	Weight	Measure
Flour	25 lb	25 qt
Baking powder	1 lb 4 oz	3 3/4 c
Salt	8 oz	3/4 c
Cream of tartar	2 1/2 oz	2/3 c
Sugar	10 oz	1 1/4 c
Shortening [a]	10 lb	5 1/2 qt

Directions for mixing: Stir the flour, baking powder, salt, cream of tartar, and sugar until blended. Sift three times. Turn into the mixing bowl of a large mixer. Cut the fat into six or eight portions and put on top of dry ingredients. Use the flat paddle to blend the ingredients. Start mixer on "low" speed. Mix 45 seconds. Scrape. Mix 45 additional seconds. The mix should now be well blended and somewhat like cornmeal in consistency.

[a] *Shortening which does not require refrigeration.*

A master mix can be adapted for use in products that have similar basic proportions by modifying recipes to include the mix instead of the dry ingredients and the fat. The mix is flexible and can be used for biscuits, muffins, cakes, and cookies, and can also be adapted to other types of baked goods. The amount of shortening included in the mix should approach the upper limit advisable for such products as biscuits and muffins and the lower limit for cakes and cookies.

Baking Pans. The size, shape, and type of material of the baking pans definitely affect the quality of flour mixes.

During baking, factors that make heat penetration faster often improve cake quality. For this reason cakes baked in shallow pans tend to be superior to those baked in deeper pans. Heat penetration is more rapid in pans with

[17] *Edith Kirkpatrick and Gertrude Sunderlin, "The Master Mix in Quantity,"* Journal of the American Dietetic Association, 25, *54 (1949).*

dark color and/or a dull finish than in pans with bright surfaces that reflect heat.[18]

Products baked in pans with a dark color or dull finish generally have a larger volume and better crumb quality than those baked in pans with shiny surfaces, but the center tends to be more rounded. Cakes baked in tinned steel and aluminum pans have been found to be comparable in size and quality, but a longer time for baking is required with the aluminum. Glass pans produce a cake with slightly darker crust, but their use in most institutions would be impractical because of their weight, breakability, and the amount of storage space required. Aluminum baking sheets with low sides produce the most nearly standard cookies.

Wheeler [19] investigated the effect of the use of baking pans made of two slow-baking materials, stainless steel and aluminum, on the time and rate of baking cornbread in quantity. Pans of the same size and gauge and an oven temperature of 350°F and 400°F were used. The aluminum pan at the 350°F temperature gave the best volume and grain, although the time for cooking was greater. That baked at 400°F in aluminum gave poorest quality. Cornbread baked in stainless steel pans at both temperatures resulted in a product that ranked between the two extremes of aluminum.

Vail et al.[20] state that "shallow pans produce larger and more tender cakes with flatter tops than do deep pans. In deep pans, the batter near the sides of the pan becomes firm during the early part of the baking period, and the softer center of the batter expands to form a humped crust that usually shows a crack." Too large a pan allows the batter to spread so thin that excessive browning results. Aluminum pans that are shallow and not shiny on the outside are a good choice. A baking sheet 18 x 26 inches and 1 1/2 inches deep with straight sides is a frequently used size for cakes, cookies, and some quick breads. Some foodservices use baking pans 12 x 18 inches or 12 x 20 inches, with 2 1/2- to 3-inch sides. Since these

[18] *Ruth M. Griswold*, The Experimental Study of Foods, *Houghton Mifflin, Boston, p. 439, 1962.*

[19] *Madelyn L. Wheeler, "A Comparison of Certain Qualities of Cornbread Baked in Stainless Steel and Aluminum Pans at Two Oven Temperatures," unpublished Master's Thesis, The Ohio State University, 1961.*

[20] *Gladys E. Vail, Jean A. Phillips, Lucile Osborn Rust, Ruth M. Griswold, and Margaret M. Justin,* Foods, *Sixth Edition, Houghton Mifflin, Boston, p. 328, 1973.*

pans are deeper than the 18 x 26 baking sheets, special attention must be given to the amount of batter in the pans. Recipes should be standardized for the pan sizes in use and the weight of the batter for each pan indicated on the recipe. Loaf pans for pound cakes and quick breads and tube pans for foam cakes vary in size and should be selected according to the size serving desired.

BEVERAGES AND FOOD ADJUNCTS

The enjoyment and satisfactions of eating often depend in part on that "perfect" cup of coffee as an accompaniment to the main menu items, or to the seasonings or flavorings used in the preparation of foods to enhance or accent their natural flavors.

BEVERAGE PREPARATION

Certain conditions common to the preparation of both tea and coffee are necessary for the attainment of a highly acceptable product. Both beverages are infusions and, as such, require boiling water to begin with, but water must be *below the boiling point* thereafter to favor optimum infusion of the volatile oils. Freshly boiling water free from excessive mineral content should be used. If the hot-water supply in the institution is softened, use cold water and heat. All equipment should be absolutely clean, and nonmetallic unless of stainless steel. Accurate measurements of the tea or coffee and water are necessary and, once determined, the same proportions should be used each time the beverage is made. Serve immediately after making in preheated cups so it will be piping hot when received by the guest.

Coffee. The best coffee may be ruined in the making. In institution foodservice it is better to make coffee often and in small quantities than to make it in a large quantity and let it stand indefinitely. There are several methods of brewing coffee, any of which may be successful if correctly done.

In addition to conditions previously given, a blend of coffee pleasing to the clientele and of the correct grind for the type of coffee maker must be selected. The proportion of 1 pound of coffee to 2 or 2 1/2 gallons of water usually gives the most desirable strength. Best results are obtained when full capacity of the coffee maker is used, and never should it be less than two thirds full. Once made, coffee should not be allowed to boil; under such conditions oxides are precipitated that change the flavor, make the coffee bitter, and increase the extraction of caffeine. Coffee needs to be served immediately after it is made, since reheating melts the waxy, resinous, insoluble fats of the ground bean into the brew, making it less palatable.

A brew of double strength for iced coffee is best made by using half the amount of water to the usual amount of ground coffee. Doubling the usual amount of ground coffee and using the same amount of water causes underextraction and overflowing of the coffee basket.

The accepted standards for coffee are: a clear, dark amber liquid free from sediment and bitterness, a pleasant aroma, and steaming hot when served. Reactions and comments by the clientele are the basis for determining quality acceptance in most foodservices.

Coffee makers for institution use are of three general types: the urn for large batches, the automatic brewer for frequent smaller batches, and the vacuum maker that brews a small decanter of coffee at a time. Frozen concentrated coffee is now available. A dispenser proportions a mixture of coffee concentrate and hot water as each cup or decanter is drawn. The type of coffee maker selected will be determined by the serving problems of a specific foodservice operation. Directions for use of the coffee maker could well be posted near it so that the employee responsible for making the coffee will have a constant reference to the procedure to be followed. Proper supervision of the workers will do much to ensure good quality coffee in a foodservice.

Tea. Tea contains little or no food value, and so, like coffee, its consumption depends on the flavor and refreshing, stimulating effect. Accepted standards for tea are: clear, mild in flavor, and free from leaves.

Tea is never boiled. Freshly boiling water is poured over the tea leaves in a scalded and heated earthenware, china, or glass jar, and the infusion is covered and allowed to steep from 3 to 5 minutes, the time depending on the desired strength of the infusion. The infusion is then decanted, and the tea is ready to serve immediately. A practice commonly followed in institutions is the use of individual tea bags, each of which contains enough tea for making 1 or 2 cups. The guest removes the tea bag from his cup or teapot when the beverage has reached the preferred strength.

A tea-making machine is now available in which powdered tea combines with freshly boiled water in the machine, and a cup of hot, fresh tea is dispensed at the touch of a lever. This has become a standard piece of equipment especially in self-service units.

Iced tea is a popular summer beverage. Usually a special blend of green and black tea is used, although the usual hot-tea blends may be acceptable for this purpose. Tea bags for making 1 or 2 gallons of infusion for iced tea are commonly used in institutions to save the time of measuring or weighing bulk tea. Their use also ensures a much more standard product. The recommended proportions for making iced tea are one 2-ounce bag of tea to each gallon of freshly boiling water. Steep 6 to 10 minutes and serve in well-filled glasses of chipped ice. One-half ounce of instant tea may be substituted for the 2-ounce tea bag.

Cocoa and Chocolate. Although cocoa and chocolate are used in institution foodservices for other purposes as well as for beverages, their importance as beverages is great enough to merit their consideration along with tea and coffee. The accepted standard for cocoa or chocolate beverage is a thoroughly homogenized mixture free from sediment, rich brown in color, glossy, and not bitter. The making of beverages from cocoa and chocolate involves the incorporation of the whole substance instead of the infusion of part, as in tea and coffee.

Cocoa and chocolate contain appreciable amounts of carbohydrate and fats and must be cooked so as to ensure even dispersion of starch particles and the freeing of essential oils. Cocoa or melted chocolate is combined with sugar and enough hot water to make a thin paste, which is cooked until thick and glossy. The cooked mixture is added to heated milk, beaten briskly for thorough mixing, and seasoned with salt and vanilla if desired. Cocoa and chocolate may be kept hot or reheated without great deterioration. For such a purpose a double boiler or steamer, not direct heat, should be used. Frequent stirring or whipping is necessary to prevent the formation of a thin skin over the top of the cocoa or the settling out of solids in the bottom of the kettle. Cocoa or chocolate may be stored for serving in a hot counter insert, an insulated jug, or a heated urn. Individual packets of instant cocoa are available where the demand for cocoa is irregular.

FOOD ADJUNCTS

The term "food adjuncts" is given to the substances used in the preparation of foods to enhance or accent their natural flavors or impart a special taste. In most cases essential or volatile oils are responsible for the aromatic or savory qualities that make these substances popular for flavoring and seasoning. These essential oils are made available for use in food preparation as flavoring, spices and herbs, condiments, and other seasonings.

Flavorings. The palatability and enjoyment of many foods, particularly bakery products, ice creams, and other desserts, depend on the addition of some type of flavoring during their preparation.

A good quality flavoring extract from natural sources is often difficult to obtain and high in price. Hence, although such extracts are preferred, it is sometimes necessary to accept as alternates the synthetic flavorings available—for example, vanilla, maple, and lemon.

Some fruits and fruit juices may advantageously replace flavoring extracts. Lemons and oranges are perhaps the most commonly employed for this purpose. Their use gives a desirable flavor and adds somewhat to the food value of the product.

The addition of flavoring extracts that are alcoholic solutions of volatile oils should be made as late in the preparation of food as possible to insure that the flavoring is not volatilized. Flavoring extracts are concentrates and should be used as such if desired effects are to be obtained. Each shipment should be tested for strength and used accordingly. Often smaller amounts of strong extracts than are called for in a recipe can be used, and a saving will be effected. Long-continued cooking of food following the addition of flavorings or vinegar tends to drive off the characteristic taste and odor and results in a somewhat flat product.

Spices and Herbs. A wide field for experimentation is open in American cookery for use of spices that have wide acceptance in other lands, some of which may be regarded as exotic. In addition to the large number of individual spices, several mixtures blended to meet seasoning needs in the preparation of certain dishes—for instance, pumpkin pie spice, seasoned salts, barbecue sauce seasoning, and poultry seasoning are available. Among newer developments in the spice industry are dehydrated vegetable seasonings such as onion, garlic, mint, parsley, peppers, and mixed vegetables, usually in flake form. These are labor savers, because they do not require reconstituting before use in most recipes.

Spices are parts of plants in which the volatile or essential oils are held enmeshed in the dried plant tissue (Table 4.9). It is these essential oils that make them desirable for imparting aromatic or savory seasoning to foods. Application of moisture and heat for an effective period of time facilitates release of the oils and thus makes possible the imparting of flavor and aroma of the spice to the food mass. Because they are usually purchased in the dried form, their inclusion early in the cooking process is recommended. Spice is often cooked in liquid to extract its flavor, and then the spice itself is

TABLE 4.9 SPICES AND HERBS: THEIR DESCRIPTION AND CHIEF USES

Name	Description and Chief Uses
Allspice (spice)	Dried unripe pea-size fruit of pimento tree grown in Jamaica; flavor resembles a blend of cinnamon, cloves, and nutmeg. Use: whole—pickles, meats, consommé, sauces; ground—baked goods, puddings, relishes, preserves.
Anise (seed)	Small aromatic licorice-flavored fruit from Spain, India, Mexico. Use: coffee cake, sweet rolls, cookies, candy, sweet pickles; flavoring for licorice products.
Bay leaves (herb)	Aromatic smooth shiny green leaves of laurel tree grown in eastern Mediterranean countries. Use: soups, chowders, roasts, stews, fish, tomatoes, pickles.
Caraway (seed)	Aromatic and pungent fruit of caraway plant grown in Holland, Russia, Poland, Africa. Use: rye bread, cheese spread, pickling spice, sauerkraut, sprinkled on pork, liver, kidneys before cooking.
Cardamon (seed)	Dried immature fruit of tropical reedlike bush grown in Ceylon, India, Central America. Use: whole—(in pod) pickling spice; ground—(seed only) Danish baked goods, cakes, candies, curries, sauces, soups, sausage.
Cassia (spice)	Ground thick bark of Cassia tree, commonly called cinnamon; darker and more pungent flavor than true cinnamon; grown in China, Indochina, Indonesia. Use: see Cinnamon.
Cayenne (spice)	Small fire-hot red peppers ground fine; grown in Africa, Mexico, Japan, India. Use: meats, fish, cheese and egg dishes, salads, sauces, pickles.
Celery seed	Tiny seedlike fruit of vegetable plant similar to cultivated celery grown in southern France and India. Use: whole—sauces, salads, pickles, sprinkled on rolls; ground—soups, fish, stews, salad dressings, cheese spreads.
Chili powder (blend)	Ground Mexican chili-pepper pods and blended spices. Use: chili con carne, tamales, meats, stews, hash, scrambled eggs, Spanish rice, gravy, pickles.
Cinnamon (spice)	Aromatic thin inner bark of cinnamon tree grown in Ceylon. Use: stick—pickles, preserves, stewed fruits, tea; ground—fruit, pastries, puddings, toast.
Cloves (spice)	Nail-shaped flower bud of clove tree grown in In-

Name	Description and Chief Uses
	donesia, Madagascar, Zanzibar; highly aromatic and pungent. Use: whole—hams, pickles, spiced sweet syrups, tea; ground—baked goods, preserves, pickles, fruits, sweet potatoes, tomato sauce.
Cumin (seed)	Small dried seedlike fruit of low shrub grown in Mexico, Syria, India; an ingredient of curry and chili powders. Use: soups, cheese spread, stuffed eggs, stews, sausage.
Curry powder (blend)	Blend of spices including turmeric, which gives characteristic color. Use: meat, fish, poultry, eggs, vegetables, fish chowders, rice dishes, French dressing.
Dill (seed)	Small dark seed of dill plant grown in India; aromatic slightly sharp taste resembling caraway. Use: pickles, sauces, salads, soups, gravy, spiced vinegar, cauliflower, cabbage, turnips.
Ginger (spice)	Palmate-shaped root of herbaceous perennial from Asia and East Indies; strong piquant flavor. Use: cracked—chutneys, pickles, preserves, dried fruits, tea; ground—cakes, cookies, breads, canned fruits, pot roasts, soups.
Mace (spice)	Orange-red fleshy covering of nutmeg kernel, smooth nutmeg-like flavor, grown on nutmeg trees in Indonesia. Use: blades—fish sauces, pickles, preserves; ground—fish, oyster stew, fish and meat stuffings, cakes, cherry pie, whipped cream, chocolate dishes.
Marjoram (herb)	Dried leaves and flowering tops of aromatic herb of mint family, grown in southern France, Chile, North Africa; fragrant odor, delicate flavor. Use: lamb, stews, soups, sausage, poultry seasonings, cottage cheese, French dressing, lima beans, peas.
Mint (herb)	Leaves of spearmint plant grown in most localities. Use: lamb, sauces, peas, iced tea.
Mustard (seed)	Small round smooth seeds of annual herbaceous plant of watercress family, common in United States and England; pungent tangy flavor. Use: whole—salads, pickled meats, fish; dry—meats, sauces, gravy, salad dressings; prepared—(blended with other spices, salt, vinegar) sauces, sandwich fillings, meat accompaniment.
Nutmeg (spice)	Dry, hard, wrinkled seed or pit of nutmeg fruit grown in Indonesia; aromatic warm slightly bitter flavor. Use: whole—grated as needed; ground—sausage, cakes, doughnuts, puddings, eggnogs, custards, soups, cream sauce for vegetables.

295

TABLE 4.9 SPICES AND HERBS (*Continued*)

Name	Description and Chief Uses
Oregano (herb)	Dried leaves of a perennial herb of the mint family grown in Mexico and Italy; aromatic odor, slightly bitter flavor, ingredient of chili powder. Use: soups, meat and egg dishes, chili con carne.
Paprika (spice)	Dried, ripe red sweet peppers grown in middle Europe, United States, Chile, Argentina; pleasant odor, mild sweet flavor. Use: fish, shellfish, stews, salad dressings, sandwich fillings, tomato dishes, garnish for salads.
Pepper (spice)	Dried small round berry (peppercorn) of climbing tropical vine grown in Indonesia, Malaya, India; aromatic penetrating odor, pungent flavor; black—whole immature berry; white—mature berry with black center coating removed; usually ground. Use: most generally used of all spices.
Poppy seed	Tiny slate-colored seeds of annual herbaceous plant of poppy family grown in Holland, Poland, Germany, England, United States. Use: topping for breads, rolls, cookies, cakes; oil used for salads and margarines.
Sage (herb)	Dried whitish-green leaf of low-growing garden herb; common in the United States and Yugoslavia; fragrant, slightly resinous flavor. Use: meats, poultry, salads, soups, egg dishes.
Sesame (seed)	Small, flat, oval high-oil seed of sesame plant; common in India, China, Central America; flavor resembles that of toasted almonds. Use: rolls, breads, cookies, candies.
Sweet basil (herb)	Dried aromatic leaves and stems of small annual plant grown in India and along the Mediterranean; clovelike flavor. Use: tomato paste, meat pies, stews, soups, peas, squash, French dressing.
Tarragon (herb)	Pungent aromatic anise-flavored leaves of tarragon plant. Use: vinegar, pickles, sauces, mustard, salads, soups.
Thyme (herb)	Aromatic leaves and stems of small garden perennial, common in the United States and France; clean warm slightly pungent flavor. Use: stews, soups, poultry stuffings, meat loaves.
Turmeric (spice)	Ground dried aromatic root of turmeric plant, similar to ginger; grown in the Orient; slightly bitter flavor; bright-yellow color. Use: important ingredient in curry powder; meat and egg dishes; adds coloring to food and other spices.

discarded. Dehydrated vegetable seasoning flakes are added directly to liquid foods or those containing enough liquid to rehydrate them while cooking.

Condiments and Other Seasonings. New developments in food technology and methods of food preparation have greatly increased the number of items that have gained popularity in institution kitchens. No attempt will be made to discuss other than a few that enter into the production of flavorful foods.

Condiments are used extensively in quantity food preparation as well as in the home. They are made up of a combination of spices and other ingredients and usually are in a liquid or semiliquid form. Examples are catsup, chili sauce, pepper sauce, prepared mustard, and meat sauces. Standard specifications have been established for certain items and all must list ingredients on the labels. *Vinegar* is the principal important condiment that does not depend on essential oils for its characteristic flavor.

Salt is more commonly used to season foods than any other condiment. Cooking salt as well as table salt is purified and, in its many forms, provides a convenient way to introduce mild flavor into foods. For those people restricted to a low-sodium intake it is possible to substitute quite satisfactorily certain of the sodium-free salt compounds like potassium chloride for the regular sodium chloride.

The use of salt, plain or modified, serves to accent instead of conceal the original flavors of foods. In some recipes they are added with other dry ingredients; with foods such as meats, they are added after cooking; and with vegetables, they are added to the cooking water.

Monosodium glutamate is a neutral sodium salt of glutamic acid derived from wheat or corn protein and may be used as a seasoning agent in certain foods. It has been reported as improving the flavor appeal of meats, sea foods, and cooked vegetables particularly. Fruits, fruit juices, cakes, breads, cereals, and dairy products generally are not considered improved by its use. The principal effect is to balance, blend, and round out total flavor of the product.

Soluble concentrates of chicken, beef, and other extracts to which tomato, spices, and other ingredients may have been added are now readily available. Such products may be used to intensify the flavor in a given food preparation or form the base for soups or other stocks and gravies. Although they are expensive, these items do have considerable merit as food adjuncts.

SELECTED REFERENCES

Charley, Helen, *Food Science,* Ronald Press, New York, 1970.

"Cooking Meat in Quantity," National Live Stock and Meat Board, Chicago.

Demler, Louise, *Food Preparation: Study Course,* The Iowa State University Press, Ames, Iowa, 1971.

Food, The Yearbook of Agriculture 1959, U.S. Department of Agriculture, 1959.

Food for Us All, The Yearbook of Agriculture 1969, U.S. Department of Agriculture, 1969.

Fowler, Sina Faye, Bessie Brooks West, and Grace S. Shugart, *Food for Fifty,* Fifth Edition, Wiley, New York, 1971.

Griswold, Ruth M., *The Experimental Study of Foods,* Houghton Mifflin, Boston, 1962.

"Handbook of Food Preparation," The American Home Economics Association, Seventh Edition, 1975.

Institution Management Department, Iowa State University, *Standardized Quantity Recipe File for Quality and Cost Control,* Iowa State University Press, Ames, Iowa, 1971.

Kotschevar, Lendal H., *Standards and Principles of Quantity Food Production,* Third Edition, Cahners, Boston, 1974.

Levie, Albert, *Meat Handbook,* Third Edition, Avi, Westport, Connecticut, 1970.

Morgan, William J. Jr., *Supervision and Management of Quantity Food Preparation,* McCutchan, Berkeley, California, 1974.

Myers, Lillian, *Food Chemistry,* Reinhold, New York, 1960.

Paul, Pauline, and Helen H. Palmer, *Food Theory and Applications,* Wiley, New York, 1972.

"Quantity Recipes for Type A School Lunches," PA-631, U.S. Department of Agriculture, 1971.

Smith, Evelyn, and Vera C. Crusius, *A Handbook on Quantity Food Management,* Second Edition, Burgess, Minneapolis, 1970.

Terrell, Margaret E., *Professional Food Preparation,* Wiley, New York, 1971.

"The Science of Meat and Meat Products," American Meat Institute Foundation, W. H. Freeman, San Francisco, 1960.

Tressler, Donald K., Wallace B. Van Arsdel, and Michael J. Copley, *The Freezing Preservation of Foods,* Fourth Edition, Vol. 4: Freezing of Precooked Foods, Avi, Westport, Connecticut, 1968.

"Turkey Handbook," National Turkey Federation, Mount Morris, Illinois, 1961.

Vail, Gladys E., Jean A. Phillips, Lucile Osborn Rust, Ruth M. Griswold, and Margaret M. Justin, *Foods,* Sixth Edition, Houghton Mifflin, Boston, 1973.

5.
DELIVERY AND SERVICE OF FOODS

New delivery and service systems for foodservice organizations have developed in recent years due, primarily, to the increased use of foods prepared centrally, off-premises. A distinct separation of preparation from service of food, both in time and distance, has been the result. Two major factors seem to have precipitated this change: (1) spiraling labor costs, and (2) technological developments from both food and equipment research. Dietitians and foodservice managers faced with high labor costs provided a ready market for the new forms of food with built-in "convenience" or labor-saving features. These foods, in their various forms and stages of preparation, which appear on the market in increasing numbers each year, have led to the need for specialized equipment for delivery and making the food ready for service.

Technological research and development have helped to mold new foodservice systems. This, however, does not relieve dietitians or food managers from making the many decisions required to adopt one particular system appropriate for their institutions' specific needs.

FOODSERVICE SYSTEMS

In order to understand the delivery and service systems available, it is necessary to have some knowledge of total foodservice systems. From the maze of reports and differing terminology found in the literature, Unklesbay, Knickrehm, and Cremer [1] have identified and described four major or basic foodservice systems: Conventional, Commissary, Ready Prepared, and Assembly/Serve. Definitions and descriptions of these four systems will help to identify the components of each as they will be used in this text. In addition, the term "delivery system" is used to mean the equipment needed to transport food from place of preparation to the service area, then to the consumer.

CONVENTIONAL FOODSERVICE SYSTEM

As the name implies, this is the type of foodservice that most establishments have used over a period of many years. Foods are purchased by the individual foodservice in various stages of preparation, but all preparation is completed and foods made ready for service in a kitchen on the premises where the food is to be served.

The feature that all conventional operations have in common is that following food production, the time for product flow is shorter than for commissary and ready-prepared operations. Following food production, foods are held hot or chilled and served as soon as possible. [1]

Rappole [2] has identified the conventional food system as:

The conventional food system traditionally includes a butcher shop, bake shop, vegetable preparation area, kitchen with direct-production people, and service and clean-up personnel. Food of all types is purchased raw and processed on the premises shortly before serving.

He adds a subsystem or variation that he calls:

The "semi-conventional system" defined as the one in which the butcher and bake shops are eliminated and the system minimizes food preparation through purchasing pre-portioned meat cuts, frozen vegetables and desserts, and some prepared salads. Thus only direct production, service, and cleanup personnel are required. [3]

---

[1] *Nan Unklesbay, Marie Knickrehm, and Marion Cremer, "Quality and Safety of Foods Served in Mass Feeding Systems," NC 120 Regional Research Project Bulletin, in preparation, June 1975.*
[2] *Clinton L. Rappole, "Institutional Use of Frozen Entrees," Cornell HRA Quarterly, 14 (1), 72 (May 1973).*
[3] *Clinton L. Rappole, "Institutional Use of Frozen Entrees," Cornell HRA Quarterly, 14 (1), 72 (May 1973).*

Delivery. Foods prepared in the conventional kitchen, on-premises, may be distributed for service directly to an adjacent serving area as a cafeteria, dining room, or lunch counter. Or, in hospitals or other health-care facilities where tray service to patients is required, the service of the food onto the trays may be centralized or decentralized.

Centralized Service. Centralized service means serving the individual portions of food onto the trays that have been assembled and set up at some central point in or close to the kitchen. All trays are so prepared under common supervision. They are then distributed by carts or vertical conveyors to patient floors; from there they are carried to the patient's bedside.

Decentralized Service. Decentralized service means the distribution of bulk quantities of food in sufficient amount to serve a given number of patients in one section of the facility. This system requires some means of transporting the food, for example, in heated or refrigerated trucks or carts, to serving pantries located throughout the building.

Trays for the patients are set up in these serving pantries, usually on a conveyor belt, and food is served onto the trays at the several locations instead of all at one place, as with the centralized service. Decentralized service requires duplication of some equipment for service; often dishes are also washed in the decentralized pantries.

More employees are needed to serve in the various pantries than for centralized service. A greater number of supervisors is also required unless serving times can be staggered so that one supervisor could move from serving area to another as the food arrives for service. Usually decentralized service is more practical for use when the building structure is low and sprawling, making it difficult to serve centrally and have the food hot on arrival if it must travel one-half mile of corridor.

Examples of these methods of distribution will be discussed under the heading Service for different types of foodservices.

Automated Cart Transport System. An automated cart transport system (often known as the monorail) may be built into the facility for use by all departments, including dietary. It can carry trays to patient areas in a few seconds in its own specially built-in corridors, out of the way of other traffic in the building. This is a costly system that must be designed and built in at the time of building construction; it cannot be added to a facility already constructed.

This delivery system is particularly suitable for hospitals or other large facilities with more than one department to utilize it. It is effectively used with any of the on-premises production systems.

Advantages of the conventional system are many. Usually it is more adaptable to individual preferences, and foods are more easily prepared to satisfy various cultural and socio economic backgrounds of the consumers. From an economic standpoint, it is often possible to take advantage of price fluctuations and seasonal items unless bids are let too far in advance.[4]

Other advantages include greater flexibility in menu planning without restrictions imposed by the availability of commercially prepared entrees and other menu items. This gives individuality to the food of the establishment also.

Distribution costs are minimal, which is a real consideration in times of fuel and energy shortages. There is no out-of-building delivery required.

Disadvantages to this system have to do with the peaks and accompanying stress caused by meal period demands. Work distribution is uneven and so productivity is lower than desired. Labor costs are therefore high. Foodservices that offer three or more meals a day or are open for continuous service may have overlapping shifts of employees, which adds to the labor cost if the number on duty at one time is more than necessary. Labor cost is the one major factor primarily responsible for the gaining popularity of other systems.

COMMISSARY FOODSERVICE SYSTEM

Foodservice organizations with many serving units have sought ways to curtail labor and other costs by centralizing production and other activities. A commissary is one solution. It is a large production kitchen, usually equipped with sophisticated, automated equipment.

Commissary foodservice systems have centralized food procurement and production functions with distribution of prepared menu items to several remote areas for final preparation and service. The actual food product flow varies with different commissary adaptations. The common feature of all commissaries is that the food production center and service areas are located in separate facilities. Therefore, the function of food distribution

[4] *Charles Eshbach, Editor,* Food Service Trends, *"Satellite System Recommended for a College Health Center After Study of Three Kinds of Systems," by Cathryn J. Louis, Cahners, Boston, p. 161, 1974.*

must receive considerable emphasis for the effective operation of these foodservice systems.[5]

Another centralized facility for food production is a central kitchen. This is thought of as smaller than a commissary and with more conventional equipment, but it is separate from the serving unit, as is the commissary.

The term "satellite" foodservice is sometimes used synonymously with commissary. If there can be a distinction drawn between the two, it is that a satellite kitchen is used to refer to an existing kitchen adapted for use to produce for several like-units in the same geographical area. It is thought of as being smaller, less sophisticated, and not built especially for large-scale centralized production. Prepared food is trucked to other schools in the area. This interpretation of a satellite kitchen has not been generally used, however, and so satellite is considered a variation of the commissary system. A satellite *serving unit,* however, is any facility where food prepared centrally is delivered for service.

Delivery. Menu items processed in the commissary "may either be held in bulk or portioned before storage. Three alternatives for storage following food production are available: frozen, chilled or hot-held. Each method requires different types of foodservice equipment and careful managerial monitoring for quality and microbiological consideration."[6]

Bulk foods may be placed in counter-size pans for freezing. Or, if they are to be transferred to serving units in the chilled or hot state instead of frozen, they are placed in heavy containers with lids that clamp on securely. Otherwise, spillage may result during transportation to the foodservice facility. Individual portions may be placed in casserolelike dishes, onto TV-like portioned aluminum tray plates, on plastic or paper plates, or wrapped in wax paper as sandwiches for a school foodservice lunch.

Carriers (Fig. 5.1, for example) to hold the portioned food in their containers are filled at the commissary. At scheduled times each day, other types of carriers, which may be heated or refriger-

[5] *Nan Unklesbay, Marie Knickrehm, and Marion Cremer, "Quality and Safety of Foods Served in Mass Feeding Systems," NC 120 Regional Research Project Bulletin, in preparation, June 1975.*

[6] *Nan Unklesbay, Marie Knickrehm, and Marion Cremer, "Quality and Safety of Foods Served in Mass Feeding Systems," NC 120 Regional Research Project Bulletin, in preparation, June 1975.*

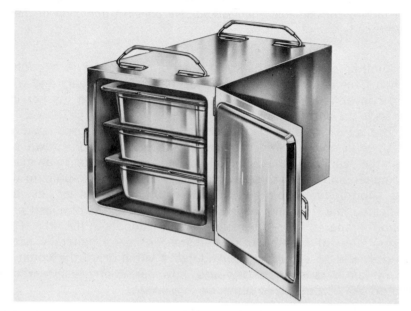

FIGURE　5.1　*Insulated pan carrier for bulk food has Underwriters Laboratories, Inc. (UL) approved heating element to maintain 165° F temperature during transport from commissary to serving units; recessed covers and eutectic lids eliminate need for pan slides making carriers easy to clean yet hold pans firmly during transport. Courtesy, The Vollrath Company.*

ated or not, whatever is appropriate to maintain optimum food temperature, are loaded onto a truck for transfer to the service unit. In many cases, the driver is responsible for unloading the truck and taking the food carriers to the storage or service area as required. Carriers from the last delivery are collected and returned empty to the commissary on the delivery truck.

The fleet of trucks required by the commissary will depend on geographic distances to be traveled and number of deliveries to be made by each truck driver. Timing can be crucial, especially in those situations where the food is delivered hot just at meal times. School foodservices or college residence hall service may utilize the hot food delivery system to a greater extent than other foodservices. Finishing kitchens may not be available in the individual schools or dining halls; if not, distances for food to be transported should be short.

Delivery of frozen foods requires well-insulated carriers to maintain food in the frozen state during the time it is being transported. If the service facility has adequate space for holding frozen food, there is little problem with delivery time, since meals can be sent a day or two ahead. If there is no storage space for these, timing of delivery must be correlated with meal periods and time for rethermalizing and assembling the menu items.

Advantages of the commissary foodservice system may readily be seen. The economics of the system mentioned have been the benefit of centralized, large-volume purchasing, no need for duplication of equipment and personnel for each unit as would be required in the conventional system, and reduced amount of supervision required. Another advantage is the uniformity of quality of products for all units. With the conventional system, quality sometimes varies considerably, causing complaints from the consumers, college students, for example, who believe that the food is better at one dining hall over another. Yet all pay the same board rate.

Another advantage pointed out in one case study of 15 state institutions sharing a central commissary system is that productivity increased from 50 percent when the units operated independently to 90 percent after centralization. "The greatest saving has resulted from a major reduction in overtime costs. Because frozen foods are available from the central plant, the institutions need only minimal foodservice staffing on the weekends and holidays."[7] Another advantage noted by these authors is the ability, with centralized procedures, to determine accurately all costs, especially overhead, operating, and delivery costs. These costs are difficult to prorate fairly when the dietary department is one section of a larger facility. Realistic charges for prepared food to the cooperating institutions is now possible, and the bills include all of the production costs so the commissary can operate on a self-sustaining annual budget.

With the consolidation into one facility, it is usually possible to purchase more sophisticated equipment, such as computer-controlled, automated foodservice equipment. Although initial investment of such equipment is expensive, the savings that can be realized over a period of time through use of it can be sizable.

Many central commissaries are equipped with a small test kitchen for product development and evaluation. For large organizations this is highly desirable and may be considered an advantage to this system. However, it is not unique to these organizations; any

[7] *Dorothy T. Bailey and Margaret M. Bonivicin, "Central Source for State-wide Sharing,"* Hospitals, JAHA, 47, 57 *(November 1, 1973).*

foodservice may have such a feature and employ a qualified person to develop and standardize recipes for the organization.

Disadvantages to the commissary foodservice system relate primarily to delivery and safety of the food. First, it must be transported in such a manner that it is of good quality and appearance and maintains correct temperature for safety when received for service. This requires specialized equipment for delivery. Poor weather conditions, delivery truck breakdowns, or other such catastrophies may result in the food arriving late at its destination, causing irritating delays in meal service. The cost of gasoline for delivery may become a high cost factor if distances to be traveled are great.

READY-PREPARED FOODSERVICE SYSTEM

This foodservice system is one in which foods are prepared on the premises, then frozen immediately and held for use at some later time. The term "ready foods" was first introduced at Cornell University School of Hotel Administration Research Department. They mass-produced their own foods for chilling or freezing. Thus, foods are "ready" prepared well in advance of time of service. The terms "cook-freeze" and "stored labor concept" are sometimes used for this system.

A variation of the cook-freeze system is the "cook-chill" system. In this system, the food is prepared, plated, chilled and rethermalized just prior to service. . . . Some facilities prepare, chill and plate the patients' food at night. Trays are stored in the refrigerator and rethermalized in the patient area in microwave ovens. [8]

Extreme care must be maintained in food handling procedures to assure microbial safety of products by this system. Rappole [9] describes this system as "ready foods."

The "Ready Foods" system produces precooked frozen entrees on the premises for use later on. Typically, this system also eliminates the butcher and bake shops and vegetable preparation areas. Direct production people manufacture the frozen and fresh food items. Service and cleanup people

[8] Nan Unklesbay, Marie Knickrehm, and Marion Cremer, "Quality and Safety of Foods Served in Mass Feeding Systems," NC 120 Regional Research Project Bulletin, in preparation, June 1975.

[9] Clinton L. Rappole, "Institutional Use of Frozen Entrees," Cornell HRA Quarterly, 14(1),71 (May 1973).

are needed, of course. This system provides tighter control over the quality of frozen entrees than does the total convenience system.

This system requires a blast freezer for quickly freezing the foods, an essential for preserving quality of textures, flavors, and safety of foods. Someone with a technical knowledge of food science and food microbiology should be on the staff to develop or adjust standardized recipes. Compensation must be allowed for structural changes that may occur with some foods during freezing. This is essential to assure good quality when foods are reheated.

Another requirement of the ready-prepared system is adequate freezer and refrigerated storage to accommodate the volume of prepared food deemed necessary. Also, raw products must be stored until processed.

Consideration must be given to equipment for rethermalizing food with the ready-prepared system. Products frozen in bulk are generally tempered in a refrigerator just before serving time, then heated in convection ovens for cafeteria or dining room service.

For tray service several options are available for distribution and rethermalization of preplated meals. One is a central tray line with plates of chilled foods transported to serving areas throughout the facility for heating. Generally it is desirable to reheat the food quickly. Microwave ovens are the fastest for preplated portions (either frozen or chilled) but, unless the institution invests in the tunnel-type microwave oven, only one portion can be heated at a time. An alternative, of course, is to purchase a fleet of microwave ovens, which may become very costly.

Convection ovens are used by many institutions, particularly hospitals, for the rethermalizing process. Small units, patterned after those used in airline galleys, and called flight-type convection ovens, meet the need for reheating several meals at a time. This provides fast total service and less handling of individual plates than with the single microwave oven. Needs of the institution must be weighed and equipment appropriate for desired output purchased.

The model illustrated in Fig. 5.2 is designed so that preplated food served in the central serving area may be loaded into oven inserts and transported to the patient area, placed in the ovens as a single unit for reheating.

The *Integral Heat* system "developed by the 3M company converts electric energy to heat through the use of thin-coat carbon composition resistors fused to the bottom of individual dishes which transmit the heat to the food they contain. This means that meals

FIGURE 5.2   *Galley Station (9½ linear feet) includes flight-type convection oven with capacity for reheating 24 frozen or chilled preplated meals. Courtesy, Crimsco, Incorporated.*

can be served in the same dishes in which they have been prepared." [10] (See Figs. 5.3 and 5.4.)

Dishes for the system are in two parts. The interior is porcelain ceramic and the outer section is a high-quality polysulfone plastic shell on which the metal buttons or contact points for the electric current are placed. A resistor is fused to the bottom exterior of the inner dish. A cabinet with sliding removable metal racks is the unit into which the dishes are placed for cooking or heating of frozen or chilled items.

Push button controls on the integral heat unit send electric current pulsing through the electrodes to the metal buttons on the bottom of the

[10] *Bernard Schukraft, "Integral Heat System for Volume Food Preparation," Food Technology, 27, 27 (September 1972).*

outer shell of the dish. The current is passed through the resistors on the inner dish. There the electric current is converted to heat and transmitted through dishes to the food. Thus the food rather than the air or walls of the unit receives the heat. In fact, the integral heat unit and the outer thermal shell remain cool to the touch.[11]

Delivery. Cabinets may be transported to any area for use and service. Thus foods are hot when they reach the consumer. The manufacturer states that 24 chilled meals can be heated in 11 minutes in one oven, 20 minutes if frozen. Also, 90 percent of the unit's heat energy (as opposed to 30 percent for electric range) is directed to the food, which means more efficient use of electric power.

FIGURE 5.3   *Heating cabinet for 3M Company's integral heating system. An electronic "memory unit" in the integral heating control module permits variable programming. This means that different kinds of foods— some requiring more or less heating time than others—can be prepared in the same module at the same time. Courtesy, Integral Heating Systems, 3M Company.*

[11] *Bernard Schukraft, "Integral Heat System for Volume Food Preparation," Food Technology, 27, 27 (September 1972).*

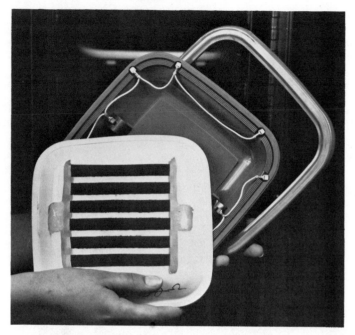

FIGURE   5.4   *Dish in two parts for use with the integral heat system. Special resistive coating (dark areas) on bottom of porcelain ceramic inner shell of "dish-oven" in which food is both heated and served. Inner and outer shells are thermally sealed with gasket (top). Dish always remains cool to the touch. Courtesy, Integral Heating Systems, 3 M Company.*

Advantages of the ready-prepared system are those related primarily to reducing "peaks and valleys" in preparation, as described under the commissary type. Production scheduling for menu item inventory prevents the stress of a last minute rush to complete preparation at a certain time.

The establishment has close control over menu items selected for production, the quality, quantity, and portion size of foods, and should realize considerable savings in labor costs. A normal workday schedule with fewer early morning and late evening shifts and weekend hours on duty should result.

Labor costs may be reduced by utilizing less skilled personnel in the kitchen to reheat foods for dining room or cafeteria service instead of having high-paid cooks to do this task.

One advantage over the commissary system is the lack of worry over delivery schedules from the central production kitchen. With foods prepared on premises, menu items are available on call and no waiting time is involved.

Disadvantages could be the high cost of installing the blast freezer equipment and lack of adequate freezer storage space. Equipment costs for reheating foods would be no greater than with the commissary system using frozen foods. However, highly skilled pantry workers are required to operate and maintain the reheating equipment, which may boost labor costs.

ASSEMBLY-SERVE SYSTEM

This system is the one in which completely prepared foods are purchased from the food processing industry (purveyor prepared foods). Only the "finishing" processes as tempering, (thawing) or rethermalizing, portioning and merchandising the food for service are required on premises. This concept of foodservice is also known as "total convenience" and "minimal cooking." Its objective is to curtail the expenditure of labor time and other management resources by divorcing the manufacturing process from the distribution process.[12]

Merrick and Sutton [13] stated that three forms of food may be procured for assembly-serve systems.

1. Completely prepared foods; ready-to-serve.

2. Completely prepared foods; ready-to-serve after simple preparation method as thawing or rethermalizing.

3. Partially prepared foods; ready to combine with one or more ingredients prior to heating or chilling.

"These foodservice systems tend to procure smaller, more uniform sizes of food items than the other types of foodservice systems. This allows effective storage and handling procedures." [14]

Another feature often, although not always, associated with the assembly-serve system is the use of single-use or disposable table-

[12] *Kathleen Zolber, Ph. D., "Research on Assembly-Serve Systems,"* Hospitals, JAHA, 45(2), 83 *(January 16, 1971).*

[13] *M. Merick and P.J. Sutton, "Minimal Cooking Concept,"* Hospitals JAHA, 46(11), 92 *(June 1, 1972).*

[14] *Nan Unklesbay, Marie Knickrehm, and Marion Cremer, "Quality and Safety of Foods Served in Mass Feeding Systems." NC 120 Regional Research Project Bulletin, in preparation, June 1975.*

ware. This reduces labor costs still further by elimination of a dishwashing unit and equipment necessary for this task.

Delivery. Distribution of meals for the assembly-serve system may be any one of those described for the other three foodservice systems. Most often in the assembly-serve system, menu items are received frozen and preportioned and are tempered in a refrigerator and assembled in the chilled state for either cafeteria or tray service. Carts convey the trays to patient areas, where meals are rethermalized by microwave ovens.

For cafeteria or dining room service, convection ovens or microwave ovens are commonly used.

Advantages of this totally convenient assembly-serve foodservice system are its labor time-cost saving. Zolber[15] reported in a study of hospitals that: "(1) significantly less total time was expended in two of the three assembly-serve systems than in the 11 conventional production systems, and (2) total direct labor time was sizeably less in the three assembly-serve systems than in the 11 conventional production systems."

Minimal investment in equipment is another major advantage, and the operating expenses such as gas, electricity, and water will be reduced. Portion control is absolute and little if any waste will occur.

Disadvantages are the limit on menu items as determined by availability of products in the geographical area.

The higher cost of food purchased commercially may not offset the labor savings realized in this system. Dietitians and food managers must carefully weigh the overall cost effect by such a conversion.

Another disadvantage in some situations may be the quality of available products and customer acceptability of them. The proportion of ingredients, especially protein food, to sauce or gravy, must be considered in relation to the nutritional requirements of the clientele. For example, 2 ounces of protein is required for school foodservice with Type A meals; many frozen entree items may contain much less protein than this.

Catheryn J. Louis[16] made a study of three kinds of foodservice

[15] *Kathleen Zolber, Ph. D., "Research on Assembly-Serve Systems,"* Hospitals, JAHA, 45(2), 86 (January 16, 1971).

[16] *Charles Eshbach, Editor,* Food Service Trends, *"Satellite System Recommended for a College Health Center After Study of Three Kinds of Systems," by Catheryn J. Louis,* Cahners, Boston, p. 161, 1974.

systems as a basis for recommending one for a college health center. Part of this study involved cost. Her cost comparisons of three types of service for a 2-week period is presented below. Although actual costs are soon outdated, the relative costs involved in each may be of interest.

COST COMPARISON OF THE THREE TYPES OF SERVICE
FOR A 2-WEEK PERIOD

	Standard Food Preparation and Service	Convenience Foods and Disposables	Food Prepared Elsewhere
Food	$529.17	$ 589.90	$660.01
Personnel	406.60	231.60	226.80
Supplies	4.91	438.35	4.91
Utilities	7.52	6.00	3.14
Depreciation	19.60	19.60	19.60
Transportation	—	—	33.58
Totals	$967.80	$1285.45	$948.04

In summary, foodservice systems, with their production and delivery systems, may be outlined on a continuum from conventional to total convenience, assembly-serve as shown on p. 316.

To illustrate the use of these systems and some modifications and variations, examples of foodservices in several types of organizations are given. First, a description of types of service will be discussed.

SERVICE OF FOOD

The ultimate objective to be achieved with whatever foodservice system is used is that the food be of good quality, attractively served, and of the correct temperature for customer acceptability and microbial safety. Also, it must be a system economically compatible with the goals and standards of the organization. The appearance of the food when served contributes to the customers' acceptance and enjoyment of it. Likewise, the courtesy and efficiency of those serving the food contribute to the guests' sense of complete satisfaction with the meal. The continued achievement of this standard becomes more and more difficult in this age of speed, do-it-yourself service and, in some cases, unwillingness on the part of the consumer to devote time to leisurely dining.

Type	Characteristics	Delivery Methods
1. Conventional	Total production on-premises from raw state and served at once.	Short-time holding in heated cabinets for cafeteria service, or chilled for use in short time.
a. Semiconventional	Production of most items on premises but purchase portion ready meats, mixes, and some other convenience items.	Centralized service: on conveyor line with various types of equipment for temperature retention; food portioned all in one place for service. Decentralized service: bulk quantities of food sent by heated or refrigerated carts or open carts to various serving units throughout the facility; food portioned at these unit kitchens for distribution.
2. Ready foods	On-premises preparation; food chilled or frozen for some later time service. Production can be equalized over a normal work day; peaks and valleys of production eliminated. Food is reheated and made ready for service at meal time. Usually suitable for large foodservices; requires a good amount of freezer storage space.	Blast freezer or other fast-freeze equipment necessary. Microwave ovens often used on floor or unit kitchens for reheating. Steamers, steamjacketed kettles, and convection ovens or steamers also used for bulk quantity reheating. Methods of food distribution for service may be the same as for the conventional type.
3. Commissary (also known as central kitchen)	Owned and operated by the foodservice organization. Mass production of food for distribution to many service facilities. Often utilizes automated equipment and sophisticated techniques; central kitchen is thought of as a smaller production kitchen with more conventional type of equipment. Food may be hot, chilled, or frozen in bulk or individual portions for delivery to service units.	A fleet of trucks needed to deliver food to various facilities. Temperature controlled containers as carts or carriers required for safety of food and to prevent spillage enroute. Type of equipment must be suitable for bulk or individual pack system.
4. Assembly/serve	Foods purchased totally prepared from a commercial company. Stored, reheated, and made ready for services on premises. Adequate freezer and other storage space required.	Delivered to institution by the wholesaler. Reheated and delivered to consumer by any of the methods previously described.

The service of food to achieve these objectives should be a major concern of every administrative dietitian and foodservice manager. There are many types of service, differing widely among insititutions, but each has common requirements to be met through whichever style is selected. The basic types of service to be discussed are:

1. **1.** Self-service.
   a. Cafeteria: traditional; free flow or scramble; food bank or electronic cafeteria.
   b. Machine vended.
   c. Buffet and smorgasbord.

2. **2.** Tray service.
   a. Centralized.
   b. Decentralized.

3. **3.** Waiter-waitress service.
   a. Counter.
   b. Table: American; French; Russian; Banquet;
   c. Drive-in.

4. **4.** Portable meals.
   a. Home delivery.
   b. Mobile carts or trucks on premises.

More specifically, there are many types of service, differing widely, among institutions, but each has common requirements to be met.

SELF-SERVICE

The simplest provisions for foodservice are those made in a self-service unit where the guest selects his own food, and often the silver, water, and napkin, and carries them to a dining table. The cafeteria is the best known example of self-service, although buffet, smorgasbord, and vending are popular also.

Cafeterias are of three types: the *traditional* one where the employees are stationed behind the counter to serve the guest, encourage him in his selections, and give a friendly word of greeting as he moves along a counter displaying the food choices. There are many configurations for counter arrangement from the straight line to parallel or double line, zig zag, and others. In each case, however, the patrons follow each other in line to make their selections.

This traditional self-service style is used in colleges and other residences, cafeterias open to the public, school lunchrooms, in-plant foodservices, and commercial operations. The emphasis is on standardized portions and speedy yet courteous service. The rate of flow of people through the cafeteria line varies according to the number of choices offered and the patrons' familiarity with the setup. From 3 or 4 per minute in a commercial cafeteria to 12 to 15 in a school cafeteria with a limited number of items from which to choose are typical.

Another type of cafeteria design is known variously as the *hollow square, free flow, or scramble* system. Whatever the name, it is one in which separated counters for hot foods, sandwiches and salads, and desserts usually are placed along three sides of a room. Customers can go directly to the section desired without having to wait in line for their food. This is a confusing system for the first timer, but it provides speed and flexibility and relieves the pressure on those who do not want to hurry. As many as 25 people per minute can be served in this type of foodservice, once the customers learn the routine. In order for it to be successful it is necessary to have repeat business and a mechanism for controlling the number of people who enter at one time.

The third type of cafeteria is the *"cook-it-yourself" electronic* cafeteria. It was first used in in-plant feeding, but has been expanded for use by highway travelers stopping in restaurants along freeways and turnpikes and by other organizations. The customer selects a precooked frozen meal from a freezer display case. The meals are sealed and color coded. He places the meal of his choice into a microwave oven that has color coded, automatic timer buttons to match the colors on the meal packages. In this way the meal will be heated the correct number of minutes for proper serving temperature. Dining areas are provided for the patrons. Disposable dishes and eating utensils are used so there is no dishwashing required unless it is for trays that may be provided for the customer's use. This type of service is speedy although very impersonal and has had somewhat limited use.

Vended Foodservice. Machine-vended foodservice skyrocketed in use and popularity in the 1950s and 1960s, since it seemed to meet the demand expressed by the American people for speedy service and availability of food at any time of day or night.

The history of vending extends over a period of many years. Although food vending is considered a development of modern times, it has been noted [17] that vending dates back as far as 215 B.C. At that time a coin-operated machine that dispensed holy water was installed in front of a Greek temple!

Beginning with the penny gum machine, other items such as cigarettes, coffee, and cold drinks soon were dispensed from vending machines. Today, complete meals are vended through automatic cafeterias with some hot food machines that not only serve but actually cook or reheat the meals. (See Figs. 5.5 and 5.6.)

Acceptance of vending by the general public has made it an important supplement to manual types of service. Schools, residence halls, hospitals, industrial plants, and office and transportation terminal buildings have used this mode of service for coffee breaks, after-meal-hour snacks and, in some, as the sole means of providing meals.

Food for the vending machines may be prepared by the institution using them. In institutions having no kitchens, foods are provided by an outside catering company that delivers fresh foods at frequent intervals and keeps the machines supplied and in good working order. Fast turnover of food and a good supply service are requisites for safety and success of vended foods. However, the impersonality of machine-vended food is an influencing factor in its acceptance by some individuals. Cooperative effort has been made by those concerned with packaging, production, merchandising, transportation, storage, and sanitation, and improvements have followed in the quality and variety of the food offered. Probably, in the future, new types of automatic merchandisers and electronically controlled money systems will make possible payment for all items selected rather than payment at each machine, as is necessary today.

Vending machines offer 24-hour service, 7 days a week, and are used in many institutions to supplement the regular type of foodservice. Hospitals find vending service a good solution for providing food to guests, night employees, and visitors to the hospital at off-meal times. They are used in residences, schools, and office buildings to provide snacks or supplements to lunches brought from home, or to provide food for overtime employees who might other-

[17] R. L. Ottenad, "Role of Vending Equipment in Food Service Industry," Proceedings of the 7th Conference of the Society for the Advancement of Food Service Research, p. 25, November 1962.

FIGURE 5.5 *Vending machine layout. Courtesy, J. E. Welty.*

FIGURE 5.6 *Vending units may be combined to meet the needs of specific operations.*

wise be without catering facilities. In order to be successful, the foods offered must be fresh and displayed attractively. Glass-front display cases are found to be far superior to metal-front machines for this purpose. Cleanliness and adherence to city health and sanitation codes are important factors in the success of vended foodservice.

Buffet or Smorgasbord Service. Buffet service such as the smorgasbord is a means for dramatically displaying foods on a large serving table. Guests move around the table to help themselves to foods of their choice. Selections usually are numerous and more elaborate than in a cafeteria, and eye appeal is an all-important factor in the foods offered. Foods that "stand up" during the meal hour and the proper equipment to keep them hot or cold, as desired, are essential to the success of this type of service. One concern that may be met through local health department regulations is for the protection of foods on the buffet table against patron contamination. Portable sneeze guards placed around the foods give some protection, yet allow the customers to serve themselves, as in Fig. 5.7.

FIGURE   5.7   *Portable serving units for hot and for cold foodservice may be set up in various combinations to provide an attractive buffet service. Courtesy, Precision Metal Products, Inc.*

TRAY SERVICE

Tray service or carrying food on a tray to persons unable to utilize other dining facilities deserves special attention on the part of the dietitian or food manager. Usually the persons served in this manner are ill or infirm, and attractive trays do much to tempt their appetites and so help to restore their health. Attention should be given to details such as color coordination of the tray covers, dishes, and other appointments used. Employees who serve the trays to the patients or others should be trained to present a pleasant manner and to offer friendly encouragement to those who are to consume the meal.

The two types of tray delivery, *centralized* and *decentralized,* have been described earlier in this chapter. The trend is toward centralized service, where trays are set up in a central serving area in, or adjacent to, the kitchen. Here proper food items for each patient are placed onto his tray as it moves along an assembly line. Various types of equipment may be employed to transport the served trays to the bed patient. Figure 5.8 illustrates one type of food cart. The use

FIGURE   5.8   Hospital food cart.

of fast-moving conveyors to the different floors and a cooperative group of employees to serve the trays to the patients is one procedure. Speed is essential for ensuring that the food is of proper temperature and good flavor and appearance when it reaches the patient.

Decentralized service is used in many hospitals, particularly those that are built horizontally instead of vertically, and where the distance from the kitchen to the patients' room is great. The problem of retaining the proper temperature of the food during the time it is transported is always one of great concern to the dietitian. Bulk quantities of food taken in heated trucks to various pantries for serving, located near the patients' rooms, help to solve this problem.

Most airlines utilize tray service for meals served in-flight to their passengers. Methods used to accomplish this service are discussed under examples given for various types of organizations (p. 334–336.

WAITER. WAITRESS SERVICE

Counter. Lunch counter and fountain service is perhaps the next thing to self-service in informality. Here guests may sit on stools at a counter table that makes for ease and speed of service and permits one or two attendants to handle a sizable volume of trade. Covers are laid and cleared by the waiter or waitress from the back of the counter, and the promixity of the location of food preparation to the serving unit facilitates easy handling of food. The U-shaped counter design often used utilizes space to the maximum, and personnel have limited steps to take to serve many customers.

Table Service. Restaurants and hotel-motel dining rooms use more formal patterns of service than the counter service, although both employ service personnel. Many degrees of formality (or informality) may be observed as one dines in commercial foodservice establishments around the world. Generally, there are four major styles of service classified under table service: American, French, Russian, and banquet service.

The *American* service is that generally used in the United States, although all styles are used to some degree. A host or hostess greets and seats the guests and provides them with a menu card for the meal. Waitresses or waiters place fresh table covers, take the orders, bring in food from the serving pantry and serve the guests, and remove soiled dishes from the tables. Characteristic of this type of service is that food is portioned and served onto dinner plates in the kitchen. Bussers may carry trays of soiled dishes from the dining room, fill water glasses, and serve bread and butter. Checkers see that the food taken to the dining room corresponds with the order and also verify prices on the bill.

French style service is used in exclusive and high-cost restaurants. It is sometimes considered "old-fashioned" but elegant. In this style, portions of food are brought to the dining room on serving platters and placed on a small heater (*rechaud*) that is on a small, portable table called a *gueridon.* This table is wheeled up beside the guests' table and here the chief waiter (*chef de rang*) completes preparation, for example, boning, carving, flaming, or making a sauce. He serves the plates, which are carried by an assistant waiter (*commis de rang*) to each guest in turn.

This style is expensive, since two professionally trained waiters are needed to serve properly and extra dining room space is required for the *gueridon.* It is slower than other methods, but gracious and leisurely and much enjoyed by the patrons who receive individual attention.

Russian service is the most popular style used in all of the better restaurants and motel dining rooms of the world. Because of its simplicity, it has replaced to a high degree the French style that seems cumbersome to many. In Russian service, the food is completely prepared and portioned in the kitchen. An adequate number of portions for the number of guests at the table are arranged on serving platters by the chef. A waiter or waitress brings the platters, usually silver, with food to the dining room along with heated dinner plates and places them on a tray stand near the guests' table. A dinner plate is placed in front of each guest. The waiter then carries the platter of food to each guest in turn and serves each a portion. This is done by using a spoon and a fork as tongs in the right hand and serving from the left side. This is repeated until all items on the menu have been served. Although this service has the advantage of speed, one waiter only required, and no extra space needed in the dining room, it has the possible disadvantage that the last person served may see a disarrayed unappetizing serving platter. Also, if every guest orders a different entree, many serving platters would be required. For further details of these styles of service, see "Essentials of Good Table Service," included in Selected References at the end of this chapter.

Banquet service, unlike other types discussed, is a preset service and menu for a given number of people for a specific time of day. Some items, such as salads, butter, salad dressings, or cocktails may be on the table before guests are seated. Either the American style or the Russian style may be used.

For American style, dinner plates filled in the kitchen may be transported to the guests in several different ways: preheated carts are filled with up to 96 plates and taken to the dining room before guests arrive. Service personnel remove plates from these carts to serve their guests. Another way is for each waiter to go to the serving area, obtain two dinner plates, one in each hand and, as a group, go to the dining room and serve one table completely. Several trips back and forth are required to finish this service. Still another method is to use bussers to carry trays of dinner plates to the dining room, place them on tray stands, and return for another load. Service personnel working as a team remain in the dining room to serve the plates as bussers bring them in. Guests at one table are served before they move on to another table. In each case, the head table is served first; then the table furthest from the serving area should be served next, so that each succeeding trip will be shorter.

The Russian style, if used at banquets, is used as it was described for restaurant service.

Drive-In Service. Drive-in service requires waiters or waitresses (usually called carhops) to serve patrons who drive up to the restaurant and remain in their cars to be served. This service was most popular in the 1950s and 1960s; today many patrons seem to prefer going into a restaurant instead of having to eat in their cars. A majority of drive-ins have provided dining space inside, although many still enjoy good business as they were.

PORTABLE MEALS

This type of service is that of delivering meals to the residences of aged, chronically ill, or infirm individuals not requiring hospitalization. This plan, sometimes called "meals-on-wheels," attempts to meet the need for nutritious meals for those persons who are temporarily disabled or for the aged, who usually are living alone and unable to cook for themselves. In communities where such a plan is in operation, meals are contracted and paid for directly by the individual in need of the service, or some community agency or volunteer organization may provide funds for persons unable to pay. Desirably, the menus are planned by a dietitian or nutritionist working cooperatively with the organization providing the meals. Food is prepared by restaurants, hospitals, or other foodservices and may be delivered by them or by volunteer workers.

Federal legislation under the Older Americans Act, Titles IV and VII, provides funds for meals for the elderly who are isolated and in need of improved nutrition. Although primarily allocated for bringing these people to central dining rooms for socialization as well as food, a certain percent of the funds could be used for home-delivered meals. This project has given impetus to the portable meals program. New designs in equipment for carrying the meals (see Fig. 5.9 for an example) have been made to assure food safety during transportation.

Another example of portable meals is that often used for industrial or business office foodservice. In some industrial plants, foods are distributed to workers at their workplace by mobile carts that move throughout the plant. Carts are equipped with heated and refrigerated sections for simple menu items such as soup, hot beverages, sandwiches, and snack items.

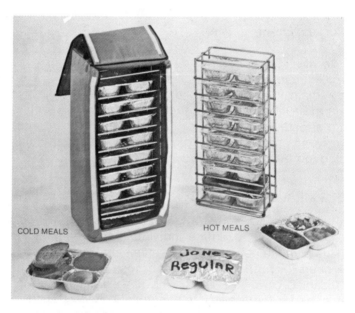

FIGURE 5.9 *A lightweight insulated carrying case for transporting home delivered meals; meal-ready temperatures can be maintained for up to two hours. Courtesy, Dietary Products Division American Hospital Supply Corporation.*

Catering companies may be employed to bring a truck to the yard of the plant and set up a canteen-type service that in itself, is portable. Workers must leave their stations, however, to take advantage of this service. Catering companies also service office employees with meals delivered to them on a contract basis. One company [18] in New York City offers an office-delivered, diet lunch-only program for those who wish a calorie-restricted meal service. This service has been so popular that the company is expanding to other cities.

Many variations of these basic styles of service are to be found in today's innovative foodservice systems. A brief review of some of these are given for selected types of organizations.

FOODSERVICE IN SELECTED TYPES OF ORGANIZATIONS
HOSPITALS AND EXTENDED CARE FACILITIES

In hospitals and extended care facilities such as nursing homes, tray service is generally used for patients' meals. One of the more common practices in large hospitals is to send the prepared food to serving pantries on the various floors, where it is arranged on trays and carried to patients. Cold foods such as bread, salads, and desserts may be sent to the pantries 20 to 30 minutes before serving time. Hot food is taken from the main kitchen to the pantries in heated food trucks a few minutes before serving time. Dishes and trays are washed and stored in each pantry. This is the decentralized service described earlier in this chapter. Many hospitals have central tray service; that is, all trays are set up in one place and sent directly from there to the patients by vertical conveyor from which they are picked up by aides and carried to the patients. The use of a portable conveyor belt, as shown in Fig. 5.10, provides a serving area that can be moved away if space is needed for other purposes.

Research conducted recently has attempted to determine the most efficient methods for patient foodservice in terms of labor cost, personnel usage, and food quality. Results have led to the adoption by many hospitals of the method whereby trays are assembled in a central commissary and delivered to the hospital with food in a chilled state. Trays are distributed to floor pantries or kitchens, where the food is reheated in microwave ovens. Figure 5.11 shows one such setup. This is sometimes considered an adaptation of air-

[18] *"Desk-delivered Diet Lunches Take Off (Pounds),"* Restaurant Business Magazine, 74, 80 (June 1975).

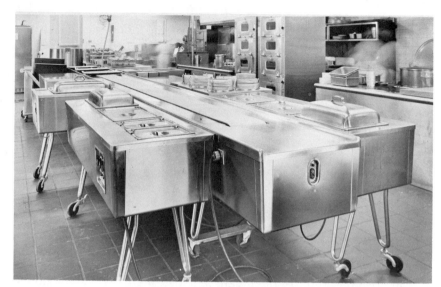

FIGURE 5.10 Wheel-away conveyor belt and mobile hot and cold food units for hospital tray assembly provide flexibility in arrangement. Courtesy, S. Blickman, Inc.

FIGURE 5.11 A bank of microwave ovens for rethermalizing preplated, chilled food in a hospital serving pantry. Courtesy, Hobart Corporation.

328

line foodservice. The Ready-Prepared System may be used in the same way for service.

Electronics and automation have replaced older traditional methods of serving in some hospitals. In one, a Ready-Prepared system was utilized with the added feature of having individual portions of frozen food ordered electronically from

plastic loading devices called cassettes. Each cassette holds 20 to 28 portions of food. The cassettes are then fitted into ejection devices called magazines, each holding nine cassettes or 180 portions of food.

Food is ordered electronically from the magazines from a console located at the assembly area in the dietary department. The console is equipped with 24 numbered buttons to correspond to the 24 magazines. Beside each menu item selected is a number that also corresponds to a button on the console and a magazine.

The person operating the console picks up the tray and the menu, then pushes the buttons corresponding to the patient's selections. He then pushes another button marked "Delivery," places the menu on the short conveyor, and sends the tray to the next person, whose task is to place the ordered portions on the tray. This procedure is repeated until every tray has been ordered.[19]

Another system [20] (VOSS Optacon developed by Vosswerke, Hanover, Germany) "incorporates automatic preparation and handling of foods, continuous processing equipment, streamlined materials flow, and efficient distribution with electronically controlled guidance and data processing for various functions." Space savings of 30 percent in a 1000-bed hospital and reduction in personnel requirements of 33 percent have been effected by this system.

Integral heating, which has previously been described, has proved to provide piping hot food of good quality to patients. This system, combined with monorail delivery, provides excellent but somewhat expensive service. At present integral heat units are available on a lease basis only.

Some hospitals are now charging patients separately for meals or food consumed during their hospital stay. Realistic charges for board based on actual meals consumed gives the dietary department a firm basis for cost accounting and usually gives the patient a

[19] Barry D. Brown and Paul R. Doyon, *"An Automatic Electronic Food System,"* Hospitals, JAHA, 47 (21), 63 (November 1, 1973).

[20] Norbert Nicolaus, *"Automated Food Preparation and Service,"* Hospitals, JAHA, 44 (6), 108 (March 16, 1970).

break if he is not able to eat certain meals. Charges are calculated for each type of diet.

Balsley [21] discussed the increase in hospital mergers and the development of multihospital units as a possibility for the future. She warned, "Dietitians and educators in the dietetic field might well give thought to the management skills needed for centrally controlled, large scale, more diverse and dispersed organizations." Undoubtedly new and emerging systems will be the result.

Another method of serving patients is in patient dining rooms for those who are ambulatory or in wheelchairs. They are found in all types of hospitals, including those for the mentally ill. The therapeutic values of social contacts at mealtime have been recognized, and provisions have been made for such patient dining in a majority of hospitals. Either self-service or table service may be used.

Meals for hospital staff and employees are usually provided in a pay cafeteria. Vended food often supplements regular cafeteria service and is available to all hospital personnel and visitors on a 24-hour basis. A few hospitals provide private dining rooms where certain patients may dine with family or friends.

SCHOOL FOODSERVICE

Over the years, the major objective of school foodservice has been to provide a nutritious meal for children at as low a cost as possible and to provide some nutrition education through the program. Dietitians may use the meal hour to teach good nutrition as shown in Fig. 5.12. Schools use many different systems, each locality utilizing its resources to best advantage. The geographical location, degree of student participation, and local support in addition to federal funding all help to determine the system to be used.

In 1970, the U.S. Department of Agriculture granted authority to schools to use commercial contracting firms to supply school lunches without jeopardizing their federal financial support. As a result, a number of school districts have contracted for their meals.

Other innovative systems have been inaugurated to provide meals to students in schools without foodservice facilities. Moskowitz [22] reported the advantages and disadvantages of a sandwich

[21] Marie Balsley, "Hospital Mergers and Multi-Hospital Units: Impact on Foodservice and Dietetics," Journal of American Dietetic Association, 66 (6), 609 (June 1975).

[22] Ruth B. Moskowitz, R. D., "Mission Impossible," School Foodservice Journal, XXVII (10), 28 (November/December 1973). Copyright © American School Food Service Association (1973).

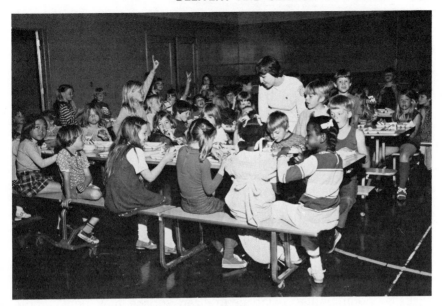

FIGURE 5.12   *School foodservice programs offer excellent opportunities for the promotion of nutrition education.*

lunch provided from either a vendor or from the school district's central kitchen. This is a complete lunch in a plastic-wrapped tray and contains a sandwich, fruit, and salad, plus milk. A variation of this is an infrared hot sandwich meal with sandwiches heated in their wrappers in portable equipment supplied by the commissary vendor. Children can heat their own entree; milk, salad, and fruit will complete the meal.

Other systems reported are the hot, preplated meal delivered in insulated trays either by an outside company or the school's commissary; a cup-can system with the main entree in a can, which is heated onsite and the contents eaten from the can; and a freeze-dried casserole that requires hot water and reconstituting on premises. With each of these systems, fruit, salad, milk and bread complete the meal.

The Chicago school system [23] uses a combination of centralized production, with bulk delivery to the schools, the nutripack system of prepacked bag lunches, and a hot and cold pack system all under contract.

[23] *"School Foodservice in Chicago,"* Cooking for Profit, 42 *(274), 46 (October 1973).*

Tom Farley,[24] director of Milwaukee, Wisconsin's school food-service program, holds the view that on-premises preparation best suits the needs of children and can be economically sound because of their high student participation. "We do not get one complaint a year from 160 schools in which we serve 75,000 meals daily. The secret of our success is that for the past 10 years, we have tailored our menus to students' tastes." A student council of 66 members meets seven times a year to taste test new food items, discuss menus, and become involved in menu planning itself. A single selection is offered and is the same in every school.

Many schools have adopted the satellite system: using one school in an area to prepare meals for several other schools close by. Food is usually distributed hot, in bulk, to be served in the other schools that ordinarily have preparation facilities available, but these facilities are not in use in order to economize.

When the foods arrive at the satellite schools, hot foods are reheated and finishing touches are given to make the food "table-ready" and attractive before the children come for lunch. Managers in other communities using centralized service may find it more desirable to have lunches packaged into individual portions at the preparation center. This eliminates the need for rehandling at the school. Specially designed and equipped trucks and an exact time schedule for deliveries are necessary for the success of this type of school foodservice.

COLLEGE AND UNIVERSITY FOODSERVICE

The National Association of College and University Food Service (NACUFS) has drawn a profile (1974) of average college foodservice operations throughout the country. The average college has a student enrollment of 12,000 students, of whom 4233 live on campus. It operates four dining halls, two snack bars and two miscellaneous units. It employees an average of 118 full-time workers, 35 part-time nonstudent workers and 267 student workers on each campus. Nationwide, minimum starting rate is $2.22 an hour and maximum wage is $3.77. Student workers start at $1.80 an hour. Average food cost is $.722 per meal and labor cost is $.498 per meal. An average of 9.6 meals per man-hour are produced.[25]

[24] *"School Foodservice at the Crossroads?"*, Cooking for Profit 44 *(295), 19 (July 1975).*
[25] *News Note.* School Foodservice Journal, XXVIII, 4 *(March 1974). Copyright © American School Food Service Association (1973).*

College foodservice has had many changes in recent years, as have other foodservice organizations. Residence hall dining is meeting student requests for extended meal hours (some are open continuously or nearly so for a 12-hour span), for more menu choices, and for greater intimacy in the dining areas. (See Appendix A, for more details.)

Free flow cafeterias, self-service of many items, and the installation of grill-snack bars that are open at off-meal hours are other trends. In some colleges, students may use their meal ticket to eat at any one of the residence halls on campus. See Fig. 11.27 for an example of a free flow cafeteria design.

Student union foodservices are resorting to many solutions to the competition they face with commercial foodservice operations close by. Some have leased space for fast food chain companies to operate a unit in their union building. Others have instigated many novel ideas to keep up with current "in" trends in foods to retain student trade and a desirable volume of business.

INDUSTRIAL PLANTS

Often the industrial plant operates 24 hours a day and serving units must provide continuous and rapid service. Certain simple devices and techniques have been found helpful in extending the services of the industrial cafeteria to capacity, and they are widely used to this end. They include staggered-line service, that is admission of groups of persons at 5- to 10-minute intervals; the serving of a plate lunch, with the possibility of adding certain items as desired; the installation of several short counters; the simplification of serving, using as few side dishes as possible; the employment of adequate help for the service; and the use of prepaid meal tickets to relieve delay at the cashier's desk.

Types of service other than cafeteria are used to replace, supplement, or extend industrial foodservices to employees. In large plants particularly, mobile carts are used to carry a limited number of items such as soup, milk, coffee, sandwiches, fruit, cookies, and pie. The carts are moved throughout the plant to reach the workers at their stations, thus allowing them maximum time for lunch. Canteens, lunch counters, or vending machines located at various points in the building are also used to assure a quick meal and adequate food at the time and place it is most needed by the personnel.

Executive dining rooms are provided by some companies to permit more leisurely dining and a place to entertain business guests and visitors. Table service is generally used when such dining facilities are available.

AIRLINE FOODSERVICE

Ever increasing use of airlines as a common mode of transportation has focused attention on the major competitive factor among airlines—foodservice. It is estimated by Inflight Food/Services Association (IFSA) that the 12 large airlines, 10 regional, and about 5 local airlines together spend close to $1 billion annually on foodservice expenses including food, beverage, and equipment. Foods served range from the complimentary beverage service on short flights to gourmet meals served on fine china, crystal, and linen on certain airlines' flights.

The type of menu offered changes frequently to meet customers' preferences, for example, a lunch-type menu at noon instead of a full dinner meal and a variety of special diet and other special meals such as kosher, soul food, vegetarian, and children's menus. Airlines cater to regional likes and habits and to the type of customer ordinarily using a particular flight—business persons, vacationers, or students. Over the years, the passenger mix has changed considerably from the once predominantly business traveler to the average American pleasure tourist; this has influenced the foods offered.

Food is supplied to airlines either from their own or subsidiary commissaries, or on contract from caterers. Many airlines use a combination of both in order to have meals available at the many locations along their routes.

Food for the planes generally is preportioned at the commissary. (See Fig. 5.13). Those to be served hot are handled in one of three ways: preplated and chilled, frozen, or held hot for loading aboard. The chilled or frozen meals are rethermalized on the plane in either small convection ovens or in microwave units. Some airlines control part of their inflight cooking in conduction ovens with energy input to produce temperatures up to 500°F in a short time. These two procedures are suitable for flights long enough to allow time for reheating the number of meals required and for serving and dining. One airline rethermalizes foods for hot holding in huge rack-type convection ovens, as shown in Fig. 5.13.

Meals that are hot when put onto the planes may have been frozen and reheated just before flight time or served hot and, in both cases, placed in an insulated holding cabinet or "buffet" that is

FIGURE 5.13 *Airline commissary utilizes industrial assembly line techniques.* (a) *Preplated portions are loaded onto racks.* (b) *Racks are rolled into specially designed convection ovens for fast heating just before flight-time loading. Courtesy, Cooking For Profit.*

335

transported directly to a plane. The meals are for short flights and must be served soon; they do not lend themselves to longer flights or to the desire of the passengers to eat now or wait until later.

Airlines have expanded their use of cold plates, salads, sandwiches, and snacks to help economize and to provide a variety of meals. In some cases, with economy-rate flights, passengers may purchase a meal on board, but meal service is not a part of the fare.

On some of the newer very large planes a galley and kitchen are included to "permit a smooth integration of foods and supplies from production to packing and serving stages. On the L1011, the galley is located below the main cabin, so food and supplies are packed below deck, where meals are prepared away from passengers. Finally, food is transferred to serving areas throughout the cabin." [26]

The trend in airline foodservice seems to be for the use of commissary-produced foods operated either by the airline or a catering company and a desire to meet passengers' wants yet operate on a sound, economical basis. Good food merchandising techniques will continue to help meet the competition for business among airlines.

[26] Phillip B Fitzell, "Sky's the Limit on Airline Foodservice," Restaurant Business Magazine, 74, 45 (July 1975).

SELECTED REFERENCES

Bard, Bernard, *The School Lunchroom: Time of Trial,* Wiley, New York, 1968.

Dahmer, Sandra J., and Kurt W. Kahl, *The Waiter and Waitress Training Manual,* Cahners, Boston, 1975.

Eshbach, Charles E., Editor, *Food Service Trends,* Cahners, Boston, 1974.

"Essentials of Good Table Service," Revised Edition, The Cornell Hotel and Restaurant Administration Quarterly, Ithaca, New York, 1968.

"Food Service Manual for Health Care Institutions," Second Edition, American Hospital Association, Chicago, 1972.

Glew, George, *Cook/Freeze Catering An Introduction to its Technology,* Faber and Faber, London, 1973.

Jacobs, H. Lee, and Woodrow W. Morris, *Nursing and Retirement Home Administration,* The Iowa State University Press, Ames, Iowa, 1966.

Jernigan, Anna K., and Lynne N. Ross, *Food Service Equipment: Selection, Arrangement, and Use,* The Iowa State University Press, Ames, Iowa, 1974.

Kahrl, Willaim L., *Foodservice on a Budget,* Cahners, Boston, 1974.

Kahrl, William L., *Planning And Operating A Successful Food Service Operation,* Chain Store Age Books, an affiliate of Lebhar-Friedman, Inc., New York, 1973.

Kotschevar, Lendal H., *Management By Menu,* National Institute for the Foodservice Industry, Chicago, 1975.

McKenna, Francis X., *Starting and Managing A Small Drive-In Restaurant,* The Starting and Managing Series, Volume 23, Small Business Administration, Superintendent of Documents, U.S. Government Printing Office, Washington, D.C., 1972.

Millross, Janice, Alan Speht, Kathleen Holdsworth and George Glew, *The Utilisation of the Cook-Freeze Catering System for School Meals,* Cater-

337

ing Research Unit, Procter Department of Foods and Leather Science, The University of Leeds, W. S. Maney and Sons Ltd., Leeds, England.

Pinkert, M.S., *The Ready Foods System for Health Care Facilities,* Cahners, Boston, 1973.

SECTION 2
ORGANIZATION AND ADMINISTRATION

6.
ORGANIZATION AND MANAGEMENT

The foodservice industry is commonly ranked fourth in the dollar volume of sales among the major industries in the United States and employs approximately 2 million people. The successful operation of an industry of such magnitude or of any one enterprise is dependent to a large extent on the organization structure, the application of the principles of scientific management, and the effectiveness of its personnel.

In today's economy, external and internal environmental factors are having an impact on the foodservice industry as they are on all industries in this country. Blaker [1] cited some current trends facing foodservice operations, such as rising costs, decreasing productivity, governmental control, unionization, increasing size and complexity, technological advances, and the food factory concept. Change has, and will continue to have, an important impact on foodservice and requires not only a basic knowledge of organization and management but an awareness by dietitians and foodservice managers of changing philosophies in management.

[1] *Gertrude G. Blaker, "Annual Administrative Reviews—Food Service,"* Hospitals, JAHA, 47, *129 (April 1973).*

ORGANIZATION

THEORIES OF ORGANIZATION

Dale [2] tells us that organization for management is as old as human society and grew out of a common interest and combined effort to accomplish a common goal. Since that time, many theories have been proposed, particularly since the early part of the twentieth century. Most of them fall into three categories: classical or traditional, human relations, and modern or systems approach.

Classical. Classical organization theory rests on several premises— that division of work is essential for efficiency, that coordination is the primary responsibility of management in the organization of work, that the formal structure is the main vehicle for organizing and administering work activities, and that the span of control sets outside limits on the number of people responsible to a given manager.[3] Other principles that emerged during this period were: (1) scalar principle, in which authority and responsibility flow in a direct line vertically from the highest level of the organization to the lowest; (2) delegation, in which decisions are delegated to the lowest competent level; (3) unity of command, which specified that each person should be accountable to only one superior; (4) functional principle, based on specialization of work; and (5) line and staff principle, in which support and advisory activities were provided for the main functions of an organization. Classical organization theory continues to have great relevance to basic managerial problems, but it has been criticized as being too mechanistic and not recognizing the interaction of groups and the decision-making processes in the formal structure.

Human Relations. The human relations theory evolved from the effort to compensate for some of the deficiencies of the classical theory. Where classical organization advocates focused on tasks, structure, and authority, the human relations theorists introduced the behavioral sciences as an integral part of organization theory. They viewed the organization as a social system and recognized the existence of the informal organization, in which workers align them-

[2] *Ernest Dale, "Planning and Developing the Company Organization Structure," American Management Association Research Report No. 20, pp. 14–15, 1952.*
[3] *Theo Haimann and William G. Scott,* Management in the Modern Organization, *Second Edition, Houghton Mifflin, Boston, p. 121, 1974.*

selves into social groups within the framework of the formal organization. Many human relations theorists held that employee participation in management planning and decision making yielded positive effects in terms of morale and productivity.

Systems Approach. The systems approach applies to organization and management the general systems concept that has been used in the physical and biological sciences for some time. Kast and Rosenzweig [4] define a system as "an organized unitary whole composed of two or more independent parts, components, or subsystems and delineated by identifiable boundaries from its environmental suprasystem."

In this context they define an organization as:

1. A subsystem of its broader environment, and

2. Goal-oriented—people with a purpose; including

3. A technical subsystem—people using knowledge, techniques, equipment, and facilities;

4. A structural subsystem—people working together on integrated activities;

5. A psychosocial subsystem—people in social relationships, and coordinated by

6. A managerial subsystem—planning and controlling the overall endeavor.

The term systems approach has a broad connotation, and Johnson, Kast, and Rosenzweig [5] identify these three areas of current usage: as a systems philosophy, which is described as a way of thinking about phenomena in terms of wholes—including parts,

[4] From Organization and Management, A Systems Approach, *Second Edition by Fremont E. Kast and James E. Rosenweig. Copyright © 1970, 1974 by McGraw-Hill Inc. Used with permission of McGraw-Hill Book Co., p. 20.*

[5] From The Theory and Management of Systems, *Third Edition, by Richard A. Johnson, Fremont E. Kast, and James E. Rosenzweig. Copyright © 1963, 1967, 1973 by McGraw-Hill, Inc. Used with permission of McGraw-Hill Book Co., p. 19.*

components, or subsystems and with emphasis on their interrelationships; systems analysis, as a method for problem solving or decision making; and systems management, as the application of the systems theory to managing organizational systems or subsystems.

The systems theory is still in its early stages of development but, according to Beach: [6]

Unquestionably it has made major contributions to the study of organization and management in recent years. Systems theory aids in diagnosing the interactive relationships among task, technology, environment, and the needs of organization members. When viewing an organization as a social system, the behavior and attitudes of the members are seen as interdependent. Practitioners have adopted the system's conceptualization in designing, building, and operating management information systems and automation processes. There have been many applications in aerospace and weapons systems planning, design, fabrication and procurement. In partnership government and business are now building entire transportation systems not just individual vehicles and individual highways.

The application of the systems approach to foodservice has been limited, but a review of the current literature reveals an increase in the systems approach as a way of viewing foodservice. The identification of the systems and subsystems varies with the different authors, but perhaps the major contribution so far has been in thinking of the foodservice as a subsystem operating within the larger system, for example, within a health care, school, or university system.

Space does not permit an indepth discussion of the many contributions that have been made to the present body of knowledge in organization theory, but many of the references listed at the end of the chapter include comprehensive discussions on this subject.

ORGANIZATION STRUCTURE

Beach[7] defines an organization as "a system, having an established structure and conscious planning, in which people work and deal with one another in a coordinated and cooperative manner for the accomplishment of recognized goals." The formal organiza-

[6] *Dale S. Beach,* Personnel, The Management of People at Work, *Third Edition, Macmillan, New York, p. 169, 1975.*
[7] *Dale S. Beach,* Personnel, The Management of People at Work, *Third Edition, Macmillan, New York, p. 161, 1975.*

tion is the planned structure that establishes a pattern of relationships among the various components of the organization. The informal organization refers to those aspects of the system that arise spontaneously from the activities and interactions of participants.[8]

In the management literature, according to Dale,[9] the term organization is:

> Used in two somewhat different senses: to designate a process and to describe the results of that process. Considered as a process, then, organization includes (1) breaking down the work necessary to achieve the objective into individual jobs and (2) providing means of coordinating the efforts of the jobholders. . . . The result of the process of organizing is the "organization"—the people employed and the network of relationships among them.

Certain steps are necessary in developing the framework of an organization structure if goals of an enterprise are to be accomplished and the workers' talents developed to their fullest potential. These steps may be summarized as follows:

1. *Determine and define objectives.* The purpose of every organization dealing with manpower is to accomplish with the efforts of people some basic purpose or objective with the greatest efficiency, maximum economy, and minimum effort, and to provide for the personal development of the people working in the organization.

Specifically, a foodservice has as its goal the production and service of the best food possible within the financial resources. It is important that these objectives and the plans and policies for their achievement be presented in writing and understood by all responsible.

2. *Analyze and classify work to be done.* This is accomplished by dividing the total work necessary for the accomplishment of overall goals into its major parts, and grouping each into like, or similar, activities. Examination

---

[8] *From* Organization and Management, A Systems Approach, *Second Edition, by* Fremont E. Kast *and* James E. Rosenzweig. *Copyright © 1970, 1974 by McGraw-Hill, Inc. Used with permission of McGraw-Hill Book Co., p. 208.*
[9] *From* Management: Theory and Practice, *Second Edition, by* Ernest Dale. *Copyright © 1969 by McGraw-Hill, Inc. Used with permission of McGraw-Hill Book Co., p. 178.*

of the work to be done will reveal tasks that are similar or are logically related. Such classification may be made by grouping activities that require similar skills, the same equipment, or duties performed in the same areas. There are no arbitrary rules for grouping. In a foodservice the activities could be grouped as purchasing and storage, preparation and processing, housekeeping and maintenance, and service and dishwashing. Each of these groupings might be broken into smaller classifications, depending on the type and size of the enterprise. With the increasing complexity of foodservice organizations and the trend toward centralization of certain functions, the organization structure takes on new dimensions and must consider the total management structure as well as the organization of its individual units.

3. *Describe in some detail the work or activity in terms of the employee.* This step will be discussed in more detail in this chapter under "job description."

4. *Determine and specify the relationship of the workers to each other and to management.* The work should be grouped into departments or other organizational units, with responsibility and authority defined for each level. It is generally understood that each person assigned to a job will be expected to assume the responsibility for performing the tasks given him and that he will be held accountable for the results. However, he can be accountable only to the degree that he has been given responsibility and authority. Responsibility without authority is meaningless. An assignment should be specific and in writing. For an organizational structure to become operational, of course, requires the selection of qualified personnel, provision of adequate financing and equipment, and a suitable physical environment. No successful organization structure remains static. It must be a continuing process that moves with changing concepts within the system and with changing conditions in its environment.

Application of the principles of organization and administration to a specific situation should precede any attempt at the operation of a foodservice unit. A detailed plan may be outlined for use as a guide in initiating a new foodservice of any type or reorganizing one previously in operation. To illustrate, organization plans for two college residence halls are given in Appendix A. The same basic principles exemplified there would apply in formulating plans for other types of foodservices, such as cafeterias, hospital foodservices, restaurants, and hotel dining rooms.

TYPES OF ORGANIZATIONS

Two types of authority relationships most often found in foodservice systems are line and line-and-staff relationships. Large, complex operations may be organized on a functional basis.

Line. In the line organization, lines of authority are clearly drawn, and each individual is responsible to the person ranking above him on the organization chart. Thus, authority and responsibility pass from the top-ranking member down to the lowest in rank. In such an organization structure each man knows to whom he is responsible and, in turn, who is responsible to him.

Organization line structure can grow in two directions, vertically or horizontally. Vertical growth occurs through the delegation of authority, in which the individual at the top delegates work to his immediate subordinates, who redelegate part or all of this work to their subordinates, and so on down the line. For example, the director of a growing cafeteria operation may add an assistant manager, thus creating another level in the chain of command. When the distance from the top to bottom becomes too great for effective coordination, the responsibilities may be redistributed horizontally through departmentalization. In establishing departments, activities are grouped into natural units, with a manager given authority and accepting responsibility for that area of activities. There are several ways of dividing the work but, in foodservices, the most usual are by function, product, or location. The work may be divided into production and service; in dietetics, by administrative, clinical, and education; in a central commissary, by meat, vegetable, salad, and bakery departments; or by individual schools in a multiunit school foodservice system.

Advantages of the line organization include expediency in decision making, direct placement of responsibility, and clear understanding of authority relationships. A major disadvantage is that the person at the top tends to become overloaded with too much detail, thus limiting the time that he can devote to planning and research necessary for development and growth of the organization. There is no specialist to whom one can turn for help in the various areas of operation.

Line and Staff. As an enterprise grows, the line organization may no longer be adequate to cope with the many diversified responsibilities demanded of the person at the top. Staff specialists, such as personnel director, research and development specialist, and data processing coordinator, are added to assist the lines in an advisory capacity. The line positions and personnel are involved directly in accomplishing the work for which the organization was created; the staff advises and supports the line. A staff position also may be an assistant who serves as an extension of a line officer. The potential for conflict exists between line and staff personnel if there is not a clear understanding of the lines of authority. For example, if a staff specialist recommends a change in procedure, the order for the change would come from the line staff. Friction may arise if a strong staff person tries to overrule the manager or if the manager does not make full use of the abilities of the staff.

Functional. Some writers consider functional authority as staff and others consider it a distinct type in itself. Functional authority exists when an individual has delegated to him a limited authority over a specified segment of activities. In a multiunit foodservice company, for example, the responsibility for purchasing or for menu planning and quality control may be vested in a vice-president who then has authority over that function in all units.

MANAGEMENT

What is management? Allen [10] tells us that:

Definitions and interpretations vary widely. Some see management as a complex of personal and administrative skills. Others view it as a technique of leadership. Still others define it as a means of coordination or cooperation. These are part of the picture, but they are inadequate to our needs. For our purpose, we must be able to identify management as a body of systematized knowledge, based on general principles which are verifiable in business practice.

According to this author, "If we are to consider management a profession, a key problem is to decide what a manager is."

[10] *Louis A. Allen,* Management and Organization, *McGraw-Hill, New York, pp. 3 and 5, 1958.*

Strong [11] answers this by saying:

The manager plans, organizes, motivates, directs and controls. These are the broad aspects of his work. He adds foresight, order, purpose, integration of effort, and effectiveness to the contributions of others. That is the best use of the word "manage." That is the work of the manager.

What do managers "manage"? What do they plan, organize, motivate, direct and control? In general terms, the six M's: men, money, materials, machinery, markets, and minutes—the resources common to any organization, be it a church, a lodge, the government, or a business firm.

FUNCTIONS OF MANAGEMENT

The functions of management in an organization are commonly classified as planning, organizing, delegating, actuating, and controlling. Some writers add staffing as a major function. That there is a degree of overlapping is evident in the functions themselves and in the efforts to classify them.

Planning. Planning is the basic function, and all others are dependent upon it. The objective of planning is to think ahead, determine clearly objectives and policies, and select a course of action toward the accomplishment of the goals. Day-to-day planning of operational activities and short- and long-range planning toward department and institution goals are part of this function. Overall planning is the responsibility of top management, but participation at all levels in goal setting and development of new plans and procedures increases their effectiveness.

Forecasting is an important factor in effective planning for the future operating program of any company. Predictions of trends for the immediate and distant future based on objective study of past and present situations usually are more reliable than mere guesses. Outside or external factors such as social, economic, political, and other environmental conditions are involved in forecasting, as are internal factors such as size of plant and productivity of the personnel. A study of the interrelationships of such factors and their effects on the business, from data such as personal incomes, population growth, cost of living, and technological developments in food and equipment, should help the food manager to interpret his possible future needs for personnel, physical facilities, and other budgetary

[11] *Earl P. Strong,* The Management of Business, *Harper and Row, New York, p. 5, 1965.*

items. A high degree of accuracy in forecasting is difficult to attain because of the uncertainties of the future. However, forecasting has merit in that it requires creative thinking, provides some helpful information, and may call attention to current problem areas within the organization.

Organizing. The organizing function identifies activities and tasks, divides tasks into positions, and puts like tasks together in order to take advantage of special abilities and skills of the worker and use his talents effectively. Perhaps the chief function of the organizing process is the establishment of relationships among all other functions of management.

Delegating. Delegation of responsibility is essential to distribute work loads to qualified individuals at various levels. Whoever delegates a responsibility should not fail to do so with detailed instructions as to what is expected of the subordinate and the necessary authority to carry out the responsibilities. If a subordinate is not given sufficient authority the job is merely assigned, not delegated. Andrew Carnegie, who it is said built a fortune on the principle of delegation, once remarked, "It marks a big step in a man's development when he realizes that other men can help him do a better job than he can do alone."

Actuating. Actuating is getting work done with people. It is concerned with employees as human beings. Studies have shown that most people work at only 50 to 60 percent efficiency, and some investigators place this figure as low as 45 percent. The alert manager is aware that through careful, intelligent guidance and counseling, and by effective supervision, the worker's productivity may be increased as much as 20 percent. This may mean the difference between financial success and failure of an enterprise.

Controlling. Control tends to ensure performance in accordance with plans and is a necessary function of all areas of foodservice. This necessitates measuring quantity of output, quality of the finished product, food and labor costs, and the efficient use of workers' time. Through control, standards of acceptability and accountability are set for performance. A good control system prevents present and future deviation from plans and does much to stimulate an employee to maintain the standards of the foodservice director. The control function should be one of guidance, not command. It is concerned with employees as human beings with interests to be stimulated, aptitudes and abilities to be directed and developed, and comprehension and understanding of their responsibilities to be increased. Records and evaluations of the results of work done are kept as the work progresses in order to compare performance with the yardstick of acceptability. Noting deviations from the established standard and making necessary corrections in work schedules and procedures are all a part of the manager's control responsibilities.

TOOLS OF MANAGEMENT

The director of a foodservice commonly uses the organization chart as a means of explaining and clarifying the structure of an organization. He also uses job descriptions, job specifications, and work schedules as devices for the clear presentation of personnel and their responsibilities to top management and to employees. These mechanical means are indispensable in the able direction and supervision of a foodservice and for convenience may be called tools of organization and management. Performance appraisal as a tool of management is discussed in Chapter 8.

Organization Chart. The chart of an organization may be considered the first tool of management. It presents graphically the basic groupings and relationshsips of positions and functions. The chart presents a picture of the formal organization structure and serves many useful purposes but does have some limitations. While lines of authority are depicted on the chart, the degree of authority and responsibility at each level is not shown. Informal relationships between equals or between people in different parts of the organization are not evident. For this reason, job descriptions and organization manuals are valuable supplements to the organization chart.

The organization chart usually is constructed on the basis of the line of authority but may be based on functional activity or a combination of the two. Functions and positions are graphically presented by the use of blocks or circles. Solid lines connecting the various blocks indicate the channels of authority. Those persons with the greatest authority are shown at the top of the chart and those with the least at the bottom. Advisory responsibility and lines of communication often are shown by use of dotted lines. Organization charts for a small and a large hospital are shown in Figs. 6.1 and 6.2.

Another method of presenting an organization structure is by a circular chart, as illustrated in Fig. 6.3. The supreme position in this arrangement is the center of concentric circles. Functions making

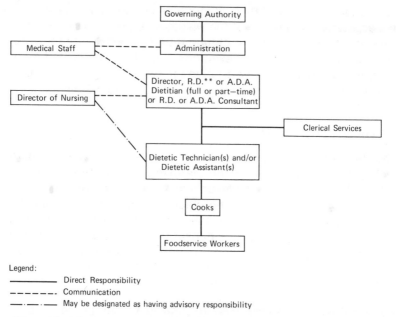

Legend:
——————— Direct Responsibility
— — — — —. Communication
—·—·— May be designated as having advisory responsibility

*The need for full—time, part—time, or consultant R.D.(s) and lines of communication will be dependent on type, complexity of patient care. and the systems of food service provided by the health care facility.
**R.D. The registered trademark for Registered Dietitian

For a group care facility of 100 or more beds a full—time Director, R.D. is reommended. A part—time Director, R.D. for 75—100 beds facility and for less than 75 beds an R.D. or A.D.A. Consultant are also recommended. The Director usually assumes the responsibilites assigned to Clinical and Administrative R.D.s.

FIGURE 6.1   *Organization chart for the department of dietetics in a hospital or other group care facility of less than 150 beds.* Courtesy, The American Dietetic Association (revised 1975).*

up the structure are clustered around this center; the closer the position is located to the center, the more important the function. Positions of relative equal importance are located on the same concentric circle. Solid lines joining the blocks representing functions indicate the channels of formal authority, the same as in conventional organization charts.

Job Description. A job description is an organized list of duties that reflects required skills and responsibilities in a specific position. It may be thought of as an extension of the organization chart in that it shows activities and job relationships for the positions identified on the organization chart. Job descriptions are valuable for matching qualified applicants to the job, for orientation and training of em-

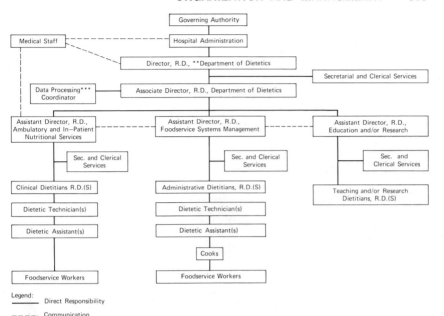

FIGURE 6.2 Organization chart for the department of dietetics in a large hospital (500 beds or more), health center or other group care facility.* Courtesy, The American Dietetic Association (revised 1975).

ployees, for performance appraisal, for establishing rates of pay, and for defining limits of authority and responsibility. They should be written for every position in the foodservice and should be reviewed and updated periodically. In many organizations, the job descriptions are incorporated into a procedure manual or kept in a looseleaf notebook for easy access.

Job descriptions may be written in either narrative or outline form or a combination of the two. The format probably will vary according to the job classification; for example, the work of the foodservice employee is described in terms of specific duties and skill requirements, but the job description for the professional position is more likely to be written in terms of broad areas of responsibilities. Most job descriptions include identifying information, a job summary, and specific duties and requirements. The initial job descrip-

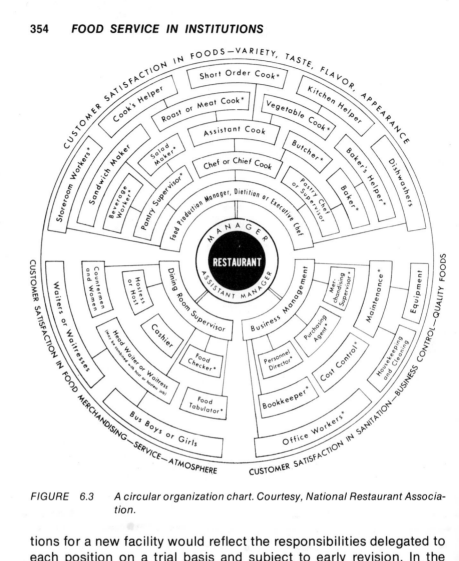

FIGURE 6.3   A circular organization chart. Courtesy, National Restaurant Association.

tions for a new facility would reflect the responsibilities delegated to each position on a trial basis and subject to early revision. In the case of an established unit, they are developed from information obtained from interviews with employees and supervisors and from observations by the person responsible for writing the job description. A *job analysis,* in which all aspects of a job are studied and analyzed, may be conducted first to collect information for the job description.

The following job description may be useful as a guide. The exact content and format, however, will vary according to the posi-

JOB DESCRIPTION

Job title: First Cook   *Date:*   September 2, 19___
Job code: 2–26.32 Dept. 10   *Location:*   Kitchen of University Cafeteria

Job summary
  Prepares meats and main dishes, soups and gravies for noon meal.
  Cleans and washes small equipment used in cooking.
  Keeps own working area clean.

Performance requirements
  Responsibilities: responsible for the preparation of meat and main dishes, soups and gravies to be served at a stated time.
  Job knowledge: plan own work schedule, know basic principles of quantity food cookery and how to use certain equipment.
  Mental application: mentally alert.
  Dexterity and accuracy: accurate in weighing and measuring of food ingredients and portions.
  Equipment used: food chopper, mixer, ovens, ranges, steam cooker, steam-jacketed kettle, fryer, broiler, meat slicer.
  Standards of production: preparation of foods of high quality in specified quantities.

Supervision
  Under general supervision of dietitian.
  Gives some supervision to assistant cooks.

Relation to other jobs
  Promotion from: Salad maker or vegetable preparation worker.
  Promotion to: Foodservice supervisor (if education and ability warrants).

Qualifications
  Experience desirable but not required.
  Education and training.
    Technical or vocational training: none.
    Formal education: grammar school.
    Ability to read, write, and understand English.

---

tion being described and the needs and complexities of the institution.

Job Specification. A job specification is a written statement of the minimum standards that must be met by an applicant for a particular job. It covers duties involved in a job, the working conditions peculiar to the job, and personal qualifications required of the worker to carry through the assigned responsibilities successfully. This tool is used primarily by the employing officer in the selection and placement of the right person for the specific position. Many small institutions use the job description as a job specification also.

JOB SPECIFICATION

Payroll title: First Cook
Department: Preparation Department   *Occupational code:* 2–26.32
Supervised by: Dietitian
Job summary: Prepares meat, main dishes, soups, and gravies for noon meal.
Educational status: Speak, read, write English. Grammar school graduate or higher.
Experience required: Cooking in a cafeteria or restaurant 6 months desirable but not required.
Knowledge and skills: Knowledge of basic principles of quantity food preparation; ability to adjust recipes and follow directions; ability to plan work.
Physical requirements: Standard physical examination.
Personal requirements: Neat, clean; male or female.
References required: Two work and personal references.
Hours: 6:30 a.m. to 3:00 p.m., 5 days a week; days off to be arranged; 30-minute lunch period.
Wage code: Grade 3.
Promotional opportunities: To foodservice supervisor.
Advantages and disadvantages of the job: Location, environment, security.
Tests: None.

Work Schedule. A work schedule is an outline of work to be performed by an individual with stated procedures and time requirements for his duties. It is important to break down the tasks into an organized plan with careful consideration given to timing and sequence of operations. Work schedules are especially helpful in training new employees and are given to the employee after he has been hired and training has begun. This is one means of communication between the employer and employee. Work schedules should be reviewed periodically and adjustments made as needed to adapt to changes in procedures.

An example of a work schedule for a cafeteria worker is given in Fig. 6.4. For food production employees, the individual work schedule would outline in general terms the day's work routine, but would need to be supplemented by a daily production schedule giving specific assignments for preparation of the day's menu items and pre-preparation for the next day. A more detailed discussion of production scheduling is included in Chapter 4.

Van Egmond [12] suggests three basic types of work schedules:

---

[12] *Dorothy Van Egmond, School Foodservice, Avi Publishing Co., Westport, Connecticut, p. 77, 1974.*

WORK SCHEDULE FOR CAFETERIA COUNTER WORKER

Name: _____

Position—Cafeteria Counter Worker—No. 1
Days off: _____

Hours: 5:30 to 2:00 p.m.
30 min for breakfast
15 min for coffee break

Supervised by: _____
Relieved by: _____

5:30 to 7:15 A.M.:
1. Read breakfast menu
2. Ready equipment for breakfast meal
   a. Turn on heat in cafeteria counter units for hot foods, grill, dish warmers, etc.
   b. Prepare counter units for cold food
   c. Obtain required serving utensils and put in position for use
   d. Place dishes where needed, those required for hot food in dish warmer
3. Make coffee (consult supervisor for instructions and amount to be made)
4. Fill milk dispenser
5. Obtain food items to be served cold: fruit, fruit juice, dry cereals, butter, cream, etc. Place in proper location on cafeteria counter
6. Obtain hot food and put in hot section of counter
7. Check with supervisor for correct portion sizes if this has not been decided previously

6:30 to 8:00 A.M.:
1. Open cafeteria doors for breakfast service
2. Check meal tickets, volunteer lists, guest tickets, and collect cash as directed by supervisor
3. Replenish cold food items, dishes, and silver
4. Notify cook before hot items are depleted
5. Make additional coffee as needed
6. Keep counters clean; wipe up spilled food

8:00 to 8:30 A.M.:
Eat breakfast

8:30 to 10:30 A.M.:
1. Break down serving line and return leftover foods to refrigerators and cook's area as directed by supervisor
2. Clean equipment, serving counters, and tables in dining area
3. Prepare serving counters for coffee break period
   a. Get a supply of cups, saucers, and tableware
   b. Make coffee
   c. Fill cream dispensers
   d. Keep counter supplied during coffee break period (9:30–10:30)
4. Fill salad dressing, relish, and condiment containers for noon meal

10:30 to 11:30 A.M.:
1. Confer with supervisor regarding menu items and portion sizes for noon meal
2. Clean equipment, counters, and tables in dining area
3. Prepare counters for lunch:
   a. Turn on heat in hot counter and dish warmers
   b. Set out tea bags, cream, ice cups, glasses
   c. Place serving utensils and dishes in position for use
4. Make coffee
5. Fill milk and clean dispensers
6. Set portioned cold foods on cold counter

11:30 A.M. to 1:30 P.M.:
1. Open cafeteria doors for noon meal service
2. Replenish cold food items, dishes, and silver as needed
3. Keep counters clean; wipe up spilled food
4. Make additional coffee as needed

1:30 to 2:00 P.M.:
1. Turn off heating and cooling elements in serving counters
2. Help break down serving line
3. Return leftover foods to proper places
4. Serve late lunches to doctors and nurses
5. Clean equipment and serving counter as directed by supervisor

2:00 P.M.
Off duty

FIGURE 6.4   *Work schedule for cafeteria counter worker. Courtesy, American Hospital Association.*

357

individual, daily unit, and organization. Because the individual schedule on a daily basis would be too time consuming for most managers, she recommends the daily unit schedule, shown in Fig. 6.5. The organization work schedule gives the standing assignments by half hour periods for all employees in chart form. It does not relate specifically to the day's menu. This type of schedule shows graphically the total work load and its division among employees, but would not be effective unless accompanied by daily assignments or a production schedule.

SCHEDULING OF EMPLOYEES

Workers may be scheduled successfully only after thorough analysis and study of the jobs to be done, the working conditions, and the probable efficiency of the employees. The menu pattern, the form in which food is purchased, the method of preparation, and the total quantity needed are important factors in determining the amount of preparation time and labor required to produce and serve meals in a given situation. Good menu planning provides for variation in meal items and combinations from day to day, with a fairly uniform production schedule. Workers cannot be expected to maintain high interest and to work efficiently if they have little to do one day and are overworked the next.

Analysis of several sample menus in terms of total labor hours and the time of day required for the amounts and types of preparations is a basic consideration in determining the number of employees necessary in any foodservice. The total estimated work hours required to cover all activities within the organization divided by the number of working hours in the day would give an indication of the number of full-time employees needed. However, careful attention must be given to time schedules so that each employee will be occupied during his hours on duty. Certain preparations or service duties may require a reduction in the estimated number of full-time workers and the addition of some part-time ones during peak periods, in order to maintain the desired standards at an even tempo. A graphic presentation of the estimated work hours needed for each job assists to clarify the problems of scheduling and the distribution of the work load (Fig. 6.6).

Working conditions such as the physical factors of temperature, humidity, lighting, and safety influence the scheduling of personnel and affect their performance. Of particular importance is the amount and arrangement of equipment. The distance each employee must

WORK SCHEDULE

MENU:
LASAGNA CASSEROLE   BUTTERED FRENCH BREAD
TOSSED SALAD   MILK
CHILLED PEACH HALVES

Time	Manager 7 1/2 hr	6-Hr Assistant	5-Hr Assistant	4-Hr Assistant
7:30– 8:00	Make coffee or tea for teachers			
8:00– 8:30	Help with lasagna sauce	Prepare lasagna		
8:30– 9:00	Lunch count—Tickets		Dip up fruit and refrigerate	
9:00– 9:30				
9:30–10:00	Teachers' salads		Wash vegetables for salad	
10:00–10:30	Cut bread and butter	Prepare bread crumbs for fried chicken tomorrow		Cut up vegetables for salad
10:30–11:00			Put out desserts	Set up line—napkins, straws, dishes
11:00–11:30	Eat lunch—20 min Put food on steam table	Eat lunch—20 min Put food on steam table	Eat lunch—20 min Wash pots and pans	Mix salad for first lunch
11:30–12:00	Cashier	Serving Set up for next line	Serving Help in dishroom	Back up line Dishroom
12:00–12:30	Serving	Serving Set up for next line	Cashier Help in dishroom	Back up line Dishroom
12:30– 1:00	Serving	Serving Put away food	Cashier 10 min break	Back up line Dishroom
1:00– 1:30	Count money—10 min break Help to clean tables	10 min break Clean tables	Clean steamtable	Eat lunch (eat on own time)
1:30– 2:00	Prepare reports	Clean up		Clean dishroom
2:00– 2:30	Place orders			Help with kitchen cleanup
2:30– 3:00	Take topping out of freezer and put in refrigerator for tomorrow			

FIGURE 6.5   *Sample elementary school work schedule. Example of a daily unit schedule. Courtesy, Dorothy Van Egmond, School Foodservice, Avi Publishing Company, Westport, Connecticut.*

359

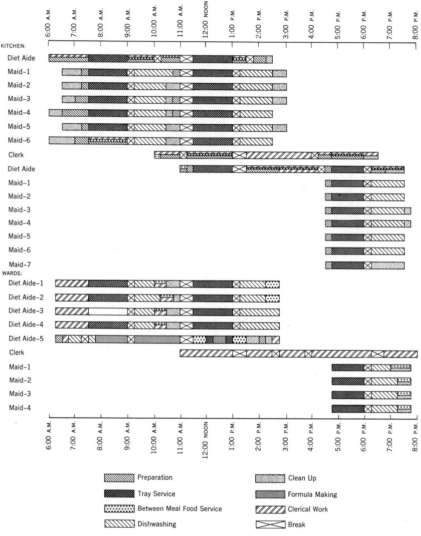

FIGURE 6.6 Bar graph showing employee time schedules and task assignments for patients' foodservice. Courtesy, King County Hospital System, Unit I, Seattle.

travel within his work area should be kept at a minimum in order to conserve his energy and time. Use of mechanical devices in the processing and service of food may decrease the total labor hours needed and increase the degree of skill and responsibility of employees. Arrangement of work areas for efficient operation cannot be overemphasized.

A work-distribution analysis chart of the total activities within a department will show where tasks may be eliminated, combined, or modified in the overall picture. One must be sure that the activities are so organized and combined that efficient use is made of the labor hours of each individual worker. Studies may be made to determine a good standard for each procedure, such as the time required for the average worker to combine and shape 25 pounds of ham loaf mixture into loaves in pans for baking. The standards set for each procedure should be such that the workers in a particular organization will be able to maintain them. The standard time should be established at a level that the average employee could do 20 to 30 percent more work without undue fatigue.

Written schedules clarify the responsibilities of workers and give them a feeling of security. It is wise to include a statement indicating that additional duties may have to be assigned from time to time. However, work schedules must be kept flexible and adjustments made as needed to adapt to the daily menu. Also, the introduction of new food products may decrease the amount of time needed for prepreparation as well as the time of cookery; likewise, additional processes may become necessary.

WORK IMPROVEMENT

Organization charts, job descriptions, job specifications, and detailed work instructions are invaluable aids in establishing standards of work, clarifying responsibilities, and selecting the right persons for jobs. However, the successful and efficient day-by-day operation of a foodservice is a constant challenge to its management group. No foodservice system can afford to remain static for long, but must keep pace with the socio-economic changes and technological developments in food and equipment and their effects on the overall pattern of operation.

Increased production with less human effort has been an objective in industry for years. Interest in the designing of work systems to convert human work practices to machines was a contributing factor to the Industrial Revolution. Since then the development has not been steady but, today, we rely heavily on mechanization and automation to increase productivity and develop manpower effectiveness. Current high material and labor costs make it imperative that every effort be made to study the work design and perfect efficient operation if high standards of production and quality of products are to be maintained at a reasonable cost. Simplification of tasks and techniques designed to decrease fatigue of workers are effective aids to good management that are accorded wide recognition and attention by both managers and workers in the foodservice field.

Factors Affecting Fatigue. The manager of a foodservice may find that fatigue or tiredness of some workers, with a resultant drop in their energy, enthusiasm, and output of production, is due to external factors beyond his control, such as irregularities in the home situation, extraordinary physical exertion away from the job, or a nutritionally inadequate food supply. However, within the organization and while the workers are on the job, there are unlimited opportunities to study causes of fatigue and correct them if possible.

Certain psychological factors such as attitude because of disinterest in and boredom with the job, dislike of the supervisor, or a low rate of pay may contribute to the fatigue and low output of some workers, but such situations often can be improved through changes in personnel policies and their administration.

Emphasis in this section of the text will be relative to the environmental and physical factors on the job affecting fatigue and work improvement methods.

With a given set of working conditions and equipment, the amount of work done in a day will depend upon the ability of the worker and the speed at which he works. . . . The fatigue resulting from a given level of activity will depend upon such factors as (1) hours of work, that is, the length of the working day and the weekly working hours; (2) the number, location, and length of rest periods; (3) working conditions, such as lighting, heating, ventilation, and noise; and (4) the work itself. [13]

The amount of reserve energy brought to the job varies with individuals. Some workers can maintain a fairly even tempo throughout the day, whereas others tire rather quickly and need to rest peri-

[13] *Ralph M. Barnes,* Motion and Time Study, *Sixth Edition, Wiley, New York, p. 573, 1968.*

odically to recoup nervous and physical energy. Short rest periods appropriately scheduled tend to reduce fatigue and lessen time taken by employees for personal needs.

Lighting, heating, ventilation, and noise are environmental factors that often contribute to fatigue of workers. Satisfactory standards for the lighting of kitchen areas is 35 to 50 foot-candles on work surfaces with reflectance ratios of 80 for ceiling, 35 to 30 on equipment, to a minimum of 15 for floors. Temperature and humidity influence worker productivity. A desirable climate for food preparation and service areas is around 75 to 80°F with relative humidity 50 to 60 percent. Higher temperatures tend to increase the heart rate and fatigue of most workers. Air-conditioning in hot and humid locales is considered a necessity, whereas in some parts of the country a good fan and duct system is satisfactory to give an air change every 2 to 5 minutes. Hoods over cooking equipment provide for the disposal of much heat and odor originating from these units. Noise has a disturbing and tiring effect on most people. Effective control of the intensity of noise within a foodservice area is possible through precautionary measures such as installation of sound-absorbing ceiling materials, the use of rubber-tired mobile equipment and smooth-running motors, and training the employees to work quietly.

Much has been written about the values of the study of physical facilities and the procedures followed in specific jobs, aimed at increasing efficiency in the operation of a foodservice. A thorough analysis of a floor plan, on paper or in actuality, would provide facts on which to base decisions regarding changes needed in order to make the most compact arrangement possible, yet provide adequate equipment in an efficient arrangement.

Work Simplification. Detailed studies of activities within an organization often reveal that cost and time requirements are high because of unnecessary operations and excess motions used by the workers in performance of their jobs. When proper adjustments are made in both the physical setup and the work procedures, the conservation of energy of the workers, increased production, and a reduction in total man hours should result. Such studies have proved highly effective in the simplification of effort in both repetitive and nonrepetitive activities and apply either in a new situation or where long-established procedures have become accepted practices.

The term *work simplification* is familiar to the foodservice manager, although various designations are used by writers on this subject. Niebel [14] says:

The terms "operation analysis," "work simplification," and "methods engineering" are frequently used synonymously. In most cases the person is referring to a technique for increasing the production per unit of time, and consequently, reducing the unit cost.

Another writer [15] states:

Work simplification is a way of getting something done, step by step, by breaking a problem into simple segments. It is an organized, commonsense attack upon the way in which work is done now, with a view to doing it better. It makes use of the techniques of method improvement, but it goes beyond a series of techniques. Work simplification "stretches the mind" by introducing and solidifying a new concept of what is useful work. It changes habits of thinking about what must be considered as waste work.

It does not stress working harder or faster, but the emphasis is on elimination of the unnecessary parts of a job and those that add no value to the product. This may involve changes in equipment and its arrangement or merely in work procedures, either or both of which make it possible to do better and usually more work with minimum effort. Conservative estimates are that through an effective work-simplification program, foodservice worker productivity can be increased as much as 20 to 50 percent.

Employee interest, understanding, and cooperation are essential to the successful operation of a work-simplification program. Thinking through and planning before starting any task is necessary if it is to be accomplished efficiently and in the simplest manner possible. The elimination of wasted effort is easy once the worker becomes *motion conscious*, learns to apply the simple principles that may be involved, and sees objectively the benefits of changed procedures. Such benefits may be evidenced by lessened fatigue of workers, safer and better working conditions, better and more uniform quality production, and possibly higher wages through increased production. Agreement and understanding of the objectives and realization that benefits will be shared mutually by workers and

[14] *Benjamin W. Niebel,* Motion and Time Study, *Sixth Edition, Richard D. Irwin, Homewood, Illinois, 1972.*
[15] *W. Clements Zinck,* Dynamic Work Simplification, *Reinhold, New York, p. 3, 1962.*

management are factors for success. The solicitation and incorporation of suggestions for job-improvement methods from the workers are conducive to enthusiastic interest and participation by them. Usually any employee resistance to change in established work routines can be overcome by the proper approach of management before and after the inauguration of a work-simplification program. The selection of personnel qualified by personality and training for leadership in this work is of prime importance to its implementation.

Motion Economy. The same principles of motion economy adopted by engineers many years ago are applicable in a foodservice operation. Analysts and supervisors need to have an understanding of these principles and the ability to interpret them to workers effectively before job breakdown studies and revision in procedures, arrangement of the work area, and equipment are inaugurated. A listing of these fundamental principles of motion economy follows on p. 366.

Practical application of most of these principles can be made easily in the foodservice field and will lead to increased efficiency, that is, reduction in the motions and time required for the job, and to a steady output of production with less fatigue on the part of the worker. A few specific examples of application follow.

Principles 1, 2, and 3. To serve food onto a plate at the counter, pick up plate with left hand and bring to a center position while right hand grasps serving utensil, dips food, and carries it to the plate, both operations ending simultaneously; when panning rolls, pick up a roll in each hand and place on pan.

Principle 6. Stir a mass of food easily and with minimum fatigue by grasping the handle of a wire whip (thumb up) and stirring round and round instead of pushing the whip directly back and forth across the kettle. Principles 5 and 7 are applied also in this same example, since greater force may be gained easily at the beginning of the downward and upward parts of the cycle.

Principle 8. Gain and maintain speed in dipping muffins or cupcakes through the use of rhythmic motions; use regular and rhythmic motions in slicing or chopping certain vegetables and fruits with a French knife on a board.

PRINCIPLES OF MOTION ECONOMY

A check sheet for motion economy and fatigue reduction

Use of the Human Body	Arrangement of the Work Place	Design of Tools and Equipment
1. The two hands should begin as well as complete their motions at the same time.	10. There should be a definite and fixed place for all tools and materials.	18. The hands should be relieved of all work that can be done more advantageously by a jig, fixture, or a foot-operated device.
2. The two hands should not be idle at the same time except during rest periods.	11. Tools, materials, and controls should be located close to the point of use.	19. Two or more tools should be combined wherever possible.
3. Motions of the arms should be made in opposite and symmetrical directions, and should be made simultaneously.	12. Gravity feed bins and containers should be used to deliver material close to the point of use.	20. Tools and materials should be pre-positioned whenever possible.
4. Hand motions should be confined to the lowest classification with which it is possible to perform the work satisfactorily.	13. "Drop deliveries" should be used wherever possible.	21. Where each finger performs some specific movement, such as in typewriting, the load should be distributed in accordance with the inherent capacities of the fingers.
5. Momentum should be employed to assist the worker wherever possible, and it should be reduced to a minimum if it must be overcome by muscular effort.	14. Materials and tools should be located to permit the best sequence of motions.	22. Levers, crossbars, and hand wheels should be located in such positions that the operator can manipulate them with the least change in body position and with the greatest mechanical advantage.
6. Smooth continuous motions of the hands are preferable to zigzag motions or straight-line motions involving sudden and sharp changes in direction.	15. Provisions should be made for adequate conditions for seeing. Good illumination is the first requirement for satisfactory visual perception.	
7. Ballistic movements are faster, easier, and more accurate than restricted (fixation) or "controlled" movements.	16. The height of the work place and the chair should preferably be arranged so that alternate sitting and standing at work are easily possible.	
8. Work should be arranged to permit easy and natural rhythm whenever possible.	17. A chair of the type and height to permit good posture should be provided for every worker.	
9. Eye fixations should be as few and as close together as possible.		

Source. *Ralph M. Barnes,* Motion and Time Study, *Sixth Edition, Wiley, New York, p. 220, 1968.*

Principles 8 and 10. Equip and arrange each individual's work area so that body movements are confined to a minimum in his job performance.

Principle 11. Store mixing-machine attachments and cooking utensils as close as possible to place of use; remove clean dishes from washing machine directly to carts and lowerator units that fit into serving counter; store glasses and cups in racks in which they were washed; cook certain foods in containers from which they will be served.

Principle 12. Install vegetable peeler at end of preparation sink so that peeled potatoes can be dumped directly into the sink; install water outlets above range and jacketed kettles so utensils may be filled at point of use.

Principle 14. For breading foods, arrange container of food to be breaded, flour, egg mixture, crumbs, and cooking pan in correct sequence so that no waste motions are made.

Principle 16. Provide some means of adjusting height of work surface to the tall and short worker; include one or two adjustable-height stools in list of kitchen equipment.

Principle 18. Provide knee lever-controlled drain outlets on kitchen sinks; install electronic-eye controls on doors between dining room and kitchen.

Work Improvement Program. Improvement in any work program is contingent on a study of the environmental factors and the activities of the workers in meeting the objectives of the organization. Such a study may involve one or more jobs in an organization. The usual approach for analysis and revision of a job method is:

1. Select the job to be improved. Begin on a job that needs attention, such as one that requires much time, movement, or backtracking, is often repeated, and is not too big. For example, the scrapping of trays in the food-service pantry of a hospital is a repetitive task at which considerable time is spent, with variable degrees of efficiency.

2. Break down the job in detail. Analyze each operation, noting procedure, equipment used, distance moved, and time required.

3. Question each detail. *What* is being done? *What* can be done? *Which* operations are necessary to produce what is wanted? *Why* is it being done? Is it essential? *When* is the job being done? Is it the correct time for the result desired? *Where* is the task being performed? Is the equipment adequate for the job? Is the equipment placed to produce a smooth flow of operation? *Who* is doing the job? Is the person doing the job the one to whom it was assigned? *How* is the job being performed? *How* could the method be changed to make for greater efficiency?

4. Work out a better method. The process- or activity-analysis chart affords opportunity to study any job objectively and to evaluate the efficiency of performance. Checks can be made easily to determine the necessary and the excess operations, where and how delays occur, the distances either product or worker must travel, and where changes can be made.

5. Put new method into effect. Teach new method and follow up with proper supervision. Continue to seek new and better ways to do the job.

Much of the analysis or breakdown of jobs is accomplished through motion and time studies. Barnes defines *motion* and *time study* as

the systematic study of work systems with the purposes of (1) developing the preferred system and method—usually the one with the lowest costs; (2) standardizing this system and method; (3) determining the time required by a qualified and properly trained person working at a normal pace to do a specific task or operation; and (4) assisting in training the worker in the preferred method.[16]

Methods for Work Improvement Study. The breakdown of job activities may be made in various ways and recorded appropriately for analy-

[16] *Ralph M. Barnes*, Motion and Time Study, *Sixth Edition, Wiley, New York, p. 4, 1968.*

sis, study, and evaluation. Among the possibilities are work sampling, pathway or flow diagram, operation and process charting, and micromotion studies. The objective is to be able to gain a complete and detailed picture of the process, regardless of the method of recording.

Work sampling is a tool for fact finding and often is less costly in time and money than a continuous study. It is based on the laws of probability that random samples reflect the same pattern of distribution as a large group. The primary use of work sampling is to measure the activities and delays of men or machines and determine the percentage of the time they are working or idle instead of observing the detailed activities of a repetitive task. The shorter and intermittent observations are less tiring to both the worker and the observer than continuous time studies; several workers can be observed simultaneously; interruptions do not affect the results; and tabulations can be made quickly on data-processing machines, although neither management nor workers may have the knowledge of statistics involved. This process is sometimes known as random ratio-delay sampling.

Reports of studies of work sampling made in foodservice enterprises have been limited, but the possibilities of successfully using this technique are indicated by Wise and Donaldson,[17] who conducted a study to establish a procedure that could be used for analyzing the work activities of hospital foodservice employees.

A pathway chart or flow diagram is a scale drawing of an area on which the path of the worker or movement of material during a given process may be indicated and measured, but with no breakdown of time or details of the operation. Measurement of the distance traveled as the worker moves about in the performance of his task is made by computing the total length of lines drawn from one key point to another simultaneously with his movements and multiplying by the scale of the drawing. A more convenient method is to set up pins or string supports at key points on a scale drawing of the worker's area and wind a measured length of string around the supports as the worker progresses from one position to another.

Operation charts may be used as simple devices to record, in sequence, the elemental movements of the hands of a worker at a given station, without consideration of time. A diagram of the work

---

[17] Blanche Irons Wise and Beatrice Donaldson, "Work Sampling in the Dietary Department," Journal of The American Dietetic Association, 39, 327 (1961).

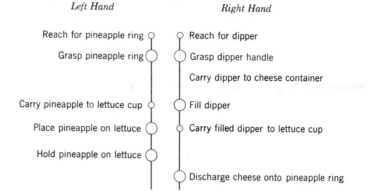

FIGURE 6.7　*Operation chart showing movements of the two hands in making pineapple and cottage cheese salad.*

area might head the chart with the observed activities of both hands listed in two columns—left side for left hand, and right side for right hand. In such a chart, small circles usually are used to indicate transportation and large circles to denote action. Analysis of the chart gives a basis for reducing transportation to the lowest degree possible and for replanning the work area and procedures. It is important that both hands be used simultaneously and effectively. A chart showing the procedures used in making a pineapple and cottage cheese salad is given in Fig. 6.7. The lettuce cup had been prearranged on the plate.

The *process chart* is a fairly simple technique for recording and analyzing the breakdown of a job. It presents graphically the separate steps or events by the use of symbols for a given process so that the entire picture of the job can be condensed into compact yet easily interpreted form. A process chart may present either *product analysis,* which shows in sequence the steps that a product goes through, or *man analysis,* which is a study of what the person does. Many different symbols were used by the Gilbreths when they devised this method of recording job activity years ago. Today, for most practical purposes, only four or five symbols are used that simplify and list quickly the steps or activities in a process. The symbols often used are:

○ = operation or main steps in the process.

⟹ = transportation or movement.

D   =delay.

▽   =storage or hold.

□   =inspection such as examination for quality or quantity.

Symbols may be arranged in a vertical line in sequence or, as in the activity-analysis charts (Figs. 6.8 and 6.9), with lines drawn from one symbol to another in each succeeding step. This method of charting makes for ease in checking time and in determining the number of repeats in any process as a basis for their reduction through revision of the method.

Without benefit of an elaborate process-chart form, a simple listing of the procedures and times used in the preparation of a menu item can be made and used to improve either the physical setup or the method, for example, the observance of the cook mixing and portioning meat balls, beginning at the worktable.

Approximate Distance (ft)	Time (min)	Description of Operation
6	9:00	Fasten bowl and beater in position on mixer
15	9:01	Go to refrigerator for milk, ground meat, and other weighed recipe ingredients (use cart)
15	9:035	Return to mixer
3	9:04	Place seasonings, eggs, milk, and cut-up bread in mixer bowl
	9:05	Mix slightly (observe)
	9:06	Add meat and mix to blend (observe)
3	9:075	Remove beater and take to wash sink
5	9:085	Lift bowl of meat mixture to low bench near work table
50	9:09	Assemble portion tools and pans
	9:10	Portion onto pans with number 12 dipper
	9:25	Complete portioning

Micromotion study is a technique whereby movements of the worker may be photographed and recorded permanently on film. This method affords a more accurate presentation of detail than others, and projection for analysis may be made at different rates of speed. In addition, the time of each movement may be recorded.

Process Chart

Present ☒ Proposed ☐

1951 - H.Q. Davidson FILE NUMBER page

SUMMARY		No.	TIME ( )		
OPERATIONS	○	1,546		TASK or JOB:	Dishwashing Procedure, Operations I Scrapping Trays
INSPECTIONS	□	0		DEPT.:	10th Floor Pantry
MOVES	⇨	99		EQUIPMENT, TOOLS' etc.:	Scrapping counter, prerinse counter with disposal unit, trash can, carts, cloth
DELAYS	D	70			
UNITS PRODUCED: 70 trays			1½ hr.	OPERATOR	Pantry Maid A
TOTAL DISTANCE MOVED				ANALYST	DATE March 20, 1963

Descriptive Notes	Activity	Dist.	Time	Analysis Notes
Rinses cloth at sink.	(X) □ ⇨ D			Damp cloth is used to wipe trays
Carries cloth to scrapping table.	○ □ (X) D	8' 6"		
Brings loaded cart into pantry from hall.	○ □ (X) D	5' 6"		Positions cart at left of operator. Each cart holds 6-9 trays.
Moves to side of table.	○ □ (X) D			
Takes tray from cart and places on scrapping table.	(X) □ ⇨ D			
Moves around in front of table.	○ □ (X) D	1' 0"		Convenient position for working.
Changes position of tray.	○ □ ⇨ (X)			
Places tray on stack of empty trays.	(X) □ ⇨ D			
Pulls menu from tray.	(X) □ ⇨ D			
Places name card on tray at extreme right of scrapping table.	(X) □ ⇨ D			Name cards in stacks by sections.
Picks up salt and pepper with left hand.	(X) □ ⇨ D			
Places salt and pepper on tray with name cards.	(X) □ ⇨ D			
Empties coffee pots into disposal.	(X) □ ⇨ D			
Places empty coffee pots on prerinse counter.	(X) □ ⇨ D			
Picks up plate and scrapes waste into disposal.	(X) □ ⇨ D			
Adds plate to stack on prerinse counter.	(X) □ ⇨ D			
Picks up creamer and empties contents into disposal.	(X) □ ⇨ D			
Places creamer on prerinse counter.	(X) □ ⇨ D			
Places cup and saucer on prerinse counter.	(X) □ ⇨ D			Saucers stacked.
Removes glasses from tray and empties contents into disposal.	(X) □ ⇨ D			
Places empty glasses upside down in wash rack on prerinse counter.	(X) □ ⇨ D			
Picks up bowl with right hand.	(X) □ ⇨ D			
Transfers bowl to left hand.	○ □ ⇨ (X)			Unnecessary handling.
Scrapes waste food from bowl with spoon into disposal.	(X) □ ⇨ D			Rubber scraper better tool.
Stacks bowls on prerinse counter.	○ □ ⇨ D			

DEPARTMENT OF INDUSTRIAL ENGINEERING—THE OHIO STATE UNIVERSITY

FIGURE 6.8 *Process chart of tray scrapping as observed in a hospital floor-service pantry.*

PROCESS CHART

Present ☐ Proposed ☒

1951 - H.Q. Davidson — FILE NUMBER — page

SUMMARY		No.	TIME ( )	
OPERATIONS	○	1,024		TASK or JOB : Dishwashing Procedure, Operation I Scrapping Trays
INSPECTIONS	□	2		DEPT. : 10th Floor Pantry
MOVES	⇨	13		EQUIPMENT, TOOLS' etc. : Scrapping counter, prerinse counter with disposal unit, trash can, carts, pan, rubber scraper
DELAYS	D	0		
UNITS PRODUCED: 70 trays			1 hr. TOTAL	OPERATOR : Pantry Maid A
TOTAL DISTANCE MOVED 117 feet				ANALYST : DATE: April 3, 1963

Descriptive Notes	Activity	Dist.	Time	Analysis Notes
Rinses cloth at sink and fills pan with water.	⊗ □ ⇨ D			Cloth is rinsed several times during operation.
Carries cloth and pan to scrapping table.	○ □ ⇨(x) D	7' 0"		Pan of water at counter reduces trips to sink.
Goes to silver storage unit.	○ □ ⇨(x) D	4' 9"		
Gets rubber spatula from drawer.	⊗ □ ⇨ D			
Returns and places spatula on scrapping table.	○ □ ⇨(x) D	5' 0"		
Brings loaded cart into pantry from hall.	○ □ ⇨(x) D	5' 6"		Pre-positioned tray on scrapping counter facilitates placement of name cards, and salts and peppers.
Takes tray from cart and places on scrapping table.	⊗ □ ⇨ D			
Picks up salt and pepper and places on tray at extreme right of worker.	⊗ □ ⇨ D			
Places name-card holder with menu on same tray.	⊗ □ ⇨ D			Menu pulled after name-card holder is on tray while hand is in position. Drops menu on table; all menus later put into trash can at one time.
Scrapes waste food from bowl with rubber scraper.	⊗ □ ⇨ D			
Stacks bowls on prerinse counter.	⊗ □ ⇨ D			All refuse from one tray scraped into one dish; then, into disposal.
Places silver in rack on prerinse counter.	⊗ □ ⇨ D			
Removes glasses from tray, empties contents into disposal.	⊗ □ ⇨ D			
Places glasses upside down in wash rack on prerinse counter.	⊗ □ ⇨ D			
Empties coffee pot and creamer into disposal, transfers directly to dish rack.	⊗ □ ⇨ D			Both hands used simultaneously. Movements combined or continuous wherever possible.
Removes paper tray-cover, folds once and places in trash can.	⊗ □ ⇨ D			
Wipes off bottom of tray, places on stack than wipes off top of tray.	⊗ □ ⇨ D			Handling of each tray reduced to a minimum.
Reaches to cart for next tray.	⊗ □ ⇨ D			
Operations repeated until all trays are scrapped.	○ □ ⇨ D			
	○ □ ⇨ D			

DEPARTMENT OF INDUSTRIAL ENGINEERING—THE OHIO STATE UNIVERSITY

FIGURE 6.9 Process chart of same operation as Fig. 6.8 after a study and revision of the original procedures had been made. By changing the sequence of operations and moving the tray cart near the working area, the operations, moves, and delays were reduced materially.

A detailed motion breakdown of the activities portrayed on micromotion film is easily made and recorded in graphic form by use of *therbligs,* expressed through letter, line, or color symbols. The word thereblig, formed by spelling Gilbreth backward but retaining the original order of the last two letters, was coined by Frank Gilbreth at the time he introduced the system of breaking down, into 17 subdivisions or elements, basic hand movements employed in job performance. The therbligs are: search (Sh), select (St), inspect (I), transport empty (TE), grasp (G), hold (H), transport loaded (TL), release load (RL), position (P), pre-position (PP), assemble (A), disassemble (DA), use (U), avoidable delay (AD), unavoidable delay (UD), plan (Pn), and rest (R).

Most often letter symbols are used in recording the breakdown of a procedure, for example, cutting a cake.

P	Place cake on table in position to cut.
TE	Move right hand toward knife rack.
Sh	Look over supply of knives.
St	Decide knife to use.
G	Take knife in right hand.
TL	Move knife to cutting position above cake.
U	Cut cake.

Any human activities may be analyzed by this system as a basis for eliminating the unnecessary and excess motions in the formulation of an improved method of procedure.

The *chronocyclegraph* is a photographic technique to show motion patterns of hands in performing rapid repetitive operations. It is made by attaching lights to the hands, which show as dotted lines on the finished photograph. The entire workplace must be included in order to study the relationship of the worker and direction of his hand movements to the work setup. Complete calculation of velocity and acceleration of hand motions is limited by the two-dimensional factor in this technique.

Suggestions for Application. Analysis of the data accumulated in the study of the work situation and the methods used in a foodservice may show that certain changes could be made immediately, while others involve time, money, and an educational program for the workers. No one set of rules can be used to bring about the desired improvements but, through the cooperative effort of management and worker groups, many things can be made possible. A few suggestions for making improvements follow.

One of the first steps in a job improvement plan is to try *to eliminate the unnecessary operations, delays, and moves* without producing deleterious effects on the product or worker. Habit plays an important part in the work routines of people, and it is easy for them to continue in the old pattern; for example, even though the improved methods of processing dehydrated fruits eliminates the necessity of soaking before cooking, some cooks might continue to soak them. A common example of good practice is to have one person fill and deliver storeroom requisitions once a day instead of each cook going to the storeroom for single items as need. *Operations may be combined* as in the making of certain types of sandwiches when the butter could be combined with the spread mixture and all applied in one operation instead of two. Other examples of simplified practice are the one .bowl method of combining ingredients for cakes and cutting a handful of celery stalks at one time on a board instead of singly in the hand. A *change in sequence of operations* to make the most efficient use of time and equipment and to reduce distance is important. Instead of struggling to pare and cut dry hard squash, it may be steamed for a short time until the hard covering softens; then it can be pared and cut quickly and easily.

The *selection of multiple-use equipment* reduces to a minimum the items needed. A mixing machine with all of the chopper, slicer, and grinder attachments might be more desirable for a given situation than the purchase of a chopping machine in addition to the mixer without attachments. Where and when the item will be used will determine its best location. A mixing machine to be used in one department only should be located convenient to that center of activity, whereas a machine shared by two departments would be located between the two but nearest and most accessible to the department requiring the heaviest and most frequent usage. Duplication of some equipment may be compensated in reduced labor hours required for certain jobs.

Equipment may be relocated or removed entirely to facilitate a more direct flow of work in any area. To reduce "searches" a definite place should be provided for every item, and in a well-regulated foodservice everything will be kept in the designated location except when in use. This storage location or prepositioning of the items should be convenient to the center of their first use; for example, the bowls, beaters, and attachments for the mixing machine should be stored next to or underneath the machine, the cook's cutlery stored in a drawer or on a rack at the cook's table, and clean water glasses returned to the water cooler in the wash racks for storage. Some kitchens may have retained a meat block, even though pan-ready meats are now used. Others may have more range space than is needed for modern cookery. In either case, the removal of certain equipment would provide space for more efficient utilization. Some kitchens may need additional equipment to provide adequate physical facilities for satisfactory operation. Most kitchen machines are designed as labor-saving devices and can do many times the amount of work that could be accomplished by hand in a comparable time and should be used whenever feasible. Improvements in design and operation of kitchen machines influence the method of operation. Automatic timing and temperature-control devices release the worker for other duties more than was possible when frequent checking and manual control were necessary.

The *reduction of transportation* or movement of materials and equipment often can be made through rearrangement of equipment, mobile equipment, and the use of carts to transport many items at one time. The relation of the receiving, storage, and preparation areas requires careful planning to be sure that the flow of the raw product through preparation and service is kept direct and in as condensed an area as practicable. Some delays in operation may be avoided by the installation of additional equipment, by a change in the sequence of operation, such as the assembly-line technique in pie making, by the training of the workers to use both hands at one time and to practice certain shortcuts in preparation, or by a better understanding of the timing standard for various processes.

The use of a different product could become a deciding factor in changing the method of procedure. The present tendency is toward the increased use of preprepared foods. Peeled carrots, processed potatoes, peeled and sectioned citrus fruit, frozen fruits and vegetables, basic mixes for baked products, freeze-dried shrimp, and pan-ready poultry are only a few such items that definitely change the preliminary procedures necessary in many food-production jobs.

Consideration of these suggestions and other factors peculiar to the situation provides a basis for outlining an improved method that can be tried and reevaluated for further streamlining. An example of the advantages to be gained from such a revision are indicated in the summaries at the tops of Figs. 6.8 and 6.9.

Information pertaining to the broad subjects of organization and management is voluminous. Only basic concepts with limited application have been included in this chapter. The following chapters discuss some special areas of concern to persons in the management of foodservices. Supplementary reading of current literature is advised to become acquainted with newer developments as they evolve.

SELECTED REFERENCES

Albers, Henry H., *Principles of Management, A Modern Approach,* Fourth Edition, Wiley, New York, 1972.

Argyris, Chris, *Management and Organizational Development,* McGraw-Hill, New York, 1971.

Barnes, Ralph M., *Motion and Time Study,* Sixth Edition, Wiley, New York, 1968.

Barnes, Ralph M., *Work Sampling,* Second Edition, Wiley, New York, 1957.

Beach, Dale S., *Personnel: The Management of People at Work,* Third Edition, Macmillan, New York, 1975.

Carroll, Stephen J. Jr., Frank T. Paine, and John B. Miner, *The Management Process,* Macmillan, New York, 1973.

Dale, Ernest, *Management: Theory and Practice,* Second Edition, McGraw-Hill, New York, 1969.

Drucker, Peter F., *Management: Tasks, Responsibilities, Practices,* Harper and Row, New York, 1974.

Eckles, Robert W., Ronald L. Carmichael, and Bernard R. Sarchet, *Essentials of Management for First-Line Supervision,* Wiley, New York, 1974.

Food Service Manual for Health Care Institutions, American Hospital Association, Chicago, 1972.

Haimann, Theo, and William G. Scott, *Management in the Modern Organization,* Second Edition, Houghton Mifflin, Boston, 1974.

Hicks, Herbert G., *The Management of Organizations: A Systems and Human Resources Approach,* Second Edition, McGraw-Hill, New York, 1972.

Job Descriptions and Organizational Analysis for Hospitals and Related Health Services, U.S. Government Printing Office, Washington, D.C., 1971.

Johnson, Richard A., Fremont E. Kast, and James E. Rosenzweig, *The Theory and Management of Systems,* Third Edition, McGraw-Hill, New York, 1973.

Kast, Fremont E., and James E. Rosenzweig, *Organization and Management: A Systems Approach,* Second Edition, McGraw-Hill, New York, 1974.

Kazarian, Edward A., *Work Analysis and Design,* Avi, Westport, Connecticut, 1969.

Koontz, Harold, and Cyril O'Donnell, *Principles of Management,* Fifth Edition, McGraw-Hill, New York, 1972.

Krick, Edward V., *Methods Engineering,* Wiley, New York, 1962.

Likert, Rensis, *New Patterns of Management,* McGraw-Hill, New York, 1961.

Likert, Rensis, *The Human Organization, Its Management and Value,* McGraw-Hill, New York, 1967.

Litterer, Joseph A., *The Analysis of Organizations,* Second Edition, Wiley, New York, 1973.

McGregor, Douglas, *The Professional Manager,* McGraw-Hill, New York, 1967.

"Methodology Manual for Work Sampling: Productivity of Dietary Personnel," Institution Management Laboratory, Department of Foods and Nutrition, University of Wisconsin, Madison, 1967.

Moore, Russell F., Editor, *AMA Management Handbook,* American Management Association, New York, 1970.

Mundel, Marvin E., *Motion and Time Study,* Third Edition, Prentice-Hall, Englewood Cliffs, New Jersey, 1960.

Nadler, Gerald, *Work Design,* Richard D. Irwin, Homewood, Illinois, 1963.

Niebel, Benjamin W., *Motion and Time Study,* Fifth Edition, Richard D. Irwin, Homewood, Illinois, 1972.

Odiorne, George S., *Management by Objectives,* Pitman Publishing Corporation, New York, 1965.

Odiorne, George S., *Management Decisions by Objectives,* Prentice-Hall, Englewood Cliffs, New Jersey, 1969.

Peterson, Elmore, E. Grosvenor Plowman, and Joseph Trickett, *Business Organization and Management,* Fifth Edition, Richard D. Irwin, Homewood, Illinois, 1962.

Scott, William G., and Terrence R. Mitchell, *Organization Theory: A Structural and Behavior Analysis,* Revised Edition, Richard D. Irwin, Homewood, Illinois, 1972.

Terry, George R., *Principles of Management,* Sixth Edition, Richard D. Irwin, Homewood, Illinois, 1972.

"Handbook for Analyzing Jobs," U.S. Department of Labor, U.S. Government Printing Office, Washington, D.C., 1972.

Van Egmond, Dorothy, *School Foodservice,* Avi, Westport, Connecticut, 1974.

7.
ADMINISTRATIVE LEADERSHIP

Those individuals who assume the management of foodservice organizations find themselves in a leadership role. As administrative leaders they will be successful to the degree that they are willing to assume responsibility and are able to maintain good human relations. Goals and objectives of the department cannot be attained by the administrator alone; working satisfactorily with and through other people constitutes the major part of his job. Persons in foodservice management positions should accept as a personal philosophy that their human resources are their greatest assets and that to improve their value is not only a material advantage but a moral obligation as well. Good leaders provide incentives and actively guide and develop employees to their highest potential so they may better share in realizing group accomplishments.

This type of leadership requires thinking, planning, and doing. It begins with the development of a philosophy at top management level, includes supervisory personnel, and permeates down through the entire organization. The philosophy should be so well established and understood by all that the objectives expressed in it will be certain to be achieved.

LEADERSHIP

Cribbin states that leadership is a management tool for accomplishing goals. "No manager is paid to lead; he is paid to accomplish organizational goals through his people and leadership is but one of the instruments that he has available for doing so." [1] *"Leadership* is defined as behavior which induces energetic, emotionally committed, cooperative followers. People follow a leader because they see reason, both emotional and rational, for following. Leadership finds the reasons and makes them more appealing. It encourages average people to achieve above-average results." [2]

LEADERSHIP ROLE

"Role is the pattern of actions expected of persons in their activities involving others. . . . The managerial role requires different conduct with different people rather than uniform conduct." [3]

Leadership role expectations of those in the organizational group may vary according to their own needs and goals and, at the same time, their perception of what a leader should be. Good leaders are found to be those who give support to their workers instead of making them feel threatened or alienated. Workers are more productive when they feel or sense this type of support and in situations where the leaders are able to build group loyalty and good teamwork. Established goals and objectives that are clearly understood help managers to achieve this type of role with their subordinates. Results of research studies "demonstrate that on the average, pressure-oriented, threatening, punitive management yields lower productivity, higher costs, increased absence, and less employee satisfaction than supportive, employee-centered management which uses group methods of supervision coupled with high performance expectations." [4] To the extent that manager-leaders recognize these differing expectations and capably meet them through their own leadership styles or manner of dealing with workers and their characteristics will they be successful administrators.

A person may have the traits that cause others to follow his lead, yet that person may not know how to manage—his time, en-

---

[1] *James J. Cribbin,* Effective Managerial Leadership, *American Management Association, Inc., New York, p. 68, 1972.*

[2] *From* Business and Society: Environment and Responsibility, *Third Edition, by Keith Davis and Robert L. Blomstrom. Copyright © 1975 by McGraw-Hill, Inc. Used with permission of McGraw-Hill Book Co., p. 110.*

[3] *From* Business and Society: Environment and Responsibility, *Third Edition, by Keith Davis and Robert L. Blomstrom. Copyright © 1975 by McGraw-Hill, Inc. Used with permission of McGraw-Hill Book Co., p. 100.*

[4] *Rensis Likert, "Measuring Organizational Performance,"* Harvard Business Review *(March–April 1958), p. 45.*

ergies, and things. Therefore, leaders are not necessarily good managers, but managers must always be leaders. Management *is* leadership and it is hoped that those who enter the foodservice field as administrative dietitians and managers will be good managers as well as good leaders.

LEADERSHIP STYLES OR PATTERNS

Each manager has a style of leadership that, to a large degree, is a reflection of his own personality. It includes the prior experiences he has had, the attitudes or habitual way of reacting to things or people, and the knowledge, skills, and abilities he possesses. A manager acts the way he does because of his own physical condition and emotional balance in relation to situations that arise and the personalities of the individuals with whom he works.

The range of possible leadership patterns is based on the degree of authority used by the manager and the amount of freedom allowed the employees in the decision-making process. Owens [5] names five leadership styles:

Autocratic, Bureaucratic, Diplomatic, Participative and Free Rein. These exemplify: the leader who knows what he wants done and how, tells the workers what their assignments are and demands unquestioning obedience; the leader who administers "by the book" and follows procedures and policies to the letter, allowing workers little or no freedom; the leader who is persuasive and "sells" his ideas thus motivating the workers to achieve desired results; the leader who encourages his workers to participate or share to some degree in decisions, who remains the democratic or consultant leader and allows his people a high degree of freedom; and finally, the free rein leader who sets policies and allows subordinates to operate with a minimum of direction or control.

The classic article by Tannenbaum and Schmidt [6] provides further understanding of leadership patterns based on their continuum of leadership behavior, presented in Fig. 7.1.

Managers lead, using a range of behavior styles represented somewhere along this continuum from the strictly autocratic, authoritarian type to the entirely free rein. Some situations require an immediate decision and command; a fire in the kitchen does not

[5] *James Owens, "The Art of Leadership,"* Personnel Journal, 52(5), *393. Reprinted with permission of the* Personnel Journal, *Copyright © May 1973.*
[6] *Robert Tannenbaum and Warren H. Schmidt, "How to Choose a Leadership Pattern,"* Harvard Business Review *(March–April 1958), p. 96.*

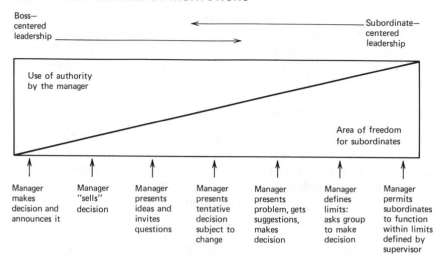

| Boss—centered leadership | ←————————————————→ | Subordinate—centered leadership |

Use of authority by the manager

Area of freedom for subordinates

| Manager makes decision and announces it | Manager "sells" decision | Manager presents ideas and invites questions | Manager presents tentative decision subject to change | Manager presents problem, gets suggestions, makes decision | Manager defines limits: asks group to make decision | Manager permits subordinates to function within limits defined by supervisor |

FIGURE 7.1   *Continuum of leadership behavior. From* How to Choose a Leadership Pattern, *by Robert Tannenbaum and Warren H. Schmidt. Courtesy, Harvard Business Review.*

require a meeting of the group to decide what to do! On the other hand, a needed change of policy or procedure that will affect employees directly should call for some group participation in effecting such change.

An understanding of these leadership styles may help the food-service manager to assess his own behavior on the job and to modify it as needed to keep negative effects to a minimum and so become more successful in the leadership role. The emerging trend, according to Montag,[7] who traced the patterns of managerial leadership from the beginning of the twentieth century to the present, is the participatory style of leadership. Dietitians and foodservice managers should watch for further research on this style, which involves workers in establishing their own goals and managing their part of the operation, and whether or not it continues as a preferred pattern.

Foodservice managers must realize that their own behavior pattern and style of leadership affect not only their employees, but also their customers.

The business of understanding needs and feelings of individuals

[7] *Geraldine M. Montag, "The Dietitian and Patterns of Managerial Leadership." Journal of the American Dietetic Association, 64(6), 630 (June 1974).*

works at all levels, since the responsibility of the foodservice manager does not stop with personnel management. The end point of production and service of food is the person who is lying in a hospital bed, seated at a table or counter in a restaurant, or waiting in a cafeteria line in a school lunchroom. These people, too, have special feelings and often are demanding and unreasonable. It requires well-adjusted leadership to establish and maintain a "climate" so that all workers will perceive the underlying feeling of the consumer and cater to him as a hungry human being.

Terry [8] as well as others have said that "The leader's role and the degree of its acceptance by the group condition the leadership" and that "the style of leadership and the situation affect the results obtained." Since these observations from research in behavioral science indicate the importance of the role of the manager as a leader, real consideration should be given to the leadership styles, traits, and qualifications needed by those who seek management positions in foodservice. To be aware that there is an increasing need for better human relations in management is not enough. To translate this knowledge into everyday dealings with sensitive, thinking, and feeling employees requires skill and diplomacy.

QUALIFICATIONS AND SKILLS

Personal Qualifications. Individuals who are considering a career in foodservice management or dietetics or who wish to improve their abilities as leaders will be interested in the personal as well as professional characteristics deemed necessary in executing their responsibilities. The task requires administrative ability and can be successfully accomplished only by an executive. There is little agreement among educators, business executives, and personnel directors as to the specific characteristics that make a good manager. Indeed, some believe that it is the mix of characteristics and the way a person uses his abilities that is important. However, behavioral scientists continue to provide some answers about desirable characteristics and traits, and there seem to be some that are common among successful leader-managers. Neuschel [9] says "that

[8] *George Terry,* Principles of Management, *Sixth Edition, Richard D. Irwin, Homewood, Illinois, p. 462, 1972.*
[9] *Robert P. Neuschel, "Analyzing Leadership,"* Passages (*Northwest Airlines Inflight Magazine*), 1(2), 20 (May–June 1970). Air Publications, Inc., New York.

while each manager has his own style and individuality, all seem to have these qualities in common:

Unusual energy.

Self-discipline.

Enthusiasm.

Total commitment to the goals of the organization.

A talent for swift, cool action when the "heat is on."

A desire to study and keep updated.

Involvement in outside social, political and civic activities.

Terry [10] adds these as among the more common traits associated with successful managers.

Intelligence—up to a certain point beyond which individuals tend to prefer the abstract.

Initiative of two types—ability to act independently and start action, and capacity to see courses of action not seen by others.

Energy or drive—both mental and physical.

Emotional maturity that includes—dependability, persistency, and objectivity; can spread enthusiasm; is consistent in action; refrains from use of anger; has a purpose in life and knows what he wants to accomplish.

Persuasiveness.

Communicative skill—a leader is able to talk and write clearly and forcefully.

[10] *George Terry,* Principles of Management, *Sixth Edition, Richard D. Irwin, Homewood, Illinois, p. 470, 1972.*

Self-assurance—has confidence, is well adjusted, and has belief in his own ability to meet most situations that confront him.

Perceptiveness and empathy.

Creativity.

It is generally recognized that managers' performance depends not so much on personality traits possessed but, instead, on three basic skills: technical, human, and conceptual. *Technical skill* involves facility in the use of tools and techniques as well as proficiency in the use of proper methods, procedures, and processes necessary to accomplish a given task. It involves some specialized knowledge and some analytical ability to perform effectively. Most on-the-job training and vocational preparation is concerned with these technical operations and has its greatest application at the entry and lower-level positions in the organization.

Human skill is the ability to work harmoniously with others in the group in order to accomplish the work to be done in an effective and efficient manner. It involves understanding what others mean by their words and actions, and the ability to communicate one's own ideas and behavior to others. Human skill implies recognition of the worth and dignity of individuals and a sensitivity to the beliefs and feelings of others.

Conceptual skill is the highest level of skill and is required of all successful managers. As the name implies, it is having an overall concept of the enterprise or organization as a whole and how the independent parts are related to and affected by the whole. It is the ability to relate activities of the business to the total industry, and to relate the trends of the economic, social, technological, and political forces in the nation to one's own enterprise. It means the ability to visualize, create, coordinate, and react to changes and to determine future directions for the department. The degree of conceptual skill that a manager possesses is likely to be related to the overall success of the business.

For Foodservice, Specifically. Some time ago Northrop wrote of the dietitians's work as creative work. She said:

Dietitians neither produce by the work of their hands nor by the use of business machines, but by creative thinking. This means doing the job to which one has been assigned efficiently, thoroughly and well, and then going beyond the routine to find some way to improve oneself and the job. It means reading and thinking, dreaming if you like, as well as just working. It means stretching to one's full capacity and reaching to one's full height. This can be fun. In itself, it makes the job more interesting and so is, in part, its own reward. Moreover, this creativity is a basis for promotions.[11]

In restaurant and business management particularly, innovative, creative persons are much in demand as managers. Original works or ideas are needed to meet the competition and to make the enterprise successful; mere hard physical work is no longer sufficient.

Gleiser,[12] in speaking of the dietitian as an executive, has named five characteristics necessary in a "quality" dietitian. These are: creative and analytical thinking, good judgment in thought and action, initiative, confidence or the ability to act with assurance, and vision.

Good judgment in thought and action implies that the executive has the basic facts and knowledge about situations so he can make correct decisions quickly. The good executive can then translate his thoughts into action. This requires the *initiative* mentioned earlier, the ability to be one's own self-starter. Enthusiasm on the part of the leader can motivate those working with him, so that the plans and programs initiated will gain momentum and cooperative effort. He must be an "innovator" and an "energizer."

Confidence in one's own ability is necessary in order for the executive to inspire those around him; however, he must be genuine and have "know-how" in order to gain their respect. Willingness to admit to mistakes and then correct them is an indication of maturity, another attribute to managerial efficiency.

Maturity implies acceptance of responsibilities, obligations, and consequences of one's own acts, ability and willingness to make decisions and to defend them, open-mindedness, and a capacity to overcome the frustration that seems to accompany the accomplishment of many an objective. A good sense of humor can carry one over many a rough spot.

Vision means taking a long look ahead, to anticipate accelerated change and to forecast and adjust plans for operation to meet the evolving situations. Whereas *vision* implies looking ahead, it

[11] *Mary W. Northrop, "Which Road for Dietitians?", Hospitals, Journal of the American Hospital Association, 34(5), 68 (1960).*
[12] *Fern Gleiser, "The Dietitian—An Executive," Journal of the American Dietetic Association, 36(2), 103 (1960).*

must be accompanied by versatility and flexibility within the executive to make him ready and willing to change. He will view change as an opportunity for growth and development and not as an upset to comfortable routines of today. He will recognize that meeting the competition of today's fast-moving age requires keeping abreast of change and new developments by continuous study and learning. Advanced academic study, attendance and participation in professional and trade association meetings, workshops, and seminars, and reading of new literature in the area of specialization are a few of the ways of accomplishing this.

Specifically, those interested in a career in foodservice management and dietetics should have a strong aptitude for science. Dietitians should have scientific curiosity and a desire to find the reasons for things happening, curiosity about food, enthusiasm for its preparation, and an artistic flair in handling it. Good health and the ability to maintain an average weight without becoming "too fat or too lean" are most important; if those in charge are to influence others to control weight, they must be able to do so themselves. The foodservice administrator must have an eagerness to be of service to people and an interest in promoting good health, and so work toward a better world.

DIETITIANS AND FOODSERVICE MANAGERS; SUPPORTIVE PERSONNEL
ACADEMIC PREPARATION

Persons who assume the responsibility for the management of a foodservice may be professionally prepared either as administrative dietitians or as foodservice directors. Basically, both groups have a bachelor's degree from an accredited college or university with a major in foodservice systems management, administrative dietetics, or restaurant management. Those who become qualified dietitians follow a curriculum that includes certain subject areas required for membership in The American Dietetic Association, the national organization of dietitians.

University curricula generally ensure students a liberal education. Approximately one half of the credit hours required for graduation are in broadening cultural courses in humanities, social and natural sciences, and in English. The other half are courses in the area of specialization and basic supportive courses.

Administrative dietetics and restaurant management are fields of specialized knowledge, built on natural sciences, especially chemistry, microbiology, and physiology, and on social sciences, such as economics, sociology, psychology, and human relations. It requires preparation in the science of food and nutrition, meal management, and institution administration. Business and personnel management and communications courses are also basic. Out-of-school work experience during vacations and holidays or part-time work during college years provides opportunity for the student to supplement his background and develop certain skills not attainable in the college classroom. Such experience gives the student a knowledge of how to work with many types of people and the point of view of an employee.

Often the undergraduate program includes on-the-job work experiences known as field or clinical experience. This type of coordinated experience gives the student the opportunity to put into practical application the theoretical aspects of classroom teaching and makes information more relevant than when experience comes after the degree is earned. However, that is not always possible and, if not, an apprenticeship with a commercial foodservice organization or an approved dietetic internship is highly recommended as an important step between college and the responsibilities of a first position. The internship or apprenticeship provides experience in all phases of the work of a staff member yet under expert guidance and supervision. It is a period for the recent graduate to gain confidence in his or her own ability, to learn to work as a member of a professional team, and to acquire new insights into opportunities for employment and service.

The new situation gives stimulus toward maturity and happiness in life, with the patient or guest as the focal center instead of self, or one's personal interests and desires. The chance to share in a profession cannot be granted without assurance of personal adequacy, maturity, and competence. Professional mindedness is fostered in many ways during the period of internship or executive apprenticeship. Accessions of knowledge and increased skills are nicely balanced by the awareness that learning is not enough—it must be sustained by a professional attitude, a desire to serve, and a sense of obligation.

TERMINOLOGY, DEFINITIONS AND SPECIFIC RESPONSIBILITIES

In order to understand the terminology related to the professional foodservice manager and supporting personnel, the following definitions and outline of responsibilities are presented. (From "Report of Committee to Develop a Glossary on Terminology for the Association and Profession," *JADA,* 64 (6), 661–664, 1974, reprinted with permission).

Dietitians

GENERIC TITLES

A.D.A. DIETITIAN

A specialist educated for a profession responsible for the nutritional care of individuals and groups. This care includes the application of the science and art of human nutrition in helping people select and obtain food for the primary purpose of nourishing their bodies in health or disease throughout the life cycle. This participation may be in single or combined functions; in foodservice [2] systems management; in extending knowledge of food and nutrition principles; in teaching these principles for application according to particular situations; or in dietary counseling.

Registered Dietitian (R.D.)®. This is a person who meets all requirements for membership in The American Dietetic Association, who has successfully completed the examiniation for registration, and who maintains continuing education requirements. On the job, the R.D. has the same responsibilities as the ADA member.

FUNCTIONAL TITLES, DEFINITIONS, AND SUGGESTED POSITION RESPONSIBILITIES

ADMINISTRATIVE DIETITIAN, R.D.[4]

The administrative dietitian, R.D., is a member of the management team and affects the nutritional care of groups through the management of foodservice systems that provide optimal nutrition and quality food.

---

[2] *"Foodservice" is used as one word in deference to the Foodservice Systems Management Education Council, which feels there is a distinct connotation in one word which is not implied in "food service" as two words.*

[4] *Job titles may change, depending on the place of employment.*

Responsibilities—Administrative R.D.[5]

1. Plans, develops, controls, and evaluates foodservice systems.
2. Develops short- and long-range department plans and programs consistent with departmental and organizational policies.
3. Manages and controls fiscal resources and recommends budget programs.
4. Utilizes human effort and facilitating resources efficiently and effectively.
5. Coordinates and integrates clinical (sometimes known as therapeutic) and administrative aspects of dietetics to provide quality nutritional care.
6. Establishes and maintains standards of food production and service, sanitation, safety, and security.
7. Maintains effective written and verbal communications and public relations, inter- and intradepartmentally.
8. Compiles and utilizes pertinent operational data to improve efficiency and quality of foodservice systems.
9. Plans, conducts, and evaluates orientation and in-service educational programs.
10. Interprets, evaluates, and utilizes pertinent current research relating to nutritional care.
11. Develops menu patterns and evaluates client acceptance.
12. Develops specifications for the procurement of food, equipment, and supplies.
13. Plans or participates in the development of program proposals for funding.
14. Plans layout designs and determines equipment requirements for new or renovated foodservice facilities.
15. Administers personnel policies as established by the department and organization.

CONSULTANT DIETITIAN, R.D.

The consultant dietitian, R.D., with experience in administrative or clinical dietetic practice, affects the management of human effort and facilitating resources by advice or services in nutritional care.

Responsibilities—Consultant R.D.

1. Evaluates and monitors foodservice systems, making recommendations for a conformance level that will provide nutritionally adequate quality food.

[5] *Responsibilities listed for each title are designed to serve only as a guide and should not be considered all inclusive.*

2. Develops budget proposals and recommends procedures for cost controls.
3. Plans, organizes, and conducts orientation and in-service educational programs for foodservice personnel.
4. Plans layout design and determines equipment requirements for new or renovated foodservice facilities.
5. Recommends and monitors standards for sanitation, safety, and security in foodservice.
6. Develops menu patterns.
7. Assesses, develops, implements, and evaluates nutritional care plans and provides for follow-up, including written reports.
8. Consults and counsels with clients regarding selection and procurement of food to meet optimal nutrition.
9. Develops, maintains, and uses pertinent record systems related to the needs of the organization and to the consultant dietitian.
10. Develops, uses, and evaluates educational materials related to services provided.
11. Consults with the health care team concerning the nutritional care of clients.
12. Provides guidance and evaluation of the job performance of dietetic personnel.
13. Interprets, evaluates, and utilizes pertinent current research relating to nutritional care.
14. Maintains effective verbal and written communications and public relations, inter- and intradepartmentally.

Shared Dietitian, R.D. The shared dietitian, R.D., with some experience in administrative and clinical dietetic practice, affects the management of human effort and facilitating resources with direct responsibility, on a part-time basis, for each of two or more foodservices, usually small hospitals or other health care facilities.

Responsibilities—Shared Dietitian, R.D. Responsibilities are the same as those listed under consultant dietitian, except the shared dietitian has direct authority for carrying out departmental responsibilities instead of just making recommendations, as is the consultant's role. (See consultant dietitian, R.D., above.)

Foodservice Manager. This term is used for those who assume responsibility for the administration of a foodservice department in any type of organization but who do not have the professional credentials of a registered dietitian. The responsibilities as outlined for the administrative dietitian are essentially those of every foodservice manager. Unless the foodservice manager is employed by a hospital or other health care facility, he would not have the responsibility of coordinating and integrating clinical and administrative aspects of dietetics. (See administrative dietitian, R.D., above.)

Supportive Personnel. Every profession has a group of supportive personnel on whom managers rely to help "extend the arm" of the professional. Some of the more routine supervisory responsibilities are delegated to this well-trained, important auxiliary group. In the field of dietetics these people are known as dietetic technicians, and dietetic assistants or foodservice supervisors. In other types of organizations the supportive personnel may have these same titles, or they may be those employees who have attained the upper levels on the career ladder. Their qualifications and usual delegated responsibilities are outlined below.

DIETETIC TECHNICIAN

A technically skilled person who has successfully completed an associate degree program which meets the educational standards established by The American Dietetic Association. The dietetic technician, working under the guidance of an R.D. or an A.D.A. dietitian, has responsibilties in assigned areas in foodservice management; in teaching foods and nutrition principles; and in dietary counseling.

Responsibilities—Dietetic Technician

1. Plans menus based on established guidelines.
2. Standardizes recipes and tests new products for use in facility.
3. Procures and receives supplies and equipment following established procedures.
4. Supervises food production and service.
5. Monitors foodservice for conformance with quality standards.
6. Maintains and improves standards of sanitation, safety, and security.
7. Selects, schedules, and conducts orientation and in-service education programs for personnel.
8. Participates in determining staffing needs, in selecting personnel, and on-the-job training.
9. Develops job specifications, job descriptions, and work schedules.
10. Plans master schedules for personnel.
11. Maintains a routine personnel evaluation program.

12. Understands and supports personnel policies and union contracts.
13. Assists in the implementation of established cost control procedures.
14. Gathers data according to prescribed methods for use in evaluating foodservice systems.
15. Makes recommendations which may be incorporated into policies and develops written procedures to conform to established policies.
16. Recommends improvements for facility and equipment.
17. Submits recommendations and information for use in budget development.
18. Compiles and uses operational data.
19. Obtains, evaluates, and utilizes dietary history information for planning nutritional care.
20. Guides individuals and families in food selection, food preparation, and menu planning based on nutritional needs.
21. Calculates nutrient intakes and dietary patterns.
22. Assists in referrals for continuity of patient care.
23. Utilizes appropriate verbal and written communication and public relations, inter- and intradepartmentally.

DIETETIC ASSISTANT

A skilled person who has successfully completed a high school education or equivalent and a dietetic assistant's program which meets the standards established by The American Dietetic Association. The dietetic assistant, working under the guidance of an R.D., or an A.D.A. dietitian, or a dietetic technician, has responsibility in assigned areas for foodservice to individuals and groups.

Responsibilities—Dietetic Assistant

1. Assist in standardization of recipes and testing of new products.
2. Receives deliveries and checks receipts against specifications and orders.
3. Assures correct storage and inventory of food and supplies.
4. Prepares food production work sheets and assists in the supervision of food production and service.
5. Supervises personnel in sanitation, safety, and security practices in accordance with established standards.

6. Instructs personnel in use, care, and maintenance of equipment.
7. Assists in orientation, on-the-job training, and in-service educational programs for personnel.
8. Plans daily personnel schedules based on a master rotation plan, monitors and makes necessary adjustments in daily personnel coverage, and maintains attendance records.
9. Participates in personnel evaluation programs.
10. Understands and supports personnel policies and union contracts.
11. Collects operational data as requested.
12. Assists in implementing cost control procedures.
13. Makes recommendations which may be incorporated into policies or procedures.
14. Recommends improvements for facility and equipment needs.
15. Processes dietary orders, menus, and other directives related to patient care.
17. Writes modified diets according to established patterns.
18. Utilizes appropriate verbal and written communications and public relations, inter- and intradepartmentally.

CAREER LADDERS IN COMMERCIAL FOODSERVICE

The National Restaurant Association [13] has proposed and is promoting the use of career ladders within the industry to identify for potential managers and supervisors the promotional opportunities available through experience. These lower-scale positions are known as "support function positions," and the people who fill them as "support personnel." Figure 7.2 presents a model of a potential career ladder system for a foodservice organization employing a large number of employees. It is an illustration only, and is not intended to be applicable to all types of organizations. This integrated career progressions chart relates four functional areas, sanitation, production, control, and service, to each other.

For the career ladder concept to be successful, the jobs must be structured so that the skills developed at one level will be utilized and expanded at the next higher level. This requires an ongoing training program within the organization, and/or some additional

[13] *"Career Ladders in Food Service,"* The Cornell HRA Quarterly, 12(*1*), 84 (*May 1971*). Part III, A Model for Career Progression.

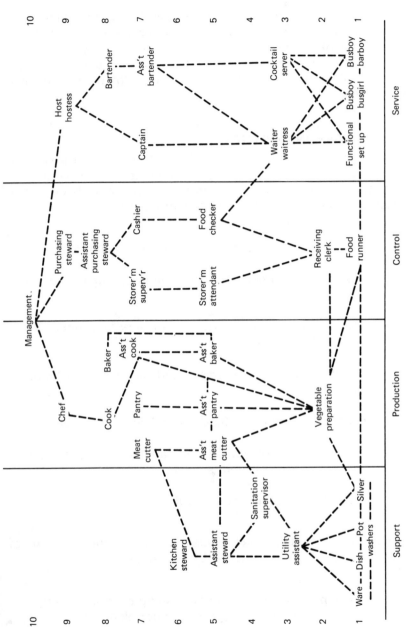

FIGURE 7.2 Functionally integrated career progression model for a foodservice facility. Courtesy, Cornell Hotel and Restaurant Administration Quarterly.

formal education at some levels for progression up the career ladder. Even though this model was proposed for the restaurant industry, it is adaptable for use in many types of foodservices.

It is hoped that each organization will develop a career progression plan that is suitable for its own particular conditions, policies, and type of service.

GENERAL RESPONSIBILITIES

Certain basic responsibilities are common to all foodservice administrators in whatever type of organization they may be employed. Most of the ones that are specific to foodservice have been or will be discussed in detail in other chapters of this book. They include:

Establishment of goals, objectives and standards.

Personnel selection, education, and welding an effective staff.

Overall planning and delegation of work to be done; scheduling of workers.

Purchase of food, equipment, and supplies according to specification.

Planning for physical facilities and equipment needs.

Supervision of all technical operations: production, delivery and service of food; sanitation; safety; security.

Financial planning and control.

These responsibilities may be classified under the functions of management given on pages 349–351, which are:

Planning—departmental policy and procedure making; menu and production planning; floor planning and equipment arrangement; establishment of standards to be maintained in food production, service, sanitation, and safety.

Forecasting—estimating numbers of people to be served; determining quantities of food needed to purchase and prepare; budget making; predicting future needs for staff and department based on trends and change.

Organizing—identification of activities and tasks and dividing them into positions; personnel selection to meet the table of organization chart; welding together of an effective staff without overlapping or duplicating responsibilities.

Delegating—assignment of responsibilities and authority to each staff member through work schedules and job descriptions.

Actuating—training, supervising, directing, motivating, and disciplining the workers.

Controlling—financial control through the use of a system of records and reports; supervision of all activities.

The American Dietetic Association's [14] position on the administrative dietitian includes similar responsibilities. Directors of specific types of foodservices may have additional responsibilities that are peculiar to that type of organization. For example, a hospital dietitian may choose to specialize in clinical dietetics (therapeutics) or teaching instead of administration. In this case she will work closely with the physician, nurse, and others as a member of the medical team to improve the health of the patient. She will visit and instruct patients and their families about diet and its modification, teach medical students, nurses, or employees about nutrition and diet therapy, or work with the doctor on some aspect of metabolic research.

A college or university residence hall dietitian may be responsible also for teaching dietetic and restaurant management majors quantity food production and other institution management courses. The student union foodservice manager must help to build a good image for the university in the eyes of the community. The school foodservice manager usually is responsible for a nutrition education program for the students. She works with parents and others in the

[14] *"Position Paper on the Administrative Dietitian,"* Journal of the American Dietetic Association, 67 (5), 478 (*November 1975*).

community to let them know the importance of the school meals to the total educational program.

The restaurant or hotel foodservice director may spend considerable time in catering to the public and participating in civic and legislative activities of the community. In all cases the responsibilities are largely administrative and are undertaken to render a service to humanity and to direct resources and efforts toward the successful accomplishment of a desired goal.

Many of the responsibilities mentioned have to do with teaching or training. Much of the working day of the foodservice director and the dietitian is devoted to this activity, either formally or informally, and anyone wishing to enter foodservice management because he does not wish to teach should be forewarned. However, this activity should prove challenging and rewarding.

Not to be forgotten among the list of foodservice managers' responsibilities are those common to all in management positions. These include:

Establishment and implementation of policies.

Effective communications at all levels.

Planned continuing education for self and staff.

Decision making.

Building good public relations.

Evaluation.

Of these Drucker [15] states that:

> Managing is specific work. As such it requires specific skills. Among them are: making effective decisions, communications within and without the organization, the proper use of controls and measures, and the proper use of analytical tools, that is, of the management sciences. No manager is likely to master all of these skills. But every manager needs to understand what they are and what they can do for him, and what in turn, they require of him. Every manager needs basic literacy with respect to essential managerial skills.

[15] *Peter F. Drucker,* Management: Tasks, Responsibilities, Practices, *Harper and Row, New York, p. 464, 1974.*

ESTABLISHMENT AND IMPLEMENTATION OF POLICIES

A policy is a guide for future action. Policies serve as directives under which managers dispatch their responsibilities. Policies may come from owners of the business or from top administrative officers of the organization.

The owners, for example, may have definite policies concerning wages, ethics, social obligations, and public relations that are quite different from those commonly accepted. These policies may create in the service a unique situation inimical to sound business, or they may indicate managerial leadership. Those in authority may decree that the school lunchroom is to operate without profit or that the club dining room must carry the load of refurnishing the living quarters. In either event the set of directives is effective down through details of organization and cost control. Other policies may be the result of a decision required by a middle-level manager.

Also, policy formulation must be within the bounds of legislation, which affects what managers may or must do, such as the fair employment practices act or the minimum wage law among others. Externally imposed policies also may come from labor unions and trade associations. Whatever the source, all policies are broad guides to direct the thinking of those who make decisions. These directives plus those departmental policies relating to specific standards that foodservice managers wish to uphold are the guides for operational procedures to be followed.

Once formulated, policies should be put into written form and disseminated throughout the organization. Often an employees' handbook is the means for communicating policies to the staff and workers. Policies must be clearly stated and discussed in order to be clearly understood. Only then do they truly serve as a guide for action.

COMMUNICATIONS

Communication is the process of transmitting and receiving information, and its purpose is to bring about some desired action, either concrete or intangible. The intangible action may be a change in attitudes, acceptance of a change in policy or a rule, or understanding of a situation or problem.

The elements of communications include a source (sender), a message (form), and a destination (receiver). Whether or not the correct message has been received depends on the response or "feedback." It appears to be a simple enough procedure, but there are many barriers to effective communications that should be realized and removed. Words or semantics are not always mutually understood or may have different meanings for different people. The sender should be certain that the vocabulary used is on the level of those who are to receive the message.

Some physical barriers exist that prevent effective communication, such as poor voice quality, illegible handwriting, or the message sent to the wrong place or person. Also, sociological and psychological barriers may exist such as lack of common experiences on which to base information, differences in values and motives of the sender and receiver, "mind sets" against change, or emotional involvements in situations. All of teaching and learning is dependent on skill in communicating, and improved ability in this on the part of the manager will save time and money for his department. People expect to receive explicit directions and orders so that they may work effectively and intelligently.

It should be remembered that half of communicating is *listening* and that to be a good listener requires skill and concentration. It is estimated that 45 percent of a dietitian's communicating time is spent listening. The manager especially must be attuned to his staff and workers by hearing what they wish to say.

The lines of communications within an organization should be clearly established. The modes of communicating are many and varied; a variety of them will be used within a foodservice department. An employees' handbook, which has been mentioned, is a good starting point for managers to communicate with their personnel. Group meetings to discuss policies, rules, and procedures are important and effective when well planned. Bulletin board notices, memos, and posters provide another means of communication, but must be kept up to date and must be changed frequently to provide the desired impact.

An informal means of communicating found in every organization is the "grapevine." If managers do not communicate adequately or give complete information to employees, particularly in regard to an anticipated change, rumors begin. "What you do not tell me, I assume to be bad" is the usual attitude of those who are not "in the know." To avoid misapprehension, mistrust, and fear that can arise from false rumors, managers should be as frank and open as the situation allows. This helps build confidence, loyalty, and good morale among the working group.

At the administrative level, much of communicating is accomplished through the use of analytical tools of management science. Routine reports generated for managers' analysis, simulation techniques as a basis for decision making, and certain planning and other functions may be carried out through use of a computer. Operations Research (OR), Performance Evaluation and Review Techniques (PERT), and Management by Objectives (MBO) are a few of these tools used by managers for communicating data and information at upper levels in the organization.

PLANNED CONTINUING EDUCATION

Executive obsolescence is a term heard frequently in business management circles. Some professions have estimated that within five to ten years a member may become entirely outdated if no attempt has been made to keep up with developments in the field. Thirty to forty years ago that which was learned lasted a long time. New developments and resultant changes came slowly; managers had time to contemplate revisions that would be required. Not so today. Change, as the result of new developments, is fast and immediate and demands some planned program for updating staff as well as employees.

Continuing Education is defined as that education of an individual beyond the basic preparation required for the profession or for a specific position. One such plan with a built-in requirement for continuing education is the registration process for dietitians. On June 1, 1969, The American Dietetic Association became a pioneer among professional organizations when it began its voluntary program of registration. In 1976 registration became independent of membership in The American Dietetic Association. Among other requirements for initial registration is passing an examination; for continuing the registration status the completion of 75 clock hours of continuing education every five years is required.

The registration program was formulated to upgrade professional competency by evidence of self-improvement through continuing education of the registrant, thus serving to improve the status of professional dietitians. Stimulation of continuing education for members of the American Dietetic Association was and is the heart of the method for encouraging high standards of performance by dietetic practitioners.[16]

[16] *Margaret L. Bogle, "Registration—the Sine Qua Non of a Competent Dietitian,"* Journal of the American Dietetic Association, 64(6), 618 (June 1974).

Although membership in The American Dietetic Association is no longer a requirement for registration, it is expected that every professional person will keep up to date. Attendance at professional and trade association meetings, graduate study or enrollment in specific college or university courses, seminars, workshops, conferences, and other similar types of approved activities provide the necessary update. The American Management Association maintains one of the most comprehensive programs of seminars and self-study materials for its members of any organization. Other organizations [17] have similar if less extensive programs. Indeed, it is not difficult for every individual who truly wishes is avoid obsolescence to find a continuing education program of the educational level, length of time, location, and cost constraints to meet his or her own needs. It is hoped that top administrators will, through company policy, encourage staff to participate in such programs by allowing time from the job to attend and, to the extent possible, provide financial support.

Dietitians and foodservice managers have a similar obligation to their employees. Opportunities for their development and skill improvement make possible promotions from within the organization as well as mobility for the worker with potential to move up the career ladder. A planned, ongoing, in-house training program is a highly desirable first step. Many community colleges and vocational schools offer night classes for foodservice workers, which makes it possible for them to combine full-time employment with some formal education. State departments of continuing or distributive education offer related courses in many localities. Foodservice managers often encourage their employees to participate in such programs by paying the tuition or fees for them to attend. Return benefits to the organization usually more than offset the investment made.

PUBLIC RELATIONS

Every dietitian and foodservice manager speaks for his profession. Attitudes and manners displayed when dealing with the public create good or poor impressions for the organization that may be long lasting. The example set by the manager is reflected throughout the entire organization, and his adherence to the standards and

---

[17] *Publications Reprint List, The American Dietetic Association, 430 N. Michigan Ave., Chicago, Illinois, 60611.*

rules required of other workers is essential for good human relations. The dietitian who is unable to control her own weight is apt to have little influence on patients who are attempting to bring their weight under control. The foodservice manager who is unwilling to devote some time to community affairs will likely receive little support for his own business from the public.

Three major factors concerning the operation of a foodservice are rated high among the demands of the public. They are a clean sanitary facility, courteous helpful employees, and good food. Good public relations can be achieved by the foodservice that is able to provide these things for its patrons. Also, methods of creating interest in and interpreting the goals of the organization to the public should be carefully planned. For example, the school foodservice program and its importance in the total educational system should be made known to parents and others in the community through newspaper publicity, talks given at parent meetings, and the enthusiasm generated by the children themselves for the meals they are served. Additional interest has been created in some communities where foodservice facilities of the school are extended to provide meals for the elder citizens of the area. Other types of foodservice operations also promote their services through advertising or day-by-day contacts with the public.

Interdepartmental contacts provide another avenue for building good public relations. The ability of the dietitian or foodservice manager to work cooperatively with those in other departments of the organization creates a desirable atmosphere for accomplishing mutual goals. The individual who is courteous, emotionally mature, and generous with his time to be of assistance to others will, indeed, create good will and prove to be an asset to his own department, organization, and profession.

EVALUATION

Evaluation is a means for determining whether or not goals have been reached. It implies that something has to be "measured" and, therefore, there must be some criteria for judging or comparing in order to have a valid evaluation. Measurable standards in terms of quantity, quality, time, and cost objectives provide such a basis. Predetermined objectives for all phases of foodservice operation stated in specific terms is the beginning of a planned evaluation program. It should be a continuous ongoing activity and an integral part of the management function. Planned evaluation leads to the discovery of strengths and weaknesses of individuals or operations. It should help to solve problems by identifying them and motivate improvement and self-understanding. Evaluation of self and department is one of the most important procedures to be inaugurated by the dietitian or foodservice manager. Only by "taking stock" and seeking ways to improve can progress be made.

Recent legislation relating to the health professions requires evaluation of health care delivery programs. The Social Security Amendments of 1972 (PL 92-603) provides for establishing Professional Standards Review Organizations (PSROs) and a program for qualifying health care personnel through proficiency examinations. To meet this mandate, The American Dietetic Association and its affiliated state associations have established Professional Standard Review Committees to develop measurable levels of performance, criteria for the process of screening, assessment, and evaluation by peer review for the dietetic segment of the Allied Health professionals. The plan will also include development for a change in programs including continuing education to meet identified deficiencies in areas of dietetic practice.

Specific methods of evaluation have been discussed in the chapters on Personnel Management, Sanitation and Safety, and Cost Control, as well as in Menu Planning and Food Production. The use of the evaluation procedures presented in those chapters should be a part of the overall planned program.

Results of a planned evaluation program, which is continuously ongoing, are many. Among them are improved productivity through a known standard to be achieved; increased job satisfaction on the part of the employee who knows exactly what is expected, what was achieved, and how to improve, as discussed in performance appraisals; training programs improved or broadened in light of evaluated performance; and cost reduction in all areas because of careful evaluation of all expenditures.

PROFESSIONAL AND TRADE ASSOCIATIONS

Affiliation with an organization whose membership is limited to those with mutual objectives and concerns is highly desirable. Membership affords opportunity for professional and personal development through participation in the activities of state, national, or local associations. It provides the stimulation to keep up to date with developments in the field through contacts with leaders, attendance at conventions, workshops, and participation in other programs of work. Many services are available to members that are of benefit to them. In turn, the members have an obligation to the organization to support its programs and work actively toward attaining its goals.

The statement of Francis Bacon (1561–1626) merits citing on this point, "I hold every man a debtor to his profession, from the which as men do of course seek to receive countenance and profit, so ought they of duty to endeavor themselves, by way of amends, to be a help and an ornament thereunto." [18]

Professional associations have specific academic standards as well as other definite requirements for membership, because a professional person is one who has specialized knowledge, conceptual ability, integrity, and allegiance to established codes of ethics.

The founding of The American Dietetic Association in 1917 marked the real recognition of dietetics as a profession in the United States. The early members were true pioneers with vision for the future, for they established high standards for membership that are maintained today. Minimum requirements include a bachelor's degree from an accredited college or university with a major in food, nutrition, or institution management, and completion of an approved internship *or* specified experience requirements.

Trade and other associations have less specific academic requirements but skill in a particular type of work is a basis for membership. The American School Food Service Association is a national organization made up of state affiliates, and membership is open to those associated with school foodservice programs. Membership in the National Restaurant Association, which is a trade organization, is open to: [19]

Any person who is the owner or manager of a restaurant or an executive officer or acts in a supervisory capacity of a restaurant operating company is eligible to membership in this Association. The restaurant he represents must be of good reputation and known to be controlled in conformity with the standard of service, quality, and sanitation of the NRA. Owners, managers and executive officers of companies rendering catering and banquet or curb service shall be eligible to membership on the same basis.

---

[18] *Russell M. Wilder, M.D., "The Profession of Dietetics,"* Journal of the American Dietetic Association, 26, *497–502 (1950).*
[19] *By-Laws of the National Restaurant Association, Article III.*

Two other organizations whose memberships include foodservice personnel are The Hospital, Institution, and Educational Food Service Society (HIEFSS) and the Council on Hotel, Restaurant, and Industrial Education (CHRIE). The HIEFSS Society provides membership to foodservice workers who have completed prescribed, approved educational-experience requirements, usually offered in vocational or adult educational programs or as correspondence courses for the Dietetic Assistant or the Foodservice Supervisor; the Dietetic Technician whose program follows a two-year course offered in an accredited community or junior college is also eligible for membership.

Members of CHRIE are committed to improving the education at all levels for the hospitality industry. Educators in technical and trade schools, junior and community colleges, and in bachelor's degree programs are invited to membership. Many future leaders of the foodservice industry undoubtedly will come from these programs. All that can be done to upgrade the programs that prepare these leaders will, in turn, improve the industry as a whole.

In *summary,* persons who will successfully administer foodservice departments in the future are those who are committed to a philosophy of service, who will refresh and utilize their knowledge and skills to keep pace with ever-changing situations by improving conditions for their organization and its personnel.

A colorful challenge was presented by Davis [20] in 1948 that is applicable today to responsible persons in the foodservice industry.

TO   THE   DIETITIAN

You hold in your menus the shape of the human figure, whether those at your tables are to be too fat or too lean. You can, by the essence of food, turn a wan face into a healthy, smiling countenance. By careful, scientific planning you can transmute the copper pennies of a limited budget into the golden nutrition of well-being. You work with something of which everyone partakes at least three times a day, that babies and children think about almost continuously, and that never satiates a much too large portion of the hungry creatures of the earth. The feasts you prepare are solace for the lonely, the ill, the loveless. The calories, odors, and tastes are too frequently a substitute for affection and human understanding, causing the guests of your tables to wax fat upon their unhappiness. A pinch of this vitamin or that a day keeps depression away. This factor builds healthy bones and that sharpens the eyes to rival those of the proverbial cat.

[20] *Watson Davis, from an address given at the Annual Meeting of the American Dietetic Association, Boston, 1948.*

You practice the art of culinary camouflage to foil the gastronomic foibles of finicky humans. You help the doctor prescribe and the nurse to woo back to health. You discover the useful and unusual in strange fruits, exotic viands, and disdained by-products. You can change the mores of the stomach and of the palate. To the butcher, the baker, and the vitamin maker, you are the consultant and the customer. You, dietitians of this modern era, are the high priests and efficient engineers of food, and the energy substance of the human earth.

SELECTED REFERENCES

Appley, Lawrence A., *Management in Action,* American Management Association, New York, 1956.

Cribbin, James J., *Effective Managerial Leadership,* American Management Association, New York, 1972.

Davis, Keith, *Human Behavior at Work,* Fourth Edition, McGraw-Hill, New York, 1972.

Davis, Keith, and Robert L. Blomstrom, *Business and Society,* McGraw-Hill, New York, 1972.

Day, David R., and Ralph M. Stogdill, "Leader Behavior of Male and Female Supervisors: A Comparative Study," The Ohio State University, Division of Research Reprint Series, College of Administrative Science, Columbus, Ohio, 1972.

Drucker, Peter F., *Management: Tasks, Responsibilities and Practices,* Harper and Row, New York, 1974.

Eckles, Robert W., Ronald L. Carmichael, and Bernard R. Sarchet. *Essentials of Management for First Line Supervisors,* Wiley, New York, 1974.

Fiedler, Fred E., *A Theory of Leadership Effectiveness.* McGraw-Hill, New York, 1967.

Fuller, Don, *Manage or Be Managed,* Cahners, Boston, 1970.

Gellerman, Saul, *Management By Motivation,* American Management Association, New York, 1968.

Haimann, Theo, and William G. Scott, *Management in the Modern Organization,* Houghton Mifflin, Boston, 1970.

Huse, Edgar R., and James L. Bowditch, *Behavior in Organizations,* Addison-Wesley, Reading, Massachusetts, 1973.

Jennings, E. E., *An Anatomy of Leadership,* Harper and Row, New York, 1969.

Keister, Douglas, and Ralph D. Wilson, *Selected Readings for an Introduction to Hotel and Restaurant Management,* McCutchan, Berkeley, California, 1971.

Likert, Rensis A., *Human Organization: New Patterns of Management,* McGraw-Hill, New York, 1967.

Lundberg, Donald E., and James P. Armatas, *The Management of People in Hotels, Restaurants, and Clubs,* Third Edition, Wm. C. Brown, Dubuque, Iowa, 1974.

McGregor, Douglas, *The Professional Manager,* McGraw-Hill, New York, 1967.

Scott, William C., and Terrence P. Mitchell, *Organization Theory,* Richard D. Irwin, Homewood, Illinois, 1972.

Selected Reprints from American Management Periodicals, American Management Association, Inc., New York:
"Communication Within the Organization."
"Communication With Subordinates."
"The Use of Communication Tools."
"Controlling The Computer. Management of EDP Problems."

8.
PERSONNEL
MANAGEMENT

Good human relations within the organization play a major role in the sucess of any enterprise. The ability of managers to understand people, recognize their potentials, and provide for their growth and development on the job is of inestimable worth in helping to create good will. Also, realization by workers that they are useful and important to efficient functioning of the business contributes to their sense of responsibility, proprietorship, and pride in the organization. Increase in pay alone does not buy good will, loyalty, or confidence in self and others. Often only simple changes or considerations such as beautification of the work area, elimination of safety hazards, rearrangement of equipment, modification of work schedules, or even cheerful words of appreciation and encouragement produce incentives with resultant increased and improved quality output. Mutually understood and accepted objectives and policies of the foodservice and well-defined channels of communications also contribute significantly to high-level employer-employee relationships.

A detailed plan of organization for a foodservice indicates the number and types of units of manpower needed, presents their distribution among the various work areas of the service, and shows the time of their comings and goings, the provision made for their training, and the responsibilities assigned to each. Far more difficult than the formulation of such a plan on paper is its inauguration in actuality. Then all the neat little blocks on the chart designating individuals assigned certain responsibilities become persons with diverse energies and loyalties, egocentric ideas, and unclarified codes of values, some skillful, others not, some with acceptable food standards, and others apparently wholly lacking in this regard. Left to chance, the introduction of the human element into an orderly plan is likely to plunge it into chaos. With wise selection, intelligent and adequate direction, and careful supervision, the human element vitalizes and enriches the plan.

Foodservices in many large companies have personnel departments responsible for the administration of manpower. In such organizations the dietitian or food director works closely with the personnel department. However, in many small foodservices, personnel management responsibilities are assumed by the director of that department. Thus he may be responsible for the organization plans, the procurement, placement, induction, on-the-job training, and supervision of all employees under his jurisdiction.

Management of the human resources presents unique problems that can be solved only by persons with an understanding of human nature, a respect for the personality of others, and an appreciation of the labor requirements and employment opportunities of the company. Insight into and respect for the rights of all individuals in an organization is the responsibility of the person in charge. These time-honored rights are the right of every man (1) to be treated as an individual and respected as a person, (2) to have a voice in his own affairs, which include his right to contribute to the best of his abilities in the solution of common problems, (3) to recognition for his contribution to the common good, (4) to develop and make use of his highest capabilities, and (5) to fairness and justice in all his dealings with his supervisors.

As soon as a worker is employed he becomes a member of the group and begins to share in forming that intangible but all-important element termed group morale or group spirit. If he is understanding, cooperative, and helpful he contributes to group morale; if he is irritable, carping, complaining, and obstructive he destroys it. Many organizations have learned through sad experience how very great a destructive force one malcontent member can exert on group spirit. That the monks long ago recognized the problem and dealt with it in their own way to preserve the peace of the monastery is indicated by this ancient admonition.

BENE DICTUM, BENEDICTE!

If any pilgrim monk comes from distant parts, if with wish as a guest to dwell in the monastery, and will be content with the customs which he finds in the place, does not perchance by his lavishness disturb the monastery, but is simply content with what he finds, he shall be received for as long a time as he desires. If, indeed, he find fault with anything, or expose it reasonably, and with the humility of charity, the Abbot shall discuss it prudently, less perchance God had sent him for this very thing. But, if he have been found gossipy and contumacious in the time of his sojourn as guest, not only ought he not to be joined to the body of the monastery, but also it shall be said to him, honestly, that he must depart. If he does not go, let two stout monks in the name of God explain the matter to him.

—SAINT BENEDICT.

Today neither the discipline of the worker who is a disturbing force nor yet his elimination from the group can be handled quite so directly and forcibly. For this reason the selection of those who will build morale rather than destroy it is of great importance in the choice of staff.

The skill, craftsmanship, dependability, and regularity of a worker and his contribution to group morale may determine his selection as a present worker. Certain other things indicate his probable contribution in the future. His capacity for growth, desire for self-improvement so that he may render greater service, ambition for promotion, and identification with the firm are all important in the selection of manpower for tomorrow. However, not all people are equally desirous of assuming responsibility and carrying a project to conclusion. This is true also of workers who are unwilling to face problem solving. Some people are overdependent and eager to avoid directing themselves or others.

After the food director has considered manpower needs of the foodservice under his charge, he may well consider what the service has to offer in return. Part of the recompense will be made in wages. Adequate compensation and steady employment are basic to any satisfactory employer-employee relationship. Another part of the recompense may be intangible; that is, just as the employee contributes to the morale of the group spirit of the service, so the administration will contribute to his sense of personal satisfaction. A third part of the compensation will be the opportunity to do a good job. Full instructions as to accepted procedures and standards and adequate on-the-job supervision are vital to satisfactory performance by the worker. Only then will he experience pride in his accomplishments and attain and maintain a high performance on his job.

The job should provide opportunity for growth and a reasonable chance for promotion. The worker should have an opportunity to make his service a creative experience. He should be encouraged to regard improvement in techniques as possible and welcome and to feel that suggestions toward this end will be cordially received. He has a right to expect fairness in his dealings with management, freedom from misrepresentation and misinformation about the organization that employs him, a reasonable opportunity for continued education, promotion when earned, and provision for satisfying recreation.

The food director should synthesize the two points of view—the employer's and the employee's—into an adequate, functioning personnel program. Such a program should be characterized by wise selection, careful placement, adequate supervision, and education for the present job and for the future; fair employment policies; services desirable for the comfort and welfare of employees; and the keeping of records that will facilitate the evaluation and revision, if needed, of the management program.

THE EMPLOYMENT PROCESS

Organization charts indicate the number of workers needed in each department of a foodservice, and job descriptions and job specifications outline the specific conditions under which each employee will work, the requirements that the job will make of him, and the training and other personal qualifications deemed desirable. Such information affords the food director charged with personnel management an inventory of employment needs.

RECRUITMENT

The next step is to survey the sources of labor supply and determine which one or ones shall be used to bring the best qualified prospective employees to his attention. There should be active recruitment of minority group members if the institution is to stay in line with public policy. Labor sources are many and varied, dependent somewhat on which sources are available locally and on the general labor market. Most sources may be classified conveniently as either internal or external.

Internal Sources. Promotion of employees to a position of higher level, transfer from a related department or unit, and rehiring of a person formerly on the payroll are examples of internal sources. Promotions or transfers within an organization help to stimulate interest and build morale of employees when they know that on the basis of measured merit they will be given preference over an outsider in case of a good vacancy. Caution must be taken to ensure that the individual has the necessary personal attributes as well as training and experience for the position open and that equal opportunity employment regulations have not been violated.

An indirect internal source of labor is a present employee who notifies friends or relatives of vacancies and arranges for an interview with the employer. This means of recruiting labor has advantages and disadvantages. Present employees usually recommend only those who are congenial, and a pleasant spirit within the group may be built by utilizing this source of labor supply. On the other hand, personal ties may be stronger than business loyalties, and inept, unskilled workers may be highly recommended by relatives and friends. Futhermore a strongly clannish feeling among the workers may lead to an unfortunate generalized reaction against any disciplinary measure, however well justified. The many phases of the matter should be considered before extensive use is made of this source of labor.

External Sources. Some foodservice organizations may plan to fill many vacancies by promoting from within, but eventually replacements will be needed to fill the depleted ranks. The most common external sources are the press, employment agencies, schools, and labor unions.

Advertising. Newspaper advertising is a means of reaching a large group of potential applicants. Such advertisements cite the qualifications desired; otherwise a mass of applicants may respond, none of whom are qualified. Definite statements as to desired training and experience in the foodservice field tend to limit the applicants to possible candidates. Details concerning salary, sick leave, time schedule, and vacations are much better left until the personal interview. The advertisement should state whether application is to be made first in person or by letter.

Employment Agencies. Private employment agencies have long served as a means of locating labor. They are supported by a registration fee charged those seeking employment. Usually they provide a preliminary weeding out of would-be applicants, eliminating the obviously unfit from consideration. Often these agenices tend to deal with specialized groups in the professional or technical areas and are of most value to those seeking employees on the managerial level.

The growth of public employment agencies, federal, state, and local, has been relatively rapid, and they are now considered of significant importance as a labor source. The value of these agencies has increased, since they have studied the employer's needs and set up machinery to test aptitudes and skills of the workers. Such procedures have benefited the foodservice managers endeavoring to reduce turnover to a minimum and develop stability of employment.

Schools. In some localities vocational and technical schools offering training for the food industry have excellent prospects from among the senior graduates. The adequacy of their specific preparation for this work may greatly shorten the period of preliminary training necessary.

Another source, important in the foodservices of colleges and universities, is the student employment office of the college. Utilizing this type of labor offers financial assistance to worthy students and often provides experience to students majoring in food systems management. Perhaps the greatest advantage of student employees to the college dietitian is their availability for short work periods during the peak of the service load. However, the labor cost is high because of the inexperience of the workers, and the labor turnover is great, thus requiring the expenditure of much energy in introducing new workers to the jobs. The short work periods necessitated by the students' classroom assignments make the planning of work far more complicated than when full-time employees are used. The immaturity and inexperience of the worker may result in waste of food supplies and labor hours unless constant and thorough supervision is provided. The maintenance of high food standards and acceptable service is often much more difficult with student employees than with carefully chosen, well-trained employees of long-time service.

Labor Unions. In institutions where employees are unionized, the labor union may be an important source for workers.

SELECTION

After the prospective workers have been recruited, the next step is for the employer to select the most able person available for the particular opening. The cost of hiring, training, and discharging or transferring a worker is too great to allow many mistakes in the employee procurement. Failure at this point is far more expensive than is commonly recognized.

Recognition of the heavy initial cost of employment means, when the labor market permits, a trend toward careful selection of each appointee.

Application Form. In the employment of any worker the application form plays an important role. The information requested should be phrased in direct simple statements pertinent to the particular job in which the applicant showed interest, and questions raised should be easily answered by him. Obviously, quite different information would be required of the person applying for the position of administrative dietitian than for one who expects to be a counter worker. However, both application forms, when filled in, must contain biographical data that will provide the employer with all the facts necessary for him not only to determine the fitness of the applicant for the job, but also to compare the qualifications of all applicants. The Fair Employment Practice laws adopted by many states make it illegal to ask questions that would be discriminatory because of race, religion, sex, or national origin. After the employee has been hired, such information can be obtained for the individual's personnel records. The dietitian or manager should check with the personnel department or other authoritative source regarding restrictions in the application form and the interview. References of former employment usually are requested and should be checked.

Interview. The purpose of the selection interview is twofold; it helps to determine fitness of the applicant for the opening, and it also provides information that helps the applicant determine his interest in the position and in the company. Usually the initial interview is the first contact of the worker with the organization. Just as the management appraises the applicant for a job, so he evaluates the company by his initial experiences with it.

The *direct* personal interview is advantageous in that the interviewer has opportunity to become acquainted with the applicant and to observe personal characteristics and reactions that would be impossible to learn from an application form or letter. Also, the great majority of the employees of a foodservice are persons relatively untrained, whose qualifications cannot be ascertained in any other way than by a personal interview and possible communications with previous employers. Documents that could be termed credentials are rarely available; therefore the personal interview becomes of great importance in making a wise choice. In filling administrative positions the personal interview serves as a final check on the fitness of a person whose credentials have been considered carefully.

The environment for interviewing should be conducive to a sense of friendliness and ease. Privacy and freedom from tension are essential to the office atmosphere where personality traits are to be evaluated. The person conducting the interview must be cognizant of the details of the job and its requirements of the worker as described in the job specifications. Recognition of the qualities of the applicant to meet demands of the job requires skill on the part of the interviewer.

The applicant should be treated as a person whose concern with the decision is as real and vital as that of the employing agency. He should see his job in relation to other jobs in the foodservice to which his job might lead. Reasonable hopes for promotion should be discussed and fringe benefits should be presented. Appraisal of the job specifications in terms of his own fitness should motivate self-direction toward either self-placement or self-elimination.

The development of a successful technique in interviewing requires thought, study, and experience. The interview should be planned and questions directed toward obtaining information about the applicant.

The interviewer may find it helpful to develop an interview evaluation form on which to summarize the impressions made by an applicant. Form 8.1 is an example.

Personnel Records. After an agreement on employment terms has been reached, a record of appointment is made. This becomes the nucleus of the records of the activity and progress of the worker within the organization. Records may be kept on data-processing cards, in card files, or in loose-leaf form. Included among the items listed on the forms are name, address, name of wife or husband, number of children, other dependents, educational background, former employment (including company and length of time), the date of hiring, the job assigned, the wage rate, whether or not meals are included, absences with reasons, adjustments in work and wages, promotions, demotions, or transfers with reasons, and information concerning insurance. Such complete records are useful in indicating the sense of responsibility and the serious intent of employees, and as a basis for merit ratings, salary adjustments, or other benefits.

Tests. Impressions of the prospective employee gained in the interview and from the follow-up of references are admittedly incomplete. They may be checked or replaced by tests of various types, the most common of which are intelligence, trade, and aptitude. Any type of testing, to be of value, must be done by a person well qualified by education and experience for this specialized function of personnel management.

Interview Evaluation

Rating: 1 2 3 4   M
Job: F
Date:

Name _____

Address _____ Transportation _____

Why interested in a job with this company?
Kind of work preferred?
What previous experience would qualify him for this work?
Would other work be considered on a temporary basis?

Employment record:	*Last Employment*	*Previous Employment*	*Previous Employment*
Name of company			
Kind of work			
How was job obtained?			
Beginning wage			
Wage at separation			
Did he like his work? (if not, why not?)			
Was attendance record good?			
(if not, are reasons sound?) Why terminated?			

(are reasons justified?)

Other Work Experience

Name of Company	Work Performed	Wage	From	To	Why Left

Education

What grade did he complete in school?   Year   Age at leaving
Did he graduate?   Grammar   High   College
  (is education ample for job?)
If not a graduate, why not?
  (are reasons for not finishing good ones?)
Did he help finance his education?   P.T. Work   Vacations
  (does this show industry?)
Does he have any physical disabilities?

Analysis

When rating consider: Motivation   Loyalty
                  Stability   Ability to get along with others
                  Industry   Health
                                 Interviewer: _____

FORM   8.1   *Evaluation of applicant following a personal interview.*

The physical fitness of an applicant for a foodservice appointment is highly important. A health examination should be required of all foodservice workers. Only a physically fit person can do his best work. Quite as important is the need for assurance that the individual presents no health hazard to the foodservice. Managers are well aware of the devastation that might result from the inadvertent employment of a typhoid carrier or those with other communicable diseases.

THE WORKER ON THE JOB

ORIENTATION

The induction of the newly employed worker to his job is a most important phase of personnel management. It is necessary first to acquaint him with the goals or objectives of the service in such a way as to challenge his interest and elicit his support. Identification of individual objectives with those of the foodservice is necessary to avoid conflicting interests and loyalties. Presentation of the goals or objectives sought by the organization should be made to the employee by both the spoken word and printed materials. A friendly discussion of the history of the foodservice, including a review of its traditions and present policies, is regarded by many as the best possible initiation of an employee.

The use of printed material affords more lasting stimulus than that conveyed by oral instruction. A policy manual, clearly and attractively written, can present effectively not only the objectives and policies, but also the regulations in regard to hours of work, wage scales, social and welfare provisions, and penalties attached to absence or tardiness. Some organizations use booklets available on the market instead of attempting individual publication, although a simple handbook prepared for use by the employers and employees is considered by most managers and supervisors an indispensable tool of management. Such a manual, when properly designed, presented, and discussed with newcomers in a foodservice, will tend to give them a sense of belonging.

Another effective method of introducing the new employee to his work is that of taking him on a personally conducted tour of the building or buildings and discussing with him en route the interrelation of the departments visited. The bird's-eye view so gained is valuable in developing an understanding of the sequence of work and the interdependence of all employees.

When a new worker reports, he should be introduced to the person in charge, such as the production manager or the foodservice supervisor, and to his co-workers. In some instances a well-oriented fellow employee may be assigned to sponsor a newcomer, assisting him to become acquainted with the facility and his co-workers.

A complete job description will aid the worker to gain efficiency through a thorough understanding of his assignment. Also, a statement of specific responsibilities prepared by the supervisor, accompanied by a work schedule and a list of necessary equipment to be used, the sequence of tasks, and the procedures and time allotment approved by the organization.

TRAINING

After the indiviual worker has been properly introduced to his job, there still remains the need for training through qualified supervision, especially in the initial period of employment. Familiarity with established operational policies and procedures, presented by management in a well-organized manner, can do much to encourage the new worker and help him to gain self-confidence. Generally, advantages of a good training program include reduction in labor turnover, absenteeism, accidents, and production costs, and an increase in the maintenance of morale, job satisfaction, and efficient production at high levels.

Group Training. Often training can be given efficiently and economically through group instruction. This type of teaching saves time for the instructor and the worker, and also has the further advantage of affording the stimulus that comes as the result of group participation. In a foodservice, basic group instruction concerning the policies of management is practical and valuable. Among the areas that might be included are the history and objectives of the organization, relationships of departments and key persons within the particular department, the operational budget as it affects the workers, the preparation and service of food, the sanitation and safety program, and the principles and values of work improvement programs.

Perhaps the most important psychological principle of group training is the use of well-prepared teachers instead of a fellow worker who may have had successful experience in a limited area. Often the stimulation and the inspiration given to the employee by an able instructor are highly motivative and more important in the development of the individual worker than the immediate mastery of routine skills. Tools found to be of value in such an instructional program are audio and visual aids, including films and television, illustrative material, such as posters, charts, and cartoons, and demonstrations in which both the instructor and the employees participate. It is wasteful to spend time and money merely showing films in group training classes unless the workers have been alerted to the points of emphasis, time allowed for discussion after the presentation, and follow-up through application on the job. Other psychological principles of group education cannot be considered here, although they should be understood by those in charge of such programs.

On-the-Job Training. Some large foodservice organizations have inaugurated rather extensive programs to provide on-the-job training of employees, with highly satisfactory results. Important among the objectives of such programs are: to reduce time spent in perfecting skills for the production and service of attractive, wholesome food of high quality at reasonable cost, to avoid accidents and damage to property and equipment, and to promote good understanding and close working relationships among employees and supervisors. In these programs emphasis is given to certain requirements common to all good job instruction, such as job knowledge, manipulative skills, human relations, adaptability, and ability to express oneself. Unless these requirements characterize the instructor, he is an ineffective teacher, unable to do a satisfactory job of instruction.

Teacher preparation for instruction to be given on the job and the teaching steps include the following.

First—to Get Ready to Instruct
1. *Break down the job*—list principal steps, pick out the key points.

2. *Have a timetable*—how much skill you expect your pupil to have and how soon.

3. *Have everything ready*—the right tools, equipment, and materials.

4. *Have the work place properly arranged*—just as the worker will be expected to keep it.

Second—to Instruct
1. *Prepare the worker*
    Put him at ease. A frightened or embarrassed person cannot learn.
    Find out what he already knows about the job. Begin where his knowledge ends.
    Interest him in learning the job.
    Place him in correct position.

2. *Present the operation.*
    Tell, show, illustrate, and question carefully and patiently.
    Stress key points. Make them clear.
    Instruct slowly, clearly, and completely, taking up one point at a time—but no more than the trainee can master.
    Work first for accuracy, then for speed.

3. *Try out the worker's performance.*
    Test him by having him perform job under observation.
    Have him tell and show you; have him explain key points.
    Ask questions and correct errors patiently. Continue until you know the worker knows.

4. *Follow up worker's performance.*
    Put worker on his own.
    Check frequently, but do not take over if you can give the help needed.
    Designate to whom he goes for help.
    Encourage questions.
    Get him to look for key points as he progresses.
    Taper off extra coaching and close follow-up until he is able to work under usual supervision.
    Give credit where credit is due.

A *job breakdown* is the analysis of a job to be taught and a listing of the elemental steps of *what* to do and the key points of *how* to do them. This serves as a guide in giving instruction so that none of the necessary points will be omitted. Figure 8.1 is an example of a job breakdown for making change.

Job Title _____ Making Change _____

Equipment and Supplies _____ Money and Cash Register _____

Important Steps	*Key Points*
REGISTER FIRST—WRAP AFTERWARDS	
1. Accept money from customer.	1. State amount of sale* "out of" amount received from customer.
2. Place customer's money on plate.	2. Stand in front of cash register. Do not put bill in drawer until after change has been counted.
3. Record the sale on cash register.	3. Check amount recorded on viewer.
4. Count change from till.	4. Begin with amount of sale picking up smallest change first up to amount received from customer.
5. Count change carefully to customer.	5. Start with amount of sale—stop counting when amount is the same as the customer gave.
6. Place customer's money in till.	6. Close the drawer immediately.
7. Deliver change, receipt or sales slip, and merchandise to customer.	7. Say *Thank You.* Let her know you mean it.

* Including tax (state and federal).

FIGURE   8.1   *Job breakdown for making change at the cash register.*

Slide-tape programs for individual instruction in work methods and procedures have proven to be satisfactory and, while their preparation is time consuming, the results appear to justify their use. Slides showing correct techniques are accompanied by oral explanations on tape. Special equipment is available in which the audio and visual aspects are coordinated, but an ordinary slide projector and tape or cassette recorder may be used. For techniques involving motion or rhythm, a film taken with an 8 mm movie camera may be helpful.

Encouragement of the worker by his supervisor during the first days on the job and the period of his training alike is important in stabilizing his interest and sustaining his sense of adequacy. Informal interviews may serve as a desirable means of determining points on which he needs help, as well as those in which his ability is most marked. Every expression of friendly, courteous interest is appreciated by the worker and aids in his successful adjustment to his new environment.

In addition to the satisfaction attained by establishing pleasant employer-employee relations, right induction of the new worker has a dollar-and-cents value that cannot be overlooked. If an employee is unhappy, disinterested, and discontented, he will tend to look for placement elsewhere after a short experience with the company. Then all the money, time, and effort spent in obtaining him and introducing him to the job will have been lost, and a similar expenditure must be made before another worker can be assigned the task.

WORK STANDARDS AND PRODUCTIVITY

Training *does* pay dividends to the organization, and highest dividends will be realized when specific standards for achievement have been met. "A very important part of the personnel manager's responsibility . . . is the establishment and maintenance of many standards by which performance can be judged. A *Standard* can be defined as an *established criterion or model against which actual results can be compared.* Standardization is merely the process of determining and maintaining these standards in order to produce a measure of uniformity." [1]

Foodservice managers and administrative dietitians have responsibility for determining the standards for their own department, standards of time, quantity, quality, and cost. How much work of what quality is to be accomplished in what length of time and at what cost? Managers *must* be able to answer these questions realistically and provide the information for the workers if any degree of competence and high productivity are to be achieved. Otherwise, employees develop their own standards and may never reach their own potential nor produce at an acceptable level. Managers who allow this to happen have lost control of operations; events then control the manager.

Standards are derived from objectives, the statements of what is to be achieved. Behavioral objectives relate specifically to what an individual should be able to do as a result of the learning process. Such objectives usually form the basics of a training program and give specific measures for trainee attainment. And, while workers learn proper techniques and procedures through a training program, actual work experience usually is necessary for them to de-

[1] *From* Principles of Personnel Management, *Third Edition, by Edwin B. Flippo. Copyright © 1971 by McGraw-Hill, Inc. Used with permission of McGraw-Hill Book Co., p. 79.*

velop speed and accuracy in completing a given task. This is where preestablished standards are necessary so the employees will know exactly what is expected of them and so a goal is provided for them to attain.

Time and quantity studies must be made within a given foodservice department in order to establish desirable standards for that department with its own equipment, space arrangement, facilities, and procedures. These variables make it difficult if not impossible to have universal standards among foodservice organizations. The employee who knows he is expected to make 45 sandwiches in 15 minutes, or 3 sandwiches per minute, is much more apt to respond to and meet the challenge of a goal to be reached than the employee who is told to "just work as fast as you can."

Each operation or task to be performed requires similar questions to be asked and answered. Actual time studies may be made in order to arrive at realistic time-quantity standards. Quality and cost standards come from the knowledge of the dietitian or foodservice manager, who must have acquired this from his basic education and preparation for the position. Standards for personnel to which applicants can be compared include minimum acceptable qualities necessary for adequate performance of the job duties. These standards or qualifications will be stated in job specifications for use by those who select personnel. (See page 355 for more on job specifications.)

Although no one can set standards for someone else's department, results of some research studies may prove helpful as a guide to foodservice managers undertaking a standards-setting project. Pedderson [2] gives a formula for determining how long it takes to accomplish a given task, using the following symbols.

a = the *least* amount of time to do a given task
b = the *most* amount of time to do a given task
m = the most *likely* time to do a given task

To calculate the most *probable* (allowable in the schedule) amount of time it will take to do a given task, use the formula:

$$\frac{a + 4m + b}{6} = \text{Probable time required}$$

[2] *Jule Wilkinson, Editor,* Increasing Productivity in Foodservice, *Section on Motivation and Worker Productivity by Raymond Pedderson, Cahners, Boston, p. 46, 1973.*

Let us say, for instance, that we want to know how much time should be allowed to mop a heavily obstructed 1600-square foot institutional kitchen:

A sloppy, cursory job will take 20 minutes.
$a = 20$ (minutes) *
An extremely thorough job will take 120 minutes.
$b = 120$ (minutes) *
The job, done adequately, will most likely take
45 minutes.
$m = 45$ (minutes) *
Using the formula,

$$\frac{a + 4m + b}{6} =$$

$$\frac{20 + (4 \times 45) + 120}{6} = \frac{320}{6} =$$

$$\frac{20 + 180 + 120}{6} =$$

$$53\frac{1}{3} \text{ minutes}$$

Knowing that the most probable time to mop the floor is 53 1/3 minutes, we will allot that amount of time daily to that task.

Derived from actual time study of cursory, thorough, and adequate sampling.

Bartscht and co-workers [3] made comprehensive time studies of tasks performed in hospital dietary departments. The methodology that they developed can be used as a formula by other hospital dietary managers to calculate the amount of time required to perform a task in their own department, based on distances to be travelled.

[3] *Karl G. Bartscht, F. H. Bayha, D. G. Molhoek, and G. J. Kausler, "Hospital Staffing Methodology Manual, MM-3 Dietary," Ann Arbor: Community Systems Foundation. Performed under Contract No. PH-86-83-231 and Grant No. HM-00406-01 by the Hospital Systems Research Group at the Institute of Science and Technology, University of Michigan, Ann Arbor.*

Other studies throughout the years have given suggested standards in terms of number of labor minutes required for one meal served. These ranged from a low of 4 or 5 minutes for some school foodservices, to 9 or 10 minutes for college and industrial cafeterias, up to 18 to 20 labor minutes per meal including supervisory time in hospitals. Greater efficiency (lower number of minutes required) is usually achieved when a larger number of meals are served as compared with a small organization serving few meals. Foodservice managers may wish to make a study of their own operations and develop a standard for themselves based on number of labor minutes needed for each meal served.

School foodservice standards for personnel staffing have been suggested.[4] These are stated in terms of number of employees needed for number of meals served, as follows.

Number of Meals Served	Number of Employees
300–600	4–6
600–1000	6–10
1000–2000	10–20
2000–3000	20–25

Worker efficiency in foodservices is estimated to be from 40 to 55 percent. Although the nature of the work involved in preparing meals for specified periods of the day, causing uneven work loads, may be part of the reason for such low productivity as compared with that in other industries, foodservices can no longer afford the luxury of inefficiency. Labor costs are too high, and every means possible should be used to improve productivity.

Many definitions have been given for productivity but, essentially in foodservice management, it is a measure or level of *output* of goods produced or services rendered in relation to *input* in terms of time (labor hours, minutes, or days), money spent, or other resources used. Productivity is sometimes equated with efficiency. Welch and Hockenberry[5] proposed this formula for expressing work efficiency.

[4] *Design Criteria—School Food Service Facilities.* State of Florida, Department of Education, Tallahassee, Florida, p. 32.

[5] *John M. Welch and George Hockenberry, "Everything You Always Wanted to Know About Work Sampling,"* School Foodservice Journal, 29, 71 (January 1975). Copyright © American School Food Service Association, 1975.

$$\frac{\text{Time the worker performs necessary work}}{\text{Time for which employee is paid}} \times 100 = \frac{\text{Worker efficiency}}{\text{percentage}}$$

Time the worker performs necessary work may be determined through use of the management tool, work sampling. (See page 369.)

It is hoped that every dietitian and manager concerned with the administration of a foodservice will establish and use standards that are realistic and that will be of benefit both to the employee and to organization.

PERFORMANCE APPRAISAL

For maximum effectiveness from the work force, every employee should know what is expected of him and how he is performing on the job. He is entitled to commendation for work well done and to the opportunity to earn greater responsibility, either with or without increased remuneration. One of the responsibilities of management and supervision is the performance appraisal, and then management has an obligation to communicate this information to each individual regarding his progress. The personal development of and efficient production by each worker is of concern to management, but an individual worker cannot be expected to improve if no evaluations are made known to him or counsel made available to assist him. Performance appraisals are used to determine job competence, need for additional training or counseling, and to review the employee's progress within the organization. Ratings made objectively and without prejudice furnish valuable information that can be used in job placement, training, supervision, promotion, and replacement. Careful selection and placement and proper training of employees for their particular responsibilities are prerequisites to a successful evaluations program. The performance appraisal may be accomplished by several methods, including rating scales, check lists, narrative evaluation, personal conferences, or management by objectives.

There are few if any objective standards that can be used for measuring subjective personal characteristics such as character, reliability, and initiative. Yet these traits, as they relate to the capabilities, efficiency, and development of each employee, are important to an organization. These characteristics must be appraised in some way if management is to have an intelligent basis for classifying workers according to rank or grade and thus help to provide a standard for salary increases, promotions, transfers, or placement into a job for which the worker is well suited.

Rating procedures have been developed that provide a measurement of the degree to which certain intangible personality traits are present in each worker and of his performance on the job. Care should be taken to design the scale to meet the objective desired. Will this estimate of the relative worth of employees be used as a basis for rewards or recognitions or as a tool for explaining to workers why they may or may not be making progress on the job? In the hands of competent administrators, the rating form could be designed to obtain information to accomplish both purposes.

Distinguishable personal traits most likely to affect performance might be honesty, initiative, judgment, and ability to get along with other workers. Examples of qualities on a rating chart are: quality of work, quantity of work, adaptability, job knowledge, and dependability.

These so-called rating scales, from which the variously known merit, progress, development, or service ratings are derived, are not new in industrial management, although few are directly applicable to institution foodservices. Some administrators prefer a system of gradation checking where each quality, factor, or characteristic may be marked on a scale ranging from poor to superior, or the reverse, with two or three possible levels within each grade. For example:

Factor I | Superior | Good | Fair | Poor |

Another format might describe the grade for each factor listed.

Form 8.2 is an example of a rating scale with definitions of the various factors attached for use of the rater.

Clinton[6] devised a successful numerical rating system with a different form and breakdown of points for each classification of workers. (See Form 8.3.) In this organization each individual worker was rated at 3-month intervals by the immediate supervisor, the department head, and the manager most closely associated with the worker's activity. The average of their totals for each quality evaluated became the final composite numerical rating. Those persons whose ratings fell below 75 were given special counseling and supervision and placed on probation; failure of an individual to show improvement by the next rating period made him subject to transfer or replacement.

[6] *Edmond J. Clinton, "Rate Your Employees Fairly,"* Restaurant Management, 83(5), 62 (1958).

EMPLOYEE PERFORMANCE REVIEW RATING

NAME_____DATE _____

PRESENT JOB _____DEPARTMENT_____

PAY RANGE_____ TO _____

CURRENT RATE_____ NEW RATE _____

REVIEW PERIOD FROM_____TO_____
        Date   Date

REASON
FOR REVIEW: ☐ PROBATIONARY ☐ ANNUAL ☐ SPECIAL_____
                                             Explain

Date to be returned to Personnel Department _____

PART I
The purpose of the Employee Performance Review is twofold.

1. To identify the areas in which the employee is proficient, to encourage more effective utilization of known and demonstrated strengths, and to apply these proficiencies to the best advantage in accomplishing the objectives of the job and the department.
2. To identify areas in which improvement is desirable and to assist the employee to plan and execute a program of study, practice and/or discipline to develop total competency in the job.

It is the responsibility of the employee's supervisor to do the utmost to see that these purposes are accomplished. With this in mind, make every effort to state your comments so that they are constructive and positive.

It is important to remember that a rating of "Successful Performance" represents the performance level of a fully competent employee who is successfully performing all job duties and responsibilities and is doing a good job. Performance levels either above or below "Successful Performance" should be fully documented in Part II with regard to what was done to merit the rating given.

Indicate your evaluation of the employee's performance on each of the factors below by placing a (√) at the proper place on each scale.

FORM 8.2 Scale for review of employee performance. Courtesy, Lincoln General Hospital, Lincoln, Nebraska.

For your convenience the midpoint on the rating scale has been indicated *but* it is important to remember that the evaluations criteria
have been weighted. Therefore, the relationship between the score
checked on the rating scale and the amount of the merit increase is
minimal (a score of 5 on the rating scale does not mean a 5 percent
increase).

KNOWLEDGE OF WORK: Consider the knowledge and understanding the employee has regarding the job. Does the employee
know the methods or techniques to be used? Does the employee
know the reasons for the procedure to be followed? Does the employee know the purpose of the job and what is required to be accomplished and how it contributes to the objectives of the department?

Evaluate:

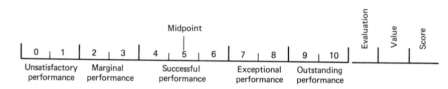

QUALITY OF WORK: Consider the accuracy, thoroughness and neatness with which the employee accomplishes the assigned work. Does
the employee approach the work methodically? Is the employee economical with work time and materials used?

Evaluate:

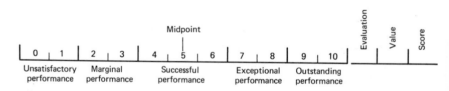

QUANTITY OF WORK: Consider the volume of work done under everyday conditions. Does the employee normally complete the work
schedule or assignments? Does the employee work fast enough to
accomplish the assigned share of the work? More than the assigned
share?

Evaluate:

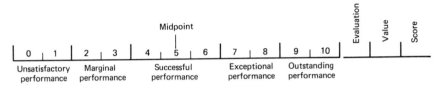

| 0 | 1 | 2 | 3 | 4 | 5 | 6 | 7 | 8 | 9 | 10 |

Midpoint

Unsatisfactory performance | Marginal performance | Successful performance | Exceptional performance | Outstanding performance

Evaluation   Value   Score

DEPENDABILITY: Consider the extent to which the employee can be depended on in the job. Is the employee punctual? Is the employee on the job when scheduled? To what extent does the employee require supervision? Does the employee inform the appropriate person if late, absent, or unable to complete the assigned work task?

Evaluate:

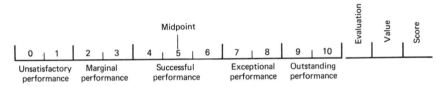

| 0 | 1 | 2 | 3 | 4 | 5 | 6 | 7 | 8 | 9 | 10 |

Midpoint

Unsatisfactory performance | Marginal performance | Successful performance | Exceptional performance | Outstanding performance

Evaluation   Value   Score

COMPATIBILITY: Consider the extent to which the employee's attitude toward the work, the responsible supervisor, and the hospital are compatible with the objectives of the hospital. Is the employee cooperative, easy to work with? Is the employee's attitude toward patients and fellow employees friendly and cooperative? Where contacts outside the hospital are required in fulfilling job responsibilities, does the employee represent the hospital with confidence and discretion? Does the employee conform to the personal grooming standards?

Evaluate:

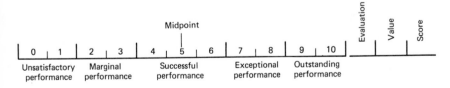

| 0 | 1 | 2 | 3 | 4 | 5 | 6 | 7 | 8 | 9 | 10 |

Midpoint

Unsatisfactory performance | Marginal performance | Successful performance | Exceptional performance | Outstanding performance

Evaluation   Value   Score

INITIATIVE: Consider how well the employee applies the knowledge of work. Is the employee a self-starter who makes frequent practical suggestions? Does the employee proceed on assigned work voluntarily and readily accept suggestions? How much does the employee rely on others in getting started on assigned work? How effectively does the employee share acquired skills with others?

Evaluate:

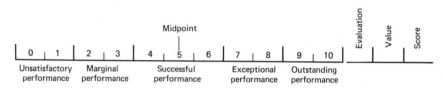

SAFETY: Consider the extent to which the employee is aware of unsafe practices and conditions in the work setting. Is the employee quick to sense possible hazards and then to take the appropriate steps to get them corrected? How careful is the employee insofar as safe work practices are concerned with regard to regular work assignments? Does the employee always follow the established work procedure for assigned tasks?

Evaluate:

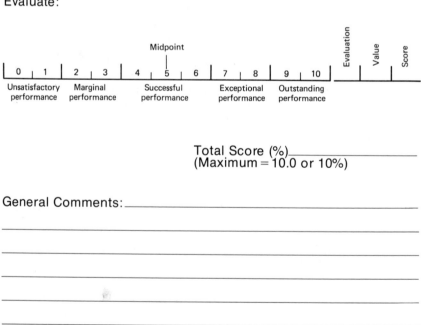

Total Score (%)_____
(Maximum = 10.0 or 10%)

General Comments:_____

_____

_____

_____

_____

PART II

The purpose of this section is to present the employee a well-conceived and workable program for:

1. Optimum application of known and demonstrated strengths and;
2. Study, practice, and/or discipline to develop competency in the areas requiring improvement. Be specific. Formulate benchmarks, attainable objectives so that the employee can recognize accomplishment and be aware of growth.

Knowledge of Work: ————————————————————

——————————————————————————

——————————————————————————

——————————————————————————

——————————————————————————

Quality of Work: ————————————————————

——————————————————————————

——————————————————————————

——————————————————————————

——————————————————————————

Quantity of Work: ————————————————————

——————————————————————————

——————————————————————————

——————————————————————————

——————————————————————————

Dependability: ————————————————————

——————————————————————————

——————————————————————————

——————————————————————————

——————————————————————————

Compatibility: ————————————————————

——————————————————————————

——————————————————————————

_____

_____

Initiative:_____

_____

_____

_____

Safety:_____

_____

_____

_____

Prepared by _____ _____ _____
             Name   Title   Date

Department head _____ _____
                       Name   Date

FOR EMPLOYEE: My signature on this form indicates that I have reviewed my performance evaluation as presented on this form and a copy has been given to me.

For Probationary Rating ONLY
Recommended for:

☐ Permanent Status

☐ Extension of Probation

_____

Signature   Date   ☐ Termination

ASSOCIATE RATING FORM: KITCHEN WORKER

1. *Job Skill* (Max. points: 25)
   Consider job performance and skill. Does he keep up with his work and keep his station clean, make all products uniformly; is he waste conscious, economical; does he work quietly and reasonably fast, refrain from visiting with fellow associates while on duty?

Excellent	25
Good	20
Average	15
Fair	10
Poor	5

2. *Cooperation* (Max. points: 25)
   Consider attitude. Does he respond quickly to a call for assistance from a fellow associate? Does he have a spirit of willingness? Is he receptive to change and new ideas? Will he accept new suggestions regarding his work?

Excellent	25
Good	20
Average	15
Fair	10
Poor	5

3. *Sanitation* (Max. points: 10)
   Consider health regulations: "No Smoking—Wash Hands When Leaving Rest Rooms." Does he keep: paper, trash, liquids, vegetable leaves, and other foreign materials off floor, hot foods hot, and other food under refrigeration?

Excellent	10
Good	8
Average	6
Fair	4
Poor	2

4. *Care of Equipment* (Max. points: 10)
   Does he: keep equipment clean and everything returned to proper place, know correct way to operate ovens, steamers, mixers, and other appliances?

Excellent	10
Good	8
Average	6
Fair	4
Poor	2

5. *Safety* (Max. points: 10)
   Does he work safely and is he safety conscious? Does he correct or report all hazards that may cause an accident? Does he know whereabouts of fire extinguisher and how to use it?

Excellent	10
Good	8
Average	6
Fair	4
Poor	2

6. *Appearance* (Max. points: 10)
   Consider personal cleanliness and neatness. Does he seem to enjoy his work? Is he clean of body? Are clothes clean and appropriate?

Excellent	10
Good	8
Average	6
Fair	4
Poor	2

7. *Attendance* (Max. points: 10)
   Consider regular daily attendance and promptness. Does he return from 10 minute breaks and meal periods on time?

Excellent	10
Good	8
Average	6
Fair	4
Poor	2

FORM 8.3   *Rating card for kitchen worker. Comparable forms could be made applicable for each classification of workers. Courtesy, Restaurant Management (now Institutions Volume Feeding Management).*

Management by objective (MBO) was designed to overcome the limitations of the more traditional performance appraisal. This approach emphasizes the setting of measurable performance goals that are mutually agreed on by the employee and his immediate superior. At stated intervals the progress of the employee toward this goal is assessed by the employee and his supervisor.

Regardless of the rating systems selected, the person to make the rating should be well qualified for the responsibility of evaluating people. Usually the immediate supervisor is in a position to do the best job, since he can observe activities continuously. However, he needs adequate instructions as to the purpose and values of the program so that he will follow through with assistance when needed, through his supervision. Also, he must have a thorough explanation and understanding of the factors to be rated so that he cannot misinterpret the forms or fail to meet the intended standards. The abilities to be objective and evaluate the individuals in terms of the factors to be rated, to be guided by the pattern of performance instead of isolated happenings, to communicate fairly and accurately what he observes, and to be consistent from time to time are prime requisites of the person who is charged with the responsibility of rating employees.

PROMOTION AND TRANSFERS

On the basis of sound ratings by members of staff, the dietitian or foodservice manager is fairly able to predict the probable future development of various members of the organization. In the application of a rating scale one group may stand high. In it will be found the people deserving the stimulus and encouragement of promotion. The term promotion commonly implies an increase in responsibility and salary. Sometimes promotion carries only the opportunity for experience in a desired field. It may mean shorter hours and greater assurance of security. Regardless of the nature of the promotion, it is an expression of appreciation of the worth of the individual.

Often a worker found unfit for one job may do well in another. The apparent lack of fitness may arise in the supervisory relationship or in his contact with his co-workers. It may be a personal prejudice against a particular type of work or physical inability to do the job. In some cases a minor shift may enable him to become a contented and valuable employee. Transfer of an employee who is not finding satisfaction in his job to another opening within the organization offering a different challenge or opportunity has served to salvage many workers. Different jobs may present wide variation in skill requirements, which makes possible the transfer of workers if necessary. Relative levels of difficulty should be considered in placement and in replacement. The use of training techniques that serve not only to extend the preparation of the worker but to relate him to the whole organization are also important.

DISMISSALS

If employment is terminated without the consent of the employee, the act is termed dismissal. An individual may be discharged because of failure to perform assigned duties, but this should be the final step and should follow counseling, warning, or possibly disciplinary layoff. Each person discharged from a foodservice should be given a terminal or "exit" interview in which his strong points are recognized and the reasons for his dismissal are dispassionately reviewed. If the situation merits his being recommended for another position, aid should be given him in his placement problem. In any event the discharged employee should not leave the service without having had a chance to express himself in regard to his dismissal and without being made aware, if possible, of the fair deal given him by the supervisor.

Opinions differ regarding the discussion of a dismissal with other employees. If there is a possibility that the incident may foster a sense of insecurity among the group, a presentation of the facts, not necessarily full and complete, may be desirable from the standpoint of group morale. Often employees understand far more of such situations than the director believes.

SUPERVISION

Supervision encompasses the coordinating and direction of the work of employees to accomplish the organization's goals. In small foodservice systems, the total supervisory function may be the responsibility of the dietitian or manager. In larger systems, the supervision of the day-to-day technical operations may be delegated to foodservice supervisors, dietetic technicians or assistants, or cookmanagers. The dietitian or manager is thus able to concentrate on planning, policy and goal setting, and interdepartment relationships, and on solving overall problems of the department. In a large department, the director, chief dietitian or other administrator may delegate these management functions in part to other professionally trained staff.

When responsibility and authority are delegated, management must provide some sort of guidance. The supervisor must understand the limits of authority, that is, what decisions can be made without consultation and what actions can be taken on his own. Management has a responsibility for training supervisors so they can solve problems and meet emergencies.

The supervisor represents both management and employees. In a foodservice unit, as with industry in general, the supervisor is one of the key persons in the organization. He is the one to whom the persons under his supervision look as a representative of management, whereas to management the supervisor represents the working force. Both groups, therefore, are interested in the quality of the supervision as represented by this staff member. He must be able (1) to interpret the objectives and policies of the company to the employees in such a way as to encourage their cooperation and elicit their confidence, and (2) to inspire and lead employees as evidenced through fair and intelligent dealing with them and through the personnel program.

Throughout an employee's term of service from the first days to the last, supervision should play a large part in relating him to his task and to his co-workers. When the probation period is past and the employee is regarded as a member of the permanent staff, familiar with his task and able in its performance, supervision is still necessary to maintain interest and provide for personal growth. To a large extent, recognition and approbation by superiors remain potent incentives to the average worker. The supervisor must accept the responsibility of finding and using incentives that lead to sound development. Adjustments in work assignments to meet changes in the individual's abilities and interests are wisely made only when supervision is adequate, both in kind and amount.

ROUTINE SUPERVISION

Routine supervision will vary with the situation, but it is, for the most part, a matter of personal contacts reinforced through checking by observations, records, and charts. It may consist each day of greeting employees by name, checking for cleanliness, appearance, and state of health, checking menus and work schedules, making work assignments, explaining to employees any instruction they seem not to understand, checking continuously for quality and quantity of production and service, inspecting for sanitation of work areas and equipment and, in general, maintaining good working conditions. The supervision of personnel is too often left to chance or to the "free time" that never seems a part of the food manager's busy day. To avoid the hit-and-miss contact with employees, the wise supervisor sets aside a certain time each day for checking on the work in progress and for stimulating interest and cooperation in the individual and in the group. Schedules are needed for checking daily, weekly, and periodic jobs. Checking at the end of the day to see that the work as scheduled has been carried out completes the "routine" supervision.

DECISION MAKING

Much of the supervisor's time is spent in making decisions and solving problems. Eckles et al.[7] define decision making as "the process of choosing a course of action or activity designed to solve a specific problem or set of problems." These authors further state that

many of the problems faced by the supervisor may be routine or may occur frequently. These situations can be routinized or systematized, or a policy can be established that would provide a ready solution. In these repetitive situations the decision-making process is used at the beginning and then the solution is repeated every time. Exceptions to these established routines or policies become the difficult decisions that have to be made by the supervisor. This is called management by exception. These are individualized or nonroutine decisions or courses of action that someone in management must determine.

Decision making is a skill that can be learned through understanding of the decision-making process and practice in its application. The steps in decision making are: [8] (1) recognition and analysis of the problem, (2) determining workable solutions, (3) identifying key uncertainties, (4) gathering data, (5) estimating the value of each alternative or workable solution, (6) choosing a solution, (7) taking action, and (8) following up the action.

[7] *Robert W. Eckles, Ronald L. Carmichael, and Bernard R. Sarchet,* Essentials of Management for First-Line Supervision, *Wiley, New York, pp. 159, 160, 1974.*

[8] *Robert W. Eckles, Ronald L. Carmichael, and Bernard R. Sarchet,* Essentials of Management for First-Line Supervision, *Wiley, New York, p. 160, 1974.*

HANDLING GRIEVANCES

The wise supervisor gives active supervision; that is, he does not sit at a desk waiting for employees to come to him with problems. He foresees and is prepared to meet possible difficulties instead of merely waiting for something unpleasant to happen. Grievances are not always expressed in verbal or written form. Supervisors should be alert for symptoms of unexpressed dissatisfaction such as excessive absenteeism, decline in quantity or quality of work, change in attitude, or indifference.

"There are many reasons why an employee may not express his complaint verbally," according to Eckles et al.[9]

He may be hesitant because of embarrassment over inability to frame his complaint in clear terms. The lack of verbal skills is particularly common among members of some minority groups, although it is found in all categories of workers. Other reasons include the feeling that uttering a complaint may do no good, fear of some kind of retaliation, or the hope that the problem may go away if left alone.

It is here that the skills of the supervisor come to the fore. Supervisory practices play a vital role in establishing the work climate. The supervisor must have gained the confidence of his work groups so that they feel free to approach him. They must know from past experience that they will receive a fair and understanding hearing, without fear of punitive action. The supervisor's empathy, his ability to analyze human factors, and his interviewing skill will enable him to help those employees who cannot express themselves clearly.

Equally important in handling both expressed and unexpressed complaints is the leaderships style of top management. The supervisor's superiors must give him the authority to decide and to act in appropriate situations.

Many grievances can be settled by the supervisor and employee on an informal basis. If the employees are unionized, the contract includes formal grievance procedures, which usually include presentation of the grievance in writing (see Form 8.4) and an attempt to settle the dispute at the first-line supervisory level. If this is not possible, the grievance moves through higher levels of authority until settled.

[9] *Robert W. Eckles, Ronald L. Carmichael, and Bernard R. Sarchet,* Essentials of Management for First-Line Supervision, *Wiley, New York, pp. 518, 519, 1974.*

LINCOLN GENERAL HOSPITAL
LINCOLN, NEBRASKA

GRIEVANCE CONTROL FORM

1. _____
   (Name)   (Position Title)   (Dept.)   (Employment Date)

   _____   _____
   (Supervisor)   (Department Head)

2. *Nature of Dissatisfaction:* (Be specific in writing up the dissatisfaction. Be sure to state who is involved, what happened, where
   did it occur, what were the circumstances, how did it happen, and
   what is the solution being sought.) _____

   _____

   _____

   _____

   _____

   _____

   _____

   _____

   _____

   _____

   _____

3. *The Final Settlement Was:* (Resolution at what step; what was the
   recommended solution and all other pertinent information significant to the solution.) _____

   _____

   _____

   _____

FORM 8.4   *Form for written presentation of grievance. Courtesy, Lincoln General
Hospital, Lincoln, Nebraska.*

FORM 8.4 (Continued)

4. Action Taken:

*Work Days	Step	Date	Action Taken By:	Schedules Met (Yes/No)	**Work Days	Resolved (Yes/No)
2	I	___	(Supervisor, Verbal)	___	2	___
2	II	___	(Department Head, Verbal)	___	2	___
5	III	___	(Grievance Committee, Written)	___	2	___
4	IV	___	(Administrator, Written)	___	2	___

Comments: (Regarding any exceptions made at any step) _____

_____

_____

_____

_____

_____

_____

* *Any of the time limits specified in the procedure may be extended by mutual agreement of the parties involved.*

** *In the event that the employee fails to appeal the decision to the next step in the grievance procedure within two (2) working days, the employee will be deemed to have accepted the decision and waived the right to further appeal.*

STAFF CONFERENCES

Regular staff conferences, department meetings, and the use of rating scales are all valuable in personnel direction. Continued effort to relate workers to their tasks and to the organization as a whole is often expressed in conferences scheduled at regular intervals by the supervisor. At these conferences, points of general interest are presented and suggestions for improvement of the foodservice are exchanged. Knotty problems, such as waste, breakage, and low production, that have not been mastered by direct supervisory approach may yield to solution as the interest and awareness of the whole group is focused on them. Never should a staff conference be used for disciplinary action for certain members of the group. The adult worker, like the school child, rarely benefits from public reprimand and unkind ridicule.

In addition to group contact, time should be taken by the supervisor for a talk with each individual worker at least once a week. Everyone likes to feel that someone is interested in him as a person and recognizes his present and potential worth to the organization.

LABOR POLICIES AND LEGISLATION

Policies, as stated below are guides for future action. They should be broad enough to allow some variation in management decisions at all levels yet offer guidelines for consistency in interpretation, and commit personnel to certain predictable action. Policies should not be confused with directives or rules. Policies are adopted to provide meaning or understanding related to a course of action; directives and rules are aimed at compliance.

An important aspect of personnel management is the labor policies accepted and put in force. This statement is true regardless of the size of the organization. There is an old saying that when two men (or women) meet, there is a social problem; when one undertakes a task at the other's behest, there is a labor problem; and when wages are paid for this labor, there is an economic problem. The policies controlling the approach to these problems have slowly developed as our civilization has grown and as the number of workers has increased. They have been formed, reformed, and revised due, particularly in recent years, to legislation enacted at federal, state, and local levels.

Policies relating to personnel are known as labor policies. According to Flippo,[10] these policies have to do with procurement, development, compensation, integration, and maintenance of personnel. More specifically, *procurement* policies may be related to preferred sources to be used for obtaining applicants, instruments such as tests to be used in selection, or a ratio of employees, such as women to men or minority to majority racial groups to be hired.

Policies for *development* of personnel may concern the type of training programs the company will offer, whether or not fees or tuition for continuing education will be paid, time to be allowed from

[10] *From* Principles of Personnel Management, *Third Edition, by Edwin B. Flippo. Copyright © 1971 by McGraw-Hill, Inc. Used with permission of McGraw-Hill Book Co., p. 79.*

work for personnel to attend classes or meetings, and the bases for promotions and transfers.

Those policies regarding *compensation* have to do with wage scales to be followed, vacation, sick leave and holiday time pay to be given, bonus or profit-sharing plans to be offered, and group insurance or other benefits available to the personnel.

Integration policies refer to a recognition or not of labor unions, the way that grievances and appeals will be handled, or the degree of employee participation to be permitted in decision making.

Maintenance policies are about the services to be provided for employees' physical, mental, and emotional health. They may be related to safety measures, compensation for accidents, retirement systems, recreational programs, or other services, all of which are a part of the institutional plan.

Once policies have been developed and accepted, they should be written. The wise employer of today makes available to every worker a copy of his labor-management policies presented in a company handbook. This publication may be an impressive volume of many pages and elaborate illustrations or a few mimeographed sheets but, whatever its format, the contents should include information that the worker wants to know about the organization and that the employer wants him to know. No employee is interested in cooperating as a member of a team without understanding the policies, especially as these affect him and his co-workers. He wants to know what is expected of him and to be kept informed of his accomplishments, the basis for promotion, for wage increases, fringe benefits, opportunities for steady work, and the possibilities of any seasonal layoffs.

From the standpoint of the employee, labor policies should be explicit in their provisions for a fair rate of pay, for promotions and transfers, for stabilization of employment, and for ways of keeping jobs interesting so that life will not become mere dull routine. They should offer provisions for fair disciplinary action among employees, recognition of industrial health hazards and provisions for their control, participation in the formulation of future plans and policies of the company, usually expressed by demands for collective bargaining, and certain fringe benefits.

Managers wish to have employees informed of policies about the goals and objectives for which the organization is in business, the products and services offered, the effect of high productivity as a benefit to both the employee and the company, cost-expenditure ratios and how it affects profits and resulting benefits, and the relationships desired with the public and with other departments of the organization.

There is general agreement on the list of topics that the employer has found must be covered in labor policies conducive to productive management and those desired by employees as vital to satisfactory working conditions. The ones cited by both—wages and income maintenance, hours of work, schedules and overtime provisions, security in employment including transfers and promotions, safe and otherwise satisfactory working environment, insurance, retirement, or pension plans, equal employment opportunities, and fair employment practices and civil rights—may be regarded as the major issues in labor policies for most foodservice operations.

Those topics will be grouped under four headings for discussion: Wages and Income Maintenance, Hours and Schedules of Work, Security in Employment, and Employee Services and Benefits. Major federal legislation applicable to employment in the private sector will be included as appropriate under each heading.

WAGES AND INCOME MAINTENANCE

From the point of view of the worker, the most important characteristic of his wage, the take-home pay he receives for his labor, is its purchasing power. This represents the measure of the wants that he is able to satisfy and largely determines the adequacy of his standard of living, his sense of financial security, and identification of himself as a worthy and responsible member of the community. In the past, foodservices, like other industrial organizations, accepted as the rule an annual wage rate below that necessary for a fair standard of living. This situation has been improved only as the desirable policies on wages have been adopted and as state and federal legislation have been enacted.

The formulation of satisfactory policies regarding wages and other income maintenance is contingent on many factors, among them (1) the desire and intent of the company to pay fair wages to all employees and at the same time to maintain just control over labor costs; (2) recognition of the relationship between the duties and responsibilities of various jobs within the organization and the wages paid; and (3) acknowledgement of individual differences in experience, ability, and willingness to take responsibility. Management has the obligation to reflect such differences in the wage scale established for a particular job and to communicate freely with the workers on these points. Policies based on such considerations will lead to a systematic classification of jobs and wages that could be developed jointly by the employer and the employees. It would then be possible to express the value or worth of each job in terms of wages.

The application of the wage policy to kitchen and dining room personnel would lead to certain groupings, such as:

1. Bussers, pot and pan washers, dishwashers.

2. Workers in preliminary or prepreparation.

3. Food service group, including counter workers and waiters or waitresses.

4. Cook's assistants and second cooks.; dining room host or hostess, cashiers.

5. Cooks, including meat, vegetable, salad, and pastry cooks.

6. Supervisors on the nonprofessional level.

A wage differential will be found to exist between groups. Civil service and labor unions as well as many other organizations have established steps within each wage level or grade so that employees who merit wage increases may be given such recognition for superior service although not qualified for advancement to a higher grade or job category.

The Fair Labor Standards Act. This Act of 1938, also known as the Federal Wage and Hour Law, was first enacted to help eliminate poverty, to create purchasing power, and to establish a wage floor that would help prevent another depression. The minimum wage set at that time was 40¢ per hour! Gradually, over the years, the base was increased. The Act was amended in 1966 and, under new provisions, most foodservice employees were included for the first time. The minimum wage that year was $1.60, and the law included provisions for gradual increases that would continue until a minimum wage rate of $2.30 was reached in 1977. The Act applies equally to all covered workers regardless of sex, of number of employees, and whether they are full-time or part-time employees.

The Equal Pay Act, a 1963 amendment to the Fair Labor Standards Act, prohibits employers from discriminating on the basis of sex in the payment of wages for equal work for employees covered by the Act. It requires employers to pay equal wages to men and women in their employ doing equal work on jobs requiring equal skill, effort, and responsibility that are performed under similar working conditions.

Another provision of the FLS Act of special interest to commercial foodservice managers relates to wages for tipped employees. Tips received by an employee may be considered by the employer as part of the wages of the employee, but cannot exceed 50 percent of the applicable minimum rate. A "tipped" employee is a worker engaged in an occupation in which he customarily and regularly receives more than $20 a month in tips.

Many foodservice operations employ student workers; this is especially true in colleges and universities, schools, retirement homes, and other homes for congregate living. Minimum wage laws adopted by various states may make provision for compensation at an adjusted rate below the federal standard. Usually students who work less than 20 hours per week are not affected by provisions of such laws.

Unless specifically exempt by this law, all employees must be paid at least one and one half times the employee's regular rate of pay for all hours worked in excess of 40 hours in a work week of 7 days. Extra pay is not required for Saturday, Sunday, holiday, or vacation work.

All foodservice managers should become familiar with the state and federal laws regulating minimum wages for their various classifications of employees. Information may be obtained from the nearest office of the Wage and Hour Division of the U.S. Department of Labor.

Unemployment Compensation. In addition to regular pay for work on the job, income maintenance is partially assured by another piece of federal legislation, unemployment compensation. This nationwide system of insurance to protect wage earners and their families against loss of income because of unemployment was first established under the Social Security Act of 1935. The purpose of this insurance is to provide workers with a weekly income to tide them over periods of unemployment between jobs. Persons covered must have been employed for a specified period of time on a job covered by the law, who are able and willing to work, and who are unemployed through no fault of their own.

Unemployment insurance is a joint federal-state program, operated by the states with assistance of the U.S. Department of Labor. Each state has its own specific requirements and benefits. Basically, employers pay a tax based on their payrolls. Benefits to unemployed workers are paid out of the fund built up from these taxes. In most states firms employing three or four or more workers during 20 weeks in the year must participate. Each state law specifies conditions under which workers may receive benefits, the amount they receive, and the number of weeks they may draw benefits. In most states, the employer alone contributes to this fund; in only a few do employees make payment to it. Thus, unemployment compensation is an added payroll cost for many foodservice managers and an added benefit to the employees.

HOURS AND SCHEDULES OF WORK

The 40-hour work week established under the Minimum Wage and Hour Law is generally in use throughout the United States. Some organizations have adopted a 37 1/2 or a 35-hour week and, some such as nursing and rest homes, which are exempt under this legislation, may have a 48-hour week. Time worked beyond this and within a 7-day or a 14-day period as specified under the law requires extra compensation, as previously noted.

The schedule of specific hours of the day when each employee is to be on duty should be carefully considered by all foodservice managers. As discussed, a good many different factors enter into the planning of satisfactory schedules. Employers have a responsibility for scheduling their employees so that their time at work will be as needed and will be used to best advantage to help control labor costs. Split shifts are almost a thing of the past; straight shifts are usually preferred. An 8-hour day, 5 days a week is common practice also. However, some organizations have experimented with variations, notably a 10-hour day and 4-day week to allow a 3-day off-duty period for the employees. Most foodservice organizations have not found this scheduling practical because of the nature of the work to be done.

In addition to the needs of the employer and the organization, consideration is given also to the employee and his needs and to stipulations in union contracts, if in effect, when planning scheduled time on and off duty for each member of the staff. Most state labor laws require break times for meals and between-meal rest periods for employees, which is a further consideration when planning schedules to cover work that must be done. Familiarity with these regulations is a necessity for the manager.

SECURITY IN EMPLOYMENT

One of the major concerns about the world of work in recent years is that every person who wishes it may have equal opportunity for employment for which he is qualified. Equal employment opportunity has been the topic of much legislation, beginning with consideration of civil rights.

The Civil Rights Act of 1964 stipulates that "No person in the United States shall, on ground of race, color, or national origin be excluded from participating in, be denied the benefits of, or be subjected to any program or activity receiving Federal Financial assistance." Title VII under this Act extended the provision to include prohibition of discrimination "by employers, employment agencies and labor unions." [11]

Thus, employees who are in covered positions are entitled to be free of unlawful discrimination with regard to recruitment, classified advertising, job classification, hire, utilization of physical facilities, transfer, promotion, discharge wages and salaries, seniority lines, testing, insurance coverage, pension and retirement benefits, referral to jobs, union membership, and the like. All potential employees have equal opportunity, regardless of background.

The *Age Discrimination in Employment Act of 1967* promotes the employment of the older worker, based on ability instead of age. It prohibits arbitrary age discrimination in employment and helps employers and employees find ways to meet problems arising from the impact of age on employment. The Act protects most individuals who are at least 40 but less than 65 years of age from "discrimination in employment based on age in matters of hiring, discharge compensation or other terms, conditions, or privileges of employment." [12]

[11] *"Federal Labor Laws and Programs,"* Employment Standards Administration, Division of Employment Standards, U.S Department of Labor, Bulletin 262, p. 133, revised September 1971.
[12] *"Federal Labor Laws and Programs,"* Employment Standards Administration, Divison of Employment Standards, U.S. Department of Labor, Bulletin 262, p. 128, revised September 1971.

Legislation has been effected also in many states and cities to prohibit discriminatory employment practices against persons because of their race, color, religion, national origin, or ancestry. These are designated as fair employment practice laws and have as their intent the barring of undemocratic practices in American industry. A Public Accommodations law, when in effect, requires that service be given in an equal manner to anyone.

As may be seen, our economic society is characterized by many areas of friction in industry. Students of labor are quite generally agreed that in no area is there an economic problem more important to human beings than security of job tenure, which means assurance of the satisfaction of physical needs, a place in the esteem and affection of others, an opportunity for self-expression, and a chance to enjoy leisure. The three risks that more than any others tend to make the position of most wage earners in industry insecure are unemployment, physical impairment, and old age. The definition for unemployment used by the U.S. Bureau of Census in making its enumeration is, "Unemployment may be described as involuntary idleness on the part of those who have lost their latest jobs, are able to work, and are looking for work." This definition is obviously narrow, because it excludes all those persons who are unwilling to work, are unemployable because of physical or mental defects, or are temporarily idle for seasonal causes. However, the definition covers the group whose unemployment usually arises from conditions inherent in the organization and management of industry.

Problems of tenure must concern all persons charged with the direction of the foodservice industry. Fortunately, foodservices on the whole lend themselves to steady employment, and many managers take pride in the long tenure of large numbers of their workers. Sometimes, however, the workers' acceptance of tenure, as a matter of course, brings definite problems such as laxity and inefficiency in the performance of assigned tasks and lack of interest in improved practices. Standards of performance in some instances have been lowered as security of employment has been assured. Personnel policies should cover such contingencies.

EMPLOYEE SERVICES AND BENEFITS

Benefits that employees receive often represent 15 to 25 percent of wages earned. Some of these are so taken for granted that they are scarcely realized or appreciated by those who receive them. Yet, if such services were not provided, the lack would be acutely noticed. Managers recognize the humanistic desirability of making available certain programs and services in addition to a fair wage for their employees' comfort and well-being. A less altruistic point of view may cause managers to offer those same benefits in order to compete in the job market and attract desirable applicants.

Extra benefits, sometimes called "fringe" benefits, fall into three general groups: health and safety, economic, and convenience and comfort. The first, *health and safety,* is an important basic factor in all personnel problems. This matter affects social and economic life, being of interest not only to the employee but to the employer and the public as well. Time lost because of illness and accidents is expensive for both management and labor, results in lowered production and increased losses for the employer, and directly affects the income of the employee. Maintaining the good physical condition of employees is economically desirable as well as necessary for achievement of the many goals of the department. Also, dietitians and managers of any foodservice recognize that the health of the worker may affect the health of the public through both direct and indirect contact. Additional discussions regarding the importance of good health for the foodservice employee are given in Chapter 10.

Safe working conditions are of first importance to employer and employee alike. A foodservice does not present the identical hazards found in any other industry, but duplicates some of those found in several. Falls, burns, shocks, and cuts are possible, as they are in any other place where mechanical equipment is used. It is the responsibility of the manager to see that safeguards are maintained, that the equipment is kept in safe condition, and that all working conditions are safe and clean.

The Occupational Safety and Health Act (OSHA) of 1970 has forced managers to look critically at working conditions and to bring any that are undesirable up to a standard demanded by law. See page 621 for further information on OSHA.

Another benefit for employees is that provided for in the *Workmen's Compensation Insurance* program. This legislation is administered by the states, and the liability insurance premiums are paid for by employers. Workmen's compensation laws are based on the theory that the cost of accidents should be a part of production costs, the same as wages, taxes, insurance, and raw materials.

This insurance covers employers' liability for the costs of any accident incurred by an employee on or in connection with his job. The worker must show that he was injured on the job and the extent of his injuries. Compensation laws state the specific amount of payment allowed for each type of injury in addition to hospital, surgical and, in case of death, funeral expenses. All foodservice directors will need to determine, through their state department of labor, who can be covered by Workmen's Compensation, the methods of payment, and the amount of benefits to which the worker is entitled.

It is estimated that

on the average, these premiums cost about one percent of the total payroll. When an employer has to write a check for these premiums and knows that he can reduce them by preventing accidents, he becomes acutely aware of the out-of-pocket cost of the accident. . . . As the employer becomes fully educated in regard to the true cost of an accident, he becomes more concerned with its prevention.[13]

Health and accident insurance plans provide some assistance to employees who may become ill or who are injured off the job. Fear of injury or illness is the cause of much worry, even when an insurance plan is available to employees. Without it, many workers would be in financial straits, trying to pay medical and hospital bills on their own.

Many forms of health and accident insurance are available for groups. In some cases the company alone pays for it for the employees; in others it is jointly borne by the company and those who participate in it. Through labor union efforts and the efforts of concerned managers, more and more health services are being made available to employees, many at employer expense. Some of these include dental care, mental health counseling, vision care, and prescription drugs.

The extent to which foodservices provide these benefits to employees usually depends on the size of the organization and the facilities it has available, for example, the emergency room of a hospital, and the concern of those at the decision-making level.

The second group of employee services and benefits are those labeled *economic*. Most of the programs discussed so far provide some economic benefit to workers, even if indirectly. All insurance plans undoubtedly could be put under this classification instead of putting some under health and safety. However, benefits to be discussed in this economic group have a direct monetary value in re-

---

[13] *From* Principles of Personnel Management, *Third Edition, by Edwin B. Flippo. Copyright © 1971 by McGraw-Hill, Inc. Used with permission of McGraw-Hill Book Co., pp. 515–517.*

turns to the employee; the employer carries the cost of some, and others are shared by the employer.

Social Security benefits are provided by the Social Security Act, a nationwide program of insurance to protect wage earners and their families against loss of income due to old age, disability, and death. A designated percentage of the salary of each employed person must be withheld from his wages and the same amount from the business added to the Social Security Fund, or to a comparable retirement-system fund if a nonprofit type of organization is involved. Provisions and benefits of Social Security change from time to time, so details soon become outdated. Managers must keep in touch with their local Social Security Office to be informed of current changes.

Other economic benefits offered by some organizations to their employees may include group life insurance programs, profit-sharing plans, and pensions or retirement plans. All of these add to the economic security of those who continue in the service of a particular organization long enough to build a fund that is significant for them after regular employment ceases, either because of retirement or death. Vacations, holidays, and sick leave, all with pay, are other forms of fringe benefits for personnel. Properly administered, they are of advantage to the organization as well.

Employee convenience and comfort benefits make up the third group of fringe benefits. Services provided for the comfort or convenience of employees comprises a long list and includes, among others: adequate rest and locker rooms, meal service available to employees often at reduced or at-cost levels, free medical service on an emergency basis, credit unions, and recreational facilities. Educational tuition or fees for personnel to attend workshops or classes for self-development and skill development are also among these. Various foodservices participate in many of these or in different ones for their employees. In turn, these benefits help in building a loyal, contented working group with high morale.

Labor legislation, as discussed, is directed toward establishing socially desirable channels of behavior to be observed by labor and management. Whatever the purpose of labor legislation may be, the federal, state, and local laws have been the chief means by which an enlightened public conscience has expressed its concern with the health, safety, and general well-being of the worker on the job. The method of expressing this interest differs among the states. Full information on each specific situation is important because requirements for various industries may differ widely. For the most part, foodservices are controlled through state laws. They become subject to federal laws when they engage in interstate commerce or under conditions just discussed. Local laws may regulate the sanitation standards, but they seldom take labor policies under their scrutiny.

Although many of the labor laws enacted are directed toward the protection of specific groups, the regulations applicable to all workers are well established. Familiarity with federal, state, and local laws applying to foodservice employees is obligatory for every foodservice administrator and manager. Only then can labor policies be of benefit to both the worker and his organization and be put into action for implementation.

LABOR-MANAGEMENT RELATIONS

Dietitians and foodservice managers are concerned with problems arising from directing employees' activities, that is, in handling the people who must translate the policies, procedures, and plans into action. When groups of people work together, there is always potential for conflict. Some people must manage and some must carry out the technical operations. Everyone wants more of whatever will improve his position. The closer the relationship between the employee and manager, with open and free discussion on both sides, the less danger there is for grievances to arise.

Many foodservices are so small that the relationship between employer and employee is immediate and direct. Under such circumstances discussion of points of mutual concern is possible right in the place of work. Direct face-to-face contact tends to develop a sense of real association and mutual interest. The employee with a somewhat complete picture of a relatively small business may see his job in relation to the whole. Many services, on the other hand, are so large that there is limited personal contact between employer and employee. The worker may feel there is little chance for the individual to be recognized as an important person in the organization. Also, he may not have an overall view of the business that would make possible self-evaluation of his own job in terms of the whole. The worker engaged in a limited phase of total large-scale production may find that he lacks the direct contact that tends to humanize employer-employee relationships in a small foodservice.

Managers who are not attuned to these concerns of employees, who do not recognize that a small complaint or conflict that may arise is probably a symptom of a deeper problem and fail to investigate and correct the situation, are opening the door for labor unions to come in to represent the employees better.

Over the years much legislation has been enacted to attempt to balance the power between labor and management. The *National Labor Relations Act* of 1935 was pro-labor in its intent; workers in many situations had been exploited by management during depression years just preceding passage of the bill. Terms of the Act regulate unfair management practices, and prohibit management from interference with their employees joining a union and from discrimination against those who do join.

The *Taft-Hartley Labor-Management Relations Act* in 1947 was pro-management, to offset the power and unfair practices that labor unions seemed to have acquired since 1935. Among other things, it prevents unions from coercing employees to join, outlaws the "closed shop," and makes it illegal for unions to refuse to collective bargaining. The law created the National Labor Relations Board (NLRB) to administer the provisions of the Act, to remedy unfair labor practices whether by labor organizations or employers, and to conduct secret ballot elections in which employees decide whether unions will represent them in collective bargaining.

Further legislation in 1959 was the *Labor-Management Disclosure Act,* which is in the interests of both labor and management, but is especially pro-individual labor union member. It contains a Bill of Rights for union members and requires disclosure of union trusteeship practices through a specified reporting system.

Employees of hospitals operated entirely on a nonprofit basis were exempt from the original National Labor Relations Act. However, the recent amendment to the NRLA brings nonprofit hospitals under the provisions of the act. In such situations dietitians may be called on to defend their positions as "management" instead of as "labor."

Van Cleve [14] has said that "for numerous reasons employers may become the target of union organizing attempts or employees may turn to a union. Chief among these reasons are poorly developed or administered personnel policies and practices, or a breakdown in some facet of employer-employee relations." He outlines a list of steps that should be taken by managers long before organizational attempts begin. Most important among them is a review of personnel policies and employee relations, making every effort to

---

[14] *William Van Cleve, "Information About Organizing Attempts by Unions,"* ADA Courier, XIV (5), 5, *The American Dietetic Association, by permission of William Van Cleve, 1975.*

maintain good personnel practices, put policies into writing, and communicate them to employees with frequent reviews and discussions. Countering union organizing attempts, unfair practices in such countering attempts, and union organizing techniques are also described by Van Cleve.

Weinmann [15] points out that there are many instances where an employer is faced with unionization, even though his company has the best conditions in the area or in the industry. When inquiries are made as to why his company has been singled out to be unionized, the union frequently has no answer except that it was the employees who asked for it. He says that

. . . it would appear that legally, morally, and practically, the choice is not for management to make as to whether it will have or not have a union in the first place instance. This opinion is qualified by the exception that to the extent employees are made satisfied, to that extent they are less likely to seek unionization, although as we have indicated there are no guarantees.

The impact of unionization on foodservices may be great for those who are naive in the ways of collective bargaining. Legal counsel to assist in negotiating a fair, workable contract for both labor and management is to be encouraged. If unionization is to become a reality, it is important to create a favorable climate for co-operation, to make sure that the negotiator understands the economic as well as the administrative problems of a foodservice operation, such as scheduling required to cover meal hours, the services necessary, especially to patients in health care facilities, the equipment to be used, and the prices charged in relation to the labor costs.

It should be recognized that certain rights of management *may* be lost when unionization takes place, since some of the authority but little of the responsibility will be shared with the union. Some of the freedoms lost are the right to hire, discharge, change work assignments and time schedules, set wages and fringe benefits, change policies without appeal, discipline workers without being subject to appeal to the union, and receive and act on grievances directly. The loss of right to use volunteer workers in the department may also be realized.

It is imperative, therefore, that the collective bargaining agree-

[15] *Richard Weinmann, "Unions: What Choice?", Cornell Hotel & Restaurant Administration Quarterly 14(2), 13 (1973).*

ment contain a management's rights clause. "There are two major catagories of management rights clauses. One is a brief, general clause not dealing with specific rights, but with the principle of management rights in general. The other is a detailed clause which clearly lists areas of authority which are reserved to the management." [16]

Certain cost increases will be noted also: for time loss from the job by the person selected to be the union steward, and the cost of management support to the union based on a given sum per member per month in contributions.

The history and background of hotel and restaurant employees' unions is described by Lundberg and Armatas. (See Selected Readings at end of chapter.) The union representing the commercial segment of the foodservice industry is the Hotel and Restaurant Employees and Bartenders International Union. The rights and duties of members of that organization are spelled out in their leaflet for new members, "Your Union." [17] Managers may be interested in exploring the information presented, and would do well to prepare such a leaflet describing the company for which their employees work.

The nature of labor organizations and the methods they use differ according to the understanding and goals of the leaders and members, their convictions as to remedies needed, and by legal and other forms of social control. Ordinarily, management and organized labor have different approaches to solving their problems. This often leads to long hours of negotiations before a satisfactory mutual agreement can be reached. It is important that each group try to see the other's viewpoint with fairness and with an honest belief in the good faith of the other.

[16] Norman Metzger and Dennis D. Pointer, "Labor-Management Relations in the Health Service Industry," Science-Health Publications, Inc., 1740 N. Street N.W., Washington, D.C. 20036, p. 167, 1972.

[17] "Your Union: What It Is . . . How It Operates," The Hotel and Restaurants Employees and Bartenders International, Cincinnati, Ohio.

SELECTED REFERENCES

Beach, Dale S., *Personnel: The Management of People at Work,* Third Edition, Macmillan, New York, 1975.

Bellows, Roger M., *Psychology of Personnel in Business and Industry,* Third Edition, Prentice-Hall, Englewood Cliffs, New Jersey, 1961.

Black, James M., and Guy B. Ford, *Front-Line Management,* McGraw-Hill, New York, 1963.

Carroll, Stephen J. Jr., and Henry L. Tosi Jr., *Management by Objectives,* Macmillan, New York, 1973.

Cribbin, James J., *Effective Managerial Leadership,* American Management Association, New York, 1972.

Davis, Keith, *Human Relations at Work,* Third Edition, McGraw-Hill, New York, 1967.

Flippo, Edwin B., *Principles of Personnel Management,* Third Edition, McGraw-Hill, New York, 1971.

Gellerman, Saul, *Management by Motivation,* American Management Association, New York, 1968.

Hepner, James O., and John M. Boyer, and Carl L. Westerhaus, *Personnel Administration and Labor Relations in Health Care Facilities,* C. V. Mosby, St. Louis, 1969.

Hersey, Paul, and Kenneth R. Blanchard, *Management of Organizational Behavior Utilizing Human Resources,* Second Edition, Prentice-Hall, Englewood Cliffs, New Jersey, 1969.

Jucius, Michael J., *Personnel Management,* Seventh Edition, Richard D. Irwin, Homewood, Illinois, 1971.

Knudson, Harry R. Jr., *Human Elements of Administration,* Holt, Rinehart and Winston, New York, 1963.

Latham, James L., *Human Relations in Business,* Charles E. Merrill, Columbus, Ohio, 1964.

Lundberg, D., and J. P. Armatas, *The Management of People in Hotels, Restaurants and Clubs,* Third Edition, Wm. C. Brown, 1974.

McGehee, William, and Paul W. Thayer, *Training in Business and Industry,* Wiley, New York, 1961.

McGregor, Douglas, *The Human Side of Enterprise,* McGraw-Hill, New York, 1960.

Metzger, N., and D. D. Pointer, *Labor Management Relations in the Health Services Industry,* Science and Health Publication, 1740 N. St., NW, Washington, D.C., 1972.

Meyers, M. Scott, *Every Employee a Manager,* McGraw-Hill, New York, 1970.

Nierenberg, G. T., *Fundamentals of Negotiating,* Hawthorne Books, New York, 1973.

Odiorne, George, *Personnel Administration by Objectives,* Richard D. Irwin, Homewood, Illinois, 1971.

Pigors, Paul, Charles A. Myers, and F. T. Malm, *Management of Human Resources,* Second Edition, McGraw-Hill, New York, 1969.

Pigors, Paul, and Charles A. Myers, *Personnel Administration,* Sixth Edition, McGraw-Hill, New York, 1969.

Strauss, George, and Leonard Sayles, *Personnel: The Human Problems of Management,* Third Edition, Prentice-Hall, Englewood Cliffs, New Jersey, 1972.

Terry, George R., *Principles of Management,* Sixth Edition, Richard D. Irwin, Homewood, Illinois, 1972.

Yoder, Dale, *Personnel Management and Industrial Relations,* Sixth Edition, Prentice-Hall, Englewood Cliffs, New Jersey, 1970.

9. COST CONTROL

Control as a management function is an absolute necessity in the financial operation of any successful foodservice. Controlling has been defined [1] as:

Determining what is being accomplished, that is, evaluating the performance and, if necessary, applying corrective measures so that the performance takes place according to plans.

In the foodservice industry the term cost control has come to mean control over all items of income and expense concerned with the functioning of the foodservice system. Applying the definition of control to this specific operation, the manager is concerned with the setting of goals or standards for financial achievement usually through a planned budget; knowing what is being accomplished through a system of records that gives pertinent data on current operations; evaluating the data of daily, monthly, and yearly reports that compare the actual achievement with the standard; and, finally, taking corrective measures to bring operations in line with expected standards. This may involve, among other things, a change in menu to include lower or higher food costs, greater supervision or training of employees to prevent waste and provide better quality food, or better merchandising of the food to increase volume of sales.

The common approach to cost control in a foodservice all too frequently has been increasing the selling price of the food, lowering the quality of food served, reducing the size of portions, and

[1] *George R. Terry,* Principles of Management, *Sixth Edition, Richard D. Irwin, Homewood, Illinois, p. 535, 1972.*

465

tolerating unacceptable service. Professional training is not required of the person following such a procedure. Anyone can do this. But to provide meals at the lowest cost possible consistent with the policy of the institution in regard to quality and quantity of food served requires good management. There is no substitute.

Administrative dietitians and managers of foodservices of all types are facing the cost-price squeeze and know that in order to realize any profit or just to break even requires control of every phase of the operation. The necessity for information concerning income and expenditure is recognized as essential to efficient cost control. No longer can a food manager operate on the theory that the department is a success as long as the business shows an excess of income over expense in the profit and loss statement. No foodservice is too small to require accurate accounting of transactions.

And no manager can consider himself entirely informed about the position of his company, his competitors, or his industry unless he understands financial statements and the information they contain. He cannot rely on general impressions of financial structure or vague notions of the competitive climate to provide him with an adequate background for making the exact decisions which successful operations demand.[2]

Good cost control is based on a system of records that serves as a tool to operate a business or department within predetermined financial limits. Wise and effective use of these records will give ready answer to such questions as:

What are the sources and amount of income?

What are the food and true payroll costs?

What is the value of the inventory and of the accounts receivable?

What is the amount of the accounts payable?

What is the amount of the profit or loss?

What are the trends in sales, expenses, and profits?

[2] *Donald E. Miller,* The Meaningful Interpretation of Financial Statements, *Revised Edition, American Management Association, Inc. New York, p. 1, 1972.*

Answers to these questions will give bases for evaluation and comparison with other food systems of a similar type.

The function of cost control then is to provide a constant pressure in order to maintain efficiency, expose unfavorable trends, and prevent "hit-or-miss" operation. Its purpose is to assist in obtaining the highest possible gross profit consistent with the operating policies of the organization.

Any system of cost accounting should be simple enough to be kept accurately yet provide adequate data to make evaluation possible. The system chosen depends on the size and complexity of the organization and the amount of clerical help available to keep the records. It should assist the operation by furnishing only the information necessary for effective operation and control of the business and should not strangle it in a network of detail.

A review and examination of existing policies of the organization that affect financial management is the first step in putting a cost control system into operation. Policies relate to overall goals of the organization, whether it be to provide a service or to operate for profit. The policies should be stated clearly and should be understood and accepted before the manager will know what is expected of him and the business. Next, decisions will have to be made regarding the information essential for the food director to have about the financial transactions and position of his department. Forms can then be designed to provide the necessary data.

There is increasing demand for up-to-date records and accurate reports of food and other costs in all types of institutions. As a result, automatic data processing is used by an increasing number of institutions each year. Also,

Control can be greatly helped by the computer. Not only may more control procedures be employed, but the results can become available in time to take corrective action.[3]

In the past, many foodservice organizations believed they could not afford data processing time. The number of transactions and paperwork was limited and did not seem to warrant utilizing this management tool. However, with the decreasing costs of automatic data processing (ADP) and the opportunity to share programs and equipment in many localities, the use of computerized data has become possible. Information that may be obtained is almost limitless;

[3] James Keiser and Elmer Kallio, Controlling and Analyzing Costs in Food Service Operations, Wiley, New York, p. 209, 1974.

almost any computer can be used to adapt tasks presently done by hand. In relation to cost control, these information systems may include menu planning within cost, nutrient, and customer preference and other constraints, inventory and purchasing control, analysis of sales by time periods or other ratios desired, sales forecasting, employee payroll and check writing, and budgeting and financial reports.

Employees concerned with keeping records, including those for computerization, must be informed and instructed as to their use and value to the overall financial picture of the organization. Data obtained from the records are routed to the food manager's desk each day in summary form for study, analysis, and interpretation. The use of this information to improve operations and provide the best possible financial report completes the cycle of a cost control system. Major items of expense included in the monthly financial report, such as, food, labor, operating, and overhead costs, will be considered here.

FACTORS AFFECTING COST CONTROL

FOOD COSTS

Food is the most readily controlled item of expenditure and the one subject to greatest fluctuation in the foodservice budget. If control of food costs is to be effective, efficient methods must be employed in planning the menu, purchasing, storing, preparing, and serving food. The expenditures for food vary greatly from one type of institution to another and often for institutions of the same type because of the form of food purchased, the amount of on-premises preparation, geographic location, and delivery costs.

Food cost, usually expressed in terms of percent of the income spent for food, may range from 18 to 20 percent to 70 or 80 percent of the income. These wide variations are due to many causes and, with the rapidly changing foodservice systems, it is difficult to give percentage figures that are typical for any type of organization.

In luxury restaurants with elaborate service and high overhead costs, only about 18 to 20 percent of the guests' food dollar may be spent for food. In college cooperative residences for students where much of the labor is provided by the residents and some of the overhead is often paid by the school, the food cost may be as high as 70 to 80 percent of income.

The large state university without adequate support to finance building of new residences may issue bonds for this purpose and call on the food service to make enough "profit" to pay the bond debts as they come due. Food costs in this situation may be as low as 30 to 35 percent of the board income. The debt retirement may take from 10 to 30 or 35 percent of the income. In other college residence halls where this type of financing for new buildings does not exist, 40 to 50 percent of the income may be spent for food.

It is the responsibility of every food director to understand his own situation and to know within narrow limits the percentage of the income that should wisely be spent for food under existing conditions. This percentage may be determined by analyzing past expenses and watching the daily reports and monthly profit and loss statements.

Each foodservice manager should establish a level of expenditure for food that is right for that particular establishment with its own characteristics and expense items. Whatever level of food cost percent is established, it should be based on careful analysis of past expenditures and on other costs that must be met. It also should reflect a fair return in the form of food that is satisfying to the customers who provide the income. Consideration must be made for some excess of income over expenditure to the extent that the goals and philosophy of the organization expect.

In spite of the variation in the amounts spent for food, the underlying bases of food cost control are the same for all types of foodservice units. The menu, type of service offered, the purchasing, receiving, storage and storeroom control procedures, methods used in the production of food including prepreparation, cooking, and serving, the use of standardized recipes and portions, the method of pricing and forecasting, and the cost of employees' meals all determine the effectiveness of this control.

Menus. Menu planning is the first and perhaps the most important step in the control of food costs. The menu determines what and how many foods must be purchased and prepared. A knowledge of these food costs and the *precosting* of the menu to determine whether or not it is within budgetary limitations is an essential control procedure.

The extent of the number of choices of each menu also influences food costs. Menus that provide extensive choices require preparation of many kinds of foods, several of which may not be sold in quantities sufficient to pay for their preparation. If a widely diversified selection is offered, the investment of too large a sum in food or labor for its preparation may result.

Today, however, there is such a wide selection of commercially prepared frozen foods available for institutions and restaurants to buy that a wide menu selection may be possible without adverse effect on overall costs. Keeping a variety of frozen items on hand for use when needed allows a wider selection on the menu than is possible when all fresh foods are used.

School foodservices offering a plate lunch and a limited number of other foods usually are better able to stay within their limited budget than are those that offer a large selection of a la carte items.

Menus, although they are made some days or even weeks in advance, must be adjusted daily to the inventory of food on hand and to local market conditions. Waste can be prevented only by wise utilization of available supplies, which helps to keep food costs under control and adds to variety of the menus.

Type of Service. The type of service offered may be a factor in determining the food costs. For example, university residence halls used all table service for many years. The change to cafeteria-style service for breakfast, lunch and, finally, at dinner also, lowered both food and labor costs. Today, self-service is commonly accepted for many foods, except meat items, to allow students freedom of portion size and to further reduce labor costs. Savings have been realized by this method, since each individual is best able to determine the quantity he prefers and so reduces waste.

The selective menu offered by many hospitals provides a choice to appeal to the taste of the patients. This not only reduces plate waste and, therefore, food cost, but also provides more satisfaction to the patient.

Purchasing Methods. Food costs begin at the time of purchase, and controlled procedures are an effective step for wise buying.

The person ultimately responsible for food quality for financial stability of the foodservice is the one who should have charge of food buying. In some establishments, the buying is done directly by this person; in large organizations that have a purchasing agent or department, food orders must go through that channel. Close cooperation and good working relations between these two are essential.

Recently there has been a growing trend toward group purchasing by schools, hospitals, and other health care institutions as a means of keeping costs as low as feasible. By banding together and pooling food and supplies orders, considerable savings can be achieved through greater volume buying. Although saving can be shared, other things must be shared also; jointly agreed on specifications for quality, form of food, and size of units to purchase are among them. Success depends on this type of cooperative decision making.

Purchasing organizations to represent the cooperating institutions have been established. In addition to actually coordinating the food orders, negotiating prices, and placing orders, purchasing organizations offer other services to their member organizations. These have included information about new products, their quality and potential uses, legal contract advice, can-cutting demonstrations and evaluations for canned goods, taste panel evaluations of new products, and standardization of product specifications.

As one example of group purchasing, 16 rural school districts in one state that had excessively high charges for food because they were not on regular delivery routes organized for group purchasing. Cooperatively they purchased 155 food items costing $40,238 for a savings of from 5 to 7 percent by the various districts over the cost of purchasing independently.[4] Other studies indicate similar results. This method seems to be most successful when those participating are in a close geographic area for a "manageable" delivery zone.

A rigid set of specifications for quality of food to be purchased, detailed enough to make competitive bidding possible, statements of exact amounts needed and, finally, a report on the condition of the foods received are requirements for successful control of costs at this point, whatever the purchasing method.

Purchasing procedures differ from institution to institution because of the policies of management, the money available for food at any time, the amount and type of storage, and the proximity to large market centers and local sources of supply. However, the food director responsible for the satisfaction of the clientele and for the successful operation of the service must be aware of the interrelations of quantity, quality, and price, and of the importance all have in controlling food costs. The importance of knowing quality and quantities of food needed can scarcely be overstressed in an effective cost control plan, and intelligent buying becomes a problem of "what" and "how much" instead of "what price." There is general agreement that the quantity and quality of food purchased are far more important in cost control than the price paid per unit.

The purchasing activity is a constantly changing one, and the

[4] M. Brokaw, "Why Not Cooperative Purchasing?" School Foodservice J. 26, 31 (July 1972). Copyright © American School Food Service Association, 1972.

buyer must study to keep abreast of developments in the field if he is to meet the competition. The person who knows the market and searches for foods best suited to his own operation will be the most successful. And so it is that costs are controlled through wise purchasing by an informed, capable buyer who is alert to the everchanging market conditions and has a knowledge of new products available to him. (See Chapter 3 for more details on wise buying.)

Receiving Control. The next step in food cost control is proper receiving of the foods purchased. It is management's responsibility to make certain that exactly what was ordered is received, both as to quantity and quality. The actual counting of all items delivered, even to the last hard roll or bunch of radishes, will make purveyors aware that the manager is alert and so exercise more care in filling orders properly. On large orders one case of each product should be unpacked and carefully examined; cases of eggs should be weighed to see that they are of standard weight; milk and cream should be tested often to see that the butterfat is up to standard.

A chart showing the average weights of all perishable food items as usually received should be posted in the receiving room near the scales. This aids in speedily checking deliveries, and the use of it should prevent loss that may result from the case of eggs from which one layer is missing, the 100-pound sack of potatoes that weighs in at 90 pounds, or the tomatoes that show a weight shortage. Likewise, a listing of standard container weights is helpful in checking quickly a lug, hamper, bushel, or box of any product purchased by weight.

Weighing of foods as they are received may make the difference between an acceptable food percentage and one that is out of line. Meat, the most costly of all items in the food budget, is an example in point. If 100 pounds of round steak are ordered and paid for at the rate of $1.89 per pound and 98 pounds are delivered, the loss is $3.78, or 2 percent. This loss may seem small at the time, but should it continue to occur daily throughout the year, the annual cash loss would amount to well over $1200. The use of a receiving scale would quickly detect such a loss and should be used while the deliveryman is present to verify it. Figure 9.1 shows an efficient arrangement for checking deliveries. The company should be notified at once and correction made either through an adjustment in the bill or delivery of the additional amount needed to complete the order.

It is true that in the matter of weights and measures the buyer has some legal protection. However adequate these regulations may

FIGURE   9.1   Weighing-in scale with dial visible from both sides. Courtesy, Dietary
Department, Ohio State University Hospital.

be, they do not relieve the buyer of the responsibility of intelligent
selection, careful checking of orders and weighing of foods when
received. Scales are an important item of equipment in any foodservice and should be used to weigh every article of food as delivered in the same careful manner and for the same reason that one
counts change after having paid for a purchase. Losses that occur
when food of poor quality is delivered or items are short weighed
are no less than those in situations in which cash is directly involved.

In summary, Keiser and Kallio [5] have listed a good set of procedures for receiving food to be followed in every foodservice.

1.   All items are counted, weighed and marked.

2.   All pieces of meats, fish and poultry are weighed and
inspected individually, and their tags are prepared.

[5] James Keiser and Elmer Kallio, Controlling and Analyzing Costs in Food
Service Operations, Wiley, New York, p. 72, 1974.

3. Cartons of fruits and vegetables are opened at random to inspect for quantity and quality.

4. All items are checked against purchase specifications.

5. Invoices prices are checked against the purchase order or the buyer's quotation sheet.

6. All receiving invoices, after verification, are stamped and signed by the receiving clerk.

7. All merchandise, food, and supplies are written on the receiving report.

8. The unit price is put on each item and then placed in storerooms or refrigerators.

9. Management periodically checks its receiving procedures.

Storage and Storeroom Control. Protection of the company's large investment of money in the food after it is purchased and received contributes greatly to overall cost control. It has been said that one should buy only the amount that can be used at once or stored adequately. Furthermore, one should store only what is essential for limited periods of time because unnecessarily large inventories tend to increase the possibility of loss through spoilage, waste, pilferage, or theft.

Correct temperatures and humidity for optimum storage of various perishable foods, fresh, frozen, and cooked, have been discussed at length in Chapters 3 and 10, and need not be repeated here. Suffice to say that storage areas for canned and staple foods must be well ventilated and cool if spoilage is kept at a minimum. Canned foods can be damaged by high temperatures. Other foods, such as flour, need adequate circulation of air to retain their good quality and flavor. The use of covered metal containers for rice, dry beans, and similar products to prevent infestation by rodents and insects is also essential for waste reduction and cost control.

Rigid control over storeroom items is essential. A controlled storeroom is one in which one person is held accountable for the merchandise it contains. It is kept locked, and issues are made only upon written requisition, signed by the person to whom authority for ordering has been given. No one should be permitted to enter the storeroom except the people who work there.

Storeroom organization and arrangement are important to efficient operation in terms of convenience and motion and time economy. The items may be arranged according to groups and foods in each group placed on the shelves in alphabetical order—for example, *canned fruits,* apples, apricots, and so on. This system facilitates counting at the time of inventory taking and gives an orderly appearance to the storeroom, and each item can be located easily when filling requisitions for storeroom issues.

A chart of storeroom arrangement may be posted near the door. A suggested classification follows.

FOOD STORES INDEX

A. Beverages
B. Cereals, prepared
C. Cereals, flour, cereal products
D. Crackers, cookies
E. Chocolate, cocoa
F. Condiments, seasonings, spices
G. Extracts, colorings
H. Fats, oils
I. Fish, canned and freeze dried
J. Fruits, canned
K. Fruits, dried or dehydrated
L. Fruit and vegetable juices
   (includes ginger ale, beer)
M. Gelatin, prepared desserts
N. Leavening agents

O. Meats and poultry, canned and
   freeze dried
P. Milk products
Q. Nuts, nut products
R. Pickles, olives, relishes, sauces,
   salad dressings
S. Prepared mixes
T. Preserves, jams, jellies, candied
   fruit
U. Soup and soup bases, canned
   and dehydrated
V. Sugar, syrups, candy
W. Vegetables, canned
X. Vegetables, dried, dehydrated,
   freeze dried

CLASSIFICATION OF PERISHABLE FOODS

Bread, rolls, other baked products
Butter, margarine
Cheese
Eggs, fresh, frozen, and dried
Entrees, frozen
Fats, oils
Ice cream, ices, sherbets
Milk, cream
Meats: beef, lamb, pork, ham,
   bacon, veal, variety meats

Poultry, fresh and frozen
Fish, fresh, frozen, and smoked
Shellfish, fresh and frozen
Fruits and fruit juices, fresh
Fruit and fruit juices, frozen
Vegetables, fresh
Vegetables, frozen

Daily checks of the refrigerator by managers assure prompt utilization of food so that it never becomes unsafe. This one routine procedure alone can effect untold savings of leftover food that should not be held over 24 hours. Correct handling and storage of cooked foods are not to be forgotten as another phase of food cost control.

Production of Foods: Preparation, Cooking, and Leftovers Control. The quality and form of food purchased has a direct bearing on the amount of waste in the process of preparation and cooking. The actual cost of food is influenced by not only the relationship between amount or weight of the edible portion and that of the waste or inedible portion, but also by the quality of the edible portion. Experienced food production managers are well aware that the initial unit price is not the basis on which food costs should be figured; instead, the cost of the edible portion determined after preliminary preparation and cooking losses have been accounted for is what matters. For example, an 18-pound ready-to-cook turkey is priced at 68¢ per pound. The purchase cost is $12.24. After cooking and slicing, the amount of edible meat is 9.9 pounds or a yield of 55 percent. The other 8.1 pounds is inedible bones, evaporation, and other cooking losses. The 9.9 pounds of edible portion costs the same as the original turkey, $12.24, which when divided by 9.9 pounds is a cost per pound of $1.24!

Excess waste in preliminary preparation of foods may result from leaving vegetables in a peeler too long and therefore wearing away edible portions of that food, cutting off too much of the tomato ends, or trimming meat carelessly. Such waste cuts into profits and should be avoided. Those losses may be due to unskilled, inexperienced personnel who have not been trained, inadequate supervision, or lack of proper equipment; these are all *management* caused, and yet they are management responsibility. These preparation losses are examples of seemingly small channels of waste but, by the end of a month, they make a large contribution to an unsatisfactory financial statement.

The proper use of standardized recipes will do much toward reducing errors in preparation that could result in financial losses. Ingredients inaccurately weighed and measured may yield unsatisfactory products that cannot be sold. Slight excesses in nonbasic ingredients above actual requirements, a few additional pieces of fruit, an extra spoonful of nut meats or olives, or a little more cream than is necessary soon make an appreciable difference in the total cost of a product. Some foodservices have found good control resulting from the use of a *central ingredient room.* This requires one person trained and responsible for weighing and measuring all ingredients to be processed by the cooks. Since only these amounts are issued to the kitchen, it reduces to a minimum the possibility of the cooks using incorrect amounts.

Natural losses due to shrinkage of foods during the cooking period should not be overlooked; however, these can be reduced to a minimum by controlled oven or cooking temperatures. The cook who sets the thermostat at 400°F to "speed up" the cooking of the roast produces a loss in volume as well as in quality of food and therefore a loss of dollars in sales.

These situations can be cut to a minimum by adequate training of employees in the use of desired procedures and of the recipes provided, and by adequate supervision to assure continued accurate use of them. The provision of proper and adequate equipment for the employees to use is a management responsibility.

Management's use of sales records that show quantities of prepared foods sold as a basis for determining production needs should reduce leftovers to a negligible amount. The greater the success in accurately forecasting quantities that will be sold, the better the financial picture will be.

Loss of profit in food service business often stems from overproduction, which may result when managers leave the decision making to the cooks who have inadequate knowledge of how much food is needed at specified times. Too often cooks like to have all food ready at the beginning of the serving hour to "avoid the rush" instead of cooking smaller quantities as the need arises, resulting in poor quality or leftover food.

Standardized Portions and Serving Wastes. Standardized portions or portion control is important not only in the control of costs but also in creating and maintaining guest or customer satisfaction and good will. No one likes to receive a smaller portion than other customers for the same price.

Portion control does not necessarily mean a smaller portion for the patrons any more than food control means lowering the quality of food in order to stay within the budget. One or more portions less from a can of fruit, a few servings less than the estimated number from a pan of scalloped oysters, and a few bowls less of mushroom soup may lower the money return from these various dishes to a figure below cost. Twelve servings of creamed chicken may be the estimated yield from 1 quart of diced chicken meat. If only 10 servings

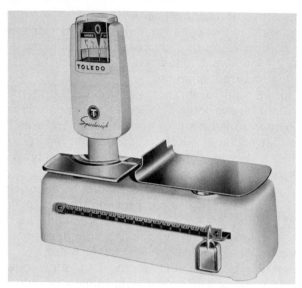

*FIGURE   9.2   An accurate, easily read scale simplifies portion and cost control.
Courtesy, Toledo Scale Company.*

are obtained there is an appreciable loss that cannot be tolerated in a well-managed business. Uniform portions based on weight and measure will prevent waste of this type. A portion scale as shown in Fig. 9.2 is essential for control of portion weight.

Portion control begins with the purchase of foods according to definite specifications so that known yields can be obtained from each food. Meats, fresh fruits to be served raw, canned foods of a certain grade for definite number of pieces per can of peach or pear halves, or pineapple slices are examples.

The establishment and use of standardized recipes to include the number and size of each portion the recipe will yield is the next step in portion control. Each food director will determine the size portion to be served and its selling price in relation to the total volume and cost of the recipe. This is of little value if, after the food is prepared, the person who is serving it does not know or does not follow the directions for obtaining the exact number of portions from a given quantity of prepared food. An overly generous employee can raise costs appreciably without detection.

One means of assuring standardized portions is to know size and yield of all pans, measures, ladles, and other small equipment used in the serving. For example, if 1 quart of gravy is to yield 16 servings, there must be accurate measurements both of the original quantity of gravy and the amount taken up in the ladle. Dippers sized from 6 to 40 are convenient tools for measuring exact portions of foods in the preparation and serving units.

No two foodservices may sell exactly the same size portions but, for each situation, the food director should post a list of foods most commonly served, the size of the portion, and the anticipated yield per unit. (See Fig. 9.3.)

KITCHEN (FOR COOKS)

Item	Size of Portion
Grilled meat patties	Number 10 dipper
Grilled cheese sandwiches	1 3/4 oz cheese, 2 slices bread
Stuffed peppers	Number 10 dipper
Stuffed wieners (2)	1/2 slice bacon, 1/2 oz cheese, 1/2 pickle
Tuna salad	Number 12 dipper
Cheese balls and pineapple	1 slice pineapple, 2 balls, Number 40 dipper

BAKE SHOP (FOR PASTRY COOKS)

Bakery Products	Pan Size	No. to Serving	Size Serving (No. cuts)	Amount in Pan
Brownies	18 x 26 in.	2	8 x 16 in.	8 lb 5 oz
Layer cake	9 in.	1 slice	16 cuts	1 lb 1 oz batter/layer
Pie crust	9 in.	1 piece	6 cuts	7 oz, bottom; 5 oz, top
Fruit for pie filling	9 in.	1 piece	6 cuts	1 lb or 1 qt prepared filling

SERVING PANTRY (FOR SERVERS)

Item	Size of Portion
Chili	6-oz ladle, 1 sack crackers
Creamed sweetbreads and ham	Number 8 dipper
Ham and egg scallop	Number 10 dipper
Heart, dressing	2 oz meat, number 16 dipper dressing
Corn pudding	1/20 counter pan size, 12 x 20 in.
Ranch style beans	4-oz ladle
Sundae sauce	1-oz soufflé cup
Ice cream	Number 16 dipper, 9/qt

FIGURE 9.3   Standard portion lists, to be posted in the proper production and service area.

Methods of Pricing. One of the important responsibilities of any food-service manager is to determine a sound basis for establishing the selling price for food. Haphazard methods can lead only to financial disaster, dissatisfaction of the patron, or both. Perhaps this lack of intelligent planning is one of the major factors contributing to the high percentage of failures in the foodservice business each year.

Some foodservices, especially commercial operations, must establish a selling price for the individual items or for a combination of items to be served together. These are the prices posted on a menu board or on a printed menu card so customers may know what they will have to pay. For these establishments, pricing involves two considerations: the precosting of standardized recipes and the predetermination of food-cost percentage level that the institution hopes to achieve.

An illustration of a standardized recipe that has been costed is shown in Fig. 9.4. Note that this recipe serves 48 portions of a 7-ounce size. Therefore, the total cost, $8.422, is divided by the number of portions to give the cost of one serving.

Food-cost percentage is that percent of the income spent for food. It varies with the type of foodservice, each determining its own in relation to other known costs.

Traditionally, the selling price for an item of food is based on raw-food cost plus a markup suitable for the type of organization. The markup is determined by dividing the desired food-cost percent into 100 (representing total sales or 100 percent). The resulting number is called the *mark-up factor.* To illustrate: if 40 percent is the desired food-cost percentage, it is divided into 100, with the resulting mark-up factor of 2 1/2. Each portion cost or other raw-food cost multiplied by 2 1/2 equals the desired selling price. Thus, a piece of pie with a raw-food cost of 12¢ would have a selling price of 30¢.

If the overall food-cost percentage is to be maintained within the desired percent-of-income level, the mark-up factor cannot be used alone to calculate the selling price. The many free foods given to the customer such as salt, pepper, sugar, cream, mustard, catsup, and sauces, must be accounted for in the sale price of the foods. Also, it is imperative that the food manager know not only the raw-food cost of menu items but also the cost of the many hidden losses in preparation, cooking, and serving which if not controlled, add appreciably to the total food cost. Overproduction and unavoidable waste likewise add to the costs, and the wise manager will analyze all of these, control what is possible, and consider the other in the establishment of selling prices. Obviously, prices cannot always be

Name of Product _Quiche Lorraine_   Size of Pan _12 × 20 × 2_

Yield (Total Quality) _2 pans_   How Portioned _4 × 6 : 24/pan_

Size Portion _7 oz._   Date Prepared _5-19-75_

No. of Portions _48_   Prepared by _K. L._

NUMBER OF SERVINGS: _48_

INGREDIENTS	E. P. Weight	Measure	A. P. Weight	Measure	Unit Price	Cost
Flour, Pastry				3 lbs.2 oz	.112/lb	364
Salt, Cooking				2 oz	.044/lb	001
Shortening				1 lb 12 oz	.494/lb	.8645
Water		2½ c				—
Onion, Chopped	4.2 g.		4.5 oz		.155/lb	0456
Milk		1 gal.			1.07/gal	1 07
Swiss Cheese, Grated			2 lb		1.35/lb	2 70
Eggs, fresh, whole		3 doz			.55/doz	1 65
Mustard, dry			½ oz		.73/lb	022
Ham, ground (optional)	1 lb 4 oz				1.38/lb	1 725

Procedure:

Total Cost $8.4421

Portion Cost .176

FIGURE 9.4   A costed standardized recipe.

481

within the exact bounds of the mark-up figure. To equalize the small-profit items included on the menu for variety and customer appeal, some high-profit foods should also be included. Meats usually yield the lowest profit: soups, salads, and some desserts yield the highest profit. Pricing of a table d' hote, selective, or elective menu follows the same procedure except that all items on the menu are costed and totaled before the mark-up figure is used to obtain the selling price.

This conventional method of establishing a selling price has been questioned by some managers in these times of soaring labor and operating costs. Overhead costs remain about the same regardless of the menu and do not vary from day to day. Preparation time and therefore labor cost are affected by the menu and are different for each item of food. Roasts and steaks, for example, usually have a high food cost but require relatively little labor time to prepare. Stew and hash, traditionally low-cost items, require much more time to prepare. It seems logical, therefore, to establish selling prices on the basis of labor time and cost as well as raw-food cost for each item on the menu. In this way all customers share equally in the general expenses of the foodservice.

By this method, it is necessary to calculate for the meal period the amount of income needed to cover all costs: food, labor, operating and overhead, plus the desired amount for profit. The total of these costs divided by the anticipated number of customers gives the selling price per person. Accurate data to provide information on these costs on a per meal basis is essential to this system of establishing a selling price for a meal.

Stokes has reported another method. Operators of steak, lobster and chop houses, where high cost items are the principal menu offering, often price their menus in terms of dollar gross profit. . . . A steak for example may cost $1.25 a portion. If this price is multiplied by 2, 2 1/2, or 3 (mark-up figures), the resultant price would be too high, they feel, to draw sufficient volume. Consequently, it may be priced as a special item at $1.95, thus giving them 70 ¢ gross profit. If they can sell 100 steaks at a meal, the resulting net profit will amount to $70.00. This method emphasizes the contribution made by each item rather than focusing on an overall percentage.[6]

The prime cost method of menu pricing was initiated by Harry H. Pope of the Pope Cafeteria in St. Louis, Missouri. It is an attempt

[6] *John W. Stokes,* How To Manage a Restaurant or Institutional Food Service, *Second Edition, Wm. C. Brown, Dubuque, Iowa, p. 251, 1974.*

to include not only the raw-food cost but also the cost of the labor directly involved in the preparation of the menu item. This equalizes the true cost of producing the food among the various menu items and distributes the charges among the customers in a more equitable way than the conventional method of pricing. The "prime cost," then, is the cost of the raw food plus the cost of labor time involved in the preparation of that food item.

To utilize this system, accurate records of time spent in preparing the various foods must be kept. The amount of labor time used multiplied by the employee's wage rate will give this cost of labor. This cost, plus the raw-food cost, usually calculated from the standardized recipe, is the basis for establishing the selling price. Since the prime cost usually averages 70 percent of income, the mark-up factor would be 1 1/4 or 1 1/2 (70 into 100) instead of the 2 1/2 or 3 or more used in the conventional method of pricing. An example of pricing by each method is shown below.

	Conventional Method at 40 Percent Food Cost		Prime Cost Method	
STEAK	Raw-food cost × markup	$1.10 2 1/2	Raw-food cost + labor time/cost of 3 min @ $4/hr Prime cost × markup	$1.10 .198 1.298 1 1/2
	Selling price	$2.75	Selling price	$1.95
STEW	Raw-food cost × markup	.65 2 1/2 1.63 or	Raw-food cost + labor time/cost of 30 min @ $4/hr Prime cost × markup	.65 2.00 2.65 1 1/2
	Selling price	$1.65	Selling price	$4.98

In these examples, the cost of preparing a stew versus that of preparing a steak is reflected in the selling price. The customer gets a break, pricewise, with the steak and the demand for food with the lower labor cost is evident. With today's high labor cost, this may be preferable.

Today, with so much "built-in" labor in the foods purchased, it does seem that the customer should not have to be charged twice for the labor cost as he would be with the conventional method where the markup does include an allowance for labor costs. The prime cost method is fairer when ready foods are purchased for use.

Institutions having a fixed income, such as board paid in advance in a residence hall, are not concerned with selling prices for the food they serve. Instead, the board rate divided by the number of operating days gives a per diem allowance or income figure.

The desired distribution of the food dollar serves as a "method of pricing" guide also. If according to a predetermined budget 35 percent of the food dollar is to be spent for meat, fish, and poultry and the allocation for food for the day is $700, the purchase price of these items should not exceed $245.

Employees' Meal Costs. Providing meals for employees is necessary and desirable in most foodservices. Many workers not only are needed during the meal hours, but employers believe it wise for the employees to become familiar with the foodservice by participating in it. The philosophy of the management regarding employee meals generally indicates a desire to maintain effective employer-employee relationships. By providing wholesome, nutritionally balanced meals at reduced rates or free of charge as a convenience to employees, management extends a fringe benefit to them and, at the same time, hopes to build and maintain a healthy, happy, and efficient working force.

The policy regarding the kind and quantity of food served and the amount and method of payment for such meals varies with individual situations. The establishment of rates to be charged the employees for their meals is based, in most cases, on the raw-food cost alone. Meals may be charged "at cost," or with the addition of a mark up as decided on by the organization. In other cases, a discount of a given percentage (30 to 50 percent) of the retail selling price is the basis used to determine the rate. In other situations a flat charge per meal, such as 85¢, is set as the policy, or a deduction is made from the paycheck, perhaps $15 to $20 a month, for one meal per day.

Whatever the method adopted in providing meals for the employees, a definite time and place for eating should be designated. Such a plan provides not only a pleasant meal hour for the personnel, but makes it easier to control their selections of food, if limited, and hopefully helps to eliminate eating while on duty.

The value of food consumed by employees should be of real concern to management in attempting to better control both food and labor costs. On the average, the expense of providing meals for employees may be estimated as 4 to 5 percent of total food cost. Although 4 to 5 percent of total food cost or 1 to 3 percent of total sales may seem an insignificant figure, these amounts can have a decided bearing on a financial statement.

When employees' meals are included as part of their wage, the cost of the meals should be charged to the labor budget and not to food cost. This separation of the cost of food consumed between that served to guests and to employees is made so that employees' meal cost is reflected as a labor cost instead of as a food cost item.

An accurate record of number of employee meals served must be kept, and this figure multiplied by the cost per meal decided on will equal the total cost of employees' meals. Employees' meals are a part of the conditions of employment and are, as such, an operating expense and not a sale or income to the foodservice organization. They should be shown in this light in the profit and loss statement.

Labor Costs

Labor costs in foodservice organizations have been spiraling upward over the last few years until this item of expense has become one of the most controversial in the overall budget. Many foodservices find that their labor costs are almost as high and, in some situations, higher than the food cost percentage. Food costs have been controlled to a fine point, but until recently less concern has been given to controlling labor costs. They are less controllable than food costs, and the percentage of payroll costs to sales will fluctuate with sales. It is impractical if not impossible to change the number of employees or their scheduled times of duty day by day in proportion to the number of customers, patients, or students, as one might change the menu to meet fluctuating needs. Therefore, it is necessary to consider ways to get full returns from the payroll dollar.

Labor cannot be considered a fixed expense, because it is influenced by many conditions, some of which can make for greater productivity, reduce costs, and give management a "full day's work for a fair day's pay." These conditions include: the type of operation and extent of services offered; the hours of service; the menu pattern and the form in which the food is purchased; the physical plant—the size and arrangement of the preparation and serving units and their relation to each other, and the working conditions; the amount, kind, and arrangement of labor-saving equipment; the personnel program and policies regarding selection, training, and scheduling of employees, the amount and adequacy of supervision, the wage scale and fringe benefits given, and rate of turnover; and the standards that are to be maintained in production and service.

Type of Service and Extent of Services Offered. Because the amount of the income spent for labor varies according to all of the mentioned conditions, there is no clear cut, average figure for labor cost in general. Commercial operations with full table service in luxurious surroundings may have a labor cost of 40 to 50 percent, whereas those of a vending or do-it-yourself type of operation or restaurants using prepackaged ready-to-heat entrees and a limited number of menu items may have only 5 or 10 percent of sales as the labor cost percentage. Varying numbers of fringe benefits given to employees in different organizations and ways of reporting these make it even more difficult to arrive at comparable figures.

Certain labor costs, such as the salaries of the director, assistants, office employees, and regular kitchen and dining-room employees, do not vary directly with volume and may be considered fixed labor expenses. For example, a director may be able to supervise a foodservice for 200 to 300. With the increase to the larger number no additional office help would be required. Some additional employees would be needed in the kitchen, but not in direct proportion to the increase in the number to be served. Kitchen workers can absorb an increase in volume of production up to a point with little extra time or energy required. Therefore, the greater the volume of business, the greater the returns on labor dollars spent.

The extent of service offered within the organization will affect total labor costs. In cafeterias, for example, the patron may carry his own tray and bus his own soiled dishes, as on some college campuses or in industrial plants, or there may be a waitress available to perform these services in commercial cafeterias. Where table service is used, the ratio of waiters to guests will vary as will the cost of labor. If the menu and service are simple as might be true in residence halls, homes of various types, or low-cost restaurants, one waiter is able to serve many guests. When the formality of dining calls for personalized service and several echelons of dining room employees from the maître d' to the head waiter, waiter, wine steward, coffee server, and bus boy, it is easy to understand the high cost of labor in such establishments.

Hours of Service. The hours of service will determine the number of "shifts" of personnel as well as total number of labor hours required to accomplish the work to be done. The hospital cafeteria for personnel that is open 7 days a week and serves 4 or 5 meals daily, breakfast, lunch, dinner, night supper, and a 3 A.M. lunch for the night workers will demand a larger complement of employees than the school lunchroom that serves only 1 meal per day for 5 days. The restaurant open 24 hours a day, 7 days a week will have a different labor scheduling than the one that is open for business 10 or 12 hours a day for 6 days a week. Each situation will result in a different labor cost expense.

Menu Pattern and Form in Which Food Is Purchased. As the menu is the center of activity of the institution kitchen and service areas, so it is a major controlling factor in determining the number of employees required and the skill they must possess in order to produce and serve the food. The amount of skill required of a cook in a school lunchroom with its simple food and limited menu selection varies considerably from that expected of the chef in an exclusive restaurant with gourmet foods and elaborate preparations demanded by its clientele. The labor time required in each case would be quite different, as would the wage rate demands.

Careful analysis of menu items and their popularity and sales appeal serves as the basis for eliminating items that will result in leftover wastage as well as the labor costs involved. The cutting, chopping, recombining, and other processes involved to make the product salable a second time adds significantly to total labor costs.

The menu determines not only the number of labor hours for its preparation but also the number of dishes and pieces of silverware required to serve it and hence to be washed. The diswashing labor hours will be increased when difficult-to wash dishes are used, such as individual custard or casserole dishes that require soaking and special handling. This is a real consideration in total labor cost in operations like college foodservices where part-time student workers may be employed on an "as needed " basis.

The amount of "built-in" labor purchased with the food will further influence the labor hours required for preparation within the foodservice department. The purchase of peeled potatoes and carrots, sectioned oranges and grapefruit, and ready-to-cook, preportioned meats in addition to the convenience foods such as mixes, prepared soups, sauces, and gravies, as well as the extensive list of prepared, frozen entrees certainly change the labor requirements and also add to the food cost.

Some questions have been raised about actual savings effected through the purchase of labor-saving products, particularly preportioned foods, such as packaged crackers, jellies and jams, catsup, mustard, and dressings and sauces. Often there are "lull" times in certain employees' schedules that could be utilized to good advantage to portion such items on the premises. Studies to determine the exact labor time and cost involved in the preparation plus the raw-food cost of both forms of the food and a careful comparison of the two total costs give a preliminary basis for decisions on which form to buy. An example of such a study follows.

POTATO COST STUDY

	Peeling Potatoes on Premises		*Purchasing Dehydrated Potato Granules*	
Purchase Price	100-lb sack	$9.70	30-lb bag	$8
Preparation time and cost	Peeling and eyeing: labor time = 1 hr 20 min or 80 min @$3/hr	$ 4.00	No preparation required	
Peeling loss	Average, 20%		None	
Total cost	For 80 lb E.P.	$13.70	For 30 lb	$8
Cost per pound, E.P.		$ .171		$ .267
Cost per serving	(100/30 lb E.P.)	$ .051	(100/3.5lb granules)	$ .0093

One hospital dietitian says she knows they could peel their own potatoes for less cost than buying them ready peeled, *if* they had adequate supervision to make certain the potatoes were not left in the peeler too long. Since they have insufficient supervisory help, they buy ready-peeled potatoes! However, further analysis of work schedules, labor time available, and amount of supervisory time required must be made before determining which form of food will be more profitable and acceptable in a particular organization.

The Physical Plant: Size and Arrangement. Efficient kitchen arrangement is another major factor in labor cost control. Plans that provide large areas of floor space, poorly arranged for the convenience of the worker, are common sources of disproportionate expenditures for labor. Inconvenience and waste of human energy may also be caused by poor planning of departments and by poor placing of equipment within a department.

In one research project [7] it was found that "Of the total productive time, employees in all the restaurants studied spent approximately 27 percent of the working day in walking. This average represents the equivalent of more than seven people walking continuously." The data presented showed that 18 percent of the average annual payroll cost was spent for walking. "These costs point out the need for improved layout of foodservice facilities as the average employee spends more than 2 hours out of every 8 in walking an average of 6.5 miles." [8] This is readily recognized as an example of a hidden payroll waste.

The placement of the food preparation unit in relation to the serving unit is a feature for which the food director may not be responsible. However, if the arrangement is not efficient it will result in a labor expenditure out of proportion to the usual allowance. Bakeshops in the basement, far removed from food subveyors, may entail the handling of baked food five or more times before it finally reaches the point of service. Central kitchens in the main building of a group of college buildings with foodservice for special occasions on the second floor of an adjacent building may double the cost of service of a special meal.

Additional employees may be required to lift, handle, and carry or move materials in such poorly arranged kitchens. A test for efficiency of a proposed floor plan can be made by using a typical week's menu to trace the pathway the raw materials and finished products must travel. The layout should minimize distances to be traveled and the equipment placed for convenience and efficiency. (See Chapter 11).

Equipment and Its Arrangment. Adequate equipment conveniently arranged for the use of the worker is important if an unnecessary load to labor costs is to be avoided. A saving is evident not only in labor costs but also in the energy and the increased satisfaction of the workers when units are designed for efficient operation.

---

[7] *"Labor Utilization and Operating Practices In Table Service Restaurants,"* USDA Marketing Research Report No. 931, Superintendent of Documents, Washington, D.C., p. 1, 1971.
[8] *"Labor Utilization and Operating Practices In Table Service Restaurants,"* USDA Marketing Research Report No. 931, Superintendent of Documents, Washington, D.C., p. 11, 1971.

The amount and adequacy of available labor-saving equipment bears a relationship to the number of labor hours required to accomplish a given piece of work.

It must be questioned, however, whether *all* labor-saving equipment really reduces labor cost. Even though large volumes of food can be processed more quickly with the use of power equipment, certain hand operations may be more efficient when small amounts are involved. The time required for using and cleaning an electric cutting machine, for example, may be much greater than that required for chopping a few onions by hand.

The complexity of some equipment may require the services of highly skilled and well-trained employees to operate it. Although the use of the equipment reduces the number of labor hours, the wage rate for the operator may be so high as to increase the total labor cost.

Labor-saving methods often are more profitable than either machinery or physical arrangement. The application of the principles of motion economy discussed on page 365 and an effective training program for the employees can result in a highly efficient working force.

Personnel Policies and Productivity. Labor is a commodity that cannot be purchased on short notice. And no organization can expect to have an efficient working force if the people in it are not carefully selected and placed in positions for which they are best fitted by native ability, training, and experience. The determination of the work to be done and the number of labor hours needed to do it have been discussed in Chapter 8 and are basic to control of labor costs. In addition to the initial cost involved in finding, selecting, and training an employee, the investment of several thousand dollars a year in his wages should be an incentive to the manager to select employees with great care. By so doing, turnover should be kept at a minimum and costs for replacement should be reduced; in one study [9] it was reported that "turnover costs could exceed $12,600 a year in a firm with 35 employees and a turnover rate of 13% a month."

Keiser and Kallio [10] have said: "probably the most important ele-

---

[9] *"Labor Utilization and Operating Practices in Table Service Restaurants,"* USDA Marketing Research Report No. 931, Superintendent of Documents, Washington, D.C. 1971.

[10] *James Keiser and Elmer Kallio,* Controlling and Analyzing Costs in Food Service Operations, *Wiley, New York, p. 3, 1974.*

ment in labor cost is productivity of employees. A high wage rate can be justified by employees' productivity but the foodservice industry has generally lagged behind other industries in improving productivity."

Industrial engineering studies indicate that employees work at 40 to 50 percent efficiency. They tend to adjust to the amount of work to be done by speeding up or slowing down according to the demands. To make employees more productive and to utilize their time to best advantage is the aim of management in helping to control the cost of labor.

To do a job properly and efficiently an employee must know exactly his share of the work and how to do it. "Training pays dividends" is a truism, but management must, first of all, determine *how* the work is to be done and set the standards to be maintained.

Standards are needed for tasks in order to encourage better performance by individuals. For example, in a cafeteria a fair standard for wrapping silver is six sets per minute. If an employee is made aware of the standard, it is not difficult to get the employee to meet or better the standard. If no standard is communicated to the employee, the productivity may be one-half or one-third as much.[11]

The determination of standards of production can be made only by research studies within a given organization. The number of pies that can be produced in one kitchen in a given period of time, for example, will not be the same as in another because of conditions already discussed. Dietitians or supervisors cannot rely entirely on published standards, which are necessarily averages, or on comparing theirs with those of another operation of a similar type. These may serve only as guides for establishing one's own standards.

Freshwater and Bragg[12] participated in several research projects with the foodservice industry to improve productivity and reduce costs. An analysis of scheduled time versus productive time in the 20 foodservice establishments included in one study and a graphic presentation of savings in labor cost through scheduling is given in Figs. 9.5 and 9.6.

[11] *Jule Wilkinson, Editor,* Increasing Productivity in Foodservice. *Cahners, Boston, p. 194, 1973.*
[12] *John F. Freshwater and Errol R. Bragg, "Improving Food Service Productivity."* Cornell H.R.A. Quarterly, 15(4), 16 (February 1975).

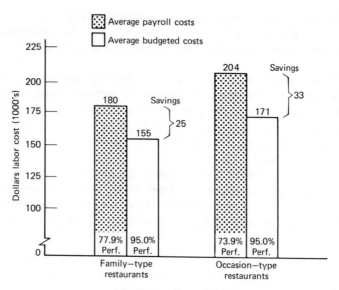

FIGURE 9.5   *Annual potential savings in labor cost through scheduling in family- and occasion-type restaurants.*

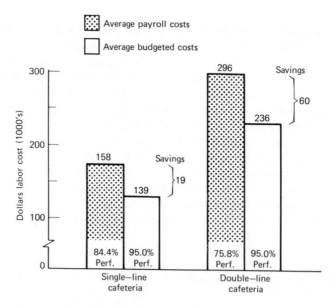

FIGURE 9.6   *Annual potential savings in labor cost through scheduling in single- and double-line cafeterias.*

Figure 9.5 shows the average annual potential savings in labor costs in the family and occasion-type restaurants that participated in this research. The average payroll cost in the "family-type" restaurants was $180,000 at a performance level of 77.9 percent. If the performance level were increased to 95 percent this cost could be reduced to the budgeted cost of $155,000, for an annual saving of $25,000. If the performance level in occasion-type restaurants were increased from 73.9% to 95%, the payroll cost of $204,000 could be reduced to the budgeted cost of $171,000, for an annual saving of $33,000. This labor cost reduction could be realized by reducing nonproductive time through improved scheduling of part-time employees.

Figure 9.6 summarizes the potential labor cost saving in single- and double-line cafeterias. The performance in each department of cafeterias is comparable to that in each department of restaurants; therefore, payroll and budgeted hours by department are not shown. As shown in the figure, a potential labor cost saving of $19,000 is possible in single-line cafeterias by reducing nonproductive time. This saving is the difference between average payroll costs of $158,000 per year and the budgeted cost of $139,000. A potential labor cost saving of $60,000 per year is possible in double-line cafeterias. This saving is the difference between average payroll costs of $296,000 and the budgeted costs of $236,000.

The potential savings that are possible by reducing nonproductive time are significant. The annual saving of $25,000 in family-type restaurants is equivalent to a reduction in the payroll cost ratio of 5% in both family- and occasion-type restaurants (from 32% to 27% in family-type restaurants and from 29% to 24% in occasion-type restaurants). The annual saving of $19,000 in single-line cafeterias is equivalent to a reduction in the payroll cost ratio of 4% (from 30% to 26%). The annual saving of $60,000 in double-line cafeterias is equivalent to a reduction in the payroll cost ratio of 7% (from 34% to 27%).

Many administrative dietitians and other researchers have attempted, over the years, to establish a standard for labor needs in various types of establishments, based on number of labor minutes per meal. Other standards for labor time-cost requirements are expressed in terms of percentage of income spent for labor, customers per labor hour, labor cost per customer, minutes of labor per customer, income per labor hour, and income per employee per day. These have been discussed in the chapter on personnel management. They are mentioned here to remind the reader that such "standards" are available and suitable only as a guide for those who wish to compare and analyze their scheduled labor time, or to help determine labor needs (time-cost) for newly organized foodservices. Variables are too numerous within each foodservice and from place to place to allow the use of any one set of "standard" figures, but managers should be aware of the need for analyzing their own labor costs in an attempt to keep them as low as feasible.

The number of guests, students, patients, or other types of patrons served per 8-hour employee or the number of hours worked and wages earned by employees in various production and service units expressed in terms of per cent of total and compared with hours and earnings of the entire unit, may be used as guides to operational trends. Recording these figures day by day is one means for seeing at a glance whether or not improvements are being effected. (See Form 9.1.)

It is well known that in general the larger the institution, the lower the total number of labor minutes required. One employee can produce a large volume of food with little more time expenditure than it would take for a smaller quantity. Anything that can be done to increase the number of meals served within the physical limits of the institution and with the existing complement of personnel will improve the labor cost percentage.

Supervision. Supervision is one major factor in the final labor cost picture that cannot be over looked if labor costs are to be kept at a minimum. Dardarian said many years ago that:

The effects of good or bad supervision on payroll costs, or on any costs for that matter, cannot be underestimated. Good supervision occupies an essential place in control and reduction of payroll costs. Tighter production schedules, greater utilization of labor and equipment, more compact functioning layouts and more rigid adherence to menu standards and specifications are impossible to achieve without the assistance of constant, close, and understanding supervision . . . and, considering their influence on costs and profits, management should endeavor to create an atmosphere in which good supervision may thrive.[13]

The truth of that statement has not changed. Supervision is sometimes regarded as an expensive item in labor costs. Not infrequently the first attempt at reduction of such costs by administration is the replacement of a competent, well-trained director with an immature, inexperienced, and incompetent one at a much lower wage. Sometimes an experienced but untrained person is promoted from the ranks, again at a relatively low salary. Rarely does such replacement prove satisfactory. Neither the inexperienced nor the experienced untrained worker is able to see the full view of the foodservice

[13] *Leo Dardarian, "10 Ways to Cut Your Labor Costs," Part II,* Restaurant Management, 80(2), 43 (1957).

Unit	Number of Employees	Labor Hours	Per cent of Total	Wages	Per cent of Total
Receiving, storing, issuing					
Pre-preparation					
Cooking					
Service					
Dishwashing, including pot and pan washing					
Cleaning					
Managers and supervisors					
Total					

FORM 9.1   Suggested form for use in making comparison of hours worked and wages earned in relation to specific units and to the entire foodservice department.

operation. Usually the costs begin to rise until any slight saving entailed in the employment of an untrained director is absorbed many times over. Money spent for efficient supervision brings high returns in economic value to the organization. There is no substitute for good supervision.

One final word about control of labor costs has to do with overtime work-pay. Unless some control procedures are followed, overtime work may be "abused," and the costs resulting from this practice may throw the labor budget out of balance. An advance requisition authorizing overtime work should be required. This way the supervisor will know how much overtime costs will be, and he can try to minimize this type of expenditure through better scheduling or redistribution of work loads.

In summary, it may be said that the combined cost of food and labor has made up approximately 70 percent of the income for many years and is probably about the same today. However, only by careful analysis of these two groups of costs can the manager know what action would be necessary to bring operations in line with a desired level.

OPERATING AND OTHER EXPENSES

Control should not end with consideration of food and labor costs only; 12 to 18 percent of the departmental budget probably will be used for other items classified as overhead and operating expense. These include utilities, laundry and linen supplies, repairs, replacement and maintenance, telephone, printing, paper goods, office supplies and cleaning materials, depreciation, rent or amortization, and insurance and taxes.

In addition, there is a real concern for conservation of energy resources within all foodservice establishments. Not only does conservation meet a national need, but it also helps to reduce departmental operating costs.

Many innovative suggestions for saving resources have been made in the last few years. Ideas presented relate to better utilization of existing equipment by finding new or extra uses for it and loading to full capacity each time it is used. The development of new equipment has been designed to save energy such as the integral heating unit built into a serving plate for hospital foodservice. A planned maintenance program with a full-time maintenance engineer has prevented breakdowns and extended the life of equipment and so has paid dividends in some institutions.

Adherence to specific practices for the conservation and control of energy use can affect notable savings in food and operating costs in any foodservice. A special report by Avery [14] on energy saving presented in *Institutions/Volume Feeding* magazine lists many suggestions for reducing common energy wastes. Included were charts compiled in late 1973 by one hotel system, showing daily utility costs for operation of kitchen equipment when different fuels were utilized. (See Fig. 9.7.) These charts may give clues to managers for study of their own operations and for finding additional energy-saving procedures.

A condensed sample energy-saving checklist adapted from one prepared by Hyland [15] follows; a complete listing applicable to a particular foodservice should be compiled to aid the manager in reducing and controlling his operating costs.

SUGGESTIONS FOR CHECKING ENERGY-SAVING CONTROLS FOR (1) REFRIGERATORS AND FREEZERS AND (2) OVENS

Refrigerators and Freezers:

Install pilot lights on walk-in refrigerator light switches to show if lights have been left on inside.

[14] *Arthur C. Avery, Ph.D., "You Can Save Energy,"* Institutions/Volume Feeding, 74, 41 (March 15, 1974).
[15] *Mary Rose Hyland, "Energy Saving Checklist for Institutions,"* Hoosier Chef, Indiana Restaurant Association, December 1973.

Doors should be self-closing and kept closed as much as possible.

Check gaskets on doors for leaks.

Check coils in walk-in and reach-in refrigerators and freezers for ice buildups.

Check defrost cycles periodically to make sure of proper functioning.

Defrost regularly (if not automatic).

Set controls for each unit at proper temperature for storage of particular foods or food groups.

Use reliable thermometer to check temperature settings in each unit.

Store frozen and refrigerated foods immediately upon delivery.

Unpack shipping cartons and crates before products are stored, if practicable.

Trim and discard unusable parts of products before storage, if feasible, to reduce volume and hasten chilling.

Store products on portable racks or carts to reduce labor of handling.

Avoid leaving empty trucks and carts in refrigerators and freezers.

Thaw meats and vegetables from freezer, in refrigerator before cooking.

If external surfaces of a unit are excessively cold, check insulation for possible replacement.

Check compressors periodically for leaks and level of refrigerant. Place condensers where they get maximum cooling.

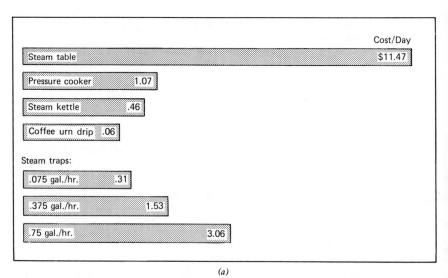

Cost/Day

(a)

	Cost/Day
Steam table	$11.47
Pressure cooker	1.07
Steam kettle	.46
Coffee urn drip	.06

Steam traps:

.075 gal./hr.	.31
.375 gal./hr.	1.53
.75 gal./hr.	3.06

Cost/Day

	Cost/Day
Electric ranges	$9.60
Bake oven	9.60
Dishwasher	4.80
Exhaust fan	3.36
Griddle plate	2.88
Coffee urn	1.92
Deep fat fryer	1.92
Food—warming cabinet	.96
Garbage disposal	.96
Rotary toaster	.58
Light bulb (100 watt)	.05

(c)

FIGURE 9.7 Average daily utility costs for operation of equipment as computed by one hotel foodservice system: (a) Oil. (b) Steam. (c) Electricity. (d) Gas.

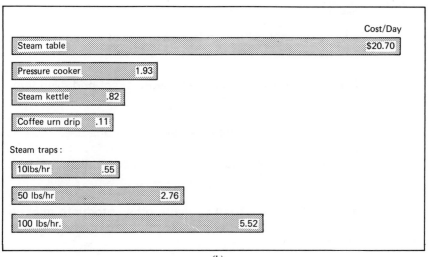

	Cost/Day
Steam table	$20.70
Pressure cooker	1.93
Steam kettle	.82
Coffee urn drip	.11

Steam traps:

10lbs/hr	.55
50 lbs/hr	2.76
100 lbs/hr.	5.52

(b)

	Cost/Day
Steam table*	$11.25
Pot wash sink*	11.25
Bake oven	2.25
Heating cabinets	1.50
Ranges	1.20
Broilers	1.20
Deep fat fryer	1.20
Griddle plate	1.20
Roasting oven	1.20
Steam kettles*	.45

*Gas used to heat the water in this system.

(d)

Ovens:

Select compact oven with least amount of waste space for the intended use.

Calibrate controls regularly to insure exact and even temperature.

Schedule ovens for capacity and continuous use.

Use lowest temperature setting to accomplish the task satisfactorily.

Preheat ovens for baking; many other products may be placed in cold oven and begin to cook during the preheating time.

Keep oven doors closed (estimated heat loss is 1°F drop in temperature each second oven is open).

Turn off oven early so excess heat in walls and racks will finish the baking.

Install special meat thermometer in roasting oven through oven wall with external temperature recorder to indicate, without opening the door, when meat reaches desired degree of internal doneness.

If external surface of oven becomes exceedingly hot, check for need to replace insulation.

Consideration has been given also to recommended lighting level standards with the thought that they may be higher than necessary. In some facilities energy savings have been effected by lowering their lighting levels without impairing worker efficiency. Clark [16] suggests that lighting might be reduced 20 percent in some areas of hotels and restaurants to save energy dollars. His recommended values for kitchens is 70 footcandles for inspecting, checking, and pricing and 30 footcandles for general lighting. Many institutions have

[16] *Jack Clark. Utilities Management: Part I—"Shedding Light,"* The Cornell H.R.A. Quarterly, *16(1), 19 (May 1975).*

used higher levels. It is important to check light intensity and, if it is too high, cut down.

The recognition that such problems exist is the first step in eliminating them. Some have been discussed previously. Other wastes are incurred through lack of attention to the care of equipment such as leaky faucets, noisy electric motors, gas burners with improperly adjusted flames, or thermostats out of control, or through failure to turn off lights, ranges, and ovens when not in use. A two-fold program set up by the manager will aid in reducing such wastes. First, make a definite time schedule for checking all equipment and for having it serviced; second, solicit the aid of employees in reporting immediately anything that is in need of repair, and have it fixed promptly.

Breakage of glassware and china can be reduced by proper sorting and stacking at the dishwashing machine, as well as through a training program for employees in proper dish handling. Charts giving the prices of each piece of china and glassware posted for the employees to see may make them more aware of the cost of breakage and the need for care in their work. Laundry costs can be kept at a minimum by issuing at scheduled times a given number of towels, aprons, uniforms, and cleaning cloths for employees' use instead of giving them access to the whole supply.

Proper amounts of cleaning supplies and compounds are more likely to be used when managers issue given quantities or set up a written chart of proportions required for various jobs than if left to the discretion of the employee. Too often they go by the rule, "If a little is good, more is better," resulting in much waste.

These are only a few suggestions of the many ways that foodservice managers themselves are responsible for control of costs. Efficient management and adequate supervision are, in truth, the essence of the whole matter. Finally "from time waste there is no salvage. It is the easiest of all wastes and the hardest to recover because it does not litter the floor," said an anonymous writer.

RECORDS FOR CONTROL

Complete and accurate records are among the basic requirements for control of costs. A foodservice operation, no matter how small or how large, cannot long exist without the definite information that records can provide to guide present operations and as a basis for future financial planning.

Records, like all forms of control, vary with the type, size, and policies of the institution, so that the management must ascertain what information is desired and how it may be obtained with the least expenditure of effort, time, and money.

Many foodservice organizations today utilize the computer for much of their record keeping and reporting. Data required for computer input is essentially the same as that for noncomputerized record keeping; forms and procedures vary. Good manual control and decisions on what information should be provided by computer are prerequisites to a good computerized control system. Designing appropriate forms for data organization is the next step in planning conversion to a computer-assisted program for greater cost control. Assistance in designing appropriate forms may be obtained from published reports of research by those who have pioneered in this field, especially Balintfy,[17] and Moore and others at the University of Missouri Medical Center[18] who have generously shared the results of their work.

No records, however carefully designed, will be of value unless they *are kept daily, are accurate, and are used by management.*

Records deemed essential for a noncomplex foodservice operation include those for controlling the major phases of the operations. These essential records may be classified as those for procurement and receiving, storage and storeroom control, production and service of food, number of people served, cash transactions, operating and maintenance, and personnel.

Illustrations of many of these record forms are given here as examples only. Each foodservice director will want to design forms for his own department according to the specific situation. However, these may aid in determining what information should be included.

PROCUREMENT AND RECEIVING RECORDS

Purchase Order. This is a written record of items ordered by telephone or by mail. It is a listing of items, quantities desired, and specifications. It may contain the price quotations and date and time of delivery. Form 9.2 shows a purchase order form for a college cafeteria designed for its own specific use and lists the items ordered by

[17] *Joseph Balintfy, Computerized Dietary Information System, Volume I: Data Organization and Collection Procedures, Research Paper 14. Computer System Research, Tulane University School of Business Administration, New Orleans.*
[18] *Aimee N. Moore and Byrdine Tuthill, Editors, "Computer-Assisted Food Management Systems," University of Missouri-Columbia Technical Education Service, Columbia, Missouri, 1971.*

POMERENE REFECTORY

Date_____

ON HAND		ORDER
Dairy:		
_____	gal whole milk	_____
_____	cs ½ pt	_____
_____	cs ½ pt choc	_____
_____	cs ½ pt B. milk	_____
_____	gal skim milk	_____
_____	gal 10% cream	_____
_____	gal XX cream	_____
_____	lb cot. cheese	_____
_____	Ice cream	_____
Bread:		
_____	White bread	_____
_____	Wheat bread	_____
_____	Rye	_____
_____	Sandwich white	_____
_____	Sandwich wheat	_____
_____	Sandwich rye	_____
_____	Crumbs	_____
Sweet Rolls:		
_____	Raisin bread	_____
_____	Cinnamon	_____
_____	Butterscotch	_____
_____	Raised donuts	_____
_____	Bismark	_____
_____	Twist	_____
_____	Pecan strip	_____
_____	Stick donuts	_____
_____	Jelly donuts	_____
Meats:		
_____		_____
_____		_____
_____		_____
_____		_____
_____		_____
_____		_____
_____		_____
_____		_____
_____		_____
Fish:		
_____		_____
_____		_____
_____		_____
Miscellaneous:		
_____		_____
_____		_____
_____		_____
_____		_____
Potato Chips:		
_____		_____
_____		_____

ON HAND		ORDER
Fresh Vegetables:		
_____	Cabbage	_____
_____	Carrots	_____
_____	Cauliflower	_____
_____	Celery	_____
_____	Celery cabbage	_____
_____	Cucumbers	_____
_____	Egg plant	_____
_____	Head lettuce	_____
_____	Leaf lettuce	_____
_____	Onions	_____
_____	Parsley	_____
_____	Peppers	_____
_____	Potatoes	_____
_____	Spinach	_____
_____	Squash	_____
_____	Tomatoes	_____
Frozen Vegetables:		
_____	Asparagus	_____
_____	Green beans	_____
_____	Lima beans	_____
_____	Broccoli	_____
_____	Brussel sprouts	_____
_____	Cauliflower	_____
_____	Peas	_____
Fresh Fruits:		
_____	Apples	_____
_____	Bananas	_____
_____	Berries	_____
_____	Cantaloupe	_/_
_____	Grapefruit	_____
_____	Grapes	_____
_____	Lemons	_____
_____	Oranges	_____
_____	Peaches	_____
_____	Pineapple	_____
_____	Plums	_____
_____	Watermelon	_____
Poultry:		
_____	Chicken	_____
_____	Turkey	_____
_____	Eggs	_____
Frozen Fruits and Juices:		
_____	Apples	_____
_____	Cherries	_____
_____	G. fruit sections	_____
_____	Lemon juice	_____
_____	Orange juice	_____
_____	Peaches	_____
_____	Rhubarb	_____
_____	Strawberries	_____

FORM 9.2   *Daily purchase order form.*

503

telephone. It is printed and bound in a notebook and is simple to use, since only the amounts need to be filled in. Although this is not considered a permanent record, it is used by management as a check against deliveries to be certain that what was ordered is received. If there is no written record of what was ordered, it is difficult to prove that a delivery is or is not what was specified.

Purchase orders may be mailed to a vendor, usually for staple goods. Orders by mail should be made in triplicate with one copy retained by the person ordering and two sent to the vendor. Usually one is returned with the delivery for further check on correctness of the order.

Invoices. The delivery slip that accompanies an order is the invoice. It is prepared by the vendor and lists the items purchased with the unit price and total cost of each item purchased. This invoice or delivery slip is checked against the items received and against the purchase order for correctness. Prices, extensions, and totals are checked for accuracy of mathematics. Items from the invoice should be posted to a permanent purchase record that shows the quantity, description, unit cost, and the vendor.

Daily invoices, after being checked for correctness and approved, usually are filed in the foodservice manager's office. File folders with the names of the firms with whom the organization does business can be set up for holding the invoices until the *weekly* or *monthly statement* arrives. Statements are checked with the invoices before being signed for payment. The canceled check is the receipt for payment received.

Receiving Record. A list of goods received is recorded in a ledger-type book under the date received. No attempt is made to classify the items. It is merely a listing for verification that the order was received and on what date. Large organizations with central receiving use this record more frequently than the small foodservice operation that does its own purchasing and checking in of merchandise.

Purchase Record. This is a permanent record of date of purchase, vendor from whom goods were purchased, quantity received, and price paid for each individual item. A form for a purchase record usually is set up on individual cards for a cardexlike file drawer, or on a single, short-sheet page for a ring-binder notebook. One card or sheet is used for each item carried in stock. It may be combined

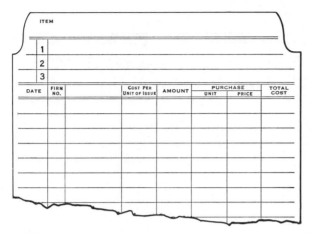

FORM   9.3   Purchase record.

with a perpetual inventory but is illustrated in Form 9.3 as a single record form.

The primary purpose and uses of this record of purchases received are: to have information on prices for costing recipes and storeroom issues and inventories, and for use in watching trends in prices as a guide to buying. Comments on the brand purchased may be noted also for future reference.

Summary of Purchases Record. This is designed to show the total amount of each item purchased each month. Quantities purchased for a given period of time can be determined quickly and easily from this record. The summary is helpful for managers when forecasting quantities of foods or supplies needed for future use.

The purchase record and purchase summary may be "housed" with a physical inventory form, as illustrated in Form 9.4. Having these three records together simplifies their use and make record keeping easy and faster than if they were in separate locations.

STORAGE AND STOREROOM CONTROL.

Storage Records. Control of goods received cannot be effective if "everyone" has access to the storeroom. The storeroom should be kept locked and authority delegated to one person to have control over the merchandise. Even if the foodservice is too small to justify the employment of a full-time storekeeper, an employee may be

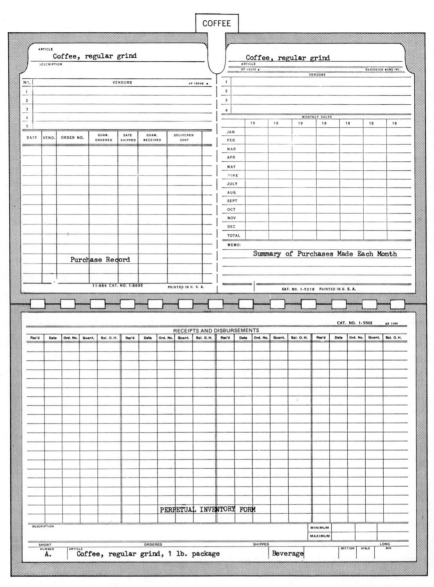

COFFEE

ARTICLE Coffee, regular grind
DESCRIPTION

NO.	VENDORS	KP 13348
1		
2		
3		
4		
5		

DATE	VEND.	ORDER NO.	QUAN. ORDERED	DATE SHIPPED	QUAN. RECEIVED	DELIVERED COST

Purchase Record

11-886 CAT. NO. 1-8895   PRINTED IN U. S. A.

Coffee, regular grind
ARTICLE
KP 15156   REMINGTON RAND INC.
VENDORS

	19	19	19	19	19	19	19
	MONTHLY SALES						
JAN							
FEB							
MAR							
APR							
MAY							
JUNE							
JULY							
AUG							
SEPT							
OCT							
NOV							
DEC							
TOTAL							
MEMO:							

Summary of Purchases Made Each Month

CAT. NO. 1-5218 PRINTED IN U. S. A.

CAT. NO. 1-5502   KP 1104

RECEIPTS AND DISBURSEMENTS

Rec'd	Date	Ord. No.	Quant.	Bal. O. H.	Rec'd	Date	Ord. No.	Quant.	Bal. O. H.	Rec'd	Date	Ord. No.	Quant.	Bal. O. H.	Rec'd	Date	Ord. No.	Quant.	Bal. O. H.

PERPETUAL INVENTORY FORM

DESCRIPTION		MINIMUM	
		MAXIMUM	

SHORT		ORDERED	SHIPPED		LONG

NUMBER	ARTICLE		SECTION	AISLE	BIN
A.	Coffee, regular grind, 1 lb. package	Beverage			

FORM 9.4   Suggested form for purchase and summary records combined with perpetual inventory.

made responsible for receiving, putting away, and issuing goods from the storeroom in addition to some other duties that can be assigned.

Each institution must decide what items will be locked in storerooms and issued on requisition and which ones will be delivered directly to the kitchen for the cook's use. This will vary from place to place, depending on the size and complexity of the organization, the amount of clerical help available, and the extent of control desired by management.

Storeroom Issue or Requisition Record. No merchandise should be removed from the storeroom except on written order of the dietitian or production manager. This written order of items to be issued from the storeroom to the kitchen is known as a storeroom issue or requisition sheet.

Storeroom Requisition

Issue following items to   Date:

_____ Department   Signed:

Item	Description	Quantity Ordered	Quantity Received	Unit Price	Total Cost	Signature of Person Checking Out Food

FORM 9.5   Requisition for storeroom issues.

All requisitions for the issuing of merchandise from the storeroom should be numbered and made out in duplicate or triplicate, as the situation requires. In large food units interdepartment requisitions (Form 9.5) may also be necessary. On the suggested form for a storeroom requisition, the items relating to cost are to be filled in by the storeroom clerk so that when the order is delivered the dietitian has the necessary data to be used in determining meal costs.

The information from the storeroom issue sheet is posted each day as a deduction from the balance on hand in the perpetual inventory. This cost of the goods issued is necessary also for determining the daily food cost report.

The Perpetual Inventory. This is a "running" record of the balance on hand for each item of goods in the storeroom. The items received are posted from the invoices and added to the previous balance on hand: the items issued are posted from the storeroom requisition sheet and are subtracted as explained. The perpetual inventory may be "housed" in different ways—a card file with cards for each item properly classified and indexed could be used by a very small foodservice such as a school foodservice. Often a cardex-type drawer file is used so each food item name can be seen at a glance. The file should be set up in the same order or classification as is used for the physical inventory form for ease in checking the two against each other. If the goods in the storeroom can be arranged in the same order, this will further facilitate inventory taking. Thus, at all times, the total quantity of each item on hand can be ascertained by a quick check of the perpetual inventory file. (Form 9.6)

Colored riders may be attached to the card to indicate items low in stock or those that need to be used at once. This is an aid to the manager when making out orders for food or supplies. One can also quickly tell what quantity of an item was used in a given time. The total of the "issued" column serves as a basis for determining quantities to purchase for the future. A third value of the perpetual inventory is that it serves as a double check against the monthly physical inventory and helps to prevent losses in stock.

In some small storerooms in which a perpetual inventory does not seem feasible, marking the price on all case goods is an aid to good cost control. The cost per dozen or case may be applied with colored crayon on the box as it is received. When cases are opened, the unit price is stamped on each can or package before it is stored on the shelves. This is a convenience for recording the price onto

SPECIFICATIONS

NO.	FIRMS		NO.	FIRMS
1			4	
2			5	
3			6	

Date	Firm	Brand	Size	Amt. Rec'd	Cost Doz	Cost Uni	Date	Firm	Brand	Size	Amt. Rec'd	Cost Doz	Cost Unit

PERPETUAL INVENTORY

Date	In	Out	Bal.	Date	In	Out	Bal.	Date	In	Out	Bal.	Date	In	Out	Bal.

PERPETUAL INVENTORY

Food Classification	Item	Description	Size	Maximum/Minimum

FORM 9.6   Perpetual inventory card.

the storeroom requisitions at the time the issues are made, and also provides a means for quickly distinguishing like items of different prices. This system is not limited to use by small organizations but is equally efficient in any foodservice.

The Physical Inventory. This is an actual count of all goods on hand at the end of the accounting period, usually a calendar month. If possible, two people work together to take inventory, one of whom should be in a supervisory position. When time permits, the director may occasionally participate in the taking of the physical inventories. There is no better way of keeping informed about storeroom control. For best control the storeroom personnel should not have sole responsibility for this activity. If there were a tendency toward dishonesty, it would be simple to juggle figures to cover up pilferage. As one person counts the number of each item on hand, he calls the information to the other person, who properly enters it on the inventory form. Prices may also be recorded on the inventory sheet at this time to facilitate the costing procedure.

If the institution keeps a perpetual inventory file, the physical inventory count may be recorded or checked against the total or balance on hand for each item at the time the count is made. This provides a simple means of comparing the two inventories, which should be in agreement. Minor differences may be expected, but major discrepancies should be investigated. Carelessness in filling requisitions or in bookkeeping are the most common reasons for these errors. After the physical inventory has been taken and reconciled with the perpetual inventory, it is costed and the total value determined. This inventory figure is used to calculate the "cost of food used" in the profit and loss statement.

The procedure for taking a physical inventory is simplified by having a form set up and duplicated or printed, on which are listed the items normally carried in stock and their unit sizes. This eliminates the need for handwriting the items each time inventory is taken. As noted previously, for convenience and efficiency in recording, the items on the inventory form should be classified and listed in the same order as they are arranged in the storeroom and in the perpetual inventory. Space should be left on the form between each grouping to allow for new items to be added as they may be purchased. The suggested food-stores index and classification of perishable foods given on page 475 has been used to develop the inventory sheet suggested in Form 9.7.

Inventories of food in the kitchen and the refrigerators in the

The Student Union Food Division

Physical Inventory ＿＿＿＿＿＿ 19 ＿＿   Page 1

Classification	Item	Unit	Quantity	Unit Price	Total Cost
Beverages:					
	Coffee	14 oz pkg			
	Hot chocolate powder	¼#			
	Tea, iced	1 gal			
	Tea, individual	100/Box			
Cereals, Prepared:					
	All Bran	1# Box			
	All Bran, individual	50/cs			
	Assorted individual	50/carton			
	Barley	1# pkg			
	Corn Flakes	100/cs			
	Cream of Wheat	1# 12 oz box			
	Hominy grits	1# 8 oz box			
	Oats, Rolled	3# box			
	Ralstons	1# 6 oz box			
	Rice, white	1# box			
	Wheatena				
Cereals and Flour:					
	Cornmeal	Bulk/lb			

TOTAL PAGE 1 ＿＿＿＿＿

FORM 9.7   Physical inventory sheet.

511

preparation units are usually not included when determining the daily food cost. However, an inventory at the end of the month should include all stock on hand in the kitchens as well as that in the storerooms. It is customary in foodservices to use the original purchase cost of the items instead of the current market price in calculating the value of the inventory. The practice of marking the unit purchase price on the package of incoming goods aids in this procedure.

Both perpetual and physical inventories should be kept of china, glassware, and silverware. These items should be revalued at least once a year on a basis of physical inventory, although often it is desirable to revalue them at more frequent intervals. Other equipment and furniture, such as that of kitchen and dining room, may be divided into groups and an inventory taken once each year. The rate of depreciation depends on the kind of equipment.

Management of inventory both as to quantities to keep on hand and the security methods used to control the stock influences overall foodservice costs. Each organization should decide on maximum and minimum quantities desirable to maintain in the storeroom. This decision is based on storage facilities and capacities, delivery patterns, and the volume of business. Established standards for quantities desirable to keep on hand aid in purchasing—both as to quantity to order and when to order (that is, when the stock approaches the minimum).

One should remember that carrying an inventory is costly and some thought should be given to the total value of such an investment. "Carrying costs normally range from 15 to 35 percent of the inventory value, but can be as high as 50 percent. Fast food operations with a minimum of inventory and rapid turnover may be as low as two to four percent of the inventory value." [19] Buchanan names the following elements usually included in inventory carrying costs:

Obsolescence of items no longer to be used.

Deterioration and spoilage.

Taxes imposed on inventories in some states.

Insurance on this asset.

[19] Robert D. Buchanan, *"How To Up Your Profits and Productivity with Inventory Management,"* Foodservice Marketing, 36, *56 (September 1974).*

Storage costs of space, personnel, materials handling, records and utilities.

Capital invested in inventory prevents use of money for other purposes.

An inventory turnover ratio may be used as a guide for evaluating one's investment in inventory. Fay, Rhoades, and Rosenblatt [20] state that "Inventory turnover ratios are designed to relate the size of inventories to the sales volume of the business. This relationship shows the number of times that the inventory is turned, that is, used up and replenished, during the year. Inventory turnovers are calculated by dividing the total cost of goods sold by the average inventory for the period." As an example,

$$\text{Food inventory turnover} = \frac{\text{Total cost of food sold}}{\text{Average food inventory}} : \frac{\$400,000}{\$16,000} = 25$$

(25 is the number of times per year that the inventory turns over)

In analyzing this figure, remember that "a low turnover when combined with a food cost higher than budgeted may be an indication of poor sales forecasting and purchasing policies and waste through spoilage and leftovers. However, a high turnover could indicate that the inventory is too small and the operation continually runs out of menu items which can lead to lost business through dissatisfied customers." [21]

Foodservice managers should evaluate their own storeroom and inventory procedures and analyze this aspect of financial responsibility in light of desired profit or service goals.

PRODUCTION AND SERVICE RECORDS

Menu. Records important for controlling costs in food production and service are the menu, standardized recipes, and a production

[20] Clifford T. Fay, Jr., Richard C. Rhoades, and Robert L. Rosenblatt, Managerial Accounting for the Hospitality Service Industries, Wm. C. Brown, Dubuque, Iowa, p. 127, 1971.

[21] Clifford T. Fay, Jr., Richard C. Rhoades, and Robert L. Rosenblatt, Managerial Accounting for the Hospitality Service Industries, Wm. C. Brown, Dubuque, Iowa, p. 128, 1971.

Food Code Number	Description	Cost/ Buy	Buy Unit	Buy C.N.	Issue Unit	Conv.	Cost/ Issue	lb/Issue Unit	Issue C.N.	Cost/ A.P. lb.
Dairy										
2200	Eggs Grade A Large	$10.80	Case	251	Doz.	30	$ .360	1.500	373	.240
2500	Milk, whole 5 gal	4.05 1.0125	5 gal 1 gal	176 0.2531/qt	5-gal can 0.063 mp	1	4.050	43.200	176	.094
Fruit										
3163	Pineapple, (6) crushed	$ 6.48	Case	531	Can	6	$1.080	6.690	131	.161
3710	Apples, Jonathans, Fresh 113 ct.	6.10	Crate	352	Each	113	.054	.332	270	.163
Vegetables										
4420	Lettuce, head 24 ct. Calif.	$ 4.50	Crate	355	Crate	1	4.50	40.000	355	.112
4410	Carrots	1.75	Sack	471	Sack	1	1.75	25.000	471	.070
Groceries										
5510	Gelatin, cherry 12/24 oz	$ 9.54	Case	319	Box	24	.397	1.500	319	.265

FIGURE 9.8 Sample items from computer printout sheet of food inventory; to be used for food costing, either manually or by computer.

report. The first two of these have been discussed and illustrated in Chapter 2. Both should be considered permanent records, since they are important tools for reference and forecasting.

Costed recipes should be updated frequently so that the production manager has current information on the cost of the food that is to be served according to the menu. This is one task that can be accomplished quickly by computer after the data have been collected and programmed. Figures 9.8 and 9.9 are examples of forms suitable for data input for recipe costing by computer.

Manual costing of recipes is slow and arduous, but once the initial task is completed, it is simple to recheck prices and recipe costs each time before the recipe is used. It is especially important to do so for items that are high in cost and whose prices fluctuate often.

SNELL HALL	OREGON STATE UNIVERSITY
09/30/74	DEPARTMENT OF INSTITUTION MANAGEMENT

RECIPE COSTING

170100
CLAM CHOWDER
DINNER/SUPPER   SOUP   NUMBER OF SERVINGS 100

ATTRIBUTES—   WHITE   MILD   LIQUID   hot
               4 DAYS SEPARATION

ESTIMATED—   WEIGHT OF A SERVING   7.69 OZ
               VOLUME   6.00 FL OZ
               RECIPE YIELD   75.00 LB

Food No.	Ingredients	Quantity	Unit	Weight Cooked	Cost/ Ingredient
2500	Milk, whole	3.00	gallon	12.00	1.125
2400	Margarine	3.75	pound	3.75	.560
5290	Flour	1.75	pound	1.75	.119
4354	Potatoes frozen	3.00	pound	3.00	.630
4426	Onions chopped	2.50	pound	2.50	.133
1200	Clams canned	28.75	pound	28.75	12.123
0	Water	3.00	gallon	10.80	0
5482	Salt	1.00	ounce	.06	.002
5470	Pepper	7.50	gram	.02	.016
Calculated recipe yield		62–63 lb	Total food cost		$14.71
Calculated weight of a serving		10.02 oz	Food cost per serving		$ .15

FIGURE   9.9   Recipe costing data card for clam chowder.

Costed recipes that are updated show at once whether a given dish is economically possible for a menu of a certain price range. Precosting a menu through use of standardized recipes will give a good indication of the probable food cost for that meal.

Standardized Recipes and Menus. These are used for instituting a precost, precontrol system that minimizes food costs and helps managers to keep within desired budgets. Standardized recipes are costed; the cost of the menu is then determined by adding the cost of all recipes to be used to the cost of the other "free" foods such as butter, cream and sugar, condiments, and sauces. Precosting allows opportunity for menu changes *before* production if costs are out of line instead of finding out after the food has been served that the cost of it was excessive. One must remember, however, that standard procedures in cooking, portioning, and serving must be followed or a precosting system will be of little value. Notations on menus about their acceptability serve as a control for future menu planning and forecasting of quantities to be prepared.

Production Schedule. This record of amounts of foods to be prepared, the resulting quantities of cooked foods available to be served, and the actual number of servings obtained from a given amount of food, together with a list of quantities left over, provides precise, specific information on which to base forecasting. Form 9.8 is an example of one such record. The more closely the food manager can predict the number of each item that will be selected by the diners and control the number of portions obtained from given quantities

PRODUCTION SCHEDULE

Name of Institution:.. Date:...

Number to Prepare	Menu Item	Quantity to Prepare	Yield	Amount Left	Servings Used

FORM 9.8   Sample production schedule form.

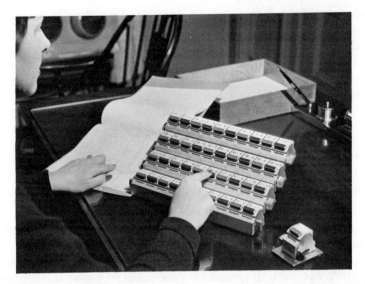

FIGURE   9.10   Multiple tally machines give accurate count of portions served, help locate waste and losses, and tabulate food preferences. Courtesy, Denominator Company.

of prepared food, the more highly successful financially will be the department. All information that can be acquired about cooking and preparation losses and yields will help the manager to become more skilled at controlling food costs. These records provide data for control; it is management's responsibility to study and use them to improve operations.

Menu Tally. Commercial foodservices especially keep a tally of menu items sold. This may be prepared by the cashier from the sales slips as customers pay their bills or from a tally machine as shown in Fig. 9.10. This tally may be checked with the production record of number of servings used, which gives some information about, and control over the food produced and not sold. For tight cost control, the accountability for leftover, unsold portions and use of them to bring in additional income is not to be ignored. Such records also provide information for forecasting amounts to be prepared in the future.

DINING ROOM AND PATIENT COUNT RECORDS

A record of numbers of people served, classified into suitable groupings, is used for many purposes. First, it provides a base to predict numbers to be served in the future. For example, such records over a period of time will provide information on percentage of expected absenteeism in a college residence hall for each meal of the day and for each day of the week; the dietitian will know more accurately the number of patrons to expect on "football" Saturdays when the game is played at home or away; the restaurant operator soon learns the dining-out habits of his customers and can better predict the numbers to expect when certain conventions are meeting in town; the hospital administrative dietitian soon learns from this record the expected bed occupancy at various times of the year and the numbers of patients on special and regular diets, as well as numbers of staff, employees, and visitors who may eat in the cafeteria.

Census Record. A form for recording the meal count is called a census record. It can be designed to meet the needs of each individual foodservice operation. It is desirable to have the information for the entire accounting period on one sheet of paper if possible. The page could be divided horizontally into the number of days in the operating period, vertically into the meal periods per day with a breakdown or classification of groups to be served under each meal. Form 9.9 is an example of a meal census form for a hospital. If more detailed information is desired, the patient meals could be separated into regular and modified diets, and personnel meals could be divided into staff and employee meals, or other groupings as deemed

MONTHLY MEAL CENSUS												
Hospital												
	Patient Meals					Personnel Meals					Patient and Personnel	
				Total Meals					Total Meals		Total Meals	
Date	Break-fast	Lunch	Dinner	Today	To Date	Break-fast	Lunch	Dinner	Today	To Date	Today	To Date
1												
2												
3												
—												
30												
31												

FORM 9.9   Meal census summary sheet.

desirable by the dietitian. This record then serves as a valuable guide for planning amounts of food to buy and prepare without fear of underproduction or costly overproduction. The meal census record also is vital in determining per meal costs, average sales per person and, as in some of the other research studies previously mentioned, as a means for setting operating standards.

Special Meals Records. A record of details of *special meal functions* is necessary for foodservices that cater to special groups in addition to their own regular meal service. A hospital, college residence hall, or industrial food service may be requested to cater for an occasional special group, whereas it is a common occurrence for several parties to be scheduled for meals at the same time in a hotel or student union. Each may have a different menu and demand specialized service, for which they pay accordingly. In all cases it is necessary to have definite policies and procedures outlined that can be followed through from the planning to the billing of the charges in order to insure successful and satisfactory operation. Form 9.10 is a typical agreement form for special group meetings and meals with record of price and total charges.

CASH TRANSACTION

A permanent record of cash transactions, both from sales or income and from expenditures or disbursements, in an absolute essential in accountability for the financial management of the foodservice department. Even small school lunchrooms may handle cash sales to pupils, teachers or outside guests, and a businesslike procedure should be set up for an accounting of this money.

A cash register is recommended for every institution. It is not only a relatively safe place for money during serving hours, but it also gives accurate data on the total number of sales and total cash received. Complex organizations may have a multipurpose register to provide additional data, as shown in Fig. 9.11.

Other specialized cost registers may be designed for individual foodservice establishments. One hospital [22] reports obtaining a register that was adapted for their needs that:

Provides a total customer count, regardless of the type of payment.

---

[22] *L. L. Walker and Morris H. Gunter, "Controlling Cafeteria Costs,"* Hospitals, JAHA, 44, *122 (August 16, 1970).*

College Union

Organization _____   Function _____

Date _____ Time _____   Arranged by _____

Room _____   Address _____

Number Guaranteed _____ Served _____   Phone No. _____

Price _____   Booked by _____ Date _____

Total Charge _____   Approved by _____

Menu	Details
	Setup
	Speaker's Table
	Flowers
	Music
	Public Address
	Tickets
	Misc.

Guarantees are not subject to change less than 24 hours in advance of party. We are prepared to serve 10% in excess of the number guaranteed.

Copies: Manager
Food Director
Catering
Maintenance
Kitchen
Accounting

Accepted _____

Union Office _____

FORM 9.10   *Data for a special meal. Courtesy, Union Building Food Service, Michigan State University.*

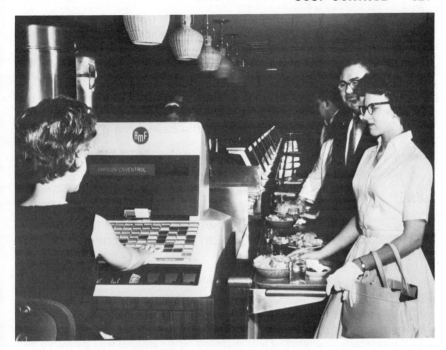

FIGURE 9.11   *Electronic development system registers customer's "tab" with a printed itemized ticket and gives correct change automatically. Food items are registered on an inventory control board while simultaneously itemizing the bill. Courtesy, American Machine and Foundry Company.*

Adds the total number of servings for each type of food, such as entrees, vegetables, desserts, salads, and beverages.

Accumulates and prints the dollar volume for each type of food.

Itemizes and prints a receipt for each customer.

Calculates automatically the change to be returned to the customer and prints the transaction on the receipt.

Accepts four separate ledger cards for meals purchased by guests and by personnel in several different categories.

Prints a detailed audit tape of each transaction and uses a system of ascending numbers for each customer. A symbol system prints on the audit tape to record the type of transaction, such as cash, meal ticket, or ledger card.

Accumulates a total customer count of those who paid by cash and a count by number of those customers who received meals other than by the cash system.

Accepts the student meal ticket system and prints a receipt for the meal purchased, prints a new value on the ticket, accepts portions of two or more meal tickets if the tickets do not have sufficient value for the meal selected, and accepts one meal ticket and cash if one ticket does not have sufficient value for the meal selected.

In discussing the benefits derived from the use of this equipment, Walker and Gunter noted that:

Although it seems elaborate and complicated, the cash register did not detain the cafeteria line when it was installed. The machine was delivered two weeks before it was placed in the cafeteria. This period was sufficient to train operators, write procedures, and provide training for other hospital personnel.

After each meal, the cash register is cleared and information is recorded in duplicate on a summary form. The first copy is retained by the food service manager; the second copy is sent to the business office and ultimately to the hospital comptroller and is used as the control and the record for cash from the cafeteria.

This total system gives the food service manager accurate and necessary information to make management decisions regarding the kinds of products to serve, staffing patterns, and pricing, and the hospital comptroller has the information necessary for cost accounting and for an accurate control system for cash.

Cash should be proved at the end of each day when the register is emptied and the cash report is made, regardless of the number of times during the day that a cash register reading may be taken.

Cash Receipts Record. The amount of cash received is entered on a form known as a cash receipts record. Form 9.11 is an example of one for use in a college cafeteria where the cash is proved after every meal period. Totals from this daily record can be posted to an accumulative cash-receipts record. This may be a simple two-column cash book, one column for the daily income figure and the other for the total to date for the month. If desired, another column for recording the income for the same day last year may be added as a good means for comparing operations from year to year.

Sources of income other than from cash sales should be classified and recorded also to give complete details about the income.

Form 7158

FOOD SERVICE

REPORT OF CASH RECEIVED

Report No._____

Dep't. No._____

Page_____of_____

Period from_____to_____Incl.

_____
(Unit)

Present Reading	Less: Previous Reading	Difference	Void	Register Sales	Tax on Register	Over Short	Description	Validated Receipt	Code
							REGISTER 1		
							TOTAL 1		
							REGISTER 1		
							TOTAL 2		
							REGISTER		
							TOTAL 1		
							REGISTER		
							TOTAL 2		
							REGISTER		
							TOTAL 1		
							REGISTER		
							TOTAL 2		
							TOTALS		

Receipt No.	Received from (Name and Description)	Date of Charge or Period Covered	Received on Account (Tax Incl.)	Other Receipts		
	TOTAL CASH RECEIVED					

Signed_____
Supt. or Manager

Total Deposit_____

FORM 9.11   Cash report form. To be filled in by cashiers using cash registers.

Special parties served, supplementary vending machine or snack bar sales, sale of bottles, boxes, and fats may constitute other sources of income. Many states have a sales tax that must be collected from the customer and accounted for separately.

If money is taken from the cash register for any purpose except making change, a receipt of this is written on a *petty cash voucher* form, which is placed in the register. This is a simple receipt showing the date, amount, item of expense or purchase, name of firm and signature of the person receiving the money, and the signature of the person removing the money from the register. This record is essential, not only for good control of money in the cash register, but also for purposes of balancing and accounting for cash at the end of the day. A typical voucher used in a school foodservice is shown in Form 9.12. Cash usually is banked daily into a checking account, and major payments are made by check.

A record of *cash disbursements* for all expenses may be kept on columnar paper with headings for each classification of expenses, such as food purchases, labor, supplies, rent, and utilities. As payments are made, the date of payment, name of firm, total amount paid, check number, and the distribution of the payment under proper headings are entered.

Even though an organization may have a central business office where checks are written to pay the bills, bank the money, and prepare financial reports, it is to the advantage of the food manager to have his own records of income and expenses so that he has infor-

---

Office of Lunchroom Manager

PETTY CASH VOUCHER

School _____   Date _____ 19 _____

      Amount: _____

      Paid to: _____

      For: _____

Approved by: _____   Received by: _____
      (Principal/Manager)

FORM 9.12   Petty cash voucher form.

mation available in his own office at all times to which quick reference can be made for future planning and decision making.

OPERATING AND MAINTENANCE

Laundry Records. Institutions not operating their own laundries should keep a record giving detailed information of the number of items sent to and returned from the commercial laundry and the costs involved. This record is planned to give a separate accounting of each department within the institution if laundry is sent from more than one department. If the institution operates its own laundry, this record should be kept and, in addition, checks should be made on operating costs such as wages, overhead, and outlay for soap and other cleaning materials. As a check on the quality of work, many institution laundries also make a daily test of tensile strength loss, maintenance of whiteness, and the completeness of soil removal.

Other Controllable Costs. A separate written record of each item of expense provides a ready source of information for the manager who is watching and analyzing cost trends with his department. As monthly statements for utilities, administrative and office expenses, repairs and maintenance, and other charges for operating the foodservice are paid, the total for each is posted to a ledger account sheet. Deviations from previous months can readily be noted. Although the expense may be perfectly legitimate, the manager will be aware of it, be able to justify it, and be certain that the effects of the expenditure will not be out of line with budget allocations.

PERSONNEL COST CONTROL RECORDS

A multiplicity of records are required of the foodservice director today. Those related to selection, scheduling, appraisals, and other employment-related details have been discussed in Chapter 8. Records related to labor cost are included here.

Time Card-Payroll Record. Included in the personnel records, which are important for financial accounting and control, is some device such as the time clock recorder, which affords an impersonal and accurate report of the hours each worker has spent on duty. The use of such a recorder is particularly helpful in checking the time spent by employees working at irregular hours, as is common with student help, although it should be used by all employees. From this record payrolls are prepared.

The scheduling of each of the entire staff by hours of the day is a valuable record for use in the control of personnel. Such a record, in graphic form, is shown on page 527.

Records of various types, including payroll data and payroll checks, are now generated by automatic data processing methods in many institutions. For organizations that have access to computer time, savings can be substantial through use of this "tool" of management over the labor hours devoted to preparing these reports manually.

Analysis of labor expenditures may be undertaken several different ways; one of them will assist managers to evaluate the situation and decide where corrective action, if needed, should be taken. One such method is a graphic presentation of labor hours worked in relation to sales by hour of day. Figure 9.12 illustrates how such a graph was prepared and used by one commercial foodservice operation. Noting peak time of sales may aid in better scheduling of employees' time; ways of spreading the flow of customers to level out the peaks may be sought to relieve those times of pressure in the kitchen and to give better customer service.

The usual analysis of labor cost is to express it as a percentage to sales (income) ratio. Percentages serve as a good guide to trends, but many managers believe that dollars mean more. As income levels change, so do labor cost percentages, since labor cost is relatively fixed. Stokes [23] points out that:

Like food cost, the labor cost drops percentagewise when prices are increased. Increases or decreases in volume affect food and labor cost percentages quite differently. To illustrate this point, let us assume a food service where the average check is $1.00, the food cost 40 percent, and the daily labor cost is $350. The effect of volume on cost percentages would be as shown below.

Effect of Volume Upon Food and Labor Cost Percentages

Meals Per Day	1,000	%	800	%	1,200	%
Sales @ $1.00 Avg. Check	$1,000	100%	$800	100%	$1,200	100%
Food Cost @ 40%	400	40	320	40	480	40
Gross Profit	$ 600	60%	$480	60%	$ 720	60%
Labor Cost	350	35%	350	43.75%	350	29.16%

[23] John W. Stokes, *How To Manage A Restaurant or Institutional Food Service, Second Edition,* Wm. C. Brown, Dubuque, Iowa, p. 268, 1974.

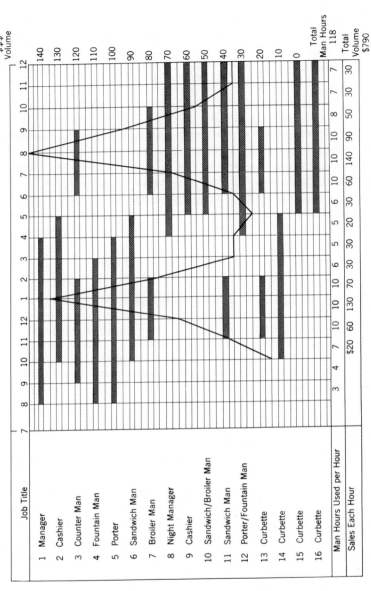

FIGURE 9.12 An evaluation of employees' time schedule in relation to volume of sales in one restaurant. Courtesy, Ohio State Restaurant Association.

This demonstrates that food cost generally remains the same, percentage-wise, regardless of volume. The labor cost percentage, on the other hand, increases as volume drops and decreases as volume rises. In other words, labor cost percentage tends to vary inversely with the sales volume.

Another analysis may be made that shows the labor cost of a department in relation to sales from food produced in that department. For the nonproduction units, administrative and supervisory, sanitation and warehousing, and service, a percentage of their payroll cost would be prorated on some logical basis to each of the production departments and added to their labor cost to get a true total. Or, for easier calculations and comparison, only the payroll costs of the department may be used.

For more detailed analysis of labor costs, see the references at the end of this chapter.

In summary, it should be reemphasized that:

Each foodservice organization is unique in and of itself. The customers served by the operation have a "group" or "mass" taste all their own; the foodservice staff at each operation has its own special character. Because of this, accurate long-term records of all major, as well as some of the minor, activities of the foodservice organization should be kept. Such records will not only serve as research material on which to base future activities of the organization, but also will provide for continuity when a changeover in management takes place." [24]

REPORTS: A MANAGEMENT TOOL

Accountability for expenditures made with the company's money is not complete by merely keeping records. The data and information provided by the type of records just described will be of no value unless they are utilized by managers in ways to evaluate and improve the financial situation of the department.

Records of past events, the historical data of the company or organization, become the basis of planning for the future. Forecasting needs, probable activities and their expected costs, and the sources of anticipated income should be prepared in an organized, orderly way. Such a plan is known as a budget.

[24] Raymond B. Peddersen, Arthur C. Avery, Ruth D. Richard, James R. Osenton, and Harry H. Pope, Jule Wilkinson, Editor, Increasing Productivity in Foodservice, Cahners, Boston, p. 29, 1973.

BUDGETS

A budget has been defined in many different ways but, essentially, it is "an estimate of future needs, arranged according to an orderly basis, covering some or all of the activities of an enterprise for a definite period of time." [25] Ordinarily it is thought of as financial planning for the future, but budgeting should include other forecasts, such as number of meals to be served and labor hours required. Budgets are made up of factual data from past records, the anticipated income, and a consideration of any changes to take place that may affect future operations, all in light of the policies of the organization.

Too often the term "budget" has carried the connotation of a "statistical strait jacket" or of curtailed spending and, therefore, of undesirability. This should not be true; instead, a budget should be viewed as a flexible management tool, used to compare with actual expenditures and to give a basis for control. A budget has been likened to a road map that gives an accurate route to be followed and serves as a guide to the traveler. However, there are many alternate routes from which to choose to arrive at the same destination. Some routes may be devious and costly; others are direct and easily followed. Whatever the choice, those involved must be able to justify their decision and make certain that funds are available to pay the cost. The manager of a foodservice needs a budget just as a traveler needs a map to indicate the general direction and the important points along the way.

For budget planning, all of those in the organization with decision-making power should be involved. Loew [26] says:

You may have mixed emotions on committees, but for budgeting, the committee is a must. It gives each member an understanding of the impact of his actions on others. Committees should include representation from each major area or division of the company. . . . Each area or division head would have the responsibility of approving and presenting the budget for his area to the budget committee, and would also have the responsibility of reporting to the committee on variances from the budget in his area.

[25] George R. Terry, Principles of Management, Richard D. Irwin, Homewood, Illinois, p. 561, 1960.

[26] John H. Loew, "The Selling of the Budget," Administrative Management, 33 (4), 72 (1972). Republished with permission from Administrative Management, copyright © 1972 by Geyer-McAllister Publications, Inc., New York.

Small foodservices may have only two or three persons involved. However, adequate time and thought must go into this planning activity in order to make the budget realistic and "workable." The following steps are ordinarily followed in planning the *financial budget.*

1. Record every source of income. The income is the sum total of all earnings for a definite period of time, such as 1 year. It may represent earnings on capital resources as well as cash from sales. The income anticipated for the ensuing year is based on the total income during the past year, allowances being made for variations caused by changing conditions. The following form is one suggested for a college foodservice for recording income items, the figures from actual operations during the last year, anticipated increases and decreases, and the final anticipated income.

Sources of Income	Income Past Period	Anticipated Increase	Anticipated Decrease	Anticipated Income
Board fees				
Cafeteria receipts				
Guest meals				
Special meals				
Catering				
Special food orders				
Miscellaneous				
Total				

2. Classify the items of expense. Expenses of the foodservice usually include food, labor, overhead, and operating costs. These major divisions are then broken down into individual items for which payment is made. The grouping of separate items of expense under certain main headings is desirable in order to obtain a complete picture of the dispersion of expense for the service.

The separate headings under which the items are grouped will vary somewhat with the kind of institution. College residence halls, which must pay every cost of operation, may include all or part of the items shown on Form 9.13.

UNIVERSITY RESIDENCE HALLS, CAMPUS A

BUDGET WORK SHEET-INCOME AND EXPENSE

	Estimated Last Year		Actual Last Year		Estimated Next Year	
	Total	%	Total	%	Total	%

Income

Expenses
1. Food

2. Salaries and wages
   Regular employees
   Student or part-time employees
   Social security tax
   Other taxes
   Fringe benefits

   Total

3. Services
   Laundry
   Utilities
   Telephone
   Exterminator
   Garbage and trash disposal

   Total

4. Supplies, repairs, and maintenance
   Cleaning supplies
   Paper supplies
   Office supplies
   Equipment repairs
   Miscellaneous supplies
   Physical plant

   Total

5. Housing
   Amortization or rent
   Taxes
   Interest
   Depreciation
   Insurance
   Repairs

Excess of income over expenses

FORM 9.13   *Income and detailed expense budget plan.*

A suggested chart of accounts for a commercial foodservice has been prepared for the National Restaurant Association.[27]

3. Study the operations of the department based on previous records. A thorough knowledge of all of the operations of the department is essential before accurate forecasting can be achieved. Keiser and Kallio [28] list the following as desirable information to collect and review while budget making:

The Department's actual operating and budget variance figures from previous years.

The department's goals.

The department's sales experience, sales reports, and sales statistics.

The department's future operating policies.

National and local economic conditions.

Sales and expense trends.

Menu prices, customer selection, portion sizes, and food cost per portion.

Such payroll statistics as the number of employees, their duties, their hours, and their wage rates.

4. Set priorities and make decisions. In establishing budgetary priorities the director should weigh the relative desires and needs of each unit, search for nonessentials, decide if any items may be provided at a lower cost, keep in mind the needs for upkeep and expansion of the plant, and provide for the development and increase of personnel. Even though the income may remain approximately the same year after year, careful appraisal of past expenses should be made whenever a new budget is prepared, in order to prevent overspending for some items to the neglect of others quite as important. In a period of rising costs some allowance should be made to take care of

[27] Uniform System of Accounts for Restaurants, *prepared by Horwath and Horwath for the National Restaurant Association, Fourth Revised Edition, Chicago, 1968.*

[28] *James Keiser and Elmer Kallio,* Controlling and Analyzing Costs in Food Service Operations, *Wiley, New York, p. 237, 1974.*

replacement of furnishings and equipment, since depreciation is calculated on the original cost of these items.

The *financial budget* must reflect the objectives and policies of the organization for which it is planned. The school foodservice that has as its objective the serving of good food at a minimum cost to the pupils may be required by the board of education to pay for food, labor, and laundry only. In such a case, the percentage of the income spent for food is, rightly, very high. The foodservice budget of a college residence hall that is being paid for by retirement of bonds from income is necessarily quite different from one whose physical plant and equipment are gifts. A hotel dining room that must show a profit to its stockholders and the industrial cafeteria maintained for the benefit of employees will each plan a budget as the first requisite of sound business procedures. In each situation, the proportion of the income spent for various expense items will vary with the size and type, objectives, and policies of the individual foodservice.

The budget planning committee has responsibility for making decisions as to what expense items can be included in the budget with a fixed income, or how the income can be expanded, if it is a variable income, to cover the cost of the items of expense deemed essential. Foreward-looking managers establish priorities and plan an orderly way of achieving these goals, even if it means looking beyond the next year's budget.

5. Write the budget for presentation. There is no established format for the formal write-up of the budget. It contains the listing of expected income, the classification of sources, and the classified list of expense items. If the budget is to be forwarded to a higher administrator for approval, an explanation of items included and a justification for them are usually attached.

6. Use the budget. Regardless of the system used for budgeting, it can be stated firmly that if after the budget is made it is not used to compare with actual expenditures, the value of the budget is lost. Form 9.14 is an example of a comparative statement showing actual costs against budgeted ones. This statement provides a ready tool for further evaluation of operations by the manager.

Name of Food Service

Month _____, 19 ____

	Number of Meals	Food Cost		Payroll Expense		Other Costs and Expenses	
	Total for month	Total for month	Per meal served	Total for month	Per meal served	Total for month	Per meal served
Budgeted							
Actual							
Over + − Under							
Cumulative for Year to Date							
Budgeted							
Actual							
Over + − Under							

FORM 9.14 Comparative statement of budgeted and actual expenditures.

The Concept of Budgetary Control. Operations controls may be exercised only where a comparison is made. Performance can only be determined to be satisfactory or unsatisfactory relative to a predetermined standard. This budgetary control process consists of three steps.

1. Comparison of actual operating results with planned results to disclose significant variations.

2. Detailed analyses to determine the problem and its probable cause.

3. Prompt action to correct the problem.

Comparison of actual operating results with those planned is the bridge connecting profit planning and budgetary control.[29]

[29] Clifford T. Fay, Jr., Richard C. Rhoades, and Robert L. Rosenblatt, Managerial Accounting for the Hospitality Service Industries, Wm. C. Brown, Dubuque, Iowa, p. 431, 1971.

Labor Budget. Many institutions prepare a labor budget, that is, a forecast of labor hours needed. Such a budget is more often planned on a weekly or monthly basis rather than for a fiscal year. A labor-hour budget outlines the number of hours of labor to be scheduled each day by employee category and meal period. It is based or planned on predicted volume of business and a standard of productivity determined by the manager for his own employees. Once the number of labor hours needed has been decided on, the wage rate is multiplied by the total hours for each employee category to give a total labor-cost figure. This, of course, does not include any of the fringe benefits to be added to the total cost of labor, but these figures do give support for budgetary requests for wages and salaries. See Chapter 8 for additional consideration of labor needs and standards.

Nutritional Budget. Institutions providing three meals a day to the same group of people, and other foodservices also, could well exercise nutritional control as well as cost control by establishing their own standard for expenditure of the food dollar. The management of the food purchase dollar through use of a food group classification system such as shown on Form 9.15 serves as a guide to nutritional adequacy of meals served. Dietitians as well as other foodservice managers are vitally interested in this aspect of food expenditures and carefully watch the distribution of the food dollar spent for food in the various groups. An established standard for each category of food, such as meat, fish and poultry, fruits and vegetables, cereals and breadstuffs, fats and oils, and so on, provides a measure against which to evaluate actual expenditure.

To keep food costs within the desired percentage range, it is necessary to establish simple, effective control measures that are economically sound, neither entailing undue expense nor creating any interference with the kitchen routine. One measure is to serve a set menu, nutritionally adequate. When a fixed menu is served, it is to be anticipated that a stable relationship will exist between daily cost of each item and the total. For example, in a school foodservice, 18 percent of the total food cost may be spent for dairy products and 35 to 40 percent for meat, and there will be little fluctuation in this ratio from period to period. However, in commercial cafeterias or wherever an a la carte menu is offered and there is a changing clientele, a constant relationship between the sales of a given food group and total sales may not develop, and analysis of the sales on this basis is not a valid means of food cost control.

Daily Food—Cost Distribution Sheet

NORTH HALL

Month of _____ 19 ___

Date	Meats, Poultry, Fish	Eggs	Milk, Cream, Ice Cream, Cheese	Butter	Fresh Fruit and Vege- tables	Pota- toes	Frozen Fruit and Vege- tables	Canned and Dried Fruit and Vege- tables	Cereals and Cereal Prod- ucts	Fats	Staples	Daily Total Cost	Total Cumu- lative Cost	Aver- age Daily Food Cost
1														
2														
3														
...														
30														
31														
Totals														
Percentages														
Cumulative Cost														

FORM 9.15   Food-cost summary sheet showing distribution of the food dollar spent for various foods by groups.

In times of high inflation and fluctuating food prices, higher-cost items such as meat may be substituted in the menu with other foods to provide nutrients required, but at a lower cost. Therefore, standards for percentage distribution of food expenditures do change.

An interesting comparison between Parsonson and Bryan's findings from an early study [30] made of the distribution of the food dollar spent for nutritionally adequate meals (higher than recommended allowances of the National Research Council) is shown below.[31]

	1951 (Bryan) (%)	1963 (Parsonson) (%)
Meat, fish, poultry, eggs, cheese	36	40.6
Milk and ice cream	20	13.2
Fresh vegetables and juices	22	26.0
Fats and oils	6	6.1
Cereals, bread, and staples	16	14.1
	100	100.0

The higher percentage for the meat, fish, and poultry, and fruits, vegetables, and juices in later figures is offset by the lower percentage for milk and ice cream, and the bread, cereals, and staples group of 12 years earlier. This points at the need for changing the standards from time to time and for continual evaluation of the situation.

The values of budget planning and of the budget are many. Those involved in this planning help to establish priorities and so are usually cooperative in staying with the limits that they were responsible for setting. Budget planning forces those in management positions to consider seriously the future directions and development of the department and to analyze past performance. It requires looking at specific needs of the total department and to equitably allocate available funds to the various units within it.

[30] Violet M. Parsonson, "A Comparison of Food and Labor Costs on the Basis of Quantities Used and Type of Service Provided in a Men's and a Women's University Dining Hall," unpublished master's thesis, Washington State University, 1963.
[31] Mary deGarmo Bryan, "Food Service Picture in College Field in 1951," College and University Business, 11 (10), 45–47 (1951).

A budget is used as a goal for achieving the desired income level for profit-making organizations and as a measure for control by comparing actual operations against those anticipated (budgeted) to reveal deviations from the standard desired. If differences are found, that should trigger action of some sort on the part of the manager to correct or justify the situation.

Finally, a budget helps to prevent problems from arising that could cause financial chaos: problems relating to what the organization can or cannot afford to purchase, for which unit a purchase should be made, whether or not salaries and wages can be adjusted, and many more such concerns related to the financial operation of any foodservice organization. In fairness it should be said that the budget must be flexible and adjustable according to changing situations. A budget that is rigid will likely be ignored and so lose its value as a guide or plan for financial action and control.

FINANCIAL REPORTS

The data and information provided through the use of records previously described should be used by management to improve the department. Records that are kept for the sake of having records and are allowed to accumulate in a file are of no value. From the records, three types of reports are prepared: the daily, monthly, and annual reports. In addition they provide data to be used as a basis for preparing the departmental budget, as just discussed.

The Daily Food Cost Report. This is the most valuable of the three reports as a management tool, because it provides up-to-the-minute information about sales, food costs, and number of people served. Expenses other than food usually are not included in the daily report, since they do not fluctuate as greatly as food costs. Food is the item of expense that needs to be watched most closely by the dietitian or manager.

The relationship between food cost and income expressed in terms of percent is the most significant single figure to be observed. The food cost percentage is found by dividing the food cost figure by the income. For example, if the income is $640 and the food cost is $265:

$$\frac{\text{Food cost: \$265.00}}{\text{Income: \$640.00}} = .414 \times 100 = 41.4\% = \text{The food cost percentage}$$

Every foodservice organization has its own standard or level of percent of income to be spent for food, as discussed on page 468. If the food cost percent figure varies from day to day within reasonable limits, there is little cause for concern. It is the cumulative or average figure, calculated each day, that should be in line with the desired food cost percentage. Variations in it indicate the need for investigation to determine the reasons.

A simple daily food cost report as illustrated in Form 9.16 is prepared from four records: the cash receipts record of total income from sales for the day, the census record of number of people served, the storeroom issues record, and the invoices for perishable foods, issued directly to the kitchen and not kept on inventory (known as direct purchases). A total of storeroom issues and direct purchases gives the cost of food for the day. In addition to the daily food cost calculation, cumulative figures for the month are shown also. The cumulative figures are used to determine the food cost percentage, because they tend to average out the "ups and downs" of a single day's operation and give the picture of operations to date.

If a more detailed daily report is desired, expense items such as the payroll for supervisors and regular employees, the operating expenses, depreciations, repairs and replacements, and the cleaning supplies may be prorated. For example, if the employees' monthly payroll is $5000 and the staff works 24 days in a month, the daily charge for this item would be $208. Other items for which charges may not be so definite, such as cleaning materials, may be approximated by using the actual figure of the amount spent for a preceding period. A weekly cumulative record of food and labor costs is shown in Fig. 9.13.

A report of daily food costs by production units is used frequently, especially in commercial foodservices that wish to analyze the costs of food as used in several units, such as pastry, salads, and meats. On a form to obtain such data are recorded the amount and cost of the storeroom issues and direct purchases of each food item for the different preparation units. (See Form 9.17.)

A record of charges for food prepared centrally and distributed to various units, as in large hotels and medical centers, is a good accounting procedure and should be a part of the daily food cost calculations. In a hotel these units may include a coffee shop, public dining rooms, catering of banquets and other parties, and room service. In a medical center complex there may be a general hospital

UNIVERSITY COMMONS
DAILY FOOD-COST REPORT

Year____

Day and Date	Tuesday May 1		Wednesday May 2		Thursday May 3		Friday May 4		Saturday May 5		Sunday May 6	
Income and Census:	Census	Sales	Census	Sales	Census	Sales	Census	Sales	Census	Sales	Census	Sales
A. From cafeteria sales (Cash register report)												
B. From parties (Charges)												
C. Total today												
D. Total to date												
E. Cumulative total for month												
Food Cost:												
F. Food cost today												
G. Total food cost to date												
H. Cumulative total for month												
Food-cost percentage												

FORM 9.16 A daily food-cost report form, used continuously for one accounting period, usually a calendar month. The food cost percentage on the last day is the average for the month.

Weekly Income and Cost Sheet
NORTH HALL

Day	Monday	Tuesday	Wednesday	Thursday
Date	8	9	10	11
No. of days this semester	1	2	3	4

Income				
Residents	750.00	750.00	750.00	750.00
Guest meals	6.50	19.50	25.00	—
Other income	3.00	—	22.00	—
Employees, prorated	11.00	11.00	11.00	11.00
Total income today	770.50	780.50	808.00	761.00
Accumulated income today	—	770.50	1,551.00	2,359.00
Total income to date	770.50	1,551.00	2,359.00	3,120.00
Average daily income to date [a]	770.50	775.50	786.33	780.00

Food Cost				
Food cost total today [b]	350.00	300.00	270.00	280.00
Accumulated food cost to date this semester	—	350.00	650.00	920.00
Total food cost to date	350.00	650.00	920.00	1,200.00
Average daily food cost to date this semester	350.00	325.00	306.66	300.00

Labor Cost and Other Expense				
Regular employees per day	90.00	90.00	90.00	90.00
Student part-time employees per day	75.00	75.00	75.00	75.00
Prorated salaries and wages	45.00	45.00	45.00	45.00
Other expenses (estimated) [c]	120.00	120.00	120.00	120.00
Average total expense per day	680.00	655.00	636.66	630.00

[a] *Divide total income to date by number of days served.*
[b] *Average daily food allowance (budget) $300.00.*
[c] *Other expenses include housing (amortization, taxes, interest, rent); services other than personal; supplies other than food; laundry; capital outlay and replacements, such as equipment.*

FIGURE 9.13   Cumulative operating record.

SUMMARY OF DAILY FOOD COST EXPENSE BY PRODUCTION AND SERVICE UNITS

Month_____, 19____

Day and Date		Main Production Unit	Vegetable Preparation	Salad Unit	Bakery	Serving Counter	Totals
	Direct purchases						
	Storeroom issues						
	Total						
	Total to date						
	Cumulative total						

FORM 9.17 Charges for food issued to various preparation and service units may be accounted for by use of this record form.

with cafeteria for staff and personnel as well as patient foodservice, and rehabilitation, psychiatric, and children's units.

The charge for food prepared and sent to these units may be based on the number of portions issued, or on total weight or volume of the food. In either case, precosting with current prices of the various menu items is the preliminary step. A form for recording these daily issues and charges may be developed by the dietitian or foodservice manager so that the appropriate transfer of charges may be made.

The daily food cost report, although more or less approximate, usually is sufficiently accurate to pinpoint trouble spots before serious financial reverses can occur. If a detailed breakdown of costs each day is important to the manager, a computer program may be planned to make such information available quickly. A computer printout of essential data from the previous day's transaction can be on the manager's desk each morning for study and evaluation. As with all reports, the daily food cost report, of whatever form, provides a working tool for foodservice managers, who are expected to know how to use it.

The Profit and Loss Statement. This report is a summary comparison in dollars and cents of the income with *all* expenses of the department to determine the amount of profit or loss for a given period. Usually it is prepared at the end of each calendar month. In schools, however, the accounting period may be the number of operating days per year divided into equal periods of about 20 to 25 days each. This gives a basis for better comparison of operations from period to period. The profit and loss statement shows the true cost of food used based on purchases, adjusted with inventories, and all other actual expenditures.

The figures for preparing this statement are taken from the cash book, income and disbursements, and from the beginning and ending physical inventory figures. A simple summary of the profit and loss statement is:

	Sales
Less:	Cost of food sold
Equals:	Gross profit
Less:	Labor and operating costs
Equals:	Net profit or loss

The cost of food sold is determined by adding the beginning inventory (taken the last day of the preceding month) to the cost of all food purchased during the month (obtained from the monthly statements checked against invoices). The total of these two gives the value of all food available to be used. However, some foods will be left in the storeroom at the end of the month, which necessitates subtracting the value of the ending inventory. A complete profit and loss report is shown in Fig. 9.14. Percentage ratios of the major items of expense and of the profit to the sales are included for better interpretation of operations.

If this report is to be effective it must be completed and available as early in the month as possible, and certainly no later than the tenth of the month. Reports coming to the food manager's desk a month or 6 weeks after the end of the operating period will have little or no control value at that late date. The amount of profit or loss should be no surprise, however, to the manager who has used the daily reports to "keep a finger on the pulse of operations."

The cost and expense figures in the profit and loss report must reveal such data as will enable management to review the stability of the operation and to institute further studies where deficiencies are found. Sudden changes in ratios between items in the profit and loss statement should be investigated. It is not enough to know that there has been a change; the manager must analyze operations and know *why*. Perhaps the volume of business and sales have dropped off, or a new employee, poorly trained, is serving too large a portion of food and so increasing food costs, or the food production manager estimated poorly and overproduction resulted. It is management's responsibility to seek the facts that may point the way towards greater efficiency in operations, and halt extravagance before it has reached the danger point.

ANNUAL REPORTS

No discussion of reports would be complete without mention of a yearly or *Annual Report* of the dietary or foodservice department. Such a report usually is prepared for higher administrative officials and provides a resume of the activities and accomplishments of the year just completed as well as plans and hopes for future developments. Although an annual report contains statistical data, it should be much more than a mere listing of facts and figures. It is the interpretation of these data that make the report significant to those who read it.

April, 19___

(Operating days, 22)

			Per cent of Sales
Sales	$26,476.72		
Less: sales tax	1,040.00		
Net sales		$25,436.72	100.00
Cost of food sold			
Inventory—April 1	1,976.05		
Freight	35.16		
Purchases	10,632.07		
	12,643.28		
Less: inventory April 30	2,258.99		
Net cost of food sold		10,384.29	40.82
Gross profit on food		$15,052.43	59.18
Labor:			
Regular employees	4,651.48		
Student employees	3,081.51		
Supervision	2,479.53		
		10,212.52	40.15
Operating expenses:			
Social security tax	386.96		
Other taxes	291.16		
Maintenance and repair	590.06		
Utilities	757.56		
Supplies (cleaning, paper, office)	766.73		
Laundry	527.39		
Depreciation on equipment	600.00		
		3,919.86	15.41
Total labor and operating expense		14,132.38	
Excess of income over expenses		$ 920.05	3.62

FIGURE 9.14   Monthly profit and loss statement for one college commons.

545

The preparation of such a report usually requires staff participation and planning together as a group. It calls for creative thinking and provides opportunity to dream while forecasting ways in which the department can be improved, not just next year but 2, 5, or 10 years hence.

Steps in preparing an annual report have been outlined by Strenski.[32]

> **1.** Determine what the central theme will be, that is, the message that managers wish to convey besides profit and loss, for example, research and development, sales and facilities. Build the report around the theme for continuity and maximum impact.
>
> **2.** Set up an annual report committee who will be responsible for obtaining information, the copy, graphics, and so forth.
>
> **3.** Prepare a page-by-page outline as a guide to follow in writing.
>
> **4.** Establish a timetable for completion.

The cumulative profit and loss statements, census reports, and other records of income and expenses are the bases for the financial part of an annual report. Comparisons should be made of the actual and budgeted figures for the year and explanations given for increases or decreases. Often the presentation of these data in graphic form, such as a pie chart illustration of the expenditure of the income dollar, will be more quickly understood than the mere statement of words. The use of bar graphs to show comparisons and the plotting of income or census figures month by month on a graph are other examples of effective reporting.

Information on the personnel situation should be included also, since the cost of labor is high. Administrators are interested in percent of turnover, promotions, length of service, and outstanding achievements of the staff and employees. Reasons for terminations

---

[32] *James B. Strenski, "Annual Reports That Pull Their Weight,"* Management Review, 61(*1*), 22 (*1972*).

of employment are important, too; they may help to point out some weakness in the organization. Interpretations of labor hours worked in terms of ratios to meals served, income received, or other comparisons of special significance may well be included.

The physical plant and the equipment changes or repairs that have been made as well as anticipated needs in all areas of operation should be reported. Any situation that calls for a major expenditure of money requires explanation and justification.

The annual report also includes a summary of accomplishments or goals reached during the period. Special problems encountered and solved, unusual occurrences or service rendered, and the projected plans for the future complete an annual report.

"Ten Commandments of A Good Report" were written some time ago but are pertinent today and should be helpful to foodservice managers in preparing annual reports. They are:

1. Organize record keeping so the information can be used to make up reports *on time* and in time to be meaningful.

2. Practice the art of being brief and to the point.

3. Learn to distinguish between important and unimportant data.

4. Be accurate both in narrative as well as in graphic presentation.

5. State the case clearly and concisely in language which will be understood.

6. Employ techniques which will simplify the data—if in statistical form, use small unit which has more meaning.

7. Reports for top management will have little meaning unless related to a standard for comparison as a budget or pre-established goal.

8. Have the courage to report all facts both favorable and unfavorable and be honest in giving them.

9. Do not be afraid to dramatize reports by using:
Arrows or symbols to point out significant facts
Colored pencil to underline
Red type to emphasize important points
Charts and graphs to make data more meaningful.

10. Keep in mind that the value of the report will be balanced against the data it contains. The report should be such that it will motivate the right person to take the right action at the right time.

Cost control of the dietary department belongs to the dietitian or foodservice manager. The extent to which he can carry this responsibility and exercise the controls outlined in this chapter will determine to a large degree the financial success or failure of the organization. Knowing *what* is to be accomplished and what *has been* accomplished and then having the ability to analyze operations and make improvements are requisites of a good financial manager.

SELECTED REFERENCES

Brodner, Joseph, Howard M. Carlson, and Henry T. Maschal, *Profitable Beverage Operation,* Fourth Edition, Ahrens, New York, 1962.

Dukas, Peter, and Donald E. Lundberg, *How to Operate A Restaurant,* Ahrens, New York, 1960.

"Energy Management and Energy Conservation Practices for the Food Service Industry," MRI Project No. 3985-D for the National Restaurant Association, Chicago, Midwest Research Institute, 425 Volker Blvd., Kansas City, Missouri 64110, December 1974.

Establishing and Operating a Restaurant, U.S. Department of Commerce, 1957.

Fay, Clifford T., Jr., Richard C. Rhoades, and Robert L. Rosenblatt, *Managerial Accounting for the Hospitality Service Industries,* Wm. C. Brown, Dubuque, Iowa, 1971.

Frooman, A. A., *Five Steps to Effective Institutional Buying,* Second Edition, Lakeside Press, Chicago, 1953.

Guides for Business Analysis and Profit Evaluation, U.S. Department of Commerce, 1959.

Guide to Energy Conservation for Food Service. Federal Energy Administration, Office of Industrial Programs in cooperation with FEA Food Industry Advisory Committee. October 1975.

Horwath and Horwath, *Uniform System of Accounts for Restaurants,* Fourth Revised Edition, The National Restaurant Association, Chicago, 1968.

Kahrl, William L., *Foodservice on a Budget for Schools . . . Senior Citizens . . . Colleges . . . Nursing Homes . . . Hospitals . . . Industrial . . . Correctional Institutions,* Cahners, Boston, 1974.

Keiser, James, and Elmer Kallio, *Controlling and Analyzing Costs in Food Service Operation,* Wiley, New York, 1974.

Keister, Douglas Carlyle, *How to Increase Profits with Portion Control,* Ahrens, New York, 1957.

549

"Labor Utilization and Operating Practices in Table Service Restaurants," USDA Agricultural Research Service, Marketing Research Report No. 931, Superintendent of Documents, U.S. Government Printing Office, Washington, D.C. 1971.

Levings, Pat, *Profit From Foodservice,* Cahners, Boston, 1974.

Lundberg, Donald E., and James Armatas. *The Management of People in Hotels, Restaurants, and Clubs,* Third Edition, Wm. C. Brown, Dubuque, Iowa, 1974.

O'Leary, Joseph A., *Accounting for the Small Restaurant,* Ahrens, New York, 1957.

Small Business Administration: Starting and Managing Series, Superintendent of Documents, Washington, D.C.
Zwick, Jack, *Handbook of Small Business Finance,* Seventh Edition, SBMS No. 15, 1965.
Sanzo, Richard, *Ratio Analysis for Small Business,* Third Edition, SBMS No. 20, 1970.
McKenna, Francis X., *Starting and Managing a Small Drive-In Restaurant,* SBMS No. 23, 1972

Stokes, John W., *How to Manage a Restaurant or Institutional Food Service,* Second Edition, Wm. C. Brown, Dubuque, Iowa, 1974.

Wilkinson, Jule, Editor, *Increasing Productivity in Foodservice.* Cahners, Boston, 1973.

Witzky, Herbert K., *Practical Hotel-Motel Cost Reduction Handbook,* Ahrens, New York, 1970.

Woodman, Julie, *Encyclopedia of the Foodservice Industry,* The International Foodservice Manufacturers Association (IFMA), Chicago, 1972.

10.
SANITATION
AND SAFETY

Sanitation and safety are closely related environmental factors in the planning and operation of a foodservice. Provision for the maintenance of high standards in both are strategic to the health and well-being of the community population, especially to the workers and persons served in the particular food establishment. Also, sanitation and safety contribute immeasurably to the aesthetic satisfactions of individuals and give a feeling of personal security.

Minimum standards for sanitation and safety in foodservices are established and enforced by city, state, and national legislation. Agencies such as the U.S. Public Health Service, organizations like the National Sanitation Foundation and the National Safety Council, university and other research centers, dietitians and foodservice managers and food and equipment manufacturing companies conduct research and recommend many standards. They also cooperate in the preparation, distribution, and interpretation of pertinent information in publications and exhibits and participate in programs and seminars for various interested and concerned groups and the public. Dietitians and managers are responsible for the maintenance of high sanitation standards in their respective foodservices.

SANITATION

The word sanitation is derived from the Latin word *sanus*, meaning "sound and healthy," or clean and whole. The modern interpretation of the term is broad, including knowledge of health and of sanitary conditions as well as the full acceptance and effective application of sanitary measures. The gradual broadening of the concept of sanitation that followed increased knowledge of microbiology, botany, chemistry, zoology, and engineering makes a fascinating story that takes one back centuries and centuries. When the children of Israel first received the law, it gave them dietary rules stressing the relationships between the way of life of living creatures and their acceptability, as well as their power of contamination. The Book of Leviticus states:

This is the law of the beast and of the fowl and of every living creature that moveth in the water and of every creeping thing that creepeth on the earth; to make a difference between the unclean and the clean and between the beast that may be eaten and the beast that may not be eaten.

In just as specific terms were phrased the laws requiring that food coming in contact with the living body or the "carcass" of creatures declared unclean be regarded as unclean and unfit for human consumption; that earthen utensils so polluted, whether bowls or ranges, should be broken and discarded, and that persons showing signs of unhealthfulness in their bodies should be barred from food handling and from direct contact with their own kind until declared sound by the priests. These regulations were primarily sanitary in character, although enforced as religious sanctions and prohibitions. By the time of the Greeks and the Romans, an urban way of life had replaced the earlier nomadic one, and the state sought to insure the health of the people through extensive provisions for public baths by which personal cleanliness was encouraged. The builders of aqueducts to provide pure mountain water were hydraulic engineers who knew the laws of flowing water but nothing of its quality except in terms of temperature and clarity. They sought also to dispose of sewage and other wastes regarded as menaces to public health, all of which are significant contributions from that period in history.

Many centuries intervened before the bacteriological work of Pasteur in the "world of the infinitely small." Only then was the way possible to an understanding of infection as the cause of communicable diseases. The route of infection was found to be from person to person, from person to spoon, cup, or plate to person, or from person to food to person. In most cases the human element is found in the pattern. Somewhat later than Pasteur, the joint efforts of bacteriologists and chemists led to the discovery of ways of breaking the chain of infectious contacts such as the avoidance of gross pollution by employees, sterilization of food and its subsequent proper storage, and sanitary washing of mouthed dishes and utensils. A sound basis now exists for control of sanitary conditions in food plants and foodservices. Legal measures not known in earlier days are widely accepted by producers and public alike as necessary for general safety and security.

The National Sanitation Foundation, a nonprofit, noncommercial organization with headquarters in Ann Arbor, Michigan, proclaims in these words that sanitation is more than religious sanctions or a code of laws:

Sanitation is a way of life. It is the quality of living that is expressed in the clean home, the clean farm, the clean business and industry, the clean neighborhood, the clean community. Being a way of life, it must come from within the people; it is nourished by knowledge and grows as an obligation and an ideal in human relations.[1]

This Foundation has brought into sharp focus the importance of environmental sanitation and its bearing on "quality living" for the American people. The objective of the Foundation is to increase knowledge in sanitation through research and to distribute that knowledge through education. Activities extend from research on practical problems such as dishwashing, detergents, and sanitizers to the establishment of a testing laboratory where products like food preparation and serving equipment can be tested and approved as meeting desirable sanitation standards.

The U.S. Department of Health, Education and Welfare, through its Public Health Service, also is concerned with prevention of foodborne illnesses in order to promote a high level of health for every person in the United States. It is charged with responsibility to identify and help control health hazards. For many years the Public Health Service has supported research dealing with the purity and wholesomeness of food. One of its centers, the Center for Disease Control in Atlanta, Georgia, also maintains records of foodborne outbreaks and publishes an annual summary of these. The Center also prepares and disseminates excellent training materials for use by schools and foodservice managers.

Since 1966 the Center of Disease Control (CDC) has maintained surveillance of outbreaks of foodborne disease with the objective of preventing

[1] *National Sanitation Foundation, Ann Arbor, Michigan.*

such outbreaks through an understanding of the responsible etiologic agents and contributing factors. In 1968 a standard form for reporting outbreaks to the CDC was made available to all state health departments. Since then over 300 outbreaks have been reported each year. Participants in surveillance of foodborne diseases with the CDC are local and state health agencies and two federal regulatory agencies, the Food and Drug Administration, and the Department of Agriculture.[2]

MICROBIOLOGY AND FOOD

Sanitation in any foodservice is influenced by the understanding of the dietitian or manager and the members of his or her staff of food microbiology and food sanitation. The presence and growth of bacteria in food is the result of their introduction at some stage of the food handling, delivery, or service, on the presence in the food of the nutrients and moisture necessary for bacteriological growth, and the maintenance of favorable temperatures for an adequate period of time. The hazard in their presence depends on the type of the organism and possible by-products from its growth. Learning basic facts about microbiology and prevention of contamination of food by harmful bacteria during food preparation, handling, delivery, and service should be required of every foodservice manager. An outbreak of foodborne illness caused by contaminated food or workers within a particular foodservice has devastating effects on the reputation of that organization and, therefore, on the success or failure of the establishment.

In brief review, bacteria are microscopic in size. Those whose forms are recognizable under the microscope are *cocci,* round in shape; *bacilli,* rod-shaped; and *spirilla,* or corkscrewlike. Viruses too small to see with the light microscope may also be transmitted through foods. Certain conditions are necessary for growth of bacteria: food, moisture, proper temperature, and time. Most bacteria grow best in low-acid food, a few in acid food. Some grow best if sugar is present in the food, others if proteins are present. Some need air for growth, and others thrive in its absence. The temperature most favorable to the growth of pathogenic bacteria is body temperature of about 98°F; temperatures below 45°F inhibit their growth markedly, and temperatures above 140°F for a period of time are lethal to many varieties of organisms. Time required for growth

[2] *Michael H. Merson, W. H. Baker, and A. Taylor, From the Center for Disease Control, J. of Infectious Diseases, 129 (3),365 (1974), University of Chicago Press, Publisher.*

and multiplication depends on the other conditions present and the type of food. The foods of greatest concern in foodservices are those defined by the United States Public Health Service as potentially hazardous.

Potentially hazardous food shall mean any perishable food which consists in whole or part of milk or milk products, eggs, meat, poultry, fish or shellfish, or other ingredients capable of supporting rapid and progressive growth or infections or toxigenic micro-organisms.[3]

Certain of the organisms are able to invade the human body, the resulting infection causing more or less severe illness and hazard to life. If passed from one person to another directly or indirectly, the resulting disorders are termed communicable diseases. According to the Public Health Service, there are at least 62 different communicable diseases, each caused by a specific kind of organism (see Table 10.1).

The means of transport or the channels of infection by which bacteria are communicated merit consideration. One common route is from person to person through *direct contact.* This direct contact of man with man in which carriers or infected persons harbor the disease-causing bacteria and convey them to other human beings accounts for a large part of the spread of communicable disease. A *carrier* is defined as a person who, without symptoms of a communicable disease, harbors and gives off from his body the specific bacteria of a disease. An *infected person* is one in whose body the specific bacteria of a disease are lodged and produce symptoms of illness. Another route is the inclusion of fecal matter from an infected person in the water, milk, or other food consumed. Still another route of infection is by drinking raw milk drawn from cows with infected udders. A now rare source of infection is from muscle tissue of hogs infested with the parasitic organism *Trichinella spiralis.*

An infectious disorder of the respiratory system such as the common cold may be spread by the droplet spray of infected discharges of coughing and sneezing without safeguard. An *indirect route* of infections spread through respiratory discharges is the used handkerchief, the contaminated hand, and the subsequent handling of food or plates and cups in serving a patron.

[3] United States Department of Health, Education and Welfare, Food Service Sanitation Manual, *Public Health Service Publication No. 934, p. 39, Washington D.C. 1962.*

TABLE 10.1 CONTROL OF FOODBORNE DISEASES IN FOODSERVICE ESTABLISHMENTS

Germ (Disease in parenthesis)	Source	Factors that contribute to outbreaks	Preventive Measures
Staphylococcus aureus (Staphylococcal food poisoning)	Workers' noses, hands, hair, intestines, boils Infected sores and cuts	Workers touching cooked foods Keeping food at room temperature Storing foods in large pots in refrigerators Holding foods at warm (bacterial growing) temperatures	Wash hands after coughing, sneezing, smoking, going to the toilet Practice good personal hygiene Cool foods rapidly Put foods in shallow pans in refrigerators Keep cold foods at 45° F or below Keep hot foods at 140° F or above Cover infections with waterproof dressing or band-aid Restrict workers with diarrhea or colds from touching foods
Salmonella (Salmonellosis)	Intestinal tract of man and animals Surfaces of meat and poultry Unpasteurized egg products	Inadequate cooking Cross-contamination of cooked foods from raw foods by contact with common equipment or with hands Keeping food at room temperature Storing foods in large pots in refrigerators Holding foods at warm (bacterial growing) temperatures Inadequate cleaning of equipment Inadequate reheating of cooked foods	Cook foods to internal temperatures of 165° F Use separate equipment for raw and cooked products Cool foods in shallow pans in refrigerators Keep cold foods at 45° F or below Keep hot foods at 140° F or above Reheat leftover foods to 160° F Clean and disinfect kitchen utensils and equipment Wash hands after visiting toilet and handling raw foods of animal origin Restrict workers with diarrhea or fever from touching foods

Clostridium perfringens (*Clostridium perfringens* gastroenteritis)	Intestinal tract of man and animals Surfaces of meat and poultry Soil Dust	Keeping foods at room temperature Storing foods in large pots in refrigerators Holding foods at warm (bacterial growing) temperatures Workers touching cooked foods Inadequate reheating of cooked foods	Cool foods rapidly Put foods in shallow pans in refrigerators Keep cold foods at 45° F or below Keep hot foods at 140° F or above Reheat leftover foods to 160° F Wash hands after going to toilet, handling raw meat, and doing activities other than food preparation Clean and disinfect kitchen equipment Restrict workers with diarrhea from touching foods

The modes of transmission or locomotion for various microorganisms are listed in Table 10.1. It should be noted that human wastes, particularly fecal material, are especially hazardous. An individual who has used the toilet is certain to have contaminated hands. If careful and thorough handwashing is ignored, the worker's hands can be a dangerous "tool" in the kitchen.

The greatest number of common foodborne diseases is caused by bacterial infections. In this group, typhoid once ranked high, but improved sanitation (especially in relation to water and milk supplies and close control over typhoid carriers), and education of food handlers and the general public in high standards of personal hygiene have all but eliminated this disease in the United States.

A differentiation between foodborne *infections* and food *poisoning* or intoxication should be made. The term *"foodborne infections"* means an illness caused by the ingestion of harmful living organisms into the body, usually on food consumed. Two organisms in this classification that are especially prevalent and for which special care in food handling must be exercised are salmonellae and streptococci.

Salmonellae infections account for numerous cases of gastrointestinal disorders. The causative organism may be any one of the 1300 known serotypes of salmonellae, of which the three most common are *S. enteriditis, S. typhimurium,* and *S. newport.* Infected foods most commonly reported include dairy products, custards, meats, protein salads, and eggs. Contamination of the food may occur through human carriers and animal carriers, including cats, dogs, rats, mice, and pet turtles, or it may result when edible animals infected with salmonellae are slaughtered and their flesh marketed through channels that bypass meat inspection. Milk from cows with udders infected with salmonellae or eggs from ducks and less frequently chickens may carry the infection to human beings. In countries where duck eggs are used extensively, consumers are urged to cook them well done. A precautionary measure in this country, even with the pasteurization of egg solids, is the recommendation that the use of dry egg solids be restricted to their inclusion in oven-cooked dishes where the time-temperature relationship is sufficiently high to destroy any salmonellae that might have been present.

Vibrio parahaemolyticus has been the cause of the majority of foodborne illnesses in Japan, but only recently has been recognized as a cause in many countries. Since this microorganism lives in salt water, contamination of fish and shellfish may occur. Most outbreaks have resulted from eating undercooked seafood or cooked seafood that has come into contact with raw products or contaminated containers.

Streptococcus faecalis (Group D) is another microorganism that may cause foodborne infection. The symptoms produced are mild as compared with other foodborne illnesses, and cases of this origin may not be reported.

Group A streptococcus, which causes upper respiratory infections with fever, has been spread from food handlers who were ill with a streptococcal infection through food to consumers, causing large outbreaks of illness.

In addition to the foodborne infections caused by the entry of harmful living bacteria and parasites into the human body with ingested foods, there is still another group of foodborne diseases of great concern. These are classed as *food poisoning* or *food intoxications* and differ from foodborne infections in that bacteria growing in the food prior to its ingestion by the body have produced certain toxins or poisonous substances.

The microorganisms themselves are quite harmless, but the toxin they form causes the problem. Illness occurs more quickly from the toxin than from infection with living bacteria, which take a longer time in the body to cause symptoms of illness. In both cases, however, cramps, nausea, diarrhea and sometimes vomiting will occur. Microorganisms in this group include *Staphylococcus aureus* and *Clostridium botulinum.*

Staphylococcal food intoxication, the most frequent type of food poisoning, results from the contamination with *Staphylococcus aureus* of dishes high in protein, meat, eggs, milk, and cream pie and cream-puff fillings. This organism is commonly found on the human skin and is abundantly present in pimples and suppurating wounds.

Certain conditions are necessary for an outbreak of staphylococcal food intoxication; first, the food must be contaminated with the enterotoxin producing *Staphyloccus aureus;* second, the food must be a medium in which this organism can grow; third, the food must be held at a favorable growth temperature for a period of time long enough to permit growth of the staphylococci and the attendant production of the toxin that causes this disorder.

Major points of attack in control of this food hazard include the following. Workers plagued with pimples, pus pockets, or suppurating wounds should be excluded from the service so that gross contamination of food may be avoided. Foods known to be potentially susceptible to the organism should be kept under refrigeration. Most reported cases of staphlococcal food intoxication are traceable to violation of one or more of the above.

General estimates are that a large majority of the cases of "food poisoning" are due to staphylococcal organisms. The illness is not fatal, but causes extreme pain and nausea to its victims for several hours. Usually the symptoms are evident within 1 to 7 hours after the ingestion of the infected food, which may have shown no visible indications of the contamination at the time of consumption.

In contrast with the food intoxication just described is the far more serious food poisoning, botulism, which results from a toxin produced in various media under anaerobic conditions by the spore-forming *Clostridium botulinum*. This organism is not pathogenic for man, but the toxin produced by it under certain conditions is highly poisonous and usually fatal. Commonly, foods contaminated with botulism show more or less marked changes from normal. The toxin can be destroyed by boiling vigorously for 20 minutes. Fortunately, botulinum poisoning is an uncommon occurence in institution food-services. Commercially processed foods are usually fully sterilized at high temperatures under pressure. However, the hazard is great enough to stimulate constant watchfulness of food condition and quality.

Clostridium perfringens, which is an anaerobic, spore-forming bacteria, is often also placed in this group of organisms causing food poisoning. However, the toxin is produced in the intestinal tract instead of having been present in the food. The incubation period varies between 8 and 20 hours, when illness then occurs.

The organism is found widely distributed in the soil, water, dust, sewage, and manure, and is also found in the intestinal tracts of human beings and healthy animals. Many foods purchased by institutions, especially meats, are probably contaminated with *Clostridium perfringens.* Also, foodservice workers may carry this organism into the kitchen on their hands. Extreme care must be taken to keep hands and equipment clean, especially meat slicers. Meats to be sliced should never be left in the slicer to be "cut as needed" over a long serving period. *Clostridium perfringens* grows rapidly, faster than almost any other of the bacteria discussed here. Gravy, a frequent offender, should be held above 140°F.

In summary it may be noted that, according to the Center for Disease Control: [4]

[4] *"From the Center for Disease Control: Surveillance of Foodborne Disease in the United States, 1971–1972,"* J. of Infectious Diseases, 129 (3), 365 (1974), University of Chicago Press, Publisher.

In 1972 and 1971, salmonellae and Staphylococcus aureus *together were responsible for over 50% of confirmed outbreaks.*

Next in number of outbreaks were those caused by *Clostridium perfringens.*

The food vehicles most commonly causing illness in decreasing order of frequency in both 1971 and 1972 were pork and pork products, beef, poultry, and fish. Staphylococcal disease was most often associated with pork products; outbreaks of salmonella involved a variety of animal and dairy products. Clostridium perfringens *outbreaks generally involved meat products.*

A detailed study of Table 10.1 will indicate the potential health hazards that foodborne diseases and poisonings present. Consideration of the sources, factors that contribute to outbreaks, and the suggested preventive measures show clearly that the responsibility for safe food is no simple matter. Unclean foods or those containing certain pathogens may be found on the market with no associated outbreaks of illness. However, such foods are more likely to cause disease than clean foods. Food as purchased must be fit for human consumption. Even then it will not remain safe if handled by employees infected with one or more of the various communicable diseases, if prepared or served by helpers with unclean personal habits on contaminated utensils or dishes in unsanitary surroundings, or if stored under conditions favorable for bacterial growth.

Chemical poisoning results from the ingestion of food to which toxic chemicals have been added accidentally. Such cases usually occur because these toxic substances have been mistaken for sugar, salt, or flour and hence have been included in the preparation of a product. Careful labeling of all poisons and their storage in a place apart from foods are helpful safeguards and aid in stimulating employee awareness of an ever-present danger.

SOME LEGAL SAFEGUARDS FOR FOOD SAFETY

The vital importance of safe food to the public has found expression in legal safeguards enacted to provide protection to the consumer. The regulatory agencies contributing to this important program include the U.S. Public Health Service and the related state and municipal departments of health, the U.S. Food and Drug Administration, the Animal and Plant Health Inspection Service of the

U.S. Department of Agriculture, and the Bureau of Commercial Fisheries, U.S. Fish and Wildlife Service, Department of Interior. Each of these agencies establishes and supports that standard of sanitation that seems consistent with the existing public opinion from which it draws its support. When standards of sanitation, once acceptable in a municipality, state, or region, are regarded with dissatisfaction by the people, new ones evolve and find expression in regulatory acts that provide more nearly adequate protection for the consumers. Often attendant on these expressions are more exacting interpretations of existing laws bearing on sanitation.

Pasteurization of Milk. Among some of the early efforts to obtain safe food were those of certain municipalities directed toward improvement of the milk supply. As early as 1835, Robert A. Hartley of New York publicized the filthy conditions under which cows were milked in the shadows of breweries in that city. Finally the medical profession became aroused, and the cattle were moved to the country. There milk production was continued under the haphazard conditions then prevalent, with no assurance of safety or purity. A new problem, that of the sanitary distribution of milk, was added to those already awaiting solution. The first milk ordinances, passed in 1856, were directed toward preventing adulteration, which was then rampant. A. L. Rice of New York City reports that as recently as 1880 half of all milk samples collected in that city were adulterated.

Concern with safe milk was stimulated by Pasteur's epoch-making research on bacteria and ways and means of controlling them. In 1893 certification regulations were adopted, and the first pasteurization in this country was undertaken. The next 3 decades saw much work under way in health departments and related agencies on measures needed for controlling the bacterial content of milk during the process of production, on milkborne diseases, and later on pasteurization times, temperatures, and equipment. The list of milkborne diseases is impressive and includes tuberculosis, typhoid, undulant fever, diphtheria, salmonellosis, dysentery, and streptococcus infections. The hazards that an unguarded milk supply can present to a foodservice and its clientele are, therefore, evident. Protection is usually afforded through municipal adoption of adequate milk laws. In 1923 the U.S. Public Health Service formulated a milk ordinance designed to provide a safe milk supply and to standardize, as far as possible, milk sanitation requirements. Today, minimum standards for milk and milk products are designated by city or state ordinance that assures means for its sanitary marketing to the consumer. Every effort should be made by the food manager to purchase only pasteurized milk and milk products—cream, butter, cheese, and ice cream.

Pasteurization of Liquid Eggs. The Egg Products Inspection Act (United States Public Law 91–597, 1970) was enacted to help safeguard against salmonellae. This federal law requires that all liquid eggs for freezing and drying be pasteurized. Also included in the law is provision for inspections to be made during the processing, and no egg processing plant may sell eggs or egg products unless they are processed under the required inspection. Now, all cake and other mixes that include eggs must contain only those that are free of salmonellae; in other words, only pasteurized eggs are permitted to be used in mixes.

Meat Inspection. The Meat Inspection Bill passed in 1906 provided for government inspection at government expense to insure that only safe meat from sound animals free from disease and slaughtered and prepared for market under sanitary conditions should be sold in interstate commerce.

Today the stamp "U.S. Government Inspected" with its assurance that the meat so labeled is from a healthy animal slaughtered under sanitary conditions is familiar to all. Acts and ordinances similar to the Wholesome Meat Act of 1967 and the Wholesome Poultry Products Act of 1968 authorize federal help to the states to extend strict inspection to plants that process products for sale only within state lines. It is the responsibility of the food buyer to select only those meats, poultry, and fish of known quality and from reliable sources as a safeguard for the health and well-being of those whom he feeds. Likewise inspected fresh and processed fruits and vegetables should be selected, whenever possible, to insure their safe usage.

Pure Food and Drug Legislation. Further efforts to provide a degree of consumer protection led to the passage in 1906 of the Pure Food and Drug Bill, which purposed to control certain merchandise sold in interstate commerce. This bill was directed toward the elimination of some of the gross abuses in food production and marketing, particularly adulteration and misbranding. Adulteration was defined in the Pure Food and Drug Bill as "lowering in quality or in strength by the mixture or substitution, in whole or in part, of other substances, or if any valuable constituent had been removed, wholly or in part, or if it were mixed, colored, powdered, watered or stained in order to conceal damage or inferiority." Misbranding was likewise defined: "bearing any false or misleading statement or design, device or label, as to contents or as to the place in which it was manufactured or produced."

Extensions to the Pure Food and Drug Act that carried consumer protection still further included first the Net Weight Act of 1913, which required that all foods and drugs shipped in interstate commerce be marked to indicate clearly the quantity contained in the package in terms of weight, measure, or numerical count. Later the regulation was made applicable to hams, sides of bacon, and other cuts or pieces of meats marketed wrapped. Allowances for shrinkage, normal deviations, and possible errors were found necessary in the enforcment of the act, but even when these adjustments were made, the total gain to the consumer was great. Later, the passage of an amendment to the Pure Food and Drug Act in 1930 was followed by the Food, Drug and Cosmetic Act in 1938, which extended the scope of the definition of adulteration to include: "A food shall be deemed to be adulterated (1) if it bears or contains any poisonous or deleterious substance which may render it injurious to health; (2) if it consists in whole or in part of any filthy, putrid, or decomposed substance, or if it is otherwise unfit for food; or (3) if it has been prepared, packed, or held under insanitary conditions whereby it may have become contaminated with filth, or whereby it may have been rendered injurious to health."

Thus, if a food is shown to contain a deleterious substance (staphylococcus, toxin, salmonellae, etc. among other things) it can be proceeded against under Federal law. Also, if it was known to have been prepared, packed, or held under insanitary conditions whereby it may have become contaminated, it can also be proceeded against. Both of these conditions apply to foods that were adulterated after shipment in interstate commerce.

In both situations the law provided for prosecution of the one responsible for the violations, as well as seizure of the adulterated food. It is interesting to note that these sanctions permit legal sanctions against foodservice operators who handle interstate foods in an insanitary manner, even though they do no interstate business.[5]

All types of foods are under constant scrutiny of this agency to insure safety of the food supply to the nation. Investigations and inspections, definitions and standards of identity, modifications and

[5] Curtis Joiner, "Legal Requirements for Food Safety", Cornell HRA Quarterly, 13 (1), 34 (May 1972).

interpretation of regulations, adjustments in tolerances for acceptable additives, and approvals for new products and their labeling and packaging are only a few of the activities of the Food and Drug Administration. Emphasis in the program of this agency is on the avoidance of contamination and adulteration of the food supply and on the assurance to the public that the many items of food found in the market are safe when processed and packed.

No discussion of food safety would be complete without some mention of food additives. In 1958 a food additives amendment to the Food, Drug and Cosmetic Act was made and requires the food industry to prove that the additives are safe before they can be added to foods. Additives are classed as functional ingredients and include both those that are legally food additives and those that are *generally regarded as safe* (GRAS).

This refers to the wording of the Food, Drug, and Cosmetic Act, which says in effect that any substance which is a component of food is a food additive unless it is generally recognized as safe by experts qualified through training and experience to judge its safety.[6]

The amendment states that substances generally recognized as safe need not be cleared through the food additives clearance procedure. Some 500 of these functional ingredients comprise the GRAS list and include items such as spices, flavorings, emulsifiers, and leavening agents. All of the items on the list have been under study and review to be certain that each is still considered safe. Scientific review and changes in the amounts and uses of the GRAS substances may result in change of status of certain of them. "This is based on the amply demonstrated fact that safety is not an absolute attribute but is related to level of intake." [7]

Cyclamates were under this scrutiny a few years ago, and it was determined that they no longer were generally recognized as safe. Now their use in the food supply is not permitted; however, additional evidence may result in review at a later date. This may be true for other substances from time to time.

State and Municipal Regulations. Most states and municipal governments have passed laws and ordinances intended to extend the pro-

---

[6] *Virgil O. Wodicka, "FDA's View of Food Safety," Reprint from* FDA Consumer, *October 1973, p. 4; DHEW Pub. (FDA) 74-2016, 1974.*
[7] Ibid.

tection of the federal law to food sold in local rather than interstate commerce. More and more, the sanitation of the raw food to be processed, the processing equipment and plant, the distribution of the product are under sharp scrutiny of inspectors and consumers alike. Cleanliness, purity, and freedom from contamination are widely accepted as expected attributes of desired food products, and the trend is toward correspondingly high sanitary standards.

Local health department regulations cover in detail such things as definitions, safe source of food, and the various aspects of the operation of markets and food processing and serving establishments. Also included are items such as licensing, inspections, approval of floor plans and equipment for new and remodeled installations, and food handlers permits, certain of which will be discussed later in this chapter.

Federal Regulations. It has long been recognized that there is a need for greater uniformity in sanitation standards throughout this country. The great variation that exists in regulations from state to state makes it difficult for organizations engaged in interstate business to keep track of what is expected.

In October 1974, the FDA [8] proposed new uniform requirements relating to foodservice sanitation for state and local regulatory agencies. The model ordinance and federal regulations in regard to interstate shipment are, of course, to be in agreement.

The purpose of the proposed regulations and model ordinance is to provide foodservice establishments with standards and state and local governments with a comprehensive model law for the regulations of foodservice sanitation.

It is hoped that these requirements will be approved and then adopted by all states so that there will be uniform standards of performance throughout the country. Such a model code is useful to both the government and the foodservice industry.

SAFE FOOD

Every person who eats away from home in a foodservice operation has the right to expect that the food served is safe for human

[8] *Food Service Sanitation—Proposed Uniform Requirements. Dept. of HEW, Food and Drug Administration,* Federal Register, 39 *(191), 35438, Part II, October 1, 1974.*

consumption. Likewise, every foodservice manager has the responsibility for assuring that all food served in his establishment is safe and wholesome. However, many new problems have been created for the manager by the rapid increase in the foodservice industry, by the vast number of new developments in the technologies of processing and handling foods, and by the overwhelming number of new products on the market from which to choose. Producers, marketing specialists, processors, microbiologists, dietitians and nutritionists, public health officials, and consumers are all deeply concerned about the safety of food in this time of rapidly changing situations. They are working together to coordinate research efforts and to discuss mutual concerns and their solutions for safe food prepared in quantity.

A thorough discussion of foodservice sanitation and safety is given by Longree [9] and readers are encouraged to use that reference for detailed information. A briefer review of desirable procedures for use in food production and service is given here together with some research reports of special significance for the foodservice manager.

Food Preparation, Handling, Distribution, Service. Data reported by Bryan,[10] who studied factors responsible for outbreaks of foodborne illness, most of which occurred from foods prepared in foodservice establishments, reveal that:

Inadequate refrigeration practices *were the chief operational procedures that have contributed to these outbreaks. Other procedures that have contributed to a large number of outbreaks are* preparing foods far in advance of planned services *with improper storage during the interval before serving,* infected persons touching foods *after the final heat processing, and* holding foods in warming devices *at temperatures that favor bacterial growth.*

Foodservice personnel must be trained to exercise particular care in use of safe procedures related to all four of these areas of concern. Management, too, has responsibility for providing adequate refrigerated and heated storage space for the kind and amount of foods to be prepared.

[9] *Karla Longree,* Quantity Food Sanitation, *Second Edition, Wiley, New York, 1972.*
[10] *Frank L. Bryan, "Microbiological Food Hazards Today—Based on Epidemiology Information,"* Food Technology, 28, 52 (*September 1974*).

Temperature controls on walk-in and other refrigerators should be in good working order and checked daily to make certain that temperatures *are* maintained below 45°F, as appropriate for the specific foods stored in them. Equally important is the use of a thermometer *inside* the refrigerator, placed in the warmest section of the box. Daily checks should be made of this also to assure that desired temperatures are maintained in the area where the food is stored.

As has been noted in earlier discussions of microbiology and food, and as shown in Fig. 10.1, the danger zone favoring bacterial growth is the temperature range of 45 to 140°F, and the period of time during which food is allowed to remain in this critical temperature zone largely determines the rate and extent of bacterial growth. It is imperative, therefore, that potentially hazardous foods be held *below* 45°F or *above* 140°F to assure their safety.

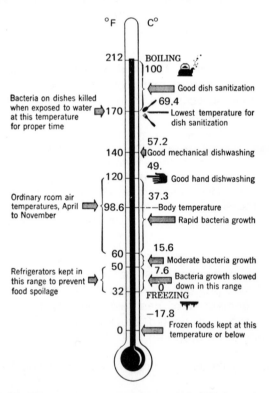

FIGURE 10.1 *Temperature and food sanitation guide. Adapted from Klenzade diagram.*

Practices in an institution kitchen relate to three categories of food whose preparation and storage require special procedures to assure their safety:

1. Frozen foods including partially and fully cooked menu items purchased for institutional use.

2. Food requiring preliminary preparation, possibly including cooking prior to the final steps in their preparation. This includes items such as sandwich and salad mixtures; sliced, chopped, cut, boned, and hashed cooked poultry and meats; ground, mixed, and shaped cooked meats; cream pie fillings and puddings; and sliced ham and similar items.

3. Leftover foods, fully prepared and cooked, and offered for service but in excess quantity over demand.

Likewise, three categories of equipment to store, hold, or transport food and maintain it within the safe temperature zone deserve special mention. These are:

1. Refrigerator and freezer storage.

2. Heated holding cabinets and serving counters for cooked foods.

3. Refrigerated and heated carts and trucks used to deliver prepared foods from a central production unit to various facilities or units where food is served.

Each of these will be discussed in some detail.

Research studies indicate that one must not assume that because heat kills bacteria or that freezing seems to inactivate them that any food product that has been heated or frozen will be free from contamination, or that a low bacterial count in a product means safe food. Different types of organisms vary in their degree of resistance to high and low temperatures, and recognition must be given to this fact when procedures for food handling are developed.

Peterson and Gunnerson [11] state that an understanding of the effect of temperature on microbial growth is of utmost importance. Consideration is first given to low temperature or frozen food products.

Any discussion of the microbiological considerations of frozen food, especially frozen prepared, or convenience foods, must begin with the recognition that such foods receive no terminal sterilizing heat treatment by either the processor or the consumer.

Furthermore, they state that:

Preservation of food by freezing is based on the retardation of microbial growth to the point at which decomposition due to microbial action does not occur—this is generally at or below 32°F (0°C). Pathogenic organisms do not grow below 35°F (about 2°C). Although there is a general die-off of microbes during frozen storage, especially some sensitive types of microorganisms, processors are well aware that the freezing process is not lethal and cannot be expected to sterilize food products.

It should be noted that while a large number of bacteria may be killed in the freezing process, a considerable number remain alive even after long periods in freezer storage, and they can cause spoilage when the food is thawed and heated for serving. Figure 10.2 summarizes the low temperature limits on microorganisms.

In order to better protect consumers of precooked frozen foods, the National Association of Frozen Food Packers has proposed a trial standard of allowable bacterial count of 100,000 bacteria per gram in precooked frozen foods. This figure is still under debate, and a precise standard has not yet been accepted. Also, the Food and Drug Administration inspects processing plants and analyzes samples of their products for microbiological quality. This inspection further assures foodservice managers that the product that they purchase is safe at the point of production.

It is the responsibility of the manager, however, to specify that any such products purchased shall be held at a temperature of 0°F or lower from the time of processing through delivery to the institution. Adequate freezer space maintained at a maximum of 0°F and, preferably, −10°F must be available on the premises to assure qual-

---

[11] A. C. Peterson and R. E. Gunnerson, "Microbial Critical Control Points in Frozen Foods," Food Technology, 28, 37 (September 1974).

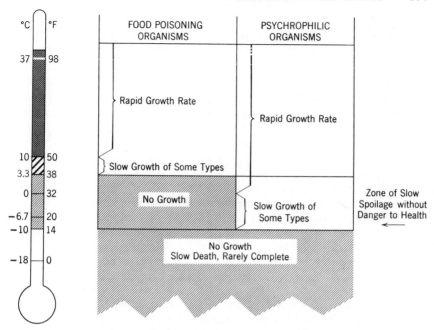

FIGURE 10.2   Low-temperature limits on growth of food poisoning and psychrophilic organisms. Courtesy, Paul Elliott and Horace K. Burr, U.S. Department of Agriculture.

ity and safety control. Frozen products should be stored immediately upon delivery; any that show signs of thawing should not be accepted, but should be returned to the purveyor.

Although foodservice establishments purchase and use frozen, precooked entree items, some institutions prepare or may consider preparing their own entrees to freeze for later reheating and service. The latter practice may be dangerous unless facilities for quickly freezing the large mass of food are available.

Freezers must be available which are capable of freezing food in a very short time, preferably within one-half hour. Many institutional freezers would not be capable of performing that efficiently although they might be very adequate for the storage of food already frozen.[12]

[12] Karla Longree, Quantity Food Sanitation, *Second Edition, Wiley, New York, p. 354, 1972.*

Thawing and heating of frozen, potentially hazardous foods are additional steps in food preparation where care must be taken to prevent contamination. Time-temperature controls are especially important considerations in handling these food items. Bryan and McKinley [13] reported a study of use of frozen turkeys in school lunch kichens. Turkey is served frequently in institutions of all types and is often found to be the source of foodborne illnesses for three reasons.

In the first place, raw turkeys are often contaminated with Salmonella, Staphylococcus aureus, *and* C. perfringens *when they are received in kitchens. Inadequate cooking may allow these bacteria to survive. Secondly, turkeys require considerable handling, such as deboning and slicing, before they are served. Cooked turkeys are handled in the same general area as the raw ones, by the same personnel who previously handled the raw ones, and sometimes on or in the same equipment used for the raw ones. This handling not only increases the chances for recontamination with* Salmonella *from raw turkey, it also increases the risks of contaminating the product with* S. aureus *or* C. perfringens *from human sources. Thirdly, and perhaps most important, turkeys are almost always prepared at least a day before serving. In this amount of time, foodborne pathogens that got into the turkeys during handling or those that survived cooking can multiply in the meat or stock if the foods are not cooled rapidly to 45° or less and held at that temperature.*

Unfortunately, cooling is seldom accomplished rapidly enough. Turkey meat and stock cool slowly when refrigerated in a conventional manner, and, very often school kitchens do not have enough refrigerator space to store the number of turkeys needed to serve the students. Large pots and pans are frequently used for refrigerator storage of the meat and stock. Sometimes, turkeys are even left overnight in ovens which are warm but have been turned off. Both practices provide ideal conditions for bacterial growth. On the day of serving, turkey meat, gravy, or dressing are often not heated or are only warmed to a temperature less than 165°F, or hot gravy is often poured over cold meat. Such practices will kill neither cells of C. perfringens *that have emerged from spores nor any post-cooking contaminants that have multiplied during storage.*

In this study, 20-pound frozen turkeys were thawed either in a refrigerator, at room temperature in paper bags, or at room tempera-

[13] Frank L. Bryan and Thomas W. McKinley, "Prevention of Foodborne Illness by Time-Temperature Control of Thawing, Cooking, Chilling and Reheating Turkeys in School Lunch Kitchens" J. of Milk and Food Technology, 37, 420 (August 1974).

ture with no bag covering. Turkeys were prepared for cooking either by making a roll of the raw turkey meat wrapped in the skin or by cutting them in half through the breast bone. Some were roasted whole. Various cooking methods, equipment, and temperatures were used in this experiment. Range ovens, and steam kettles were employed. Cooling methods experimented with were: cooled at room temperature for 1 to 3 hours then refrigerated; deboned while warm and cut into bite-size pieces; whole turkeys stored overnight in a walk-in refrigerator; a half turkey left overnight in an oven that had been turned off; and a half a turkey roll placed in a plastic bag and then covered with ice and refrigerated, the other half wrapped in aluminum foil and refrigerated. Also, stock was cooled by various methods for testing. Methods of reheating the turkey meat and stock were studied. Temperature recordings were taken at frequent intervals throughout the entire experiment, and microbiological analyses were likewise conducted at each stage.

Based on this investigation the following recommendations are made for preparing, cooking, cooling, and reheating turkeys in a school kitchen:

Thawing

1. Always thaw frozen turkeys completely before cooking them. Too much time is required to adequately cook large, frozen turkeys to be practicable in school food service operations.

2. Thaw plastic-wrapped turkeys in refrigerators whenever possible. The refrigerator temperature should be 45 F or below. (For 20-lb. turkeys, 3 days or more are required.)

3. If turkeys must be thawed within 24 h or if refrigerator space is not available, enclose wrapped, frozen turkeys in double kraft paper bags, tape the bags shut, and thaw at room temperature. When thawing in bags, do not allow them to remain at room temperature more than 1 h per pound if one, double-layer bag is used or 1-1/4 h per pound if two, double-layer bags are used.

Cooking

1. Cook turkeys to internal temperatures of at least 165 F. (180 to 185 F and 170 to 180 F are recommended for thigh and breast internal temperatures, respectively.)

2. Test turkeys for doneness by inserting a thermometer into the center of turkey rolls.

3. Bake dressing separately until it reaches an internal temperature of at least 165 F.

4. When baking turkeys in ovens, set thermostat at 325 F or higher. Baking turkeys at temperatures of 225 F or lower requires too much time for the turkeys to reach an internal tem-

perature of 165 F to be practicable in a school food service operation.

Holding and cooling

1. *Never allow cooked turkeys to stay in unheated ovens (such as for overnight holding).*
2. *Never refrigerate cooked whole turkeys for overnight storage without first reducing their bulk.*
3. *Wear disposable plastic gloves when deboning cooked turkeys.*
4. *As soon as the turkeys cool to a temperature at which they can be handled, debone them and slice or cut meat into small pieces.*
5. *Put pieces of cut-up, cooked turkeys directly into cold pans (pans setting in pans of ice).*
6. *Do not pile turkey meat more than 3 inches high in pans.*
7. *Never store turkey meat and stock in the same containers.*
8. *Never refrigerate large batches of turkey stock in large stockpots.*
9. *Rapidly chill stock by immersing containers, such as 2-1/4 gal in a 5-gal stockpot, in an ice bath or a water bath, or by mixing with a vertical mixer before storing in a refrigerator.*

Reheating

1. *Boil stock on the day it is to be used either before or during gravy preparation.*
2. *Reheat turkey meat to 165 F in steamers, in boiling gravy, in covered pans on a range, or in open pans in ovens. (This last procedure, heating meat with gravy in ovens, requires considerable time.)*

Cleaning and personal hygiene

1. *Thoroughly wash and disinfect all equipment that touches raw turkeys before it is used for cooked meat or stock.*
2. *Wash hands after handling raw turkeys and before handling cooked turkey or other foods.*[14]

These suggestions are equally appropriate for any foodservice that prepares and serves turkey and other poultry and meat items requiring similar preparation.

[14] *Frank L. Bryan and Thomas W. McKinley, "Prevention of Foodborne Illnesses by Time-Temperature Control of Thawing, Cooking, Chilling and Reheating Turkeys in School Lunch Kitchens,"* J. of Milk and Food Technology, 37, 428 *(August 1974).*

The Public Health Service [15] recommends a minimum internal temperature of 165°F for cooking stuffings, poultry, and stuffed meats with no interruption of the initial process, and at least 150°F for the internal temperature of pork and pork products that have not been specially treated for trichinae.

Ordinary cooking of foods destroys many pathogenic organisms that may be present. Those that cause diseases such as typhoid, salmonellosis, tuberculosis, brucellosis, tularemia, dysentery, sore throat, scarlet fever, and diphtheria are easily destroyed by boiling. It should be noted also that although a 165 to 170°F temperature in the center of the food mass is lethal to viable staphylococci and salmonellae, it cannot be relied on to destroy spores or staphylococcal enterotoxin if they are reformed in the food.

Roast beef and gravy made from its drippings have been the cause of several reports of *Clostridium perfringens* outbreaks. Although the raw meat may be contaminated before it is received in the institution kitchen, the contamination may readily occur after cooking. Too often roasts may be held on the meat slicer for a considerable period of time waiting for individual orders before slicing. Or, several large roasts put into the refrigerator at one time to chill, may raise the temperature to the point where roasts cool so slowly that the time period in the danger zone (between 45 and 140°F) is long enough to allow for growth of *C. perfringens.*

The workers themselves can cause this microorganism to spread through careless personal habits or failure to adequately sanitize equipment that was used for raw foods and then for the cooked foods. This cross-contamination by a worker or equipment that has been in contact with raw meat or poultry and then with cooked is a serious problem and is a practice to be avoided in every foodservice operation.

The practice of cooking, chilling, and then reheating beef roasts is also a potentially hazardous practice because reheating may not be to a temperature high enough (165°F) to destroy any bacteria that may have survived in the meat.

In a study of *C. perfringens* related to roast beef cooking, storage, and contamination, Bryan and Kilpatrick [16] give 18 recom-

---

[15] *United States Department of Health, Education and Welfare,* Food Service Sanitation Manual, *Public Health Service Publication No. 934, p. 44, 1962.*
[16] *Frank J. Bryan and Edward G. Kilpatrick, "Clostridium Perfringens Related to Roast Beef Cooking, Storage, and Contamination in a Food Service Restaurant,"* American J. of Public Health, 61(9), 1883 (1971).

mendations for establishments preparing and serving roast beef sandwiches. Many of the practices have been discussed previously. Emphasis should, however, be given to six of these that, briefly stated, are:

1. Frozen beef should be thawed in a refrigerator with a temperature below 45°F;

2. The weight of each roast should be limited to six pounds, to speed cooking and reheating times;

3. Hold cooked roast in a heated cabinet for no more than two hours, preferably much less;

4. Avoid leaving meat on the slicing machine for extended periods of time;

5. Reheat roasts to an internal temperature of at least 160°F and serve them as soon as possible; and

6. Wash, rinse, and disinfect al kitchen equipment after it has been used. Give special care to sanitizing thermal pins, thermometers, slicing machines, scales, and all other equipment that touches cooked roasts. Disinfect all meat-contact surfaces by immersing into water that is at least 170°F for 30 seconds, or into a solution containing an equivalent of at least 50 ppm available chlorine for at least 1 minute. Use a chemical disinfectant (at twice the above-mentioned strength) on equipment, such as the slicing machine blade and base, that cannot be immersed in water. Use brushes and disposable cleaning fabrics rather than washable cloth rags and towels.

Preparation of potentially hazardous foods that must be cooled before further combining into the finished product presents some real problems for the production manager. Cream pie fillings and puddings and other prepared or semiprepared foods should be refrigerated as soon as possible, but not later than one-half hour after their preliminary preparation has been concluded. Attempting to cool at room temperature in order to save refrigeration is a practice to be discouraged. Every effort should be made to lower the temperature of the food to a degree unfavorable to bacterial growth in the shortest possible time.

Masses of hot food cool slowly, even in large walk-in refrigerators. Current recommendations are that for hot food to be cooled quickly, it should be no more than 2 inches deep in shallow containers, and the center of the food mass should reach 45°F within a maximum of 4 hours, and preferably less. (See Fig. 10.3.) Other suggestions for cooling large amounts of food quickly include agitating or stirring the food and putting the pan of food into an ice "bath" or vat of *cold* (40°F or less) *running* water.

The importance of food refrigeration is outranked only by the condition of the food itself and by the health and sanitary practices of the personnel who prepare and serve it. Foodservice workers must be reminded constantly that in order to remove a clean wholesome product from storage, it had to be in that condition when placed there. They must be instructed that food and containers of

FIGURE   10.3   Portable wire racks facilitate rapid cooling of food in shallow pans. Courtesy, Metropolitan Wire Goods Corporation.

food to be refrigerated should be shallow and placed to permit free circulation of cold air throughout the storage unit. If cooked and raw foods must be stored in the same refrigerator, be certain that cooked foods are placed on top shelves and raw foods on lower ones. This arrangement prevents any contamination of cooked foods from leakage or drippings from raw foods.

Following cooking, some foods are held heated pending service and during the service period. Staggered production of certain items throughout the service period is a desirable practice. Protein dishes to be served in a sauce such as turkey a la king and creamed ham and eggs can be combined in small batches and heated as needed.

Baked meat, fish, or poultry casseroles and other potentially hazardous foods may be held in hot-holding cabinets or sent by truck in heated or hot containers to serving units. These foods should have an internal temperature of 165 to 170°F when put into the serving counter, hot-holding cabinet, or truck for distribution in order that the temperature of the food will not go below the 140°F mark before it is consumed.

Any holding or delivery time required should be as short as possible, preferably not more than 20 minutes. It should be remembered holding cabinets are not designed for heating, and temperatures will never go above that of the food when it is put into them. Therefore, the use of a thermometer to check internal temperatures of those potentially hazardous foods before they are taken for distribution and service is the only way the manager can be certain that they will be hot and safe when served.

Preliminary preparation of items such as sandwich and salad mixtures, turkey a la king, and other potentially hazardous foods such as ground cooked meat for croquettes requires that they must be mixed, shaped, sliced, ground, chopped, boned, or cut. These handling processes provide ample chance for contamination from the air, the utensils and equipment, and the foodservice personnel. The heating of the foods may be incomplete for sterilization, and the room temperatures at which they are held may be high enough and for a long enough period of time to favor bacterial growth and attendant food spoilage.

Foods that have been fully prepared and held on the serving counter without being sold and then, as leftovers, are finely subdivided, mashed, or otherwise prepared for incorporation in a "made" dish and stored for some hours present similar opportunities for bacterial contamination and growth. Leftover foods constitute a hazard as far as food safety is concerned because of the "double" handling they must have; they are twice exposed to human and storage contamination. Longree [17] makes the following recommendations in regard to leftovers.

Plan to have no or little food left over. Leftovers can be wasteful and are a bacteriological hazard. They are handled often and are thus subjected to many chances for contamination. Moreover, leftovers are usually subjected to various cycles of holding, cooling, and warming and are often held for many hours at temperatures at which bacteria may multiply.

Before storage, reheat lukewarm leftovers to boiling, if possible, to destroy contaminants; precool and refrigerate. This rule applies in particular to items that have not been served and are returned from counters and patient floors in bulk quantities. Precool and refrigerate leftover items following the methods stated previously. Use leftovers within a day.

A summary of basic standards for safeguarding the preparation and storage of food follows:

1. Select clean, wholesome food from sources approved or considered satisfactory by the health authority.

2. Specify that frozen products be maintained at 0°F or lower during delivery.

3. Wash thoroughly all raw fruits and vegetables before using.

4. Scour and sanitize all cutting boards, knives, and electric slicers immediately after use with raw or cooked meats, fish, or poultry.

5. Maintain all potentially hazardous foods at *safe* temperatures, 45°F or below, or 140°F or above, except for brief necessary periods for preparation and service.

6. Check internal temperature of cooked foods to be held on a serving counter or in a holding cabinet: should

[17] *Karla Longree, Quantity Food Sanitation, Second Edition, Wiley, New York, p. 379, 1972.*

be 165 to 170°F before taking to the serving unit in order to maintain 140° during serving period.

7. Refrigerate immediately any cooked foods to be used later; refrigerate in shallow containers; center of food mass should reach 45°F within 4 hours. Place pans in refrigerators so that air circulation is not blocked.

8. Discard any questionable food.

9. Protect food from contamination or cross-contamination during preparation, service, and storage through precautionary measures such as: use of clean properly sanitized equipment; optimum refrigerator temperatures; proper handling of food by healthy personnel who wash hands thoroughly after touching any food or objects that may be contaminated; and storage and use of poisonous or toxic materials away from the food.

Table 10.1 summarizes practices observed in institution kitchens that contribute to foodborne diseases. Administrators of foodservice departments would do well to use a checksheet, as suggested in Fig. 10.4, to inspect and identify foodborne disease risks associated with a foodservice operation or as a supplement to a routine sanitation checklist to indicate the items that, if deficient, need immediate correction. Also, it may be used to determine priorities in setting up control activities or a training program for employees.

PERSONNEL

The importance of good personal habits on the part of foodservice employees cannot be overemphasized. The Center for Disease Control reported [18] that "infected employees who practice poor personal hygiene" ranked fourth in relative order of frequency of causes of foodborne outbreaks in the United States between 1961 and 1970. "Poor employee hygiene" was listed first among frequent complaints of what annoys customers most in restaurants as surveyed by Restaurant Business.[19]

[18] Frank L. Bryan, *"Identifying Foodborne Disease: Hazards in Food Service Establishments,"* J. of Environmental Health, 36 (6), 537 (1974).
[19] *"Sanitation: Customer Demand,"* Restaurant Business Magazine, 73, 39 (December 1974).

Food should be handled only by healthy individuals. Physical and medical examinations may or may not be a requirement in the selection of foodservice workers, although most health authorities require at least tuberculin tests, chest x-rays, and blood tests before issuing food handlers' permits. Additional checks depend on the local health service regulations and the individual food operation. Constant observation of the health of employees and attention to their work habits are important functions in supervision.

Only healthy persons should be permitted to participate in the foodservice operation. Although this sounds ridiculously trite, personnel practices today reward a person for coming to work while ill. To many, the concept of health obviously is the ability to show up at work. It is difficult to believe that this concept is valid for any position or occupation, but it is particularly damaging when foodservice or other health care professions are considered.[20]

Sanitary conditions in any foodservice can be effective only insofar as the owner or manager believes that high standards of sanitation are essential, assumes responsibility for creating this desirable philosophical climate, and imparts a sense of urgency about the matter to his employees. In spite of the sincere interest of owners, managers, or operators of foodservice departments in developing and carrying through an adequate sanitary program, inadequate employee training and consequent lack of group concern has too often hindered their efforts, and the results have fallen far short of meeting the accepted standards. An intense educational program that emphasizes the responsibilities of the worker to the customer and to himself is essential.

A *continuous* educational program for foodservice personnel is obligatory if a high standard of sanitation is to be maintained. This program should keep the employees aware of sanitary procedures and practices advocated in legislative measures and why they are important. Also employees must continually realize the heavy responsibilities that they, as foodservice personnel, assume for the health and well-being of the people whom they feed. Keen awareness of the importance of their own good health, personal hygiene, and work habits, and the inherent dangers in improper care and handling of food should be emphasized.

[20] Lee D. Stauffer, "Sanitation and the Human Ingredient," Hospitals, JAHA, 45, 62 (July 1971).

FIG. 10.4   EVALUATION OF FOODBORNE DISEASE HAZARDS IN FOOD SERVICE ESTABLISHMENTS

Item	*Deficiency*
Inadequate Cooling	
Failure to reduce temperatures of leftover foods or foods cooked in advance of planned service to 70°F within an hour (unless served immediately or held at 140°F or above)	_____
Foods in refrigerated units at internal temperatures above 45°F (unless put into unit within 3 hrs)	_____
Storing nonliquid, leftover or prepared foods so that they have a vertical cross section of more than 3 in. or storing them in containers that have a height of over 4 in. (such as storing foods in stock pots)	_____
Inadequate Hot Holding	
Foods in warming or hot holding devices at internal temperatures below 130°F	_____
Inadequate Cooking or Reheating	
Failure to reach temperatures of 165°F in the internal portion of poultry or dressing (this practice frequently occurs when turkeys are cooked in the frozen state)	_____
Failure to reach temperatures of 150°F in the internal portions of pork or pork products	_____
Failure to reheat cooked, leftover food to internal temperatures of at least 160°F	_____
Using Contaminated Foods	
Obtaining foods (including water, milk and milk products, shellfish, canned goods, meat and meat products, mushrooms) from unsafe sources (underscore unsafe item or specify: _____)	_____
Using potentially contaminated ingredients in uncooked foods (such as cracked or checked eggs in egg nog or ice cream—specify situation: _____)	_____
Contamination by Workers	
Workers who have diseases that are transmitted by foods or diseases or symptoms that promote the spread of foodborne pathogens (diarrhea, fever, colds, rhinorrhea, jaundice, sore throat, sinusitis) or who are infected with certain pathogens (such as *Shigella* spp. and *Salmonella typhi*) that may be transmitted by foods (underscore or specify situation: _____)	_____

The low standards of personal hygiene and the questionable work habits of many foodservice personnel reflect a limited knowledge of the proper care of the body and of food microbiology in relation to the dangers of contaminating the food with which they work. To the extent that the educational program can be made to combine the "why" with the "how-to-do," it may be said to be a well-organized, systematic, and functioning program. Teaching ma-

Item	Deficiency

Contamination by Workers (continued)

Infected lesions (boils and other pus-containing lesions) on workers who touch cooked or prepared foods ⎯⎯⎯⎯

Failure to wash hands after visiting the toilet, smoking, coughing, sneezing, blowing nose, touching sores or bandages, or touching raw foods of animal origin (underscore poor practices) ⎯⎯⎯⎯

Touching cooked foods with hands ⎯⎯⎯⎯

Other poor personal hygiene practices which may serve to spread contamination to foods (such as working in street clothes, dirty appearance, smoking or chewing tobacco in food areas—specify: ⎯⎯⎯⎯

⎯⎯⎯⎯⎯⎯⎯⎯⎯⎯⎯⎯⎯⎯⎯⎯⎯⎯⎯⎯⎯⎯⎯⎯⎯⎯⎯)

Contamination by Equipment

Cooked foods processed on or with the same equipment or stored in the same containers that had been used for raw foods without thorough intermediate cleaning—cross contamination (specify pieces of equipment involved: ⎯⎯⎯⎯

⎯⎯⎯⎯⎯⎯⎯⎯⎯⎯⎯⎯⎯⎯⎯⎯⎯⎯⎯⎯⎯⎯⎯⎯⎯⎯⎯)   ⎯⎯⎯⎯

Kitchen equipment and utensils not effectively washed, rinsed, and disinfected ⎯⎯⎯⎯

Contamination by Chemicals

Storing acid foods in containers or conveying them in pipes that contain toxic metals (such as antimony, cadmium, copper, lead, or zinc) or packaging them in materials in which toxic products may migrate to the foods (specify food, metal, and container: ⎯⎯⎯⎯)   ⎯⎯⎯⎯

Addition of chemicals or food ingredients that produce toxic reactions in man during food preparation to levels that exceed culinary requirements (specify chemical and amount: ⎯⎯⎯⎯⎯⎯)   ⎯⎯⎯⎯

Contamination During Dry Storage

Storing poisonous substances in the same room as foods ⎯⎯⎯⎯

Stored foods subjected to sewage drippage, or overflow, or backflow ⎯⎯⎯⎯

Other poor dry storage practices (such as exposing foods to water or other forms of moisture—specify: ⎯⎯⎯⎯⎯⎯⎯⎯⎯)   ⎯⎯⎯⎯

FIGURE 10.4   Evaluation of foodborne disease hazards in food service establishments. Courtesy Frank L. Bryan, "Identifying Foodborne Disease Hazards in Food Service Establishment," Journal of Environmental Health, 36(6), 539 (May–June 1974).

chines have been used effectively in some organizations for self-learning of the requisite sanitation procedures.

The demand for better sanitation in foodservice establishments has led to formal training programs for foodservice managers and operators in many sections of the country. These programs have been voluntary until recently when, in some cities, they have been made mandatory.

New York City already requires that all new applicants for restaurant or other eating place permits successfully complete the city health department's Food Protection Course, before the permit is granted. New York also requires course attendance for those managers whose establishments are cited for serious health violations, and who do not have a valid food sanitation certificate. [21]

Florida has had a voluntary manager certification program and is expected to be the first state to make this cerification mandatory. The Oklahoma Restaurant Association deserves credit for initiating its own certification program for foodservice employees and is one of the first states to require certification of managers as well as workers. A planned training program, self-study, and tests are required before certification is given.

Organized classes in sanitation may be held satisfactorily either within an organization or by an outside agency such as a city health department, as well as the continuous on-the-job training and supervision. Eight 1-hour sessions or six 1 1/2-hour sessions are recommended and outlined by the U.S. Public Health Service [22] for presentation to groups of foodservice personnel. These may be repeated as often as necessary to give all workers an opportunity to attend, or as refresher courses. The amount of training will be determined somewhat by rate of turnover of personnel and the existing sanitary conditions needing further improvement. The classes should be taught by well-qualified persons who know and can explain the technical phases of the program to the employees on a level that will be meaningful to them. There are many visual aids in the form of films, slides, and posters that may be used to add interest and emphasis. The National Restaurant Association [23] distributes many such materials. Also, training materials may be obtained from the Center for Disease Control [24] and from the National Sanitation Foundation, [25] among others.

[21] *"Food Sanitation Certification,"* Restaurant Business Magazine, 73, 41 (*December 1974*).

[22] Instructors' Guide—Sanitary Food Service, *PHS Pub. 90, U.S. Government Printing Office, Washington, D.C., reprinted 1960.*

[23] *National Restaurant Association, P.O. Box 92558, Chicago 60690.*

[24] Training Bulletin, *U.S. Dept. HEW Publication 74-8005 PHS, Center for Disease Control, Atlanta, Georgia 30383.*

[25] A Reference Manual of Food Service Sanitation Educational & Training Materials, *National Sanitation Foundation, NSF Building, Ann Arbor, Michigan 48104.*

In summary, certain standards should be met by employees in the preparation for foodservice work. These standards should be included in an ongoing training program and follow-up with supervision on the job. The wearing of hair restraints by women and men is a protective measure to be observed by all food personnel. Clean aprons, clean uniforms, and comfortable, well-fitted shoes are essential; elimination of jewelry and nail polish and avoidance of excessive makeup are common requirements of the worker. A checklist for use in inspection of food personnel usually covers the following points: general good appearance; clean, well-kept nails; clear skin with no pimples, boils, or blemishes; clean teeth, nonoffensive breath; lack of any body odors; and freedom from colds or other respiratory difficulties.

Correct work habits of employees and sanitary food handling procedures to be followed by the foodservice personnel include:

Wash hands with soap and water on reporting for work and after handling raw poultry and meat, smoking, sneezing, and use of handkerchief and, above all, after each visit to the toilet.

Keep work surfaces clean and the work area well organized and orderly so that each part of the work may be carried through to completion without hazard.

Refrigerate unused foods and clean up any spillage promptly.

Use only clean utensils in preparing, cooking, and serving food.

Keep fingers and hands out of food as much as possible. Use spoons, forks, tongs, or other appropriate utensils. Wear disposable gloves for handling food that will not be further cooked before serving.

Always grasp utensils such as spoons, spatulas, tongs, and forks by the handles.

Pick up and convey glasses by the bases, cups by their handles, and plates by the rims, being careful to avoid possible contamination of the serving surface.

Use a clean spoon each time for tasting food.

Observe the "no smoking" rule in the preparation and serving areas.

PHYSICAL PLANT AND EQUIPMENT

Certain points merit careful consideration in the selection of a building that will meet basic standards in the operation of a sanitary foodservice. These include: the adequacy and safety of the available water supply; the adequacy and regularity of garbage and trash disposal; and the suitability of the structure and equipment to the sanitary requirements of the foodservice and to the activities involved in all its varied departments.

It is relatively easy to check on the assured pressure and volume of the water and its safeness from the reports of the department of health. The adequacy of the hot water supply can be checked against the existing standards of consumption. At least 1.8 gallons should be allowed for each meal served. Food preparation activities require approximately one fourth of this total; dishwashing takes one half to one fifth and kitchen cleanup takes one fifth or less. The remainder is spent on hand washing and other sanitation needs. These demands are not made simultaneously, but extend over several hours during which time there will be several well-defined peaks.

The source of heat and the capacity of the hot water storage tank determine the quantity of hot water that can be supplied in most small institutions. Rapid heating with a high recovery rate reduces the storage requirement greatly. With a good source of heat a 50-gallon storage tank should supply adequate hot water within the meal preparation, service, and cleanup period to provide a meal for 100 persons. However, the storage capacity of a tank heated slowly must be greater to provide adequately for the same number of patrons, because the recovery rate would be relatively slower. Some type of booster heater system may be installed to insure a ready supply of water for heavy or unusual demands and when water of a higher temperature than 120 to 140°F is required. Water above this temperature in the pipe lines of a building would be a hazard to the safety of the workers. Larger institutions usually have an unlimited supply of hot water provided by means of the steam heating system.

Other information that may be desired is the relative hardness of the water, since this will have a bearing on the detergents selected and perhaps on the predicted life or time span of useful service of necessary equipment such as that in the dishwashing area, most of which is fairly expensive to replace. If the hardness or ratio of carbonates or sulphates to water exceeds the usual maximum tolerance of 250 parts per million, undesirable precipitation may be expected and deposition on equipment will occur. If there is an unpleasant taste or odor, the quality of coffee and other foods may be impaired. If iron and manganese are present in excess, staining and discoloration will occur, with probable alteration in the flavors of food. Any organic matter present may be regarded as bringing the safety of the water under question.

Provisions for the disposal of garbage are commonly made by the city although, in some instances, they are regarded as a responsibility of the operating firm. In either case, any garbage not eliminated through mechanical means should be removed daily. Until such disposal is made, garbage should be stored temporarily in metal cans with tight-fitting lids, in a well-ventilated and chilled place. The containers should be scrubbed daily, rinsed, and steam treated.

Heavy-duty mechanical food waste disposer units have proven indispensable in many foodservice installations where allowed by city ordinance. Food waste from preparation and the after-meal plate scraps is ground fine and flushed down the drain instead of left around to become unsightly and often unpleasant. Units are located advantageously where waste originates in quantities, as in vegetable and salad preparation units, main food preparation center, and the dishwashing area. (See Fig. 10.5.) In this area it may be incorporated as a part of the scrapping and prewash unit. Some kitchen managers prefer to use containers in the kitchen for the collection of food refuse and transport it often to one large central machine for final disposal. This procedure gives good control over what is thrown away.

Many institution foodservices have electrically powered compactors with can and bottle crushers (Fig. 10.6) to reduce appreciably the volume of trash, including items such as disposable dishes, food cartons, bags, and crates.

The structure of the building itself should be fitted to its intended use. This means that smooth, nonskid floors with all crevices and cracks sealed are so laid that good drainage is assured after washing. Adequate, well-placed floor drains are essential. Glazed tile walls or other smooth impervious surfacing make cleaning easy.

The structure should be one in which an adequate ventilating

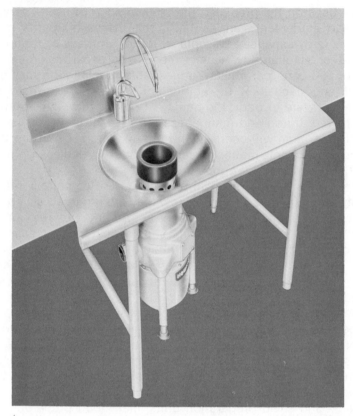

FIGURE 10.5 The installation of mechanical disposers near sources of waste eliminates unsightly garbage cans and their cleaning. An important factor is to select motor power adequate to carry the anticipated loads.

system has been installed if needed, and the ducts and fans should be accessible for easy cleaning. Adequate lighting should be provided so that all tasks may be performed in well-illuminated areas. Cleaning procedures are usually performed more satisfactorily when there is ample light to show up the areas to be cleaned. Further information on ventilation and lighting is found in Chapter 11.

Adequate sanitary facilities for employees are basic requirements that must be provided in the physical plant of any food or related service. Most states have made legal specifications as to the kind and number of facilities to be provided and what shall be deemed as satisfactory standards in use. Standards generally regarded as reasonable include separate toilet facilities for each sex in the general ratio of one toilet to each 10 or 12 persons. Floors of toilet rooms to be of cement or tile laid in cement, or other nonabsorbent materials. Toilet rooms to be separate and apart from the space devoted to production and serving, yet of a maximum distance of 150 to 200 feet. All toilet rooms to be adequately equipped with toilet paper and holders, and those for women sanitary napkin holders.

Washrooms affording adequate hand-washing facilities should be maintained adjacent to the toilet rooms. These should be supplied with running hot and cold water, soap, and paper towels or air-drying facilities.

Rest rooms must be provided for all work places with cots available for anyone who may become ill at work.

Toilets and washrooms should have self-closing doors and outside windows completely screened. Individual lockers of adequate size, well-ventilated and well-lighted, should be provided to em-

FIGURE 10.6   *Waste equipment system capable of reducing volume of food scraps and disposable materials into semidry pulp as much as 85 percent. Product of Hobart Corporation.*

ployees for storage of clothing and personal effects during the working day. Complete shower facilities, equipped with hot and cold running water, should be available adjacent to the locker space.

Drinking fountains and hand-washing facilities, separate and apart from other sinks, should be so placed as to be readily available to all employees in all parts of the kitchen. Their location should be such as not to create cross lines of traffic into any planned production line. Managers cannot expect employees to maintain clean hands if a lavatory where they may wash is a long distance from their work station.

Rodent and Insect Control. The importance of rodent and insect control cannot be minimized. Rats, mice, flies, roaches, grain insects, fruit flies, and gnats all facilitate the transmission of communicable diseases, as noted previously in Table 10.1 (page 556). It becomes essential in any foodservice to try to effect complete elimination of resident pest infestations and then to correct conditions within the establishment so that such pests cannot gain entrance in the future.

Two conditions, food and a place to "harbor" or hide and live, are required for these pests to survive. Adherence to strict rules for proper food storage and maintainance of high standards for cleaning the nooks and corners, such as drawers in cooks' tables, around sink pipes and drains, as well as the general overall sanitation and cleaning program, provides good preventive maintenance against pests.

Constant attention and alertness to signs of the intruders and an effective program for their destruction by a trained person within the organization or an outside agency are usually required.

Ratproofing of the building to make it impossible for rodents to gain entrance is the best preventive measure for maintaining a rat-free foodservice. This means the closing of openings as small as 1/2 inch in diameter, placing ratguards on all wires on both inside and outside of pipes leading into the building, and careful joining of the cement walls and foundations of the building. It is estimated that rats can jump vertically or horizontally 36 inches from a flat surface, reach 18 inches horizontally or vertically, drop 50 feet, or burrow 4 feet vertically into the earth. Trapping or the use of rodenticides are parts of a rodent-control program and are used either inside or outside the building. However, the most effective rodenticides are also the most dangerous to men and pets; therefore they must be used with care and caution.

Many roaches and other insect pests gain entrance to a building on incoming foodstuffs and packages, which makes their control difficult. Their reproduction is rapid, and they thrive in the warm, damp hiding places afforded them in many foodservices. Screens to help keep out flies, covered garbage cans, closed cracks and crevices in walls and around equipment and areas around pipes, and clean storerooms are preventive measures to try to block the entrance and reduce the hiding places of such pests. The use of certain residual insecticides is effective treatment when there is no danger of polluting food, whereas the use of less toxic insecticides is recommended for contact spraying. More often than not the actual eradication of these pests is made the responsibility of competent and reliable specialists in rodent and insect control.

These specialized entomological services may be scheduled as often as once a month. The effectiveness of such effort depends on its scope, regularity, and intelligent administration of a cleaning program and proper care of foodstuffs to eliminate the environmental factors conducive to the harboring of pests.

Maintenance. The total housekeeping program of the foodservice department must reflect concern with sanitation as "a way of life" if this philosophy phrased by the National Sanitation Foundation is to pass from words into reality.

The organization of a plan for housekeeping and maintenance begins with a list of duties to be performed daily, weekly, monthly, and occasionally. Most organizations believe that "sanitation is a part of every person's job," and that daily cleaning of the equipment and utensils used by each is his responsibility. General cleaning of floors, windows, walls, lighting fixtures, and certain equipment is assigned to cleaning personnel. Drake [26] has outlined a typical job assignment rotation for heavy-duty cleaning in a hospital foodservice department. This may serve as a guide for other managers who are setting up a cleaning schedule. See page 592.

These duties should next be developed into written work sheets or job breakdown sheets, one for each task to be performed. These constitute the procedure to be used by the worker. They should ininclude his tools, equipment, and materials to be used and the step-by-step list of what to do and how to do it. The development of such well-defined procedures reflect the standards desired for sanitation in a foodservice operation, and the technique is highly recom-

[26] *Richard L. Drake, "Control as a System Function,"* Hospitals, JAHA, 46 (15), 73-75 (August 1, 1972).

Typical Job Assignments for Heavy-duty Cleaner

MONDAY | Filter grease in snack bar
| Clean left side of cafeteria hot-food pass-through
| Clean all kitchen windows
| Clean all kitchen table legs
| Vacuum air-conditioner filters; wipe exterior of air conditioner
| Wash all walls around garbage cans
| Complete high dusting around cooking areas
| Clean diet kitchen steam kettles
| Wash kitchen carts
| Clean cart-washing area

TUESDAY | Snack bar: Wash inside of hood exhaust
| Clean all corners, walls, and behind refrigerator
| Empty and clean grease can
| Wash garbage cans
| Main range area: Clean sides of ovens, deep-fat fryers, grills, drip pans, and hood over ovens

WEDNESDAY | Clean two refrigerators in cooks' area
| Clean right side of cafeteria hot-food pass-through
| Clean kettles, backs of steamers, and behind steamers
| Clean diet kitchen ovens
| Clean walls around assembly line and pot room

THURSDAY | Clean all ovens in cooks' area, bottoms of ovens, and between ovens and stoves
| Clean long tables in cooks' area, including legs and underneath
| Clean and mop storage area

FRIDAY | Clean stainless steel behind kettles and steamers
| Clean main range and tops of ovens
| Clean legs of assembly line tables
| Clean vents in all refrigeration equipment
| Clean cart-washing area

---

mended for maintaining efficient and economical cleanliness at the desired level. Longree and Blaker [27] have developed a guide for maintenance that provides a valuable reference for foodservice managers. An example of the detailed daily care necessary for one major piece of institution equipment is outlined on page 598.

[27] *Karla Longree and Gertrude C. Blaker,* Sanitary Techniques in Food Service, *Section III, Wiley, New York, 1971.*

WORK LOAD DETERMINATION FORM

AREA _PROP MGMT. DEPT. 1570 SQ. FT._   QUALITY STANDARD _88_ _____

ITEM TO BE CLEANED	CLEANING METHOD (DESCRIBE)	STANDARD TIME PER ITEM	AMOUNT OR NUMBER OF THE ITEM	TOTAL TIME (MINUTES)	CLEANING FREQUENCY	YEARLY TIME (HOURS)
WASTE BASKETS	_EMPTY_	_17 SECONDS_	_15_	_4.3_	_DAILY_	_18.6_
ASH TRAYS	_EMPTY & DAMP WIPE_	_10 SECONDS_	_11_	_1.8_	_DAILY_	_7.8_
STD. DESK GROUP-	_DUST-WHISK_	_42 SECONDS_	_12_	_8.4_	_DAILY_	_36.4_
DESK, CHAIR,	_UPHOLSTERED CHAIRS_					
TELEPHONE,						
MAIL BASKET, FILE						
ASPHALT TILE FLOOR	_DUST MOP_	_8 M/1000_	_1570 SQ.FT._	_12_	_DAILY_	_52_
ASPHALT TILE FLOOR	_COMPLETE BUFFING_	_20 M/1000_	_1570 SQ.FT._	_30_	_WEEKLY_	_25_
PROJECT WORK	_WAXING,_	_7 M/1000_	_1570 SQ.FT._	_11_	_DAILY_	_47.6_
	FURNITURE WASHING,					
	SPOT WASHING, ETC.					
				TOTAL YEARLY TIME (Area Work Load):		

FORM 10.1   Summary form work load. Courtesy, Nationwide Insurance Company.

A chart of total work load based on items to be cleaned, the amount of space, types of materials used in construction of building and equipment, and the methods and time standards to be used, is next translated into man-hour requirements for cleaning. A suggested chart for this calculation is given in Form 10.1. From these data, schedules for when the work is to be done and directions for doing the work are made for each "sanitor."

Training employees in correct, efficient methods of cleaning, providing adequate tools and materials, and having established time standards for completing the work are all essential responsibilities of management. Conservative estimates of budget allocations for sanitation maintenance in public buildings indicate only 8 percent is spent for supplies, while 92 percent is spent for the labor. With this investment in labor cost, management has a real responsibility for good returns for money spent. According to Drake,[28]

[28] Richard L. Drake, "Control as a System Function," Hospitals, JAHA, 46 (15), 73-75 (August 1, 1972).

On the basis of our experience, good sanitation results can be obtained through setting of high standards, rigid scheduling of assignments, constant training, control of cleaning supplies, and frequent, meaningful inspections and performance review.

Design and Placement of Large Equipment. One of the major activities of the National Sanitation Foundation has been to help establish definite acceptable sanitation standards for materials used in food-service equipment and for its design, construction, installation, and maintenance. These standards are based on scientific research and are agreed on by joint committees made up of qualified representatives from research, industry, education, and the public health profession. Publications are available from the Foundation in which such minimum standards are defined clearly and specifically. The standards are adaptable to various geographical areas. Attention will be called to certain of the standards in this text, but it behooves each foodservice director to have access to a complete set of the publications for reference. (See suggested references at the end of this chapter.)

Manufacturers who meet the standards are privileged to use the stamp of approval of the Foundation on their products, and the purchaser is assured of acceptable design, materials, constructions, and performance, if the equipment is properly installed and operated. Recommended standards have given much attention to the proper conditions for installation and use of equipment as well as construction in the factory.

Much is done to publicize the recommended standards through publication and distribution of booklets and posters. Local and state public health departments make wide use of the standards in formulating and enforcing codes for physical facilities and the operation of foodservices under their jurisdictions. Emphasis in the work of the Foundation is on the positive approach to good health in the prevention of disease through knowledge and practice of high standards of sanitation for the community, especially in the foodservice industry.

Each piece of stationary equipment, the use of which involves contact with food, should be so designed and constructed that the food contact surfaces are nonabsorbent (like stainless steel), continuous and smooth, free from open seams, cracks, chipped places, exposed junctions, and sharp corners. All junctions should be rounded or coved. Not only should the food contact surface be readily cleanable, but it should also be readily accessible for cleaning and maintained in complete cleanliness. (See Fig. 10.7.)

FIGURE 10.7   Smooth-welded joinings, rolled edges, rounded corners, sloped-to-drain bottom, mixer faucet, knee-lever control drain are conducive to good sink sanitation. Courtesy, S. Blickman, Inc.

The placement of the pieces of large fixed equipment should be determined thoughtfully to allow the worker space for necessary activity and to avoid such things as accident and spillage. Adequate space beneath and behind heavy equipment is necessary for mopping and cleaning if such items are not built into the floor or wall with proper fittings and joinings (see Standards, page 737). Figure 10.8 is an illustration of equipment of simple design and good arrangement for work to assure that high sanitation standards are maintained.

Care of Equipment. All equipment used in food preparation, service, and storage should be maintained in excellent condition to assure sanitation and help avoid the development of off-flavor in foods. A usual recommendation is that all containers and all utensils be

FIGURE 10.8 Simple design and good construction of equipment facilitate ease of maintenance and contribute to beauty of a modern food service. Courtesy, Southern Equipment Company.

cleaned thoroughly *after each use.* This is especially true of meat slicers, cutting boards, and knives to assure safety against C. perfringens and salmonellae contamination.

The thorough cleaning and sanitizing of stationary equipment are even more difficult but quite as necessary, as is the cleaning of dishes and small portable equipment. No piece of large equipment should be purchased unless the operating parts can be disassembled easily for purposes of cleaning. Dishwashing machines, mixers, peelers, slicing machines, and stationary can openers are examples of equipment that should be cleaned after each use. The standard practices for hand dishwashing should be followed in the routine cleaning of such equipment. An example of the detailed daily care necessary for one major piece of fixed equipment is given on page 598.

DISHWASHING

The purposes of dishwashing are to clean and to sanitize the dishes and utensils. It requires a two-part operation, that is, the cleaning procedure to free them of visible soil, wash water and detergent, and the sanitizing or bactericidal treatment to eliminate the health hazard. Dishwashing for public eating places should and has become subject to rigid regulations.

The two groups of equipment and utensils that are commonly considered for discussion under *dishwashing* are: the kitchen uten-

METHODS OF HAND DISHWASHING

Preferred Method

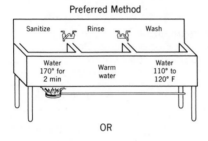

OR

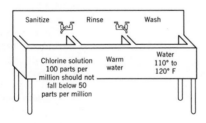

Accepted Method

FIGURE 10.9   *Sink arrangement and recommended temperatures of water for hand dishwashing. Courtesy, U.S. Health Service.*

HOW TO CLEAN A FOOD SLICER

Equipment and supplies needed:
  Three cloths:
    One to wash
    One to dry
    One to apply rust preventative
  One-gal container for detergent
  One container with sanitizer
  One table knife

Cleaning products needed:
  Hand detergent
    In amount needed to make one
    gal of solution
    Usual proportion: 1 oz to 1 gal
    of water
  Sanitizer:
    Usual proportion: 2 oz chlorine to
    1 gal water
  Rust preventative:
    In amount needed to moisten cloth
    for application of thin film to speci-
    fied metal surfaces

Approximate time: 20 min
Frequency of cleaning: Daily
Approximate cost: Labor _____
                Supplies _____

What To Do	*How To Do It*
1. Remove parts	1. *a.* Remove electric cord from socket.
	b. Set blade control indicator at zero.
	c. Loosen knurled screw to release; remove meat holder and chute.
	d. Grasp scrap tray by handle; pull away from blade; remove.
	e. Loosen bolt at top of knife guard in front of sharpening device; remove bolt at bottom of guard; remove guard.
	f. Remove two knurled screw nuts under receiving tray; remove tray.
2. Clean knife	2. *a.* Wash circular surface with hot hand-detergent solution; rinse; dip in sanitizing solution; dry. DANGER: Keep clear of knife edge.

What To Do	How To Do It
	b. Wring out cloth dipped in hot detergent solution, bunch thickly and wipe entire circumference of blade, wiping from center toward edge of blade; rinse; dip in sanitizing solution; dry with bunched cloth.
3. Clean and replace guard	3. a. Wash knife guard in hot detergent solution; rinse; sanitize; dry.
	b. Replace knife guard.
	c. Tighten bolt at top; insert and tighten bolt at bottom. DANGER: Replace knife guard as quickly as possible to prevent injury.
4. Clean other parts	4. a. Immerse in hot detergent solution: 1. Meat holder and chute. 2. Receiving tray.
	b. Wash; rinse; sanitize; dry.
5. Clean beneath receiving tray	5. a. Wash surface below receiving tray with hot detergent solution; rinse; dry.
	b. Apply *very thin* film of rust preventative to any exposed metal *under* receiving tray.
6. Clean frame and base	6. a. Wash frame with hot detergent solution, rinse, dry.
	b. With table knife, push damp cloth under knife of slicer; pull cloth through to remove food particles.
7. Replace parts	7. a. Replace meat holder and chute; tighten knurled screw.
	b. Replace scrap tray.
	c. Replace receiving tray; replace and tighten two screw nuts under tray.

sils such as pots, pans, strainers, skillets, and kettles soiled in the process of food preparation; and the dishes, glassware, spoons, forks, knives, and other eating and drinking utensils.

Mechanical pot and pan washing equipment is relatively expensive, so that in many foodservices this activity still remains a hand operation. A three-compartment sink is recommended for any hand-washing setup. (See Fig. 10.9.) Public Health authorities recommend that sinks used for manual washing and sanitizing operations shall be of adequate length, width, and depth to permit the complete immersion of the equipment and utensils.

The soil may be loosened from the utensils by scraping and then soaking them in one compartment of the sink, well filled with hot water, previous to the time of washing. After the surface soil has been removed, the utensils are washed in a hot detergent solution in the first compartment; rinsed well in the second compartment, the outlet and inlet of which are so adjusted as to keep the water level constant if hot water is kept running throughout the process; and sanitized in the third compartment. A forced-flow pump system unit, such as shown in Fig. 10.10 facilitates the ease of cleaning pots and pans. It can be installed onto the end of any sink and is relatively inexpensive to install and operate, and highly effective in the loosening and removal of cooked-on food.

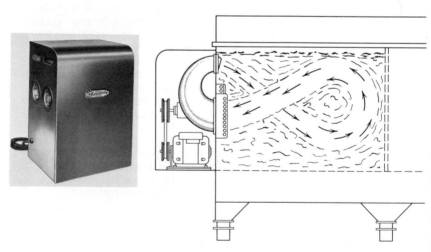

FIGURE   10.10   Pump-forced flow of water loosens food particles from cooking utensils in few minutes. May be installed on end of regular pot and pan sink. Courtesy, Kewanee Washer Corporation.

One recommended method for sanitizing both dishes and cooking utensils is by immersing them for at least 1 minute in a lukewarm chlorine bath containing a minimum of 50 ppm available chlorine. Dishes and utensils must be thoroughly clean for a chlorine rinse to be an effective germicidal treatment. Another method of sanitizing handwashed dishes or utensils is immersion in clean hot soft water at 170°F for 2 minutes or in clean boiling soft water for 1/2 minute. The desired temperature of the water may be maintained by use of a booster heater on the hot water line or by a thermostatically controlled heater arrangement (180–195°F), by burners placed directly under the sink compartment, or by the installation of steam injectors into or closed coils within the vat. Another successful method of sanitizing utensils is to subject them to live steam in an enclosed cabinet after washing and rinsing (Fig. 10.11). The hot, clean utensils should be air-dried before stacking upside down on racks or hanging for storage.

FIGURE   10.11   *Washed utensils may be sanitized by steam under pressure in a metal cabinet near pot and pan sink. Courtesy, Kansas State University.*

Dishwashing may be accomplished by hand or by use of mechanical washers. In either case, prewashing or preflushing of all dishes and utensils is recommended as an important part of the dishwashing operation to prevent food soil in the wash water. This term is applied to any type of water scrapping of dishes before washing. The usual types of water-scrapping equipment include (1) a combination, forced water stream and food waste collection unit built into the scrapping table, by use of which dishes are rinsed under the stream of water before racking; (2) a hose and nozzle arrangement over a sink for spraying the dishes after they are in racks; and (3) a pre-wash cabinet through which the racks of soiled dishes

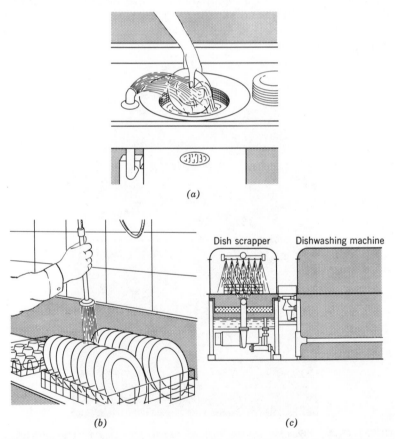

FIGURE 10.12   Preflush arrangements. (a) Forced water spray. (b) Hose and nozzle. (c) Water scrapping cabinet.

pass and are jet sprayed to remove food particles prior to their entering the wash section of the dishmachine (see Fig. 10.12). The wash cabinet may be built in as a part of the large model machines or, in small installations, it may be a separate unit attached to the wash machine in such a way that the water used is the overflow from the wash tank. The prewash water should be at a temperature of 110 to 140°F to provide for the liquefying of fat and the non-coagulation of protein food particles adhering to dish surfaces. The installation and use of a prewash system lessens the amount of organic waste and the number of microorganisms entering the wash tank, removes fat that might otherwise result in suds formation, reduces the number of washwater changes, cuts the cost for detergents, and results in cleaner dishes.

There are many dishwashing machines on the market. Various types are discussed in Chapter 12, but Fig. 10.13 illustrates the general principles of *how* dishes are washed in a single-tank machine. Larger machines have divided tanks (see Fig. 10.14) so that the wash and rinse waters are kept separate and the dilution of the wash water is less rapid.

The installation of elaborate equipment offers no real security for good sanitation, since the efficiency of the machines depends almost wholly on the operator, the availability of an adequate supply of hot water of the proper temperature and pressure, the selection and concentration of detergent used for the hardness of the water, and the length of time the dishes are subjected to treatment. In the small, hand-operated, single-tank machines, the process and length of washing time is under the control of the operator and is followed by the rinsing process, also under his manual control. Other machines have automatic controls that regulate the length of times for washing and rinsing. Thermometers that record the temperatures of both wash and rinse waters and thermostatic controls, except for the final rinse, are now included as standard parts of dish-washing machines. Booster heaters with temperature controls are available and necessary to provide the sanitizing rinse temperature, because 180°F water in the pipe lines of a building would be a hazard to safety of the personnel. The installation of electronic detergent dispensers makes it possible to maintain optimum detergent concentration in the wash water. Each of these mechanical aids is most helpful in reducing the variables due to the human element and assures clean, properly sanitized dishes and pots and pans. See Fig. 10.15 for an arrangement of machines for washing dishes and pots and pans in the same area.

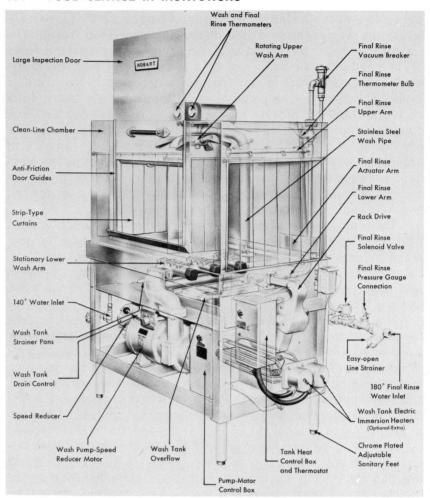

Wash and Final
Rinse Thermometers

Rotating Upper
Wash Arm

Final Rinse
Vacuum Breaker

Large Inspection Door

HOBART

Final Rinse
Thermometer Bulb

Final Rinse
Upper Arm

Clean-Line Chamber

Stainless Steel
Wash Pipe

Final Rinse
Actuator Arm

Anti-Friction
Door Guides

Final Rinse
Lower Arm

Strip-Type
Curtains

Rack Drive

Final Rinse
Solenoid Valve

Stationary Lower
Wash Arm

Final Rinse
Pressure Gauge
Connection

140° Water Inlet

Wash Tank
Strainer Pans

Easy-open
Line Strainer

Wash Tank
Drain Control

180° Final Rinse
Water Inlet

Wash Tank Electric
Immersion Heaters
(Optional-Extra)

Speed Reducer

Chrome Plated
Adjustable
Sanitary Feet

Wash Pump-Speed
Reducer Motor

Wash Tank
Overflow

Tank Heat
Control Box
and Thermostat

Pump-Motor
Control Box

FIGURE 10.13   Design of a single-tank dishwashing machine. Product of Hobart
Corporation.

Soiled dishes must be loaded into the racks or onto conveyor
belts so that all surfaces of each piece will be subjected to the wash-
and-rinse treatment. Cups, bowls, and glasses must be inverted, and
the overcrowding or nesting of pieces must be avoided if the dishwashing process is to be effective. The clean rinsed hot dishes
should air dry at least 45 seconds before they are removed for
storage.

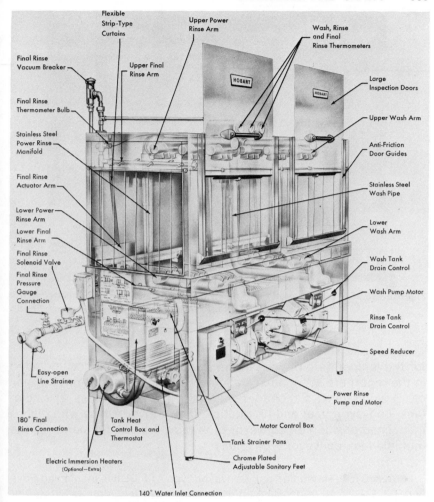

Flexible Strip-Type Curtains

Upper Power Rinse Arm

Wash, Rinse and Final Rinse Thermometers

Final Rinse Vacuum Breaker

Upper Final Rinse Arm

Large Inspection Doors

Final Rinse Thermometer Bulb

Upper Wash Arm

Stainless Steel Power Rinse Manifold

Anti-Friction Door Guides

Final Rinse Actuator Arm

Stainless Steel Wash Pipe

Lower Power Rinse Arm

Lower Wash Arm

Lower Final Rinse Arm

Final Rinse Solenoid Valve

Wash Tank Drain Control

Final Rinse Pressure Gauge Connection

Wash Pump Motor

Rinse Tank Drain Control

Speed Reducer

Easy-open Line Strainer

Power Rinse Pump and Motor

180° Final Rinse Connection

Tank Heat Control Box and Thermostat

Motor Control Box

Tank Strainer Pans

Electric Immersion Heaters (Optional—Extra)

Chrome Plated Adjustable Sanitary Feet

140° Water Inlet Connection

FIGURE   10.14   Phantom view of a two-tank dishwashing machine. Product of Hobart Corporation.

Public Health Service [29] recommends that "the wash-water temperature shall be at least 140°F and in single-tank conveyor machines shall be at least 160°F." Washing at a minimum of 150°F is the standard set by the National Sanitation Foundation as desirable

[29] "Food Service Sanitation Manual," Public Health Service Publication 934, U.S. Government Printing Office, Washington, D.C., p. 56, 1962.

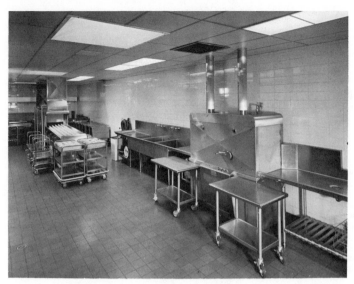

FIGURE   10.15   Dish and pot and pan washing in same area makes possible the efficient use of manpower in the small kitchen. Courtesy, Southern Equipment Company.

for the temperature of wash water in spray-type machines. Included in the report are acceptable standards for the wash and rinse cycles of (1) single-tank, stationary-rack: hood and door types; (2) single-tank, conveyor type; and (3) multiple-tank conveyor type with dishes in inclined position on conveyor or in rack. The requirements for the multiple-tank conveyor type follow:

Wash Cycle—Multiple Tank Conveyor Type with Dishes in Inclined Position on Conveyor or in Rack: *Machines for washing prewashed (water scrapped) dishes, either in racks or in an inclined position on conveyors, shall be so constructed that each lineal inch of conveyor shall be effectively sprayed from above and below with not less than 1.65 gallons of pumped wash water at a minimum of 150°F. It shall require a minimum of 7 seconds for a given point to traverse the wash spray area. The pump delivery capacity shall not be less than 125 gallons per minute when installed in the machine. The pressure and spray pattern of wash water delivered during the washing operation shall be sufficient to remove physical soil from all portions of the racked dishes. The above mentioned 1.65 gallons per lineal inch is based upon a wash area width of 20 inches. For widths of more or less than 20 inches the volume shall be proportionate; for example, 1.48 gallons for 18 inches width; 1.82 gallons for 22 inches width, and 1.98 gallons for 24 inches width. For other conveyor widths multiply the width of the conveyor in inches by 0.0825. An adjustable device shall be provided for automatically adding makeup water to the wash tank in sufficient quantity to maintain a constant level and run off any grease which may be present. Not more than 2 gpm may be supplied from the final rinse supply.*

Pumped Rinse—Multiple Tank Conveyor Type: *Machines of this type shall be so constructed that each lineal inch of conveyor shall be effectively sprayed from above and below with not less than 1.65 gallons of pumped rinse water at 160°F or more. It shall require a minimum of 7 seconds for a given point to traverse the rinse spray area. The pump delivery capacity shall be not less than 125 gallons per minute when installed in the machine. The pressure at the jets and the spray pattern during rinsing shall be such as to thoroughly rinse all portions of the dishes. The above-mentioned 1.65 gallons per lineal inch is based upon a rinse area width of 20 inches. For widths of more or less than 20 inches, the volume shall be proportionate; for example, 1.48 gallons for racks 18 inches wide, 1.82 gallons for racks 22 inches wide and 1.98 gallons for racks 24 inches wide. For other conveyor widths multiply the width of the conveyor in inches by 0.0825. Sufficient space shall be allowed between the rinse sprays and wash sprays, or adequate baffles shall be provided, to prevent intermingling of wash and rinse water.*

Final Rinse-Multiple-Tank Conveyor-Type: *A final rinse shall be provided from nozzles above and below distributed evenly across the conveyor so as to cover a space of at least 3 inches measured at a height of 5 inches above the conveyor in the direction of travel. The temperature of such water shall be maintained at not less than 180°F nor more than 195°F at the entrance of the manifold. The flow shall not be less than 4.62 gallons per minute at a flow pressure of 20 psi. The rinse volume of 4.62 gpm is based on rack or conveyor width of 20 inches. For units of greater width, the rinse volume shall be increased proportionately. The conveyor speed of the machine shall not exceed 15 feet per minute.*

Note: *The flow pressure shall not be less than 15 pounds per square inch on the line adjacent to the machine and not in excess of 25 pounds per square inch.*[30]

China, glassware, and silver may be washed in the same machine, but it is preferred wherever possible to subject glasses to friction by brushes so that all parts of the glass are thoroughly cleaned, which means the use of a special machine designed for that purpose. (See Fig. 10, 16.) A suitable detergent for the washing of silver is advised and also in the final rinse a drying agent with high wetting property to facilitate air drying with no water spotting is desirable. The introduction of a drying agent with low foam characteristics into the sanitizing rinse promotes rapid drying of all types of tableware.

[30] *"Standards—Commercial Spray-Type Dishwashing Machines,"* National Sanitation Foundation, *Standard 3, pp. 29–31, amended, April 1965.*

FIGURE   10.16   Glasswasher unit incorporated in back-of-counter setup.

Provision for the storage of clean glasses and cups in the racks or containers in which they have been washed eliminates the possibility of much hand contamination.

Any machine can fail in its function if it is not kept clean and properly maintained, and dishwashing equipment is no exception. Corrosion or lime deposits in nozzles can alter the jet or spray materially. Also, detergent sanitizers can be inactivated by contact with soiled surfaces and lose their power of penetration. The removal of microbial contamination is necessary; otherwise the washed surfaces of dishes will have deposited on them bacterial populations and soil proportionate to that in the washing solution.

Procedures for the cleaning and care of dishwashing machines are as follows:

> The dishwashing equipment should be cleaned thoroughly at the end of each washing period.
>
> Clean dish tables using detergent and rinse with fresh water. During this operation scrap trays shall remain in place in machine.
>
> Turn off heat on wash or rinse tanks.

Drain water from tanks and pumps.

Remove racks from door-type machines and curtains from curtain-type machines.

Remove wash arms or end caps where arms are not removable, and clean with brush provided for this purpose.

Check and clean, if necessary, final rinse sprays.

Remove and clean scrap trays.

Close tank drain and hose and scrub the entire inside of machine thoroughly. Refill tank and then flush out pump and pump lines by running the machine at least one minute. Then drain tank.

Scrub and wash down curtains and hang in place for drying.

Replace scrap trays, wash arms, and rinse arms.

Check machine for next operation, leaving all inspection doors open.

Clean and refill detergent dispenser.

Check filler opening, final rinse and pump-packing glands for leakage.

Periodic checks should be made by authorized manufacturer personnel or manufacturer's authorized distributor every six months.

Good maintenance also includes frequent examination and lubrication where needed by a qualified maintenance man to insure the continuing satisfactory operation of motors, nozzles, pumps, thermostats, thermometers, and all moving parts of a dishwashing machine.

Hand and machine dishwashing as summarized in the *Instructor's Guide* [31] are given below.

[31] *"Instructor's Guide—Sanitary Food Service,"* Public Health Publication 37, *Washington, D.C.,* pp. 70–71, reprinted 1960.

HAND DISHWASHING

Important Steps (in Doing the Job)	Key Points [a]
1. Get ready (materials and equipment)	Sinks Hot water Washing powders (chlorine, or other bactericidal treatment, if used) Scraper Garbage can Drying racks
2. Scrape dishes and prewash	Use scraper Garbage in can or disposer
3. Wash dishes	Each piece separately Hot water, 110–120° F Use detergent (washing powder)
4. Rinse	Place in basket Set in hot rinse water
5. Sanitize	Place basket in vat In hot water (170° F for 2 min or 212° F for 30 sec) [b] 2 min in chemical solution (chlorine of approved strength)
6. Dry	Lift out basket Place on drain board Air dry
7. Store	Cups and glasses bottoms up Stack dishes on mobile carts In clean protected place
8. Clean vats	Stiff brush Washing powder
9. Use separate baskets for dishes, cups, and glasses	
10. Silver may be air-dried or by use of clean towel	
11. Fingers should not touch surfaces which come in contact with food or drink	
12. All multiservice eating and drinking utensils must be thoroughly cleaned after each usage	
13. Single-service containers must be used only once	

[a] Key points are those things which will make or break the job, injure the worker, or make the job easier to do.
[b] This standard may vary with local or area regulations.

MACHINE DISHWASHING

Important Steps (in Doing the Job)	Key Points [a]
1. Get ready (materials and equipment)	Sort dishes, cups, glassware, and silver Water temperature: 140° F wash, 170° F rinse [b] Check washing powder and dispenser, wash and rinse sprays
2. Scrape and prerinse	Use brush to scrape off garbage
3. Rack dishes, etc.	Place in separate racks Do not pile dishes, cups, etc. Cups and glassware bottoms up One kind at a time, separately
4. Place racks in machine	Every dish, etc., under spray
5. Wash	Start machine Turn on wash spray 140° to 160° F Do not hurry machine if it is manually operated Keep washtank water clean
6. Rinse	10 sec 170° F [b]
7. Dry	Remove racks Allow dishes, etc., to dry in racks on drain table or if flight type machine, do not remove dishes before they reach end of conveyer
8. Store	Fingers should not touch surfaces which come in contact with food In a clean, dry place above floor Away from dust and flies Dishes stacked Cups and glasses bottoms up—leave in racks in which they are washed
9. Clean machine	Take out scrap trays and clean Clean wash sprays Use clean water Add new washing powder as required

[a] *Key points are those things which will make or break the job, injure the worker, or make the job easier to do.*
[b] *This means temperature of 170° F at the dish, and requires 180° F water in the line. This standard may vary with local or area regulations.*

FIGURE   10.17   *Closed carts protect dishes while in storage or when fitted with heating elements may be used at hot food counters. Courtesy, Crescent Metal Products, Inc.*

Figure 10.17 shows a good example of a clean dish storage cart for transport to serving area.

DETERGENTS

Detergents are defined as cleansing agents, solvents, or any substances that will remove foreign or soiling material from surfaces. Specifically listed are water, soap, soap powders, cleansers, acids, volatile solvents, and abrasives. Water alone has some detergency value but, most often it is the carrier of the cleansing agent to the soiled surface. Its efficiency for removing soil is increased when combined with certain chemical cleaning agents. Basic alkalis such as caustic soda and soda ash produce saponification, but they have poor water-softening and rinsing qualities and high corrosive properties. The addition of sodium metasilicate improves the cleansing power and reduces the corrosive qualities. Tri-sodium phosphate makes a good cleaning solution and acts as a water softener, but it precipitates the calcium and magnesium salts in the water as a film on surfaces. None of the above have complete satisfactory rinsability, and all are harsh to the hands.

The development of polyphosphate detergents has provided us

with a wide variety of highly satisfactory cleaning compounds from which to choose. Film deposit from precipitation, poor rinsability, and harshness to hands no longer need to be a problem, and the selection of cleaners can be made to meet the needs for particular uses in the institution food service; for instance, a suds-producing hand wash with high-wetting action would be satisfactory as such but entirely unsatisfactory for machine dishwashing where a non-suds-producing detergent is needed.

Foodservice sanitation is concerned mainly with china, crockery, glass, and metal surfaces. Common soils to be removed are saliva, lipstick, grease, and carbohydrate and protein food particles that may adhere to dishes, glassware, silverware, cooking utensils, worktable tops, floors, or other surfaces. Some types of food soil such as sugars, starches, vegetable and animal proteins, and certain salts are water soluble. The addition of a wetting agent to hot water will readily remove most of these simple soils. The soils that are insoluble in water, such as animal and vegetable fats, organic fiber or carbon residues, and mineral oil, are more difficult to remove. Abrasives or solvents may be necessary in some cases to effect complete cleanliness.

The use of a "balanced" detergent or one with a carefully adjusted formula of ingredients suitable for the hardness of the water and the characteristics of the soil is advised in order to produce the best results. The properties of the detergent must cause complete removal of the soil without deposition of any substance or deleterious effect on surfaces washed.

Three basic phases of detergency are *penetration, suspension,* and *rinsing.* To remove soil, the cleaning solution must penetrate between the particles of soil and between the layer of soil and the surface to which it adheres. This property or ability to reduce surface tension is known as *wetting* action and permits the water to penetrate to a greasy or otherwise water-repellant surface to make removal of the soil possible. Such wetting agents may be soaps or synthetic detergents, and most of them are quick but rather fragile suds formers.

Suspension of the loosened soil in the washing solution is necessary to prevent redeposition on washed surfaces before it can be flushed away. Melted fats must be *emulsified* or broken into tiny globules and held in a homogeneous state by an emulsifying or coupling agent. Soap, highly alkaline salts, and many of the non-ionic synthetics are good emulsifiers. Certain water-soluble foods such as sugars and salts are easily converted into *solutions.* The process of dispersing solid soil particles and forming them into colloidal solutions from partially soluble soils such as proteins is called *peptizing* (also known as *sequestering* or *deflocculating*). Peptizing agents are important in the control of curd formation in hard water, exemplified in the familiar bathtub ring and dingy glassware. *Saponification* of fats with a mild alkali washing solution aids in the cleaning process if the soap formed is not precipitated immediately as insoluble calcium or magnesium soap.

Rinsing is removing soil and cleaner with clear water. To do so effectively, the detergent used for washing must have had the properties to penetrate and "lift" the soil from the surface and then keep it in suspension in the cleaning medium, thorough emulsification, peptization, deflocculation, saponification, or in solution, so that rinsing with clean, clear, hot water is effective.

Certain of the detergents have nontoxic germicidal properties, and some operate best at a relatively low temperature, because their solubility decreases with increased temperature. However, heat hastens action and makes most detergents more effective. Synthetic detergents are classified according to the production of electrically negative (anionic) or positive (cationic) charged, or neutral (nonionic) organic particles in the water. The cationic synthetics are usually good bactericides, but some have limited detergency values. The quaternary compounds come within this group. The nonionics are often in liquid form and are good wetters. There seems to be no perfect product for all conditions of use.

Selection of the right detergent for the job of cleaning in any situation is determined in large measure by the hardness of the water. The sequestering of the lime and magnesia of hard water by the polyphosphates produces a clear, not muddy, solution with insoluble precipitates, as is the case when some of the phosphates and silicates are used.

Hodges [32] explains further in regard to selection of a detergent for dishwashing machines:

The modern dishmachine detergent is a complex combination of the many chemicals required to provide uniformly good results in one pass through a high speed machine. Among other things it must soften water, provide high alkalinity, protect metal, increase wetting action, maintain PH control, suspend soil, solubilize and emulsify greases, and break down protein soils . . . (in selecting a detergent) one must look, not at price per pound of the

[32] Larry T. Hodges, "Know Your Detergent," School Lunch Journal, 23, 31 (1969). Copyright © American School Food Service Association, 1969.

detergent but as results *per pound. Results per pound are affected by these key ingredients:*

(1) *The ability to counteract minerals in the washing solution. This is a prime requirement in every dishwashing detergent.*
(2) *Defoaming action, where excess sudsing is a problem.*
(3) *Chlorination action, where a chlorine-type detergent is employed.*

Hodges further explains that it is the phosphate ingredient in the dishmachine compound that reacts with the minerals in the water. Many different types of phosphates are used, some relatively crude like trisodium phosphate (TSP) and some more refined like pyrophosphates, but the most efficient is the *highly refined polyphosphate* ingredient that completely cancels out the mineralization of the water and "conditions" the water in the wash tank for the cleansing task.

If sudsing occurs in the dishmachine from food soils, primarily from the protein-caused foam, the detergent selected should contain an effective defoaming agent. Likewise, if discoloration or staining of dishes is a problem, a chlorinated detergent is desirable. It is now possible to obtain a *high-performance* chlorinated dishmachine detergent in which the chlorine ingredient is stable. (Formerly the alkali would react with the chlorine, which was then released as a gas and became ineffective.)

These terms, high-strength alkali and highly refined polyphosphate, are not mere adjectives, they are chemical descriptions. A product either has them or does not, and you have a right to know whether or not it does.[33]

The effectiveness of the product instead of the price should be the primary factor in the selection of any cleaning compounds. In evaluating the cost of a rinse agent, for example, consider the concentration required (parts per million) for effective drying in relation to the price to get a true usage cost.

The quality of service offered by a company selling cleaning supplies is an important factor to their successful use in any organization. For example, a good salesman should and usually does know more about the operation of various dishwashing machines than the owners do. His judgment on the amount of compound to use is usually good, since he is accustomed to making the neces-

[33] *Larry T. Hodges, "Know Your Detergent," School Lunch Journal 23, 34 (1969). Copyright © American School Food Service Association, 1969.*

sary quantitative and qualitative tests. Also, he is aware that too much is as ineffective as too little, and it is to his advantage to have his product do the best job possible. It is generally recommended that dishwashing machines be equipped with automatic detergent dispensers that will keep the detergent solution at the proper determined concentration. In hard-water areas the installation of a water softener more than pays for itself in a short time in savings on equipment and detergents.

Exact reports on costs of dishwashing are difficult to obtain; there is great variation in labor rates, cost of dinnerware, amount of breakage, use of disposables, hardness of water, and the procedures followed. Some operators estimate costs with a breakdown of around 94 percent for labor, hot water, breakage, and indirect costs, and 6 percent for detergents.

The cleaning of equipment and utensils by ultrasonics is in the experimental stage. Also, in this age of convenience foods, the use of disposables is increasing rapidly in certain types of foodservices. Both will have decided effects on the foodservice sanitation problems in the future.

SANITATION CHECKS

The maintenance of high standards of sanitation is of utmost importance in all operations within the food service industry. A sound basis of understanding and cooperative effort and interest on the part of management, personnel, and control officials is necessary to carry out an effective program in food sanitation. If management fails, official control measures must be enforced. Most personnel will do only what they believe management stands for and will expect. On the other hand, management can operate successfully and happily under its own high and established standards and more than meet requirements that might be effected through legislation; hence, the emphasis on the importance of management's attitude.

Training programs in sanitary food service on both management and personnel levels have done much to make both groups aware of their responsibilities in the environmental sanitation of their community. Unpolluted water supply and good sewage, garbage, and trash disposal are a necessity. The service of high-quality food from safe sources cannot be overemphasized and implies the use of pasteurized and carefully handled and refrigerated milk and other dairy products, inspected meat and poultry, and baked products from a bakery with high standards of sanitation. The proper care in preparation and serving of the food means good work and personal habits of clean, disease-free personnel, adequate cooking, refrigeration, dishwashing, and storage facilities. A clean physical plant is one in which the building and its equipment are free from soil and pests, have good ventilation and lighting, and are kept in good order.

Inspections. Several of the programs for good sanitation previously discussed have some type of evaluative check sheet for management use in maintaining high standards of cleanliness. Also, the Federal Food and Drug Administration's Proposed Uniform Requirements for Food Service Sanitation (see page 566) serves as a model ordinance for states and local government. The details of this model code provide an excellent reference for any foodservice manager who wishes to set up standards for good sanitation and to check on them. Included in this model code are definition of terms, procedures for food care, and personnel. The intelligent food director will consider the safeguards required for health and be active in careful observance of them. A study of the inspection form recommended by the Food and Drug Administration will show points that are important in maintaining sanitary conditions. Periodic inspections of each foodservice are made by many local health authorities at least twice a year, more often if problems arise. Form 10.2 is the FDA check sheet for recording conditions found on such visits.

Some institutions have found check sheets for each separate unit of the food service useful in directing various workers' attention to the major points on which maintenance of sanitary and desirable working conditions depends.

Bacterial Count on Dishes. The cleanliness of dishes and utensils may be checked for visible soil deposited on their surfaces or, more exactly, by bacterial counts determined by the swab test, the procedures of which are outlined in *U.S. Public Health Service Bulletin 37*. Counts of 100 or less are acceptable, but those showing 30 to 100 colonies indicate that something should be done to improve the situation. Counts above 100 mean unclean dishes or utensils and indicate poor or faulty methods of dishwashing, which must be located and corrected. Such counts should be made routinely as a safeguard to the health of the people served. Form 10.3 was designed to report the bacterial counts on the dishes and eating utensils in each of the foodservice units on one campus, made monthly by the department of microbiology. Such reports indicate where procedures in dishwashing or handling need revision and are of interest to both manager and employees in maintaining a good record of clean tableware.

FOOD SERVICE ESTABLISHMENT INSPECTION REPORT

NAME OF ESTABLISHMENT	ADDRESS	CITY	ZIP CODE	COUNTY OR DISTRICT

BASED ON AN INSPECTION THIS DAY, THE ITEMS MARKED (X) BELOW IDENTIFY THE VIOLATION IN OPERATION OF FACILITIES WHICH MUST BE CORRECTED BY THE NEXT ROUTINE INSPECTION OR SUCH SHORTER PERIOD OF TIME AS MAY BE SPECIFIED IN WRITING BY THE REGULATORY AUTHORITY. FAILURE TO COMPLY WITH THIS NOTICE MAY RESULT IN IMMEDIATE SUSPENSION OF YOUR PERMIT.

ESTABLISHMENT NUMBER ☐☐☐☐☐☐☐☐ 1. 2. 3. 4. 5. 6. 7. 8.
RATING SCORE ☐☐☐ 9. 10. 11.
SEATING CAPACITY ☐☐☐ 12. 13. 14.

15. WATER SUPPLY ☐ 1. PUBLIC ☐ 2. PRIVATE
16. SEWAGE DISPOSAL ☐ 1. PUBLIC ☐ 2. PRIVATE

17. TYPE ☐ 1. COMMERCIAL ☐ 2. SCHOOL ☐ 3. TAVERN ☐ 4. DAY CARE ☐ 5. NURSING HOME
☐ 6. CLUB ☐ 7. INSTITUTION ☐ 8. OTHER

18. PURPOSE ☐ 1. ROUTINE ☐ 2. FOLLOW-UP ☐ 3. COMPLAINT ☐ 4. INVESTIGATION ☐ 5. OTHER

19. PERMIT/LICENSE POSTED ☐ 1. YES ☐ 2. NO

20. OWNER/OPERATOR CERTIFIED ☐ 1. YES ☐ 2. NO

ITEM	X	WT	DESCRIPTION
			FOOD ////
*1		5	SOURCE, WHOLESOME
2		1	ORIGINAL CONTAINER, PROPERLY LABELED
			FOOD PROTECTION ////
*3		5	POTENTIALLY HAZARDOUS FOOD MEETS TEMPERATURE REQUIREMENTS DURING STORAGE, PREPARATION, DISPLAY, SERVICE, TRANSPORTATION
*4		4	FACILITIES TO MAINTAIN PRODUCT TEMPERATURE
5		1	THERMOMETERS PROVIDED AND CONSPICUOUS
6		2	POTENTIALLY HAZARDOUS FOOD PROPERLY THAWED
*7		4	UNWRAPPED AND POTENTIALLY HAZARDOUS FOOD NOT RE-SERVED
8		2	FOOD PROTECTION DURING STORAGE, PREPARATION, DISPLAY, SERVICE, TRANSPORTATION
9		2	HANDLING OF FOOD (ICE) MINIMIZED
10		1	FOOD (ICE) DISPENSING UTENSILS PROPERLY STORED

ITEM	X	WT	DESCRIPTION
			WATER ////
*27		5	WATER SOURCE, SAFE: HOT & COLD UNDER PRESSURE
			SEWAGE ////
*28		4	SEWAGE AND WASTE WATER DISPOSAL
			PLUMBING ////
29		1	INSTALLED, MAINTAINED
*30		5	CROSS-CONNECTION, BACK SIPHONAGE, BACKFLOW
			TOILET & HANDWASHING FACILITIES ////
*31		4	NUMBER, CONVENIENT, ACCESSIBLE, DESIGNED, INSTALLED TOILET ROOMS ENCLOSED, SELF-CLOSING DOORS,
32		2	FIXTURES, GOOD REPAIR, CLEAN: HAND CLEANSER, SANITARY TOWELS/HAND-DRYING DEVICES PROVIDED, PROPER WASTE RECEPTACLES
			GARBAGE & REFUSE DISPOSAL ////
33		2	CONTAINERS OR RECEPTACLES, COVERED: ADEQUATE NUMBER INSECT/RODENT PROOF, FREQUENCY, CLEAN

PERSONNEL

No.	Wt.	Item	
*11	5	PERSONNEL WITH INFECTIONS RESTRICTED	///
*12	5	HANDS WASHED AND CLEAN, GOOD HYGIENIC PRACTICES	
13	1	CLEAN CLOTHES, HAIR RESTRAINTS	///

FOOD EQUIPMENT & UTENSILS

14	2	FOOD (ICE) CONTACT SURFACES: DESIGNED, CONSTRUCTED, MAINTAINED, INSTALLED, LOCATED	
15	1	NON-FOOD CONTACT SURFACES: DESIGNED, CONSTRUCTED, MAINTAINED, INSTALLED, LOCATED	
16	2	DISHWASHING FACILITIES: DESIGNED, CONSTRUCTED, MAINTAINED, INSTALLED, LOCATED, OPERATED	
17	1	ACCURATE THERMOMETERS, CHEMICAL TEST KITS PROVIDED, GAUGE COCK (1/4" IPS VALVE)	
18	1	SINGLE-SERVICE ARTICLES, STORAGE, DISPENSING	
19	2	NO RE-USE OF SINGLE-SERVICE ARTICLES	
20	1	PRE-FLUSHED, SCRAPED, SOAKED	
21	2	WASH, RINSE WATER: CLEAN, PROPER TEMPERATURE	
*22	4	SANITIZATION RINSE: CLEAN, TEMPERATURE, CONCENTRATION	
23	1	WIPING CLOTHS: CLEAN, USE RESTRICTED	
24	2	FOOD-CONTACT SURFACES OF EQUIPMENT AND UTENSIL CLEAN, FREE OF ABRASIVES AND DETERGENTS	
25	1	NON-FOOD CONTACT SURFACES OF EQUIPMENT AND UTENSILS CLEAN	
26	1	STORAGE, HANDLING OF CLEAN EQUIPMENT-UTENSILS	

*CRITICAL ITEMS REQUIRING IMMEDIATE CORRECTION

REMARKS

OUTSIDE STORAGE AREA, ENCLOSURES PROPERLY CONSTRUCTED, CLEAN; INCINERATION CONTROLLED ///

| 34 | 1 | INSECT, RODENT, ANIMAL CONTROL | /// |
| *35 | 4 | PRESENCE OF INSECTS/RODENTS - OUTER OPENINGS PROTECTED, NO BIRDS, TURTLES, OTHER ANIMALS | /// |

FLOORS, WALLS & CEILINGS ///

| 36 | 1 | FLOORS: CONSTRUCTED, DRAINED, CLEAN, GOOD REPAIR, COVERING INSTALLATION, DUSTLESS CLEANING METHODS. | |
| 37 | 1 | WALLS, CEILING, ATTACHED EQUIPMENT: CONSTRUCTED, GOOD REPAIR, CLEAN, SURFACES, DUSTLESS CLEANING METHODS | |

LIGHTING ///

| 38 | 1 | LIGHTING PROVIDED AS REQUIRED, FIXTURES SHIELDED | /// |

VENTILATION ///

| 39 | 1 | ROOMS AND EQUIPMENT---VENTED AS REQUIRED | /// |

DRESSING ROOMS

| 40 | 1 | ROOMS CLEAN, LOCKERS PROVIDED, FACILITIES CLEAN | /// |

OTHER OPERATIONS ///

*41	5	TOXIC ITEMS PROPERLY STORED, LABELED, USED	
42	1	PREMISES: MAINTAINED, FREE OF LITTER, UNNECESSARY ARTICLES, CLEANING/MAINTENANCE EQUIPMENT PROPERLY STORED, AUTHORIZED PERSONNEL	
43	1	COMPLETE SEPARATION FROM LIVING/SLEEPING QUARTERS LAUNDRY	
44	1	CLEAN, SOILED LINEN PROPERLY STORED	

DATE OF INSPECTION _____   RECEIVED BY _____   INSPECTED BY _____

FORM 10.2   *Food service establishment inspection report. Courtesy, Federal Register.*

REPORT OF BACTERIA COUNTS IN DINING HALLS

Date_____

Location	Date of Sample	Time Sample Taken	Storage Consult Code	*I *W Water Glass	Dinner Plate	Salad Bowl	Cereal Bowl	Coffee Cup	Silver-ware Knife	Fork	Spoon	Trays	Steam Table Inset
Baker Hall	5/26	9:00		0	0	1	25	1	0	0	0	0	
Women's Res.		9:30		0	0	S	0	0	7	4	3	S	
Neil Hall		9:50		0	0	0	0	0	0	0	0	1	
Stadium		11:50		S	S	S	0	S	1	3	0	40	
Pomerene		9:15		0	0	18	1	0	0	0	0	0	
University School		8:15		—	0	0	0	1	0	0	1	0	
Faculty Club		8:00		0	0	0	0	0	8	1	0	0	
Main D. R.		8:40		0	2	S	S	0	0	0	0	S	
Cafeteria		8:30		0	0	0	0	0	0	3	1	0	

NOTE: Code letters used in table:
S   Spreading type of colony
TMC   Innumerable colonies (too many to count on plate)
C   Closed storage
O   Open storage
*I   Water glass inverted—no air space
*W   Water glass inverted—with air space
D   Immediately after washing
     Silver racked: yes_____ no_____.

RATING according to City Regulations:
     0–10   Excellent
     11–29   Good
     30–49   Fair
     50–99   Poor   Counts by_____
     Over 100   Very poor   Approved by_____

FORM   10.3   *Summary record of bacterial counts on dishes make it easy to detect problem areas.*

All such information, regulation check sheets, and evaluation forms, if used wisely and continuously, should lead to a high standard of sanitation, safe wholesome food, and an enviable reputation for the foodservice.

SAFETY

Safety may be considered an integral part of sanitation; the institution foodservice department planned and operated to achieve the highest degree of sanitation is quite certain to be a safe place in which to work. Safety, however, can never be *assumed,* but is a major responsibility of management and workers alike. Dietitians and food managers who are aware of the advantages of safety measures and the waste resulting from accidents will seek ways of improving working conditions and employee performance to maintain a low frequency-rate and severity-rate. *Severity rate* is computed by the number of working days lost because of accidents, and *frequency rate* by the number of lost-time accidents during any selected period, each multiplied by 1 million and the result divided by the total number of man-hours worked during the same period.

Recent legislation, however, has made clear the mandate for even more concerted action on the part of management to assure safe and healthful working conditions for our nation's wage earners. The Occupational Safety and Health Act (OSHA) of 1970, which became effective April 28, 1971, makes it *illegal* not to have a safe establishment. The act provides that each employer has a duty to furnish the employees a place of employment that is safe and free from any hazards that may cause death or serious physical harm.

The organization set up to enforce this act has the authority to inspect any place of business and to penalize those that do not comply with the provisions of the law. Among other things, managers must strictly comply with correcting specific potential hazards and furnish written records of any accidents that have occurred.

National Safety Council statistics rank the food industry about midway in all industry classifications in terms of severity rates. However, in terms of frequency rates, it is nearly twice as high as the average for all industries reporting.

"Accidents don't happen; they are caused," and can be prevented. The National Safety Council has defined an accident as any suddenly occurring, unintentional event that causes injury or property damage. An accident has become a symbol of inefficiency, either human or mechanical, and usually represents a monetary loss to the organization. The injured individual will lose not only time at work and wages, but he also incurs indirect costs such as medical and insurance expense, cost of training new workers, waste production resulting from inexperienced substitute workers, administrative costs for investigating and taking care of accidents, and cost of repair or replacement of broken or damaged equipment. One company survey revealed that the average accident occurrence cost that company $252. Not only from the humanitarian standpoint therefore, but also from the economic, the food manager must organize for safety and develop a wholesome regard for safe procedures among the entire staff.

Specific steps for establishing a safety program may be centered around the "three E's" of safety: Engineering, Education, and Enforcement. The engineering aspect refers to the built-in safety features of the building and equipment, and the manner in which the equipment is installed to make it safe to use. Competent managers are constantly alert to new equipment designs and devices and will procure those that will provide for a high degree of safety for the employees. Encased motors, safety valves on pressure steamers, easily manipulated spigots on urns, and guards on slicing and chopping machines are examples of such features. An equipment maintenance program to keep it in good working order is the responsibility of management also.

A study of traffic patterns in kitchen and dining areas and the placement of equipment and supplies in locations to avoid as much cross traffic as possible, and the arrangement of equipment within a work unit to provide for logical sequence of movement without back-tracking are a part of the engineering phase of the safety program.

Education for safety is a never-ending process. It begins with the establishment of firm policies regarding safety, which then should be discussed with each new employee during his orientation period. "Safety from the first day" is an appropriate slogan for any organization.

Because safety is an integrated part of every activity, it should be taught as a component of all skills and procedures. A safety education program should be built on *facts.* The National Safety Council, the Bureau of Vital Statistics, and various community safety councils, as well as trade and professional organizations, can provide statistics and materials for planning such a program. Data obtained from records kept of accidents within the organization are invaluable.

Written records of accidents should include the kind of injuries

Board of Education
Office of Assistant Supervisor of Home Economics
in Charge of Cafeterias

Departmental Report of Personal Injury Involving
the Employees of the City Schools

School _____   Date _____

Name _____   Title _____

Address _____   Date of accident _____

Sex _____   Time of accident _____

Married or single _____   Nationality _____

Date of birth _____   Age _____ Birthplace _____

State fully in your own words how accident occurred: _____

_____

_____

Exact part of person injured and extent of injuries: _____

_____

_____

Probable period of disability _____

Was medical attention necessary? _____

Name and address of Physician _____

_____

Give location where accident occurred _____

Will employee lose any time? _____

If not able to work, give probable date of recovery _____

Are there any indications of permanent injury? _____

State monthly salary of employee _____

How long in our employ? _____

IMPORTANT: Fill out report in *duplicate* on day of accident and mail immediately to above office.

_____
                                                Employee

FORM   10.4   *Accidents should be reported immediately and a written record filed.*

623

that have occurred and to whom, when they occurred, the day and hour, and where they took place. In foodservices most accidents occur at rush hours when it is especially difficult to take care of the injured, find replacement help, and to continue efficient service to the guest. This fact alone should be incentive enough for the manager to do all possible to promote safety. (See Form 10.4.) An analysis of the cause of accidents provides further data for preventing them. Causes may be classified into "unsafe acts" and "unsafe conditions." Usually it is found that unsafe acts outnumber unsafe conditions three to one. From this there is an immediate indication of the need for proper training to reduce accidents.

Studies [34] of accidents in the foodservice industry show that falls cause the largest number of food-handling accidents, with cuts second, burns, and strains from lifting next in order. Falls and strains result in the greatest loss of time from the job and money loss to the institution.

It is estimated that 90 percent of all accidents could be prevented. It is management's responsibility to ferret out the reasons, remove the hazards, and then train the employees to prevent recurrence of the same accident. Good housekeeping procedures like storing tools and materials in proper places and keeping aisles and pathways clear, optimum lighting of work areas, prompt repair of broken tools and equipment, replacement of worn electrical cords, and proper care and removal of broken china and glassware are only a few of the things that can be done to correct unsafe conditions.

Education for safety continues each day with on-the-job training of the employee in the proper use and care of tools and equipment. Group training in precautionary procedures to be followed in everyday work and instructions in what to do in case of an accident should be a part of the overall safety program. Be certain that all employees know where and to whom to report an accident and that the phone numbers to use for emergencies are posted on the telephone. Directions for, and practice in the use of fire extinguishers, fire blankets, and other first-aid equipment, necessities in every institution kitchen, are included in training meetings for supervisory personnel particularly. Information about the various types of fire extinguishers and which should be used for grease, paper and wood, and other fires is important.

[34] *"A Safety Guide for Food Handling Employees," Industrial Commission of Ohio Division of Safety and Hygiene.*

General Restaurant Safety Rules

(please post)

- Report *every* injury *at once*, regardless of severity, to your Supervisor for first aid. *Avoid delay.*

- Report all *unsafe conditions*, broken or splintered chairs or tables, defective equipment, leaking radiators, torn carpeting, uneven floors, loose rails, unsafe tools or knives, broken china and glass, etc.

- Understand the *safe way* to perform any task assigned to you. If in doubt, see your Supervisor. Never take unnecessary chances.

- If you have to move over-heavy objects, ask for help. *Do not overlift.* When lifting any heavy object, keep your back straight, bend your knees and *use your leg muscles.* Your back has weak muscles and can easily be strained.

- Aisles, passageways, stairways must be kept clean and free from obstructions. Do not permit brooms, pails, mops, cans, boxes, etc., to remain where someone can fall over them. Wipe up any grease or wet spots from stairs or floors or ramps *at once.* These are serious falling hazards.

- Walk, do not run, in halls, down ramps or stairs, or around work areas. Be careful when passing through swinging doors.

- Keep your locker clean and the locker top free from all loose or discarded materials, such as: newspapers, old boxes, bottles, broken equipment, etc.

- Wear safe, sensible clothes for your work. Wear safe, comfortable shoes, with good soles. Never wear thin-soled or broken-down shoes. *Do not wear high-heeled shoes for work.* Ragged or over-long sleeves or ragged clothing may result in an injury.

- If you have to reach for a high object, use a ladder, not a chair or table or a makeshift. There is no substitute of any kind for a good ladder. *Never overreach.* Be careful when you have to reach high to fill coffee urns, milk tanks, etc.

- Horseplay or practical jokes on the job are forbidden.

- Do not argue or fight with fellow employees. The results are usually unpleasant and dangerous.

- Keep floors clean and dry. Pick up any loose object from the floor immediately to prevent someone from falling.

- Do not overload your trays. Trays should be loaded so as to give good balance. An improperly loaded tray can become dangerous.

- Dispose of all broken glass and china immediately. Never serve a guest with a cracked or chipped glass or piece of china. Check all silverware.

- Take sufficient time to serve your guests properly. Too much haste is liable to cause accidents to your guests and to yourself. *Haste makes waste.*

- Remove from service any chair, table or other equipment that is loose, broken or splintered so as to prevent injury.

- *Cashiers.* Close cash registers with back of hand. Do not permit fingers to hang over edge of drawer.

- Money is germ-laden. Keep your fingers out of your hair, eyes, and mouth after handling. Wash hands carefully before eating. Report the slightest cut or sore *at once* for treatment.

- Help *new employees* to work safely on the job. Show them the right way to do the job—the safe way.

FIGURE 10.18   Poster listing safety rules for employee information.

625

Clever, eye-catching posters that stimulate active thinking and give favorable impressions about safety may be used effectively to supplement other types of training. (See Fig. 10.18.) The National Restaurant Association has available for sale a series of such colored posters. Films and filmstrips are other aids to teaching safe practices.

The third "E," enforcement, represents the follow-up or constant vigilance required to prevent carelessness and to make certain that the rules and prescribed procedures are observed. Enforcement can be accomplished in many ways. In some organizations safety committees are set up among the employees who observe and report unsafe conditions and practices. Membership on this committee may be rotated so that everyone will be personally involved in a campaign against accidents. In other places, contests between departments act as an incentive for keeping accident rates low. Honor rolls for accident-free days or months help call attention to safety records. If possible, one person in each organization should have the overall responsibility for developing and supervising the safety program.

Probably the most effective overall enforcement plan, however, is a periodic inspection of the department by someone on the supervisory staff. The use of a check list as a reminder of all points to be observed is helpful. Any foodservice manager could develop a form for his own specific use. See Form 10.2.

The National Safety Council [35] has summarized the steps to safety that could be followed by any foodservice manager in developing a safety campaign.

1. *Insist on safety.* Practice what you preach; be sure you back up your policy.

2. *Assign someone to help on details.* Get advice on safety codes, health hazards, safety equipment, and special hazards.

3. *Locate trouble spots.* Watch for things that cause accidents, review causes of past accidents, and act on trends.

[35] *"Seven Steps to Safety,"* National Safety Council, 425 N. Michigan Avenue, Chicago Illinois.

4. *Make the job safe.* Remove hazards, provide protective equipment and adequate first-aid equipment.

5. *Control unsafe habits.* Teach the safe way to do the job, enforce general safety rules, and make new rules if needed.

6. *Keep simple records.* Uncover accident causes, check progress, and compare experience with others.

7. *Get employees into the act.* Get their suggestions; talk safety, and maintain interest through posters, leaflets, and other inexpensive ready-made material.

An overall safety program must be initiated by the dietitian or food manager. It involves indoctrinating each employee with the philosophy of working safely and instructing him how to do this.

A study of human nature and the behavior motives of the employees within their working environment provides further information for making a safety program real and meaningful. Provision of proper tools and equipment with safety devices and a system for checking both equipment and operations at frequent intervals are necessary for achieving a good safety record. Established policies regarding safety and a procedure for reporting and handling any accidents (see Form 10.4) will further aid in keeping injuries to a minimum and the working force at maximum efficiency.

Serat [36] summarized well the factors involved in accident prevention.

The prime factor in accident prevention is awareness, involvement, and good attitude on the part of management, and management's active communication of these concepts to line personnel. In application, accident prevention becomes a normal and intricate part of management, not something completely separate for some other person to handle.

[36] A. J. Saret, "Accidents—the Profit Thief," The Cornell HRA Quarterly, 13 (1), 26 (May 1972).

SELECTED REFERENCES

Ahern, Edwin F., *Safety Training Manual,* Ahrens, New York, 1955.

Applied Foodservice Sanitation, prepared in collaboration with the National Sanitation Foundation, published by the National Institute for the Foodservice Industry, Chicago, Illinois.

Applied Foodservice Sanitation Instructor's Guide, prepared in collaboration with the National Sanitation Foundation, published by the National Institute for the Foodservice Industry, Chicago, Illinois.

"A Reference Manual of Food Service Sanitation" (Education and Training Materials) 523, National Sanitation Foundation. Ann Arbor, Michigan.

Clawson, Augusta H., *Equipment Maintenance Manual,* Ahrens, New York.

"Clean Hands," United States Department Health, Education and Welfare, Public Health Service, Food and Drug Administration.

"Don't Be A Missing Link," filmstrip on safety for the foodservice industry prepared by the National Safety Council and the National Restaurant Association, Chicago, Illinois.

"Food Service Sanitation Manual," U.S. Department of Health, Education and Welfare, *Public Health Service Publication 934,* U.S. Government Printing Office, Washington, D.C., 1962.

Frazier, William C., *Food Microbiology,* Second Edition, McGraw-Hill, New York, 1967.

Guthrie, Rufus K., *Food Sanitation,* Avi, Westport, Connecticut, 1972.

Haskell, Dr. W. H., "Sanitation for Food Service Workers," reprinted from *Institutions Magazine,* Domestic Engineering Company, Chicago, 1959.

"Instructor's Guide—Sanitary Food Service," *Public Health Service Publication 90,* U.S. Government Printing Office, Washington, D.C., 1953.

Jernigan, Anna K., *Food Service Sanitation: Study Course,* Iowa State University Press, Ames, Iowa, 1971.

Longree, Karla, *Food Service Sanitation,* Second Edition, Wiley, New York, 1973.

Longree, Karla, and G. Blaker, *Sanitary Techniques in Food Services,* Wiley, New York, 1971.

The National Sanitation Foundation, Ann Arbor, Michigan.
Standards No. 2, "Food Service Equipment," amended 1973.
Standards No. 3, "Commercial Spray-Type Dishwashing Machines," revised, 1965.
Standards No. 4, "Commercial Cooking and Hot Food Storage Equipment," revised 1973.
Standards No. 5, "Hot Water Generating Equipment for Food Service Establishments using Spray Type Dishwashing Machines," revised 1972.
Standards No. 6, "Dispensing Freezers," revised 1970.
Standards No. 7, "Food Service Refrigerators and Storage Freezers," revised 1970.
Standards No. 8, "Commercial Powered Food Preparation Equipment," revised 1972.
Standards No. 12, "Automatic Ice Making Equipment," revised 1972.
Standards No. 13, "Refuse Compactors and Compactor Systems," 1973.
Standards No. 14, "Thermoplastic Materials, Pipe, Fittings, Valves, Traps and Joining Materials," 1973.
Standards No. 18, "Manual Food and Beverage Dispensing Equipment," revised 1974.
Standards No. 20, "Commercial Bulk Milk Dispensing Equipment and Appurtenances," revised 1973.
Standards No. 21, "Thermoplastic Refuse Containers," 1972.
Standards No. 25, "Vending Machines for Food and Beverages," revised 1971.
Standards No. 26, "Pot, Pan and Utensil Commercial Spray Type Washing Machines," 1970.
Standards No. 29, "Detergents and Chemical Feeders for Commercial Spray Type Dishwashing Machines," revised 1973.
Standards No. 31, "Polyethylene Refuse Bags," 1972.
Standards No. 32, "Paper Refuse Sacks," 1970.
Standards No. 33, "Commercial Cooking Equipment Exhaust Systems," 1970.
Standards No. 35, "Laminated Plastics for Surfacing Food Service Equipment," 1970.
Standards No. 36, "Dinnerware," 1970.
Standards No. 37, "Air Curtains for Entranceways in Food Establishments," 1970.
"Basic Criteria C-2, Special Equipment and Devices," revised 1972.

Pelcazar, Michael, Jr., and Roger D. Reid, *Microbiology,* Third Edition, Mc-Graw-Hill, New York, 1972.

"Proceedings of the 1972 National Conference on Food Protection," American Public Health Association, Superintendent of Documents, U.S. Government Printing Office, Washington, D.C., 1972.

Richardson, Treva M., *Sanitation for Foodservice Workers,* Second Edition, Cahners, Boston, 1974.

Sanitary Food Service Instructor's Guide, Department of Health, Education and Welfare, Public Health Service, Environmental Control Administration, Cincinnati, 1969.

Simonds, Rollin H., and J. V. Grimaldi, *Safety Management: Accident Cost and Control,* Revised Edition, Richard D. Erwin, Homewood, Illinois, 1963.

Weiser, Harry H., George J. Mountney, and Wilbur Gould, *Practical Food Microbiology and Technology,* Second Edition, Avi, Westport, Connecticut, 1971.

"You Can Prevent Foodborne Illness," U.S. Department of Health, Education and Welfare, *Public Health Service Publication No. 1105,* U.S. Government Printing Office, Washington, D.C., 1963.

SECTION 3
PHYSICAL
FACILITIES

11.
FLOOR PLANNING AND LAYOUTS

Physical facility requirements for the many and varied types of operations that make up the massive foodservice industry are as diverse and numerous as the individual units themselves. The range of locations, types of foodservices and their individual objectives, budgetary allowances, clientele, trained personnel, menus, and equipment is broad and may encompass operations such as the most sophisticated hotels and restaurants, universities and schools, hospitals, and a wide variety of fast-service types. There is no one plan to meet the needs of all, although some general patterns for each type can be used as guidelines by the persons responsible for planning. The ultimate goal, in any case, is to provide an appropriate and efficient facility for the production and service of high-quality, attractive, wholesome food—pleasing to the clientele and at a reasonable price.

TRENDS IN FOODSERVICE PLANNING

The general concept of foodservice systems management includes proper facilities as an important factor to success. Engineering principles of design applied to foodservice facility planning make for efficiency and saving of money for space, utilities, food, time, and human effort. A people-oriented setup contributes much to the happiness and satisfaction of both workers and consumers.

GENERAL TRENDS

Many factors have contributed to the obsolescence of the traditional and long-established procedures of food preparation and service and the facilities needed. Some of the factors contributing to change are: more people eating away from homes in specialized types of foodservices; rapid advances in food and equipment technology; increased food, labor, and operating costs; and the shortage of skilled employees. Emphasis on the use of modern management techniques and the planning of physical facilities based on the systems management concept contributes much to change and to the streamlining of foodservice operations. Also, the increased sensitivity to energy conservation and environmental problems demands much attention.

Varied plans have been designed for efficiency in performance of particular functions. Studies of successful floor plans have been made, but even operations of similar type and size are difficult to compare because of the many variables such as the menu pattern, use of prepared foods, amount of service provided, budget level, and clientele. The requirements for each foodservice must be determined and an individual plan made to meet the needs in a given situation.

Regardless of the type of foodservice, one commonality is to plan a minimum amount of space for a maximum job. This has been expedited through basic changes in equipment, food processing, and operational methods that make possible more production with less manpower. Output is speeded up through increased use of prepared food products and fast performance equipment such as the high-speed cutter-mixer, high-pressure cooker, and the convection oven. Efficient utilization of space is effected through arrangement of equipment to reduce to a minimum the movement of individual workers in the performance of their tasks and also to limit the direction and distance food must be transported through the production and service processes. Mobility of equipment affords multiple use and flexibility in arrangement; often these make possible the dual use of space at different hours of the day. Practically all types of work surfaces, cooking, serving, storage, and transportation units are available on wheels, which reduces to a minimum the handling of food, dishes, and utensils and facilitates good sanitation and easy maintenance practices (see Fig. 11.1).

The planning of matched modular units such as for range, fryer,

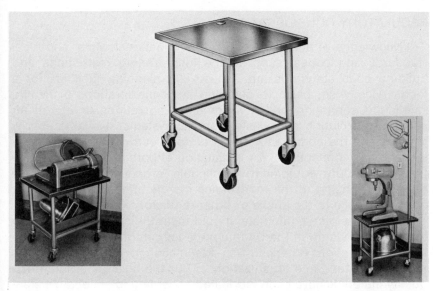

FIGURE 11.1   A sturdy, small, low table on wheels adapts itself to many uses, particularly for sharing equipment in different work areas. Courtesy, Southern Equipment Company.

broiler, and oven conserve space and simplify installation. The selection of carts, serving counters, refrigerators, and other storage units designed to accommodate the same size trays make for interchangeability and standardized procedures.

Much attention is given to design and construction of the building and equipment and its installation to insure high standards of sanitation and safety and to facilitate ease of their maintenance. Waste disposers, can and bottle openers, and compactors located at the points of waste origin have eliminated space, inconvenience, storage, and cleaning of garbage and waste containers.

Some of the other major considerations given to planning of a modern foodservice are wall and floor surfaces, ventilation, lighting, refrigeration, effective insulation; and, in equipment, to construction, fuel efficiency, exact engineering tolerances, automatic controls, arrangement, installation, and initial and operating costs. Beauty as well as function is important. Many multiple-unit operations find that centralized preparation and transportation of fully or partially cooked menu items meet their needs satisfactorily and with less space, equipment, and personnel required.

REGULATORY CONSIDERATIONS

Knowledge of and strict adherence to national, state, and local standards and codes, such as the local zoning restrictions and building code standards, are "musts" in planning facilities for a foodservice. Also, basic to planning are considerations of health, safety, fire, sanitation, and environmental regulations as regards air and water pollution and waste disposal systems; available energy sources and the codes and standards for electrical wiring and outlets and gas connections, for installation of both electrical and gas-fired heavy-duty equipment. Applicable property tax, insurance rates, or licensing of the foodservice can be affected materially by noncompliance to the above or other regulatory measures.

All foodservice equipment should meet the standards and bear the approval stamp of the Underwriters Laboratories, National Sanitation Foundation, American Gas Association, or other appropriate recognized standards organizations. Thus the buyer is assured that quality materials have been fabricated according to acceptable standards for the particular item. Installation must conform to code and is subject to authoritative inspection.

SUGGESTED STEPS TO FOLLOW FROM INITIAL PLANNING THROUGH CONSTRUCTION

The planning and construction of new foodservice facilities or the remodeling of old ones eventually become a problem with which most dietitians and foodservice managers must work. These persons are not expected to be architects or engineers, but they must be able to discuss intelligently and interpret their needs and help formulate the bases on which requests are made. They understand thoroughly the requirements of the situation, know cookery and efficient organization, and so should work actively with the architect on the detailed planning of the setup from the earliest stages. A kitchen engineer, a qualified consultant, or the equipment representative who often acts as a consultant in kitchen planning can contribute invaluable information gained through training, experience, and observation. Such persons know particularly well the materials, construction, capacity, size, and costs of the various pieces of equipment and their installation requirements. The maintenance engineer and the business manager also are important persons to assist with certain parts of the planning. Even though this group of experts formulates the floor plan and equipment specifications cooperatively, both will have to be checked many times before the final proposals are submitted for bids. It is essential that every detail is included and is so specific that no part of the architectural features or equipment specifications and arrangements are left to chance or can be misinterpreted.

Many decisions must be made prior to the actual planning of a floor layout. The objectives of the organization must be clearly defined and interpreted, a program prepared to describe the needs, the location and some of the architectural features known and, finally, a floor plan developed compatible with the known desires and the finances available.

The owner, administrator, or director in charge of the foodservice organization must take a comprehensive and long-range view to be sure that the objectives and needs will be met and that provision is made for future expansion or change. Creative thinking, objectivity, imaginative curiosity, and the ability to communicate effectively are basic to obtain the results desired. Figure 11.2 is an

FIGURE   11.2   *Both architectural features and the arrangement and installation of equipment contribute to the efficiency and ease of maintenance in an institution kitchen. Children's Hospital, Pittsburgh. Courtesy, Southern Equipment Company.*

example of a well coordinated plan. Failure of management to recognize and accept the importance of the function of effective long-range planning for foodservice layouts and neglect to allocate responsibilities for follow-up within the organizational structure, may result in a poorly coordinated and nonfunctional floor plan and arrangement of equipment.

A logical schedule to follow in planning and building or remodeling a foodservice facility is suggested below.

1. Write a clear and definite summary or *prospectus* including objectives; financial restrictions; location; architectural features preferred; predicted volume of business; menu pattern; purchasing policies; and energy, equipment, and storage needs.

2. Prepare design and layout showing space allowances and relationships and placement of equipment preliminary to preparation of blueprints by the architect.

3. Submit architect's complete set of plans including specifications to reliable interested builders, engineers, and equipment representatives for competitive bids.

4. Formulate contracts with accepted bidders.

5. Follow through with inspections on construction, wiring, plumbing, finishing, equipment and its installation, as specified on blueprints and in contracts.

PROGRAMMING FOR FOODSERVICE FACILITIES— THE PROSPECTUS

The person representing the foodservice (owner, dietitian, manager) on the planning board or committee cannot expect full understanding of the needs in space, equipment and its arrangement by the architect, professional consultant, and others with whom he works if clearly defined goals, policies, and procedures are lacking. Best results are obtained when a written program, complete with details, is prepared and used as the basis for developing plans. Research and study of all the important factors during the early preliminary programming and throughout the final planning and engineering will avert costly errors. Any manager with foresight would have begun months in advance to collect ideas and suggestions for incorporation into the project.

The program or *prospectus* should give a good picture of the physical and operational aspects of the proposed facility that might be based on many questions such as:

What type of foodservice is to be planned?

What is to be accomplished?

How many people and of what age groups are to be served? how many are to be seated at one time?

What will be the hours of service? Style of service?

What is the menu pattern?

In what form will food be purchased? How often? What storage facilities will be needed? How much refrigerated storage?

What equipment and of what capacities will be required for the preparation and service of the menus?

What are desirable space relationships?

How many employees?

Will safety precautions be incorporated?

What are the cost limitations? Projected income?

What energy sources are available? Most economical?

Obviously, the person who is to determine space and equipment needs for an institution foodservice must have authentic knowledge of the quantity of each menu item to be prepared, methods of preparation, and the schedule of preparation and service. This includes details such as customer preferences, portion sizes, quantities of prepared food to yield the number of portions needed, average preparation and cooking losses of the various foods, time required for preparation and cooking, purchase units and quantities to buy, relative serving costs of certain items in different purchase forms such as canned, frozen, or fresh green beans, storage life of foods, and abilities of personnel. Adequate space for the installation of the necessary equipment can be calculated for each area after equipment needs have been established. Also, consideration must be given to the number of workers and their work space needs, aisle and temporary storage space, and possible plans for expansion and growth in space or equipment; then, all must be combined into a workable master plan.

COSTS

Building and construction costs are affected by many factors, all of which are interrelated. They have to do with regional price of labor and materials, quality and quantity of items selected, and overall building design. The relationship of these three factors— cost, quality, and quantity—may be diagramed as a triangle. If the

cost or amount of money available to be used is preset, there will be some restrictions on quantity, quality, or both. However, if the space needs are the first and most important consideration, then the funds must be flexible to cover the cost of obtaining the size building or space required. Likewise, if the quality of features and equipment is the main determinant, the cost and quantity factors must be flexible. Thus, if one factor is changed, the others are also affected in some manner.

Since there are so many variables involved in the construction and equipping of a foodservice unit, especially during a fluctuating economy, it is difficult to suggest even average figures on which to base estimates of total costs for a project. Some architects base overall costs on cubic feet instead of square feet, or on the number of beds in a hospital, or the number of seats in a dining room of a school, restaurant, or industrial plant.

The design of the building or foodservice department determines many costs, particularly the labor costs involved in the operation of the department. A well-planned arrangement on one floor reduces to a minimum the travel distance of food and people and lends itself to good supervision. Compact work units with the proper equipment easily accessible to the workers and arranged to reduce steps, motion, and fatigue make it possible to minimize time, labor, and operating costs. In the past it was not uncommon for at least 10 percent of an employee's time to be spent in locating and assembling utensils and supplies. It has been estimated that in an efficiently planned department, perhaps only the dietitian or foodservice supervisor, storeroom clerk, dishroom supervisor, pot and pan washer, and janitor would need to walk about outside their work areas.

The total costs for cleaning materials, utilities, depreciation costs for building and equipment, and the amount of equipment needed are other costs that are in direct ratio to the amount of space allocated to the foodservice department and are often overlooked in planning.

The furnishings or items of equipment should be included that contribute to efficient operation and reflect the best design, materials, and workmanship to conform to established sanitary standards. The comfort of both guests and employees will depend on provisions made for them in early planning. Air conditioning, lighting, sound deadening, artistic incorporation of color and pleasing design, comfortable chairs and working surface heights, and clean well-ventilated restrooms are some of the things to which both patrons and employees are particularly sensitive.

The cost factor cannot be overlooked as it will necessarily influence what can be done within the budgetary allowance. The assumption will be held throughout the remainder of this book that adequate funds are available for foodservice planning on a moderate scale.

LOCATION AND SOME REQUIREMENTS FOR DIFFERENT TYPES OF FOODSERVICES

The physical environment has much to do with the successful operation of the individual foodservice establishment. No one plan is suitable for all types and sizes of institutions; however, there are general principles that are basic and applicable. Often, limitations are imposed by location and by one or several physical features of the building, equipment, and its arrangement that may cause lowered patronage or food production and lead to higher operating costs.

Commercial. The preferred location and desirable physical features of a facility vary with the type of foodservice unit. For example, the *restaurateur* who caters to downtown shoppers and business people prefers a location near the "busiest corner" with easy access from the heavy lane of pedestrian traffic. Rentals are high in such a location, so a relatively small space for preparation, service, and storage of a large volume of food must be utilized effectively. In a residential area he caters to family groups in a more spacious and relaxed atmosphere. Adequate car-parking facilities adjacent to such a restaurant are a necessity.

The *lunch-counter operator* finds that a location in or near the business areas is best for him. Many busy people demand the speedy, efficient, and inexpensive service of the lunch counter, which meets the needs of the person on a limited time and income schedule. A menu of short-order items, most of which are prepared back of the counter, requires a minimum of kitchen area and equipment but ample refrigerated storage. *Hotel and motel food units* are usually built so that the coffee shop is located in a conspicuous place with both street and lobby entrances, whereas the main dining room, party, and banquet rooms may be more secluded and accessible only through the hotel lobby, if on the same floor. Usually basic preparation is done in a central kitchen, and the pre- or partially prepared items are transported to pantries adjacent to the respective service areas. The amount and arrangement of equipment needed in each instance would depend on the particular situation.

School and University. *School lunchrooms* are preferably located on the first floor of the school building, as convenient as possible to the main hallways and locker rooms. The location should be such that, in the absence of an adequate ventilating system, objectionable odors that might lessen the appeal of food to the students and prove a nuisance to the classes will be eliminated. Foodservices for *colleges and boarding schools* are usually located in residence halls and in union or commons buildings. Most campus plans have the residence halls located on or near one side or end of the campus. The foodservice units in these halls may face a court or quadrangle. The plan of a large residence hall often includes a central kitchen and bakeshop surrounded by two, three, or four service units. A campus housing plan may include several residence halls, each with its own kitchen and diningroom, but with a central bakeshop, warehouse, and laundry. Student union or commons buildings are usually centrally located and accessible from all sides, with the dining rooms prominently and conveniently located to entrances. In school and university foodservices, large quantities of a relatively few menu items must be ready for service during a specified period of time so, even though a well-programmed schedule of preparation is in effect, several duplicate pieces of large equipment may be necessary. Also, adequate work space must be provided for the personnel required at peak production hours.

Industrial. The *industrial food service* should be central in location with ready access from as many areas in the plant as possible. Every provision should be made to expedite service so that all workers may be accommodated quickly during a fairly short lunch break. Mobile units and vending operations may be used satisfactorily in remote areas of large plants or in those too small to justify the space and expenditure for kitchen equipment, management, and labor.

Homes for Children and Adult Communities. *Homes for children and retired persons* make use of the residence hall and cottage type of planning. Because a quiet, homelike atmosphere is desirable for this type of situation, they are often found located away from the busy streets of the city and surrounded by private grounds.

Hospitals and Convalescent Care Centers. *Hospitals* and *other health care facilities* usually are located away from busy urban centers but are easily accessible to arterial streets or roadways and are situated in an attractive, pleasant, and quiet environment with a generous car-parking area.

Within a Building. The location of kitchens and dining rooms in an institution of any type depends on the use of the building and its architectural plan. In general it is practicable and preferable to have the dining rooms adjacent to the kitchen. In most institutions it is desirable to have the foodservice located on the first floor. Basement foodservice rooms present a perpetual problem of ventilation and lighting, and the psychological effect on patrons is less pleasing than in units located on the first floor or above, which have by virtue of their placement the advantage of more air and view. The location of the foodservice above the first floor has the disadvantage of inaccessibility to patrons and the problems relative to the necessary elevating of food supplies and the disposal of waste, both serious handicaps. In large cities the advantages of top floor food units, such as roof-garden dining rooms, are sometimes greater than the disadvantages. It is often more difficult to establish the popularity of such a service than to create public interest in a unit entered directly from the street. The location seems to imply a formality, not always an actuality. Particular attention must be given to the location of the foodservice department in a hospital complex because of the various types of often remote service areas.

ARCHITECTURAL CONSIDERATIONS

The architectural features that should be given detailed consideration in plans for a foodservice include the building materials and the details of construction, the kind of floors, walls, and ceilings to be provided, and the provisions for lighting, heating, ventilation, refrigeration, plumbing, sanitation, and safety.

Building Materials. There have been many changes in the appearance of buildings in recent years. Not only have architectural designs been changed and colors introduced to produce markedly different effects but also the use of improved materials by specially trained workers has been notable. Developments in the field of metallurgy, masonry, and glass have been rapid and influential in bringing about such changes. In the selection of materials for any building much depends on the type of architecture planned, the permanence desired, the geographical location, and the effect of local weather conditions on the material. Certain types of architecture, such as the extremely modern, call for materials that will help to produce striking, severe, and often bizarre effects.

If a building is to be constructed for a permanent structure, it is most important that the best possible materials and construction be obtained. The expense of building should be reckoned over a long period of time before any decision is made as to what is real economy. Often the most expensive initial cost, when prorated over the years, will mean a lower building cost as well as lower upkeep cost. The geographical location will influence markedly the type of architecture and the materials used. For example, the Spanish influence is strong in the southwestern part of the United States and may determine the choice for that area. The industrial influence is pronounced in certain cities and causes a marked similarity in building designs. Materials of local origin, such as stone of a certain kind, will naturally be used extensively because of accessibility, possible low cost, and civic interest and pride. The action of local weather conditions on materials also influences the choice and the way they are handled. For example, a roof made of material that expands and contracts appreciably would be a poor investment in a climate of extreme changes in temperature, and moisture-resistant building materials are essential for localities where the rainy season is prolonged.

Metal, stone, brick, tile, glass, cement, marble, and wood are among the materials commonly used in the construction of buildings. Supplemental materials used in public buildings include noninflammable composition material such as asbestos, rock wool, and gypsum.

Metals are used in many ways as materials in buildings, common examples of their use being structural framework, lath, doors, window and door casings, roofs, and ornamental work in iron, bronze, copper, aluminum, and stainless steel. Steel, properly treated and constructed and used as the structural part of most modern buildings, bespeaks permanence, strength, and unlimited possibilities in design.

Stone is a durable building material, highly resistant to the action of the natural elements and organic growth. Both heavy in weight and bulky to transport, it is less expensive when used near the source of supply. The use of stone is limited almost entirely to outside walls.

Brick and *tile* are made of clay that has been molded and fired. They are manufactured in many parts of the country so that transportation costs usually can be kept to a minimum. This type of building material is available in many colors and designs. Decorative brick is usually employed in exterior construction, and hollow tile and common brick are used for partitions.

Glass blocks and panels are among the relatively new building materials that have been enthusiastically received. They combine effectively with the woods and metals used for modern effects and may contribute interest and charm to a remodeling project. Huge plain, thermal or black glass panels set in a structural steel framework form the walls of many modern buildings in which foodservices are housed. They are particularly acceptable in dining rooms overlooking an attractive vista.

The field of *plastics* offers many possibilities for building and equipment uses. The acrylic resins appear to hold much promise for effective use in windows, partitions, and trims as well as in building facings.

Cement is often used for floors in heavy-traffic service areas and may or may not be covered with other materials, such as vinyl tile. It is available in colors or neutral gray and may be finished smooth or rough. Cement is highly resistant to wear and fire but, because of porosity, it readily absorbs moisture, grease, and stains.

Marble is used extensively in entrances of public buildings in the form of pillars, floors, and lower walls. It is relatively expensive and requires special care to keep it in good condition. However, it adds dignity and charm in the proper setting, and its wearing qualities are unquestioned.

Wood is most used as a finish for interiors, as floors, window and door casings, doors, and wall panels. Most woods are highly decorative and also help to soften the lines of rooms and to produce a feeling of warmth and friendliness. The use of wood is limited in food preparation units, but is extensive in dining rooms. Comparatively low structural strength and high inflammability make wood less desirable for heavy building purposes than more durable materials.

The building engineer is particularly concerned with the chemical composition of the material, the hardness, toughness, resistance to strain, and density. All are important factors in determining the material best suited to the particular structure and the type of construction that will be most satisfactory. The food director, on whom falls the responsibility of planning or remodeling a foodservice, will need to rely on the advice of experts for much of the selection of building materials and the details of construction.

Floors. Floors form a part of the background of rooms and should harmonize with walls and furnishings in color and type. They must also meet many other requirements, chief among which are utility, durability, and resiliency. Floors should be impervious to moisture, grease, and food stains; they should also be nonslippery and resistant to scratches and acid, alkali, or organic solvents. The coloring should be permanent, and the cost of maintenance and upkeep relatively low. Floors should be strong and durable to withstand the wear produced by the heavy traffic characteristic of large food units. Floors are commonly sloped to drains in various parts of the kitchen to permit easy cleaning. The floors under steam units are indented and fitted with their own drains.

Floors and floor coverings are available in many materials, designs, and colors, making possible interesting and pleasing decorative effects. Common among these are wood, concrete, and terrazzo floors, and clay, asphalt, vinyl, and rubber tile.

Wood is no longer used for flooring in institution kitchens, but hardwoods such as maple, oak, and birch, properly sealed and waxed, may be desirable in dining rooms, especially those used as social rooms for dances and receptions, as in university residence halls.

Concrete floors are most common in storerooms, receiving rooms, and laundries. The disadvantages of concrete floors are that they are fatiguing to walk or stand on, absorb grease, are cold in appearance, crack easily and, if painted, require frequent refinishing. Color may be added satisfactorily to the cement in the mixing process.

Terrazzo is a combination of cement and crushed marble, the cement serving only as a binder to hold the chipped marble in place. The marble constitutes approximately 85 percent of the surface. Brass or other metal strips are used to divide the floor into sections for the purpose of decoration and to facilitate the removal of sections for replacement if needed. Terrazzo floors are finished by grinding down and polishing. This treatment gives them a permanent smooth surface and makes them attractive, sanitary, and relatively impervious to liquids and stains. Terrazzo may be used for dining room and kitchen floors, although lack of resiliency and the noisiness of clatter on its hard surface render it less well suited to foodservice units than to entrances, corridors, and stairways in public buildings.

Clay tiles have been used as heavy-duty floorings for years and are especially satisfactory in institution kitchens. They are highly resistant to wear, nonabsorbent, color fast, easily cleaned, and give a pleasing effect. Clay floor tiles are available in a wide range of sizes, shapes, and colors that permits much choice in design and color. *Quarry* tiles are unglazed units made from natural clays by the plastic process. They have a dense body made of high-grade shales, are vitrified, formed into blocks 1 1/4 to 1 1/2 inches thick, and are highly recommended for floors in institution kitchens. They are strong enough to support the weight of heavy equipment and are impervious to staining and absorption; however, they are slippery when wet. To counteract the latter, sand may be imbedded in the surface of the tile to render it skidproof. Quarry tile so treated is more difficult to clean than smooth surface tile. A variety of shapes and colors is available, but a pleasing brick-red square is most common.

Ceramic mosaic tiles are manufactured from plastic clay, produced by dust-pressed or plastic method, are unglazed, and less than 6 square inches in area. The greatest disadvantages in their use are that they are nonresilient and slippery when wet.

Asphalt tile is often used as diningroom flooring. It is composed of natural asphalt, asbestos fiber, resin, and pure mineral pigments. Asphalt tile is available in many sizes and colors; is hard, resilient, and durable; resists abrasion, moisture, and fire; and is nonslippery even when wet. A relatively low original cost, easy installation and upkeep, high wearing qualities, and adaptability have made this type of flooring popular, particularly for dining rooms and corridors.

Plastic tile is a thermoplastic vinyl-chloride-resin compound that may be in the form of a vinyl laminate, flexible or pressed vinyl, or vinyl-plastic asbestos. In its favor are long wearing qualities, due to its resistance to alkalis, acids, grease, and weight of heavy furniture, resiliency and sound-absorbing qualities, natural luster, antislip properties, wide range of color and design, and ease of maintenance.

Rubber tile is a soft floor covering made from pure rubber vulcanized under pressure, with the addition of cotton and mineral fibers. This covering, if of the hard, firm type, is suitable for use in dining rooms because it is resilient and quiet and may be made into many attractive designs. Its wearing qualities are comparable with other types of soft floor coverings. Special attention should be given to the details of laying and to its care while in use, because deterioration is rapid if improper laying and cleaning methods are followed.

The selection of the best flooring for institution food units is a debatable matter. There is considerable difference of opinion as to which types are most satisfactory. The hard surface flooring is fatiguing for employees and causes many accidents through slipping and falling. However, this type of flooring is highly resistant to wear and soil, is comparatively easy to maintain, and is permanent. The softer, more resilient floors are likely to be less durable and more absorbent. An absolutely perfect type of floor for the institution foodservice remains to be discovered.

Care. The daily upkeep costs on floors in institution foodservice units are relatively high and, for this reason, easily cleaned floors are desirable for all work units. Good sanitary standards in upkeep include daily thorough cleaning of kitchen floors with a neutral soap or cleaner and warm water. The care of dining room floors depends on the type of floor and the kind of finish. A polished hardwood floor might need dust mopping two or three times a day and thorough cleaning and waxing every week, 10 days, or 2 weeks, whereas the tiles and terrazzo might need daily brushing and weekly washing, depending on the amount of traffic and wear. Waxing enhances the beauty and protects the floor materials from scratches, heavy traffic wear, and surface soil. Paste wax is recommended highly for wood floors and may be supplemented with a liquid polishing wax for maintenance. A self-polishing wax is recommended for asphalt, vinyl, and rubber tile and terrazzo, although a thin film of any type of wax may be used successfully on vinyl tile and terrazzo. The application of a wax containing a solvent on rubber tile should be avoided, because it causes deterioration of this flooring material.

A power scrubbing machine with vacuum attachment to remove excess wash and rinse water from floor surfaces and a power buffer are necessities where the floor area is large.

Floor Covering. Carpets have been used as floor coverings in hotel, exclusive restaurant, and club dining rooms for many years. Currently, this type of floor treatment is popular and found in many foodservice units, especially in entrances, lounges, and dining rooms.

Carpeting contributes much to the decor and atmosphere of the foodservice; it is available in unlimited design and color, absorbs noise, is comfortable to stand or walk on, lessens hazards of falling, and is an insulator against heat loss.

The carpet selected should have long wearing qualities, be resistant to soil and stain, and clean easily. Carpets made of nylon, antron, and other synthetic fibers have these characteristics. If carpets are not fire resistant they should be treated to make them so. Direct application to the floor surface is advisable to prevent rippling and permit wheels of food and dish trucks to roll easily. Outdoor-indoor carpeting is used often in entrances opening onto or near the sidewalk.

Care. Frequent vacuuming, spot cleaning, and wet, dry foam, or powder cleaning are necessary to keep carpets attractive and in good condition. The single-disc rotary brush floor scrubbing machine with solution-dispensing tank and the dry-foam shampoo machine are popular for on-location maintenance. The services of a commercial contracting cleaning company are often employed for periodic heavy cleaning.

Walls. The walls and ceilings of institution foodservice units should be planned to provide a pleasing and sanitary background. The entire wall may be plastered and finished with enamel or enamel paint. This is the least expensive of the various treatments deemed even fairly satisfactory. For food preparation rooms, walls of glazed tile or masonry at least to a height of 5 to 8 feet are commonly recommended. The remainder of the wall may then be made of a hard, smooth-finished plaster. Tile, white or colored, may be used for the entire wall if the budget permits. Regardless of the materials used, walls in all preparation units should be washable and impervious to moisture.

The amount of natural and artificial light available will determine to a great extent the wall finish selected for a given room. The colors and textures of materials that may be used as wall finishes have different reflective and absorptive qualities, which must be considered in relation to the light that the room will receive.

Rooms with walls finished in white paint or paper are easily lighted, since approximately 80 to 90 percent of the light striking them is reflected. The use of such whiteness, however, is not desirable for many rooms because of the cold and unpleasant effect produced. The lighter values of cream, pearl gray, buff, and pale green reflect approximately 80, 72, 64, and 60 percent of the light, respectively. Colors of as low a reflective factor as 50 should be avoided for interior finishes in kitchen and dining room units. Finishes that cannot be washed soon darken and lose in light-reflection value as the inevitable soil accumulates on them.

The texture of the reflecting surface has considerable influence on the amount of light reflected. The influence that the texture of a wall surface may have on the reflection factor is indicated by the fact that light-cream paint has a reflection factor of 74 and cream paper 56. Acoustical materials absorb light as well as sound, the amount varying with the material used. If such a treatment is to be given the ceiling or walls of a room, the choice of color in the finish employed must be carefully considered.

There are many possible treatments for dining room walls, varying from the mosaics found in certain commercial establishments to painted plaster, wall boards, ceramics, wood panels, or washable paper and plastic coverings. Markedly different effects are produced through the use of these various materials. The choice will depend on how permanent the service is and what one desires to express. Where there is little possibility of obtaining desirable window exposures, especially in small dining rooms, the use of mirrors is recommended. They help to make the room appear larger. Many new and novel color effects are brought out through wall lighting.

Window and door casings should harmonize with walls in type, color, and finish. Many of the new casings are made of metal, finished in the same color as the walls. Doors between preparation and serving units should be conveniently located for good traffic routing and, in most foodservices, are photoelectrically controlled so that they open as the person approaches and remain open until he passes through. Most doors are made of either wood or metal.

Walls should intersect with floors in a coved base, and all external and internal corners and angles should be rounded to facilitate cleaning and prevent chipping. Items such as pipes, ventilator fans, radiators, and wiring conduits should be concealed in the walls.

The height of ceilings in food units varies widely. Dining rooms with high ceilings usually produce a formal impression; those with lower ceilings give a more friendly and informal effect. Kitchen ceilings may vary from 11 to 20 feet in height, with 14 to 18 feet as an average. Ceilings of both kitchens and dining rooms should be acoustically treated and lighter in color than the walls.

Noise Control. Noise is a problem in any foodservice. Whether the noise comes from the careless handling of china and silver, boisterous people, or loud music, the reaction against it is of serious concern to the food director who is responsible for the well-being of the employees and for a volume of business arising from satisfied customers.

The volume of noise produced by the accumulated sounds of a kitchen, resulting from the operation of power equipment and the handling of china, silver, and cooking utensils, may be amplified by the nature of the room and readily transmitted to the dining room and other parts of the building. Noise measuring over 40 decibels is considered a nuisance and disturbing factor. The problem of reducing disturbing and undesirable sounds, beyond what can be accomplished through control of personnel, may be met through isolation of noisy equipment—such as a compactor—to a remote area, the use of noise-absorbing surfaces and furnishings at the source of such sounds, and by the use of certain types of construction that tend to break the transmission of sound. A porous surface catches sound impulses in the tiny perforations or spaces and absorbs rather than deflects them. There are many attractive, fireproof, acoustical materials available for ceilings that may be mechanically suspended from or cemented to existing ceilings, or built into new installations. In dining rooms the local noises may be minimized by the use of acoustical plaster or other sound-absorbing material as wall and ceiling finishes, by heavy draperies at the windows, and by sound-absorbing finishes, such as linoleum or rubber tile, on the floors. Some foodservices have heavy carpets on the dining room floor. Ample space, upholstered chair seats, furniture glides, tablecloths and pads, composition instead of metal trays, rubberheeled shoes for waiters and waitresses all make their contributions to the lessening of noises. Music in dining rooms should be at low volume.

The use in the kitchen of soundproof materials in wall, ceiling, and floor construction and finishes will reduce distracting noise levels. Acoustical ceiling materials suitable for kitchens have been perfected that are designed to resist deterioration from rapid temperature and humidity changes and corrosive cooking fumes. They have a low reflectance value, are fire resistant, washable, and should be given serious consideration in the planning of all new or remodeled institution kitchens. Figure 11.3 is an example of sound reduction treatment over a noisy area. Features such as automatic lubrication of the so-called noiseless power equipment that keeps it in quiet working condition, rubber-tired carts, rubber collars on openings in dish-scraping tables, and ball-bearing glide table drawers help to minimize noise in the kitchen.

Sound-absorbing materials are used not only as surface finishes in construction but also as insulators. Vents, radiator pipes, and water pipes may all act as carriers of sound, and the most effective means of noise prevention is their careful and thorough insulation with sound-absorbing material. Because of later inaccessibility and prohibitive costs, it is most important that this precaution be taken in the original construction.

Lighting. Institution food units try to utilize as much daylight as possible. The appearance of food is good in natural light, energy saving is effected, operating expense is reduced, and there is less possibility of glaring reflected light. However, many foodservice units are located in areas that have a limited amount of natural illumination and depend on artificial lighting during the day as well as at night.

Good lighting in a foodservice provides adequate and pleasing illumination for comfortable seeing in the performance of the various tasks. Much eye fatigue and general debility of workers may be attributed to improper amount and kind of light. Not only does insufficient illumination produce a gloomy and depressive atmosphere, but it impairs vision, is not conducive to accuracy in work or to cleanliness, and is a safety hazard. Glaring light is objectionable because it tends to injure vision, cause fatigue, reduce efficiency, and increase accidents.

The modern trend is definitely toward the use of better and more effective lighting with attention given to the functional and artistic aspects of the problem as well as to cost. The estimate of the amount of light needed has been based too often on watt-hour readings instead of on a comparison of efficient work units with adequate and inadequate lighting facilities as determined by satisfactions, and by foot-candle and meter measurements. A light intensity

FIGURE   11.3   Special sound-absorbing ceiling treatments above dishwashing area. (a) Removable perforated accoustical panels hung from ceiling. (b) Boxlike corrugated aluminum sheets filled with 1 inch of fiber glass insulation suspended from ceiling in metal frame.

653

of 30 to 40 foot-candles is considered adequate for general lighting in food preparation and display units, with an increase up to 50 foot-candles or more (to 90) in intensity localized on work areas such as sinks, salad tables, cookers, and where recipes are read, ingredients weighed and measured, and gauges and thermometers are located. Fifty foot-candles illumination is recommended in refrigerators for detection of food spoilage or unsanitary condition, and 70 foot-candles for inspection, pricing, and checking areas. Note Fig. 11.4 as an example of well-lighted area.

The recommended intensity of light for most institution dining rooms is 15 to 20 foot-candles, which can be supplied for about 2 watts per square foot of floor area. Hallways and corridors might have less bright (10 to 20 foot-candles) lighting. The desired intensity can usually be supplied if proper care is given to the choice of room finishes and to the selection of the types of lighting fixtures and their placement.

FIGURE   11.4   Efficient pantry arrangement for a table service operation with well-diffused overhead lighting. Courtesy, Southern Equipment Company, Inc.

Glare is caused by high brightness from large areas in a room and by reflections from shiny surfaces. Diffusion of natural light through window shades or adequate shielding of artificial light by design and position of the luminaire to direct the reflected image away from the eye of the worker is advisable. Care must be taken to keep the lighted-ceiling brightness low enough to prevent its becoming a source of glare.

Shadows on work surfaces are irritating and confusing to the worker and may be eliminated by diffusion of the light on high-reflectance room surfaces and by proper spacing of fixtures to insure as uniform distribution of light at the work level as possible.

Lighting systems may be either indirect, direct, or a combination of the two. The indirect has approximately 90 to 100 percent of the light from the luminaire directed upward, whereas the direct system has a corresponding amount directed downward. A general diffusing system has about equal amounts directed either way.

The type of fixtures and their installation should harmonize with the architectural plan of the building and be so placed that the desired illumination level and balance in brightness are assured for each particular situation. In most instances beauty is combined with utility so that in planning the lighting effects one also performs the duties of an interior decorator. Recessed louvered and luminous ceiling lighting are examples of newer developments in this area. The latter is an all-over even lighting of the entire ceiling to create the effect of natural sunlight.

The light source and its intensity selected for a foodservice has a decided effect on the general atmosphere of the place, the people, and attractiveness of the food. In discussing lighting sources Kazarian [1] states:

Since a variety of light sources are available, knowledge of their effects on color perception is important for proper lighting design. For example, the cold form of fluorescent lighting makes human skin appear pale, and makes most foods look unappetizing. Incandescent lamps or the warm fluorescent lamps enhance the red colors making people appear healthier looking and foods more appetizing. Another writer [2] on this same subject reported that:

[1] *Edward A. Kazarian*, Work Analysis and Design for Hotels, Restaurants and Institutions, *Avi Publishing Co., Westport, Connecticut, p. 80, 1969.*

[2] *Robert C. Buchanan, "College and University Food Service,"* The Anatomy of Food Service Design, *Jule Wilkinson, Editor, Cahners, Boston, p. 10, 1975.*

Yellow-white incandescent lamps present both food material and the human face in the best light. They should be used in preference to fluorescent lamps in the dining room where both food appearance and atmosphere are important. Fluorescent tube colors, in the order of desirability for use with foods were: "soft white," "white," "warm white," "cool white," "gold," "daylight," "pink," "blue," "green," and "red."

The amount and kind of lighting to plan for a foodservice represents a long-time investment and merits much study and consideration with the assistance of technical experts in this field. Items such as the adequacy, efficiency, and suitability of the system for the situation and the cost of operation are far more important than the cost of the initial installation.

Wiring is an important consideration in the planning of lighting. It is advisable to install wiring adequate to provide an economical distribution of electrical energy for future requirements instead of making additions as changes are made. When wiring is not heavy enough to carry the specified wattage, energy is lost between meter and light, light generation is lower than rated, and cost is higher.

Wiring circuits are limited in load and length. It is economical as well as convenient to have many switches and automatic circuit breakers for control of lighting. Installation of wiring, panel boards, switches, and automatic circuit breakers should be in accordance with the requirements of the National Electrical Code.

Heating, Cooling, and Ventilation. Air conditioning means more than the popularly used term "air cooling." It includes heating, control of humidity, and the circulation, cleaning, and cooling of the air. Advancement has been rapid in this field, and systems have been perfected whereby the controls for all factors are established in one central unit. The system may be set up to filter, warm, humidify, and circulate the air in winter and, with the addition of cooling coils and refrigeration, maintain a desirable and comfortable temperature in the summer. Dehumidification may be necessary in certain climates.

Perhaps, currently, the type of heating most often found in foodservices is coal, gas, oil-generated steam, or hydro-electric power. However, solar, thermal, and nuclear energy are anticipated likely heat sources in certain geographical areas in the future. Steam used for heating may be piped from an outside source or generated within the building. In any case it is transferred through well-insulated pipes to floor or in-wall radiators. Cold air is forced or passed over the radiators, warmed and circulated to all parts of the room.

Considerable attention has been given to floor and wall radiant heating for institution dining rooms particularly. Copper pipes through which hot water flows are imbedded beneath the surface and transmit the heat to the room by conduction. A constant temperature of 68°F is considered desirable, although provision is necessary for a higher temperature (72°F) in dining rooms where guests are sitting quietly. Heated air becomes dry and may prove injurious to the health of individuals unless humidified. Provision for maintaining a fairly constant relative humidity of 45 percent is possible through the addition of moisture by spray or evaporation methods or through dehumidification of air with a high moisture content. The moisture content of air is reduced by controlling the temperature of the evaporator coil through which the air passes. A low-temperature coil will absorb more moisture than a high-temperature coil. Dust particles and impurities are removed from the incoming air by mechanical filters, electric precipitation, air washers, and centrifugal devices. The air-washing method has the advantage that moisture may be added simultaneously with the cleaning process. The method of filtration selected should provide for free passage of air, the retention of dust, and easy cleaning or exchange of filters.

Cooling is effected through increased circulation of the air, which provides for rapid changes of air near the body surface, dehumidification of the incoming air, and the actual cooling or refrigerating of the air to be circulated. Refrigeration may be produced by any of the usual means. It may be desirable to install air-conditioning independent of the heating system, especially if conversion is accompanied by fans that regulate the velocity of the heated or cooled air. Average ventilation requirements for foodservices are estimated at 12 cubic feet per minute per person, or an air change in the kitchen every 2 to 5 minutes.

Adequate and satisfactory ventilation in kitchens may be provided through a fan system with a special arrangement to eliminate cooking odors and fumes, moisture, and grease-laden vapors through vented hoods located over the cooking units. Cool outdoor air may be drawn into the kitchen by fans to reduce the temperature, or direct air-conditioning may be installed. The latter is expensive and presents the problem of drafts on cooks working near heated equipment. However, their productivity is estimated to be increased 5 to 15 percent in such a controlled environment.

Automatic regulation of an air-conditioning system is necessary. Electric thermostatic control is favored for small installations, compressed-air control for larger units. The real tests of any air-conditioning system are whether or not desirable inside temperature is maintained when out-of-door temperature is extremely high or low and whether the relative humidity remains fairly constant at the desired degree. Summer cooling systems often present a health hazard by providing inside temperatures that differ extremely from those outside. An optimum difference between inside and outside temperature has been suggested as 1° for every 2 1/2° that the outside temperature goes above 70°F. This usually means that the inside temperature should be only 12 to 15°F below the outside temperature. A desirable work environment for cooks is 65 to 70°F in winter, and 69 to 73°F in summer.

Adequate and proper insulation of the building is necessary to obtain the best results with an air-conditioning system. Heat losses frequently run as high as 40 percent because of factors such as poorly constructed walls, leaky windows, and improperly fitted doors.

Air-conditioning systems are an important consideration in the planning of most commercial dining rooms and also in many other types of foodservices. It is well to make an intensive study of the local problem of the individual foodservice as affected by regions and climates before installing any particular system. It is advisable to seek the aid of specialists associated with reliable companies and to buy only from well-established firms in a position to insure good service.

Refrigeration. Institution foodservices depend on their refrigeration systems for the preservation of perishables at proper temperatures and for the attractive, appetizing appearance of fresh, cooked, and frozen foods at the time of serving. Much waste is eliminated by the successful storage of foods until they can be utilized in the regular meal service, since deterioration of many foods is common at room temperatures. A detailed discussion of the importance of food refrigeration is found in Chapter 10.

Primitive men preserved their foodstuffs in caves or cold springs. The ancient Egyptians cooled water in porous jars at night, and early Romans transported from the mountains snow and ice to cool fruits, fish, and wines for their banquets. Much later ice was cut from ponds and rivers and used in food storage chests. Still later commercially frozen ice was used for this purpose. Cooling by means of ice proved an inefficient and expensive method for large-size food units, so that when mechanical refrigeration became available it readily found a place in these services.

The development of *mechanical* refrigeration has effected many changes in the industrial world. New machinery has been designed and manufactured, experts have been trained to install and manipulate the systems, and the problem of transportation and storage of perishables has been practically eliminated. It has made possible an increased availability of perishable foodstuffs regardless of geographical location. Owing to the rapid development of refrigeration, an ample supply of fresh meats, fruits, and vegetables is now found in all parts of the United States at practically all seasons of the year. Refrigeration has not only solved the problem of transportation regardless of distance and climate that once complicated distribution but also, through better storage facilities, has helped to level the price curve of perishable commodities.

Cold is the absence of heat. Refrigeration by mechanical means in a foodservice is the removal of heat from food or other products in an enclosed area such as a refrigerator, freezer, ice maker, holding cabinet, or water cooler. The use of certain refrigerants (chemical compounds), and a system of coils or evaporator, a compressor, condenser, thermostatic expansion valve, and controls are incorporated. Warm air rises from the food and moves toward a cooler surface, which is the "evaporator," or coils within the refrigerator or freezer, which contains liquified gas when at low temperature. In the beginning of the cycle, the refrigerant in liquid form flows into the coils, where it is vaporized and pressure is built up by the heat it absorbs. This starts a "compressor," which pumps the heat-laden gas out of the evaporator and compresses it to a high pressure. The compressed gas flows into a "condenser" that is air or water cooled, the heat is released, the gas is reliquefied, and the refrigerant is stored until the temperature in the fixture rises above the control level. A sensor opens a "thermostatic valve" to admit more liquified gas to the "evaporator," and the cycle repeats itself as often as necessary to reach and maintain the desired temperature in the refrigerator, freezer, or other equipment.

Some of the common refrigerants used are sulphur dioxide, methyl chloride, dichlorodifluoromethane, known as "Freon" or "F-12" and "F-22" or "Isotron." These have a relatively low condensing pressure. Desirable characteristics of refrigerants are: low boiling point, nontoxicity, nonexplosiveness, noninflammability, noncorrosiveness, stability, harmlessness to foods, inoffensive odor, high miscibility, high latent heat, and reasonable cost.

Regrigerator systems may be central, multiple unit, and single unit. The size of the foodservice, the arrangement of the storage and preparation units, the needs, and the amount of money available are determining factors in the selection made. In a central system of refrigeration one machine supplies refrigeration in adequate amount for all cooling units throughout the building. Such a system is rarely used, since it presents the problem of trying to maintain desirable temperatures in the different units and, in case of a breakdown, all refrigeration is gone. In a multiple system of refrigeration there is a compressor for a series of coolers, the compressor being of the proper capacity to carry the load required to maintain the desired temperature in the series of coolers.

The best results will be obtained if refrigeration loads are divided among units that are operated at or near the same storage temperatures. A single-unit or self-contained refrigerating system has only one box or unit, the temperature of which is reduced, regulated, and maintained directly through the attached compressor. This type is found mainly in small institutions and in salad counter units, water coolers, ice cream storage cabinets, ice makers, and low-temperature storage units.

Any system of refrigeration selected should insure reliable, safe, quiet, and efficient operation. It should be flexible to serve changing needs, located to save steps, and designed to do a specific job with maximum efficiency. *Flexibility* is achieved through preplanning for possible conversion from standard (36 to 40°F) to low temperature (0 to −10°F) or vice versa, through dual controls or interchange of compressors. It is important that such an arrangement be incorporated in the initial installation instead of making revisions at inconvenience and greater expense. Further planning for flexibility is to provide portable shelf sections in walk-ins; also slide-in and roll-in sections fitted with glides for adjustable stainless steel wire shelves or trays are advised. (See Figs. 3.18 and 11.5.) The above should accommodate the usual standard tray or pan (14 inches x 18 inches or 18 inches x 26 inches). The selection of some portable self-contained refrigerators or freezers makes it possible to relocate units quickly to meet changing needs.

In walk-ins the floors should be made of strong, durable, easily cleaned tile, made level with the adjoining floor to permit easy transport of food on carts. Walls should have a washable finish impervious to moisture or should be covered with stainless steel, anodized aluminum, or vinyl. The unit should be fitted on the inside with a safety door opening device. An outside wall mounted recorder or gauge to indicate inside temperature of the box eliminates opening the door for checking. Complete modular walk-in refrigeration

FIGURE   11.5   *Examples of portable refrigerated storage units. (a) Mobile refrigerated cabinets are available with interchangeable interiors to accommodate different size trays, other food containers, or banquet
plated cold foods; mounted on 5-inch swivel casters. (b) Roll-in
racks may be custom made to fit major refrigerators; engineered to
utilize maximum space within refrigerator. Courtesy, Cres-Cor,
Crescent Metal Products, Inc.*

boxes assembled on the site have largely replaced former built-in
insulated rooms. Such assemblies are available in various dimensions and with a variety of finishes, colors, doors, and hardware from
which to make a selection.

    Stainless steel is the most durable and easily cleaned material
used for reach-in cabinets, but it is also the most expensive. Anodized aluminum and the colored vinyl finishes offer considerable
variation and choice of materials. Good insulation and proper-fitting
doors are of prime importance to successful refrigeration. Common
insulating materials are glass or vegetable fiber, cork board, mineral
wool, and foamed glass or plastic, any one of which must be of suitable thickness and pack for the material, and sealed against moisture. The current use of polyurethane foam has made compact models possible by lessening the thickness of walls and doors. Also,
doors are lighter in weight; many are fitted with glass windows.

Hinges, latches, and handles are points of wear and should be made of durable material. Reach-in refrigerators located in hot kitchens and opened often to place and remove items for short storage should be held at around 34°F. Reach-in boxes usually vary from 20 to 60 cubic feet in capacity and often are self-contained units, as are water coolers and ice makers.

The amount of refrigeration space necessary for any foodservice is a debatable question and one for which there is no established standard. Each operation is an individual situation with specific requirements. The type of menu, kind of service, clientele, size and seat capacity, form in which food is purchased, and the frequency with which perishable food supplies are delivered are some of the factors that must be considered in determining the refrigeration equipment needed.

Various estimates for refrigeration space have been suggested

FIGURE 11.6   Ice-maker units are a necessary part of the refrigeration system in modern foodservice installations. Courtesy, S. Blickman, Inc.

 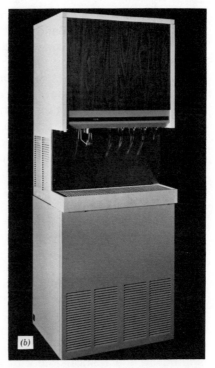

FIGURE   11.7   (a) *High volume ice flaker on top of storage bin.* (b) *Flake ice and drink dispenser on stand. Courtesy, Queen Products Division, King-Seeley Thermos Company.*

such as 1 1/2 to 2 cubic feet per meal served per day; 1 square foot per meal per person; or on the basis of the amount of space to store 2 pounds of food per person per meal or 6 pounds per day. Another estimate is that 25 to 30 pounds of food can be stored per cubic foot. Obviously, such estimates can be used only as a guide in planning.

Self-contained ice-makers (may be portable) and water coolers are advised for each area as near the point of use as possible. (See Figs. 11.6 and 11.7.) Ice makers are available with various capacities and capabilities, such as the production of flakes, cubes, or tubular forms.

The efficiency of a refrigeration system depends greatly on the capacity of the equipment in relation to the load carried and the arrangement of food on the shelves, the construction, insulation, and installation of the cabinet, and the care and upkeep given the entire setup. Proper air circulation both inside and outside the cabinet is essential. This may be either natural or forced by use of a fan and duct system large enough to permit even distribution of air from top to bottom and to affect automatic self-defrosting. The storage of food in shallow containers, placed on slatted shelves or tray slides to permit good circulation of the chilled air, is a requirement for both long- and short-time storage. Food in large masses or deep containers cools slowly, and much bacterial damage could be done before the interior temperature is reduced below the danger point. The contents of refrigerators must be checked often to see that no foods are pushed aside and held longer than acceptable. Storage of the newest food to the back is an added safeguard to the accumulation of aging items.

Care. The selection of adequate and suitable refrigeration, its cleanliness, proper use, and care cannot be overemphasized. The preservation of the quality and appearance of food, prevention of waste through shrinkage and spoilage, possible savings through quantity buying, and convenience are some of the advantages of good refrigeration to any food operation.

Routine care of all mechanical parts of the refrigeration system such as motors, compressors, condensers, and coils or plates should be the responsibility of an engineer or a qualified person who understands fully the various mechanisms. Even so, the food director should be familiar with the operating characteristics and at least know the manipulation of controls so that he can take care of an emergency situation until the engineer arrives on the scene. Regular periodic inspection and check of temperature inside each box is necessary in order to detect inadequacies in the operation, to provide proper storage conditions, and to prevent undue waste of food. Immediate replacement of worn door seals and repair of hinges, handles, and latches are necessary to prevent possible heat leakage into the refrigerator.

The cleanliness and care of the refrigerated equipment in the kitchen or other areas are the responsibility of the food director who in turn delegates these duties to various employees. Refrigerators should be completely and thoroughly cleaned at least twice a week to maintain good sanitary conditions and eliminate odors. All shelves, or other accessories should be removed and washed the same as any cooking utensils. Inside walls should be washed down and the floor mopped or washed according to the size and type of refrigerator. Water and a mild cleansing agent should be used for washing, followed by wiping with a cloth wrung from clear water or a solution of baking soda and water for the walls.

Most large units are automatically defrosted, but a close check should be made to insure this is happening. Moisture condensation on the outside of boxes and cabinets may occur when there is a large temperature difference between room air and the refrigerator, in cases where the humidity of the air is high, or when the insulation of the box is poor. Such moisture should be wiped off with a clean cloth as often as necessary.

Doors of refrigerators should be opened as seldom as possible when taking the food in and out of storage. Any great amount of warm moist room air rushing into the box affects the holding temperature and humidity within the fixture. This may cause condensation of moisture on the food or freezing on the cooling unit, either of which affects the efficiency of the system.

Safety and Sanitation. Provision for safety and sanitation must be built into the foodservice plans during the blueprint stage. These include prevention against fire, accident, and health hazards and are regulated to a great extent through established codes for building construction, wiring, plumbing, and sanitation standards. Safety precautions should be made obvious to patrons as well as employees in a foodservice to avoid accidents and to protect the management from unwarranted liability charges. Much falling, slipping, and tripping of individuals can be prevented by: weather-protected entrances; adequate lighting; the selection of nonslippery flooring; the use of ramps, elevators, or well-lighted easy-tread steps with handrails between floor levels; clear passageways free from debris, pipes, or broken flooring; high electric outlets for equipment; the use of conspicuous signs near hazardous spots; and the provision of safety ladders and conveniently placed receptacles for trash and broken glass.

Sprains and strains often occur when heavy loads are lifted or carried. These could have been avoided by better arrangement of working or storage heights or by transporting on wheels, conveyors, and subveyors. Many bumps or collisions can be averted by such arrangements as wide traffic aisles and well-lighted passageways of adequate width, double doors, photoelectric-controlled doors in heavy traffic areas, glass inserts in doors, and heavy or tight door checks. Cut fingers are kept at a minimum through proper storage of sharp cutlery in racks and the selection of mechanical equipment with guards. Burns are prevented through control of hot water temperatures, recessed pipes and radiators, hot water connections direct to cooking units such as steam-jacketed kettles, tilting fry pans, and coffee stations. The selection of equipment with steam shut-off valves that operate automatically when doors are opened and of heat-resistant material for handles of heated units reduces the hazards of injuries to employees. Also, provision for "quick disconnects" at each piece of power or steam equipment is important.

The ease of maintaining high standards of sanitation is an important factor in planning a foodservice. Cleanability is affected by the selection and proper installation of washable walls, ceilings, and floors, coved bases and rounded corners, floor drains under steam equipment, wall-or platform-mounted fixed equipment or mobilized so it can be moved for cleaning, easily disassembled equipment so parts can be removed for washing, and adequate hot water and refrigeration. Traps, drains, pipes, and equipment on legs should be 6 to 8 inches above the floor level to permit cleaning under them. Utility connections should meet standards recommended by the National Sanitation Foundation. Sanitation is discussed in detail in Chapter 10.

LAYOUT DESIGN

The designing of an attractive and functional foodservice merits serious consideration of scientific facts, experiences, and observations, and their application to the particular situation. The provision for adequate facilities for all anticipated activities and regard for future growth and development of the foodservice are involved. A real understanding of the problem is necessary in order to make an equitable division of floor space into areas for a satisfactory working relationship. Also fitting these areas into the architectural plan of a building calls for time, effort, imagination, resourcefulness, judgment, and skill in manipulation of detail on the part of those responsible for developing the complete plans.

A good balance of beauty and utility in the structure and furnishings and equipment must be maintained in successful foodservice planning. Colorful walls and floors, modern lighting, streamlined heavy-duty kitchen equipment fabricated of well-finished metals, machines with mechanical parts and motors enclosed, and the use of light woods and metals in dining room furniture are a few of the many features that contribute materially to the beauty of modern foodservice areas. Sanitation, ease of maintenance, and comfort must also be considered along with efficient use of manpower, cost of operation, and the objectives of the food system.

SPACE ALLOWANCES

Adequate space for the preparation and service of meals for the number of people to be served is a necessity for maintaining quality food and service and high standards of sanitation. However, inefficiency and lost time and effort may result from too much space. It is the responsibility of the food manager to make compatible the maximum area available for foodservice and the minimum area required for the type of facility desired. The space allowance for kitchens and dining rooms is often estimated exclusive of the area needed for activities such as dishwashing and the receiving and storing of food and for employees' restrooms and locker rooms.

Developing a good layout for a food facility is not a simple task. It is complicated by the diversity of functions to be performed, the control of quality and cost in a highly perishable product, the social and psychological aspects of food, in addition to the specific needs of the individual facility. New foods bringing marked changes in quantity food preparation and service . . . demand that the facilities be designed to operate at high efficiency as future changes are effected in food facility operation.[3]

One procedure often followed by architects or food facility consultants is to block out the dining room location and space allowance first, then the production area in good relationship to it, followed by the planning of other areas such as receiving, storage, and dishwashing. The amount of floor space required and how it should be divided must be determined for each individual foodservice. There is no one formula for allowances to meet the needs in all situations. Fairly accurate estimates for dining areas can be calculated if the type of service and number of persons to be seated at one time are known. Likewise, the seating capacity of a given area can be determined by use of the generally accepted standard number of square feet per seat for the different kinds of institution foodservices. The larger allowances permit room for easy waiter service and increased table space and comfort for the diner. Variations from the chart below will depend on the sizes of tables and chairs and whether spacious arrangement is possible. The suggested standards are given in the accompanying tabulation.

[3] *Lendal H. Kotschevar and Margaret E. Terrell,* Food Service Planning: Layout and Equipment, *Wiley, New York, p. 3, 1961.*

	Square Feet per Seat
School lunchrooms	9–12
Hotel and club banquet rooms	10–11
Commercial cafeterias	16–18
Industrial and university cafeterias	12–15
Residence halls	12–15
Restaurants and hotels (table service)	14–16
Lunch counters	18–20

Kitchen area requirements are much more complex and less definite than those for dining areas. An estimate for kitchen area on the basis of either the number of meals served, income per seat, or dining room seats alone would be unsound and unreliable. The relationship of kitchen to dining space for different types of foodservices necessarily differs. A cafeteria and residence hall serving the same number of people have entirely different requirements in both areas. A cafeteria may have an average turnover of 3 customers per hour for each seat during the peak service period, whereas the residence hall would expect to seat half of the group at one time. Larger capacity kitchen equipment would be required to prepare a greater quantity of each kind of food for the less varied menu than in the cafeteria. In the cafeteria there would be continuous preparation of a number of items in small amounts for which the total space requirement would be less. A hospital has a unique problem in that only staff, personnel, and guests, or approximately half of the people fed, are served in dining rooms. Consequently, kitchens in hospitals are large in relation to dining areas in order to provide adequate space in which to prepare and distribute the quantity and variety of food needed for patients, in addition to that served in dining rooms.

The allocation of space to dining and kitchen areas by percentage figures based on total area and a similar division of kitchen areas into major units have been used as a guide by some kitchen planners. However, it is generally agreed that any data on the relative sizes of kitchens and dining rooms have to be modified to fit the particular operation. For instance, consideration of only one or two variables, such as the type of menu or the inclusion of a bakeshop, would influence the final decision of the overall space needed in the kitchen. Formerly, when percentage distribution estimates were made, they may have varied from 25 to 35 to 50 percent of the total area, dependent somewhat on the type of foodservice.

The present trend is toward reducing the kitchen area in relation to the size of dining rooms in all types of foodservices. This change has been brought about by factors such as greater attention to the systems planning concept, less preparation of foods in the individual kitchen, utilization of specialized multiuse time and labor saving equipment, and arrangement of equipment for efficient coordinated activity of a minimum number of employees to produce and serve the amount and type of food to meet the objectives of the foodservice. Perhaps the two areas most affected would be a reduction in the production department with cooking processes confined to a concentrated area, and an increase in storage space, especially in the number and location of refrigerator and freezer units.

Avery [4] comments that

Food facility designers are human engineers. They design dining rooms that relax the patron and make it possible for him to see his food at its best and enjoy it to the fullest extent. Then the designer plans the kitchen, serving and dishwashing areas so that the workers can prepare food for the patron at the quality level and at the time he desires it. This is done with minimum expenditure of labor and with the least discomfort to the worker.

Menu Analysis. Many of the early writers agreed that the menu is basic in determining space and equipment requirements in a foodservice. Comments of two such recognized leaders are given below, which emphasize that quality food is the commodity in question and that much of the success or failure of the enterprise depends on the physical setup based primarily upon the menu pattern.

The menu pattern must be interrelated with the design of the layout. The size and capacity of each type of equipment must be determined not on the basis of the total number of persons served, but on the size of the individual batches and the frequency with which they recur. . . . The major goal of intelligent kitchen planning is the specification and arrangement of equipment and facilities so that excellent food, well prepared, with good flavor as well as eye appeal, may be produced with minimum effort and without confusion or waste. The menu, if well balanced and carefully analyzed in the production area, is the master blueprint that must be followed to achieve their goal.[5]

[4] *Arthur C. Avery, "Overview of Design,"* The Anatomy of Foodservice Design I, *Cahners, Boston, p. 3, 1975.*
[5] *Arthur W. Dana,* Kitchen Planning for Quantity Food Service, *Harper and Brothers, New York, pp. 8, 24, 1949.*

Terrell [6] wrote:

A study of the menu pattern, characteristics of the proposed service, and volume for a specific production unit will give indication of the requisite equipment. It will lead to an analysis of a desirable flow of work and will show labor and equipment loads. It will give a basis for determining the number of persons to work in an area and the pieces and size of equipment needed.

Translating space and equipment needs from the analysis of several typical menus is an arduous task at best, but results more than compensate for time and efforts spent. Montag and Tamashunas [7] say:

Requirements for equipment to meet production and service needs should be based on a production point or figure which is a downward modification of peak requirements. . . . These requirements are determined by analyzing the menu in regard to equipment usage. The total servings to be prepared are correlated with the equipment required to produce the food in accordance with a specified time schedule. . . . Several analyses based on menus typical of the institution provide a realistic estimate of equipment needs. The steps for making this type of study are: a) Determine portion size; b) Determine total production needs; c) Determine frequency and size of cooking batches; d) Record cooking time for each batch; e) Draw a tentative production schedule; f) Transfer information to bar chart; g) Translate information on bar chart into size and amount of equipment.

Literature from equipment manufacturing companies is an invaluable aid in determining selection of models best suited to meet the needs of the foodservice as found in the menu analysis data. Size and capacity charts, floor space and utilities required for installation, capabilities of each piece of equipment and other pertinent information is included therein. A sales representative of the company can answer many of the detailed and related questions of the prospective buyer.

Estimating the total space needs for a kitchen is best accomplished by grouping the required equipment into areas with rea-

[6] *Margaret E. Terrell, "Common Sense in the Kitchen,"* College and University Business, *4, 31 (March 1948).*

[7] *Geraldine M. Montag, Ph.D. and Victor M. Tamashunas, "Engineered Kitchen Layout Planning and Design,"* Journal of the American Dietetic Association, 55 (2), 128 (1969).

sonable space to make efficient workable units for equipment, food, storage, and people who work in them. Traffic aisles, space for opening refrigerator doors, and storage of and passageways for loading and moving carts must be included.

Allowances for space in other than the dining room and kitchen include areas such as entrances, dishwashing, waste disposal, storage, engineer's area, employee locker and rest rooms, and public rest rooms.

Fortunate is the dietitian or foodservice manager who has the opportunity to plan a facility in accordance with projected needs instead of being restricted by space limitations as in some remodeling situations or by an ultraconservative budget.

DESIGN DEVELOPMENT

A basic principle in planning foodservice facilities for efficient operation is the assembly line concept, with patterned traffic from receiving room to dishwashing unit. The purchasing, receiving, storing, issuing, preparing, processing, and serving of food, with the attendant removing, cleaning, and storing of dishes, washing and storing of utensils, disposal of trash and garbage, and the sanitation and maintenance of all features of the setup are the purposes that must be kept in mind when planning the detailed arrangement within a foodservice area. The successful fulfillment of each will depend in part on the space and facilities provided for it. Industrial plants have been designed to promote efficient operation from the time raw material is brought into the plant until the finished products are distributed. The same pattern is followed in the food industry and equipment grouped into related work areas in order to accomplish the purpose effectively and economically and to effect the continuous direct-work flow of the food from the time it is received at the service entrance until it is served in prepared form to the restaurant guest, to the hospital patient, or to the student in school or college.

Space Relationships. The first step in planning is to make a flow chart showing the steps which the work must take, their sequence, and the relations of the various working units to each other. This chart should show how the work should proceed from receiving area to storage, thence to prepreparation, preparation, service, consumption, and disposal of waste. It should also show which units of the department need contact with each other, which with the rest of the institution, and which with the outdoors.

An example of such a schematic sketch or flow chart Figure 11.8 shows the possible location and relationship of areas in a medium-size institution foodservice to facilitate the direct routing of food from receiving through preparation to service. Food is checked in and removed from receiving to dry long-time storage or refrigerated storage, from where it can be requisitioned to the prepreparation units if that is necessary. Otherwise, it can be moved directly from storage to the preparation or cooking areas. Much food is now purchased in ready-to-cook form so the prepreparation stations may be bypassed in some kitchens. If most foods are purchased after preliminary preparation, the vegetable preparation area may be reduced to a worktable, sink, refrigerator, and chopper, and the meat preparation area, other than refrigerated storage, may be eliminated entirely. Such diagrams are of assistance in planning kitchen arrangements to minimize traffic lines, backtracking, and crossing of traffic, all of which result in much confusion and inefficient use of space, time, and energy.

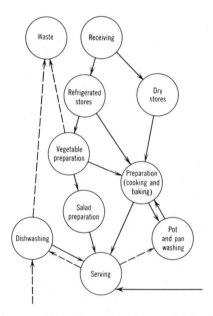

FIGURE 11.8 Chart showing location and relationship of areas to facilitate a direct flow of food from receiving through preparation to service, and the return of soiled dishes and waste. If waste disposer units are installed in preparation and dishwashing areas, waste area could be used for location of trash compactor.

It is generally agreed that more efficient service is possible if the dining room and kitchen are adjacent. A service pantry between the two is an effective means of reducing kitchen noise and confusion to a minimum in the dining room. If for any reason the dining room must be located a long way from the kitchen or on a different floor level, adequate provision should be made for mechanical means of conveying the prepared food in the briefest possible time and likewise for keeping it at the proper temperature until served. Elevators, conveyors, heated trucks, heated serving tables, and refrigerators are important aids. Rectangular or square kitchens are considered the most convenient. If possible the lengths of rectangular kitchens should not be more than twice their widths. Steps will be saved for employees if admission to the dining room is from the longer instead of the shorter side of a rectangular kitchen. An office for the manager or other person in charge should be located in direct sight of the kitchen and readily accessible to an outside entrance for the convenience of tradesmen and others. Arrangement for a counterclockwise routing of waiters through the kitchen and serving units of any seated foodservice is advisable.

The number of units to plan in a specific foodservice depends on the volume and types of food needed. A small operation may have a closely organized kitchen staffed with two or three cooks who assist each other with their work and share equipment. The shared equipment would be located nearest the area where it is used most. For example, in a small residence hall, the cook would mash potatoes or make muffins more often than the salad and dessert cook would make mayonnaise or mix a cake. Therefore the mixing machine might be located at the end of the cook's table but near the salad and dessert area. Each person may have her own work space where she performs certain duties but, generally, there are no widely separated areas. The preparation and dishwashing areas are included in the kitchen space, and a dining room and storeroom may be adjacent (see Figs. 11.9 and 11.10).

A larger foodservice may not have completely separated departments with duplicate equipment but, by careful grouping of the equipment, each cook has her own work area and may possibly share a common mixing machine and stack of ovens. Large operations are usually divided into specialized departments, each with its own equipment and short-time storage facilities. Several dining rooms may be serviced from one main kitchen. Storage space for cleaning supplies, locker rooms, and rest rooms for employees, check rooms and rest rooms for guests, and sometimes a laundry

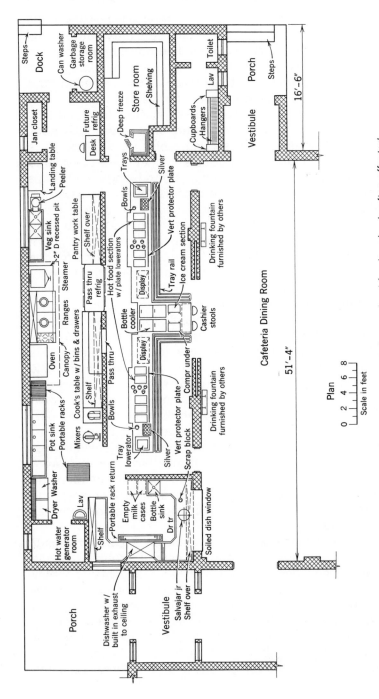

FIGURE 11.9 An efficient arrangement for a school foodservice is often effected through closely related preparation and service areas. Courtesy, Smith-St. John Manufacturing Company.

FIGURE 11.10 Elementary school service unit is separated from kitchen by partial partition in which reach-through refrigerator is installed. Courtesy, Southern Equipment Company.

and employee dining rooms are included in addition to the usual major areas mentioned earlier.

The location of areas and their relationship to each other should be conducive to the maximum output and efficient operation of the whole organization. Bottlenecks can do much to disrupt the production and service of food and should be detected in the planning stages. Direct and short routing of both food and workers is desirable. The *basic* food preparation route is the shortest distance from the storeroom or the refrigerator to the sink supplying water for preliminary cleaning, to the cook's table and range, or to the other preparation stations such as the salad area, and on to the serving area. The *actual* preparation route of the food or worker may differ from this considerably through side trips, back-tracking, or up-and-down movements. The actual preparation routes of several menu items should be followed through and measured before the final arrangement is decided on. Sometimes moving the location of a mixing machine or sink can reduce the distance traveled for either food or person, by many feet. These routes can be indicated on a floor plan by lines drawn of each movement and the total distance calculated. Long moves, many lines, backtracking, or crossed traffic lines indicate a poor arrangement. The study of such a charting is a good basis for revision and replanning of the areas concerned. Remodeling needs of existing setups may be determined through similar studies of routing and work and activity analysis charts, as discussed in Chapter 6.

The efficiency of an organization may be improved through a reduced but more capable and better-trained personnel adequately equipped with mechanical aids. In deciding on labor-saving machines and devices it is a question of increasing the investment to cut labor. A good formula is to spend one and a half or two times the annual cost of an employee to eliminate that employee. The current trend is to incorporate as much good, automatic, labor-saving and precision-type equipment into foodservice planning as the budget and space permit. A monorail system (see Fig. 11.11) is one method for fast transport of food and supplies. Chutes, conveyors, and carts are also used wherever possible to save labor and time. An intercommunication system is an invaluable time saver in large foodservices. All details that will make for high-quality output and efficient procedures to yield maximum results for minimum effort and money are of importance in foodservice planning. Every cubic foot of building space is expensive and represents a long-term investment. These facts make it imperative to utilize all foodservice areas to the best advantage, keeping in mind the volume and type of work that must be accomplished in each location.

Work Areas. Seven major phases of work must be provided for in the institution kitchen or adjacent areas. As stated before, they include checking in of food and supplies, storage, preliminary preparation, cookery, service, return of soiled dishes and dishwashing, and waste disposal. Each of these phases of work may be further subdivided; for example, cooking may be broken down into the following groupings: meats, vegetables, salads, baked goods, desserts, and beverages. Space for all or part of these units may be provided in the main kitchen. If a bakeshop is included in the plan, the baking and dessert making are removed to a separate place. Salad making likewise may be done in a separate room. In some kitchens it is found desirable to have the units separated by partitions 7 or 8 feet high. Provision must be made for proper ventilation in such cases. The

FIGURE 11.11   Provision for a monorail system of transporting food to service units should be made in the original construction of the building. Courtesy, ARA Food Services Company.

main kitchen or separate service pantries are frequently used for the work of serving. Space external to the main kitchen is often made available for preliminary preparation, dishwashing, and waste disposal. Such arrangements tend to insure a quiet kitchen and one with few sanitary hazards.

The allocation of space to various work areas is determined to a great extent by the number of workers, work surfaces, and equipment needed for the kinds and volume of food to be prepared, and the production and service schedule to be followed. Again, no one mathematical formula can be used, even for the same type of foodservice. However, as a guide (to depart from) the following distribution percentages are suggested as a possibility: meat, 4 percent; vegetable preparation, 7 percent; other cooking, 12 percent; cold food, 7 percent; bakery, 10 percent; service, 12 percent; dishwashing, 10 percent; and aisles, cart, and self-leveling storage cabinets,

36 percent. Other break-downs could be made, but space requirements change markedly with the menu and the trend toward the increased use of prepared and partially prepared foods. Mobile equipment helps to provide for flexibility in space distribution (Fig. 11.12).

Several general considerations are observed in planning an institution kitchen. The main traffic aisles should be a minimum of 5 feet, (plus 2 feet for safety), or wide enough to permit passing of hand trucks without interference with each other or with the workers in the area. Aisles between equipment and worktable must have a clearance of at least 3 feet. Three and one-half to 4 feet are neces-

FIGURE   11.12   *Wheeled equipment makes it possible to adapt the use of certain spaces to changing needs. Courtesy, Food Service Magazine.*

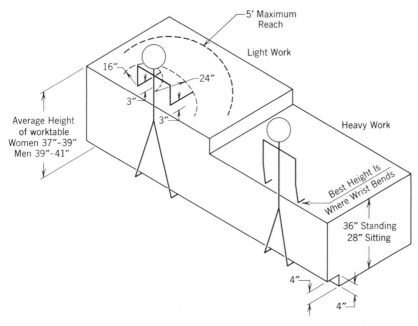

FIGURE   11.13   Optimum worktable height and working area. Courtesy, Arthur C. Avery.

sary in front of ovens or kettles where contents of the kettle are emptied into containers on a truck. Work aisles are perpendicular to the main traffic aisles or parallel with them but separated from them. Work heights are generally 36 to 41 inches for standing positions and 30 to 28 inches for sitting positions. A minimum of 4 linear feet of worktable space is recommended for each preparation employee (Fig. 11.13).

The maximum reach over a table without stretching is 20 inches, so equipment usage should come within that arc. The highest shelf should not exceed 6 feet from the floor. Tools and equipment should have adequate storage space, convenient to the point of use. Sinks, reach-in refrigerators, and space for short-time storage of supplies should be in or near the main work areas so that employees will be at one location and have everything needed to do the job. Drinking water and hand-washing facilities should be in a convenient location for all personnel. Overall integration of areas is necessary in planning.

Standards for the installation of equipment have been formulated by the National Sanitation Foundation and adopted and enforced by state and local health departments. An example is that heavy-duty foodservice equipment must be installed either on a 2-inch high cement island or have round or square closed legs with pear-shaped or round feet so there is a minimum clearance of 6 inches between the floor and the bottom of the piece of equipment. Another standard is the 12- to 24-inch clearance of heavy equipment from the wall or that equipment be sealed to the wall.

The *receiving area* includes an outside platform, preferably covered, and adjacent floor space where food is checked in, examined, and weighed or counted. The height of the platform or loading dock should be that of a standard truck floor above the driveway. The floor of the platform should be on the same level as the floor of the entrance to the building. Eight feet is suggested as a minimum width, and the length of the platform is determined by the number of trucks that might need to unload at one time. The service driveway should be easily accessible from the street or highway and provide space for trucks to back up to the loading platform or turn around. A ramp or steps at the end of the platform for pedestrians and a chute on which to slide canned goods to a basement storeroom would be advantageous. Products need to be examined for quality; weights need to be verified, and invoices checked before the deliveryman leaves; therefore, the receiving area needs to be large enough to accommodate the quantity of food and supplies that might be delivered at any one time. Also, there should be space to house hand trucks and platform scales and a desk or shelf on which papers may be placed while items are being checked off as they are delivered from the truck. Large institutions that process their own meat would find it convenient to include an overhead track with hooks for carcass meat, to extend from the loading platform through the meat preparation department to refrigerator. The outside door should be a 4- or 5-foot single or regular double size to admit hand trucks, large cartons, and any pieces of large equipment. The receiving entrance may also be used as the employees' entrance. Such an arrangement provides greater unbroken wall space and limits the hazards of open or unlocked doors that are increased with every additional outside door. A glass-walled office back of a double-face weighing-in scale would be convenient for the clerk in checking weights if someone else is responsible for examining the products for quality (see Fig. 9.1).

The *storage area* includes space for storing canned foods, grocery items, cleaning supplies, paper goods, and china, linen, and glass reserves. Also included are the walk-in refrigerators and the low-temperature boxes or rooms for perishable foodstuffs. Refrigerators used for daily supplies or leftovers in each department are usually not considered as stores. The food storage area should be as near receiving as possible and accessible to the preparation areas. In large institutions auxiliary storage space may be needed for reserve stocks of items purchased in great quantity at infrequent intervals. Dry storage rooms should be cool and well ventilated. Other requirements are moistureproof washable floors, screened windows, metal-slatted shelves for open-case goods, and covered storage bins for items such as cereal products and condiments. All should be arranged so that hand trucks may be used for convenient loading and unloading. Cases of canned goods and sacks of sugar should be stacked on racks to keep them above the floor level. A desk and possibly a file should be provided for inventory records, requisitions, order lists, or other records kept in this area. Scales are a necessity. Double doors with a good lock and wide enough to admit hand trucks should open onto a corridor leading to the preparation areas. An orderly arrangement with index posted in a conspicuous place aids in locating items without time-consuming searches.

Walk-in storage refrigerators are usually located in close proximity to the receiving and preparation areas. Mobile units of shelves that can be wheeled into the kitchen for checking and cleaning are conducive to good order and housekeeping and limited food spoilage. This type of storage was discussed earlier under "refrigeration."

The amount of storage space needed depends on the particular institution. When deliveries of supplies are made daily, comparatively little storage space is required, whereas in another institution with less frequent deliveries considerable storage space is found necessary. Also, the storage requirements will vary according to the form in which the food is purchased. Foods in prepared forms require less space but lower storage temperatures, as in the case of frozen foods. Fresh potatoes and other root vegetables should be stored in a dark, well-ventilated dry room near the vegetable preparation area.

The *prepreparation areas* include meat and vegetable preparation units and fish and poultry units in some kitchens. With the general trend toward the purchase of fabricated and pan-ready meats, peeled or frozen vegetables, and ready-to-cook fish and poultry, the need for these once necessary large and important areas has decreased. However, some institutions find it to their advantage to continue these operations in their kitchens, where the use of fabricated meat cuts does not seem advisable. A well-equipped meat preparation department would include the hard-wood meat tables, electric saw and grinder, sink, storage trays, and refrigeration facilities. If a meat preparation area is needed, it is often arranged directly in front of or at the side of the meat storage refrigerator and not far from the central cooking area.

The *vegetable preparation area* should be located near refrigerated storage and the cooking and salad areas. Often this unit in a large institution is set up in a square- or rectangular-shaped area with equipment arranged on the sides and down the center with one end open to the main kitchen. The usual vegetable preparation area is equipped with a chopper, cutter, at least two 2-compartment sinks, worktables, cart, knives, and cutting boards. A peeler, *if needed,* may be either a pedestal or a table model and placed to empty directly into a sink along a wall or at a right angle to it. A portable sink (Fig. 11.14) would be a convenience in most kitchens.

The sinks should be separated to permit unhampered use. Food waste disposer units are conveniently placed in the drainboard or the worktable near the end of the sink, or space for a garbage can must be provided. Often the prepreparation for the salad department is done in this area; therefore ample space is needed for many workers. Tables 30 to 36 inches wide and 8 to 10 feet long are adequate

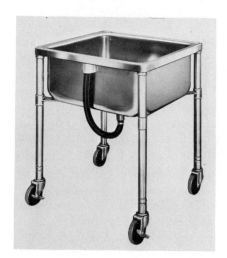

FIGURE   11.14   *Portable sink may be designed to meet size and height requirements. Courtesy, Southern Equipment Company.*

for working surfaces and convenient for moving. A 36-inch table permits workers to be on either side for most types of preparation. The inclusion of at least one table low enough for employees to sit and work comfortably is advisable. A 4 1/2-foot aisle between back-to-back workers is minimum, and 6 feet would be preferable for this area, where portable tables or carts and dollies are used in transporting foods and utensils from one area to another.

The main *cooking area* is usually the hub or center of the kitchen and is located adjacent to the meat preparation and usually the vegetable preparation areas, the pot-and-pan washing unit, the storage rooms, and back of or near the serving units. It may include range, ovens, broilers, fryers, steam-jacketed kettles, pressure steam cookers, and equipment used by the cook, such as cook's table, pot-and-pan storage rack, mixing machine, and slicers. Modern institution kitchens need much specialized equipment, such as small steam-jacketed kettles and high-pressure steam cookers for cooking fresh vegetables (Fig. 11.15); broilers; roast and convection ovens

FIGURE 11.15   *A battery of wall-hung steam-jacketed kettles with heavy-duty mixer installation in a large production unit. Courtesy, Groen Division, Dover Corporation.*

FIGURE 11.16   Convection oven. Space-saving rack shelves and forced air heat accomplish more cooking in less time than in conventional oven; Muffle-type oven seal holds in moisture and reduces shrinkage. Courtesy, Market Forge Company.

(Fig. 11.16); and tilting fry pans (Fig. 11.17); which reduce or eliminate entirely the number of heavy range units formerly required.

An island arrangement of the cooking equipment near the center of the room in large kitchens is usually favored over a wall setup, because of its relationship to preparation units, the shortened distance to the serving unit, and the sanitation factor. The grouping

FIGURE   11.17   *Tilting fry pan replaces much top-of-stove cookery. Flat bottom design gives even heat distribution for uniform browning and cooking; counterbalanced cover and pouring lip provide for flexibility in use. Courtesy, Groen Division, Dover Corporation.*

of equipment within the area varies with the size and shape of the room. Ranges and steamjacketed kettles may be set up side by side in a *straight-line* arrangement, back to back or facing in *parallel* lines, or the steam unit may be at the end and perpendicular to the line of the range unit or *L-shaped*. Other modifications are the *U-* and *E-shaped* kitchens. Broilers and fryers are placed with the range unit ordinarily. Floors under steam units are usually recessed and must be constructed to drain.

Hoods fitted with exhaust fans, vented separately, hung from the ceiling, and extending 1 foot down, over all cooking surfaces and steam units aid materially in ventilating the kitchen. Provision is thus made for carrying away odors, smoke, moisture, and gas fumes. Hoods also facilitate the installation of direct lighting fixtures by which cooking surfaces may be illuminated. Often one large hood and ventilating fan may serve the whole grouping, with consequent economy in installations. Specially designed ventilator systems with removable filters may be installed on ranges and other cooking equipment and in hoods. The filters are easily removed for cleaning, and the hazards of fire are reduced by the filtering of grease and dust from the air, the preventing of clogged greasy vent pipes, providing a fireproof filter chamber between the cooking equipment and the exhaust duct and an automatic release valve for the bypassing of any unburned gases. Such a system provides a frequent complete change of air and improves the appearance of the room.

The cook's table, usually located directly in front of the ranges, includes a rack for small equipment and, in most kitchens, a sink. Provision for keeping certain cooked foods hot during the serving period is made by the inclusion of a bain marie or hot water bath often heated by steam, a steam table, or an electrically heated food cabinet. A rack for clean pots and pans should be easily accessible to both the cooking unit and the pot and pan sink and power washer. Perhaps a mixing machine is used most in the cooking area for mashing potatoes and should be located near the pressure steam cookers. A short storage reach-in refrigerator and hand sink should be near the cook's unit. This unit requires approximately a 10-foot deep area accounted for by a 2 1/2- or 3-foot wide table, 3 1/2- or 4-foot aisle, 3-foot range and the 12- to 18-inch installation clearance for cleaning between equipment and wall or between back-to-back equipment. The length of the unit depends on the amount of equipment and the plan of the arrangement. Much of the equipment in the cooking area may be wall hung or mobile to facilitate cleaning. Flexible connections are now available with safety valves for installation of mobile gas-fired equipment.

The planning and installing of a modular utility distribution and control system has many advantages over the old plan of fixed and permanent installations that often needed to be changed after a few years. The entrance of and controls for all utilities are centered in one end support column of the system with all pipes and wiring enclosed, but with control buttons for both operation and quick-disconnect on the outside within easy reach of a worker or mainte-

FIGURE 11.18 An overhead modular utility distribution and control system facilitates flexibility in arrangement and ease of maintenance. Courtesy, Avtec Industries, Inc.

nance person. Water, steam, gas, and electrical outlets may be installed as desired in panels extending from the "one-point" control column along a wall or to a center room unit, directly back of equipment or from above (see Fig. 11.18). Also, pedestal or counter installations are possible, as shown in Figs. 11.19 and 12.22. A water outlet at each point of use, such as a swing-arm faucet between each pair of steam-jacketed kettles, above or at the side of a tilting fry pan, or at a sink, as shown in Fig. 11.19, is a great convenience and timesaver for the cook. Several gas and electrical outlets along the panel permit easy interchange of mobile equipment. It is possible to move an entire system of this type to another location in the kitchen; also, they may be custom designed for any situation.

The *salad area* is often located at one side or end of the room and as close to the serving unit as is practicable. In this unit are a liberal allowance of table space, refrigerator space, sinks, and the usual sharp knives and cutting boards. Mechanical cutters and choppers for vegetables may be used in the vegetable preparation

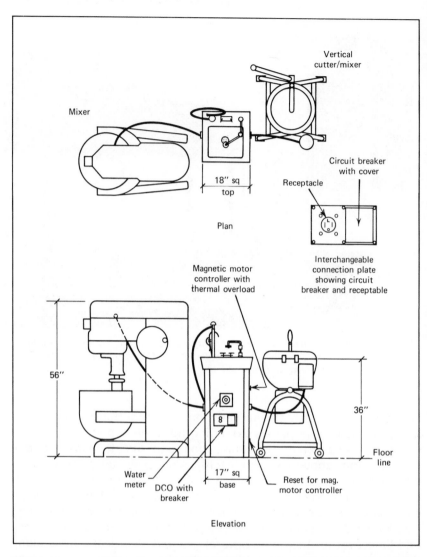

FIGURE 11.19 *Example of utility pedestal with sink. Cutter may be replaced readily by other portable equipment such as a tilting fry pan. Courtesy, Avtec Industries, Inc.*

area as a part of the prepreparation. Ingredients and dressings must be kept chilled. A refrigerated table on which to place bowls of ingredients while working helps to retain the crisp freshness desired in a salad. A refrigerated cabinet, with angle slides for trays or shelves for the storage of approximately one third of the salads needed and made up in advance, is necessary for certain types of institutions where many people are served in a limited period of time. Otherwise, it is highly desirable to make salads as late as possible before time of service. It would be advantageous to locate the salad area for a cafeteria directly back of the salad counter, with a pass-through refrigerator built into the separating wall (see Fig. 11.10). The trays of salads could be placed in the refrigerator as soon as they are made and removed by the counter attendant as needed, thus assuring a constant supply of freshly made salads and eliminating the necessity for persons to transport the finished product over a long distance from preparation to service. In a hospital or service restaurant operating on more than one floor, easy access to service elevators, subveyors, or dumb waiters is important to deliver made-up salads in good condition for service far from their source.

The *bakery and dessert area* operates as a fairly independent unit, having little direct association with the other preparation areas, and may be separated from them in location. The products are transported directly from this unit to the service unit; therefore the two units should be rather close, although the quality of pies, cakes, puddings, and rolls is not so dependent on timing and temperature for serving as are meats, cooked vegetables, and salads.

The average bakeshop equipment includes baker's table, with bins, oven, mixer, pan racks, sinks, cooling racks, stove, steam-jacketed kettle, dough divider and roller, pie crust roller, and daily refrigerator. Large units (Fig. 11.20) include additional items such as dough mixer, proof box, and dough trough. This unit requires study of routing in the performance of the tasks the same as in the main kitchen setup. Raw materials are made into finished products through weighing ingredients, combining, baking, and then distributing. The arrangement of equipment should provide for a direct line of procedure with little or no backtracking or crisscrossing. The small institution may place the baker's table near the cooking unit so that equipment can be shared.

Many institutions prefer to purchase frozen desserts, especially ice creams and ices, instead of producing them within the foodservice. If it is desirable to include this activity in the food preparation

FIGURE   11.20   Bakeshop setup for a large institution. Courtesy, Pennsylvania State Institutions.

unit, the construction of a separate room with specialized equipment must permit the techniques of handling these products to meet the highest standards of sanitation. The production of frozen desserts must conform to the regulations established by the local department of health.

The *pot and pan area* includes the space occupied by the work aisle allotted to this function, the three-compartment sink (Fig. 11.21), mechanical washer, and storage racks for both soiled and clean utensils. The location of the area should be near the cooking unit but out of any main traffic lines. Often it is conveniently located at the end or back of the cooking unit, or in an alcove. Hand-washing of pots and pans may be implemented by the use of a manually guided power scrubber and a good detergent. The three-compartment sink provides for washing, rinsing, and sanitizing either by high temperature or a chemical rinse. The installation of a steam jet in, a gas burner beneath, or an electric immersion element

FIGURE   11.21   Three-compartment, stainless steel, round-corner, wall-hung, pot
and pan sink with sliding platform. Courtesy, S. Blickman.

in the last compartment is possible. The drainboard on the right end
of the sink may be used for the temporary stacking of soiled utensils
and the left drainboard for air drying of the clean utensils. The rack
for storage of clean equipment should be near and also convenient
for the cook. Although mechanical pot and pan washers have been
installed in many large operations, sinks are still necessary for soaking or preflushing.

The dishwashing area should be compact, light, and airy. If it is
not located directly adjacent to the dining room, as in Fig. 11.22,
mechanical conveyors save time and money in transporting soiled
dishes to this work unit. It is often desirable to have the dishwashing
away from the dining room because of the noise. If this is impossible,
the area should be surrounded by acoustical material to modify the
sounds. Care must be taken in locating the unit so that the return of
soiled dishes will not interfere with the routing of service. The dishwashing unit may include a prewash arrangement, a dishwashing
machine, a glass washing machine, soiled and clean dish tables,
waste disposers, storage cupboards or carts, and carts or conveyors
for transporting dishes to and from this unit (Fig. 11.22).

The size and type of machine to select and the arrangement of
the dishwashing area depend on the number of pieces to be

FIGURE 11.22 One system for customer removal of soiled dishes to dishroom.

washed, the speed with which they must be returned for reuse, and the shape of the available area. Capacities of the different size machines and installation requirements must be studied, and the one should be selected that will best meet the needs of the organization. The setup must provide space and facilities for the smooth flow of dishes through sorting, scrapping, washing, rinsing, drying, and removal to storage. In addition to space for the fixed equipment, floor space is needed for aisles and as many conveyors, carts, and portable counter storage units as are needed to transport china, glassware, and silverware to and from this area. The length of dish tables varies with the size of the unit but, in general, the clean dish table should be long enough for three to five racks for air drying and stacking space. The usual division of space allotted to dish tables is 40 percent for clean and 60 percent for soiled dishes. Conveyor machines require comparable space for soiled dishes and adequate space for loading clean dishes at the other end of the machine.

Some form of preflushing should be provided unless a machine with a built-in or attached unit is selected. A hose and nozzle or forced spray are other possible types, neither of which requires more than about 2 feet of table space. The nozzle arrangement could be near the machine, but the forced spray should be far enough away from it to permit easy racking of dishes following the preflushing operation. Food waste disposer units could be installed with either type. Also, some method for the return of emptied racks to the soiled dish table should be provided. A power-driven conveyor arrangement is shown in Fig. 11.23.

The plan of arrangement for a dishwashing area may be straight-line, L-shape around or into a corner, U-shape, an open square, a platform, or closed-circle type. The straight-line type is often installed near a side wall in small operations. Machines are designed for either right- or left-hand operations, although the usual flow direction is right to left. The U-shape arrangement is a compact and efficient arrangement for small operations, whereas the open square might be preferred for a larger unit and could easily include a glass washer. A more complex arrangement is the platform type, where two parallel tables are connected by sliding bridges over which the loaded trays of soiled dishes may be transferred to the machine table. Usually a receiving table is located across the end or parallel with the soiled dish table, onto which the waitress may deposit silver, china, and glassware in their respective places or racks. Another arrangement is the fast-rack conveyor or closed-circle type. An example of such an arrangement is shown in Fig. 11.24. In this particular set-up the racks are moved continuously to the soiled-dish

FIGURE 11.23   *Dishwashing room shows incoming conveyor belts on left that merge on a double scrapping table with integral silver soak sink and waste disposer; convenient dish rack return. Courtesy, S. Blickman Inc.*

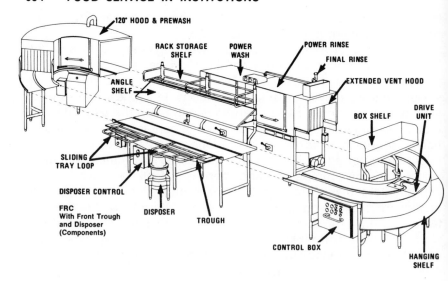

FIGURE 11.24   *Fast-rack conveyor warewashing system may be custom designed to fit the space and needs of the situation. Product of Hobart Corporation.*

end of the washer by a stainless steel chain drive. Components such as waste system for pulpable materials (see Fig. 12.20), condenser, and blower-dryer may be incorporated into the system. This type requires approximately the same amount of floor space as a straight line but fits into a more compact arrangement and is operated with fewer employees who can remain in one location.

Any type of arrangement should be installed far enough from the wall to permit ease of cleaning, and at least a 4-foot aisle is desirable if people are to work in back of the table. A hood fitted with an exhaust fan should be installed over the unit to remove steam and hot air, or exhaust ducts should be attached directly to the machines. The latter should be of rustproof material and must be watertight to prevent dripping of condensed vapor. A booster heater should be installed adjacent to the machine to increase the temperature of the rinse water from the usual 135 to 180°F. An oversize sink for washing of serving trays that are too large to go through the dishwashing machine is a necessity if they are to be returned to this area for washing. Good ventilation of the dishwashing area is essential.

The *serving area* may be in the kitchen (see Fig. 11.25) at the various preparation centers where the waiters go to have their

FIGURE 11.25   Efficient compact kitchen arrangement with serving and dish-washing units included within one room. Courtesy, Southern Equipment Company.

orders filled, in a serving unit in a room adjoining the kitchen, or even in a pantry several floors above as in a hospital. A cafeteria counter is often in a small serving room between kitchen and dining room, at the end or side of the dining room, as in Fig. 11.26, or in an alcove adjoining the dining room. The length and number of counters to be provided depend on the number of persons to be served and the speed of service held desirable. There seem to be no specific standards that relate the length of the counter to the number to be served. A 20-foot counter would be adequate for a small school lunch. A commercial establishment might find a 50-foot counter necessary to meet its needs, although newer installations tend toward the use of short counters, which are more easily supervised and require fewer workers.

Newer counter designs facilitate speedy self-service, reduce labor, and eliminate the necessity of guests waiting in long service lines. Undercounter coffee urns with dispenser faucets above and facing the guest free space for other use. Some straight counters

FIGURE 11.26   Serving counter with stainless steel top and plasticized material front reduces cost and adds color. Featured are overhead decorations, infrared lamps over hot food section, and silver dispensers at end of line. Courtesy, Paul Morrill, The Ohio State University.

are installed so guests may pass on both sides. Others have been designed into short zigzag sections. A revolving counter section centered in or near the kitchen wall in back of it is well adapted to the display of cold items such as salads and desserts and is serviced easily from their preparation areas in the kitchen. Another two-counter arrangement is a rounded U-shape with a central checkout point. Silver, napkin, beverage, and condiment bars are often located in the dining room in fast-service operations.

The hollow-square type with trays, silver, and napkins on an island arrangement in the center with counters on three sides has been modified to have separate and duplicate counters for different items with a central unit for duplicate self-serve beverage dispensers, and several checkout stations. (See Figs. 11.27 and 11.28). This is sometimes called the "scramble" or "supermarket" system.

Regardless of the length of the serving unit or type of service, it should be a well-constructed piece of equipment that keeps hot food hot and cold food cold, provides storage space for dishes, and is easily kept clean.

A desirable rate of service for the school cafeteria lunchroom is 12 to 15 students per minute. If the lunch period is limited in length it is necessary to plan for two or more counters, depending on the number to be served. The rate of service in commercial cafeterias is reported as seven to nine persons per minute. Commercial cafeterias with a seating capacity of 300 or more find it desirable to have two counters.

Steam tables, which once comprised a large part of the counter, have been replaced by electrically heated, thermostat-controlled units. In any event most hot food is displayed in the pans in which it is prepared. The containers in the counter service are small and shallow for the most part and are replaced often by other containers of freshly prepared food. The hot unit should be located as near as possible to the cooking area. Some institutions, especially school lunchrooms, prefer to place the unit for hot foods first so that the meal is selected in the order in which it is eaten. Commercial places find that desserts and salads have a stronger psychic appeal and give a greater money return; therefore, they are often placed first and the hot unit is near the end of the counter. A satisfactory plan is to arrange the counter so that the salad display counter is directly in front of the salad preparation unit in the kitchen with pass-through refrigerated cupboards between. Small-size coffee makers in which a supply of fresh coffee may be prepared continuously are often considered an improvement over giant urns in which a large quantity of coffee is made and kept hot for long periods of time. Icemakers at or near the point of use are recommended.

Commercial cafeterias find that salads and cold meats, hot meats and vegetables, desserts and beverages need about equal display space on the counter. Since a counter is usually a fabricated piece of equipment, any length desired may be ordered. Costs are computed on the basis of so much per foot of counter. Mobile units provide for flexibility in counter arrangement.

Hot food transported to serving pantries in hospitals should be taken there as late as possible in heated carts from which it is served or the containers of hot food transferred to heated counters for serving. Refrigeration facilities are usually provided in such pantries, and cold foods transported from the preparation centers are held at refrigeration temperature until it is time for serving. Trays should be served only as rapidly as they can be taken to the pa-

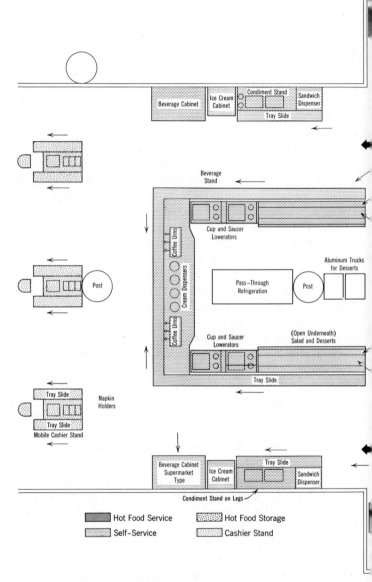

Hot Food Service   Hot Food Storage

Self-Service   Cashier Stand

FIGURE 11.27   *A schematic drawing translated into a floor diagram precedes preparation of an actual blueprint to insure an efficient arrangement. This diagram shows routes of customer traffic through serving areas planned for fast service and flexibility. Courtesy, Eastman Kodak Company.*

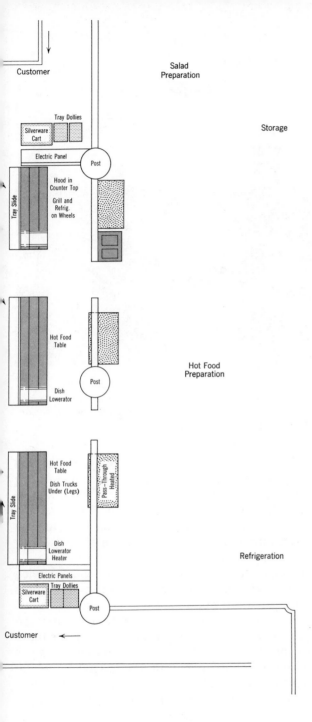

Customer

Salad
Preparation

Tray Dollies

Silverware
Cart

Storage

Electric Panel

Post

Tray Slide

Hood in
Counter Top

Grill and
Refrig.
on Wheels

Hot Food
Table

Hot Food
Preparation

Post

Dish
Lowerator

Hot Food
Table

Pass–Through
Heated

Dish Trucks
Under (Legs)

Tray Slide

Dish
Lowerator
Heater

Refrigeration

Electric Panels

Silverware
Cart

Tray Dollies

Post

Customer

FIGURE   11.28   *Picture of floor diagram shown in Fig. 11.27. Arrangement pro-*
vides both counter and self-service; three mobile cashier stands
aid in speed of service and allow for flexibility and expansion.
Courtesy, Eastman Kodak Company.

tients. Another method of serving hospital patients is by central tray service. Here the food is assembled on the trays in the main kitchen and sent to the various floors on conveyors. This removes the necessity of equipping and staffing pantries on each floor. Both systems require much supervision to insure hot and palatable food for the patients. See Chapter 5 for more details on service systems and their space and equipment requirements.

The *dining area* includes the seating facilities and small service stations. Quiet, attractive, well-ventilated, well-lighted dining areas are conducive to the enjoyment of good food and hospitality. Public dining rooms usually have many four- and two-seat tables that can be put together for groups. Dining rooms for college students more often are arranged to seat six or eight at a table. The larger tables often make for economical seating space but are difficult for waiter service and do not lend themselves to satisfactory social grouping. There should be a minimum space of 18 inches between chair backs after guests are seated, and main traffic aisles of 4 1/2 or 5 feet are advisable. Dining tables and chairs are discussed in Chapter 13.

Folding plastic or wood partitions are decorative and make it possible to close off parts of the dining room for special groups or when not in use. A separate dining room for employees is highly recommended.

Employee facilities include rest rooms, washrooms, toilet rooms, locker and shower rooms, and the traffic aisles in these units. Each employee should have a locker, and the other facilities will depend on how many people are on duty at one time. Standards for such facilities are listed in Chapter 10.

Food waste and trash storage and removal are necessary if facilities for their disposal are not possible within the building. Many institutions have incinerators in which most trash is burned, central compactors in which waste is compressed under heavy pressure to small volume, and unit food waste disposers. If no such facilities are in use, both garbage and trash must be collected and held for frequent removal. A refrigerated room near the back entrance is satisfactory for the daily storage of garbage but, when feasible, unit or central disposers should be incorporated in the system. Familiarity with and conformance to the local sanitation regulations is an important function of the dietitian or manager of a foodservice.

The smooth flow of foods from the time they enter the building until they reach the consumer depends on the equipment selected and its arrangement to make a functional layout. Although space does not permit a more detailed presentation of planning the specific areas, most of the points covered are basic and may be used as guides in foodservice planning.

Schematic Drawing. Previous decisions on the location, kind of foodservice, the budget, menu pattern and type of service, and anticipated volume of business provide background facts with which to get working drawings on paper. General space allowances and relationships, as discussed earlier in this chapter, must now be coordinated into a workable and efficient arrangement in adequate but minimal dimensions. Directing the flow of food from receiving to service departments and travel of the workers in its preparation through the shortest possible movement and distances is a challenge to the foodservice planner. Included also is the need to eliminate waste space, crisscrossing, and backtracking and to provide adequate aisle widths and the arrangement of equipment for the best possible sequence of procedures and related purposes.

Well-known and accepted principles should be followed in drawing the plans to scale, in attacking construction problems, in planning the installation of heating, lighting, ventilating, plumbing, and refrigerating systems, in selecting and applying finishes, and in choosing equipment and furnishings. Through experience and study, tentative standards for the most convenient and practical arrangement of working areas and the placement of equipment in these areas have been determined, although each unit presents an individual problem. By observing outstandingly successful features in architectural planning and construction, as reported in magazines or books and as may actually be seen in successful foodservices, and by drawing on personal experiences, a plan may be evolved for an efficient and pleasing foodservice of any type.

The mechanics of drawing the plan to scale so that the relationship of all parts may be visually depicted is most important. All details should be included to make the picture complete. It is advisable that early in the planning stages and after items and sizes of equipment for each work area have been determined that a working drawing to scale with tentative placement of each equipment item indicated is set up. Checks may be made on the steps in the preparation of several menu items by drawing lines tracing the movements of food and workers from one key work point to the next within a unit as well as from one work area or department to the next. Actual measurement of the distances can be made by passing a string over pintacks at each keypoint as the preparation of a menu item progresses and then measuring the string (usual scale is 1/4 inch to 1 foot).

Another check on the proposed space allowances and arrangement of equipment is by use of "templates" or pieces of paper designed and cut to scale to represent each item of equipment (Fig. 11.29). These should include overall measurements to cover outside controls, fittings, and installation needs as obtained from catalogs, brochures, and salesmen. The templates may be placed on the floor plan in various desirable relationships until the most satisfactory arrangement is determined and then pasted onto or drawn on the preliminary floor plan or shop drawing.

Most dietitians or foodservice managers would have been collecting a list of "do not forget to include" items that could be used as another check on the proposed floor plans. These reminders might vary from a telephone jack in the dining room to storage space for banquet tables, high chairs, reserve china, paper, and cleaning supplies; same size filters for all hoods over cooking area for easy interchange; timers on cooking appliances; steam hose by garbage can washer; tray sizes modulated for use in refrigerator and

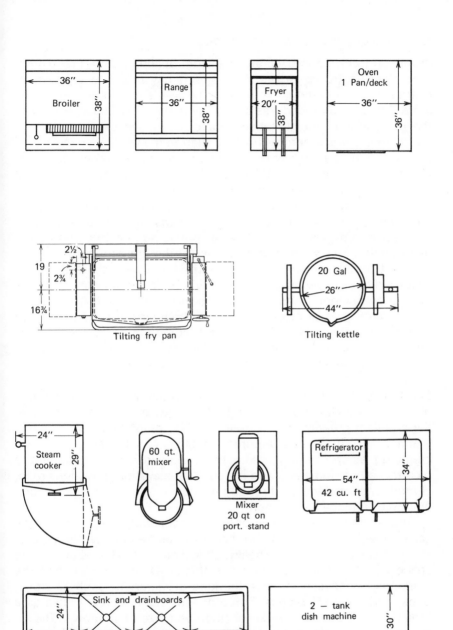

FIGURE   11.29   *Template models of sample pieces of equipment drawn and cut to scale afford an easy method of estimating floor space needed and checking for efficient and flexible arrangement of equipment.*

ovens, on trucks, dumbwaiters, shelving; bulletin board, first aid kit, time clock, extra spare parts for emergency repair of equipment; overages on carpeting, tiles, light fixtures and bulbs; and many more. The above procedures afford good checks of the adequacy of the provisions of the tentative floor plan for necessary equipment and working areas before the final plan is made. The space allowances for passageways between working areas, between tables, between ranges and cook's table, and between other major pieces of equipment should also be checked for adequacy. Changes and adjustments should be made on paper instead of after construction has begun, because it is costly to make revisions after that time.

Separate drawings are made for plumbing, electric, and equipment contractors in addition to those for the building construction. All must be coordinated and checked carefully to insure that gas, water, and waste outlets, and vents will be in the correct positions for the equipment planned. Also, the electrical wiring with convenient switch-control boxes, power and regular outlets and turn-on switches, locations and kinds of light fixtures must be noted. Telephone conduits and outlets and wiring for an intercom, public address, or TV system must be decided on and indicated.

Blueprint by Architect. After thorough checking of the preliminary plans by the dietitian or foodservice manager and others concerned, the architect prepares to accurate scale a complete set of drawings that are reproduced as blueprints. Details of construction, materials, plumbing, electric wiring, connections and fixtures, or equipment to be attached are indicated and coded. Side elevation drawings are included for such items as door and window finishings, stairways, and built-in or attached equipment.

In reading the floor plan one must constantly keep in mind the scale to which it is drawn. The scale should be sufficiently large to permit detailed study. The heavy, solid lines indicate the walls; the space between lines indicates the thickness of the wall; and the markings in between indicate the kind of materials, such as stone, brick, and concrete blocks. Three or four single parallel lines as a break in the wall indicate the position and size of windows. The direction in which doors open is shown by an arc described from the base of the line of the door, cutting it at a point equal to the width of the door (Fig. 11.30). Steps are indicated by parallel lines with an arrow and the words "up" or "down." Dimensions of all spaces are indicated and rooms and equipment labeled. All special features are shown on the plan by symbols, for example, some electrical symbols are shown in Fig. 11.31. Various architects use different designating symbols that are explained in a legend on the drawing. The schedule on the corner of the floor-plan sheet indicates wall, floor, ceiling, and woodwork finishes. The window and door schedule indicates sizes and types of these items. The use of standard-size windows and doors helps to keep their cost to a minimum.

The general considerations in making or checking floor plans are similar for different kinds of institutions, regardless of type of service, menu, clientele, and other governing conditions. The preparation and service of food are the purposes that must be kept in mind when planning a foodservice, and details that will make for increased efficiency should not be overlooked; for example, if either a monorail or an "Amscars" system for transporting supplies and food is anticipated in the future, the necessary overhead rails, under-the-floor wiring, or other requirements should be incorporated in the original construction of the building. Cost calculations and estimates must be based on scientific and practically proved facts, experiences, and observations.

SPECIFICATIONS

A set of written specifications must be compiled by the architect to accompany the blueprint when presented to contractors for bid. The specifications include details such as the location of the building, type of base construction, mix of cement, size and kinds of conduits, drains, and vents, type and installation of roofing and flooring, wall finishes, hardware, doors, windows and other construction features, brand name and model number of sinks or other attached equipment, and completion date. In large installations separate contracts may be made for electrical wiring, control switches, fixtures, and air-conditioning. Plumbing contracts would include water, sewer, and steam pipes connections and controls. Equipment would be another contract. All requirements must meet those of the local building codes, and the conditions and statements clearly worded so there can be no misinterpretations.

CONTRACTS AND BIDS

When bids are solicited on an open and competitive basis, often the contract is awarded to the lowest bidder, who then works closely with the architect throughout the construction period. The foodservice manager keeps in close contact with what is happening and

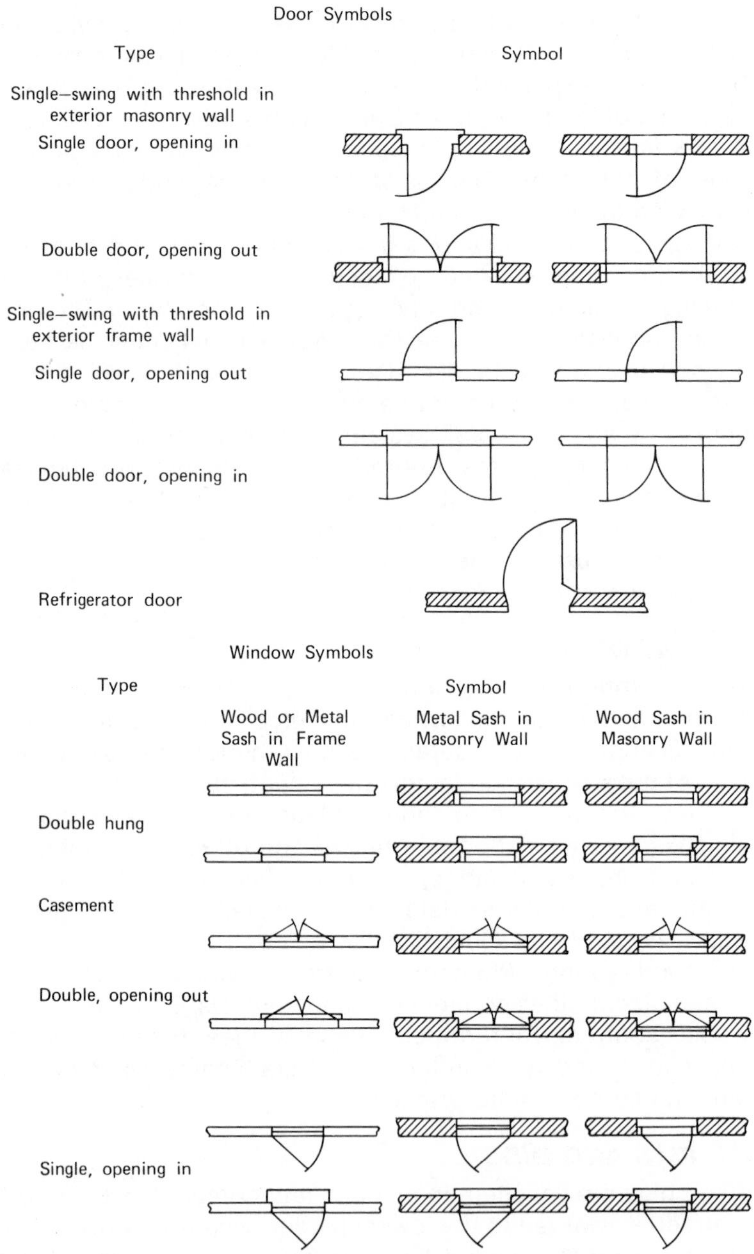

Door Symbols

Type	Symbol

Single—swing with threshold in
exterior masonry wall

Single door, opening in

Double door, opening out

Single—swing with threshold in
exterior frame wall

Single door, opening out

Double door, opening in

Refrigerator door

Window Symbols

Type	Symbol	
	Wood or Metal Sash in Frame Wall	Metal Sash in Masonry Wall	Wood Sash in Masonry Wall

Double hung

Casement

Double, opening out

Single, opening in

FIGURE 11.30 Architectural Symbols used on blue prints to show placement and arrangement of doors.

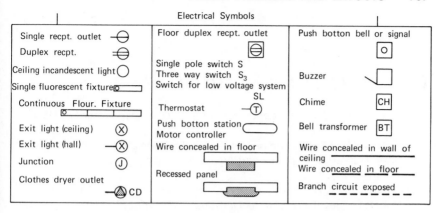

FIGURE 11.31   Symbols used to indicate locations of electrical wiring, and outlets for various types of installations.

checks often with the architect. Conditions of the contract and the individuals concerned will determine to a large extent adjustments that can be made after contracts have been signed.

CONSTRUCTION

The actual construction time will vary from weeks to several months, depending on the type and size of building and the availability of materials, labor, and equipment. Frequent checking by the architect or a qualified representative to see that construction is progressing as specified is a necessity.

All construction, equipment, and installations must be inspected and approved by the architect before the facility is accepted by the foodservice representative. Each item of equipment is performance tested to see that it meets specifications and standard claims and has been installed properly. This demonstration by a representative of the supplying company to show the proper operation, care, and maintenance of the equipment should be attended by the dietitian or manager and assistants, the kitchen supervisor, maintenance person, and the architect or his representative.

Usually the various contractors guarantee necessary adjustments and some service for a period of 1 year following the completion date. After the established date, all repairs and full maintenance are the responsibility of the foodservice management.

SELECTED REFERENCES

A Guide to Food Service Operation Planning, Ohio Department of Health.

Avery, Arthur C., *Human Engineering in Kitchen Design,* Department of the Navy, Bureau of Supplies and Accounts, Washington, D.C.

Buchanan, Robert D., Stan Adams, Robert A. Armstrong, Paul Machart, Robert E. Cleveland, Samuel Crabtree, E. A. Vargo, L. W. Kozeluh, and Arthur C. Avery, *The Anatomy of Foodservice Design I,* Jule Wilkinson, Editor, Cahners, Boston, 1975.

Cronan, Marion, *The School Lunch,* Charles A. Bennett, Peoria, Illinois, 1962.

Design Criteria—School Food Service Facilities, Department of Education, Tallahassee, Florida, 1975.

"Equipment Guide for On-Site School Kitchens," USDA Food and Nutrition Service, U.S. Government Printing Office, Washington, D.C., 1974.

"Food Storage Guide for Schools and Institutions," Agricultural Marketing Service, U.S. Department of Agriculture, PA-403, November 1959.

George, N. L., and Ruth D. Heckler, *School Food Centers,* Ronald, New York, 1960.

"Guide to Energy Conservation for Food Service," Federal Energy Administration, U.S. Government Printing Office, Washington, D.C., 1975.

Handbook of Food Service Equipment, S. Blickman, Weehawken, New Jersey.

Iuen, Richard R., *Food Facilities Planning Guide,* Cincinnati, 1960.

Kahrl, William L., *Planning and Operating a Successful Food Operation,* Chain Store Publishing Corporation, New York, 1973.

Kazarian, Edward A., *Work Analysis and Design for Hotels, Restaurants and Institutions,* Avi, Westport, Connecticut, 1969.

Kotschevar, Lendal H., "How to Use Work Simplification in Food Service, reprinted from *Institutions Magazine*, Domestic Engineering, Chicago, 1958.

Kotschevar, Lendal H., and Margaret E. Terrell, *Food Service Planning: Layout and Equipment*, Wiley, New York, 1961.

"Planning and Equipping School Lunchrooms," PA-292, Agricultural Marketing Service, U.S. Department of Agriculture, 1956.

Schneider, Nicholas, Edgar A. Jahn, and Arthur G. Smith, *Commercial Kitchens*, American Gas Associations, New York, 1962.

The National Sanitation Foundation, N.S.F. Building, Ann Arbor, Michigan. *National Sanitation Foundation Standards.* (see selected references Chapter 10).

Thomas, Orpha Mae Huffman, *A Scientific Basis for the Design of Institution Kitchens*, Teachers College, Columbia University, New York, 1947.

Current professional Journals and Trade Magazines.

Manufacturers' leaflets, brochures, catalogs, and specifications.

12.
EQUIPMENT FOR KITCHENS AND SERVING ROOMS

Foodservice equipment is defined as "machinery, appliances, equipment or supplies which are used in the storing, preparation, or serving of food in commercial establishments, as differentiated from domestic use. . . . It includes complete kitchen installations, as well as the component items such as chinaware, glassware, kitchen utensils, silverware, and service items." [1] Complete coverage of this broad subject area is quite impossible in a general textbook, but an effort will be made to include pertinent basic information that can be supplemented by current literature from the manufacturers and from observations of equipment in use.

The selection and purchase of furnishings and equipment for any foodservice are major responsibilities of the director and his or her staff, and the wisdom with which selection is made determines in a large measure the attainment of lasting satisfaction. The efficiency of work units and the beauty of environment may be marred by poor selection and placement of furnishings and equipment, and the quality of service that an organization may render is influenced, if not limited, by these features.

[1] *"Standards—Food Service Equipment," National Sanitation Foundation, Standard 2, revised, Introduction, p. vii, 1973.*

The wise selection of equipment for any institution kitchen can be made only after a thorough study of all factors affecting the particular situation has been made. A wealth of items is available in many designs, materials, sizes, and at a wide cost range, but only those items that will help to meet the specific needs of the foodservice and contribute to its efficient operation should be purchased.

FACTORS AFFECTING SELECTION OF KITCHEN AND SERVING EQUIPMENT

Equipment for any institution kitchen should be selected on the basis of a thorough study of all major considerations. Important among these are: the needs of the particular foodservice organization as determined by the menu plan and complexity of the foods included in it, the number and type of people to be served, the form in which the food will be purchased, the style of service and length of serving period, the number of man-hours available, the caliber of employees to do the work, the accessibility and cost of utilities, the budget, the amount of money allotted for equipment, and the floor plan and space allotments. Before final decisions are made, individual pieces of equipment should be considered as to design; materials in relation to suitability for the purpose, durability, and cleanability; construction and safety, size and capacity; installation, operation, and performance; maintenance and replacement of parts. Cost and method of purchase are also major considerations in the selection of equipment.

DETERMINATION OF NEEDS

Sound generalizations concerning equipment needs are difficult to formulate because each foodservice presents an individual problem with an interplay of factors not exactly duplicated elsewhere. The determination of these needs, therefore, should be one of the first and most important considerations of the foodservice manager as a basis for deciding what equipment should be purchased. Each item selected must accomplish those definite tasks peculiar to the specific situation. If the installation is new, information concerning the demands to be made of the facility and the ways in which the furnishings and equipment may help to meet these demands is of primary importance in planning the layout and selecting the equipment items. If the installation has been in operation and found to be inefficient, an analysis should be made of the layout and equipment as it exists. This study can be used as a basis to rearrange the floor plan and include any additional furnishings and equipment needed. The *menu pattern* and typical foods to be served must be known in order to determine the extent and complexity of the food preparation that will have to be accomplished. Detailed analysis of the preparation requirements of several typical menus provides the best basis for estimating kitchen and serving room equipment needs for a particular situation. This procedure was pioneered some years ago by Thomas,[2] who made application of many of the principles of industrial management to the solving of problems in the area of foodservice management. She carefully observed and recorded the processes and times involved in preparation of the various types and quantities of foods and the equipment used. Also, the capacity of each equipment item was noted as well as the hour, length of time, and by whom it was used. She employed process and equipment usage charts in recording observations. From a study of the data compiled, recommendations for desirable pieces of equipment of suitable capacities and sizes were developed for the unit under study. These same principles are followed today.

Standardized recipes that include AP and EP weights of ingredients, yields, pan sizes, and the portion size are invaluable aids to planning for efficient kitchen and serving equipment. Batch size and frequency of repeats are important considerations; for example, equipment such as a sink and oven could be utilized to capacity, a longer time allowed for large than small containers of food, and more time for the repeated use of small pressure cooker or can opener. A large mixer and both large capacity and duplicate steam-jacketed kettles or tilting fry pans might be advisable, since they are used in the preparation of many menu items. An increase in the lengths of times required for certain processes for 500 over those needed for 100 portions would be necessary but not always proportional to the increase in quantities. In general, little difference in times is required for chopping various amounts of food in less than machine-capacity quantities or for mixing or cooking an increased amount of food in larger equipment. Repetitive processes such as hand rolling of pastry requires almost proportional quantity, time, and space increases.

The *number and type of persons to be served,* the style of service, and the length of serving periods are important factors in selecting the appropriate amount and kind of kitchen and serving

[2] *Orpha Mae Huffman Thomas,* A Scientific Basis for the Design of Institution Kitchens, *Teachers College, Columbia University, New York, 1947.*

equipment for a foodservice. The equipment needs for the preparation and serving of a plate lunch to 500 children in a school lunchroom would be quite different from those of a service restaurant offering a diversified menu to approximately the same number of people three times daily. In the school foodservice there probably would be no more than two hot items on the menu for any one day, but all food would need to be ready to serve within a short period of time, whereas in the restaurant a variety of items would be ready for final preparation over extended serving periods; also, some items would be cooked in small quantities at spaced intervals according to the peak hours of service. Obviously, smaller and more varied types of equipment would be needed in the restaurant than in the lunchroom. Production schedules in a short-order operation would require duplicated equipment of items such as grills, broilers, and fryers, whereas a residence hall foodservice would need steam-jacketed kettles, steam cookers, and ovens to produce a large volume of food within a specified period of time.

The number of people to be fed determines to a great extent the total volume of food that must be prepared, but numbers in themselves cannot be used to evaluate equipment needs. Estimates of numbers of persons to be served during each 15-minute interval of the serving period will provide a guide to food and equipment needs. Amount and capacity of equipment to select is based on the number served at the interval of greatest demand in relation to cooking time required for specific items. Various *styles of service,* like self-service in a lunchroom, waiter or buffet service in a public dining room, or vended service, require particular kinds of equipment for their efficient functioning.

The *form in which the food is to be purchased* will influence greatly the equipment needs in any kitchen. The selection of fabricated meats and poultry, frozen portioned fish, frozen fruits and vegetables, juice concentrates, ready-to-bake pies, and some cooked entrees, chilled citrus fruit sections, washed spinach and other greens, and processed potatoes, carrots, and apples eliminates the need for space and equipment for the usual preparation and disposal of waste in the kitchen. Adequate facilities for short and long storage at the proper temperatures must be provided, but other equipment needs would be limited primarily to those pieces required in the final stages of production and the serving of the finished products.

The *man-hours available* and the *skill of the workers* cannot be overlooked in considering the equipment needs of any foodservice. If the labor budget or local labor market is limited, usually the selection of as much labor-saving equipment as possible is warranted. Judgment must be exercised in deciding what equipment will provide for the smooth functioning of the organization and also give the best return on the investment. Will the increased productivity of employees with automated equipment in the resulting lessened time compensate for the possible increased payroll and initial and maintenance costs? With the rising pay rates for employees at all levels, managers must weigh values carefully in selecting equipment they can man successfully, efficiently, and economically to accomplish the job to be done.

The adequacy of *utilities* for the successful installation and performance of commercial cooking and warming or power-driven equipment must be checked before the final decision is made on selections. Often the choice between gas, electric, or steam-heated cooking equipment demands considerable investigation of the continuing supply of the source of heat, replaceability of parts of the various items, relative costs of their operation and maintenance, and the probable satisfactions from their use in the particular situation. High-pressure steam is not always available, in which case self-generating steam units would become a necessary choice. Power-driven equipment is fitted with motors of the proper size for the capacity of the machine, but cycle and current would need to be designated so that the machine would operate properly for the wiring and power in the building.

Most institution foodservice kitchens include one or more each of the following: oven, range, tilting fry pan, fryer, broiler, steam-jacketed kettle, pressure steam cooker, coffee maker, refrigerator, freezer, ice-maker, mixing machine with attachments, cutter, sinks, tables, and carts. A wide variety of additional equipment may be purchased as necessity demands and money permits.

Once the equipment has been installed, care must be taken that menus are planned with consideration for its balanced use. This means that the person responsible for planning menus must be familiar with the facilities at hand and know capacities of the equipment and timing of processes for the amounts of food to be prepared. Demands for oven cookery beyond the capacity load may lead to much unhappiness between manager and cook and also encourage the production of inferior quality food or too-early preparation. Preparation time tables, equipment capacity charts, and standardized recipes that indicate AP and EP weights of ingredients, yield, and pan size for the particular setup can contribute much to effective planning for the efficient use of kitchen and serving equipment.

THE BUDGET

The budgetary allowance must cover not only the inital cost of the equipment but often the additional cost of installation. Available funds determine to a great extent the possible amount and quality of equipment that can be purchased at any given time. If the initial equipment budget is adequate, the choice among various pieces becomes mere determination of the superior and preferred qualities for each article desired. Sometimes the equipment budget is so limited that the food director is forced to decide between certain desirable articles and to weigh with serious thought the relative points in quality grades of the pieces believed to be essential. It is advisable then to list all the needed equipment so that unbalanced expenditure will not result. Lack of such thought or insistence on "the best" may lead to disastrous spending.

Consensus is that equipment of good quality is the most economical. Generally, if the amount of money is limited, it is better to buy a few well-chosen pieces of equipment that will meet basic needs and make additions as funds are available than to purchase many pieces of inferior quality that will need to be replaced in a short time. On the other hand, some consultants warn that because of the rapid change in the trend toward the use of prepared foods, it may be preferable in some installations to plan equipment for a short life span and early replacement until such developments are stabilized. The initial cost of equipment is influenced by the size, materials used, quality of workmanship, construction, including special mechanical features, and finish of the article. The limitation of funds may lead to the necessity of a choice as to which one or more of these points may be sacrificed with least jeopardy to the permanence of the article and satisfaction in its use.

Estimates of cost for foodservice equipment and furnishings are difficult to ascertain as each operation must be considered individually. Also, with the fluctuations in costs of equipment, installations, and labor, an estimated $800 to $1000 per dining room seat or hospital bed might be an unrealistic guide for current planning. It would be advisable to learn the costs of comparable situations before making tentative estimates for a new or remodeled set up.

THE FLOOR PLAN

Space allocation for the foodservice may restrict the amount and type of equipment and its placement, especially in old buildings where architectural changes are limited and in new ones where the original planning may have been ill advised regarding the functions and needs. The size and shape of the space allotted to food preparation and its relation to receiving, storage, and dining areas influence greatly the efficiency of operation and ultimately customer satisfaction, as discussed in the preceding chapter. Kitchen space either too small or too large to accommodate the equipment suitable and desirable for the volume of food production anticipated creates an unsatisfactory situation. In the first instance the overcrowding of workers and lack of space for equipment adequate in size or amount makes for confusion and frustration, limits the amount and type of preparation that can be done, and slows production. When the space is too large, much time and effort may be wasted by workers in transporting food long distances. Also, there may be a tendency to overequip with needless items simply because ample space is available. In any case a complete analysis of the real needs is necessary before an equipment investment is made.

FEATURES OF EQUIPMENT

Never has there been so much attention given to the features influencing the selection of equipment for foodservice operations as now. Owners, dietitians, managers, architects, kitchen designers, manufacturers, health authorities, and maintenance engineers have many common concerns. They relate to design, functional qualities, materials, cleanability, construction, safety, size, installation, ease and cost of operation, performance, maintenance, and replaceability of parts.

General objectives and trends in current equipment developments include an increase in the number and kind of specialized items, many of which are adaptable to multiple use; function and attractiveness in appearance; compactness and efficient utilization of space to reduce man-hour and time requirements to a minimum; speed output of quality products; modular planning of matched units as shown in Fig. 12.1; mobility and flexibility of arrangement; exact engineering tolerances, effective insulation, automatic controls for even temperatures and operation; built-in sanitation; and fuel efficiency. With the change in the type and amount of food preparation in the individual kitchen units has come a corre-

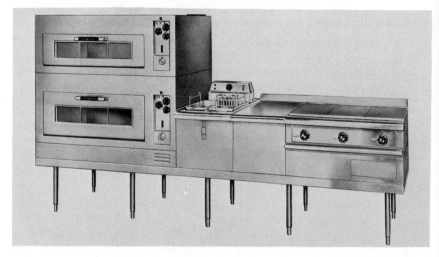

FIGURE   12.1   *A compact arrangement of modular cooking units may be fitted into a continuous framework for beauty, space-saving, operational efficiency, and maintenance of sanitation. The entire unit is adjustable to a convenient working height. Courtesy, General Electric Company.*

sponding change in equipment to meet the particular production needs.

DESIGN AND FUNCTION

The design of equipment and furnishings for the foodservice should be in close harmony with the general plan of the building, especially in the decorative features and items such as table appointments. This is particularly noticeable in summer resorts, children's hospitals, and certain types of restaurants, where not only the modern trend of kitchen planning and interior decoration has been followed, but also some specialized idea or theme has been expressed through the design and type of furnishings selected. Sensitivity to the artistic design of institution foodservice furnishings and equipment is often more acute than to the design of similar items for the home, because of the larger size of kitchen machines required and duplication in number, as in dining room tables and chairs. Generally speaking, heavy-duty kitchen equipment is designed to give a streamline effect.

The Joint Committee on Food Equipment Standards states:

*Food service equipment and appurtenances shall be designed and con-
structed in such a manner as to exclude such vermin, dust or dirt from the
food zone as may be encountered under the intended use conditions; and
be easily cleaned, maintained and serviced.*[3]

The Standard further emphasizes that design and construction must
permit easy cleaning either in an assembled position or as removable parts; and that foods can be added, dispensed, removed, or
served in a sanitary manner.

Beauty and utility may be combined in foodservice equipment
through the application of art principles and consideration of the
functions of the various items by the designer. The gadget or piece
of equipment may be beautiful in line and design, but it is of little
value if it serves no real purpose or if an unreasonable amount of
time is required for its operation or care. The design of cutlery such
as a chef's knife with a heavy wide blade shaped for cutting on a
board and a longhandled cook's fork are examples of how closely
design is related to use of an article. Also, the design may influence
the timing and efficiency of operation, such as in the shape and
weight of beaters or whips for a mixing machine.

Simplicity of design is pleasing and restful and usually means a
minimum amount of care. The manintenance of high sanitation standards in a foodservice is aided by designing the equipment so that
sharp corners, cracks, and crevices are eliminated and all surfaces
are within easy access for cleaning, as the table in Fig. 12.2. The
more complicated items should be designed for quick disassembling of parts for machine or hand washing. The Joint Committee on Food Equipment Standards has stressed the sanitation
aspect of kitchen equipment design and construction as exemplified
in the following statement regarding the material and construction
for legs and feet of kitchen pieces: [4]

*Legs and feet shall be of metal of sufficient rigidity to provide support with a
minimum of cross-bracing; and so fastened to the body of the equipment
and so shaped at floor contacts as to prevent the accumulation of dirt and
the harborage of vermin. When the outside dimension of the leg is greater
than the outside dimension of the foot by 1/2 inch or more in the same
plane, the foot shall, at minimum adjustment, extend 1 inch below the leg.*

[3] *"Standards—Food Service Equipment,"* National Sanitation Foundation,
Standard 2, revised, p. 15, 1973.
[4] *"Standards—Food Service Equipment,"* National Sanitation Foundation,
Standard 2, revised, p. 26, 1973.

FIGURE   12.2   *A well-constructed baker's table designed with features such as rounded corners, tubular legs and feet, and portable bins is attractive and easily cleaned. Courtesy, Southern Equipment Company.*

All openings to hollow sections between feet and legs shall be of drip-proof construction with no openings greater than 1/32 inch. All other openings to hollow sections shall be sealed. Legs and feet shall be of simple design, free from embellishments and exposed threads.

Gussets, when used, shall be assembled to the equipment in such a manner as to insure easy cleanability and to eliminate insect harborage. The resultant assembly shall have no recessed areas or spaces.

All equipment mounted on legs, such as the table in Fig. 12.3, should be designed to have a minimum clearance of 6 and preferably 8 inches between the floor and the bottom surfaces of equipment, shelves, pipes, drains, or traps, to permit ease of cleaning. Heavy stationary equipment such as ranges and cabinets may be mounted successfully on a raised masonry, tile, or metal platform at least 2 inches high, sealed to the floor and at all edges. Usually this type of island base is recessed to allow for toe space beneath the equipment.

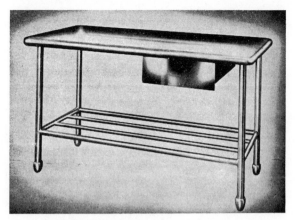

FIGURE   12.3   Kitchen worktable. Note simplicity of design, rounded edges and corners of top, smooth joinings of tubular supports, and rounded feet or may be fitted with casters. Courtesy, C. Blickman, Inc.

Specially designed mountings on wheels for specific purposes have become an important feature of foodservice planning for convenience, sanitation, and economical use of space and labor. Portable back-of-the-counter breakfast service units including toaster, waffle irons, and egg cookers can be transported out of the way during the remainder of the day. Dispenser units can be filled with clean trays in the dishwashing room and wheeled into position at the counter with a minimum of handling (see Fig. 12.4). Portable bins for flour and sugar are more convenient to use and easier to keep clean than built-in bins. Sections of shelves in walk-in refrigerators and dry-storage rooms mounted on wheels make for convenience in cleaning and rearrangement of storage. The importance of designing general utility trucks and dollies to fit into the places in which they are to be used cannot be overestimated.

Heavy-duty wheeled equipment such as range sections, tilting fry pans, fryers, ovens, reach-in refrigerators, and the many mobile work and serving units make possible their rearrangement to adapt to changing needs at minimum cost. Often the conversion of certain spaces from limited- to multiple-use areas can be effected through the inclusion of mobile designed equipment. Also, thorough cleaning back of and underneath is made easier when the equipment is movable and accessible from all sides.

One of the outstanding improvements in serving equipment has been effected through a change in the design and construction of

FIGURE   12.4   *Mobile self-leveling tray unit, filled at the dishmachine and trans-*
ported to the point of use. Courtesy, American Machine and
Foundry Company.

heated serving counters. This change from the old pattern of a given number of rectangular and round openings, far apart, in an elongated steam-table arrangement with limited fixed storage, to a condensed type with fractional size containers, has been estimated to permit up to 50 percent greater food capacity in the same amount of space. This arrangement also makes possible almost unlimited flexibility in service through the close arrangement of a few regular 18 by 12 inch rectangular top openings into which full-size or combinations of fractional-size pans of different depths may be fitted with or without the aid of adaptor bars. Hot food serving counters may be designed and constructed for two or more openings, moist or dry heat, gas or electricity, separate heat controls for individual sections or for the unit, and space below enclosed or fitted for dish storage.

The selection of inserts for this type of counter should be made to meet the demands at peak times for the best service of all the usual types of hot foods included on a menu. The number of each size and depth of pans to purchase can be determined easily by careful analysis of several sample menus, the quantities of each type of food required, and the most satisfactory size and depth of pans for their preparation and service. In most instances this will mean a relatively small number of sizes with ample duplication of those for which there will be the greatest need.

Common depths of the counter pans are 2 1/2, 4, and 6 inches with some sizes available 1 and 8 inches deep. Capacities are listed for each size as, for example, in the accompanying table. All inserts

One-Half Size		One-Fourth Size	
Depth (in)	Capacity (qt)	Depth (in)	Capacity (qt)
1	1 3/4		
2 1/2	4 1/2	2 1/2	2 1/8
4	7 1/8	4	3 3/8
6	10 7/8	6	4 3/4
8	15		

fit flush with top openings, except the 8-inch deep pans which have a 2-inch shoulder extending above the opening. Pans of one size and depth are designed to nest together for convenient storage. Since these pans are made of noncorrosive well-finished metal, certain types of menu items may be cooked in and served directly from them whereas other foods will need to be transferred to them for serving. Recipes can be standardized for a specified number of pans of suitable size and depth for a product and with the exact number of portions predetermined.

SIZE OR CAPACITY

The size or capacity of equipment to select for a given situation is determined largely by the type of menu and service offered and the quantities of different types of foods to be prepared at one time. More pieces of heavy-duty equipment of larger capacities are required for the preparation of food for a college residence hall serving a nonselective menu at a set hour than for the preparation and service for a short-order lunch counter serving comparable or even greater numbers throughout an extended meal hour. The cookery of vegetables in not more than 5-pound lots, timed at intervals to provide for a continuous supply to meet the demands of the service, is far preferable to cooking the entire amount at one time and holding the cooked products through the serving period. The latter would require one or two large steam-jacketed kettles instead of a battery of small ones and would mean less effort and time for the cook, but at the sacrifice of eye appeal, flavor, crispness, nutritive value of the food served, and the satisfaction of the guests.

Large equipment, such as ranges, ovens, tilting fry pans, mixing machines, and dishwashing machines, may be obtained in more or less standard sizes, with slight variations in the articles produced by different manufacturers. For example, range sections may vary a few inches in the overall measurements and the inside dimensions of ovens may differ, whereas the capacities of mixing machines made by most firms are comparable.

Charts are available from most manufacturers that show the capacity or output per hour for each size of machine. For example, the capacity of a dishwashing machine is measured by the number of dishes that can be washed in an hour. The size of mixer to purchase would be determined by the amount of cake batter to be prepared each mixing, the size batch of potatoes to mash, the time required for mixing or mashing each batch, and the total quantity of the produce needed within a given period of time. Obviously, the size and number of pieces of each item of equipment required will depend on the needs of the particular institution.

The articles most often fabricated are those that must conform to a given size or are desired because of special material, often made according to individual specifications. Special orders make the equipment more expensive and often delay delivery. However, to most people the satisfaction of having a piece of equipment that exactly fits usually more than compensates for these disadvantages.

Standards of uniformity in size of small as well as large equipment have become fairly well established through the experience of users and their working with designers, manufacturers, and kitchen planning consultants. Many kitchens of the past have had a multiplicity of sizes of cooking utensils, baking pans, and trays that may or may not have made economical use of range, oven, refrigerator, cabinet, or truck spaces in the particular situation. An example is the large oval serving tray that never fitted on a rack, shelf, or truck. Alert foodservice directors and kitchen planning experts have come to recognize some of these problems and to note the advantages that are gained by simplification of the whole setup through improved planning for the efficient and interrelated use of the items selected.

The selection of certain "modular" items of equipment or those of uniform size has proven advantageous in quantity food operations. When a specified size pan, tray, or rack fits easily in the refrigerator, storage cabinet, serving counter, or on racks or carts, great adaptability in and economical utilization of space are made possible. Also, manpower efficiency is increased and labor hours are reduced; less floor area is required with improved use of vertical space; the use of pans and trays of the same size or in their multiple units reduces the total number and kind to buy, their cost, and the storage space needed; the number of shelves in refrigerators, cabinets, and carts can be reduced when trays and pans can be inserted at close intervals on angle runners or glides; the rehandling or transfer of foods or dishes is reduced, since the tray rack fits into any unit, either on a shelf, on glides, or in the counter; sanitation is improved through reduced handling of food or dishes, low spillage, and machine washing of trays and pans.

Common modules are the 12 by 18 and 18 by 26 inch trays, which are easily accessible in several materials and convenient to use. The 12 by 18 inch trays fit into standard dishwashing racks or conveyor-type machines. Cabinets, shelves, refrigerators, and carts are readily available to accommodate one or a combination of such trays. Some spaces could be sized so that either one 18 by 26 bun pan or two 12 by 18 inch trays could be used. Another common module is space into which 20 by 20 inch dishracks would fit, for storage of cups and glasses in the racks in which they were washed.

This system merits careful consideration in planning kitchen equipment for simplified operation with maximum efficiency and economy. Each unit will need to continue to have a certain amount of its equipment custom built according to specification, but certainly there should be uniformity within each kitchen.

MATERIALS

Materials for the various pieces of foodservice equipment should be suitable for the purpose and give the best satisfaction possible. The materials of which equipment may be made influence price, wearing qualities, sanitation, satisfaction, and usefulness. The weight, finish, and workmanship of the materials are important factors in determining their suitability and wearing qualities.

The Joint Committee on Food Equipment Standards has established minimum requirements for materials and construction of certain foodservice equipment items.

Only such materials shall be used on the construction of food service equipment/or appurtenances, as will withstand normal wear, penetration of vermin, the corrosive action of foods or beverages, cleaning compounds and such other elements as may be found in the use environments and will not impart an odor, color or taste to the food.[5]

They further specify that surface materials in the food zone shall be smooth, corrosion resistant, nontoxic, stable, and nonabsorbent, and that they must not contribute to the adulteration of the food. Nonfood contact surfaces should be of corrosion-resistant material or be made so by coating, except with paint, which is not acceptable on parts of the equipment directly over and adjacent to the food zone. Solder must be nontoxic and welded areas must be equally as resistant to corrosion as the parent metal.

Metals. Metals have become increasingly important in kitchen planning until, at the present time, we depend on them for nearly everything, from structural features such as doors, flooring under steam units, and walk-in refrigerators to tables, sinks, dishwashing machines, and cooking equipment. A wide variety of old and well-known metals and alloys such as copper, tin, chromium, iron, steel, and aluminum was used in the kitchens of an early day, but have been outmoded by the chromium and chromium-nickel stainless steels. At one time *copper* cooking utensils and dishwashing machines were commonly found in institution kitchens. Their care and upkeep were high because they required frequent polishing and replacement of nickel or tin linings to prevent the reaction of foodstuffs with the copper. Such utensils were heavy to handle and were used mostly in hotels where male cooks were employed. *Nickel* was used considerably as a plating for equipment trim, rails of cafeteria counters, and inexpensive tableware.

Aluminum lends itself to fabrication of numerous kinds and will take a satin, frosted, or chrome-plated finish. It can be painted, etched, or engraved. It is relatively light in weight, has high thermal and electrical conductivity, does not corrode readily and, if cold-rolled, is relatively hard and durable. It is capable of withstanding

[5] *Standards—Food Service Equipment, National Sanitation Foundation, Standard 2, revised, p. 13, 1973.*

pressure at high temperature, which makes it particularly well suited for cooking and baking utensils and steam-jacketed kettles. Aluminum cooking utensils often become discolored by food or water containing alkali, certain acids, and iron. Such discoloration, which is harmless and will not discolor food, may be removed by the use of a good aluminum cleaner, fine steel wool, or it may be dissolved by lemon juice or vinegar. Strong soaps and free-alkali-containing scouring powder should not be used in the cleaning of aluminum. Many kitchen items are manufactured from anodized aluminum that has been subjected to electrolytic action to coat and harden the surface and increase its resistance to oxidation, discoloration, marring, and scratching. Anodized aluminum is often used for items such as dry-storage cabinets and service carts and trays. Its strength and light weight are factors in its favor for mobile equipment. Aluminum may be combined with other metals to produce alloys of higher tensile strength than aluminum alone.

Cast iron is used in institution equipment as braces and castings for stands and supports, for pipes, and for large pieces of equipment such as ranges. Its use in small equipment is restricted to skillets, Dutch ovens, and griddles.

Galvanized steel and iron were long used for such equipment as sinks, dishwashing machines, and tables. In the process of galvanizing, a coating of zinc, deposited on the base metal, protects it to a certain extent from corrosion. The initial cost of equipment made of galvanized material is comparatively low, but the length of life is short, repair and replacement expenses are high, sanitation is low, contamination is likely, and the general appearance is undesirable and unattractive in comparison to equipment made of noncorrosive metal.

The use of *noncorrosive metals,* mainly the alloys of iron, nickel, and chromium, for equipment in food processing plants such as bakeries, dairies, canneries and in home and institution-size kitchens has increased tremendously within recent years until, at the present time, all such units are planned with widespread usage of this material. These metals are available in forms suitable for fabrication into any desired types of equipment. If the sheets are too small for the particular item, they may be joined and welded most satisfactorily. The price is not prohibitive, so that this type of material functions in many and varied instances from decorative effects in or on public buildings to heavy-duty kitchen equipment, cooking utensils, and tableware. Improved methods of fabrication and the unprecedented emphasis on kitchen sanitation have been important factors in the high utilization of noncorrosive metals in items of equipment.

The outstanding characteristics of noncorrosive metals for foodservice equipment include its permanence, resistance to ordinary stains and corrosion, lack of chemical reaction with food, attractive appearance, ease of cleaning and fabrication, and nonprohibitive price. Tests show that with proper construction and care noncorrosive metals wear indefinitely, and equipment made from them may be considered permanent investments. The strength and toughness are so high that even a comparatively lightweight metal may be used for heavy-duty items. These metals do not chip or crack. High ductility and weldability also make for permanence of the equipment made from them; thus the upkeep costs are reduced to a minimum.

Resistance to stains and corrosion is a major feature in foodservice equipment where cleanliness, appearance, and sanitation are of utmost importance. The freedom from chemical reactions of the noncorrosive metals with foodstuffs at any temperature makes their use safe in food preparation. Tests show few or no traces of metals or metallic salts present after different foods have been heated and chilled for varying periods of time in containers made of these metals.

The appearance of noncorrosive metal equipment when well made and carefully finished is satisfying and conducive to the maintenance of excellent standards of cleanliness and order. The smooth, hard surface is not easily scratched or marred, and simple cleaning methods are all that are required. There are special metal cleaners on the market, but a good cleaner and water and the usual polishing should be enough to keep the equipment in good condition. Common steel wool, scouring pads, scrapers, or wire brushes may mar the surface or leave small particles of iron imbedded in the stainless steel to cause rust stains. Darkened areas are caused usually by heat applied either in fabrication or in use and may be removed by vigorous rubbing with stainless steel wool, a stainless steel pad and powder, or a commercial heat-tint remover. To avoid heat tinting of cooking utensils, they should be subjected to no more heat than required to do the job effectively, never heated empty or with heat concentrated on a small area.

The noncorrosive alloys manufactured most often into institution kitchen equipment are nickel-copper and the stainless steels. Monel metal is an example of the first type. It is a natural alloy that contains approminately 2/3 nickel and 1/3 copper, with a small amount of iron. The supply is fairly limited so it is seldom selected for fabrication into kitchen equipment.

By far the greatest amount of kitchen equipment is made of some type of stainless steel. Each company producing stainless steel under its own trade name may use a slightly different formula, but the important elements are practically the same. A relatively low carbon content in the stainless steels gives high resistance to attack by corrosive agents. A chromium-nickel stainless steel alloy commonly called "18-8" (number 302) is a favorite material for foodservice equipment. As its name indicates, it contains approximately 18 percent chromium and 8 percent nickel with no copper present. Manufacturers of kitchen equipment had to turn to the use of alternate types of stainless steels during the time nickel was restricted to strategic and high priority items. Chromium stainless steel (number 430) proved to be a satisfactory alternate for the chromium-nickel type. The appearance is similar and the wearing qualities are good, although the chromium stainless is slightly more susceptible to corrosion and discoloration under certain conditions, and the tensile strength and ductility are lower than in the chromium-nickel steel. The base price of the chromium stainless may be less, but the finished price could be higher than the chromium-nickel stainless steel because of great difficulty of fabrication and the longer time required for polishing. Although the corrosive penetration of these two types of metal surfaces is measurable in the laboratory, the actual damage to the same surfaces would be negligible under ordinary conditions, even after a long period of years. Observations of equipment made of the noncorrosive alloys in satisfactory use and their appearance and sanitary qualities prove the value of these materials for heavy-duty kitchen equipment.

Standard Gauge. The gauge or thickness of metals is an important consideration in selecting materials for equipment. The adoption of the micrometer caliber to indicate the thickness of sheet metal in decimal parts of an inch and the abolition of gauge numbers are strongly recommended. However, the United States standard gauge is used by most manufacturers of iron and steel sheets. This system is a weight, not a thickness, gauge. For instance, number 20 United States gauge weighs 1.5 pounds per square foot, subject to the standard allowable variation. Weight always is the determining factor. That this gauge is 0.037 inch thick is secondary in the system. Numbers 10 to 14 gauge galvanized steel or 12 to 16 noncorrosive

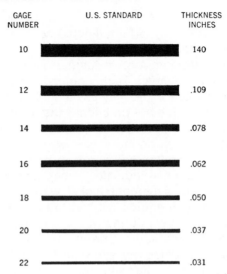

GAGE NUMBER	U.S. STANDARD	THICKNESS INCHES
10		140
12		.109
14		.078
16		.062
18		.050
20		.037
22		.031

FIGURE   12.5   *A diagram showing actual thickness of commonly used gauges of metals.*

metals are most generally used for foodservice equipment. Metal lighter than 16 gauge is commonly used for sides or parts where the wear is light (see Fig. 12.5).

Finish of Metals. The surface or finish of metals may be dull or bright; the higher the polish, the more susceptible is the surface to scratches. The degree of finish of metals is indicated by a gradation in number, the larger numbers indicating finer finish and a higher degree of polish. Standard finishes for the steels in sheet form are listed below.

Finish	Description
No. 1	Hot-rolled, annealed, and pickled
No. 2B	Full finish—bright cold-rolled
No. 2D	Full finish—dull cold-rolled
No. 4	Standard polish, one or both sides
No. 6	Standard polish, tampico brushed one or both sides
No. 7	High-luster polish on one or both sides

Numbers 4, 6, and 7 are produced by grinding and polishing the sheets of metal with different grades of abrasives. These original surface finishes are capable of being retained in the usual fabrication of kitchen equipment which requires only local forming. Materials with a number 4-grind surface are more often selected for such items as table tops, sinks, and counters than are those with shiny or mirrorlike finish.

Glass. Glass and ceramic-lined equipment, such as coffee dripolators, is most satisfactory for certain purposes. It protects against metallic contamination, corrosion, and absorption. Glass-lined equipment is highly acid resistant and will withstand heat shock. This last quality is due to the fact that the coefficient of expansion of the glass enamel is similar to that of the steel shell. Most ceramics will break readily when exposed to extreme heat or mechanical shock.

Other Materials. Items such as counter fronts and ends and food tray delivery carts made of mirror-finish *fiberglass* with stainless steel structural trim are available in many beautiful colors. The interior and exterior walls of the food delivery carts are molded in one piece, then insulated with polyurethane foam. The surfaces are strong, dent and scratch resistant, and light in weight. *Porcelain* (glass on steel) or *vinyl* covered galvanized steel may be used satisfactorily on outside walls of refrigerators and on counter fronts at less cost than stainless steel. The above materials contribute to a colorful and pleasing decor, reduce reflected glare of light, and are easily maintained. Detached well-laminated and sealed *hardwood* cutting boards are permissible in some cities and states.

Carts, racks, stands, and dollies made of *polycarbonate* are light in weight but capable of carrying heavy loads; they resist stains, dents, and scratches, will not rust or crack, and are easily disassembled for cleaning in a conveyor-type dishwashing machine. Side panels may be of a solid color or transparent, and most models are designed to accomodate 18 by 26 inch food boxes with fitted lids, trays, and bunpans (see Fig. 12.6). All items may be fitted with non-marking neoprene brake wheels, and ball bearings. Reversible non-toxic, nonabsorbent polyethylene cutting boards are available for use on the worktable topped cabinets.

CONSTRUCTION

The construction of and workmanship on equipment determines whether or not it is durable, attractive, and sanitary. High-quality material and a perfect design for the purpose do not insure good con-

FIGURE   12.6   The selection of a variety of carts for transportation, preparation, and storage of food facilitates efficient and flexible arrangements to meet the changing needs of a foodservice operation. This system provides for interchangeable parts, easy disassembling for cleaning, and items are mounted on 5-inch nonmarking neoprene swivel casters. Clear polycarbon or white high-density polyethylene food boxes with covers are available. Courtesy, Rubbermaid Commercial Products, Inc.

struction, although they contribute to it. Accurate dimensions, careful and well-finished joinings, solidarity, pleasing appearance, and ease of cleaning are important factors. Sinks, drainboards, and dishtables sloped to drain; tables and chairs properly braced; hinges and fasteners of heavy duty materials and drawers constructed to function properly; adequate insulation where needed; and safety features are a few of the points to consider under construction. It is a necessity that all parts are easily cleanable.

Welding has replaced riveting, bolting, and soldering of both surface and understructure joinings in metal foodservice equipment. Great emphasis is placed on the importance of grinding, polishing, and finishing of the surfaces and welded joints for smoothness and to insure against possible progressive corrosion. Mitered corners, properly welded and finished smooth, in items such as dishtables and sinks are superior to deep square corners or those filled with solder. The construction recommended for items of equipment used for unpackaged food is for rounded internal angles with a minimum continuous and smooth radius of 1/8 inch and internal rounded corners with a minimum continuous and a smooth radius of 1/4 inch for vertical and horizontal intersections and 1/8 inch radius for the alternate intersection.

The bull-nosed corner construction is used most often in finishing off the corners of horizontal surfaces such as worktables. The corner section of the top material is rounded off and made smooth both horizontally and vertically as an integral part of the horizontal surface. If the edge is flanged down and turned back a minimum of 3/4 inch should be allowed between the top and the flange, and the same distance should be allowed between the sheared edge and the frame angle or cabinet body to provide easy access for cleaning.

To simplify construction and eliminate some of the hazards to good sanitation, fittings and parts have been combined into single forgings and castings wherever possible, and tubular supports sealed off smooth or fitted with adjustable screw-in solid pear-shaped feet have replaced open angular bracings with flange bases. In many instances, mobile, self-supporting, or wall-hung structures have replaced external framing. Several items welded or fitted together into a continuous unit may need to be brought into the kitchen and positioned before construction of the building is complete and while there is ample space for transporting the unit into the area.

The Joint Committee on Food Equipment Standards outlines in detail permissible methods for construction of such general parts as angles, seams, finishes of joinings, openings, rims, framing and reinforcement, and body construction. Specifically, they give construction features for special items such as hoods, water-cooling units, counter guards, doors, hardware, sinks, refrigerators, power-driven machines and their installation. Many health departments use the recommended standards as a basis for approving equipment and its installation. An example of such a standard and a diagram (Fig. 12.7) follow.

COUNTER GUARDS: Display stands for unpackaged foods are to be effectively shielded so as to intercept the direct line between the average customer's mouth and the food being displayed.

Guards shall be mounted so as to intercept a direct line between the customer's mouth and the food display area at the customer "use" position. The vertical distance from the average customer's mouth to the floor shall be considered to be 4 feet 6 inches to 5 feet for public eating establishments. Special consideration must be given to the average customer's mouth height in educational institutions and other special installations.

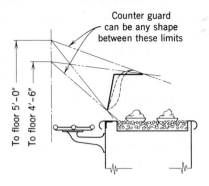

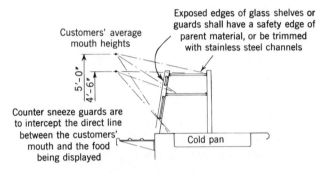

FIGURE 12.7   *Standards for counter guard construction. Courtesy, National San-*
itation Foundation.

Such guards are to be fabricated of easy-to-clean, sanitary materials
conforming to MATERIALS specifications.

Where the edges of glass or other hazardous materials are exposed,
they are to be trimmed with a smooth protective member, have a safety
edge of parent material, or be of a material which does not present a hazard
in this connection.[6]

Likewise for "food mixers—vertical," the standard reads:

Part numbers, where required on beaters, shall be located on the shank
or sleeve.

Agitators shall be constructed of stainless steel, nickel alloy, aluminum
alloy, tin-coated steel, tin-coated cast iron or equally corrosion resistant and

[6] *"Standards—Food Service Equipment," National Sanitation Foundationl,*
Standard 2, revised, p. 36, 1973.

nontoxic material. All agitators shall be readily removable for cleaning and have a simple but positive method of attachment that shall also be easily cleanable.

Agitators in the form of wire whips shall be constructed so as to hold all wires rigidly at points of attachment and support, and all other contacts between wire shall be separable . . . The space between wires at points of attachment shall be not less than two diameters of the wire. Exposed fastening devices for agitators shall be minimized. Exposed wound wire fastenings for whip handles shall not be used.

Where agitators are equipped with rubber or similar edges or scrapers, such edges shall be so attached as to avoid cracks or crevices.

Bowls, bowl covers and containers shall be constructed of stainless steel, aluminum alloy, nickel alloy, tin coated steel or equal.

Top rims of bowls shall be open and easily cleanable.

Transmissions and head assemblies shall be considered splash contact surfaces and shall be designed and constructed so as to prevent lubricant and other foreign materials therefrom from reaching the food or food contact surfaces.

Any lamp mounted on the mixer shall be enclosed or placed behind a shield of nonfriable (not subject to crumbling) material.

The bowl insulation shall be sealed in such a manner as to be water and vermin proof.[7]

Safety features for the protection of workers in the use and care of equipment and for the production of safe food are important factors in the design, choice of materials, and construction of kitchen equipment. There is also a close relationship between these and the standards and controls for sanitation in a foodservice operation. Smooth, rounded corners on work surfaces, table drawers with stops and recessed pulls, automatic steam shut-off when cooker doors are opened, temperature controls, guards on slicers and chopping machines, brakes on mixers, recessed manifold control knobs on ranges and ovens, smooth, polished, welded seams, rounded corners, and knee-lever drain controls on sinks are a few examples of built-in safety in heavy-duty kitchen equipment.

INSTALLATION, OPERATION, AND PERFORMANCE

Proper installation is a necessity for the successful operation of all equipment. The best design and construction would be worthless if electrical, gas, or water connections were inadequate or poorly

[7] *"Commercial Powered Food Preparation Equipment," National Sanitation Foundation, Standard 8, revised, pp. 21–22, 1972.*

done. The dealer from whom the equipment was purchased may not be responsible for its installation by contract, but he usually delivers, uncrates, assembles, and positions the item ready for steam fitting or electrical and plumbing connections. In many cases he will supervise the installation until he is certain that the equipment will function properly. After the installation is completed, he will demonstrate and instruct the personnel in the operation and maintenance of the equipment.

Architects, contractors, and engineers are responsible for providing proper and adequate plumbing, electrical wiring, and venting facilities for the satisfactory installation of kitchen equipment according to the standards of the local building, plumbing, electrical, and sanitation codes. Water, steam, gas, and waste pipe lines and electrical conduits must be planned for each piece of equipment so that proper joinings can be made at the time of installation to avoid the necessity of extra pipe or wiring that might interfere with cleaning or placement of other equipment items.

The sanitation and safety aspects of equipment installation are important to the convenience and safety of its use and care. Sinks that drain well, wall-hung or mobile equipment that permits easy cleaning under and around it, equipment sealed to the wall, and adequate aisle clearance so that food and supplies can be transported easily and safely on carts are but a few of the considerations to make in planning installations. An example of combining related pieces of equipment into a single continuous unit is shown in Fig. 12.1.

The National Sanitation Foundation standard regarding space behind, between, and beside units when not movable or sealed to the wall reads:

When the distance to be cleaned is less than 2 ft in length, the width of the clear unobstructed space should not be less than 6 in. When the distance to be cleaned is greater than 2 ft, but less than 4 ft in length, the width of the clear unobstructed space should not be less than 8 in. When the distance to be cleaned is greater than 4 ft, but less than 6 ft in length, the width of the clear unobstructed space should not be less than 12 in. When the distance to be cleaned is greater than 6 ft, the width of clear unobstructed space should be 18 in.[8]

[8] *"Standards—Food Service Equipment," National Sanitation Foundation, Standard 2, revised, p. 50, 1973.*

The operation of each piece of equipment must be checked many times by both the contractors and service engineers before it is ready for actual use. Full instruction for the proper operation and satisfactory performance of each piece of equipment should be given to all persons who will work with it. They must know the danger signals, such as the sound of a defective motor, so that preventive measures can be taken early.

MAINTENANCE AND REPLACEMENT

The cost of care and upkeep on a piece of equipment may determine whether or not its purchase and use are justified. The annual repair and replacement of equipment should be made with consideration of the unit as a whole, and labor and operating costs should be checked constantly. If these are too high, they limit other expenditures that might promote greater efficiency in the organization. The dispersion of outlay between care and repair is important in more ways than one. Money, attention, and effort spent on care assume the continuance of the necessary equipment in use; money and effort spent on repair are often attended by a disrupted work schedule, unpleasant stresses and strains on personnel, and sometimes definite fire hazards.

Many questions in regard to care and upkeep costs present themselves when equipment is selected. Are parts readily available, easily replaced, and relatively inexpensive? Does the replacement require the services of a specialist, or can a regular employee be trained to do the work? Should some piece of equipment fail to operate when needed, has provision been made in planning so that operations may be carried on? Are special cleaning materials needed in caring for the equipment?

The care and repair of electrical equipment represent a major item in the maintenance cost of many foodservices. The adequate care of electric motors requires expert attention by technically trained and responsible engineers. Arrangements for such care are commonly made with the maintenance department on a contract basis, covering weekly inspection and other checkups necessary for good maintenance. The competent maintenance man will have a record card for every motor in the plant. All repair work, with its cost, and every inspection can be entered on the record. If this system is used, excessive amounts of attention or expense will show up, and the causes can be determined and corrected. Inspection records will also serve as a guide to indicate when motors should be replaced because of the high cost of keeping them in operating condition.

To evaluate a piece of equipment in use, an analysis of the expenditures for care and upkeep is made, and the condition of the equipment is checked to determine if the deterioration has been more rapid than it should have been under normal usage, exposure, cleaning operations, and contacts with food and heat. A factual basis for appraising upkeep costs and depreciation of kitchen equipment can be obtained by keeping careful records on each major piece. Form 12.1 is a suggested method for keeping such records.

Successful maintenance of equipment requires definite plans to prolong its life and maintain its usefulness. Such plans place emphasis on a few simple procedures: keep the equipment clean; follow the manufacturer's printed directions for care and operation, including lubrication; keep the instruction card for each piece of equipment posted near it; stress careful handling as essential to continued use; and make needed repairs promptly. Some pertinent suggestions for the care of machines and instructions for their use are: the assignment of care of each machine to a responsible person; daily inspection for cleanliness and constant supervision by dietitian when in use; immediate adjustment of even minor repairs; thorough knowledge of operating directions; regular oiling and inspections; and repairs by competent person. Printed instructions should be easily available; directions for operation with a simple diagram should hang by the machine; and any special warnings should be printed in large or colored letters. When explaining its operation, the function and relationship of each part should be described in detail so that it is understood by the operator. There should also be a demonstration of proper use of the machine and an explanation of the value of the machine and the cost of repairs. See page 598 on the procedure for cleaning a food slicer. Similar directions should be formulated for each piece of equipment and made into a manual for use by employees responsible for the care and cleanliness of the various items.

The operating cost is an important feature often overlooked in purchasing equipment. In some localities electricity may be available for cooking purposes at a lower operating cost than gas, or vice versa. When all factors are considered, an electric range may be more economical in this particular instance, even though the initial cost may be more. Due consideration and investigation of the rela-

Name of Institution:_____

A. LARGE EQUIPMENT RECORD

Equipment or
Appliance Item: Purchase Date:

Motor Serial Number	Motor Make Model	Equipment Number	Location
Original Cost	Estimated Period of use: Months Years ☐ ☐	Make of Equipment item:	Description: Type_____ Size _____ Capacity ___ Design_____

Appraisal		Motor Specification:	Estimated	Date fully
Date	Value	W V Amp. H.P. ___ ___ ___ ___	Depreciation per Month____Year____	Depreciated

	Repairs and Replacements			
Date	Nature	By Whom	Cost	Remarks

Name of Institution _____

B. SMALL EQUIPMENT RECORD

Name of Item: Purchase   Purchased   Location:
                    Date: From:

Style Size	Amount of Original Purchase	Quality or Grade	Uses:
___ ___	_____	_____	

Appraisal		Repairs or Replacement			Amount on hand
Date	Value	Date	Nature	By Whom Cost	

FORM   12.1   *Suggested form for recording information on each piece of* (a) *large equipment,* (b) *small equipment.*

739

tive efficiency of various models and types are also necessary in selecting any piece of equipment.

METHOD OF PURCHASE

The method of purchase of equipment varies somewhat with the institution. However, regardless of whether the actual placing of the order is done by the director of the foodservice, the purchasing agent, or the superintendent of the hospital, the preliminary procedures are much the same. All available data as to the needs and requirements of the institution are collected by the director, who is responsible for the smooth operation of the service and the satisfaction of its guests. Usually representatives of different firms are willing to demonstrate equipment and to give the prospective buyer information concerning the particular piece of equipment needed. Visits may be made to various institutions to see similar models in operation. After such investigations are made and a definite idea of what is wanted is established, specifications are written and submitted to reliable firms. Written bids are then received and tabulated and a comparison is made, after which the order is placed.

The reliability of the firm from which the equipment is purchased means much to any institution. A reputable company with a record of years of successful operation usually strives to sell dependable merchandise of good quality. The company may be counted on to stand back of the guarantee and to do all possible to keep the good will and confidence of the customer. In their planning and engineering departments, equipment dealers employ experts whose services are always available to the prospective customer. Years of experience and constant contact with both the manufacturing and operating units in the field enable them to be of valuable assistance. Most companies keep records of the sale, service calls, and repairs of the various pieces of equipment. In return they deserve fair treatment and consideration from the director of the foodservice or the purchasing agent for the institution.

To be of value, a specification for equipment must be specific and definite. It covers every detail in relation to material, construction, size, color, finish, and cost, eliminating any question in the mind of either the buyer or the manufacturer as to what the finished product will be. If the equipment when delivered does not measure up to the specified order, it need not be accepted. If the buyer is disappointed but has permitted loopholes in the specification, and the product meets the requirements of the specification, it must be accepted. However, most firms are so desirous of selling satisfaction that they check orders carefully with the buyer to see that everything is included before the equipment is made or delivered.

The vague and the definite specifications given below for a particular piece of equipment illustrate the difference between the two types. Specifications may be indefinite, and yet to the casual observer all points may seem to be included. After reading the second example, one can readily see the weak spots in the first.

VAGUE SPECIFICATIONS

Item number: xx.
Name of item: Cook's table with sink.
Dimensions: 8 ft long, 2 ft 6 in. wide, 3 ft high.
Material and construction: Top of this table to be made of heavy-gauge stainless steel with semirolled edge and to be furnished with one sink, 18 in. long, 24 in. wide, 12 in. deep, fitted with drain. Sink to be located 3 in. from left end of table. The under side of this table to be reinforced with channel braces. Table to be supported by 4 stainless steel tubular standards with adjustable feet. Stainless slatted shelf to rest on cross rails 10 in. above floor. Table to be equipped with one drawer, 24 in. long, 22 in. wide, and 5 in. deep. Drawer to be made of heavy stainless steel, reinforced on front facing. All joints of this drawer to be welded, and drawer equipped with ball-bearing drawer slides. This drawer to be fitted with a white metal handle.

Price: $ . . . .

DEFINITE SPECIFICATIONS

Item number: xx.
Name of item: Cook's table with sink.
Dimensions: 8 ft long, 2 ft 6 in. wide, 3 ft high.
Material and construction: Top of this table to be made of No. 14 gauge, No. 4 grind, No. 302 stainless steel with all edges turned down 1 1/2 in., semirolled edge. All corners to be fully rounded "bull-nose" construction and integral with top. Top of this table to be fitted with one sink, 18 in. long, 24 in. wide, and 12 in. deep, with all corners and intersections fully rounded to a 1-in. radius. All joints to be welded, ground smooth, and polished. Bottom sloped to drain in center. Sink to be located 3 in. from left end of table, 3 in. from each side. Sink to be equipped with 2-in white metal drain with plug and chain complete.

The under side of this table top to be properly reinforced and braced with 4-in. No. 14-gauge stainless steel channel braces welded on. Four tubular leg standards to be welded to these channel cross braces. Standards to be made of seamless stainless steel tubing 1 5/8 in. outside diameter, cross rails and braces of the same material, fitted and welded together. Resting on these cross rails and braces will be a slatted bar shelf elevated 10 in. above floor. Slats to be made of No. 16 stainless steel, No. 4-grind, welded to 2-in. No. 16 stainless-steel supports. Slats 2 in. wide and bent down at ends and formed to fit over cross rails. Slatted shelf to be built in two removable parts of equal length. Leg standards to be fitted with adjustable inside threaded, stainless-steel, tubular, closed, smooth-finish feet.

Table to be equipped with one drawer, 24 in. long, 22 in. wide, and 5 in. deep. Drawer to be made of No. 16-gauge, No. 4-grind stainless steel throughout, reinforced on front facing with No. 14-gauge, No. 4-grind stainless steel. All joints of this drawer to be welded, ground, and polished. Each drawer to be equipped with nontilting, easy-glide roller-bearing drawer slides, and all metal tracks welded to under side of table top. This drawer to be fitted with a polished white metal pull handle.

Price: F.O.B. . . . . . . $ . . . .

Delivery date: not later than . . . .

When purchasing electrically operated equipment, it is essential that exact electrical specifications be given to the manufacturer at the time of placing the order. A motor is wound to operate on a certain voltage current and, when set up to operate on another, may run more slowly or more rapidly than was intended, causing its output to be greater or less than its rated horsepower. There is danger of overheating and a breakdown of insulation, which will result in short circuits and the necessity for motor repairs or replacements. A three-phase motor is desirable because the absence of brushes lessens the maintenance problems. Motors of less than 1 horsepower may be used equally well on 110- or 220-volt currents, but motors of larger horsepower should be operated on a 220-volt current. Manufacturers now use ball-bearing motors, fully enclosed and ventilated, which eliminate the necessity of frequent oiling. Most motors are built especially for the machines they operate. They must be adequate in power to carry easily the capacity loads of the machines.

SELECTION OF SOME BASIC ITEMS

An analysis of the basic considerations discussed thus far helps to determine whether the selection of certain items of kitchen equipment is justified and gives attention to the mechanics of buying. Standards for various types of equipment have been mentioned. The problem of selection is so important and errors are so costly that major characteristics to consider in the selection of certain types of items will be suggested. No attempt is made to evaluate or identify equipment by trade name. The buyer may need to make his selection between the products of several competitive manufacturers or jobbers, each of whom may have quality products but with a wide variance in some details. All equipment should be a sound investment for the operator, be easily cleaned, safe to operate, and accomplish the work for which it was designed. Wise selection can be made only after an exhaustive study of all available data and observation of similarly installed equipment have been accomplished.

Manufacturers' specification sheets, brochures, and catalogs, current professional and trade journals and magazines, and the representatives of the manufacturing companies are the best sources of up-to-date information on specific items. Special features may be changed fairly often so that detailed information on certain models is soon outdated in a publication like this one.

Some points for consideration when selecting foodservice equipment, other than price, cost of operation, and maintenance, are included in the following pages in this chapter to help acquaint the reader with possible features and variations of certain items. The availability of utilities and other factors might predetermine some decisions; for example, the choice between an electric or gas-heated range presents no problem if the advantages of one source of heat over the other are evident in the particular situation; instead, the problem becomes one of a choice between various models manufactured by several different firms. Space permits only a limited amount of basic information on certain fundamental items. It is expected that supplementary material will be kept up to date and made available in library or office files for students and foodservice operators.

COOKING EQUIPMENT

This equipment must conform to requirements for material, construction, safety, and sanitation established by groups such as the American Standards Association, American Gas Association, National Board of Fire Underwriters, Underwriters Laboratories, Inc., American Society of Mechanical Engineers, and the National Sanitation Foundation. One should be sure that parts are replaceable and service is available for all items selected as well as give consideration to original and operating costs, the effectiveness in accomplishing the task to be done, and the time and skill required for ordinary maintenance. The life expectancy requirement depends somewhat on the situation, but the selection of durable, high-quality equipment is usually economical.

Electric and Gas Fired Equipment. *Electrically heated* cooking equipment designed for alternating or direct current of specified voltage; rating required expressed in watts or kilowatts (1000 watts = 1 kilowatt) per hour; wiring concealed and protected from moisture; switches plainly identified; thermostatic heat controls; flues not required for electric cooking equipment but the usual hood or built-in ventilating system necessary to remove cooking vapors and odors.

Gas fired cooking equipment designed for natural, manufactured, mixed, or liquefied petroleum fuel; adapted to given pressures; rating requirement expressed in British thermal units (Btu) per hour; individual shut-off valve for each piece of gas equipment; manifolds and cocks accessible but concealed; removable burners; automatic lighting with pilot light for each burner; thermostatic heat controls; gas equipment vented through hood or built-in ventilator instead of kitchen flue to exhaust combustible gases.

Ranges. Simple design, easily cleanable; heavy, well-braced angle iron frame; sturdy riveted or welded construction; body—sheet steel with baked-on black Japan or porcelain enamel smooth finish, or stainless steel; with or without ovens and high backs; heating elements of burners with individual controls; automatic pilot; removable drip trays to prevent spillage under elements or burners; may be mounted on casters or flush-to-wall.

Types: (1) Heavy-duty ranges—durable and well suited for large volume foodservice operations with constant usage, as in hotels, large restaurants, colleges, hospitals. Approximate sizes of sections: electric—36 inches wide, 36 inches deep, 32 inches high; gas—31 to 34 inches wide, 34 to 42 inches deep, 33 to 34 inches high. (2) Medium weight or restaurant type—lighter in construction than heavy-duty and used where demands are less constant such as short-order cooking or where use is intermittent as in churches and clubs. Complete units, 6, 8, or 10 burners, or combination with fry top and/or even-heat top; 1 or 2 ovens. Approximate size 35 to 64 inches wide, 27 to 32 inches deep, 34 inches high; ovens, 26 inches wide, 22 inches deep, 15 inches high.

Tops: Polished chrome-nickel-iron alloy, high strength and heat absorption qualities; resistant to warping, chipping, and corrosion; accurate thermostats provide controlled heat surfaces as desired.

1. Open or hot plate top—Usually associated with short order preparation. Heat concentrated under kettles; heating elements and grates simple

in design, easily removable for cleaning; gas cones elevated so combustion and ventilation can be complete; burners can be turned on and off as needed; instant heat available; high Btu output by means of small blower to force air into burner.

2. Closed top—Styled for heavy duty, continuous cooking as entire surface area is heated; various burner arrangements. For gas:—*Uniform hot top:*even heat distribution from rows of bar burners set in fire brick under smooth top; depression in brick around edge acts as duct to flue in gas range. *Graduated heat:* by means of concentric ring burners with separate controls; intense heat in center (approximately 1100°F) to low heat at edge (450°F); projections on underneath side of top help direct heat to edges. *Front-fired* (gas): row of burners under front of range top; heat concentrated at front with gradation in degrees of heat intensity toward back.

3. Fry or griddle top—even heat; solid top with edges raised to prevent overflow of grease; fitted with grease trough and drain to receptacle.

Range ovens: even heat distribution, automatic pilot and heat control; high-quality insulation; walls, top, bottom, and removable racks or shelves of smooth, durable, cleanable material or finish; sturdy counterbalanced door with nonbreakable hinges, cool handle; door to support at least 200 pounds. Designed so spillage will drain to front for easier cleaning. Approximate size: 26 inches wide, 28 inches deep, 15 inches high (inside measurements).

Legs and feet: simple design; rigid support; adjustable legs; shaped at floor contact to prevent accumulation of dirt or harborage of vermin; sealed hollow sections; minimum clearance of 6 in. between floor and lowest horizontal parts unless mounted on raised masonry island at least 2 inches high and sealed to floor.

Installation: Heavy-duty range sections often joined together with other modular units as broilers and fryers to make a complete cooking unit.

Griddles. Separate griddle units to supplement or substitute for range sections; mobile griddles give use where needed, as kitchen or counter; extra-heavy, highly polished plates to hold heat and recover rapidly; even heat distribution; chromium or stainless front and ends; oversized, cool valve handles; sloped to grease drain-off. Sizes from 7 by 14 inches to 36 by 72 inches. Capacity expressed in terms of food that can be cooked at one time.

Broilers. Sheet steel of 16 gauge or better, with smooth, baked-on black Japan finish, or stainless steel; rigidly reinforced with angle support; warp-resistant heating units with radiant ceramic or alloy materials to give even heat distribution, lining of long-wearing reflective materials; spring-balanced raising or lowering device; right or left hand operation; safety stop locks; close-fitting cast-iron grids, removable for easy cleaning, adjustable over distances of 1 1/2 to 8 inches from heat source; removable drip tray; drain to receptacle; size of grid determines capacity.

Types: (1) Unit or heavy-duty broilers—designed for large volume production and fast continuous broiling; grid area varies from 3.3 to 5.0 square feet; may be same height as range section and with high shelf above or integral with an overhead oven, heated by burners in broiler below, or mounted on a conventional range-type oven and with or without overhead warming oven. (2) Combination broiler and griddle units—suitable for small kitchen where space is limited. Fry griddle forms top of broiler and both are heated by the same set of burners but simultaneous use not recommended. (3) Salamander or elevated miniature broiler—mounted above the top of a heavy-duty closed range or over a spreader plate between units of cooking equipment. Features are similar to heavy-duty broiler except for a smaller grid area of only 1.6 to 2.8 square feet. Advantage is that it requires no floor space but may be mounted on separate legs or stand if desired. Used where small amount of broiled foods are served. (4) Hearth-type or open-top broilers—utilize a heavy cast iron grate horizontally above the heat source. Charcoal, or chunks of irregular size ceramic or other refractory material above gas or electric burners, forms the radiant bed of heat. Juice and fat drippings cause smoking and flaming that necessitate an efficient exhaust fan over the broiler. Available in multiple sections of any desired length.

Fryers. Chromium-plated steel, stainless steel; automatic temperature control with signal light and timer; quick heat recovery; cool sediment zone; self-draining device; easy removal of sediment and filtering of fat; capacity expressed in pounds of fat or pounds cooked per hour; fuel input used to determine production capacity also; should fry from 1 1/2 to 2 times the weight of fat per hour.

Types: (1) Conventional instant fat fryers—sizes from 11 by 11 to 24 by 24 in. with fat capacities 13 to 130 pounds. Models are available as freestanding, counter, or built-in; single or multiple units. (2) Pressure fryers—equipped with tightly sealed cover, allowing moisture given off during cooking to build up steam pressure within kettle; cooking accomplished in approximately 1/3 normal time. (3) Semiautomatic—speed production model equipped with conveyor to permit continuous batch cooking and automatic discharge of product as completed.

Installation: Adequate ventilation necessary, venting into hood recommended; flue venting from fryer to general vent flue not desirable; table or workspace adjacent to fryer is necessary.

Tilting Fry Pan. Versatile piece of equipment—can be used as a fry pan, braising pan, griddle, kettle, steamer, thawer, oven, food warmer-server; eliminates most top-of-stove cooking and provides for one-step preparation of many menu items. All surfaces, interior

FIGURE   12.8   Small tilting fry pan for back of counter use. Courtesy, Groen Division, Dover Corporation.

and exterior heavy-duty stainless steel; contoured pouring spout; one-piece counterbalanced hinged cover; self-locking worm and gear tilt mechanism; even-heat smooth flat bottom (either gas or electric); automatic thermostatic heat controls for wide range of temperatures. Available in several sizes and capacities as floor models mounted on tubular legs with or without casters, wall mounted, or small electric table mounted (see Figs. 11.15 and 12.8); conserves fuel and labor; quick-connect installation conducive to rapid rearrangement, easy maintenance, and good sanitation. Easy to clean and reduces use of pots and pans and their washing.

Ovens. Two basic designs for heating ovens: *radiation,* in which heated air circulates around outside of heating chamber and radiates through lining, and *convection,* where heated air from heat source passes through the cabinet. All welded construction of structural steel for durable rigid frames; inner lining of 18 gauge rust proof sheet metal reinforced to prevent buckling; minimum of 4 inches of nonsagging insulation on all sides, up to 10 inches in large bakery ovens; thermostatic heat control precise between 150 and 550°F; signal lights and timer; level oven floor or deck of steel, tile, or transite (concrete and asbestos combination); well-insulated, counterbalanced doors that open level with bottom of oven to support a minimum of 150-pound weight; nonbreakable hinges; concealed manifolds and wiring; cool handles; system designed to eject vapors and prevent flowback of condensate; light operated from outside oven; steam injector for baking of hard rolls; thermocouple attachments for internal food-temperature record, and glass windows in doors available upon request.

Types: (1) Deck (cabinet)—units stacked to save space; separate heating elements and controls for each unit and good insulation between decks; decks at good working heights; 7 or 8 inches clearance for baking, 12 to 16 inches high for roasting; capacity expressed in number of 18 by 26-inch bun pans per deck; pie, cake or baking pans should be of sizes to fit multiples of that dimension; floor space requirements and inside dimensions vary with types; example of a typical 1-section oven of compact design on 23-inch legs:

Floor space requirements	60 1/2 inches wide, 39 1/2 inches deep without flue deflector
Inside dimensions	42 inches wide, 32 inches deep, 7 inches high
Capacity	Two 18×26-inch bun pans; 24 1-pound loaves of bread; 12 10-inch pies
Btu/hour	50,000

(2) Forced circulation cabinet oven—*convection* oven which employs high-speed centrifugal fan to force air circulation and guarantee even-heat distribution by an air-flow pattern over and around product in a minimum of time or from 1/3 to 3/4 of time required in a conventional oven. More cooking is accomplished in smaller space as food is placed on multiple racks instead of on a single deck (see Fig. 12.9).

Sizes vary with the manufacturers but a typical convection oven measures 36 inches wide by 33 inches deep or larger models 45 inches wide by 42 1/2 inches deep. Removable rack glides designed to accommodate 8 or 9 trays or baking sheets, 2 inches apart, thus holding more than other ovens that require greater floor space. Units may be stacked to double the output in the relatively small floor space. Convection ovens must be well insulated; may have interiors of stainless steel or vitreous enameled steel. Shelves and shelf supports lift out for easy cleaning; fitted with inside lights, timer, thermostatic heat control, glass doors or window in doors, removeable spillage pan. Quick-connect installation and addition of casters make for flexibility in arrangement. Muffle-type seal on doors for roasting and baking reduce shrinkage because of moisture retention and reduced time for cooking.

(3) Revolving tray or reel ovens—flat tray decks suspended between 2 revolving spiders in a ferris-wheel type of rotation; compact, space saving;

FIGURE   12.9   Filled baking trays placed in an oven-fitted frame may be rolled directly into the oven from a special designed dolly. Courtesy, The
G. S. Blodgett Co, Inc.

welded steel, heat-tight construction; all parts highly resistant to heat and
corrosion; main bearings and entire tray load supported independently of
side walls; trays stabilized to keep level and sway proof; each tray equipped
with individual emergency release; heavy-duty motor; smooth roller-chain
drive, self-adjusting, automatic controls; example of relative dimensions:
four trays, each 96 inches long by 26 inches wide; capacity, twenty 18 by 26-
inch bun pans; outside, 10 feet 2 inches wide, 7 feet 4 inches deep, 6 feet 7
inches high. Small units 3 1/2 feet deep and 6-pan units available for small
foodservice operations.

(4) Rotary ovens—similar to revolving tray ovens except rotation is on a
vertical axis instead of a horizontal one. Both revolving tray and rotary type
ovens are most suitable for large volume baking.

(5) Microwave ovens—electromagnetic energy directed into heating
cavity by magnetrons producing microwaves that penetrate food, create a
magnetic field, and set up friction, causing almost instantaneous cooking of

the food; energy produced at given rate is not stored nor does it heat the air surrounding or the dish containing the food (glass, china, plastic, paper); components include heating cavity of stainless steel, radio frequency generator, power supply, usually 220 volts, between 30 and 50 amperes; must pass close inspection to assure safety in use; automatic shut-off before door can be opened. Can be stacked; used extensively for fast reheating of prepared bulk or plated foods but items may be cooked quickly and served immediately on the same dish.

STEAM EQUIPMENT

Steam may be supplied from a central heating plant, directly connected to the equipment; or steam may be generated at point of use which requires water connection and means of heating it to form the steam; pressures vary according to needs, with automatic pressure control and safety valve if supply is above 5 to 8 pounds per square inch; equipment of stainless steel or aluminum for rust resistance; smooth exterior and interior surfaces for easy cleaning and sanitation; timing and automatic shut-off devices; concealed control valves; steam cookers offer fast cooking in two general types.

Cabinet Cookers. Steam injected into cooking chamber comes in direct contact with food—to insure clean steam supply may need to generate on the premises from tap water source instead from steam system for a group of buildings; door gaskets to seal; doors of full-floating type, with automatic bar-type slide-out shelves linked to doors; timers and automatic shut-off, and safety throttle valve for each compartment so doors cannot be opened until steam pressure is reduced; perforated or solid baskets for food; capacity in terms of number of 12 by 20-inch counter pans side by side each shelf or 10 by 23-inch bulk pans. Counter pans used both for cooking and serving.

Types: (1) Heavy-duty, direct connected steamers—compartments fabricated to form one piece body and entire interior of stainless steel; 5 to 8 pounds per square inch with continuous steam inflow and drain-off of condensate. One to four compartments with adjustable shelves; inside dimensions 28 x 21 inches desirable to accommodate two 12 x 20-inch counter pans on each shelf, and 10 to 16 inch high. (2) Pressure cookers—operate at 15 pound steam pressure for small-batch speed cooking; reheating frozen meals or thawing and cooking frozen foods; smaller than free-venting cabinets; self-sealing inside door cannot be opened under pressure; 15 pound safety valve and 30 pound gauge; automatic timers and cut offs. Inside

FIGURE 12.10 Self steam-generating kettles and compartment cooker designed as a single unit for a small operation. Courtesy, Columbus Gas of Ohio, Inc.

capacities, from 12 to 40 inches wide, 14 to 28 inches high, 18 to 31 1/2 inches deep; 1 to 3 cooking compartments. (3) Self steam-generating (nonpressure)—intended for installations without direct steam supply; requires water (hot preferred) connection and adequate source of heat supply to produce the steam; steam generators fit below cookers; designs and capacities similar to heavy-duty steamers.

installation: heavy-duty steamers of cabinet type may have pedestal support or be equipped with feet and have at least 6-inch clearance from floor, or be wall mounted to save space; install in drip pan or floor depression with drain; modular units available in many combinations with other steam equipment. (See Fig. 12.10).

Steam-Jacketed Kettles. Two bowllike sections of drawn, shaped, welded aluminum or stainless steel with air space between for circulation of steam to heat inner shell; food does not come in contact with steam; steam outlet safety valve and pressure gauge; direct-connected or self-generated steam supply; full or 2/3 jacketed; stationary or tilting, open or fitted with no-drip, hinged and balanced cover (note Fig. 12.11); mounted on tubular legs, pedestal, wall brackets, or set on table. Power twin-shaft agitator mixer attachment for stirring heavy mixtures while cooking, and electrically operated

FIGURE   12.11   Steam-jacketed kettle cover actuator assembly. Counter-balanced
spring tension holds cover securely tight (a), or open (b) in any
position for safe easy use; cover removable for cleaning. Suited
for all types of kettles either floor or wall mounted, stationary or
tilting.

device to automatically meter water into kettle are available; may
have cold water connection to jacket to cool products quickly after
cooking; modular design (square jacket) for easy combining with
other modular equipment to save space. Basket inserts available for
removing and draining vegetables easily (Fig. 12.12).

Types: (1) Deep kettles, fully or 2/3 jacketed—best for soups, puddings,
pie fillings. (2) Shallow kettles, always full-jacketed—suitable for braising
and browning meats, stews; prevents crushing of under layers of food as in
deep type. (3) Trunnion or tilting kettles—mounted on trunnions with tilting
device and pouring lip for easy unloading; either power-driven or manual

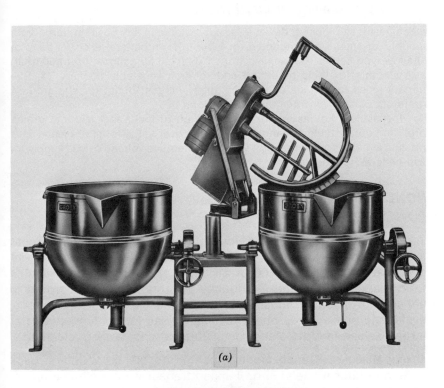

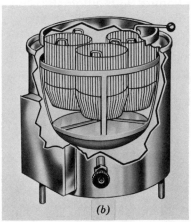

(b)

FIGURE 12.12 Steam-jacketed kettle showing (a) swivel power mixer attachment assembly mounted on extension of back leg of trunniontype kettle; (b) cross-section view of triple basket insert for holding and draining vegetables cooked in kettle. Courtesy, Groen Division, Dover Corporation.

mechanism; self-locking devices to secure kettle in any position; large floor models, or small units mounted on table to form battery; used on deep or shallow-type kettles. Capacities: from 1 quart to 80 gallons; up to 20-quart size suitable for table mounting and rotation vegetable cookery. (4) Stationary types for liquids or thin mixtures—tangent outlet for straight-flow drain-off; capacities: from 10 to 150 gallons.

Installation: kettles set for easy draw-off of food, and drip into grated drain in floor or table; mixing swivel faucet over kettle to fill or clean; table models at height convenient for workers; adequate voltage or gas supply for self-generating models.

NONCOOKING EQUIPMENT

POWER OPERATED

Modern kitchens depend upon motor-driven machines for rapid and efficient performance of many tasks. Safety precautions are necessary. Capacity charts for all types of machines are available from manufacturers and distributors. Motors, built-in according to capacity of machine, must carry peak load easily; specify voltage, cycle, and phase; three-phase is usually used for 3/4 horsepower or larger; sealed-in motors and removable parts for ease of cleaning.

Mixing Machines. Bench models for use on tables, counters, back bars, and floor models; 3- or 4-speed transmission, ball-bearing action; timed mixing control with automatic shut-off; action designed for thorough blending, mixing, and aerating of all ingredients in bowl; electrically controlled brake; possible to change speeds while

FIGURE 12.13   *Power food mixers are available in many sizes and capacities. Thorough mixing of ingredients is made possible by the planetary action of the beater or whip. Product of Hobart Corporation.*

in action on some machines; durable washable finish as stainless steel or anodized aluminum. Bowls: heavily tinned steel, or stainless steel (see Fig. 12.13).

Standard equipment: one bowl, one beater, one whip; other attachments available as bread hook, pastry knife, chopper, slicer, dicer, oil dripper, bowl splash cover, dolly, purchased separately; most models have one or two adapters with smaller bowls, beaters, and whips that may be used on same machine. Capacities: standard, 10, 12, 30, 60, 80, and 140 quarts. Example of one size: 60-quart machine, mashes 40 pounds potatoes, mixes 50 pounds pie dough, mixes 24 quart waffle batter; approximately 24 inches wide, 40 inches deep, 56 inches high.

Choppers, Cutters, Slicers. Some foodservices find their needs for chopping, slicing, and shredding are met through use of mixing machine attachments, while others need specialized pieces of equipment in certain work areas. Various sizes and capacities of such machines are available in pedestal or bench models or mounted on portable stands. A typical slicer is shown in Fig. 12.14.

FIGURE 12.14 Special slawing machine and onion slicer. Cuts up to 400 pounds per hour. Interchangeable shredder, grater, french fry, and julienne plates available. Courtesy, Qualheim, Inc.

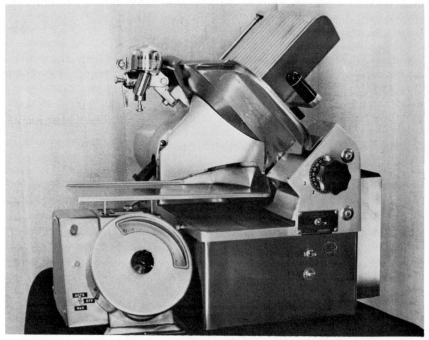

FIGURE 12.15   *Automatic portion control scale slicer is adaptable to operate with most late model gravity feed automatic slicers. It is designed to shut off the slicer when a preset weight of thinly sliced meat drops onto the scale platter. Courtesy, E. L. Sly Co., Portland, Oregon.*

All should be made of smooth, noncorrosive metals, have encased motors, safety protectors over blades, and parts removable for cleaning and should slice in horizontal or angle-fed troughs. Figure 12.15 illustrates how a slicer and portion control scale may be combined into one piece of equipment.

Vertical Speed Cutter Mixer. High-speed vertical cutter-mixer (Fig. 12.16) gray enamel cast iron base, stainless steel or aluminum bowl; blades move at 1750 rpm giving increased product yield and quality as well as speed over conventional mixing. Mixes, cuts, blends, whips, creams, grates, kneads, chops, emulsifies, and homogenizes. Counterbalanced bowl cover interlocks with motor; easy tilt design for emptying. Mounted on tubular steel frame equipped with casters for portability or permanent installations; variety of cutting blades,

FIGURE   12.16   *High-speed cutter-mixer knife blades move at 1750 revolutions per minute. Prepares foods for cooking or serving in seconds. Product of Hobart Corporation.*

shafts, and baffles for specific uses. Capacities: 25, 40, 60, 80, and 130 quarts. Forty-quart model handles 80 pounds ingredients in one load. Cuts 40 pounds frozen meat and blends for meat loaf in 40 seconds; 12 heads lettuce in 3 seconds.

Refrigerators. Detailed information in Chapter 11. Central or self-contained units; water or air-cooled compressors; walk-in, reach-in, pass-through, cabinet convertible temperatures; efficient nonabsorbent insulation; tight-fitting doors, strong no-sag hinges, strong catches; all surfaces and parts cleanable. *Reach-in:* fitted with tray glides to accommodate standard tray sizes, or removable wire or slatted stainless steel shelves (note Fig. 12.17). *Walk-in:* portable, sectional, slatted metal shelving. Some reach-in models may be detached from motor unit to provide portable, temporary refrigerated storage.

Counter units: individual compressors for salad, frozen dessert, milk storage areas; self-leveling dispensers for cold or freezer storage and service. *Ice-makers:* central and self-contained units; cubes, tubes, flakes; capacity, measured in output per hour; many models and sizes are available, (see Figs. 11.6, 11.7, and 12.18). *Water coolers:* glass filler or bubbler faucet; capacity: depends on cooling volume per hour and size of storage tank; designed for convenient storage of clean glasses.

FIGURE 12.17 *Convenient unit refrigerator: exterior surfaced with thermal bonded vinyl in choice of colors, interior silver-tone white vinyl; doors same as outside finish or sliding glass; 3-inch thick glass fiber insulation; may be fitted with pan slides or shelves and 5-inch swivel casters. Product of Hobart Corporation.*

FIGURE 12.18 *Ice cuber with easy access bin in an attractive cabinet. Makers and dispensers recommended at each point of use. Courtesy, Queen Products Division, King-Seeley Thermos Company.*

Dish and Utensil Cleaning Equipment. (1) Pot and pan cleaners. (*a*) *Manually controlled power scrubbing brush,* cleans and polishes; multiple use with accessories, extension cords, scouring brushes, buffers; requires no extra space. (*b*) *Water agitator attachment for pot soaking sinks;* loosens cooked-on food; can be installed with limited space. (2) Dishwashers, pot and pan washers, glass washers. Stainless steel, welded construction; operation control, manual or automatic. This type of equipment discussed in detail in Chapters 10 and 11 (see Figs. 10.13, 10.14, and 11.24).

Dishwashers: Bench or floor models; single or multiple tank; semi- or fully automatic operation; rack or conveyor type for continuous racking; doors or curtains; automatically timed conveyor speed; separate temperature controls for rinse, wash, and final rinse; automatic detergent dispenser; parts removable for cleaning; inspection door for easy access to wash and rinse compartments; scrapping, prerinse and blower-dryer assemblies available; water—pressure, temperature, hardness, pipe size; waste disposer.

Capacity: expressed in number of pieces washed per hour; many sizes from 1-tray bench model, 22 inches long, 23 inches wide up to heavy-duty conveyor machine, approximately 30 feet long. Trend is toward smaller units to conserve space.

Racks: chrome plated or stainless steel, plastic-coated, removable and adaptable dividers; or all-plastic, light-weight, space-saving nesting racks. Open divided racks for cups, glasses; designed for stacking in storage.

Conveyors: linked metal, plastic, or metal tipped with plastic or nylon projections to hold dishes in inclined position.

WASTE DISPOSERS

One system for the disposal of waste may solve the problem in a given situation but, in many cases, it may be feasible to combine two or more of the following methods.

Unit disposers for food waste at vegetable and salad preparation, sinks, and dish scrapping areas eliminate the need for garbage can collections, storage, and outside pickup unless their installation and use are prohibited by environmental controls. All waste paper, cardboard cartons, wood crates, plastics, tin cans, broken china, and glassware (and garbage) might need to be discharged into dumpster bins for pickup if incineration of burnable waste is restricted by antipollution regulations in the community.

Can and Bottle Crushers are capable of reducing this type of disposable bulk up to 90 percent and cut labor costs, refuse space,

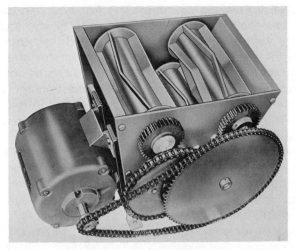

FIGURE 12.19   *Rugged crushing mechanism of can and bottle crusher. Rollers set in "v" design prevent clogging and progressively reduce cans to smallest bulk possible. Courtesy, Qualheim, Inc.*

and pick-up costs. Capacities of models vary from 50 cans and bottles per minute to 7500 per hour. Design of such a crushing mechanism is shown in Fig. 12.19.

The use of *compactors* to reduce the volume is a convenient and economical aid to the disposal of all waste in many foodservices. One model with a 7500-pound ram pressure can compact paper, milk cartons, cans, bottles, food scraps to a minimum 5-to-1 ratio or as high as 20-to-1, depending on the combination of materials. Discharge of the compacted material, up to 50 pounds, into a poly bag or carton on a dolly makes it ready for short-time storage and haulaway. Most machines operate on a 120-volt, 20-ampere outlet, have safety interlocks throughout for operating protection, and a sanitizing-deodorizing spray that may be released at each return stroke of the compaction ram to avoid any objectionable odor from the compacted mass.

The *pulping system* reduces the volume of disposable materials such as food scraps, paper, plastic, and cooked bones up to 85 percent, depending on the mix. Cans, silverware, and some glass are tolerated but are automatically ejected from the pulping tank into a trash box. Durable teeth on a rotating disc and cutters pulp the material in the tank. It is then circulated to a powerful waterpress above, reducing the pulp to a semidry form that is forced into a

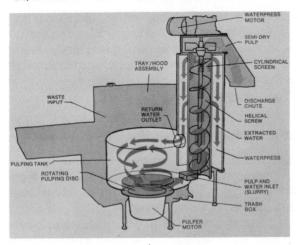

FIGURE   12.20   Diagram showing how pulpable waste may be reduced in volume
and form. Product of Hobart Corporation.

discharge chute to containers for removal as low-volume waste. The
water from the press recirculates to the pulping tank. This equipment is available in several sizes. It may be incorporated into the
dishwashing system or other area where pulpable waste originates.
(See Figs. 10.6 and 12.20.)

TRANSPORT EQUIPMENT

Usually powered equipment for transport of food and supplies
within a foodservice is kept to minimum distances by careful planning of area relationships. A thorough study of the advantages, capabilities, and maintenance factors should precede the selection of
a system for a particular situation. Also, automatic and emergency
shutoffs, enclosed but easy access to working parts, safety, and
cleanability are important features to consider.

Conveyors and Subveyors. Reverse for two-way service; emergency
brakes; safety guards; automatic stop and start with removal of tray,
or continuous flow. *Conveyors:* horizonal transportation; stationary
or mobile units for flexibility of tray or food assembly. *Subveyors:*
vertical conveying, used where space may be limited on a single
floor and work or serving units are on different floors.

Monorail and Driverless Vehicles. These require special equipment and
installations; reduce labor and hand-pushing of carts; speedy; rela-

tively expensive to install. Monorail requires overhead rail and "Amsco" system a special electronic track under the floor. Cars of the latter are monitored from a control panel; are powered by batteries; directed over the track to locations on the same floor or to a bank of special elevators that automatically open and close on signal and exit on the assigned floor.

NONMECHANICAL KITCHEN EQUIPMENT

Tables and Sinks: Often fabricated by specification order to fit space and need; stainless steel, No. 12 or 14 gauge, No. 4 grind; welded and polished joinings; rounded corner construction; seamless stainless steel tubular supports with welded cross rails and braces of same material; adjustable inside threaded stainless steel rounded or pear-shaped feet; work tables may be fitted with ball-bearing rubbertired casters, 2 swivel and 2 stationary, brakes on 2 casters.

Tables. Top of one sheet without seams; edges: integrally finished, rolled edge, raised rolled edge where liquids are used, turned up as flange or splashback and with rolled edge. Legs and feet: tubular, welded or seamless metal; adjustable; simple design; provide a minimum of 6 inches of space between bottom of unit and floor; drawers: operate on ball bearings, equipped with stop, removable. Undershelves: stationary bar, slatted, solid, removable sections; sink or bain-marie.

Dimensions: standard, length, 48, 60, 72, 84, 96, 108, 120 inches; width 24, 30, 36 inches; height, 34 inches; other dimensions by individual specification.

Types: *Baker's tables*—fitted with drawers; separate storage bins as specified. *Salad tables*—with or without refrigerated work space and storage, sinks. *Sandwich tables*—refrigerated storage for fillings; removable cutting boards. *Dish tables*—well-braced sturdy understructure; 3-inch upturned and rolled edges, higher if joined to wall; scrap block, waste drain, sinks for soaking, over-and-under shelves, rack return, tray rest; adequate space for receiving, soiled dishes, clean dishes, preflush.

Sinks. One, two, three compartments; all-welded seamless construction, drainboard and splashback integral from one sheet of metal, rolled edges; corners fully rounded with 1 inch radius, coves spherical in shape at intersection of corners; bottom of each compartment scored and pitched to outlet; outlet recessed 5 inches in diameter, 1/2 inch deep, fitted with nonclog waste outlet; partitions: two thicknesses formed of one sheet of metal, folded and welded to bottom and sides of sink; provision for overflow; drainboards pitched to drain into sink; drainboards supported by channel braces to sink legs or wall-bracketed, if longer than 42 inches usually supported by two pipe legs at end away from sink; removable strainer at waste outlet; external lever control for outlet valve; stationary or swing faucets.

Dimensions, standard single compartment, 20, 24, 30, 36, 48, 60, 72 inches long, 20, 24, 30 inches wide, 14, 16 inches deep; two-compartment, 36, 42, 48, 54, 60, 72 inches long, 18, 22, 24, 30 inches wide, 14, 16 inches deep. Others by individual specification; 38-inch height convenient for sinks.

Storage Cabinets, Racks, Carts. Cabinets and racks stationary or portable. Open or closed; shelves: attached, removable, adjustable, tray slides; sturdy construction for use; solid floor; bolted or welded; doors, hinged or side sliding, side sliding removable, suspension hung. Both stationary or portable types may be heated or refrigerated. Size determined by needs and space.

Scales. Heavy-duty *platform scale* built into floor of receiving room area for weighing in supplies and food; weight indicator should be plainly visible from both front and back. *Exact-weight* floor or table models in storeroom, ingredient room, bakeshop, and where recipes are made up. *Portion scales* for weighing individual servings where needed.

Cooking Utensils. Strong and durable to withstand heavy wear; non-toxic material; resistant to chipping, dents, cracks, acids, alkalis; cleanable; even heat spread; highly polished metal reflects heat, dull metal absorbs and browns food more readily in baking; variety of sizes of sauce pans, sauce pots, stock pots, fry pans, roast and bake pans; *aluminum heavy duty*—double-thick bottoms, extra-thick edge, *semiheavy*—lighter weight, uniform thickness, rolled edge; *stainless steel*—uniform thickness, spot heats over direct fire. Small equipment as pudding pans, pie and cake pans, quart and gallon measures, mixing bowls of lighter weight metals. Pudding and counter pans selected to fit serving table, refrigerator, and mobile racks for flexibility of use: 12 by 20 inch-size recommended. Clamped on lids cut spillage losses in transporting prepared foods.

Cutlery. High-carbon tooled steel or high-carbon chrome-vanadium steel; full tang construction; compression-type nickel-silver rivets; shapes of handles and sizes of items varied to meet needs; handle and blade weight balanced for easy handling.

SERVING EQUIPMENT

COUNTERS

Attractive, compact, efficient arrangement designed for specific foodservice; welded and polished in one piece; hot and cold units well insulated; easily cleaned; separate temperature controls for each unit of heated section; counter guard shields for open food display sections; portable or built-in self-leveling dish and tray storage may be desired; adequate tray slide to prevent accidents.

SERVING UTENSILS

Variety of sizes of ladles, long-handled spoons, perforated, slotted, and solid; spatulas; and ice cream dippers; selected to give predetermined portion size. Capacity or size marked on ladle handles and on dippers.

Special counter equipment: Convenient arrangement; easily operated automatic heat controls. Coffee maker—urn or battery vacuum makers with cup storage near; toasters, egg cookers, grills with hoods; temporary storage cabinets for hot cooked foods, rolls—controls for temperature and moisture content; freezer cabinet unit for ice creams; bread dispensers; milk-dispensing machines.

SELF/LEVELING DISPENSERS.

Counterweighted springs bring platform to uniform level upon removal of item; for foods, dishes, containers; heated, refrigerated, or freezer storage; mobile, stationary, or built-in; open or closed frames of stainless, galvanized, carbon steel or aluminum; noncorrosive springs. Tube type: for plates, saucers, bowls; chassis type: accommodates square or rectangular trays, or racks, empty or filled; adjustable to vary dispensing height. (see Fig. 12.21).

Coffee Equipment. Coffee making equipment falls into two general types: (1) urns for making large quantities of coffee when many people are served in a short period of time, and (2) small electronic automatic brewing units for a continuous fresh supply of the beverage. Requirements are fairly simple in either case but important to the making of an acceptable product: glass or stainless steel liners for urns, glass or stainless steel decanters for the automatic brewing machines; fluted paper filters; controlled hot water temperature, coffee and water measurement, infusion time, brewing speed and

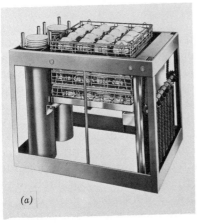

FIGURE 12.21   Self-leveling dispensers. (a) For in-counter installation, showing construction of counterweighted springs that control height of platform. (b) A mobile combination dispenser for cups and saucers for added convenience at the serving counter; cups left in racks in which washed. Courtesy, American Machine and Foundry Company.

FIGURE 12.22   Quick-disconnect system for utilities outlets provide for safety in use, convenience, and easy care of beverage equipment. Courtesy, Avtec Industries, Inc.

holding temperatures; easily cleaned. Installation with quick-disconnect utilities outlets provide for easy relocation of equipment (See Fig. 12.22). The use of freeze-dry coffee simplifies the process, reduces time and labor, and eliminates the necessity of discarding coffee grounds.

MOBILE FOOD SERVING CARTS.

Specialized equipment for transporting bulk or served food some distance to the consumer; well insulated, automatic temperature controls; engineered for ease in moving and turning; circumference bumper guards; designed for easy cleaning; may require high voltage outlets; combination heated, nonheated, low temperature and refrigerated sections; beverage dispensers and other accessories as found on serving counters. (See Chapter 5 for details.)

The selection of foodservice equipment by any arbitrary rule would be unwise and ill advised. Each operation must be studied to determine the real needs and purchases made accordingly. *The foregoing statements are suggested as a guide only in helping to recall basic considerations regarding various items of equipment.* A suggested list of equipment for a particular installation is found in Appendix A.

SELECTED REFERENCES

Clawson, August H., *Equipment Maintenance Manual,* Ahrens, 1951.

Dana, Arthur W., *Kitchen Planning for Quantity Food Service,* Harper and Brothers, New York, 1949.

Jernigan, Anna Katherine, and Lynne Nannen Ross, *Food Service Equipment: Selection, Arrangement, and Use,* The Iowa State University Press, Ames, Iowa, 1974.

Kahrl, William L., *Planning and Operating A Successful Food Operation,* Chain Store Publishing Corporation, New York, 1973.

Kotschevar, Lendal H., and Margaret E. Terrell, *Food Service Planning: Layout and Equipment,* Wiley, New York, 1961.

Schneider, Nicholas F., Edgar A. Jahn, and Arthur Q. Smith, *Commercial Kitchens,* American Gas Association, New York, 1962.

The Anatomy of Foodservice Design 1, Jule Wilkinson, Editor, Cahners, Boston, 1975.

The National Sanitation Foundation, N.S.F. Building, Ann Arbor, Michigan. *National Sanitation Foundation Standards* (see Selected References Chapter 10).

Thomas, Orpha Mae Huffman, *A Scientific Basis for the Design of Institution Kitchens,* Teachers College, Columbia University, New York, 1947.

Current professional journals and trade magazines.

Manufacturers' leaflets, brochures, catalogs, and specifications.

13.
FURNISHINGS AND EQUIPMENT FOR DINING ROOMS

It has long been a well-established fact that the furnishings and equipment for dining rooms of institutions help materially to create the atmosphere and beauty that have so much to do with the happiness and satisfaction of guests. A well-prepared but simple meal attractively served in an artistically furnished dining room may be a delightful experience. The features other than food and service that may contribute to the success of such a meal are the architecture, which has been discussed in a previous chapter, the window treatment, the selection and arrangement of furniture, and the linen, dinnerware, and tableware. The type, number, and quality of the furnishings selected depend on the clientele, the geographic location, the architectural plan of the building, the kind of service, and the funds available. All furnishings should be pleasing, durable, serviceable, and easy to maintain.

WINDOW TREATMENT

The beauty of the average institution dining room windows or group of windows is enhanced by the introduction of decorative effects produced through the use of roller, Venetian or Roman shades, glass curtains; draperies; or a combination of two or more of these.

ROLLER, VENETIAN, AND ROMAN SHADES

Window shades are used not only for the decorative effect produced but also to subdue the natural light in daytime and to insure privacy. It is most desirable that window shades be uniform in color and type from an external view. If the color of the shade that fits into the interior decorative scheme is not desirable for the outside, a two-tone material may be used.

Roller shades are available in many weights, colors, and qualities of materials. Different types and qualities of materials and treatments produce cloths of many different weights and wearing qualities. A good quality of cambric, a pyroxylin-treated cambric, and a synthetic resin, fire-retardant cambric are the types most commonly used in institutions. A good quality shade cloth shows no pin holes and does not crack easily and is semiopaque in darker colors, graduating to translucent in lighter colors. There should be no appreciable alteration in color upon exposure to light, and any shade cloth selected should be washable.

Venetian shades pleasingly combine the functional and decorative features desired in a window shade. They permit free passage of air and light at the same time that privacy is attained and help to insulate against both heat and cold. They are constructed of slats of wood or metal, usually spring-tempered aluminum, held in cloth or plastic bands and are available in many colors and combinations of colors. A pleasing variation in window treatment is obtained and straps are eliminated if the slats are installed in a vertical instead of the conventional horizontal arrangement.

Roman shades are popular in dining rooms, because they add color and texture to the decor and eliminate the need for further window treatment. They are available in solid or varicolored combinations of materials such as wood slats, reeds, bamboo, plastic, fiber glass, and cotton or synthetic yarns, woven into pleasing and artistic designs.

The initial cost of Venetian and Roman blinds is higher than that of roller shades. However, the upkeep cost is reduced, replacements are available, and the artistic values far surpass those of roller shades. Firms from which these types are purchased take all measurements and make installations.

The longevity of window shades depends on the care and attention given them. Poor adjustment, undue exposure to the elements, and careless cleaning methods will help to deteriorate rapidly the best of materials. The usual procedure in cleaning roller shades is to unroll, brush, place flat on a table, and sponge with neutral suds applied with a soft brush, rubber sponge, or soft cloth. The shade is rinsed and rubbed lightly with a dry, absorbent cloth or towel until practically dry. This process is then repeated on the reverse side, and the shade is rehung at the window to complete the drying.

The cleaning of Venetian blinds is more easily accomplished if they are left hanging at the windows than when removed. They require little more than periodic treatment with a cleaning and polishing wax (antistatic product) and regular dusting, as a piece of furniture. The dusting may be done by hand or machine. An efficient hand method is for the worker to wear washable cotton glove dusters that permit freedom of movement of the thumb and first finger to clean under the tapes. Open and slant the slats toward the worker; begin at the center tape with thumbs underneath and fingers above the same slat; move hands simultaneously to opposite ends of the slat, drop down to the slat below and dust toward the center; repeat the process to the bottom of the blind. The use of a V-shaped vacuum cleaner attachment with removable Dynel rolls is a highly effective and efficient method for dusting the slats of Venetian blinds, and use of a vacuum attachment for dusting the tapes is recommended. If washing is necessary, avoid alkaline cleaners such as ammonia since they tend to affect the finish, and washing in a vat or with a hose is not recommended for Venetian shades. Tapes and cords may be replaced easily.

Roman shades need the same careful handling and may be kept dusted by use of the vacuum cleaner attachment.

WINDOW CURTAINS

Window curtains should not interfere with the admittance of sunlight and air. Furthermore, they should serve to introduce a decorative note in color and design, to correct bad proportions in windows or walls, to relieve the severe effect of the casing, to soften the light, to insure privacy, to shut out an undesirable view, and to create atmosphere.

The selection of curtains for a dining room depends on the type of institution, the architectural features, the use of the room, the clientele, and the amount of money available. The suitability of material and style to the particular setup is most important.

The length and style of curtains influence the decorative effect. Long curtains hanging to the floor express dignity and fomality. Curtains that reach the window sill or cover the apron are informal. Those that hang straight and repeat the lines of the room are usually preferred, although the use of slightly curved lines in curtains may fit in with certain lines in the room. The proportion and type of window and room also influence the hanging of the curtains.

Window curtains or hangings for the institution dining room are divided into two groups. Sheer materials, such as net, scrim, marquisette, gauze, and voile, are obtainable in cotton, rayon, nylon, Orlon, fiber glass, and certain other of the man-made fibers. When hung next to the window, they are known as glass curtains. Heavier and more colorful fabric, such as cretonne, chintz, homespun, damask, brocade, handblocked linen, and fiber glass, are hung at the sides of the window or group of windows next to the wall, and are commonly termed draperies. The window treatment may provide for the use of either glass curtains, draperies, or both. If the draperies are hung so that they draw entirely across the window, the glass curtain is often omitted, or it may be made of a fairly heavy material hung on a second traverse rod, to eliminate the need for window blinds and to introduce a variation in the color scheme. This treatment is especially good in buildings of modern design where the windows may extend from ceiling to floor and form the outside wall of the room.

Glass Curtains. Glass curtains should give a feeling of privacy without obstructing the view; they soften but do not shut out the light. Rayon materials are used extensively but must be handled carefully. When wet their strength is decreased, and they are readily pulled out of shape. With careful handling normal strength and size are restored upon drying. Weight for weight, rayon curtains are less strong than cotton and often more sheer. Glass curtain fabrics made of certain of the acrylic synthetic fibers are highly acceptable for use in institutions because of their many fine qualities such as durability and resistance to the deteriorating effects of sunlight, heat, atmospheric gases, moths, and mildew; launderability; quick-drying properties and dimensional stability; and availability in a wide variety of colors, textures, and designs. Also, many other of the new man-made fibers and natural fibers subjected to new and improved methods of treatment have some of the same qualities and lend themselves to specific uses. Since progress in this area is rapid and continuous, it is best to seek the advice and help of qualified textile-research personnel before making the final selection of glass curtains for an institution.

Beige, ecru, cream, and the color of the wall are preferred colors for glass curtains. Standards for the average cotton or rayon glass curtain materials are 34 to 42 inches in width and 8 to 12 yards to the pound. The weights of similar fabrics made of the other fibers vary according to the denier or fineness of the yarns used. The majority of glass curtain materials are of the leno or gauze weave.

Glass curtains require frequent laundering. They may be drip-dried or partially dried and ironed, except those made of fibers such as Orlon and fiber glass, which are hung at the window to dry. Frequent laundering, followed by reversing the curtains top and bottom if hems are of equal width, helps to equalize the tendering or weakening of their parts. All sections are thus exposed equally to natural deterioration from sunlight, wind, and heat from radiators.

Draperies. Draperies play a large part in the decoration of any room. They are used to advantage in creating new proportions in rooms and in producing atmosphere. The variety and prices of materials suitable for institution draperies are almost unlimited. If the budget calls for inexpensive curtains, a good quality of material available in the price level should be selected, and the style chosen should not be elaborate. Relatively inexpensive fabrics, such as printed linens or cretonnes, adapt themselves well to this treatment, and such materials may wear several years and prove to be entirely satisfactory. The increased use of synthetic fibers in drapery materials has made available fabrics of rich and heavy appearance at reasonable cost. A furnishings budget on a higher price level will permit the use of such luxury fabrics as damasks, silks, velvets, and those made from the more expensive man-made fibers. Choice among them would depend on the nature of the other furnishings and the individual taste of the person responsible for the furnishings problem. Linings for draperies are usually sateen, in a neutral color or one that harmonizes with both interior and exterior color schemes or self-materials. They give body to curtains, make them fall into graceful folds, and protect the colors, thus increasing the life of the curtains. Inner linings are used when heavier effects are desired. Weights in hems help to make draperies hang straight. Curtains mounted on traverse rods or crane-type fixtures require less handling than those not hung in this manner. This type of curtain needs to be dusted and brushed frequently and is usually dry cleaned instead of laundered.

Fireproofing of draperies reduces the fire hazards and is required by law in most cities. Fiber glass material requires no further fireproofing treatment.

Glare from direct sunlight and deterioration and fading of curtains and fabrics in other furnishings may be lessened appreciably if black or tinted glass is used. A chemical coating of glass tint may be applied to the inside of regular glass windows. This treatment becomes relatively permanent, moisture proof, and resistant to scratches after a 30-day curing period. The degree of light deflection depends on the tint, which reduces the transfer of ultraviolet rays through the glass and also helps to insulate the room.

FURNITURE

Furniture for use in dining rooms of institutions should be suitable to the type of institution and foodservice for which it is purchased. Material, weight, design, construction, finish, and ease of cleaning are other important considerations in selecting furniture for this part of the food unit. Here, as in the selection of equipment, the consideration of available funds is necessary. It is possible to obtain different effects on the same price level through the use of various types of materials and designs and by the arrangement of the furniture in the room.

MATERIALS

Wood is the material often made into institution dining room furniture although metals and molded plastics or fiber glass have been introduced extensively. Hardwoods used in making furniture come from deciduous trees such as oak, maple, walnut, gum, birch, beech, elm, and basswood. The structural cells in the hardwoods are thick walled with much variation in size and shape, which gives a characteristic grain to the wood. The softwoods are trees that have needlelike or scalelike leaves, usually retained during the fall and winter. Pine, spruce, fir, cedar, hemlock, and cypress belong to this group. Although wide differences are found between the woods from the various sources included in each of these groups, in general, hardwood is regarded as far more desirable than softwood for furniture construction. Its points of superiority are hardness and strength that give it ability to resist wear, rigidity and permanence, the natural beauty of the grain, the capacity to take stains and finishes, and reasonable cost of upkeep.

The *metals* most often used for dining room furniture are aluminum and chromium-plated steel or brass. The advantages of aluminum are its light weight, high malleability and ductility, adaptability to a variety of finishes; also it is easily cleaned and relatively inexpensive. Chromium-plated steel and chromium-plated brass are cold in appearance. Of the two, chromium-plated brass is preferred because of its freedom from corrosion. Metals are used almost entirely in furniture of the modernistic type and often are combined with some one of the colorful and durable plastic leather or clothlike materials as upholstery on chairs, or with the hard-finished surfaces such as table tops. Well-constructed metal furniture is durable, snagproof, and requires relatively low upkeep.

Plastics and fiber glass are used extensively for dining chairs. These materials are easily molded into body contour shapes in a single-piece seat and back to which metal legs are attached. Advantages of these materials are durability, light weight, ease of cleaning, low maintenance cost, resistance to scratching and marring, and availability in a wide range of colors. The simplicity of the design of chairs made from these materials gives a modern appearance to the rooms in which they are used.

The furniture for dining rooms in institutions should be in keeping with the architectural features of the building and usually is of conservative design. Simplicity of design produces a pleasing effect and facilitates the care and upkeep of furniture where repetition of numbers of the same article is necessary, such as chairs and tables in the large dining room. Modern dining tables and seating equipment are available in a variety of weights, types, and designs that combine beauty and style with superior strength and utility.

CONSTRUCTION FEATURES

The construction features in the manufacture of wood furniture are major factors in its permanence and durability. Much of the furniture made today is of veneered construction. The advantages of this type of construction over solid wood are increased serviceability, economy, and beauty. It is estimated that a properly constructed veneered panel is approximately 80 percent stronger than solid lumber of equal thickness. Because of the scarcity and cost of the more rare and beautiful woods, it is economically impossible to construct furniture of solid woods, whereas the use of these fine woods as a veneer over a less expensive core makes a beautiful, durable, and relatively inexpensive piece of furniture.

Rigidity and solidary are important, and it is essential that good workmanship and appropriate methods of construction be followed. Strength and durability of wood furniture are obtained by firm joinings and reinforced by appropriate glue blocks and screws. The mortise and tenon and dowel joints are most satisfactory in the construction of tables, chairs, and serving tables (see Fig. 13.1). Glue that is resistant to water and washing solution, applied to the pins that fit into the sockets, increases strength, and the greater the number of dowels the more satisfactory in most cases. Corner blocks, or fitted blocks screwed to the rails, reinforce the joinings and prevent the cracking off of dowels under pressure. Close inspection of the underside of tables and chairs discloses much concerning the degree of workmanship and the method of construction.

In addition to the general construction features, special attention should be given the legs and backs of chairs. Chair legs may be sawed from a single board or be bent to form after they have been temporarily softened, or built up by gluing layers of wood together. Chairs of the first kind may split off where the post begins to slope backward if the grain of the wood is short at this point. The bentwood type is light in weight, strong and sturdy, and the grain of the wood follows the shape of the post. These chairs may change shape in an atmosphere of relatively high humidity.

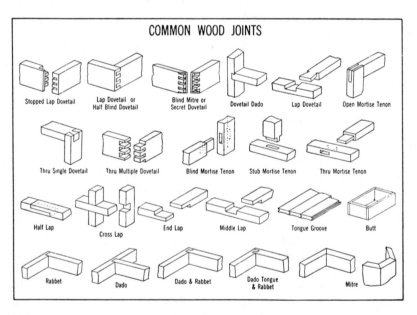

FIGURE   13.1   *Common cuts and joints in wood furniture construction. Courtesy, Stanley Tools, New Britain, Connecticut.*

A satisfactory finish for furniture made of wood is a lustrous semigloss in contrast to the glassy, shiny polish of inexpensive furniture. This finish is obtained by first sponging and sanding, then staining to bring out the color and beauty of the wood. The wood is then filled to prevent dust from entering the pores and, finally, oil, wax, varnish, lacquer, or matte finish applied to protect the wood, facilitate cleaning and enhance the beauty of furniture. Special wood table tops may be made by building up several layers of wood glued together so that the grains run at right angles to each other. This construction is known as laminated and is used to prevent warping or cracking caused by a change of size in one direction only. If the tops are made of several layers of wood with a veneer surface, the edges are usually finished by binding with a strip of solid wood, rounded at the corners and beveled on the edges to give a smooth surface. Other edges are hard finished, beveled or straight, or bound with metal stripping.

Table tops are often made of materials that may be acidproof, moistureproof, noninflammable, scratchproof, and easily cleaned, or they may be made to have these characteristics by applying certain finishes. The development of the decorative plastic laminates for table tops has made possible a great variety of long-wearing, heat-resistant, nonchip, nonpeel, or noncrack surfaces from which to choose. Such table tops are available in wood-grain patterns, plain colors, or in a multiplicity of designs and colors and are applied to wood tops or may be attached directly to the framework of the table and finished with a binding of the same material or of metal. Table tops must be mounted securely either on legs or pedestals. Often this is done by a combination of braces, corner blocks, screws, and glue to make for solidarity. Collapsible tables must have the tops well braced and be tightly hinged to the supporting structures.

Dining tables may be of many shapes and sizes and constructed of various materials. Round, square, or rectangular tables seating four, six, or eight persons are preferred in most foodservices. Long, narrow tables (5 to 12 feet by 24 to 28 inches) have been popular in school and industrial foodservices but are being replaced rapidly by smaller tables, which help to produce an atmosphere of spaciousness and permit small friendly groupings of the diners. Booth arrangements with upholstered seats are popular in public and semipublic dining rooms. Restaurants and hotels usually have most need for tables seating two or four guests, but always have facilities for larger numbers. The average table space allowance is 24 inches per person, and 30 inches is the average table height. Standard foursome tables are 30 by 30, 36 by 36, or 45 by 45 inches. Special consideration in selection of tables for a self-service unit is necessary to assure a size large enough to accommodate patrons' trays. Tables are available in an unlimited number of sizes, and selection must be made on the basis of needs of the foodservice and the available space.

SELECTIONS

Comfort is a most important consideration in the selection of furniture. Chairs too low or tables too high for the average person to use comfortably are poor investments. The seats of chairs are considered the best height when they are the same distance from the floor as the knee. Eighteen inches is accepted as a good standard, and slight deviations from this measure in either direction are scarcely noticeable. The average depth of seats from the front to the rear is 19 inches, and a 3/8-inch downward slant to the back is advisable. The standard for the top of the back support is 17 to 19 inches above the seat of the chair, with the slant of the back dependent on the slant of the seat. A good average is 3 to 4 inches downward slant. Some chairs are designed as "wall saving," with rear legs extended further than the back of the chair, thus preventing wall marking. The sitting test is the most reliable in selecting dining room chairs. A chair that supports the body comfortably, slants so that the sitter does not slide, and is easy to get in or out of is invariably the one that will give the most lasting satisfaction and comfort. Arm chairs require more space but are preferable in leisure dining situations and for older persons.

Stainless steel or brass ferrules encasing the lower part of wood table and chair legs help prevent splitting and scarring of the wood and are decorative and easily cleaned. Also, wood dining room table and chair legs should be fitted with smooth metal or plastic glides, inset in rubber, to reduce noise and increase the ease of moving them. The legs of all-metal furniture are often fitted with rubber cushioned ball-point glides to reduce noise, align with the floor, and keep the furniture in position, especially on composition flooring.

The multiple use of space in modern buildings has made folding tables and chairs and detachable table tops or stack chairs a necessity in many foodservices. Durable, well-designed, attractive, and comfortable dining room folding furniture is available in many materials. The tables may be constructed for storage in as small as 3-inch wide spaces, which is a definite factor in the planning of floor and storage spaces and their maximum utilization.

Stack chairs have largely replaced folding chairs in many food-services, especially for banquet and multipurpose rooms. Less handling and about the same amount of storage space are required as for folding chairs. They are available in many designs, colors, and materials. Usually the framework is of metal with plastic or fiber glass seat and back, or they may be upholstered with cloth, leather, or plastic material. Storage on dollies facilitates ease of handling and storage.

The tables in the average institution dining room may be kept in good condition by washing with a neutral soap, rinsing, and polishing with a soft cloth after each use. Occasional waxing or refinishing of wood tops may be necessary, depending on the permanence of the original finish and the amount of wear. Dusting the chairs with a slightly dampened cloth keeps them in good condition.

TOP OF TABLE ITEMS

LINEN

For many people much of the charm of a foodservice is conditioned, if not determined, by the use of clean table linen of good quality, freshly and carefully placed. Although table surfaces have been made that give a satisfactory effect for certain informal meals, as yet none can contribute the same interest and charm as a snowy linen cloth. Paper napkins and place mats and plastics have replaced cloth in many foodservices for convenience and economy but have had far from complete acceptance. Therefore, the choice of linen remains a responsibility of the food director, and attention to its proper maintenance is one of her tasks.

MATERIALS

Table linens may be listed as pure linen, union, rayon, cotton, cotton mercerized, or linenized damasks, and the polyester-cotton blends. The quality of linen fabrics is determined by the kind of yarn, the type of weave, the texture, durability, and clearness of color. Line yarns made of long flax fibers are used in weaving fine linens. The surface of the material is smooth and lustrous with no fuzzy ends. Yarns of different size when woven into cloth will make heavy, uneven spots throughout the material. Such variations of texture not only detract from the beauty but result in an unevenness in wear. Linen is available in half-bleached, three-quarter-bleached, full-bleached, or in pastel colors. Spots and stains are easily removed from linen, because of the characteristics of linen fibers.

Cotton fibers may be used in combination with linen or rayon in the union damasks to produce durable and satisfactory table coverings and napkins. Rayon and cotton blend table napkins are highly resistant to wear and often superior to all-cotton or all-linen napkins in appearance and breaking strength. Cotton is used alone in plain cotton, mercerized, or linenized fabrics. The last two fabrics are so treated after being woven that a permanent finish is produced that gives the cloth characteristics similar to linen. The wearing quality of cotton fabrics is better than that of linen, less loss in strength occurs through laundering, and it does not lint. Linen, on the other hand, gives greater satisfaction in use, is more attractive, and is lintless.

Table linen may be woven as single or double damask, the terms indicating the difference in the type of looms used in the construction. In the single damask the filling threads skip or float over four warp threads and go under the fifth; in the double damask, the filling threads skip over seven warp threads and go under the eighth, and in some damasks even more. Single and double damasks are sometimes known as 5- and 8-shaft linen. To compensate for the longer floats in double damask, a higher yarn count is used. Usually, single damasks have the same number of warp and filling yarns, the count ranging from 100 to 200 to the square inch. Double-damask linen has twice as many filling yarns as warp and the counts range from 165 to 400 to the inch. The weave alone, however, does not indicate quality. Although double damask formerly was thought to be superior to single, this is true only if high-quality yarns and good construction are used. Single damask of good quality is preferable because shorter yarn floats make for greater firmness and wearability. Also, small design motifs make for greater strength than large ones because of the shorter yarn floats required.

Because of the high initial and maintenance costs of both linen and cotton cloths, those of a 50-50 blend of Polyester and cotton with a no-iron finish are rapidly replacing the former in other than the most sophisticated foodservices. Polyester yarns are used in the making of lace cloths as well as the plain woven ones.

Table linen may be purchased in white, in colors, or in white with colored borders or designs. Colored linen is popular as place mats and luncheon cloths for breakfast and luncheon services. Colored linens are used to help create "atmosphere" in many dining rooms. Pink and yellow are most popular among the many colors available, but the crisp, clean white cloth is traditionally preferred by many operators and patrons. All classes of table linen including colored rayon and cotton damasks are available in a number of patterns or designs, either as made-up pattern cloths or by the yard.

SIZE

The size and shape of the tables will determine the *sizes* of cloths needed. The cloth should be large enough to hang 7 to 12 inches below the table top at both sides and ends, with allowances made for shrinkage according to the material selected. The usual sizes of tablecloths are 52 by 52 inches square, 60 by 80 inches, 67 by 90 to 102 inches or longer, depending on the length of banquet tables. Some places use a table-size top over the regular cloth for frequent changes and reduce laundry costs.

Common sizes for dinner napkins in institutions are 18, 20, or 22 inches.

SELECTION

Specifications for the selection of table linen should include thread count, breaking strength, weight per square yard, and amount of sizing and finishing material. Federal specifications for linen call for a minimum of 84 yarns in the warp and 84 yarns in the filling with a breaking strength of 100 pounds. Institutions often list 140- to 160-yarn count to the inch as a desirable standard. Higher-count linen is beautiful but may be more expensive and less durable for heavy wear. Smaller count is thin and flimsy or coarse if of standard weight. Table linen with a breaking strength of 110 pounds warp and 120 pounds filling is strong and durable for institution use. It is most important that the yarn be even and that the warp and filling yarns be similar in size and number in order to equalize the wear. A medium weight is usually preferable for institutions. Any weight less than 6 ounces per square yard is considered too light for satisfactory wear.

In purchasing linen it is well to have laboratory tests made of samples of the particular materials in which one is interested and to base selection on the findings instead of being guided by personal likes and external appearances.

The initial price ot table linen, although large, represents only part of the outlay. Other factors to be considered are the maintenance or upkeep and the replacement costs. Consideration of these costs has led many foodservices whose budgets might have provided for the initial outlay to eliminate linen and substitute finished table tops and linen or paper mats and paper napkins.

CARE

The life of linen depends more on the number of launderings than on its age. The average length of life of linen for the institution foodservice is difficult to estimate because of many factors, such as quality of material, methods used in laundering, and frequency of laundering. The average length of life of napkins has been estimated at approximately 200 washes and, of tablecloths, at 175. In terms of years this might be interpreted to mean that the life of table linen is approximately 2 or 3 years. The greatest wear usually appears near the border, owing in part to the unequal shrinkage of the warp yarns, to wear on contracted yarns in ironing, and to weakness in the yarns where the weave changes at the edge of the selvage. The first signs of wear in single-damask napkins often appear as breaks at the hem and in figured sections instead of in the plain centers. Breaks on the folds, occur less frequency than is commonly believed. It has been estimated that where linens are used, a fair average cost of replacement for them is 1.5 percent of the annual sales.

AMOUNT TO PURCHASE

The amount of table linen to purchase for any institution depends on the type of service, the laundry facilities, the numbers to be served, and the number of times the linen is changed during the day or week. In many institutions that serve three meals a day, linen cloths are used only for the evening or main meal of the day, clean linen being provided daily or as needed. Paper or cloth place mats may be used for the other meals. Daily laundry service makes it possible to keep the supply of linen at a minimum, whereas less frequent service necessitates an increased reserve supply. The number of tables in use will determine the number of cloths needed at any one time. The number of napkins is determined by the number of people to be served and by the frequency of change if used in a service other than in the commercial restaurant.

It is estimated that three to four times the amount of linen necessary for one complete service or day will meet the needs of most institutions. This supply provides one set on the table or ready to use during the day, one or two at the laundry, and one in storage. Commercial units, which make several changes during a serving period, require a large stock of linen, the exact quantity determined to a great extent by the laundry facilities.

Table pads serve as a protection to the table surface and eliminate much noise. They may be of a nonconducting composition material made in sections to fit the table tops or the quilted or felted types, the quilted ones being perhaps the most commonly used in institutions, owing to greater launderability. Table pads should be large enough to cover the top of the table but not show beneath the cloth. Ample allowance must be made for shrinkage when purchasing table pads. A resilient substance for treating table tops to give a permanent padding is now available that eliminates the need for any other type of pad.

It is possible to rent napery from a linen supply house that will furnish and launder the items needed. This may be practical for some institutions without adequate laundry facilities. However, the standards of service and work may be less desirable than could be maintained if the linen were owned and laundered by the organization.

Durable clothlike table covers of flannel with a vinyl coating are available in a variety of sizes and colors for heavy duty wear and where laundering is a problem. These covers are sponge washed on the tables, rinsed, and dried with a clean dry cloth. Their use is most adaptable to outdoor and informal fast-service operations.

DINNERWARE

The dinnerware desirable for institution food units varies with the service given. A club catering to a luxury-loving clientele may need as fine china as may be found in the homes of its patrons. On the other hand, a large school lunchroom will need durable ware that will withstand the hazards attendant on its use.

CHINA

Only *vitrified* china is recommended for foodservice table use. Vitrified china is made of an excellent quality of clay, free from iron, with flint and feldspar added. The mixture is pliable and capable of being molded into desired shapes, hardened, and fired. Thoroughly vitrified china is fired for not less than 60 hours and has a hard nonabsorbent body. Government standards for vitrified china specify that items with a maximum diameter of less than 10 inches shall absorb no more than 0.2 percent moisture and 10 inches or larger pieces to absorb no more than 0.5 percent.

The government cites specifications for three weights of vitrified institution china: thick china, hotel china, somewhat lighter in weight and with a rolled edge, and medium-weight china, sold on the market as banquet-weight china. Thick china, varying from 5/16 to 3/8 inch in thickness, is commonly used for lunch counter service or other situations where extra-heavy service is demanded of the table appointments. It is clumsy to handle and unattractive in appearance. The thickness of hotel-weight china varies from 5/23 to 1/4 inch, depending on the size of the piece. All except cups have a roll under the outer edge that gives the effect of weight and also lessens chipping on the upper side of the plate. This type of china is well adapted for use in institutions such as hospitals, residence halls, and restaurants. It is highly resistant to shock, easy to handle, and available in many designs and colors. Banquet-weight china, which is lighter in weight and usually has a straight edge, is used extensively in exclusive restaurants, clubs, and the private room service of hospitals. It resembles more closely household dinnerware. It is essential that the buyer recognize that weight does not mean strength and long life for china. Durability and strength are far more directly related to the quality of materials used and the methods of manufacture employed than they are to weight.

Tests of the durability of china used by the government are the chipping, impact, and absorption tests. In the chipping test specially constructed apparatus records the force required to chip the edge of a plate with a 6-ounce hammer. Three tests are made on the same plate and an average determined. This figure represents the relative chipping resistance of the edge of the plate. The average chipping value for rolled edges is 0.150 foot-pound; that for medium weight (hospital service) is 0.075 foot-pound. This test is used for plates and saucers. The impact test is made in a similar manner except that a 4-ounce hammer is dropped repeatedly with blows of increasing force at the same point in the center of the test piece, until a hole appears in the body or a body crack extends through the rim of plates, saucers, platters, and bakers (see Fig. 13.2). A body crack extending into any part of the foot, or the breaking away of a portion of the body, indicates the measure of force for cups and bowls. The average impact value for 7- and 5-inch plates, hotel weight, is 0.200 foot-pound, medium weight 0.180 foot-pound; for tea cups, hotel weight, 0.060 foot-pound, medium weight 0.060 foot-pound. The absorption test is made on three different samples of glazed pieces with an area of approximately 2.5 square inches. The samples are dried to constant weight at 110°C, then completely immersed and boiled in water for 5 hours and left to stand in the water for 20 hours. Excess moisture is removed with a damp cloth and the samples weighed. The absorption is determined by the formula:

$$\text{Percentage absorption} = \frac{\text{Wet weight} - \text{Dry weight} \times 100}{\text{Dry weight}}$$

FIGURE   13.2   *The resistance to breakage of china may be measured accurately.*
Courtesy, Syracuse China Company.

Vitrified heat-resistant ware of good quality is nonabsorbent, stainproof, and withstands high temperatures without crazing or breaking. Items are available in a variety of attractive colors and designs and include coffee pots, teapots, casseroles, ramekins, and individual pudding or pie dishes.

A notable improvement in the making of vitrified china has been effected through the introduction of a metallic ion "alumina" into the body materials of the china. This has enabled the industry to make a thinner, whiter, stronger piece of china than comparable bodies made of the older materials. It has a great deal more edge chip resistance than a normal body plate of comparable edge thickness, greater impact strength, and faster surface cleanability, made possible by the homogenous smoothness of the body.

The various-shaped pieces are decorated by the lining, printing, or decalcomania process, dipped into a glaze, and fired at a high temperature. When only one color is used it is applied by the printing process. Multicolors are applied by either the decalcomania, stamping, or printing process. The design and colors applied under the glaze are lasting, and the surface is smooth. It is advisable to select for institution purposes china that has the pattern applied under the glaze. The glaze is really molten glass applied as a coating and fused to the shaped, fired, and decorated dish or bisque at high temperature. This process seals the surface of the bisque, covers and protects the design, further strengthens the body, and makes the surface smooth, and it is highly resistant to chemicals and to cracking, crazing, or marring by physical shock.

Semivitrified china is a good-quality earthenware that has been fired insufficiently to obtain vitrification. This treatment results in a soft body, which is therefore porous and absorbent. Semivitrified china has been given a glaze that seals and finishes the dish, but the glaze may be sensitive to heat shocks and check easily. The design may not be permanent, as in making semivitrified and semiporcelain china, it is applied after the china is glazed and fired.

Factors in Selection. The type of china selected and the *designs* and *colors* used in its decoration affect materially the ease in creating satisfaction among the guests or patrons of any foodservice. Color schemes and motifs that fit into the general atmosphere are most pleasing. Pigments and processes have been so perfected that at the present time there is practically no limit to the color and design possibilities of china. Conservative but attractive designs enhance the beauty of any dining room and ordinarily do not detract from interest in the food. Gaudy and naturalistic designs in the centers of plates, however, seem to leave little room for food. They also create a feeling of unrest and disturbance, especially if used in the service of consecutive meals. A center design may add 5 to 25 percent to the cost of the plate. On the other hand, an inexpensive design may be created with a colored edge for the dominant note.

That the choice of china is influenced by the size of the *budget* is evident. If the budget allows only $10 a dozen for plates, there is no occasion for debate as to which design in the $15 a dozen class will be most satisfactory. Not infrequently the budget limits the choice to the china with the simple border pattern, which may or may not have artistic appeal. Fortunately, managers have become cognizant of the importance and need to weigh values of beauty and durability along with cost in the selection of china. Interest in and demand for good design in less expensive china has influenced manufacturers to produce such items.

Another factor that may influence choice is the available designs on which *replacements* may be obtained within a reasonable period of time. Stock types of patterns are usually available for immediate shipment. Specially made china, such as that having a monogram or crest, must be ordered weeks in advance. This fact must be considered along with the relatively higher cost of such special china in selecting a pattern for any specific service. Even stock types of patterns may be discontinued with limited notice; so when the initial selection is made, the possibility of replacements with identical china or that similar in type should be considered.

Plates with narrowed and flattened rims, cups shaped so that they require minimum space, and small welled saucers are popular styles or designs and contribute to a minimum of breakage. The general trend is for china with white background. This harmonizes easily with various color schemes and displays food to good advantage.

In purchasing china, *"firsts,"* the most perfect pieces that can be selected from each run of the kiln after the firing process are the most desirable. They are free from warping, chips, faults in the glaze, thin or uneven glaze, large scars on the under side from the pins on which the china was held during firing, and uneven or poorly applied designs. Other pieces are graded as "seconds" or "thirds," depending on the degree of imperfection. Warped plates are detected by rolling several plates on edge simultaneously. The warped ones show up plainly in the rolling in contrast to the first selection. Close inspection of each piece by experienced workers completes the grading process.

Sizes and *capacities* of the items may vary slightly with different potteries. Measurements for plates are usually given as factory size or the distance from the inside of the shoulder to the opposite edge, which may be approximately 1 to 2 inches less than actual overall measurement. If in doubt it is best to use overall measurements in ordering. The capacity of items such as cups, sugar bowls, and pitchers is designated in terms of ounces. In former times china orders usually included plates of five or six sizes and a variety of side dishes. The present trend is toward the limitation of the china list both as to size and number of various articles included, for example, an 8-ounce soup bowl could be used equally well for cereal or dessert. Likewise, a 6 1/4-inch plate might be used for bread and butter, salad, dessert, and underliner instead of the usual 5 1/2-inch bread and butter, and the 7 1/2-inch salad and/or dessert plate. This simplification is advantageous from the standpoint of service, inventory, dishwashing, replacement, and storage.

Amounts to Purchase. The quantity of dinnerware to be purchased for equipping a foodservice depends on many factors. Important considerations in determining quantity are: the seating capacity and total number of people to be served, the length of the serving period, the type of menu and the price of the meal, the kind of service, the dishwashing facilities and whether they are used intermittently or continuously, and the caliber and speed of the employees. Other factors not to be overlooked are the variety of sizes of each item to be stocked and the frequency of use of the piece. For example, if only one size plate is purchased for multiple use as a bread and butter, salad, and underliner, fewer total pieces would be required than if three different-size plates had been selected. Also, a larger number of coffee cups used many times a day must be purchased to provide a margin of safety than would be necessary for bouillon cups that may be used only once or twice a week.

Any listing of quantities must be determined by the needs of a particular institution and not by a set formula. The following suggestions for the number of each item of dinnerware needed per customer in a foodservice using an intermittent dishwashing cycle might be used as a basis for initial planning:

Item	Number per Customer
Cups	1.25
Saucers	1.25
9-in. plates	1.0
6-in. plates	0.66
Bowls	0.5

Table A.2 in Appendix A suggests quantities of dinnerware for a residence hall serving 300. Another guide for amounts of dinnerware to select for the average foodservice would be an allowance of three times the number of dining room seats for items such as bread and butter plates, salad dishes, dinner plates, saucers, fruit and/or cereal dishes, and four times for cups. The amounts of these and other items would depend much on the menu pattern and other conditions mentioned earlier.

Care. China will have a much longer life if handled carefully and cleaned properly. It is believed that "most breakage is caused by china hitting against china, and that 75 to 80 percent of all breakage occurs in the soiled dish and washing area." [1] Careful training and

[1] It Must Be China, *The American Restaurant China Council, East Liverpool, Ohio.*

supervision of the personnel will do much to prevent breakage and keep dishes looking bright and clean. Procedures to reduce the number of times a piece of china is handled will assist in this also. Examples are to separate soiled dishes into like kinds and stack before taking them to the dishroom for washing, and to store clean cups and glasses in the racks in which they are washed. Rubber plate scrapers and collars on openings in scrapping tables not only decrease noise but help to reduce breakage of dishes. Also helpful are the use of plastic or other synthetic coated metal dishracks and plastic or nylon pegs on dish-machine conveyors.

Suitable washing compound, proper temperature of wash and rinse waters, in addition to careful attention throughout the scrapping, washing, and the stacking and storing of clean dishes contribute to the length of life of china.

The choice of washing compound and the amount of it to use in the dishwashing machine depend on the hardness of the water. Tests are made, on request, by the manufacturers of various detergents to determine the compound best suited to the water and the quantity required. These tests may be confirmed or invalidated by others made in a local laboratory. If checking is not possible, cleaning compounds should be bought only from firms noted for reliability; brands should be chosen that have been favorably reported upon by foodservices so large that laboratory testing of supplies is a routine practice.

Temperatures recommended for the best results in dishwashing are: prerinse 115 to 120°F, wash 140 to 160°F, and rinse 180°F. A few degrees of variation one way or the other make little difference, although the temperature of the wash should not go below 140°F. Thermostats are built into machines that automatically control both wash and rinse temperatures, and automatic electronically controlled detergent dispensers are a recommended device to keep the wash water at the proper concentration for the best results.

The procedure followed in dishwashing and storage varies somewhat with the physical setup. Preliminary flushing or rinsing of dishes before they are put into the washing machine is routine except when a large model machine with built-in preflush section is used. A convenient arrangement is to have a countersunk sink over which the filled racks can slide. While in position over the sink, the racked dishes can be sprayed or rinsed by means of a hose attachment. Another common method is to rinse the dishes under a forced stream of water before racking. Regardless of the method of removing surface soil, operating costs are reduced because of the need for less washing compound, less frequent change of water, and less likelihood of washer arm and rinse spray jets becoming clogged from food particles; also cleaner dishes result.

The soiled dishes, scrapped and ready for the machine, are placed on belts or in racks, so that all surfaces are exposed. Sorting and stacking dishes into piles of the same kind and size will help to reduce breakage. The loading of one type of dishes in the racks or on the conveyor belt speeds washing at both the loading and unloading ends of the machine and insures better wash action, since there is no overlapping of larger dishes to block the spray. After the washing and rinsing, the china is air dried. Plates of like size are stacked carefully so that the bottom rim of one does not mar the surface of the plate beneath it. Cups and glasses are stored in the wash racks, and stacked on dollies, and silver is left in the containers in which it was washed. Dish-storage trucks and self-leveling mobile units have largely replaced the need to transport and transfer clean dishes to storage cupboards and out again, thus eliminating many breakage hazards and reducing labor hours.

Replacement of china may be made as breakage demands, or provision may be made for a stockroom supply ample for the probable yearly need. In this case replacement may be made of the storeroom stock following the annual inventory. As a means of reducing breakage through carelessness, it is often advisable to make a frequent inventory of stock in circulation. Thus the workers become aware that a constant check of breakage is being made. Often a price list of china is posted, and the total loss to the foodservice through breakage is made known to the workers.

Generally, breakage is highest on small plates, saucers, and fruit dishes; they are often stacked too high and slide off the trays or carts; handles are broken from cups; and the edges of large heavy plates may be chipped if stacked carelessly.

Accurate figures concerning the percentage of breakage in foodservices of various types are difficult to obtain. A large restaurant may report a china breakage of 52 percent per year while a small residence hall has an annual breakage of 10 percent, perhaps because of close supervision, and often much less handling and transporting of both soiled and clean dishes than in a large foodservice with several serving units and centralized dishwashing.

A common method of evaluating breakage and losses in commercial operations is to consider the total cost of replacement in relation to income. The average replacement of china on this basis has been found to be approximately one half of 1 percent of the total food and beverage sales. Another method is to calculate the ratio of broken dishes to the number of guest meals served. Both of the latter methods would be for a specified period of time, but neither would give numbers of each item replaced nor clues as to where controls need to be strengthened.

CORNING DINNERWARE

A popular dinnerware is made by the Corning Glass Company in which a percentage of sand is replaced by aluminum powder in the making of the basic green glass. The resulting tableware is strong, thin, well-tempered, has a smooth surface, and is highly resistant to stains, heat, scratching, and breakage. It is available in a variety of sizes, shapes, and decorative designs on a white background. The cost is slightly less than that of some high-quality vitrified china dinnerware. The amounts to order and the care of Corning dinnerware is comparable to china.

MELAMINE

The production of synthetic compounds for molded dinnerware as a competitor of china and glass is adaptable for use in some types of institution foodservices. Celluloid (1868), an early synthetic thermoplastic compound and a forerunner of modern plastics, was made of cellulose nitrate and camphor. However, its nonresistance to heat, high inflammability, and camphor odor and flavor made it unsuitable for dishware. In the next period of development (1908), phenol and formaldehyde were incorporated into a thermosetting compound that was capable of being molded under pressure and heat into forms that would retain their shapes under mechanical strains at well above the temperature of boiling water. This type of compound has had wide and varied usage but, because of its odor and unattractive brownish color, its use in the food service industry was limited mainly to counter and serving trays. The substitution of urea for phenol made it possible to produce a white compound of great strength that would take colors well. The basic cost of this material was high; therefore it was often made into thin dishes suitable only for picnic or limited use and that could be sold for a reasonably low price. During World War II, it was found that melamine could be combined with formaldehyde to give a tough strong resin that could withstand the demands on it in high-altitude flying equipment. This type of melamine plastic compound is now used in the production of dinnerware.

The first heavy-duty dinnerware made of melamine-formaldehyde compounds contained a chopped cotton cloth filler. The products had a high tensile and impact strength but were unattractive and limited to a low color range. Compounds made by blending long-fiber, high-grade paper stock with melamine resin and colorfast pigments are supplied by chemical companies to the manufacturers for the production of dinnerware at the present time. This material is known as alpha-cellulose-filled, melamine-formaldehyde, thermosetting molding compound, and the products made from it are available in a wide range of colors and designs. The differences in shape, density, and balance in design account in some measure for the price range in melamine ware. Competition is keen between the molding companies to produce items from this common basic material that are attractive in color and design and meet the needs of the food industry.

The melamine compound undergoes chemical change in the molding process under pressure of some 3000 to 3500 pounds per square inch at 335°F, which gives the pieces of dinnerware a smooth lustrous surface, resistant to scratching, chippage, breakage, detergents, and grease. Also, it is not affected by the hot water used in dishwashing. Because the color pigment is thoroughly blended with the compound before molding, there is no fading of the finished product.

The permanent decoration of melamine dinnerware was made possible by opening the press when the material has just been shaped and adding a melamine impregnated overlay, with the lithographed side placed down onto the dish. The mold is closed and, during the cure, the overlay becomes an integral part of the base material and the resulting product has a smooth wear-resistant and protective glaze over the design.

The choice between melamine or the long-accepted china dinnerware poses many problems for the prospective buyer. The light weight of melamine, which is about 1/3 that of ordinary dinnerware, minimum handling noise, and attractive colors make it especially acceptable in some hospitals, restaurants, and school lunchrooms. An early report [2] on good quality melamine ware, after a 2-year test period in a state institution, showed that material savings had been affected through breakage reduction. In this instance the breakage in 1 month was found to be about the same as it had been in 1 day

[2] *Clarence W. Winchell, "Here's Where Melmac Really Proves Its Superiority,"* reprinted from Plastics Newsfront, *American Cyanamid Company.*

for the ceramics in previous use. Also, satisfactions were high for the reduction in noise and in the negligible signs of surface wear.

The Quartermaster Corps of the U.S. Army early specified the use of plasticware after about 3 years of field and laboratory testing on the basis of acceptability by the personnel, the degree to which it met military requirements, and annual replacement cost economy. A panel of men preferred melamine to white china dinnerware; tests proved the plastics were durable and sanitary under actual conditions of use; and the annual replacement cost was approximately 1/10 and the original price 60 percent higher than that of the china in use.

An early survey of 182 large hospitals (over 300 beds) indicated that the main advantages for the use of melamine ware were resistance to breakage, lightness in weight, and minimum handling noise. The main disadvantages were staining and difficulty in cleaning. The average replacement in those hospitals reporting use of melamine was 33 percent versus 93.3 percent for those using china. Minah [3] reported, "since we have switched over to the use of melamine ware we have been able to cut breakage by about 95%."

Melamine products possess low thermal conductivity that eliminates the necessity for preheating of the ware for the service of hot foods, but these products do present a problem in air-drying after washing, because they may remain damp for storage. However, to date, bacteriological checks made by the swab-test method on such dishes have indicated no cause for alarm at this condition.

The staining of cups has been the cause of much concern and research, because by far the heaviest replacements have been for this item. The development of new washing compounds and closer attention to washing techniques have eliminated the problem somewhat. Alkaline detergents are recommended for washing, and abrasives cannot be used successfully on plastic surfaces; therefore chemical rinses must be depended on, preferably those without chlorine. Some users believe that frequent cup replacement was justly compensated by the high resistance to breaking, chipping, cracking, and crazing under ordinary conditions, the lightness of weight, the low noise level in handling, the attractive coloring and luster, and the relatively low upkeep and replacement costs. Certain manufacturers of melamine dinnerware are successfully incorporating stain-resistant compounds into the thermosetting resin, which

[3] Public Health and Melamine Tableware, *Society of the Plastics Industry,* New York.

prevents much of the objectionable staining and adds to the life of this type of dinnerware.

The final choice of dinnerware for any foodservice can be made only after an exhaustive study of the specific situation, in view of the satisfactions to be gained and the economics involved. Attractive colorful designs within a wide price range are available in the various types of ware; therefore, each product should be judged on its own merits and the one selected that will meet best the needs of the institution.

TABLEWARE

The most satisfactory type of eating utensils for institutions is that which has been designed and made especially for heavy duty. Such ware falls into two distinct classes: *flatware* of the usual array of knives, forks, and spoons; and items such as teapots, sugar bowls, pitchers, and platters, known as *hollow ware* if made of silver. All must be durable and serviceable and at the same time attractive in line and design. The decision to select silverware or stainless-steel tableware will depend largely on the type of foodservice, the tastes of the clientele served, and the amount of money available for this expenditure and upkeep.

SILVERWARE

Quality silverware is used in discriminating foodservices because of the demands for and interest of the residents or clientele in attractive service. It lends dignity and charm to dining tables, perhaps because of the association of the ideas that silver is a precious metal and hence is found where people know and appreciate gracious, comfortable living. The use of a pleasing silver service is regarded as a means of reiterating other impressions concerning the nature of the place, conveying in a very real way a sense of charming and refined atmosphere.

Blanks that serve as the basic forms for flatware and hollow ware should be strong and heavy to resist the scratching, bending, and twisting to which much institution silverware is subjected. The metal used for the blanks of institution silverware in normal times is not less than 18 percent nickel silver and has been found to meet the above requirements. Atmosphere, time, and heat control are important factors in the metallurgy of this alloy and, through years of scientific research, the various silver manufacturing companies have perfected control of these factors and have evolved satisfactory methods of obtaining the qualities and meeting the standards found desirable for the various pieces of silverware used in foodservices.

Nine pounds per gross is the standard weight of blanks of ordinary teaspoons sold for public service. The principal weights of blanks used are: heavy, 10 1/2 pounds; regular, 9 pounds; medium, 7 1/2 to 8 pounds. The 9-pound blanks are desirable for hospital tray service, whereas the 10 1/2-pound patterns may be advisable for heavy-duty silverware for certain commercial restaurants and cafeterias. The weight of the blank used influences the price of the silverware.

The design, shape, and thickness or weight of the blanks should be conducive to heavy wear and beauty. Flatware blanks are stamped, graded, and rolled until they are the corresponding size of forks or spoons. They are then placed in various presses, and the fork tines or spoon bowls are shaped. In the next step they are struck with the pattern die, after which the edges are trimmed and smoothed down so that the articles resemble the finished products. Forks should have well-designed tines, durable and heat treated, to give maximum strength, and both forks and spoons should have heavy reinforced shanks to give the best wearing qualities. After being cleaned and polished, the articles are ready for plating.

The steps in the manufacture of knives prior to plating differ from those in the making of blanks for forks and spoons. The 18 percent nickel silver base was found to produce a blade that bent easily and refused to take an edge sharp enough for practical use in cutlery. The first plated knives were made with a base of crucible steel to which a plating of 12 pennyweight of silver per dozen knives was applied. The tendency of steel to rust in the presence of moisture made its use as a base unsatisfactory. Incomplete drying of knives is all too frequent. Moisture left on the knives tends to reach the steel through the plating, and the rusting that results causes the plate to peel, revealing a black and unsightly base metal. Some less expensive knives, unfortunately, are still made with a steel base. The amount of silver plating on such knives may be comparable to that deposited on forks and spoons of like weight but, under ordinary conditions of use and care, the anticipated length of life is considerably less.

Two innovations have led to the manufacture of more satisfactory knives. Stainless steel has become widely used for knife blades, and noncorrosive alloys have been made that prove satisfactory as the base for solid-handle knives that are to be plated. The popular hollow-handle knife, made with the 18 percent nickel silver as the base of the handle, to which was welded a strip stock or forged stainless steel blade, has been replaced largely by the one piece stainless steel knife with the plated handle. The most important improvement in the design of knives in years has been the change in style from the long-blade, short-handle to the short-blade, long-handle type that permits the user to press down with the forefinger on the back of the handle instead of on the narrow edge of the steel blade. This style has been adopted in many institutions.

For better qualities of flatware there is an intervening step between the making of the blank and its plating. Reinforcements of an extra disk of silver are made on blanks at the points of greatest wear: the heel of the bowls of spoons and the base of fork tines. Such treatment increases many times the length of wear and is referred to as *overlay, sectional plate,* or *reinforced plate* (see Fig. 13.3).

The plating of silverware is accomplished by electrolysis. The pure silver bars or ingots are placed around the side of the plating tank, and the articles to be plated are hung in the solution. By means of an electric current, the silver passes from the bars and is deposited on the blanks, the length of time and the strength of the current determining the amount of silver deposited.

FIGURE   13.3   *Plated silver should be reinforced on the points of greatest wear. Courtesy, Oneida, Ltd.*

After the articles are removed from the plating tank, they are sent to the finishing rooms. Better grades of plate are burnished, or the surface of each article is rubbed under pressure with a round pointed steel tool in such a manner that the plate is hardened and smoothed out. It is then polished and colored. The better qualities of silverware are given extra burnishing. The various finishes, known as Butler, or dull finish, hotel finish, or medium bright, and bright, are obtained by using different types of buffs and polishing compounds and by carrying the polishing process to different degrees.

The plating of institution silverware is heavier than for the silverware generally used in the home, the most common institution ware being known as *triple plate* or three times full standard. In triple plate 6 ounces of pure silver have been applied to 1 gross of teaspoons, with other items in proportion—for example, tablespoons with 12 ounces of silver to the gross. A much lighter plating known as full standard carries a deposit of 5 ounces of pure silver to the gross of tablespoons and only 2 1/2 ounces to the gross of teaspoons. *Half standard,* as its name implies, carries half the amount of silver deposit of full standard. Full-standard plate quality is the lightest grade recommended for use in institutions. The leading manufacturers of silver plate recommend, and generally sell for high-grade public service under their own trade name, a better quality of silver plate than those mentioned above. The heavy finely finished metal blanks, the heavy plating standard, and the fine finish of this quality of silverware make the initial cost greater than the ordinary commercial grades of plate, but the cost is offset by the long wearing qualities and satisfactory service of the various items. An example of such silverware is heavy hotel teaspoons, which weigh 11 1/2 to 12 pounds per gross. An extra-heavy plate deposit is used on 10 1/2-pound blanks in their production. Usually the silver overlay on tips and backs of bowls and tines is invisible on any 10 1/2- and 11-pound qualities.

HOLLOW WARE

Standard-grade hollow ware is known as nickel silver (hard) soldered ware and carries a fine quality of hotel silver plate. The bodies of the various items are shaped by dies, and the many pieces of each assembled and are hand soldered by expert craftsmen. The design and quality of material and workmanship are distinguishing features of hollow ware. Pieces with sharp corners are to be avoided, short spouts are more easily cleaned than long ones, and simple designs are more pleasing than ornate. Hollow ware blanks should be made of the same base metal as that found satisfactory for flatware. Other softer metals are sometimes used in less expensive items, but they may become damaged and melt easily. Soft-soldered construction is to be avoided. Nickel silver wires or "mounts" silver soldered to the body of the article may add a decorative note and strengthen the outer edge or the side of the article. The name of the manufacturer should be stamped on the bottom of each piece.

Silver hollow ware may seem an extravagance but, when the cost is considered over a period of years, it may be more economical than china or glassware. Furthermore, the satisfaction and prestige gained through its use are not to be discounted.

Standard designs and patterns are often made individual by stamping or engraving the name, crest of the firm or organization, or a special decorative motif on the otherwise plain surface. If silverware is to be stamped, the stamping should be done on the back of the item before it is plated. It is found that plain silverware may become badly scratched with ordinary handling; hence a pleasing design that breaks the smooth surface may be more practical than plain silver, crested. Simplicity is always the keynote of good taste. The collection of dirt and tarnish is always greater on silver with deep grooves. Modern methods of cleaning have made it possible to use a great variety of designs formerly regarded as difficult to maintain at modest upkeep costs.

Since tests that the consumer may use to determine the quality of silverware are not feasible, one has to depend on a reliable firm to supply the quality specified and to assume responsibility that the articles will be found satisfactory.

The care of silverware has much to do with its appearance and wearing qualities. Careful handling prevents many scratches. The following procedure is suggested for cleaning silverware and keeping it in good condition: sort, then wash in a machine to which has been added the proper cleaning compound, at a temperature of 140 to 150°F, and rinse thoroughly. A final dip in a solution with high-wetting properties prevents spotting of air-dried silver. It is advisable to presoak flatware or wash immediately after use. If washed in flat-bottom racks, the silver should be scattered loosely over the rack surface, sorted after washing, placed into perforated dispensing cylinders, and rewashed to insure sanitization. If silver is sorted into cylinders before washing, the handles of the utensils are down so that all surfaces of knife blades, fork tines, and bowls of spoons will be subjected to the wash and rinse processes. Care must be taken not to overcrowd the containers. The washed silver is left in the cylinders to dry. This system is convenient, especially in self-service units, because clean dispensing cylinders may be inverted over those used in washing and placed on the counter without handling of the clean silver.

Constant attention is necessary to prevent and remove tarnish and stains of various kinds. Tarnish, an oxide formed on the surface of the metal, is usually composed of sulphur, silver, and oxygen. Tarnish on silver occurs much more rapidly in areas where there is considerable smoke and natural gas in the air. Contact with rubber, fiber, and certain foodstuffs also causes discoloration. Detarnishing and polishing silverware by hand are not practicable in institutions. An effective and quick method of detarnishing in a small foodservice is to immerse the silver, in a wire basket, in a solution of water and a cleaning compound containing trisodium phosphate in an aluminum kettle kept for that purpose. A piece of aluminum or zinc in the bottom of another type of container will be as effective, providing the silver touches it. The tarnish (oxide) will form a salt with the aluminum, and all tarnish will be removed through a mild electrolytic action. The cleaning compound also cuts and dissolves any grease or dirt on the silver. The silver is left in the solution *only long enough to remove the tarnish.* It is then rinsed in boiling water and dipped in a solution of high wetting qualities. Burnishing machines are used for silver polishing in large foodservices. Care must be taken to see that the machine is not overloaded and that there are enough steel shots of various sizes in the barrel of the machine to be effective in contacting all surfaces to be polished. Also, the right amount of proper detergent must be added to the water in the burnishing machine to produce the required concentration of the solution. There can be no set rule about the frequency of detarnishing and polishing; each foodservice must set up its own standards.

The quantity of tableware to purchase for a given institution depends on the number of people to be fed, the kind of service, the length of the serving period, the type of menu, the dishwashing facilities, and the help available. Flatware losses are heavy in foodservices. The replacement in commercial services is estimated to reach 7 percent of the investment in silverware annually. Other figures for commercial institutions show approximately 33 1/3 percent replacement, whereas losses in residence halls may run lower. These losses may be due to many causes, among which are discarding of silver with garbage, carelessness of employees, taking of silver as souvenirs, lack of checkup through inventories, and lack of room-service return. Losses of stainless steel flatware might be comparable in many cases, except that these pieces are regarded as less attractive as souvenirs and the original cost is less.

It is difficult to state definitely the needs of institutions for silverware. An estimate of its cost often cited is 2 1/2 percent of the total investment in foodservice equipment. A good quantity estimate of silverware for cafeterias is twice the seating capacity for all the flatware items required. Should the dishwashing facilities be limited and the turnover of patrons rapid, this quantity might need to be increased to three or even four times the seating capacity. For restaurants and residence halls 3 teaspoons per cover, 3 forks, using a dessert fork for all purposes, and 2 knives per cover usually are sufficient. All other items are estimated on the basis of 1 1/2 per cover except oyster forks, iced tea spoons, and butter knives. They are determined by the type of service and the clientele. Banquet service usually requires 2 teaspoons, 2 forks, 2 knives, and 1 bouillon or dessert spoon per cover. If the banquet is more elaborate than usual, an additional spoon and fork may be desirable. The tendency is toward the use of as few different sizes of pieces as possible. For instance, knives and forks of dessert size can be used for many purposes and are usually preferred to knives and forks of dinner size. Dessert spoons may be used for soup and serving spoons as well as for certain desserts.

STAINLESS STEEL TABLEWARE

Stainless steel tableware has gained wide acceptance for heavyduty tableware in institution foodservices. The flatware is fairly inexpensive, is highly resistant to heat, scratches, and wear, and will not rust, stain, peel, chip, or tarnish. It stays bright indefinitely with ordinary washing and offers a wide selection of attractive designs from which to choose. Flatware in stainless steel is available in *light, standard,* and *heavy* weights. Water pitchers and individual teapots of stainless steel are considered a lifetime investment, although the initial cost is high in comparison to these items in ordinary glass or crockery. The same methods of sorting, washing, and drying are recommended for stainless steel tableware as for silver. The quantity to purchase would be comparable.

GLASSWARE

Glassware may be regarded as a major item in dining room equipment for institutions. It is manufactured in many designs, colors, and shapes. However, the average institution finds a plain design in crystal well adapted to its needs, this design being usually less expensive and more readily replaced than more unusual ones. Cut crystal is considerably more expensive, but adds a note of distinction that is sometimes desirable. Colored glassware fits into certain decorative schemes and may be pleasing for certain specialized services. Tumblers are preferred to goblets for certain services because of their simplicity and relative durability, although goblets are sometimes desired despite the higher breakage attendant on their use. Often, stemmed sherbet glasses are used even though other glassware is not of this type.

Glassware may be classed as lead or lime glass, depending on the use of lead or lime oxide in the manufacturing process. Articles of glass are formed by blowing them into shape by machine or hand processes or by pressing molten glass into molds by means of a machine. The blowing method is the more expensive and produces a thinner glass of finer texture, higher luster, and clearer ring. Hand-blown lead glass is superior to all other glassware because of its brilliance, light weight, and variety of styles. Lime blown glassware possesses these characteristics in a lesser degree, is less expensive, and is used extensively in institutions. It is usually machine blown. The style, color, and decoration determine the cost of manufacture of blown glass articles. Pressed lime glass is used in many institutions. It is serviceable and better qualities of it are comparatively free from bubbles and cloudiness. Moreover, it is relatively inexpensive and may be obtained in many styles. A good quality of glassware should be selected for the institution, regardless of whether pressed glass or blown glass is to be used. Desirable characteristics are clearness, luster, medium weight, freedom from such defects as marks and bubbles, and a clear ring.

Glassware must pass boiling and shock tests without showing signs of corrosion, chipping, scumming, or cracking in order to meet federal specifications. In making the boiling test articles are suspended for 6 hours in boiling water in a closed container with vent. The shock test is made by immersing articles in tap water at $18.5°C \pm 2 \ 1/2°$ ($65°F \pm 5°$) for a 10-minute period, then suddenly transferring them into boiling water. This procedure is repeated five times. Not all the glassware sold meets federal specifications, and there is no labeling to indicate which, if any, is of that quality.

The sizes of glassware used most commonly in institutions are glasses of 4- or 5-ounce capacity for fruit juice, glasses of 9- or 10-ounce capacity for milk and water, and glasses of 12- or 14-ounce capacity for iced tea. The capacity of water goblets is usually 10 ounces, that of footed iced tea glasses is 12 ounces. The size of other items, such as dessert dishes, should be appropriate for the size of food portions to be served in them.

CARE

Glassware is often sorted and washed in a separate dishwashing machine from that used for other dishes, or in a glasswasher built for that purpose. If glassware must be washed in the same machine used for dishes, in a small operation, it should be segregated and washed first while the water is entirely free from grease and food particles, or left until after the dishes are finished and the soiled water replaced by clean. In either case, with a rack machine, all items to be washed should be placed upside down in racks after they are transported from the dining room and remain in the same racks to wash, drain, and then load into carts for transport to the point of storage or use without rehandling.

It is important that glassware be under constant scrutiny to maintain in service only those pieces that are not chipped, cracked, clouded, or scratched in appearance. Filmed glasses may be caused by low rinse pressure and volume, too short rinse cycle, nonaligned spray jets, and a hard water precipitate. Tea stains may be removed by using a chlorinated detergent in the glass washing machine. Water spots may be caused by slow drying or the need for softening the rinse water. The effect of all otherwise attractive service may be almost wholly cancelled by damaged or poorly washed glassware.

AMOUNT TO BUY

The amount of glassware needed varies with the individual situation. Basic considerations are the menu, type of service, seating capacity, rate of turnover, dishwashing facilities, and labor available for this duty at peak periods. The following items of glassware are in such constant use that it is expedient to have a reserve stock of at least 50 percent of the number of each in daily use: tumblers, glasses for fruit juice, sherbets, and iced teas. Other pieces of glassware are used less frequently, so the number in reserve need not exceed 25 percent of the number on the shelves. Typical of this group are glass salad plates.

The breakage of glassware in institutions is often high and results from careless handling and storage, choice of improper designs for heavy-service wear, use of poor quality of glassware, and subjection to high temperature during washing. The shape of the glass will have much to do with the breakage anticipated. Straight side tumblers that can be stacked are a decided breakage hazard, and there are patented shapes available that make it impossible to stack tumblers. Many items of glassware curve in slightly at the top so that the edges will not touch when they are set down together, the contact coming at a reinforced part away from the edge of the glass. Other styles have reinforced edges at the top, advertised as making them more highly resistant to chipping. This feature is also found around the foot of some stemmed ware.

Some hotels plan to replace glassware two and a half times per year, and residence halls estimate approximately 100 percent breakage annually. Breakage could no doubt be reduced through the use of heavier ware, but often this is undesirable as it would not be consistent with the other equipment and furnishings in the dining room. Plastic and aluminum drinking cups have replaced water glasses in operations such as summer camps and fast-service units (Fig. 13.4).

FIGURE   13.4   Modern dining room arrangement for industrial foodservice. Courtesy, S. Blickman, Inc.

DISPOSABLES

One-time use items for foodservices are available in everything from service employee's caps, aprons, and cleaning cloths; table covers, napkins, and mats; and cook, dinner, and tableware. However, other than paper napkins, their use is mainly in hospital isolation areas and informal dining as at drive-ins, picnics, on aircraft carriers, and for carry-out food.

Clear plastic; pressed, molded, plain, or plasticized paper; styrofoam; and aluminum foil are the materials most used in disposable items. Plastic and paper bags are used extensively, as are portioned packets and containers for foods such as sugar, condiments, milk, cream, ice cream, salad dressings, honey, and jelly.

Disposable dishware is available in many sizes, shapes, and colors. Some is made for cold food only, whereas items such as paper baking dishes and plasticized cups for hot drinks withstand considerable heat. The selection of some or all disposable dishware may well be justified, especially for certain types of less permanent food operations. Consideration would need to be given to initial and replacement costs of conventional dinnerware, space and equipment for dishwashing, and labor for handling in comparison to the initial cost of paper or plastic, its disposal and acceptability by the persons to be served. In any case, it is well for all foodservices to have ready access to some disposable dishware for times of emergency.

SELECTED REFERENCES

Bradley, L. A., *The Selection, Care, and Laundering of Institutional Textiles*, School of Hotel Administration, Cornell University Press, Ithaca, New York, 1963.

"Heavy-Duty Alpha-Cellulose-Filled Melamine Tableware," *Commercial Standard 173-50*, U.S. Department of Commerce, U.S. Government Printing Office, Washington, D.C.

It Must Be China, The American Restaurant China Council, Inc., East Liverpool, Ohio.

Kahrl, William L., *Planning and Operating A Successful Food Service Operation*, Chain Store Publishing Corporation, New York, 1973.

Kotschevar, Lendal, *How to Buy and Care For: Service Ware, Textiles, Cleaning Compounds*, published by Institutions Magazine, Chicago, 1969.

National Sanitation Foundation, *Standard No. 36, Dinnerware*, July 1970.

Public Health and Melamine Tableware, Society of the Plastics Industry, New York.

Speaking of China, Syracuse China, Syracuse, New York.

The Anatomy of Foodservice Design 1, Jule Wilkinson, Editor, Cahners, Boston, 1975.

The Manual of Paper Food Service for Restaurants and Institutions, Paper Cup and Container Institute, Inc., New York.

Current professional journals and trade magazines.

Manufacturers' leaflets, brochures, catalogs, and specifications.

Appendix A
PLANS FOR THE ORGANIZATION OF COLLEGE RESIDENCE HALLS

Residence hall foodservices continue to play a vital part in the lives of students on college or university campuses throughout the country. Trends in the national economy appear to influence student participation in residence hall living; in times of affluence, many students tend to prefer off-campus living in their own apartments. In periods of inflation, tight money, and recessions, residence halls seem more economical and therefore more popular with the students.

Many changes have occurred in recent times in the philosophy of residence hall living. Coeducational halls are the accepted pattern on many campuses. There is seldom found a dining hall segregated by sex. Alternate choices in board plans are usually available from the one-meal-a-day, five-days-a-week board rate, to the total-meals-per-week plan, and many variations in between. Extended meal hours, greater variety in menu selection, and many serve-yourself foods such as in soup, sandwich or salad bars are offered for the residents. This indicates a desire on the part of management to cater to the needs and wishes of today's students. In any event a heavy responsibility faces the director of such a food system. The complex problems to be met and solved demand a person with a broad educational and experience background, and whose personal characteristics make working with others pleasant and easy.

Unless funds are unlimited, a compromise is usually necessary as to the size of a unit that will provide acceptable living and education facilities for the residents and, at the same time, insure a sound financial program at a price the students can afford to pay. No two situations are comparable and each must be governed by local conditions.

Residence halls are larger, in general, than in former years, to take advantage of lower per unit building costs realized with the larger size units. In some situations several residence halls are built around a separate, common dining hall. This centralization of food-service is more economical than the duplication of kitchen facilities and personnel that would be required for each hall. Dining spaces in the central dining hall have, in many cases, been constructed into small units, sometimes with folding panels between to allow for flex-ibility, yet give greater intimacy that students seem to prefer over the large, open dining room. Many older dining halls have been re-modeled using decorative partitioning schemes to achieve this re-sult.

The trend today for management of college and university resi-dence hall foodservice is toward combining the responsibilities for housing and foodservice into one department with a housing direc-tor and a director of foodservice responsible to an overall manager. He in turn may be accountable to the dean of students, the business officer, or a vice-president, depending on the organizational struc-ture of the university. Although the organization may have changed with the increase in size of the food units, the need for a food direc-tor trained in and dedicated to the service of high-quality and nutri-tionally adequate food is of paramount importance. This person should also be interested in the development of the social and edu-cational phase of the residence hall program, and possibly would be called on to teach classes in foodservice management. The opera-tion of a college residence hall program must be a cooperative proj-ect between the personnel, housing, and the foodservice depart-ments. Examples of a floor plan, organization chart, and the personnel for typical small and large residence halls follow.

EXAMPLE A. A SMALL RESIDENCE HALL FOODSERVICE PLAN

Obviously any plan that might be suggested can be considered only as a guide as conditions in each situation vary with such factors as geographic location, the menu pattern, the conveniences of the foodservice layout, the amount of labor-saving equipment, the form in which the food is purchased, and the type and experience of the personnel available. Figure A.1 shows the overall organization plan of a campus residence hall food system. Figures A.2 and A.3 are the kitchen floor plan and organization chart for one of the halls serving 300. Suggested personnel with qualifications, schedules of work, and responsibilities for this size unit is indicated in Table A.1. A suggested equipment list for the same foodservice is found in Table A.2.

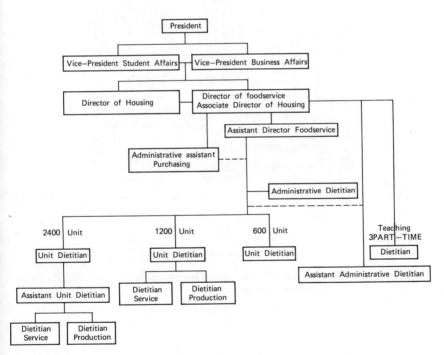

FIGURE A.1   *Organization chart for a residence hall foodservice system under the management of a home economics staff member. Courtesy, Kansas State University.*

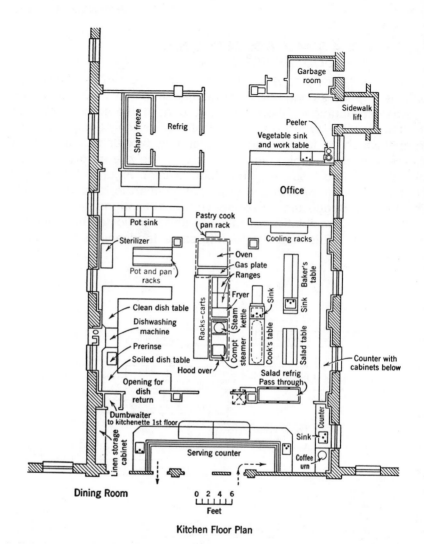

Kitchen Floor Plan

FIGURE A.2   Foodservice floor plan for a residence hall serving 300. Courtesy, Kansas State University.

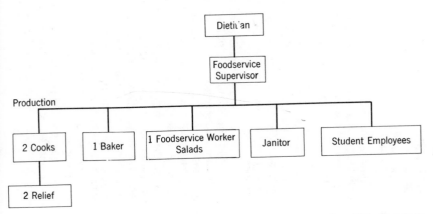

Residence Hall (300 unit)

Dietician

Foodservice Supervisor

Production

2 Cooks | 1 Baker | 1 Foodservice Worker Salads | Janitor | Student Employees

2 Relief

FIGURE A.3   Organization chart for a residence hall serving 300. Courtesy, Kansas State University.

TABLE A.1   SUGGESTED FOODSERVICE PERSONNEL [a] FOR A RESIDENCE HALL SERVING 300

Position	Qualifications	Hours	Responsibilities
Director of residence hall foodservice (if two or more halls).	Master's degree in institution management. Not less than 3 years' experience in the foodservice field as an administrator or 5 years of successful institutional experience. Meets qualifications of a good administrator.	8 A.M. to 4:30 P.M.	Outlines organization plans and policies for the department. Is responsible for foodservice in all residence halls. Works closely with head of institution management department, comptroller, dean of students, director of housing. Directs work of dietitian in each hall. Purchases all food, equipment, and supplies directly or through business manager.
Dietitian for hall, 300 capacity	Bachelor's degree in institution management. At least 1 year practical experience in addition to intern or apprentice training. Good health, high food standards, ability to work with people, good business sense.	10 A.M. to 7 P.M. Relieves assistant dietitian on day off.	Works with director of residence hall foodservice in formulating policies. Directs and supervises food unit. Supervises preparation and service of two meals. Plans menus in cooperation with director and other dietitians. Standardizes recipes for unit. Is responsible for food costs and other records. Requisitions food and supplies through the office of the director. Is responsible for order and cleanliness of the kitchens and serving units. Is responsible for work of the assistant dietitian.
Foodservice supervisor	Bachelor's degree in institution management. One-year apprentice-dietitian training course. Personal qualifications similar to those of dietitian.	6 A.M. to 2 P.M. (1 day off per week).	Supervises preparation and service of one meal. Assists dietitian in planning menus. Assists with food costs and other records.

Position	Hours	Qualifications	Duties
Morning cook	6 A.M. to 3 P.M.	Experienced cook. Good health, high food standards, good standards of cleanliness and order; cooperative, dependable and loyal; good attitude; ability to direct work of others; good disposition.	Is responsible for preparation of brea_fast and lunch. Supervises preparation and cooking of vegetables for lunch. Is responsible for all foods being ready to serve on scheduled time. Sends food to serving units as needed. Puts away all leftover hot food. Is responsible for care and cleanliness of range and cooks' table. Confers with dietitian on menu changes, amounts of food to prepare, and method of preparation. Writes requisitions for supplies for the preparation department for the following day.
Evening cook	10 A.M. to 7 P.M.	Experienced cook. Good health, high food standards, good standards of cleanliness and order; cooperative, dependable and loyal; good professional attitude.	Is responsible for preparation of dinner. Prepares meats, gravies, and cooks vegetables. Sends food to serving unit as needed. Sees that kitchen is in order. Other responsibilities same as morning cook.
Salad worker	8 A.M. to 4:30 P.M.	Good health, high food standards, good standards of cleanliness and order; cooperative, dependable and good attitude; loyal; good attitude; artistic.	Prepares salad dressings. Prepares ingredients for lunch and dinner salads. Sets up salads. Serves at salad counter at lunch. Writes request for supplies. Keeps work area and salad refrigerator clean and in order.
Pastry cook	6 A.M. to 3 P.M.	Same as salad worker. Good cook.	Prepares all desserts and hot breads for lunch and dinner. Sets up desserts.
Relief cooks (2)	According to person for whom substituting.	Need not be experienced cook. Good health, high food standards, good standards of cleanliness and order; neat, alert, able to adjust to work of others.	Assumes duties of person for whom substituting.

TABLE A.1 *(Continued)*

Position	Qualifications	Hours	Responsibilities
Storeroom clerk—pot washer	Good health, neat and clean in appearance, industrious; cooperative, loyal and dependable.	6:30 A.M. to 3:30 P.M. Relieved by student workers on days off.	Stores supplies. Issues supplies. Keeps storeroom in order. Washes cooking and serving utensils after breakfast and lunch, replaces to proper racks and drawers. Cleans kitchen floor. Keeps garbage cans clean.
Counter or service workers [b] (student employees)	Good health, alert, efficient, dependable.	6:30 A.M. to 9 A.M. or 11 A.M. to 1:30 P.M. or 4:30 P.M. to 7 P.M.	Set up serving counter or dining room tables. Serve and replenish foods as needed. Clean counter after meal. Keep dining tables clean. Fill salts and peppers, and sugar containers. Leave dining room in order.
Dishwashers	Clean, alert, dependable.	Scheduled as needed.	Scrape, rinse, rack, and wash dishes. Return clean dishes to storage areas. Clean machine and dish tables after use. Leave dishroom clean.

If adult help is available, one may employ a woman dishwasher for breakfast and lunch and supplement with student help. Such an adult can be helpful in doing miscellaneous cleaning after breakfast dishes are out of the way. Regular employees may be supplemented by student employees as needed.

[a] *Employees work an 8-hour day, 5-day week; scheduled for 8 1/2 hours if over one 1/2-hour meal period, or 9 hours if over two 1/2-hour meal periods. No Sunday evening meal served.*
[b] *Depending on style of service used.*

TABLE A.2   SUGGESTED FOODSERVICE EQUIPMENT FOR A RESIDENCE HALL SERVING 300

Item	Quantity

SMALL EQUIPMENT

Item	Quantity
Apple corer, heavy duty	6 only
Baking and counter insets	
10 × 12 × 4 in.	2 doz
20 × 12 × 8 in.	1 doz
With covers	2 only
Brushes	
Baker's, 6 in. white fiber	4 only
Pastry, round	1 doz
Pastry, 2 in. flat	1 doz
Scrub	1 doz
Vegetable	1 doz
Can opener, heavy duty	2 only
Chopping bowl, wood, 15 in. diam with double-blade mincing knife	1 only
Colander, heavy duty, 11 qt	1 only
Cookie press	1 only
Counter insets	
Round, 7 qt	6 only
Round, 11 qt	1 doz
Cutlery: hardwood handles, carbon tool-steel blades, attached with three inset rivets; full length tang.	
Forks, wooden handle	
12 in.	8 only
18 in.	4 only
Knives	
Boning, 5 in.	3 only
Boning, 6 in.	3 only
French, 8 in.	4 only
French, 10 in.	3 only
French, 12 in.	3 only
Fruit, plain, not serrated, 4 in.	1 doz
Fruit, serrated, 4 1/2 in.	6 only
Grapefruit, serrated, 3 1/2 in.	6 only
Paring, 3 in.	2 doz
Slicing, 8 in.	2 only
Slicing, 12 in.	2 only
Steak, 8 in.	2 only
Steak, 10 in.	2 only
Pan-scraper blade, 3 × 4 1/2 in.	2 only
Cutters	
Biscuit, set of 12	1 set
Cheese, no. 20	1 only

815

TABLE A.2 (Continued)

Item	Quantity
SMALL EQUIPMENT (Continued)	
Cookie, scalloped, 7 cutters	1 set
Dough, 6 in.	3 only
Doughnut, 2 3/4 in. diam	2 only
Cutting boards, solid	
16 × 10 × 1 in.	3 only
18 × 18 × 2 in.	2 only
Decorating tube set, screw type	1 only
Egg beaters, rotary type	2 only
Egg slicer	1 only
Funnels	
1 qt, 6 1/2 in. diam	2 only
2 qt, 9 in. diam	2 only
Garbage cans, 3 gal [a]	3 only
Grater, flat, heavy duty, set of 3 (large, medium, small)	1 set
Hones, 10 in.	2 only
Ice cream dippers	
No. 8	4 only
No. 10	6 only
No. 12	8 only
No. 16	6 only
No. 20	4 only
No. 24	4 only
No. 30	4 only
No. 40	4 only
Ladles, stainless steel	
1-oz solid	2 only
2-oz solid	4 only
4-oz solid	4 only
6-oz solid	4 only
8-oz solid	4 only
14-oz perforated	2 only
Measuring equipment, semi-heavy	
Measuring spoons set (1/4t, 1/2t, 1t, 1T)	1 doz sets
1-cup measures	4 only
1-pt measures	1 doz
1-qt measures	8 only
2-qt measures	4 only
1-gal measures	6 only
Mixing bowls, stainless steel	
1 1/2 qt	8 only
4 qt	6 only
6 qt	6 only
30 qt with dolly cart	2 only
Mop pails, 16 qt with wringers on casters	3 only

Item	Quantity
Paddles	
Oven, 44 in. handle	1 only
Mixing, overall 36 in.	1 only
Pans	
Bun pans, 26 × 18 in.	1 1/2 doz
Cake pans, round, 9-in. diam	4 doz
Cake pans, tubular, 12-in. diam	2 1/2 doz
Loaf or bread pans, 1-lb capacity	4 doz
Pie pans, 9-in. diam, aluminum	5 doz
Pudding or baking pans, 18 × 26 × 2 1/2 in.	3 doz
Sauce pans	
1 1/2 qt	4 only
2 1/2 qt	6 only
6 qt	4 only
8 1/2 qt	4 only
Pitchers	
2 qt	2 only
4 qt	8 only
Roaster, 16 × 20 × 4 1/2 in.	2 only
Roaster top, 16 × 20 × 4 1/2 in.	2 only
Rolling pins, freewheeling, 18 in.	2 only
Scales	
Baker's scale with scoops and weights	2 only
Bench-type scale, 20-in. diam dial, 50 lb, 1 oz with	
tare device	1 only
Platform-beam scale, 500-lb capacity	1 only
Portion scale, 5 lb × 1/8 oz	2 only
Scoops, heavy duty	
1 pt	6 only
1 qt	6 only
Scrapers, rubber	
Institution size	1 doz
Small size	2 doz
Serving utensils	
Cake turners, 8 × 3 in.	6 only
Meat servers, 2 3/4 × 6 3/4 in.	1 doz
Pie servers, 6 1/2 in.	8 only
Serving spoons, 13 in.:	
Solid, stainless steel	1 1/2 doz
Slotted, stainless steel	1 doz
Perforated, stainless steel	6 only
Tongs, hamburger	6 only
Shears, kitchen, 7 in.	2 only
Skewers, assorted sizes, set of 6	1 set
Skimmers	
4 1/2-in. diam blade	2 only
6 1/2-in. diam blade	2 only

Item	Quantity
SMALL EQUIPMENT *(Continued)*	
Spatulas, heavy duty, stainless steel	
6 in.	4 only
8 in.	4 only
10 in.	4 only
12 in.	4 only
Butter spreader, 4 in.	4 only
Stools, heavy metal, kitchen	
17 in.	3 only
24 in.	3 only
Strainers	
Chinese, 5 qt	1 only
Wire reinforced, heavy duty	
4-in. diam	6 only
8-in. diam	6 only
Thermometers	
Candy	2 only
Meat, dial type	6 only
Oven	6 only
Trays	
Composition or plastic	
14 × 18 in.[b]	30 doz
Metal, 18 × 22 in.	1 doz
Whips, piano wire (fine wire)	
8 in.	4 only
12 in.	6 only
16 in.	6 only
16 in. (French)	2 only
24 in. (French)	2 only
Whips, heavy duty	
16 in.	3 only
24 in.	2 only
LARGE EQUIPMENT [c]	
A. Preparation Areas	
Attendance-time recorder with metal card racks	1 only
Automatic ice-maker	1 only
Cooling racks, approximately 68 in. long × 24 in. wide × 70 in. high	1 only
Disposers	2 only
Exhaust hood	1 only
Food cutter, electric with dicer attachments	1 only
Freezers	as needed
Fryers, deep-fat, gas or electric	2 only

Item	Quantity
Gas or electric plate, two-burner, heavy duty	1 only
Gas or electric tilt skillet	1 only
Linen for employees	
Meat slicer, electric	1 only
Mixer, with standard equipment	
80–40 qt	1 only
20–12 qt	1 only
5 qt	1 only
Ovens	
Bake, convection	1 only
Roast, convection	1 only
Pie dough roller (optional)	1 only
Racks	
Platform racks, portable, for refrigerator storage	4 only
Portable, shelved racks for refrigerator storage	6 only
Pot and pan storage	1 only
Range unit, institution size	1 only
Refrigerators	
Pass-through, 65 cu ft capacity	1 only
Reach-in	1 only
Walk-in (as needed) with low temperature storage	
section	1 only
Roll divider	1 only
Sinks	
Handwashing	2 only
Vegetable preparation, 2 compartment	1 only
(Plus 1 in cook's table and 1 in salad preparation	
table)	
Steam jacketed kettles	
5 gal	2 only
20 gal	1 only
40-gal	1 only
Steamer, three-compartment with timer	1 only
Tables	
Baker's work table with portable storage bins (3 or 4)	1 only
Cook's work table with sink and pan rack	1 only
Portable tables	3 only
Salad work table with sink and refrigerated storage	
underneath	1 only
Vegetable preparation table	1 only
Trucks, kitchen, rubber tires	2 only
B. Serving Area	
Cafeteria counter with tray slide	1 only
Carts for dish storage (Lowerators or covered carts)	as needed
Coffee urn with stand	1 only
Counter cabinets (back bar)	1 only
Grill and stand	1 only
Toaster, rotary	1 only

TABLE A.2 (Continued)

Item	Quantity

LARGE EQUIPMENT (Continued)

C. Dishwashing and Clean-Up Area

Item	Quantity
Clean and soiled dish tables, with disposer	1 only
Compactor	1 only
Dishwasher, 2-tank	1 only
Dishcarts to transport clean dishes (Lowerators or covered carts)	as needed
Mop and broom storage closet	1 only
Pot-and-pan-washing sink, 3-compartment, with drainboards	1 only
Trash and garbage can rinser and sterilizer	1 only

CHINA

Item	Quantity
Cooking china	
Casseroles, 2 qt capacity [d]	4 doz
Custards	30 doz
Pot pies	30 doz
Teapots	3 doz
Celery dishes, 9 3/4 in.[d]	3 doz
Cereals	30 doz
Cups	40 doz
Dishes, serving, 13 1/4 in.[d]	8 doz
Fruits (sauce dishes)	50 doz
Jugs (coffee cream) [d]	6 doz
Jugs (cereal cream) [d]	4 doz
Plates, 9 5/8 in.	45 doz
Plates, 5 1/2 in.	120 doz
Salads,[d]	64 doz
Saucers	35 doz
Sugar, complete	5 doz

GLASSWARE

Item	Quantity
Juice glasses, 5 oz	48 doz
Salt and peppers with stainless steel tops	6 doz
Sherbets, low footed	36 doz
Tumblers, 10 oz	60 doz

SILVERWARE

Item	Quantity
Butter spreaders [e]	3 doz
Cold-meat forks [e]	3 doz
Forks,	70 doz
Knives	30 doz
Salad forks, individual (optional) [e]	30 doz

Item	Quantity
Soup spoons	30 doz
Tablespoons [e]	30 doz
Teaspoons	70 doz

MISCELLANEOUS AND FOR SPECIAL SERVICES AS NEEDED

Bonbon dish	6 only
Cake server	3 only
Flower bowl, oval	3 only
Flower bowl, round	2 only
Frogs, oval	3 only
Frogs, round	2 only
Glass serving plates, 16 in.	4 only
Parfait glasses	as needed
Punch bowls	as needed
Punch cups	as needed
Punch ladles	as needed
Salad Bowls, 24 in.	2 only
Salad fork, wood	5 only
Salad spoon, wood	5 only
Taper holders, glass	5 doz
Tea service and tray	as needed
Torte plate, 13 in.	6 only

[a] *If no disposers, additional garbage pails of 6 and 8 gal capacity needed.*
[b] *For self-service.*
[c] *The size, design, and materials will vary with each installation.*
[d] *Needed if table-style service is used.*
[e] *Needed if table-style service is used.*

EXAMPLE B. A LARGE RESIDENCE HALL FOODSERVICE PLAN

The organization chart of the entire foodservice system at one large university is given in Fig. A.4 and the general arrangement of one of the residence halls is shown in Fig. A.5. This six-floor hall is coeducational, the west wing housing women and the east wing men, with dining facilities in the center section. The floor plan of the octagonal-shaped dining-kitchen unit serving approximately 1150 persons per meal is shown in Fig. A.6. The organization chart for this residence hall foodservice facility is given in Fig. A.7. The time schedules and major duties of each employee are listed in Table A.3.

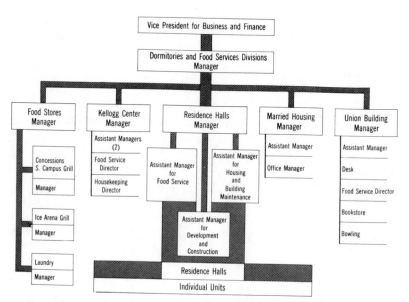

FIGURE A.4   Organization chart for large housing and foodservice system. Courtesy, Michigan State University.

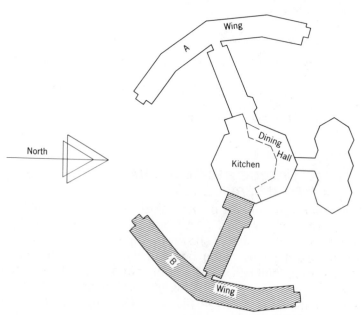

FIGURE A.5   General arrangement of floor plan for a large coeducational residence hall. Courtesy, Michigan State University.

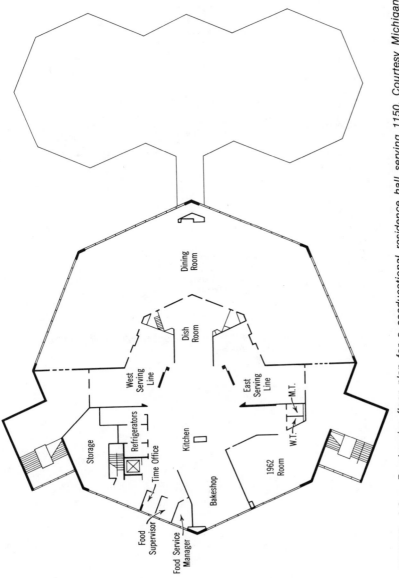

FIGURE A.6   Foodservice floor plan for a coeducational residence hall serving 1150. Courtesy Michigan State University.

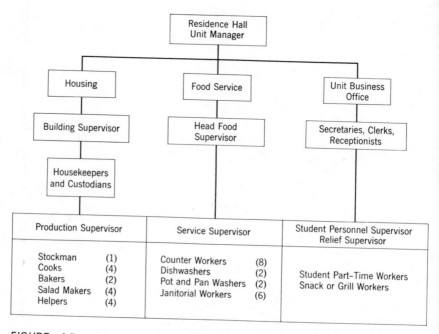

FIGURE A.7 Organization chart for a residence hall serving 1150. Courtesy, Michigan State University.

TABLE A.3 SUGGESTED FOODSERVICE PERSONNEL FOR A RESIDENCE HALL SERVING 1150

Position	Hours[a]	Responsible for
A. Production Department		
Stock clerk	7 A.M. to 4 P.M. Relieved by student worker on days off.	Receiving and issuing all food and supplies. Proper storage in stock room, refrigerators, and freezers. Cleanliness and order in storage area. Inventories and records.
Morning cooks (2)	6 A.M. to 3 P.M.	Preparation of breakfast hot cereals, main dishes, cocoa. Preparation of soups, sauces, main dishes, and vegetables for luncheon. Sending food to serving room as needed. Assisting with preparation for dinner.
Afternoon cooks (2)	10 A.M. to 7 P.M. All cooks are relieved on days off by foodservice helpers, in training for cook's jobs.	Assisting morning cooks with luncheon, especially with grilling, french frying. Preparation of meats, fish, poultry, sauces, and gravies, vegetables for dinner. Sending food to serving room as needed. Taking care of all leftover food after luncheon and dinner.
Early baker	5:30 A.M. to 2:30 P.M. Relieved by foodservice helper on days off.	Preparation of hot breads for breakfast. Preparation of buns, rolls, and desserts for luncheon. Preparation of some dinner desserts. Sending foods to serving room as needed. Taking care of leftover bakery items. Supervising helper.
Late baker	10 A.M. to 7 P.M. Relieved by part-time worker on days off.	Assisting early baker with preparation of luncheon items. Finishing preparation of dinner items. Baking hot rolls, biscuits, muffins during dinner meal. Preparation of breakfast rolls. Taking care of leftover bakery items after dinner. Supervising helper.

TABLE A.3 (Continued)

Position	Hours [a]	Responsible for
Morning salad makers (2)	7 A.M. to 4 P.M. All salad makers are relieved on days off by food service helpers.	Preparation of salad ingredients. Preparation of fresh vegetables as needed by cooks. Making salads and salad dressings. Setting up individual salads. Cleanliness and order in salad areas and salad refrigerators.
Afternoon salad makers (2)	10 A.M. to 7 P.M.	Same as for morning salad makers.
Foodservice helpers	Hours vary according to unit and employee whom they are relieving.	Filling-in for days off of regular employees in main kitchen, bakery and salad department. Learning the work of these employees and training for future openings in production areas.
B. Service Department Morning counter workers (4)	6 A.M. to 3 P.M.	Cleanliness and order in serving rooms. Reconstituting and pouring frozen juices. Dishing fruits, cutting and serving pies, cakes, and other desserts. Serving at hot and cold counters. Maintaining condiment tables. Supplying clean silver, glasses, trays, and dishes to the counter. Supervising student helpers in serving rooms.
Afternoon counter workers (4)	10 A.M. to 7 P.M.	Same as for morning counter workers.
Early dishwasher Late dishwasher	7:30 A.M. to 4:30 P.M. 10:30 A.M. to 7:30 P.M.	Cleanliness of dish room. Supervising student employees who work in dish room. Care of machine. Use of detergent. Working with university sanitarian to maintain sanitary standards. Cleanliness of dish cupboards, silver carts, glass racks, lowerators.

Position	No.	Hours	Duties
Pot and pan washers (2)	1	8 A.M. to 5 P.M.	Washing pots and pans. Sanitation of pots and pans, racks, and storage areas. Rinsing and returning milk cans to the dock.
	1	11 A.M. to 8 P.M.	
Janitorial workers (6)	1	7 A.M. to 4 P.M.	Cleaning floors, walls and windows in kitchen and serving areas. Cleaning equipment—ranges, ovens, hoods, ventilators, carts, racks, conveyor belts. Cleaning dining rooms, mopping and waxing floors, washing chairs and table legs. Assisting in dish room, pot and pan area. Disposing of rubbish, burning papers. Cleaning dock areas. Other general daily and periodic cleaning.
	2	8 A.M. to 5 P.M.	
	1	9 A.M. to 6 P.M.	
	2	3 P.M. to midnight.	
Student part-time workers		Hours assigned as needed.	Assisting regular employees at peak-load times with serving and cleanup duties.

[a] Employees take 30 min for each meal and are, therefore, scheduled for 9 hr for an 8-hr working day based on a 5-day week.

Appendix B
CONVERSION
TABLES

Regular standard United States units of temperature, weight, and liquid measurements have been used in this text. The following Conversion Tables (tables B.1 and B.2) showing equivalent metric units may be a handy reference and a useful guide for persons in the foodservice industry during the changeover period and until the use of the metric system has become commonplace in this country.

TABLE B.1   TEMPERATURE CONVERSION TABLE

The numbers in the body of the table give in degrees F the temperature indicated in degrees C at the top and side.
To convert 178° C to Fahrenheit scale, find 17 in the column headed degrees C. Proceed in a horizontal line to the column headed 8 which shows 352° F as corresponding to 178° C.

Range: −29° C (−20° F) to 309° C (588° F)

To convert 352° F to Celsius (Centigrade) scale, find 352 in the Fahrenheit readings, then in the column headed degrees C, find the number which is on the same horizontal line, i.e., 17. Next, fill in the last number from the heading of the column in which 352 was found, i.e., 8, resulting in 178° C which is equivalent to 352° F.

Conversion Formulae: $T° C = 5/9 (T° F − 32)$
$T° F = 9/5 T° C + 32$

Degrees C	0	1	2	3	4	5	6	7	8	9
−2	−4° F	−6° F	−8° F	−9° F	−11° F	−13° F	−15° F	−17° F	−18° F	−20° F
−1	14° F	12° F	10° F	9° F	7° F	5° F	3° F	1° F	0° F	−2° F
−0	32° F	30° F	28° F	27° F	25° F	23° F	21° F	19° F	18° F	16° F
0	32° F	34° F	36° F	37° F	39° F	41° F	43° F	45° F	46° F	48° F
1	50° F	52° F	54° F	55° F	57° F	59° F	61° F	63° F	64° F	66° F
2	68° F	70° F	72° F	73° F	75° F	77° F	79° F	81° F	82° F	84° F
3	86° F	88° F	90° F	91° F	93° F	95° F	97° F	99° F	100° F	102° F
4	104° F	106° F	108° F	109° F	111° F	113° F	115° F	117° F	118° F	120° F
5	122° F	124° F	126° F	127° F	129° F	131° F	133° F	135° F	136° F	138° F
6	140° F	142° F	144° F	145° F	147° F	149° F	151° F	153° F	154° F	156° F
7	158° F	160° F	162° F	163° F	165° F	167° F	169° F	171° F	172° F	174° F
8	176° F	178° F	180° F	181° F	183° F	185° F	187° F	189° F	190° F	192° F
9	194° F	196° F	198° F	199° F	201° F	203° F	205° F	207° F	208° F	210° F
10	212° F	214° F	216° F	217° F	219° F	221° F	223° F	225° F	226° F	228° F
11	230° F	232° F	234° F	235° F	237° F	239° F	241° F	243° F	244° F	246° F
12	248° F	250° F	252° F	253° F	255° F	257° F	259° F	261° F	262° F	264° F
13	266° F	268° F	270° F	271° F	273° F	275° F	277° F	279° F	280° F	282° F
14	284° F	286° F	288° F	289° F	291° F	293° F	295° F	297° F	298° F	300° F
15	302° F	304° F	306° F	307° F	309° F	311° F	313° F	315° F	316° F	318° F
16	320° F	322° F	324° F	325° F	327° F	329° F	331° F	333° F	334° F	336° F
17	338° F	340° F	342° F	343° F	345° F	347° F	349° F	351° F	352° F	354° F
18	356° F	358° F	360° F	361° F	363° F	365° F	367° F	369° F	370° F	372° F
19	374° F	376° F	378° F	379° F	381° F	383° F	385° F	387° F	388° F	390° F
20	392° F	394° F	396° F	397° F	399° F	401° F	403° F	405° F	406° F	408° F
21	410° F	412° F	414° F	415° F	417° F	419° F	421° F	423° F	424° F	426° F
22	428° F	430° F	432° F	433° F	435° F	437° F	439° F	441° F	442° F	444° F
23	446° F	448° F	450° F	451° F	453° F	455° F	457° F	459° F	460° F	462° F
24	464° F	466° F	468° F	469° F	471° F	473° F	475° F	477° F	478° F	480° F
25	482° F	484° F	486° F	487° F	489° F	491° F	493° F	495° F	496° F	498° F
26	500° F	502° F	504° F	505° F	507° F	509° F	511° F	513° F	514° F	516° F
27	518° F	520° F	522° F	523° F	525° F	527° F	529° F	531° F	532° F	534° F
28	536° F	538° F	540° F	541° F	543° F	545° F	547° F	549° F	550° F	552° F
29	554° F	556° F	558° F	559° F	561° F	563° F	565° F	567° F	568° F	570° F
30	572° F	574° F	576° F	577° F	579° F	581° F	583° F	585° F	586° F	588° F

Source. Handbook of Food Preparation, Seventh Edition, pp. 14–15. Copyright © 1975, American Home Economics Association, Washington, D.C.

TABLE B.2 CONVERSION TO METRIC UNITS

A. Comparison of Avoirdupois and Metric Units of Weight

1 oz = 28.35 g	1 lb = 0.454 kg	1 g = 0.035 oz	1 kg = 2.205 lb
2 oz = 56.70 g	2 lb = 0.91 kg	2 g = 0.07 oz	2 kg = 4.41 lb
3 oz = 85.05 g	3 lb = 1.36 kg	3 g = 0.11 oz	3 kg = 6.61 lb
4 oz = 113.40 g	4 lb = 1.81 kg	4 g = 0.14 oz	4 kg = 8.82 lb
5 oz = 141.75 g	5 lb = 2.27 kg	5 g = 0.18 oz	5 kg = 11.02 lb
6 oz = 170.10 g	6 lb = 2.72 kg	6 g = 0.21 oz	6 kg = 13.23 lb
7 oz = 198.45 g	7 lb = 3.18 kg	7 g = 0.25 oz	7 kg = 15.43 lb
8 oz = 226.80 g	8 lb = 3.63 kg	8 g = 0.28 oz	8 kg = 17.64 lb
9 oz = 255.15 g	9 lb = 4.08 kg	9 g = 0.32 oz	9 kg = 19.84 lb
10 oz = 283.50 g	10 lb = 4.54 kg	10 g = 0.35 oz	10 kg = 22.05 lb
11 oz = 311.85 g	11 lb = 4.99 kg	11 g = 0.39 oz	11 kg = 24.26 lb
12 oz = 340.20 g	12 lb = 5.44 kg	12 g = 0.42 oz	12 kg = 26.46 lb
13 oz = 368.55 g	13 lb = 5.90 kg	13 g = 0.46 oz	13 kg = 28.67 lb
14 oz = 396.90 g	14 lb = 6.35 kg	14 g = 0.49 oz	14 kg = 30.87 lb
15 oz = 425.25 g	15 lb = 6.81 kg	15 g = 0.53 oz	15 kg = 33.08 lb
16 oz = 453.59 g	16 lb = 7.26 kg	16 g = 0.56 oz	16 kg = 35.28 lb

B. Comparison of U.S. and Metric Units of Liquid Measure

1 fl oz = 29.573 ml	1 qt = 0.946 l	1 gal = 3.785 l	1 ml = 0.034 fl oz	1 l = 1.057 qt	1 l = 0.264 gal
2 fl oz = 59.15 ml	2 qt = 1.89 l	2 gal = 7.57 l	2 ml = 0.07 fl oz	2 l = 2.11 qt	2 l = 0.53 gal
3 fl oz = 88.72 ml	3 qt = 2.84 l	3 gal = 11.36 l	3 ml = 0.10 fl oz	3 l = 3.17 qt	3 l = 0.79 gal
4 fl oz = 118.30 ml	4 qt = 3.79 l	4 gal = 15.14 l	4 ml = 0.14 fl oz	4 l = 4.23 qt	4 l = 1.06 gal
5 fl oz = 147.87 ml	5 qt = 4.73 l	5 gal = 18.93 l	5 ml = 0.17 fl oz	5 l = 5.28 qt	5 l = 1.32 gal
6 fl oz = 177.44 ml	6 qt = 5.68 l	6 gal = 22.71 l	6 ml = 0.20 fl oz	6 l = 6.34 qt	6 l = 1.59 gal
7 fl oz = 207.02 ml	7 qt = 6.62 l	7 gal = 26.50 l	7 ml = 0.24 fl oz	7 l = 7.40 qt	7 l = 1.85 gal
8 fl oz = 236.59 ml	8 qt = 7.57 l	8 gal = 30.28 l	8 ml = 0.27 fl oz	8 l = 8.45 qt	8 l = 2.11 gal
9 fl oz = 266.16 ml	9 qt = 8.521 l	9 gal = 34.071 l	9 ml = 0.30 fl oz	9 l = 9.51 qt	9 l = 2.38 gal
10 fl oz = 295.73 ml	10 qt = 9.46 l	10 gal = 37.85 l	10 ml = 0.34 fl oz	10 l = 10.57 qt	10 l = 2.64 gal

Source. Handbook of Food Preparation, Seventh Edition, p. 10. C

INDEX